CRIME IN OUR CHANGING SOCIETY

CRIME IN OUR CHANGING SOCIETY

DANIEL GLASER
UNIVERSITY OF SOUTHERN CALIFORNIA

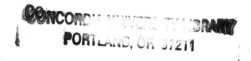
Holt, Rinehart and Winston
New York   Chicago   San Francisco   Dallas
Montreal   Toronto   London   Sydney

Photo Credits

p. 17: U.P.I. Photo
p. 59: Frank Muller-May/Woodfin Camp & Associates
p. 107: Freelance Photographers Guild
p. 176: Wide World Photos
p. 179: Constantine Manos/Magnum Photos
p. 187: Wide World Photos
p. 230: Sygma/J. P. Laffont
p. 237: U.P.I. Photo
p. 253: Bob Fitch/Black Star
p. 293: Rick Smolan/Stock, Boston
p. 301: Norris McNamara/Nancy Palmer Photo Agency
p. 334: Al Naidoff/Freelance Photographers Guild
p. 354: Marvin Newman/Woodfin Camp & Associates
p. 359: Charles Gatewood
p. 380: J. B. & Associates
p. 386: Bruce Anspach from Editorial Photocolor Archives
p. 389: Dan O'Neill from Editorial Photocolor Archives
p. 416: Peter Angelo Simon
p. 444: Culver Pictures
p. 457: U.P.I. Photo

Library of Congress Cataloging in Publication Data

Glaser, Daniel.
Crime in our changing society.

Bibliography: p. 533
Includes index.
1. Crime and criminals. I. Title.
HV6025.G54   364   77-89734
ISBN 0-03-040261-1 pbk.
ISBN 0-03-043961-2

Printed in the United States of America
890   039   987654321

PREFACE

This book relates changes in lawmaking and lawbreaking to trends in our total society, to show what crime has been, what it is becoming, and why it is changing. The objectives are to advance from accurate descriptions to sound explanations grounded in established principles of the social and behavioral sciences, and to suggest more effective public policies.

Part I provides an overview and analysis of crime definition, evolution, and measurement, and of the question "Does crime pay?" It shows that the distinction between predatory and nonpredatory offenses permits more valid statements on these subjects than can be made when referring to crime as a whole. Part II discusses general theories of crime causation and biological perspectives, then shifts to analysis of the specific offense patterns of most concern to Americans. Part III consists of a final chapter that briefly summarizes some conclusions of this volume.

This book does not undertake a comprehensive discussion of each type of criminal-justice agency (such as police, courts, and corrections) or of the criminal-justice system as a whole. Yet particular policies or practices of such agencies are examined when doing so helps to explain specific aspects of crime or illuminates policy discussion on certain types of offenses.

Of course, there is merit in a systematic study of criminal-justice organizations (the concern of another book that the author is preparing), but it is believed that readers will accomplish this task most efficiently apart from an analysis of crime. This view seems to be shared by the many universities that deal with these subjects in separate courses. No particular sequence is essential in these two pursuits, but if a choice must be made it seems preferable first to become more knowledgeable about crime. This book is offered as a contribution to that goal.

D. G.

ACKNOWLEDGMENTS

This book is my harvest from tilling many fields. When the yield seems good it is nice to take credit as the farmer, and when it is poor, to find fault with the soil of social science or the climate of criminology. If credit is due, however, the farmer should share it by pointing out his helpers.

The best of whatever is good in this writing includes much that was sowed by my wife, Pearl, whose seedlings enrich almost every page. Although some were damaged in my transplanting, most have survived, and more were added by Praeger's editor, Robert Heidel. Pearl's indefatigability in this merits a reward second only to that which she deserves for sharing our marriage with my much more demanding mate, sociology.

My crops are often hybrids, from cross-pollinating plants of many disciplines. Their nurture required help from nonsociologists. Chapter 7, on biological factors in crime, reflects very useful comments by: Professor Garth J. Thomas, Director, Center for Brain Research, University of Rochester; Dr. Saleem A. Shah, Chief, Center for Studies of Crime and Delinquency, National Institute of Mental Health; Dr. Sarnoff A. Mednick, Director, Psychological Institute, Community Hospital, Copenhagen, Denmark. Chapter 9, on violence, benefits from suggestions by Professor Albert Bandura, Chairman, Department of Psychology, Stanford University. All parts of Chapter 10, on substance abuse and crime, gained from comments by Professor William H. McGlothlin, Department of Psychology, University of California at Los Angeles. Parts of its section on opiates were improved by my correspondence on various points with: Professor Vincent P. Dole, M.D., Rockefeller University; Professor Avram Goldstein, M.D., Director, Addiction Research Foundation, Stanford University; Professor S. B. Sells, Director, Institute for Behavioral Research, Texas Christian University. In Chapter 6, the section "From Medieval to Modern Thought" follows closely the outline of lectures by Professor Ralph W. England, now of the University of Rhode Island, in a seminar on criminology that we repeatedly taught together when we were both at the University of Illinois; this outline he in turn credited to his mentor at the University of Pennsylvania, Professor (now emeritus) Thorsten Sellin.

CONTENTS

CRIME IN OUR CHANGING SOCIETY

PART ONE
QUALITY AND QUANTITY

ONE

WHAT IS CRIME?

People have always been both frightened and fascinated by crime. Many Biblical tales, Greek and Shakespearean tragedies, and other narrative classics are crime stories. The mass media—newspapers, motion pictures, radio and television—regularly portray lawbreaking, as news or as fiction, for interest in crime cuts across class, age, sex, race, nationality, religion, and era. Official statistics almost always show an increasing American crime rate, and opinion polls repeatedly confirm that crime is a leading public concern. In campaigns for political office, from local alderman to the Presidency, candidates of every persuasion list "crime in the streets" or "law and order" as a foremost problem, and each promises to do more about it.

The persistent and widespread concern with crime suggests that everyone knows what it is, and that it has always been the same. In fact, however, there is much variation over time and place in what is called criminal. Murder and robbery are almost everywhere viewed as offenses, yet even their definition varies somewhat. Many other acts, such as alcohol and drug use, are outlawed in some places while permitted in others, or have elicited both reactions in the same locales in different historical periods.

ONE   WHAT IS CRIME?

CRIME AND CRIMINOLOGY

The words *crime* and *offense* will be used here interchangeably and in their broadest legal sense, as any act for which a court may lawfully impose punishment. (In the laws of some states, however, "crime" refers just to offenses punishable by death or confinement, while those calling only for fines are labeled "infractions" and "violations.")

"Criminology" refers here to the scientific study of crime and of government reactions to it. This discipline may appear to have its boundaries determined by government, but it also investigates why governments select some types of behavior for punishment while overlooking others; thus its range of inquiry is much broader than the study of existing criminal law.

In common speech, acts that are disapproved are often called crimes even though the courts cannot lawfully punish them, and some scholars argue that criminology should also be concerned with every violation of human rights. These would include war, racism, sexism, and poverty as crimes, but not the breaking of any law they regard as immoral (see, for example, the Schwendingers, 1970). Yet such a broad conception confuses criminology with all the social sciences, impeding expertise in any, and makes the field's boundaries vary with each person's ideas on morality. Our focus on *why* governments punish some acts and not others, as well as on the consequences of government penalties, frees criminology from having its domain limited by legislative whim and possible legislative injustice.

This book's objective definition of crime as court-punishable behavior is justifiable, in a scientific criminology, partly because such a distinctive focus increases this field's ability to contribute uniquely to the solution of war, racism, sexism, poverty, and other social problems. Since criminology, as viewed here, seeks scientific explanation not only for violation of criminal law but also for past and prospective changes in this law (the topic of the next chapter), its interests include: (1) studying the relationships among what is currently defined as crime, reactions to it, and other social concerns; (2) studying the possibility of alleviating various social problems by revising criminal law (including international criminal law), or by enforcing it differently. Criminology, as thus conceived, can be a distinct complement to the other social sciences in helping to achieve a better world, precisely because of its focus on crime as behavior lawfully punishable by courts.

The Classification of Crimes

There are many ways to classify crimes, depending upon one's purpose. From a legal standpoint, for example, crimes are generally divided into *misdemeanors* and *felonies,* according to the severity of punishment that is permitted for them. In most states misdemeanors are offenses for which the maximum period of confinement is one year, to be served in jail or house of correction, while felonies call for more than a year, to be spent in prison. Yet there is considerable variation among the states in laws distinguishing between felony and misdemeanor, and courts have authority to place an act rather arbitrarily in either of these two categories.

For guiding public policy, it is useful to classify crimes by those features that most closely affect their measurement and control. Crucial for these two purposes is the distinction between offenses in which at least one party is regarded as victim and crimes in which all those involved participate voluntarily and usually do not consider themselves deprived or injured. The victimizing offenses are what we commonly think of as "crime," such as murder or theft; the so-called victimless offenses include, for example, prostitution, drug abuse, and homosexuality, wherever they violate the criminal law.

Applying the term *victimless* provokes argument, since drug abusers are often viewed as victimized by their cravings, and prostitutes by their occupation. This semantic issue can be avoided by using the terms *predatory* and *nonpredatory* ("predatory" implies preying on others). With either terminology, the separation of offenses by whether or not some people feel victimized by them has immense applications for criminal-justice policy. As Chapter 2 shows, this distinction is connected with a radical contrast in both the history and the probable future of criminal law, and in subsequent chapters its importance for understanding other problems of criminology will also be evident.

Predatory crimes—or "predations"—can be divided into *willful predations* and *criminal negligence,* according to whether the offender intended to harm another party or merely failed to take precautions against accidentally inflicting injury. *Intent,* implied by the term "willful," and specifically evil intent—denoted in law by the Latin *mens rea* (evil mind) or the English "malicious"—are parts of the legal definitions of most predations. You have to "intend to do bad" to be guilty of these crimes. In negligence offenses, however, an accused can be found guilty even if the harm done was unintended, as when someone is killed because the driver of a car was too busy caressing his passenger to notice the traffic ahead.

Predations can also be divided into crimes against persons and against property. The specific offenses they include are discussed in more detail in later chapters, but a few highlights will be given here.

Crimes against persons are acts intended to hurt, injure, or restrain, including physical attacks, forced sexual conduct, and kidnapping. They range in seriousness from the misdemeanor of *simple assault,* which may be only a slap or a shove, to the felony of *murder,* an intentional killing. Between these extremes are *nonnegligent manslaughter,* an unintended killing from an intended assault, and *aggravated assault,* inflicting bodily injury, attempting to do so, or attempting to kill. The many factors determining injuries in a brawl, or the speed and quality of medical aid may determine whether an attack proves trivial, serious, or fatal. Thus the outcome may not explain the conflict, yet be the basis for court decisions on the charge and the penalty for each combatant, often regardless of who started the quarrel.

The most common predatory sex crime is *rape,* which most states define as a male's use of force or threat of force to have sexual intercourse with a female not his spouse (the spouse exception certainly is a sexist feature). Statistics usually count both completed and attempted forced sex acts as rapes and, unless otherwise specified, include *statutory rape,* which is coitus with a female who acquiesces— perhaps even seduces the male—but whom the law classifies as too young or mentally incompetent for the responsibility of consent.

Property crimes, which include all willful predations for money or other goods, comprise over 90 percent of felonies reported to the police in urban areas. *Theft,* sometimes still called by the older term "larceny," means taking someone's property—usually just "lifting" it when no one is looking, as in "shoplifting." *Burglary* is the legal term for breaking into a building to commit a felony, but it is nearly always for the purpose of theft. *Fraud* is a misrepresentation to obtain money, property, or services. A common form is *forgery* of checks or other documents—for example, by altering them or by signing someone else's name to them, or by signing one's own name without having a bank account. Another form of fraud is *embezzlement,* a violation of trust, as when an accountant alters records to obtain money illegally. A third major type of fraud—variously called *confidence game, bunco,* or *larceny by trick*—is the use of deceit to get money or other property. The victim is usually led to expect something in exchange, which the "con artist" has no intention of providing; or he may be deceived about the use to be made of the money—for example, being duped into believing that it will go for charity or to repay a debt owed by a deceased relative. Misrepresentation in advertising and other selling is a vast area of fraud that has become routine in many businesses, from patent medicines and beauty aids to used cars and television sets; it is only slowly being defined as crime and penalized in the courts.

Robbery is the taking of money or other goods by force or threat of force. The "holdup" or "armed robbery" is its typical form, although unarmed robbery by violent assault ("mugging") injures the victims more often than does the armed variety. Robbery, clearly, is against both property and persons. Most tables in the FBI's annual *Uniform Crime Reports* combine murder, nonnegligent manslaughter, aggravated assault, rape, and robbery as "violent crimes" to distinguish them from "property crimes"; but some of its graphs categorize robbery as "crimes against property" and tag other violent offenses "crimes against the person."

Several types of willful predation are now punished by the government without recourse to the criminal courts, since they are investigated and penalized by regulatory commissions. Those who consider their penalties by the commissions unjust, however, may have them reviewed by the courts. These growth areas in the criminal law, which the courts also increasingly prosecute, include: *criminal pollution* of air, water, or food, which victimizes the general public; *criminal electioneering,* which victimizes the electorate, an area of law considerably expanded following the Watergate scandal; *criminal invasion of privacy,* which victimizes individuals by subjecting them to potential embarrassment, prejudice, or other harm by persons who secretly tap their telephones, put hidden microphones ("bugs") in their premises, or obtain illegal access to agency files about them; *cruelty to wildlife,* which extends older laws against inhumane treatment of domestic animals to laws against cruelty by hunters and trappers. Disclosures in the 1970s that the FBI and the CIA resorted to false communications, bribes, threats, and even assassinations to interfere with the political process in this country or abroad fostered calls for new criminal penalties against arrogation of congressional or presidential powers.

Criminal negligence predations cause most of the 50,000 deaths and tens of thousands of crippling or other injuries per year from auto accidents in the United States; they also cause considerable loss of life or injury from carelessness in constructing buildings, in excavating mines or tunnels, and in maintaining dangerous machinery. Much negligence is criminal even if its victims are only potential; thus we punish for speeding and reckless driving even when there is no accident, thereby presumably preventing accidents and injuries.

The nonpredatory crimes are more diverse than the predatory, but some are no longer regarded as criminal in the United States. As the next chapter elaborates and explains, the number of kinds of predatory act designated criminal continually accumulates, for technology repeatedly creates new ways in which people may be victimized, and laws against victimizing behavior seldom are repealed. Contrastingly, in the long span of human history the number and variety of nonpredatory acts designated criminal have diminished (although there were eras when they temporarily increased). The classifications of nonpredatory crimes perhaps most useful for policy purposes today are by: (1) whether they are criminal only when they have a complaining audience; (2) whether they are criminal only because of what is sold, purchased, used, or possessed.

Illegal-performance offenses may be viewed as victimizing some spectators or listeners (those who object to the performance, even feel they "can't stand it"), hence as borderline predatory, although the injuries usually are petty. One of these crimes, public drunkenness, is the most frequent basis for arrest in the United States, but is increasingly being redefined as noncriminal. Other infractions in this group include indecent exposure, vagrancy, and disorderly conduct, a vague catchall that may be used against anyone considered too loud, rude, or nude. People may legally be naked or drunk in private, but not in public. They may also be as loud as they wish if no one is likely to be disturbed, as when far out in the desert or at a football game where everyone else is yelling. If this conduct evokes complaints, however, they may be charged with a crime.

Illegal-selling offenses are crimes that involve a seller and a customer, rather than an offender and an intended victim, and there usually is no complaining audience. These crimes cater to alleged vices; they include sale of narcotics, as well as of gambling and prostitution services. The annual dollar volume of such illegal-selling crime is not known, but estimates run into the billions. They clearly entail the exchange of many times more money than the value of goods and currency taken in such predations as burglary, robbery, and theft. Sales of stolen goods and of government services (for bribes) resemble nonpredatory illegal-selling offenses because the participants do not consider themselves victimized or complain to the police; they are predations, however, because they victimize the public by selling its property or its rights, and those citizens who recognize this feel swindled.

Illegal consumption is the purchase or use of illegal goods (e.g., narcotics) or services (e.g., prostitution) or unlawful homosexual acts. These crimes usually are by consent of all participants, who naturally do not report themselves to the police and thus are not readily prosecuted. Indeed, the legal charge in these offenses often is not the forbidden behavior itself but something more easily proven that is instrumental to it. For example, it generally is not narcotic use, but illegal possession of narcotics or even of a hypodermic syringe that is the basis for arresting and punishing people to stop them from using these drugs. Similarly, in prosecutions intended to suppress gambling, illegal possession of gambling equipment may be a more frequent charge than the gambling itself. Incest and bigamy are sex crimes readily classifiable as illegal consumption if done by mutual consent, although bigamy usually is done by deceit and hence is also a form of fraud.

Disloyalty is regarded as most serious in its extreme form, treason, but it is diversely defined. Treason, although subject to the death penalty, is rarely charged in our courts, but extremist critics of our foreign policy often label their opponents "traitors." In totalitarian nations, however, and in most countries during wars, disloyalty to the state is much more frequently a basis for official punishment. In the United States, especially during the Vietnam War, an appreciable number of young men were imprisoned for avoiding compulsory military service, a crime that did not exist in periods when our armed forces consisted only of volunteers; in this period many of the punished proclaimed that it was those who opposed their views who were disloyal, so their own offense was often a public rather than a furtive act. Disloyalty is the remnant in the United States and in many other countries of a once-larger category of crime—illegal belief, not only in politics, but also in a religion not sanctioned by the state. Thus heresy and witchcraft were once common grounds for lawful trial with penalties not just of death, but of death by torture (e.g., by being burned at the stake, boiled in oil, or drawn and quartered).

Illegal-status offenses are such attributes as a specific ancestry or ailment for which, at some times and in some places, courts could impose penalties. These court actions are illegal in the United States. Among the clearest and most flagrant modern examples of status crimes were those under the Nuremberg Laws of Nazi Germany, which made it a crime to have Jewish ancestry. It often is alleged that being black or poor results in greater or more frequent punishment for crime in the United States, because charges and penalties reflect prejudice in the police or a judge. Such bias, of course, is unlawful, and our hope and belief is that it is diminishing. In most states, being of juvenile age makes one subject to lawful punishment by a juvenile court for truancy from school or home or for "incorrigibility" (being persistently disobedient to parents, teachers, or other adult authority). These are called "juvenile-status offenses" because persons past the juvenile age limit, usually 18, may no longer be lawfully punished for them. In this case, of course, it is not the status of juvenile that is punished, but an act of truancy or incorrigibility committed by a juvenile.

In 1962 the United States Supreme Court, in *Robinson* v. *California*, made a decision of far-reaching significance by declaring that a state could not properly combat illegal consumption of narcotics by imposing penalties for narcotic addiction, since addiction is a disease —hence a status—and not a willful act. (Actually, California had ignored a 1925 ruling in the *Linder* case, in which the Supreme Court had already recognized addiction as an illness by barring prosecution of physicians for prescribing opiates to addicts suffering from opiate withdrawal [see Lindesmith, 1965: 8–12].) The *Robinson* decision, however, suggested that since addiction is a disease, the opiate addicts could be committed to a mental hospital. As Chapter 10 indicates, the civil-commitment programs for addicts that followed this decision often differed from imprisonment in name only. Furthermore, although addiction was deemed a disease and not a crime, possession of narcotics without special authorization was still a crime for which addicts could be prosecuted.

The variations among crimes discussed here are summarized in Table 1-1. As the next chapter shows, important differences in the history and probable future of offenses depend on whether they are predatory or nonpredatory.

TABLE 1-1   Summary of a Classification of Crimes

TYPE OF CRIME	EXAMPLES	CLEARLY VICTIMIZES UNWILLING PARTICIPANTS?	INTENT TO COMMIT THE CRIME IS NECESSARY?	IS STILL A CRIME WHEN NOT PUBLIC?
Predatory crimes:				
Willful predations	Theft; Burglary; Rape; Murder; Robbery; Kidnapping; Assault	Yes	Yes	Yes
Criminal negligence	Reckless Driving; Speeding; Careless Construction	Yes—actually or potentially	No—if careless'	Yes
Nonpredatory crimes:				
Illegal performance	Drunkenness; Nudity; Vagrancy; Disorderly conduct	Usually Not	Yes	No
Illegal selling	Narcotics peddling; Selling gambling services; Prostitution	No	Yes	Yes
Illegal consumption	Narcotics possession for use; Patronizing a prostitute	No	Yes	Yes
Disloyalty	Treason; Heresy (formerly)	Only in wartime	Yes	Yes
Illegal status (formerly)	Lawful prosecution for being of a particular ancestry or for having a particular ailment	Yes—the accused	No	Yes

TWO

WHAT CHANGES CRIMINAL LAW?

In a world changing at a more rapid rate than ever, the criminal law is also repeatedly altered, for legislators continually modify their views on what should be defined as an offense and punished by the state. A criminology that can help to anticipate and cope with the future must identify and explain the patterns in past and current changes. As Chambliss asserts: "The starting point for the systematic study of crime is not to ask why some people become criminal . . . but to ask first why it is that some acts get defined as criminal while others do not" (1974: 7). The answer to his question depends upon the type of crime and on whether one takes a short- or a long-run view of the law-generating process.

CONFLICT VERSUS
CONSENSUS EXPLANATIONS

In criminology, as in almost all social science today, some theorists contend that *conflict* among interest groups, especially those of opposing socioeconomic classes, is the main determinant of human behavior and of government policy. They present this analysis to dispute the *consensus* approaches that ascribe causation primarily to customs and norms. Those who are called consensus theorists (e.g., Talcott Parsons, Neil Smelser, S. M. Lipset) reject that label, replying that they, too, deal with conflict and change, and more validly than their critics. As is common in controversies, each side often misinterprets the other; more important to us here, is that each describes accurately only part of the reality that affects criminal law. Conflict certainly prevails in the *short run* in almost all change, but consensus develops in the *long run* about laws on predatory crime.

Most legislation in a democracy is passed only after lengthy lobbying and debate, rather than by quick agreement. Such political argument often is self-seeking, since almost every law increases the advantages of certain people and diminishes them for others. Each change in criminal statutes not only curtails or expands the freedom of some to do as they wish, but also alters the work, size, and influence of law-enforcement, adjudication, and correctional agencies. Each legal statute is likely to pass only after considerable argument among those who speak for the various interest groups it affects, and to be agreed upon only after extensive bargaining and negotiation.

Those who make concessions to rally support for legislation tend to yield only the minimum changes necessary to gain enough votes to enact their bill. This "law of minimal winning coalitions" (Gamson, 1961; Caplow, 1968: 36–38) usually prevails in legislatures and other decision-making groups because any modification of a proposal is likely to deviate from what its initiators consider optimum. Consequently, even after enactment of a statute, conflict continues because those who sought the measure still want "something stronger" and opponents wish to weaken it. Thus, change in criminal law usually is piecemeal and protracted, especially when: (1) persons of wealth or power who victimize others resist control by the law (e.g., the sellers of questionable investments or of dubious or overpriced services); (2) the behavior is inherently difficult to regulate by criminal law (e.g., drug abuse), so that there is recurrent recognition of the ineffectiveness of prior legislation and public demand for new approaches.

Despite this case for conflict as intrinsic to enactment of criminal law, it is erroneous to assume that statutes against all offenses are forever controversial. In the definition of crime, as in other aspects of social life, much consensus does develop in the long run; thus, parts of the law are never appreciably altered, while controversy simultaneously prevails on other issues. Indeed, the conflict that divides people in one period is often followed by a growing accord on the questions that were in dispute, but new sources of discord continually emerge. Thus both conflict and consensus must be considered, if society is to be comprehended realistically (see van den Berghe, 1963).

Although conflict theories describe attitudes and behavior associated with the *initiation* of almost all criminal law, we will show that: (1) consensus has been cumulative on the need to punish many long-standing types of predation; (2) conflict tends to persist (a) whenever statutes penalize a nonpredatory offense, and (b) whenever the criminal law is extended to hitherto unpenalized types of predation. Each of these principles is valid partly because of the contrasting features of these two forms of offense, but more because of their different relationship to changes in societies.

SOCIAL EVOLUTION, CLASS, AND PREDATORY CRIMES

Four main processes of evolution are usefully distinguished in the history of modern societies: differentiation, inclusion, adaptive upgrading, and value generalization (Parsons, 1971). Although often interrupted or even reversed, in recent years they have been occurring at an increasingly rapid rate in the United States and many other countries. All four greatly affect the definition of crime. Differentiation and inclusion most directly influence predations. The other two processes we shall examine later in this chapter, when we discuss nonpredatory offenses.

Differentiation is the development of new roles and units of organization in society, the new ones generally having more special-

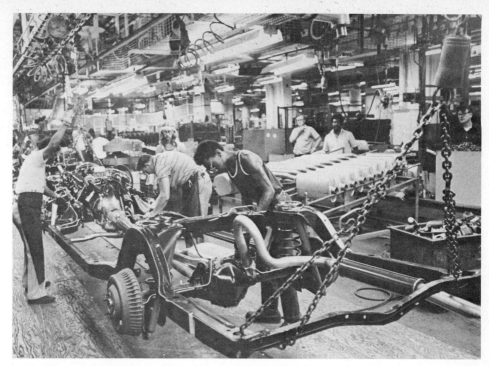

The age of specialization.

ized functions than those that preceded them. It is this process that the classic social-science works of Adam Smith (1776) and Emile Durkheim (1893) called "the division of labor."

Most contemporary organizations seem to have evolved in a long chain of successive differentiations from the extended family or kinship group. As technology develops, factories and schools assume production and education functions previously performed in the homes, and courts are established to settle disputes and to impose punishments. Comparisons of societies that are very diverse in organizational complexity suggest that: (1) institutions for religious worship and for government supplement kinship groups quite early in any series of differentiations; (2) if specialization in production of goods and services follows and trade increases, barter ultimately is replaced by some form of money, requiring financial organizations and permitting even more specialized types of business to evolve; (3) courts, police, and legal counsel accompany or soon follow financial organizations if increasing differentiation occurs (Freeman & Winch, 1957; Schwartz & Miller, 1964).

The rate of societal change in industrialized nations has been exponential, for each new specialization stimulates others. In most fields, the fastest changes occurred in the last few decades, as is readily evident in the increase of organizations, subunits within organizations, and specialized roles in education, agriculture, manufacture, selling, banking, medical care, and almost all other major institutional functions.

Technological inventions, as in the mechanization of farming and automation of industrial and clerical work by computer-controlled labor-saving devices, are the primary sources of differentiation in organizations and roles. A classic principle in economics, however, is that the division of labor depends upon the ability of the market to exchange what each produces. Therefore, rapid change requires a concentration of population or good transportation or both. Proliferation and improvement of automobiles, roads and airplanes, plus the growth of urbanized regions, have been major factors in the increasingly rapid differentiation of American society, and in consequent changes of criminal law.

Cumulative growth in the variety of predatory acts declared criminal is due largely to the cumulative nature of technological change and social differentiation. For example, the crimes of check forgery, embezzlement, and stock manipulation were impossible until the development of modern financial institutions and accounting systems. And, of course, one could not be charged with auto theft or airplane hijacking until the auto and the airplane were invented.

New inventions, occupations, or social organizations can provoke conflict whenever they shift wealth or power to new classes at the expense of those previously dominant. Therefore, new differentiations are frequently impeded by those with a vested interest in the status quo. Thus feudal and quasi-feudal landowners restricted the rise of independent businesses, professions, and skilled trades—and hence the rights and influence of a growing middle class—in seventeenth- and eighteenth-century Western Europe and in nineteenth- and twentieth-century Eastern Europe. This type of constraint was a major cause of revolutions there in these periods, and continues to provoke revolts in the developing countries.

Monopolies and cartels in restraint of trade have repeatedly blocked differentiation, at the expense of the general standard of living, in much of twentieth-century Western Europe and the United States. Although they presumably diminish somewhat after each period of intensive "trustbusting," they have impressive regenerating capacities. Today, huge new multinational corporations make the control of predatory pricefixing and of the machinations of the military-industrial complex continuing challenges for government; these control problems perhaps require international criminal law, adjudicated and enforced by multinational organizations.

Criminal legislation in the future probably will, like past laws, only be enacted as the result of backing from coalitions of interest groups with quite diverse objectives. Thus in 1906, the first law requiring federal inspection of meatpacking for cleanliness and freedom from disease was drafted and promoted by lobbyists for the largest packing firms. They wanted this government supervision not for the sake of American meat consumers, who also were demanding it, but because: (1) the overhead cost of having a federal inspector monitor operations would be less per pound of meat processed at a large plant than at a small one, thus giving the large firms a competitive advantage over the smaller ones; and (2) inspection, by guaranteeing quality, would promote the sale of American meat in foreign markets, a field pursued mainly by the larger firms (Chambliss, 1974: 16–18). In this instance, then, those who selfishly were concerned only with their profits and those who altruistically worked to protect the public from tainted meat had a common legislative goal; thus it is inappropriate that some historians regard this Federal Meat Inspection Act as purely a "triumph of conservatism" (Kolko, 1963: 98–108).

There are numerous other such examples of "strange bedfellows" in politics. Thus, in many countries and some states that remained "dry" after the Prohibition Amendment was repealed, some politicians advocating continuation of laws against the sale of alcoholic beverages were allegedly supported not only by the Woman's Christian Temperance Union, but also by bootleggers who could profit from illegal sales only while legal sales were barred. As Chapter 9 points out, gun-control advocates and gun manufacturers teamed in opposition to the National Rifle Association when seeking bans on the importation of foreign guns.

Differences in the power of various social groups to influence the government are always reflected in laws against predatory crimes, for these statutes are derived from laws on *torts*, which deal with the rights of victimized parties to sue for compensation from those who injure their persons or property (Hindelang, 1976: 1–4). Laws punishing predations enlist the state not just as arbiter of private suits, but also as advocate and punisher for one side, the side with more impact on government policy. The elite are almost always the first to get acts that injure them punished by the state, and thus to make these torts become crimes.

As Marx stressed, changes in economic production and trade that create new differentiations alter the relative power of socioeconomic classes, and hence determine who are the elites. In the middle ages, class differences were explicit in European law: for assaults and property offenses by commoners against the nobility or the clergy, the statutes prescribed severer punishment, usually corporal or capital, than for the same predations committed against commoners by members of these two highest-status classes. The British decrees on theft in the fifteenth and sixteenth centuries, however, increasingly reflected the influence of the rising capitalist class (or, bourgeoisie), for as commerce and industry grew this class gained power and that of the hereditary aristocracy diminished. These new laws protected employers rather than employees, and retail merchants rather than their customers (Hall, 1952; Jeffery, 1957; Chambliss, 1974). With the religious Reformation and the political revolutions that followed, there occurred a marked reduction in the privileges under the criminal law given to the aristocracy and clergy but denied to members of the bourgeoisie.

The rise in power of the middle classes was an early aspect of the evolutionary process of *inclusion*—growth in the proportion of a society that influences and benefits from its government. This process develops at an irregular rate, with frequent halts or reversals, depending on the unity and militancy of the conflicting groups. Inclusion is exemplified by: (1) an increase in the proportion of the population who can vote, be elected and influence democratic government (e.g., minorities, women); (2) guarantees of minimum income, medical care, and legal services to everyone; (3) any restrictions on the concentration of wealth and power through progressive-income taxes; (4) reduction of the special influence in government of those who make large political campaign contributions (by publicizing and controlling this practice, and by replacing it with government payments for campaign expenses). Most people are understandably impatient for inclusion to occur more rapidly, for much inequality persists.

As a result of the inclusion process, especially following the Great Depression, criminal law was expanded against many types of banking and investment fraud. Today's struggle is directed primarily toward increasing the public's protection from discrimination because of gender, ethnicity, or handicaps, from misrepresentation in advertising, sales, and contracts, from adulteration or other defects in merchandise, and from pollution of the environment (on these trends and their relation to the "Nader phenomenon," see Geis, 1974). Usually these measures against predation begin only as regulatory laws administered by commissions, but criminal penalties gradually increase. Such new laws are resisted by many powerful businesses, but as we noted in the example of the meat inspection bill, new statutes are occasionally backed by large corporations that can conform to restrictions at less financial loss than their smaller competitors.

Thus, concomitant with inclusion, and sometimes counteracting its accomplishments, has been the growing concentration of economic power due to the ability of large firms to absorb or eliminate smaller ones. The resulting huge conglomerates may wield political influence and maintain independence from government control, thereby creating perhaps more difficult challenges to the collective vote and organized protests of those who seek more effective penalties for polluters, careless manufacturers, and deceptive sellers. Each appreciable advance seems to be followed by new and more intensive struggles for further inclusion; although reaction sometimes occurs, slowing the rate of change for a while, consensus tends to develop on antipredation laws once they are enacted, and they seldom are repealed.

Differentiation fosters inclusion, for the more specialized businesses and occupations become, the more dependent each is on the reliability of performance by others. This interdependence creates a cumulative consensus on the need to combat predation; therefore, statutes that define victimizing acts as crimes are rarely rescinded (except when they are reformulated by new codifications of old laws). Thus, out of conflict in passing laws against predations come accord on retaining them and gradually less bias in their eventual enforcement. While differentiation creates new ways in which people can be victimized (and hence seek state penalties against those who prey on them), inclusion changes the priorities for pursuing this objective, making the state concerned with a larger proportion of the victimized. In sharp contrast to the retention of laws against predations, however, is the frequent suspension of enforcement and the ultimate repeal of laws against *non*predatory behavior. Explanation of this contrast requires another look at interest groups in society, and analysis of other processes of social evolution.

SOCIAL EVOLUTION, STATUS GROUPS, AND NONPREDATORY CRIMES

The influential German sociologist Max Weber (1922/1947: 424–29; Gerth & Mills, 1946: Chapter 7) distinguished between social classes and status groups. He defined a *social class* much as Karl Marx did, as people who share the same economic interests, for example, employers are one class and employees another. A *status group*, in Weber's usage, consists of those who conceive of themselves as sharing a common basis for claiming a unique honor or prestige, such as their religion, ancestry, artistic taste, or lifestyle.

As indicated in the preceding section, laws against predations initially reflect the influence on government of people united by the same class interests. (The laws change when differentiation and inclusion alter the relative power of various social classes.) Laws against nonpredatory offenses, however, show the political influence of status groups in trying to prevent diffusion of religious preferences, tastes, moral standards, or lifestyles that challenge their own. (Changes in this influence are related to two processes of social evolution—not yet discussed—adaptive upgrading and value generalization.)

To get the government to act against nonpredatory behavior,

the concerned status group members must stir up abhorrence of this conduct especially in that segment of the public that is influential in politics. In this agitation, which Chambliss (1974) calls "the mobilization of bias," they often portray the disapproved behavior as predatory in itself or in its consequences. Thus drinking alcoholic beverages was described by Prohibitionists as a cause of assault and theft, and the use of marijuana was alleged to turn people into assassins (drawing on the etymology of "hashish," a word with the same root as "assassin"). The mobilizers of bias—whom Becker (1963) called "moral entrepreneurs" —frequently are most successful in arousing support when they propagandize people who have had little direct experience with the conduct that is condemned, for it generally is easier to provoke fear of the unknown than fear of the familiar.

Once a criminal law is enacted, a new group—the government employees assigned to its enforcement—supplements the original proponents in mobilizing support for the law. These government functionaries have a vested interest in procuring large appropriations for their agencies and power for themselves; they thus become the new moral entrepreneurs in behalf of the law (see Chambliss, 1974: 27–34).

The leaders of a law-enforcement bureaucracy have special advantages for promulgating their views because of their ready access to the heads of the executive and legislative branches of government, their ability to issue official reports and call news conferences, and their consequent control over public information on the effectiveness of the law and the need for it (see Dunbar, 1975: 24–29). Historically, the record of the federal Bureau of Narcotics (now replaced by other agencies) is a conspicuous example of an enforcement bureaucracy that engaged in extreme and sometimes legally questionable entrepreneurial activities to expand the criminal law in the drug field and hence the size of its organization and resources (see Becker, 1963: 135–46; Lindesmith, 1965: 8–21, 64–73, 243–66; Duster, 1970; Musto, 1973: Chapters 6–9).

Table 2-1 summarizes the observation that laws making preda-

TABLE 2-1   Factors in the Initiation and Perpetuation of Criminal Law

STAGE	PREDATORY CRIME	NONPREDATORY CRIME
Initiation	Elites; organized nonelite interest groups	Moral entrepreneurs who mobilize bias
Perpetuation	Cumulative consensus	Enforcement bureaucracies

tory acts criminal are usually initiated through the influence of class interest groups on government, but are perpetuated through cumulative public consensus. On the other hand, laws against nonpredatory acts are usually initiated by moral entrepreneurs who represent status groups that feel threatened by the spread of contrasting lifestyles (see Gusfield, 1963: Chapter 1), but these laws also are extended by the zealous efforts of law-enforcement bureaucrats.

Despite entrepreneurial efforts to maintain support for the condemnation of *non*predatory conduct, the variety of such lawfully punishable behavior has *diminished,* though not at a steady rate. In colonial Massachusetts the Puritans imposed criminal penalties for blasphemy and other violation of their religious code, as well as for wearing inappropriate attire, letting hair grow too long, bragging and even talking too much (Erikson, 1966: 168). State punishment for deviant religious beliefs or practices subsequently declined greatly in the Western world, but the "Blue Laws" that banned most business and much recreation on Sundays in Pennsylvania and elsewhere in the United States were not repealed until around the middle of the twentieth century. During the 1920s and 1930s at some American beaches, males were arrested for baring their chests, and nothing nearly so exposing as a bikini was permitted for females. But in the second half of this century, there has been rapid growth in the law's tolerance of bodily exposure and of the display of sexual intimacies in films and other mass media.

Government reaction to much nonpredatory behavior—especially to illegal selling and consuming—tends to go through a cycle from permissiveness to prohibition to a renewed permissiveness, but usually under licensing or other regulation. Thus for most of its first 150 years, despite scattered local temperance statutes and ordinances, the United States had no widespread restrictions on the use of alcoholic beverages. But in 1919 the Eighteenth Amendment prohibited such use. This law, repealed fourteen years later by the Twenty-first Amendment, was followed by licensing laws to regulate manufacturers and sellers, and by age and sobriety requirements for purchasers. Our federal government was largely permissive toward opiate use until the Harrison Act of 1914 and toward marijuana until 1937, but then greatly increased the severity of penalties on both types of drug during the 1950s. However, in the late 1960s, marijuana penalties were reduced in many states and much use of methadone, a synthetic opiate, was authorized. Similarly chaotic in their historic shifts have been antigambling and antiprostitution laws: prostitution was formerly licensed in many parts of the United States and is currently legal on a county-option basis in Nevada; gambling has long been lawful in Nevada and is increasingly being legalized in other states.

Nonpredatory conduct—such as using narcotics, gambling, engaging in extramarital sex, violating religious taboos (the Sunday "Blue Laws"), being vagrant, and dressing atypically—becomes criminal when offended status groups gain state backing in their efforts to impose their standards of conduct and taste on others. For example, the now-repealed Prohibition Amendment and most of our laws against prostitution and gambling reflect primarily the organized political efforts of some Anglo-Saxon Protestants to enforce their standards on the descendants of later immigrants to the United States. More of the later immigrants were Catholics of Irish or Eastern and Southern European descent, from countries where drinking, prostitution, and gambling were more widely tolerated (on Prohibition, see Sinclair, 1962; Gusfield, 1963).

Frequently, less than a majority of the voters succeeds in having its standards of nonpredatory conduct enacted into law. This was the case, for example, with the Prohibition Amendment, whose effective supporters were well-organized, wealthy, and influential. Sometimes the penalized conduct is behavior, such as gambling, that the wealthy themselves indulge in, but consider a problem for people of limited means; they accept it for those able to attend the race track or with money to invest in the stock market, but wish to prohibit it at off-track locations.

The inclusion process, whereby a wider range of citizens affects the success of political office seekers, not only fosters laws against predations by the elite, but also reduces the power of status groups with few but influential members to impose their tastes on the majority. Drug abusers, for example, were not numerous or influential in the United States when laws against them were strengthened during the 1950s and most of the 1960s. But this situation was reversed with respect to marijuana, for by the 1970s a majority of high-school and college students in many states had tried this drug and were a rapidly growing segment of the electorate. A poll of college and high-school students shows much more consensus on the seriousness of predatory than of nonpredatory crimes, but their consensus on toleration of marijuana use increases with age (Chilton & DeAmicis, 1975). The current and prospective voting power of youth doubtless fosters the already-cited trend of decriminalizing marijuana. The repeal of many laws that define nonpredatory conduct, however, also reflects a third evolutionary process—adaptive upgrading—that is largely a consequence of the two already discussed, differentiation and inclusion.

Adaptive upgrading refers to the more efficient and effective organizations and roles that are consequences of differentiation and, usually, of an increased average education of the populace. New ways of doing things tend to survive only if they are more capable of achieving desired objectives. In most economic pursuits, the enterprises and occupations that flourish are usually those producing at a lesser cost per unit or performing new and demanded functions. These are therefore the most profitable (whether in a capitalist or other economy). In education, and in many other services, it sometimes is debatable whether quality of performance and profitability are correlated, since the units produced are hard to measure. In any case, as society becomes more technologically advanced and more interdependent, a higher average level of education is required of the general population.

With increase in education there tends to develop a more objective, analytic, dispassionate, and secular reaction to much—though not all—deviant behavior. Therefore, as the public becomes more educated it is usually more willing to reassess punishments that do not reduce the behavior they are directed against. The fruitlessness of penalties is especially evident in statutes against those nonpredatory acts that have only voluntary and private participants and hence are rarely discovered by the police. Moreover, when some form of illegal nonpredatory conduct is widespread, the unpopularity and unenforceability of laws against it and the profit of organized crime in catering to it foster corruption of criminal-justice officials. These conditions evoked support for the repeal of Prohibition and for legalization of gambling from more secular persons, even those who did not drink or wager.

Value generalization, the fourth process of social evolution, is an additional factor in reducing laws against nonpredatory conduct, for it modifies ideas of good and bad to make them more compatible with the increased variety of people and lifestyles in organizations and roles. This process leads to less concern with judging people by specific conduct—their speech, apparel, or music and cinema preference—and to more stress on general moral principles, such as honesty and dependability in meeting obligations. Thus tolerance of diversity develops as long as others are not victimized by it.

Value generalization occurs because differentiation, by placing humans in more diverse roles and organizations, makes them deal more with strangers and become dependent upon a larger number of other specialists. It is also fostered by the greater concentration of the population in urban areas, their extensive travel for work, shopping, and recreation, and the tremendous increase in college attendance, all of which brings strangers together. The mass media, especially television, are also factors in value generalization, since they make people with deviant behavior standards—"weird" dressers, homosexuals, prostitutes, drug abusers, and others—much more familiar to the larger population than ever before. Through television, especially in the "talk shows," they enter the homes of millions of people and are revealed as having ordinary human qualities. Consequently, support of criminal law on nonpredatory offenses has declined from the intensity illustrated by the burning of heretics in the middle ages, to our current slowly growing and still quite incomplete consensus on letting people "do their own thing" as long as no one else is hurt by it.

This slow shift in the law's focus, from nonpredatory crimes to predations and torts, was referred to by Durkheim (1893) as a change from "repressive" to "restitutive" law. When there is relatively small specialization of roles, he pointed out, people have similarity in norms and a sense of common identity that make them intolerant of deviation from the prevailing customs. Societies in this condition have what he called a "mechanical solidarity" that is manifest in their uniform outrage at deviance and in their cruel—thus "repressive"—punishments (e.g., not just execution, but killing by slow torture on the rack, drawing and quartering, burning at the stake). As societies develop greater division of labor—Durkheim's term for differentiation—their roles and norms become more diverse, and their specialization creates an interdependence among the members that he called "organic solidarity."

With this interdependence, Durkheim observed, there is more stress on laws for obtaining restitution from those who fail to meet their obligations—hence more tort law—and less stress on severity of punishment for most crimes. But as was indicated here (following Hall, 1952, and others), with growth in differentiation tort law on compensation for damages is increasingly supplemented by laws on predatory crime that bring the state into more of what were previously private disputes. From the standpoint of most ethical systems, but especially in a highly interdependent urban society, a predator's stealing property for which others must work, or suppressing the liberty or comfort of others by assaulting them—or, in the extreme, destroying life—gives these crimes a difference from nonpredatory offenses that may also account for their increasingly different history in the criminal law. However, with adaptive upgrading and value generalization the penalties for all offenses tend to be more oriented to changing the behavior of offenders, rather than simply making offenders suffer for the sake of affirming the punisher's morality.

With these social trends, factual questions are more frequently raised in assessing laws on nonpredatory crime, such as those on gambling, narcotics, and disorder in public gatherings (as in rock-music festivals or demonstrations by political dissidents). The arguments are now stressed in terms of expediency: they point out the financial costs, the predatory crime, the violation of rights, and stimulation of riots that often result from enforcement efforts, and the failure of these efforts to reduce the prohibited behavior. The questions thus raised include: Does the cost to society of unsuccessful attempts at enforcement exceed the social damage from the behavior that the law seeks to suppress? Can methods of public health and education be more effective than a law-enforcement emphasis in lessening the social damage from widespread nonpredatory conduct that the law has called criminal? How do the two approaches compare in cost?

FROM ABSOLUTE TO PRAGMATIC MORALITY IN PUBLIC POLICY

The focus on social costs and benefits as policy guides, a perspective ascribed to value generalization, represents a shift from *moral absolutism* to *moral pragmatism.* These terms are approximations of Weber's *Wertrationalität* and *Zweckrationalität* (1922/1947: 115). Moral absolutism is the justification of policy by uncompromising assertions on the sacredness of a particular value. Contrastingly, moral pragmatism is the guidance of policy by considerations of multiple values; it is a somewhat flexible and pluralistic perspective that creates the possibility of serving all of one's values to some degree, rather than rigidly insisting on maximum adherence to a single value.

When efforts to abolish a type of behavior are unsuccessful or create conditions that violate other values, the pragmatic person may endeavor to impose restrictions that are less severe than complete prohibition. These may reduce the social costs of an unenforceable prohibition, yet remain sufficiently restrictive to reduce social damage from the vice. In this fashion our government put large criminal organizations out of bootlegging by repealing the Eighteenth Amendment; but local authorities still regulate liquor use by licensing dealers, penalizing drunken driving, and barring sale of alcoholic beverages to minors or to persons already intoxicated. Similarly, between proponents of complete prohibition and opponents of all restrictions on narcotics are advocates of the sale of slow-acting synthetic opiates (e.g., methadone) —or even of morphine or heroin—but only under medical supervision, on a conditional basis, and just to addicts for whom prior rehabilitation efforts have failed (discussed more fully in Chapter 10).

The research orientation implicit in moral pragmatism does not yet permeate our thinking on what should be defined as crime, but whenever it prevails there is greater prospect of reaching consensus through the accumulation of evidence than when debate is rooted in assertion of values alone. For example, during the 1973 gasoline shortage due to an Arab boycott, emergency legislation defined illegal speeding as exceeding 55 miles per hour. As soon as the shortage eased, there was a strong movement to raise it back to 65 miles per hour or higher. The accumulation of evidence that a sharp drop in accidents occurred with the lower limit, however, created a predominant consensus for its retention; although drivers frequently exceed the lower limit, they drive more slowly than they did with a higher speed limit to exceed. On the other hand, conflict remains intense on whether complete nudity should be declared noncriminal on specified "clothing optional" beaches, for few facts have been used in these arguments, only speculations on psychological effects and on the morality of bodily exposure.

Debate on how criminal behavior should be punished also shifts more readily from value to factual questions with moral pragmatism than with moral absolutism. With this shift, questions of the desirability of particular penalties evoke research on their efficacy rather than just emotional support or opposition. In this spirit, for example, in a controlled experiment in Utah juvenile courts, different punishments were imposed on comparable groups of reckless-driving offenders. This experiment demonstrated conclusively that those required to write an essay on the problem (and not just copying something by rote) had fewer subsequent accidents than those given more conventional penalties (Mecham, 1968). Systematic experimentation with alternative sanctions for this or other offenses has been relatively infrequent, but with the growth of a pragmatic moral orientation one can expect such research to increase (see Glaser, 1973).

If education and medical aid prove more effective than punishment in regulating some forms of drug abuse, this finding may cause government to transfer its response to drug consumption from criminal justice to education and health agencies. Such a transfer has already occurred in many localities where detoxification centers operated by medical, social-work, and ex-alcoholic paraprofessionals replace jails for persons found drunk in a public place. These centers may be justified factually as (1) costing the public less per drunk than the police, courts and jails spend in traditional processing of public intoxication as a misdemeanor, and as (2) more effective in reducing further public drunkenness. Facts, of course, are supplemented by assessment of the public health approach from the standpoint of values—for example, as being more humane.

POLITICAL CRIMES AND PRAGMATIC VALUES

The standards for calling political dissent a crime strikingly distinguish the laws and practices of countries having representative government from those that do not. For example, in Northwestern Europe and in the United States and Canada, there routinely is tolerated a criticism of officials and of government policies which, in totalitarian countries, is punished as disloyalty to the state.

This difference in conceptions of political expression as crime results from a contrast between the basic value indoctrinations of democratic and totalitarian countries. But proponents of both systems defend their approach not only through appeals to abstract values, but also through alleged empirical consequences for economy and security. Citizens loyal to a totalitarian regime point to the virtues of quick decision making and to what they claim is a national consensus. They argue that what they presume is mass contentment with their regime compensates for the suffering imposed on dissidents. Citizens of political democracies, however, believe that greater social benefits ultimately result from their open voicing of disagreement, and that public debate and voting are more rational, orderly, and beneficial methods of changing government policies and leaders.

Another factually grounded argument for the Western system of tolerating political diversity is that there has never been a war between two countries in which even a quarter of the citizens—half the males—could freely participate in elections with secret ballots and a choice among candidates for the top legislative or executive offices of their government (Babst, 1964, 1972). Britain, for example, warred with France and with the United States only before 1832, the year the Great Reform Act finally gave voting rights to most men in Britain. Subsequent broadening of the electorates in democracies, so that men and women, minorities and dominant ethnic groups, and young and old can vote, appears to have further reduced any risk of warfare between countries with free elections.

There have, however, been civil wars within democracies, often when large segments of the citizenry would not assent to majority rule or claimed that elected officials did not represent the majority. Central to the prevention of civil wars or revolutions are freedom of political expression, increasing equality of opportunity to enhance individual status, and integration of ethnic, religious, or political minorities into the total society. With a well-established democratic election process, revolutions become impossible because they are made unnecessary; the elected officials either change their policies or are voted out of office in response to popular discontent before unrest gives revolutionary efforts prospects of success.

To have and to hold a firmly established democracy, the only acts that should be called political crimes and subject to prosecution and punishment are those of obstructing free expression of opinion, and of corrupting or impeding constitutional election, adjudication, legislation, or administration procedures.

POLITICAL CYCLES AND THE DEFINITION OF CRIME

In periods of rapid change, one finds the most intense feelings of discontent in a society, for change brings a variety of stresses, as does stagnation in defective practices and arrangements. *Liberalism* can be defined as a desire to accelerate change, especially to hasten diffusion of social benefits to those most deprived, and to foster tolerance of any nonpredatory deviance. In its more extreme form—the demand for rapid and drastic alteration of the social system—this perspective is labeled *radicalism.* On the other hand, *fundamentalism* is an extreme "resistance to value generalization" (Parsons, 1971:100); it is an appeal for restoration of the older, more specific conduct norms, for going back to the legendary "good old days." In more moderate form—calling mainly for a slower rate of change—it is called *conservatism.* Ambrose Bierce (1906) wryly defined a conservative as "a statesman who is enamoured of existing evils, distinguished from the Liberal, who wishes to replace them with others."

As indicated earlier, differentiation usually creates stress for members of established organizations who see some or all of their functions taken over by newer and more specialized social units. Inclusion creates stress for members of hitherto advantaged groups who see persons of lower class or status gaining influence and becoming more competitive with them in income or other benefits. Therefore, the two main exponents of conservatism are (1) those with a vested interest in older arrangements and (2) those accustomed to a relatively higher status than groups beginning to rise. In the past few decades in the United States, the first group consisted disproportionately of small businessmen who could not compete with chain stores or other large corporations; the second group included the white "rednecks" and "hardhats" who could no longer look down so readily on blacks, Mexican-Americans, and other minorities.

Liberalism evokes support from those who will benefit from new differentiation and inclusion, and from their sympathizers. Those who are deprived become especially impassioned when promised improvements do not materialize as rapidly as they had expected. They suffer what sociologists call "relative deprivation"—having less than they have come to expect, even if more than they formerly had. Therefore, it is often in periods that historically give lower-status groups their most rapid rates of advancement that they become most intensely militant.

This paradox, sometimes called the "revolution of rising expectations," occurs because dramatic shifts from a traditional and stable denial of equal opportunity arouse visions of the possibility of full equality. Thus in the 1960s, a decade of major urban race riots, much more intense discontent was manifest among American blacks than in the 1920s or the 1940s when their rights compared with those of whites were much less. However, the Supreme Court decisions and civil-rights bills of the 1950s evoked expectations of equality—Dr. Martin Luther King's "I have a dream!"—that were much slower in materializing than many had anticipated.

What are the implications of these political cycles for criminal law? Conservatism is associated with demands for the punishment of a larger variety of conduct (including nonpredatory deviance) and for repressive penalties (including a greater use of capital punishment), characteristic of less differentiated societies. By contrast, the response of liberalism to crime tends to be less rigidly punitive—stressing, for example, psychological services for offenders alleged to be mentally ill and job training for property offenders from economically deprived groups. This contrast was shown by the vote on two propositions on the 1972 ballot in California, one to restore capital punishment and the other to decriminalize marijuana possession for personal use. Apparently any person who voted for one measure would almost always vote against the other. (Votes on these two measures by precinct had a negative correlation beyond 0.9.) Only in the state's most liberal county, San Francisco, was the marijuana proposal passed and the capital-punishment measure defeated (Johnson & Newmeyer, 1975). (Three years later the legislature reduced marijuana penalties to a fine for amounts under one ounce.)

Neither liberal nor conservative reactions are always highly rational and scientific: both may have no objective evidence on which policy is most effective in reducing crime, and both are often emotional responses that intensify whenever there is a general discontent with society. All proposals on defining or controlling crime elicit both liberal and conservative reactions (for elaboration on this, see Miller, 1973). Most units of government—local, state, and national—seem to have cycles of liberal and conservative domination, with elements of each always present. In general, conservatives tend to favor rigid legal rules on offenses and mandatory penalties, but liberals seek primarily what Kadish and Kadish (1973) call a "checks and balances" legal system in which some law violations are tolerated if they do not seriously hurt anyone.

The difficulty of suppressing crime is so great that there are often marked swings by the public and its leaders from one position to another on criminal-justice policies, in reaction to the failure of a liberal or a conservative program to eliminate high-crime rates or unusually heinous offenses. Indeed many leaders, as well as the public at large, tend to be unstable or inconsistent with respect to criminal-justice issues, as is evident from public-opinion polls showing frequent shifts in support of or opposition to both capital punishment and psychological treatment programs. Greater public consensus, or at least increased objectivity in the expression of disagreement, may perhaps be reached by separating the types of issues involved in discussions of what should be called crime.

SUMMARY AND CONCLUSION

Laws against predatory acts originate in conflict among classes and other interest groups; but once they are enacted, extensive consensus

Table 2-2 Summary of Effects of Social Change on Criminal Lawmaking

ASPECT OF CHANGE	DISTINGUISHING FEATURES	SOCIAL EFFECTS	EFFECTS ON CRIMINAL LAWMAKING
Evolutionary Processes:			
Differentiation	Occupations and organizations become more specialized and diverse in function.	Greater interdependence of all components of society, and ultimately of all humanity.	Creates new methods of victimizing that first evoke desire for vengeance, then tort action, then accumulate as predatory crimes because victim's class can procure aid from the government.
Inclusion	More persons and groups gain influence on and hence benefit from government action.	Less actual deprivation but more relative deprivation and more public demand for change.	Lower-class power growth leads to increases in state penalties for those who victimize them.
Adaptive upgrading	Productivity per capita and average person's knowledge and training rise.	More public sophistication on other cultures; more scientific policies.	More stress on prevention, rehabilitation, and research on effectiveness in policies on crime; less stress on severe penalties as reaction to crime.
Value generalization	General values are stressed more and specific norms less in assessing personal conduct.	Greater tolerance of cultural diversity; more stress on honesty and consideration as values.	Decline in the variety of nonpredatory acts declared criminal; less emphasis on punishment and more on humaneness in state reaction to both criminals and their victims.
Poles of political cycles:			
Conservatism (fundamentalism)	Seeks to slow down or reverse value generalization and inclusion.	Creates discontent by ignoring inequities and strain in class deprivations.	Seeks return to more severe punishments and criminalization of more types of nonpredatory deviance.
Liberalism (radicalism)	Seeks to accelerate value generalization and inclusion.	Creates discontent in those losing relative status or maladapted to changes.	Seeks less stress on punishment, more criminalization of corporate predation against the poor, and decriminalization of nonpredatory acts.

TWO   WHAT CHANGES CRIMINAL LAW?

develops across class lines, making them become cumulative. Much more recurrent conflict occurs over criminal laws on nonpredatory behavior. Indeed, it is much easier with these crimes—such as prostitution, homosexuality, and narcotics offenses—to demonstrate that deviance is not inherent in the "deviant" acts, but varies with the audience that classifies the acts (Becker, 1963: 9).

All nonpredatory crimes are derived from concepts of abstract morality, from acts regarded as vices and sins even when they are not torts; predatory crimes are all derived from concepts of tort, of damage done to another. Nonpredatory crimes do not directly injure anyone, but may be perceived by certain status groups as affronts to their religion, their standards of sexual morality, the importance they attach to work, thrift, or family, or any other norm or value that they stress. Nonpredatory offenders are not publicly charged with doing tangible injury to others so much as accused of setting bad examples to children or to others who might be tempted to join or imitate them in deviant conduct. Only relatively late in legal history did deliberate injury to persons or property not of the ruling nobility legally warrant punishment by the state rather than by friends or relatives of the victims. But state penalties for nonvictimizing crimes, especially religious heresy, are very ancient.

As indicated in Table 2-2, *differentiation*, a process of social evolution resulting from technological innovation, is the creation of more specialized roles and organizational units and hence of greater interdependence among people. It thereby increases the variety of victimizing acts—predations—that the law declares criminal. *Inclusion* is the winning of influence and benefits from government by a larger proportion of the population; hence it expands criminal law against those who victimize the poor. Often independently of this process, however, moral entrepreneurs repeatedly mobilize bias against nonpredatory behavior they view as deviant, thereby promoting a shift from permissiveness to prohibition in the criminal law, and creating enforcement bureaucracies that continue to foster bias. *Adaptive upgrading* and *value generalization* are evolutionary processes in modern societies that increase the public's tolerance for diversity in belief and lifestyle. These processes promote change to the mere regulation of the prohibited forms of nonpredatory conduct, or to the total abolition of government restrictions on it.

From these trends, policy on crime is increasingly determined by a pragmatic multiple-value orientation rather than by absolute moralities, especially on nonpredatory offenses. Disagreements, therefore, more often raise purely factual questions that can be resolved by research. Such a rational resolution of differences is also enhanced by the elimination of laws against the expression of deviant beliefs, and by the enforcement of laws against interference with democratic political procedures.

SUMMARY AND CONCLUSION

As is also shown in Table 2-2, fundamentalism, the extreme resistance to value generalization, and its more moderate form, conservatism, impede efforts to change criminal law on nonpredatory conduct. Conversely, radicalism, or its more moderate form, liberalism, accelerate change. Because stresses result from both change and stability, most societies tend to oscillate between liberal and conservative domination.

THREE

WHEN IS A CRIME NOT A CRIME?

Central to the spirit of the eighteenth-century Enlightenment—the Age of Reason—was the proposition that all people are capable of rational thought and therefore have certain natural rights, such as equality before the law. This concept, identified notably with Montesquieu and Voltaire in France and John Locke in England, appealed to the growing middle classes in their economic and political struggles with the nobility, struggles that were part of the inclusion process of social evolution described in Chapter 2. The goal of equality in legal rights, although never completely attained, inspired such proclamations as our Declaration of Independence and the French Declaration of the Rights of Man.

This equalitarian thought spurred three changes in criminal justice. The first reduced ambiguity in the law. In earlier centuries, for people of all social classes, "crimes were ill defined . . . and judges exercised arbitrary powers to convict and punish for acts not legally defined as crimes at all. No one could be sure at any time that he might not be charged with such an act" (Radzinowicz, 1966: 2). The second change lessened or abolished criminal sentences for dissent (e.g., atheism, heresy, witchcraft, or criticism of the government). The third increased equality before the law, in contrast to prior exemption of the nobility from severe punishment in many offenses for which commoners received cruel corporal and capital penalties.

Abuses attacked during the Enlightenment prevailed more in Continental Europe than in Britain, where important criminal justice reform began with Magna Charta in 1215, when local areas gained some independence from the king's judges. Yet when these areas had their own gentry in judicial roles, practices such as those on the Continent often persisted. Indeed, throughout Western Europe, the growth of fairness in the courts has been sporadic and at times has even been reversed. Knowledge of the trends of the past few hundred years facilitates an understanding of developments still in progress.

CRIME AND REASON

By far the most influential person in changing European legal systems —including that of Britain and thereby of the United States—was a remarkable Italian nobleman named Cesare Beccaria. In 1764, when only 26 years old, he published anonymously in Italy a small book entitled *Dei delitti et delle pene* (*Of Crimes and Punishments*). It was promptly published throughout Europe in translations, and most of these were quickly reprinted in numerous editions.

Beccaria's effort to hide the authorship of his book was unsuccessful. His fears of denunciation by conservatives and of attempts to prosecute him proved well founded, but he was protected by liberal rulers. He had become a hero to many prominent advocates of reform throughout the Continent and Britain, as well as in the British colonies in America. Fame led to honors in many cities of Europe and to a professorship in his native Milan. In the fantastically versatile thirty remaining years of his life, he invented a metric system of measurement, wrote a treatise on demography that anticipated Malthus, expounded economic theory as an Italian Adam Smith, and founded one of the first schools of veterinary medicine (Maestro, 1973).

Of Crimes and Punishments was influential because, in brief and logical prose, Beccaria clearly argued the case against an arbitrary, cruel, and overreaching criminal-justice system. He wanted the types of behavior that were declared criminal to be limited to the minimum that is absolutely essential for assuring the greatest happiness to the greatest number of people. He pointed out, far ahead of his time, that an excessive number of prohibitions often provoke more crime than they prevent. He called for a criminal law that, in contrast to the prevailing one, would be clearly and unambiguously expressed in writing, and not readily modified by judges; in effect, he implied today's basic legal principle of *nulla poena sine lege*—no punishment without a law.

He insisted that "the great and rich should not have any advantage over the less fortunate" in the criminal courts. This is a principle honored more often as precept than as practice, but much less flagrantly now than in Beccaria's time. His essay covered many other topics, such as the presumption of innocence until guilt is proved and the elimination of torture to obtain confessions.

Sir William Blackstone credited Beccaria with helping him become more critical of the criminal law. His *Commentaries on the Laws of England,* published only a year after Beccaria's essay, guided lawmaking and adjudication in most of the English-speaking world for over a century thereafter (Radzinowicz, 1966: 20). Benjamin Franklin and Thomas Jefferson read Beccaria, as did other framers of the Bill of Rights—the first ten Amendments to the Constitution of the United States—and his principles are clearly expressed in the Fourth through the Ninth Amendments.

In early nineteenth-century Britain, Jeremy Bentham, Samuel Romilly, and others in the classical school of legal philosophy (see Phillipson, 1923), espoused, as had Beccaria, the ethical principles of utilitarianism. They held that law and other public policy should strive to create the greatest happiness for the greatest number of people, so that values are dependent on presumed factual consequences rather than on sacred dogma. A criminal law based on utilitarianism, then, would be inherently moral (Gouldner, 1970: 65–71).

Classical philosophers also stressed (indeed, in their zeal, exaggerated) the capacity of all persons to guide themselves by reason and to calculate the course of action that maximizes individual happiness. Accordingly, they undertook the detailed application of Beccaria's principles, particularly that a specific penalty for each crime be set forth in writing, and that the penalty cause only sufficient pain to clearly outweigh all pleasure that the offense might bring. If such laws were enacted and enforced, they argued, no rational person would engage in lawbreaking.

In eighteenth-century Britain, well over a hundred types of crime were subject to the death penalty, but the classical school's tremendous influence reduced this number to about a dozen by the first part of the nineteenth century. Overlooked by this school, however, was the rationality of offenses by those who do not expect to be caught, as well as the irrationality of crimes by persons too aroused to comprehend the criminality of their acts.

In recognition of unusual emotional stress that sometimes causes a rational person to engage in crime, and of the fact that many people are not as rational in contemplating crime and anticipating punishment as had been assumed, a nineteenth-century neoclassical school of criminal jurisprudence was formed. It advocated some flexibility in penalties, at the discretion of judge or jury, to permit consideration of aggravating or mitigating circumstances in each case, rather than require by statute that all perpetrators of a given offense receive identical punishment. It held that some people are deficient in reasoning capacity, either permanently or in special circumstances, and should therefore have some exemption from the criminal law. This contention will now be our main concern.

NONAGE AND JUVENILE DELINQUENCY

The tenets of the classical school, which were the foundation for American criminal law, required one qualification at the outset, to which later neoclassical restrictions were added. This earliest limitation applied to children. If a young child—for example, a five- or six-year-old —damages someone's property, or finds a loaded gun and maims or even kills another, the child is not legally regarded as a criminal, for a long-established principle of *nonage* exempts persons below a certain age from responsibility for crime. This legal innocence of a young child in European and American practice goes back to Roman law. No responsibility for a criminal act was charged to a perpetrator under seven years of age; but the court could decide whether an accused person between seven and 12 had the mentality of a child or an adult and, if the latter, the punishment would be that prescribed for an adult. Later, as a result of the neoclassical emphasis on the offender rather than just the offense, the seven-year-old age limit was raised in most jurisdictions, usually to 12.

The fact that maturation is a gradual process, occurring at different rates in different individuals, is more readily acknowledged in the criminal-justice system by the twentieth-century legal concept of *juvenile delinquency* than by that of nonage. The idea of delinquency was derived from that of *dependency;* it evolved from the practice of making children wards of the state if orphaned, abandoned, or with parents incapable of caring for them. The legal authority for such government action stems from the principle of *parens patriae* (the state as parent), which was the basis for judges acting in *loco parentis* (in place of parents) to make decisions on behalf of children whose parents were unavailable or incapable of acting as parents should.

Delinquency encompasses both behavior that would be criminal if done by an adult, and certain noncriminal misconduct, such as persistent truancy from home or school and "incorrigible" disobedience of parents or teachers. A variety of other deviations from puritanical (so-called middle-class) standards of behavior was also defined as delinquency in the first juvenile-court laws, including a child's use of profanity, smoking, drinking, and loitering in public places (see Teeters & Reinemann, 1950: 41–43, 277–92; Platt, 1969).

Justifications given for establishing the legal concept of delinquency included: (1) preventing crime by dealing with the vaguely defined varieties of noncriminal juvenile misconduct believed conducive to crime; (2) reducing the stigma of criminal convictions for children; (3) permitting the courts to avoid imposing on young teenagers the prison sentences that were then mandatory for anyone convicted of felony offenses, or the jail terms required for certain misdemeanors.

Juvenile delinquency now denotes any crime committed by a child below a specified age, most often 18. Periodic revisions in most states have tried to reduce the vagueness of original legislation on the juvenile misconduct that might justify a court's depriving a child of liberty, and to increase the formality of juvenile court procedures for fact finding. Nevertheless, habitual or extensive truancy from home or school, or incorrigibility—persistent disobedience to parents or teachers—can still lead to a juvenile's being made a ward of the court and being placed in an institution or special home. Truancy and incorrigibility are known as *juvenile-status offenses,* since they can bring no penalty to an adult; after the birthday that terminates juvenile-court jurisdiction, a person may be absent from home or school and disobey parents or teachers without thereby becoming subject to penalty by the state. There has been a strong movement to divert from the criminal-justice system to purely social work agencies those children about whom the only complaints are of juvenile-status offenses, rather than of acts that would be criminal if committed by adults.

The age limit of juvenile status in 32 states and the District of Columbia was 18 as of January 1, 1972, but it was 17 in 12 states and 16 in six. Three states had one age limit for boys and an older one for girls, but such distinctions have been held unconstitutional. Some states have variations of age for different offenses. Most jurisdictions have the option of processing youths in a given age range, such as 14 to 18, either in the juvenile or the criminal court, depending on the gravity of the charge. In a dozen states, juveniles accused of murder must be tried as adults if above a certain age (often 14) (Levin & Sarri, 1974).

In a few states and in the federal judicial system, the courts may declare convicted persons between 18 and 21 "youthful offenders" rather than either juvenile delinquents or criminals. The consequences of youthful offender status are not necessarily separation from either juvenile or adult offenders so much as greater flexibility in location and duration of confinement. This status still involves a conviction and not the clear exemption from having a criminal record that often follows adjudication as a juvenile delinquent.

We have seen that the young age of some offenders may make their crimes technically not crime, through legal concepts of nonage and delinquency. The classical legal theory's justification for these exemptions from criminal charges was the claim that children have insufficient reasoning capacity to comprehend the immoral nature of their alleged offense or the implications of punishment. As one British writer observes, however: "Only someone who has never had personal dealings with children could believe that a mentally normal boy of, say, 12 is unaware that theft is an offense or is unable to restrain himself from thieving . . ." (Walker, 1969: 176). But the history of the juvenile-court movement indicates that the usual argument for creating separate courts and a separate concept of delinquency for young offenders, as well as a separate system of correctional institutions and services, was not the classical school's notion that such children lacked reason; instead, the juvenile court reflected the neoclassical school's concern for the offender as well as the offense, and the belief that special measures would reduce the prospect of juvenile offenders becoming adult criminals. When reasoning capacity is directly questioned, however, there are other types of exemption, regardless of age, from being defined a criminal.

INSANITY

In European and American legal theory, from ancient to modern times, punishment is usually premised on the view that offenders are responsible for their offenses. *Responsibility,* in this legal sense, usually implies that the persons *freely* and *knowingly* chose to commit offenses. Thus proof of guilt must include not only evidence of criminal behavior (*actus reus*) by the accused, but also that it was done willfully.

When criminal intent, or *mens rea,* is deemed absent—for example, if it is proved to the court that the accused was forced to commit the crime, or was not aware of committing it, or lacked the mental capacity to know that it was criminal—the perpetrator may be found not guilty (see Jeffery, 1967: Chapter 1; Bassiouni, 1969: 51–67). The major exception to this *mens rea* principle is in crimes of negligence, such as reckless driving that injures or kills others. Here failure to take reasonable precaution must be shown rather than intent to commit a crime.

Insanity is a legal concept that has been given diverse meanings, but it is used most consistently as lack of mental capacity to know that one's behavior is criminal. In Britain an insane person was defined by the thirteenth-century jurist Henry de Bracton as "one who does not know what he is doing"; and in the seventeenth century, by Lord Coke, as someone who loses his memory or understanding by sickness, grief, or other accident, either completely or periodically (Goldstein, 1967: 10). The predominant definition of insanity in the English-speaking world was established in 1843, however, after a British wood-chopper, Daniel M'Naghten, killed the male secretary to Prime Minister Robert Peel, mistaking him for Peel.

M'Naghten was found not guilty by reason of insanity, for it was reported in court that he had a delusion of being persecuted by Peel's Tory party, a delusion that defense counsel contended "takes away from him all power of self-control." This acquittal so outraged many British leaders that the House of Lords addressed a series of questions to the fifteen highest criminal-court judges in the land. Their collective answer, known as the M'Naghten rule, stresses that " . . . to establish a defence on the ground of insanity, it must be clearly proved that at the time of committing the act the party accused was labouring under such a defect of reason from disease of mind, as not to know the nature and quality of the act he was doing, or as not to know that what he was doing was wrong." They added that every person accused of a crime was to be presumed sane unless proved otherwise. Also, a "medical man" who has heard the evidence presented in court "may be asked, as a matter of science, whether the facts stated by the witnesses, supposing them to be true, show a state of mind incapable of distinguishing between right and wrong" (quoted in Walker, 1968: Chapter 5). This rule, known as the "right-or-wrong test," stresses cognition, the ability to know.

Psychiatrists, from the early nineteenth-century beginnings of their discipline to the present day, have insisted that to determine insanity, we must consider the total personality of the accused, including compulsive emotions and unconscious desires as well as cognition. Their complaints about the M'Naghten approach led first to its supplementation by the "irresistible-impulse" rule, whereby persons can be found not guilty by reason of insanity if their mental states make them incapable of controlling impulses to commit acts that they know to be wrong. Goldstein (1967: Chapter 5) calls this the "control test" of sanity. He notes that in some cases the evidence of inability to control criminal impulses is the suddenness with which a criminal act follows its provocation, while in others the evidence is the long-term and chronic nature of a person's mental disturbance. The irresistible-impulse conception of insanity is accepted in less than half the jurisdictions of the United States.

The dissatisfaction of psychiatrists with the M'Naghten definitions of insanity was most completely relieved by the 1954 decision of Judge David Bazelon of the U.S. Court of Appeals for the District of Columbia, in *Durham* v. *United States*. A lower court had found Monte Durham sane when it convicted him of housebreaking, for psychiatrists said they found no evidence that he could not tell right from wrong. Judge Bazelon set aside this finding because the lower court, by relying only on the M'Naghten rule, had ignored psychiatric testimony that ascribed the offense to Durham's long history of delusions and deranged behavior. Bazelon ordered that courts in the District of Columbia use what was soon called the "product rule," that defendants are not guilty by reason of insanity if their criminal acts were "the product of mental disease or defect." This approach ignores the M'Naghten question of whether the accused knows right from wrong.

As Brooks (1974: 111–12) summarizes, insanity is an "excusing condition" for a person who has committed a crime. Under M'Naghten, he says, this excuse is "I didn't know what I was doing" or "I didn't know that what I did was wrong," under the irresistible-impulse test it is "I couldn't help it," and under Durham, "I was mentally ill when I did it."

The Durham rule makes a decision on insanity depend primarily on what psychiatrists deem the basic cause of criminal conduct in each case. The supremacy given these specialists was welcomed by famed psychiatrist Karl Menninger as "more revolutionary" than the Supreme Court's school desegregation decision of the same year (quoted in Bazelon, 1974), but lawyers complained that the Durham rule was too vague, that it created an easy loophole for too many cases, and that it presumed more validity and precision of diagnosis than psychiatrists could provide (see A. A. Stone, 1975: 224–26). The Durham rule was accepted in the courts of only a few states and in some federal judicial districts.

A synthesis of the M'Naghten, Durham, and irresistible-impulse rules was prepared in 1955 by a committee of the American Law Institute, in a Model Penal Code that asserts: "A person is not responsible for criminal conduct if at the time of such conduct as a result of mental disease or defect, he lacks substantial capacity either to appreciate the criminality of his conduct or to conform his conduct to the requirements of the law"; but "the terms 'mental disease or defect' do not include an abnormality manifested only by repeated criminal or otherwise antisocial conduct." This statement covers both cognition and emotion by requiring the offender's "appreciation" rather than simply the M'Naghten rule's "knowledge" of the criminality of the act; it qualifies the Durham instruction by specifying that criminal behavior alone does not suffice as evidence of "mental disease or defect"; and its use of "conform" reflects the irresistible-impulse theme. This ALI formulation, more than any other, pleased both psychiatrists and lawyers and was widely adopted during the 1960s and 1970s; it was even endorsed by Judge Bazelon (in *United States* v. *Brawner,* 1972) as preferable to his Durham terminology.

Both court experience and experimental research have demonstrated quite conclusively that no legal rule greatly reduces the difficulties of judges and juries in determining who is not guilty because of insanity. Before the Durham decision in 1954, only 0.2 percent of all criminal cases in the District of Columbia were adjudged insane by its courts. This proportion steadily increased thereafter—peaking at 5.1 percent in 1962—but then declined to about two percent, a figure reached also in many courts operating with only the M'Naghten or the

M'Naghten and irresistible-impulse rules. The widespread increase from 0.2 to 2.0 percent was perhaps stimulated by the extensive professional debate on the Durham decision, in which psychiatrists often addressed conferences of lawyers, and by the growing public education on mental illness.

The District of Columbia's initial increase to the 5.1 percent found not guilty by reason of insanity reflected enthusiasm of some judges and most psychiatrists for the Durham decision's medical interpretation of criminal behavior. When most of the growing number of persons committed to the District of Columbia's mental hospital as criminally insane proved much less tractable and less amenable to treatment than more typical psychotic patients, the hospital's psychiatrists lost much of this enthusiasm. As advisors to the court when the question of insanity is raised, they began to interpret the Durham decision as they did the M'Naghten rules, as applicable only to persons with symptoms resembling those of the usual patients in mental hospitals (Arens, 1967; Jefferey, 1967; Arens & Lasswell, 1969).

During this post-Durham period, in a series of experiments sponsored by the Ford Foundation at the University of Chicago Law School, thirty simulated juries were paid to hear and rule on a tape recording of the Durham case testimony and argument. The jurors were recruited by random selection from lists of registered voters, thus making them fairly typical of regular juries in that area. After they heard the recording, 10 juries were instructed according to the M'Naghten rule, 10 according to the Durham instructions, and 10 according to a "No Rule" instruction: "If you believe the defendant was insane at the time he committed the act of which he is accused, then you must find the defendant not guilty by reason of insanity." The experiment was repeated with a tape recording of an incest case, and with a larger number of juries. The proportion of these experimental juries finding the accused not guilty by reason of insanity did not vary markedly or consistently with the type of instruction they received, although there was more discussion among jurors with the Durham rule and, perhaps for this reason, more of them ended up as "hung juries," unable to reach unanimity (Simon, 1967: Chapter 3).

One major reason for the failure of various instructions to reduce markedly the difficulties of juries or judges in reaching agreement on whether a person is not guilty by reason of insanity is that accused persons who most clearly manifest mental illness are never brought to trial. As a rule, only ambiguous cases reach the court. Police or prosecutors initiate charges in almost all criminal proceedings, but they refer any arrestee they consider psychotic directly to a mental hospital or clinic for examination. If the psychiatrists recommend civil commitment to a mental hospital, the case is usually not sent to the criminal court.

A second reason for ambiguity in the notion of insanity is the fact that many psychiatric symptoms—such as swings of emotion, fantasies, extreme withdrawal, and emotional "flatness"—differ from normal behavior only in degree. Third, many severe mental disturbances are not continuous, but come and go, so that an individual may appear normal at one period but abnormal a few hours, days, weeks, or months later. For this reason, psychiatrists focus on the overall behavior record of anyone they are asked to diagnose, rather than just on the behavior manifested in a brief interview. This is their defense against the charge that the interviews on which they base their advice are often shockingly brief (see Scheff, 1964, 1966; Gove, 1970).

About 15 states, including California and Pennsylvania, seek to reduce the difficulty of deciding between sanity and insanity by employing the compromise of a "diminished-responsibility" rule. Under this rule, an offense may be reclassified to permit a lesser penalty if the mental capacity of the offender is deemed to have been partially impaired at the time of the crime. Thus in California a charge of first degree murder can result in conviction for second degree murder if the thinking of the killer is believed to have been distorted by alcohol or drugs or by other source of diminished mental capacity, though not sufficiently to constitute insanity. There has been much inconsistency in applying this rule, but its supporters endorse it as alleviating the difficulty of reaching absolute decisions on sanity and as fostering continued efforts to improve the diagnosis of mental capacity (see Brooks, 1974: 200–217).

A person found not guilty by reason of insanity is usually committed to a mental hospital as criminally insane. This occurs automatically in about a dozen states, but the rest require a separate hearing to determine whether the accused still is sufficiently mentally disturbed to warrant hospitalization (Rubin et al., 1963: 507–11).

Several investigations into prior records of mental-hospital patients found that for about two-thirds, the behavior cited as the basis for hospitalization included criminal acts (Miller & Kenney, 1966; Levine, 1970; Blankenship & Singh, 1976). Goffman (1961: 133–34) observes:

> The case histories of most mental patients document offenses. . . .Often there is also a record of some *complaint*. . . . Here is the *social* beginning of the patient's career, regardless of where one might locate the psychological beginning of his mental illness.
>
> The kinds of offenses which lead to hospitalization are felt to differ in nature from those which lead to other extrusory consequences—to imprisonment. . . . But little seems known about these differentiating factors; and when one studies actual commitments, alternate outcomes frequently appear to have been possible. It seems true, more-

over, that for every offense that leads to an effective complaint, there are many psychiatrically similar ones that never do. . . .

In interviewing experienced police officers Blankenship (1968) found that all referred some of their arrestees to mental-health agencies rather than to criminal prosecution. They based these decisions on what they regarded as illogical responses to their questions, unrestrained or unfocused aggression, or deviant sexuality. Often, however, the decision of police or prosecutors on whether to channel arrestees into criminal or mental-health facilities seems a matter of convenience or of response to pressures from complainants or from friends or relatives of the accused. The victims of crime demand penalties for the offenders, and those sympathetic to the accused urge a mental-health commitment.

Increasingly, complaints have been voiced against the long and arbitrary confinement of allegedly insane offenders in mental hospitals, often when they were charged with only minor crimes and not convicted of any. The most dramatic evidence of such impropriety was provided by an investigation of 967 persons committed to New York maximum security institutions as "criminally insane" and "dangerous," but released under the 1966 *Baxstrom* v. *Herold* decision that found they had been denied the protection by the Fifth and Fourteenth Amendments against being deprived of liberty "without due process of law." Upon release, the average length of their detention was 13 years. A four-year postrelease followup found only nine of the 967—barely one percent—convicted of new crimes (mostly just misdemeanors), but about half rehospitalized (mostly by immediate transfer). Of the latter, only two percent were in maximum security facilities (Steadman & Keveles, 1972). Such findings led to more formal procedures for involuntary hospitalization in many states, requiring proof that the patient is indeed dangerous, and providing for periodic rehearings on this issue (Wexler, 1976).

Psychiatrists have resisted being questioned in court on the validity of their advice on hospitalization. In 1972 Judge Bazelon, in *United States* v. *Brawner,* not only replaced his Durham rule by the ALI rule, but also ordered that to "prevent the experts from exercising undue dominance over the jury, . . . the expert . . . will be required to present the basis underlying his conclusions."

Further dramatic evidence on the unreliability of many psychiatric diagnoses was provided by the Rosenhan (1973) experiment in which eight sane people deliberately got themselves admitted, at various times, to 12 different mental hospitals. They would initially report that they had heard voices, but once hospitalized they behaved normally and reported no further symptoms. Although they received a wide variety of medications, they had scant other staff attention, but all were released in seven to 52 days (19 days in the average case) with diagnoses of schizophrenia in remission. Staff at a research-and-teaching mental hospital were then informed of these findings, and after they claimed it could not happen at their institution, they were told that at some time during the next three months one or more pseudo-patients would be among the cases they received. In this subsequent period the staff were asked to rate each new entrant's probability of being a pseudopatient. For 41 of 193 such admissions, one or more staff members expressed "high confidence" that the admittee was a pseudo, with 23 of these ratings made by at least one psychiatrist rather than by clinicians lacking an M.D. degree. However, no pseudopatient had been presented during this period.

In practice, the insanity defense tends to be used mostly for persons charged with serious crimes, such as murder or sexual assault, especially when their offenses are unusually bizarre and not readily explainable in terms of rage, greed, or lust alone. ". . . It is interesting to note that in Great Britain, where judges had less discretion in imposing the death penalty than they do in the United States, the number of murderers found insane—and so spared the gallows—dropped sharply after the death penalty was abolished" (Wilson, 1975: 187). Prominent cases in which insanity was debated, but not always granted, include the "Manson family" in California, the "Boston Strangler," and William Speck, Chicago's murderer of nurses. Such offenders may appropriately be called "quasi-insane" (Glaser, 1972: 59–62), because their criminal behavior seems inexplicable by causal theories that fit more common forms of either criminal or psychotic behavior. They also pose special problems for treatment or prognosis in either correctional or mental-health facilities.

Formerly a large proportion of mental-hospital patients had repeatedly been in jails or other correctional institutions for such misdemeanors as public drunkenness, disorderly conduct, or vagrancy. Frequently, in rural areas and small cities the choice between committing such persons to state hospitals for the mentally ill, state schools for the mentally retarded, or state farms for misdemeanants appeared to be either a matter of convenience for the sheriff who had to deliver them, or of trying another alternative when a previous measure had not eliminated the deviant conduct. There is now increased tolerance of these forms of behavior in many communities, however, and less willingness of the courts to order confinement on either criminal or mental grounds. Therefore, arrest rates for these misdemeanors declined each year in the United States during the late 1960s and 1970s. A decision to arrest, hospitalize, jail, or imprison is often the outcome of a negotiation process in which the accused, relatives of the accused, defense counsel, police, complainants, psychiatrists, prosecutor, and judge may all be involved. All participants seek a resolution of the case most favorable to their own interests and viewpoint, and each has different power to affect the outcome (Sudnow, 1965; Bittner, 1967a, 1967b; Scheff, 1968).

The basis for ascribing crime to insanity, under any of the rules that have been discussed here, need not be a judgment that the perpetrator was psychotic at the time of the offense, but rather an opinion that this person was too stupid to know right from wrong. Technically, low intelligence, commonly called mental deficiency or retardation can be grounds for a ruling of not guilty by reason of idiocy, since it is a mental defect impairing cognition. Mental retardation is seldom claimed by the defendant, but is ascribed to the accused by the prosecutor, defense counsel, or judge when proposing that the case be resolved by institutionalization for mental deficiency instead of by criminal prosecution. The practice is most common with the misdemeanors already discussed—public drunkenness, disorderly conduct, and vagrancy—but occurs also with prostitution and occasionally with felonies, particularly arson and child abuse by persons presumed to be of very low intelligence. Of course, these types of criminal behavior are not typical of those of low intelligence, but if the accused is mentally retarded this condition is readily (but probably incorrectly) blamed for the misconduct, and commitment to a mental institution follows.

Two or three percent of the American population is classified as mentally retarded by most intelligence tests, although every test is somewhat imprecise and the proportions vary greatly among different components of our society. Persons reared in homes where the adults had little schooling and speak a language other than English or an English dialect different from that taught in the schools often have difficulty both in reading examinations and in understanding oral instructions. Such problems can cause them to score poorly on intelligence tests even when they demonstrate shrewd judgments and quick minds in their everyday lives. Their test performance can be further impaired if they are not motivated to try to do well, as when they are hostile to the testers or expect to be humiliated by their score. Thus cultural traits and social processes may account for much of the variation in IQs. Nevertheless, some clearly biological factors are also evident in many cases of low intelligence. Mental retardation can occasionally occur even in the most advantaged homes with highly intelligent parents—for example, the mental retardation of a sister of the late President John F. Kennedy. This occurrence of deficient intelligence, atypical in such a family, is usually acribed to prenatal, perinatal, or infantile injuries, or to genetic variations and mutations.

Cultural and social factors interact with biological factors and may either simultaneously or separately cause the low test performance or the impression of stupidity that leads to confinement in an institution for the mentally deficient. It is especially difficult to distinguish biological from other factors in the "educable retarded" (formerly called "morons"), whose IQ is assessed as between 50 and 70. Biological defects are more probable in those now called "trainable retarded" (formerly called "imbeciles"), with IQs estimated at between 25 and 50. Organic mental deficiency is frequent in the "untrainable mentally retarded" (formerly called "idiots"), with IQs of less than 25 (for fuller discussion, see Farber, 1968: Chapter 3; Mercer, 1973).

Less than four percent of the estimated mentally retarded in the United States are institutionalized (Farber, 1968: 187), but this number is nearly 200,000, or almost as many as those confined in state prisons. About a half-million others classified as mentally retarded are in special school programs in the community. In both of these groups, many are removed from their homes or schools not when they manifest stupidity, but when charged with crime or delinquency. Classifying offenders as mentally deficient is, in many cases, an alternative to calling them delinquent or criminal. This classification can occur through a formal court finding that the accused is not guilty by reason of insufficient mental capacity to know right from wrong. But it occurs much more commonly before charges are pressed. Typically, consensus is reached among the complainants, the family or friends and defense counsel of the accused, law-enforcement officers, and prosecution or judicial personnel. All become convinced that the most constructive plan is to transfer the alleged offender to a mental-health agency rather than deal further with the case in the criminal-justice system.

It has increasingly been proposed that the insanity defense be abolished in criminal proceedings. Instead, all persons charged with crime would first be given court hearings with due-process rights to determine whether they did, in fact, commit the offense, regardless of whether or not anyone claims that they were insane when they did it (Morris, 1968; Morris & Hawkins, 1970: 176–81). If, at the time of these court hearings, the accused is unable to understand the charges, cooperate with defense counsel, or comprehend the significance of possible penalties—the current grounds for deferring trial because of mental incompetence—the court would still conduct trial-like hearings, with defense counsel provided (Burt & Morris, 1972). Only after such processes establish beyond a reasonable doubt that the accused committed the offense would the court conduct hearings on whether dangerousness or other grounds justify confining the offender or imposing rules and supervision in the community on release, with the prospect of confinement if the rules are violated. Decisions would also be made at this time, under appropriate legal statutes, on what type of agency—correctional or mental-health—should provide such confinement or supervision, and on its duration and other stipulations (see Goldstein & Katz, 1963, for an elaboration of some of the problems courts would still have even if the insanity defense were abolished). Michigan approached abolition in 1975 when it permitted juries to find an accused "guilty but mentally ill" (Rosenbaum, 1976).

Such proposals for abolition of the plea of insanity reflect (1) the ambiguity of this concept, (2) the overlap between mental health and correctional cases, (3) the more formal court proceedings and proof of dangerousness increasingly required to guarantee constitutional rights of due process before a person's liberty is removed on mental-health grounds (though proceedings are still far from ideal in many cases), and (4) the diminishing distinction between what is actually involved in punishment as a criminal and in treatment as a mental patient deemed dangerous. Even if treatment of those who are proved criminal and dangerous were identical in correctional and mental-health institutions, two important questions could be raised about the wisdom of eliminating the separation of these two types of agency, and of abolishing the plea of insanity as a defense against criminal charges. The first is whether a mental-health commitment is less socially stigmatizing than a criminal conviction, hence less of an impediment to rehabilitation. Parents and relatives of persons accused of crime generally assume that hospitalization as mentally ill is not only more therapeutic, but also less discrediting to the accused—or perhaps to themselves—than a jail or prison sentence. Morris and Hawkins (1970: 182) suggest, however, that criminal conviction stigmatizes offenders only as bad, whereas commitment to a mental hospital for a crime labels them as both mad and bad and, therefore, much more to be feared.

The second question raised by the proposed—and perhaps on-going—convergence of mental-health and criminal-justice reactions to crime is whether formal conviction and sentencing in criminal court deters others more than commitment to a mental hospital, assuming that the average length of confinement for offenders is the same in both cases. This does not seem very pertinent to the vast majority of criminal trials that receive little or no publicity, but it might be applicable to highly publicized cases. The issue of the deterrent effect of criminal penalties is complex; whether involuntary confinement in a mental hospital is less deterrent to others than imprisonment is unanswerable at present.

STATUTE OF LIMITATIONS AND THE FULL PARDON

A crime is not a crime if the prosecution waits too long to accuse the perpetrator. This was not always true, is not part of the British tradition known as the Common Law, and still does not apply to murder and treason or, in many jurisdictions, to such other serious crimes as arson.

Forgery is also often exempted, perhaps because of the long time that occasionally elapses before the documents involved in this offense are examined closely enough to discover their fraudulence. For most cases, however, time limits between offense and formal accusation in a court were established by legislative statutes in most American jurisdictions—usually one year for misdemeanors and three years for felonies other than murder and a few other serious crimes.

These time periods are referred to in legal literature as "limitations of action," but in law-enforcement practice and common speech the actual duration—for example, three years—is called the *statute of limitations.* The authoritative commentary on American law, *Corpus Juris Secundum,* explains:

> Such statutes are founded on the liberal theory that prosecutions should not be allowed to ferment endlessly in the files of the government to explode only after witnesses and proofs necessary to the protection of the accused have by sheer lapse of time passed beyond availability. They serve not only to bar prosecutions on aged and untrustworthy evidence, but also to cut off prosecution for crimes a reasonable time after completion, when no further danger to society is contemplated from the criminal activity (Ludes & Gilbert, 1961: Vol. 22, Sec. 223).

In calculating this time period some jurisdictions permit exclusion of any period during which the accused was not "usually and publicly a resident of the state" (see, for example, 38 Illinois Sec. 3–7a) or when the suspect was "fleeing from justice" (18 U.S.C. Sec. 583). For embezzlement or other crimes committed in public office, the statute of limitations usually does not apply while the accused is still holding such office; thereafter it is calculated from the end of the term of office rather than from the time of the alleged offense. If a person is indicted for a felony when the statute of limitations has expired for misdemeanors but not for a felony, the court cannot then convict the accused of a misdemeanor, although such reduction of charges if the accused pleads guilty is a frequent practice when time limits do not apply.

The statute of limitations has the effect of complete acquittal, so that persons who admit crimes after the statutory time limit has expired cannot be prosecuted for them. Even the most incontrovertible evidence of guilt becomes irrelevant for formal conviction and punishment if the period between the offense and a formal charge by the prosecutor exceeds the statute of limitations for the offense.

Another equivalent of acquittal for a crime, the *full pardon,* can occur even after an individual has been duly convicted in court and denied any appeal by higher courts. The chief executives of most national governments, including the President of the United States, may grant a full pardon for any offense in their own country. The governor of most states and provinces is empowered to pardon those convicted by state or provincial courts. In 10 of our states, however, this pardon power has been transferred from the governor to a special board or to the parole board (Seidman & Chambliss, 1974: 673–74).

Pardons are seldom granted for more than a fraction of one percent of a court system's criminal convictions, and most of those granted are not the full pardons to which we refer above, but are reductions of sentence that do not alter the conviction for a crime. Justifications for both full and more limited pardons have included: (1) the convicted person's exceptional display of character (as in saving someone's life); (2) suffering that the convicted person has experienced (for example, from a serious accident or disease); (3) correcting what has become noncriminal due to change in the law (for example, repeal of the Eighteenth Amendment left people in prison for liquor offenses that were no longer illegal); (4) to hasten reversal of judgment when new evidence clearly proves the person has been wrongfully convicted (this could also be obtained through the court's setting aside its earlier conviction, although procuring such a court action may be costly, uncertain, and time consuming). Sometimes, as when full pardon is based on sympathy rather than on proof of innocence, it is debatable whether this actually eliminates the conviction for a crime, although technically its effect is usually to cancel the conviction. In 1974, after President Nixon resigned and then received from President Ford a full pardon for any crimes he may have committed while in office, University of California law professor Laurence Eldredge wrote on the legality of this action:

> In 1867, Justice Field wrote for the Supreme Court this passage, which I believe accurately states the present law: ". . . A pardon reaches both the punishment prescribed for the offense and guilt of the offender; and when the pardon is full, it releases the punishment and blots out of existence the guilt, so that in the eye of the law the offender is as innocent as if he had never committed the offense. If granted before conviction, it prevents any of the penalties and disabilities, consequent upon conviction, from attaching; if granted after conviction, it removes the penalties and disabilities, and restores him to all his civil rights; it makes him, as it were, a new man, and gives him a new credit and capacity."

> Many state constitutions, including those of California, Illinois, New Jersey, and New York, specifically provide that the pardoning power can be exercised only "after conviction" (Eldredge, 1974).

The restriction of pardons to postconviction action was incorporated into these state constitutions, Professor Eldredge indicates, because of the traditional abuses of pardon power by the crown in England and by executives elsewhere, who covered up offenses by blocking prosecution of certain offenders.

SUMMARY AND CONCLUSION

The philosophy of the eighteenth-century "Age of Reason," which inspired our Declaration of Independence and our Constitution, was also the basis for the classical school of jurisprudence from which our criminal law emerged. This school assumed that people freely choose to commit a crime when they calculate that it will bring pleasure outweighing the pain of statutory punishment that might follow. Their consequent policy of prescribing a standard penalty for each type of offense was soon revised, however, by the neoclassical school, which called for modification of penalties on the basis of the mentality of the accused at the time of the offense. This is consistent with a variety of legal concepts—notably insanity, delinquency, statute of limitations, and full pardon—under which persons may sometimes not be convicted of their offenses. Details are summarized in Table 3-1.

Analysis of the first three of these exemptions raises profound questions about the borderline between normal and abnormal mentality, the difference between mental illness and criminality, and, indeed, the contrast between criminality and noncriminality. Evidence indicates that these distinctions are inconsistently made by many decision makers in the criminal-justice and mental-health systems, so that deprivation of liberty must often be based on very arbitrary classifications of people. This blurring of the boundaries between criminality and noncriminality is also a central problem in the next task that will concern us—counting offenses and offenders.

TABLE 3-1 Summary of Exemptions from Being Called Criminal for One's Crimes

TYPE OF EXEMPTION	EFFECT OF EXEMPTION	CRITERIA; OFFICIAL JUSTIFICATION FOR EXEMPTION	TRENDS IN USE OF OR VIEWS ON EXEMPTION
Nonage	Not charged with crime.	Formerly age seven, now usually 12; *hence*, incapable of exercising reason.	Replaced by delinquency concept in most criminal issues.
Delinquency	Processed in nonadult courts and correctional agencies.	Under a specific age, usually 18, with some age range in which accused can be treated as juvenile or adult; *hence*, permits flexibility, informality, preventive rather than punitive focus, and less stigma.	Increasingly formalized; differences from processing of adult crime diminishing; differences led to abuses and often did not warrant claims made for them.
Insanity	Perpetrator of crime found not guilty.	*M'Naghten*: can't tell right from wrong or that act was a crime. *Irresistible impulse*: can't control urge to commit crime. *Durham*: crime is product of mental disease or defect. *ALI*: Mental disease or defect (evinced not just in crime) impairs appreciation or control of crime; *hence*, can't learn from penalty.	A demonstrated ambiguity of all criteria of insanity, along with convergence of mental-health and criminal-justice procedures, is leading to calls for abolishing the insanity defense against criminal charges.
Statute of limitations	Not charged with crime.	Lag between offense and charge; *hence*, defense evidence gone.	Firmly established.
Full pardon	Unconvicted.	Executive grace; *hence* flexible.	Shifting to a board's decision.

FOUR

HOW MUCH CRIME IS THERE?

Any concern with public policy on crime soon leads us to ask: How much crime is there? Where is it concentrated? Whom does it involve? Is it increasing or decreasing? The difficulties in answering these questions are immense but largely surmountable.

Many assertions on the dimensions of crime are extremely erroneous; others are just wild guesses. But quite accurate estimates are available for some types of offense, and much more valid counts are possible for others than are now usually achieved. The United States in the 1970s initiated important new methods for measuring rates of offense; its crime statistics, long among the least accurate of any major industrialized nation that publishes such rates, may become the most reliable in the world. To assess crime figures, however, we must know:

Who reports what types of crime?

Who records them?

Who counts those that are recorded?

How are they reported and recorded?

These matters differ according to whether the offense is predatory or nonpredatory, and also vary for particular crimes within these two broad categories.

COUNTING PREDATORY OFFENSES BY CRIMES KNOWN TO THE POLICE

The police are the "front line" of government efforts not only to combat crime, but also to count it. Yet information on national crime rates has usually been much poorer in the United States than in other technologically advanced countries, because our police forces are fragmented into tens of thousands of autonomous municipal, county, state, and federal agencies operating under 50 separate state criminal codes and federal law. Most other countries have only one set of criminal laws and a nationally controlled police force, which makes it much easier for them to count crimes (but the USSR and several other countries do not publish their crime statistics; see Connor, 1972: 2–4).

During the late 1920s the International Association of Chiefs of Police, which despite its title is primarily an American organization, developed a plan for standard crime classification and statistical tabulation by all police forces. With the association's aid this program has been carried out in the United States since 1930 by the Federal Bureau of Investigation (FBI), which compiles submitted municipal, county, and state police data into its *Uniform Crime Reports* (UCR)—now a one-sheet quarterly announcement and a large annual volume, *Crime in the United States.*

At first, few police forces shared their records with the FBI. Indeed, even by 1940 the localities contributing to the UCR covered only half the American population, and by 1950 only two-thirds. But by 1960 the figure was 95 percent, and more thereafter. In 1967 the FBI began urging each state to establish its own uniform crime-reporting center, which with FBI monitoring and training would collect local police data and foster improved local recordkeeping. Stimulated by federal funding in the 1970s, 32 states had their own systems by July 1, 1975. The FBI now uses compilations by these states for its national totals, thus reducing its need to procure data directly from separate police forces (on UCR history, see Maltz, 1977).

The main focus of the UCR is on seven "index crimes." When initiated in 1958, these were murder and nonnegligent homicide, aggravated assault, forcible rape, robbery, burglary, larceny $50 or over, and auto theft. These "crimes known to the police" were selected by the FBI for estimating regional and national rates, because they are "considered to be most constantly reported" (FBI, 1974: 1). In 1973, "larceny $50 or over" was replaced by "larceny–theft," which encompasses all thefts reported to the police, regardless of the value of the items stolen. Thefts under $50 are excluded, however, in summaries of index-crime trends, in order to base current rates on the same offenses as those used before 1973, with which they are compared.

The FBI announced an increase in the rate of index crimes in the United States in every year except 1959 and 1972 since the beginning of this index in 1958. The increase between 1960 and 1975 was 280 percent, led by robbery with 363 percent (FBI, 1976: 49). Critics contend that these figures exaggerate actual increases, because of the following factors:

1. Increasingly Complete Recording or Counting by the Police

There is often a proper hesitation, at the police-precinct or street-patrol level, to record all crimes that citizens report. Many allegations of crime prove to be unfounded, and some duplicate information that has already been received. Also, police frequently hesitate to report criminal charges that they surmise will be withdrawn, such as those made by angry spouses or other relatives (Black, 1970). Occasionally, however, it is said that crimes not readily solvable or crimes that seem too unimportant to warrant much investigation are not recorded because a large excess of crimes known over crimes solved would discredit law-enforcement officials (see, e.g., Milakovich & Weis, 1975). The FBI, analyzing its first 10 years of the UCR, showed that several cities claimed about half the average crime rate but double the national percentage cleared by arrest, warranting "a suspicion . . . that minor larcenies and burglaries for which no arrests are made . . . are not represented in the statistical reports, thus causing a low rate and a high proportion of cleared cases" (1939: 90). However, the sudden correction of such errors creates a misleading spurt in reported crime rates.

In some instances, low crime totals reflect sloppy recordkeeping by the police, especially before electronic data-processing and efficient report forms are adopted. Indeed, one improvement in police administration is better records, and this often produces a sharp increase in the officially reported crime rate even if the actual rate stays constant or decreases. For example, following the 1959 police reforms

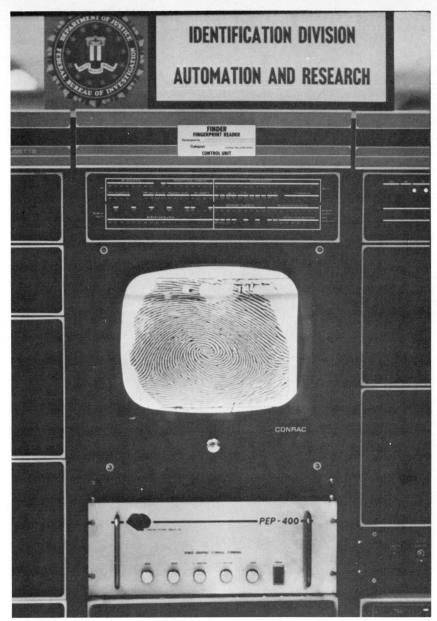

Computerized records make police crime data more complete, accurate, and readily compiled.

in Kansas City its volume of crimes increased 202 percent in two years; after improvements in Buffalo in 1961, crime totals rose 95 percent in two years; with reorganization in Chicago in 1960 the volume of crime reported by the police increased 72 percent in one year (President's Commission, 1967: 25).

That administrative changes have affected crime rates in the opposite direction also seems probable. For example, Albuquerque, New Mexico, after having for the three years 1970 to 1972 the highest rates reported to the FBI by any city with 100,000 or more population, dropped to 105th place among these cities in 1973 (and rose to twentieth in 1975). In 1969 the Nixon administration announced that the nation's capital would be the demonstration place for its anticrime program. A new police chief was appointed who allegedly threatened to replace any police commander unable to reduce the crime rate in his district. A brief decline in the city's index-crime rate soon followed, but there is evidence that this drop was mainly a change in the way offenses were described; the police started designating as "under $50" many thefts they previously would have assessed as over this amount, so that these offenses could no longer be counted as index crimes. Newspaper accounts and statistical data also suggest that some burglaries and robberies were recorded as larceny under $50 (Seidman & Couzens, 1974).

The FBI now checks for possible error whenever it receives reports indicating a phenomenal change in crime rate; in 1975 it sent out 4,000 inquiries for just this purpose (FBI, 1976: 5). When computing national trends, it adjusts totals to offset whatever figures it still finds questionable. Yet innumerable small recordkeeping improvements, in most police departments and over many years, could account for part of the national crime-rate increases announced so regularly.

2. Inflation as a Factor in Crime-Rate Increases

Inflation characterized the American economy during the 1960s and 1970s, augmenting the volume of stolen goods worth $50 or more and the frequency of thefts in which that much cash is found. Therefore, between 1958 and 1973, when "larceny over $50" was one of the index crimes, the proportion of classifiable thefts would have increased even if the total number of thefts had remained constant. Larceny over $50 was 25 percent of index crimes in 1958 and 31 percent by 1972; the new category "larceny–theft" was 50 percent of index crimes when it was created in 1973 and 53 percent in 1975.

3. Increasingly Complete Reporting to the Police

It has long been presumed, and the victim surveys (on which discussion follows) confirm, that much predatory crime is not reported to the police. There are grounds for inferring, however, that the proportion in which the police are notified has grown in recent decades, and that this could partially account for the FBI's finding of an increase in index crimes.

Such an upsurge in the reporting of crime to the police could come from the expansion since 1950 of both ownership of homes and their insurance by comprehensive policies that cover theft. More renters also carry policies with this coverage. Insurance gives people the incentive to notify the police, as a preliminary step toward making a claim on their policy, whenever their homes are burglarized and property stolen.

Another possible source of more reporting of crime during this period of burgeoning crime rates is the growing number of people who live in large metropolitan areas and who change residence frequently. Their mobility increases the probability that offenses against them are committed by strangers rather than by someone whom they know and would be reluctant to report.

Until 1967 the question of how much predatory crime is not reported to the police could be answered only speculatively. Since then, especially in the 1970s, an extremely valuable new source of statistics has developed, quite independent of information collected by the police, that provides the United States with a unique and useful check on the completeness of police statistics.

COUNTING PREDATORY CRIMES BY VICTIM SURVEYS

In 1965 the President's Commission on Law Enforcement and the Administration of Justice initiated a dramatic though simple alternative to the police counts of how much crime has occurred. It hired polling firms whose staffs of door-to-door interviewers defined the index crimes to each person surveyed, then asked whether anyone in the household had been a victim of these offenses in the previous year. After this procedure was tested in the high-crime-rate districts of a few cities, it was applied to a national sample. The findings were startling.

The seven predatory offenses in the FBI's crime index, taken together, were reported to the Commission's polltakers at about twice the rate, in relation to population, that they were reported to the police. Rape was four times, burglary three times, and robbery, larceny $50 or over, and aggravated assault about twice as frequently revealed by polling as by police reports. Probably even these crimes, especially rapes and assaults, were also not always mentioned to the pollsters. Automobile theft and homicide were the only offenses on which police figures in the UCR appeared to be as complete as those of the polls (President's Commission, 1967: 21).

Although the victim surveys show higher crime rates than the UCR, they give the regions of the United States about the same ranking on most index crimes as the regions receive from the UCR. These similarities suggest that police figures show the *relative* intensities of predatory crimes in different population groups fairly well, despite their understating the true rates (Hindelang, 1974a; Skogan, 1974).

Whenever an interviewee reported victimization, the polltaker asked whether the police had been notified, and if not, why not. The most frequent reason given for not calling the police, asserted in about two-thirds of the unreported burglaries and thefts and half the unreported robberies, was a lack of confidence that anything very effective would be done. In most unreported assaults and sex offenses, however, the victims felt that the crimes were private matters in which the police should not be involved; indeed, in many cases the known or suspected criminal was a relative, friend, or acquaintance. Less frequently given reasons for not reporting victimization to the police were unwillingness to take the time necessary for testifying in law-enforcement offices and in court if the offender were caught, and fear of reprisal (President's Commission, 1967: 22, 39–41).

The Commission found that slums have both the highest rates of index crimes reported to the police and the highest rates unreported but revealed by victim survey. The finding that residents of poor neighborhoods are least likely to call police invalidates the claim of some sociologists that peak index-crime rates are ascribed to slum areas only because police are called there most often. This evidence of not reporting crimes to the police in these districts is consistent with findings on attitudes toward law enforcement, for it is in these neighborhoods that the people most often verbalize a lack of confidence in the police (President's Commission, 1967: 99).

The President's Commission recommended frequent repetition of victim surveys as an independent source of statistics on predatory-crime trends, and as a check on variations in public confidence in the police. The Law Enforcement Assistance Administration (LEAA), established in the U.S. Department of Justice primarily to carry out Commission suggestions, funded such surveys by the U.S. Bureau of the Census. After some pilot studies, the Census Bureau initiated the National Crime Panel (NCP) in the early 1970s.

The Crime Panel's national sample includes 60,000 households (comprising 150,000 people) and 15,000 businesses, scientifically selected to maximize the probability that they are representative of the total potential crime victims in the United States. They are interviewed every six months, but at each interval a randomly picked one-seventh of the sample is replaced by a new selection from the general population and from businesses. The national sample, which covers all 50 states and the District of Columbia, will eventually provide the best data ever available on trends in predatory-crime rates.

The NCP makes separate surveys of large cities. Their first poll covered our five largest cities—New York, Chicago, Los Angeles, Philadelphia, and Detroit—plus eight "high-impact" cities in which LEAA had made large anticrime investments. In each city the interviewers contacted a sample of 10,000 households (covering 25,000 people) and 2,000 businesses. Their second survey covered 13 additional cities, and the program is continuing, including resurveys of some cities at intervals of two or more years.

Some critics ask why the NCP city samples are so large when other polls predict national election results with under one percent error from samples of 2,000 or less. It is mostly because victimization from index crimes is less frequent than voting, so that one has to query more people to find one who has been victimized in the past year. The FBI reports about one index crime per year for every 20 persons in the United States; and even though the rate revealed by victim surveys is twice as great, one must still poll about ten people to find one victim. Since robberies account for less than one of 20 index crimes, an average of about 200 persons may have to be surveyed to find one who was robbed in the preceding year. It should be noted that, by the mathematics of probability, errors in estimates from random samples are proportional to the size of the sample rather than to the size of the larger total population from which the sample was picked; thus one may need as large a sample to estimate accurately the rates of crime in one large city as in the whole nation.

The pioneer victim surveys for the President's Commission were designed to check the accuracy of the FBI's UCR, but the NCP surveys seem designed to preclude such use, and their publications advise against comparison with FBI crime statistics. Indeed, any such comparisons will be impeded for the following reasons:

1. Crimes covered by the NCP are not identical with the FBI's index crimes. Panel surveys omit homicide, but include the nonindex offense of simple assault. FBI figures include those few shoplifting and employee thefts reported to the police, but these are omitted in NCP surveys, presumably because most of them are never known to the management. Incidentally, both the FBI and the surveys include *attempts* to commit any of the index offenses, not simply the completed offenses.

2. FBI urban-crime rates are published not for separate cities, but for each cluster of adjacent cities and suburbs that has been designated a "Standard Metropolitan Area" (SMA). On the other hand, NCP city surveys cover only the central cities, excluding suburbs and other towns within SMAs.

3. The FBI computes the number of index crimes for an area by adding together all such crimes reported to the police, including offenses against persons of any age, against households, and against commercial establishments; it then divides this total by the entire population of the area to determine the crime rate. Contrastingly, from its

inquiries on victimization in a sample of an area's households and businesses, the NCP makes three separate counts of offenses and calculates three separate rates. These three rates are:

personal-victimization rates, procured by dividing the number of crimes against persons 12 years of age or older by the number of persons 12 or older in the households surveyed

household-victimization rates, calculated by adding together the burglaries of homes, larcenies of household goods, and motor-vehicle thefts (since these are often victimizations of all or several persons within the household), and dividing this total by the number of households surveyed

commercial-victimization rates, determined by adding together burglaries and robberies of commercial establishments, and dividing this by the total number of establishments surveyed.

The NCP thus provides three distinct crime rates for each city it surveys, and from its national sample it estimates three rates for the nation.

4. FBI statistics, from police reports, are based on the number of separate incidents of crimes, whereas victim-survey statistics are based on the number of individual victims. For example, if 10 people from 10 households are robbed in one holdup on a bus, and only one person is robbed in another holdup, only two robberies are recorded in police statistics. But all 10 victims of the one crime and the single victim of the other have an equal chance of inclusion in a survey sample. Thus a crime with several victims could be counted more than once in a victim survey, and would have a greater chance of being counted at least once than a crime with a single victim. Single-victim offenses, however, comprise about 90 percent of the personal crimes reported in NCP surveys.

Table 4–1 presents the first NCP findings for 26 central cities, including their dichotomy of personal crimes as either "violence" or "theft." The survey respondents were asked about crimes suffered during the preceding 12 months, so their answers covered a period that, for some of them, began in 1972. Table 4–2 suggests some of the differences between the NCP and UCR methods of counting crime by presenting the 1973 UCR rates for index crimes known to the police in the SMAs in which Table 4-1's cities were located. Table 4–2 also presents the size of SMAs and the percentage of each comprised by their central cities. The violent-crime rates are much higher in Table 4–1, not only because NCP surveys presumably elicited fuller reporting by victims than the police received, but also because they include simple assaults while UCR records only aggravated assaults.

TABLE 4-1 Rates and Ranks of Predatory Crime in 26 U.S. Cities per NCP Victim Surveys, 1972–74*

CITY	PERSONAL CRIMES OF VIOLENCE		PERSONAL CRIMES OF THEFT		HOUSEHOLD VICTIMIZATION		COMMERCIAL VICTIMIZATION	
	Rate	Rank	Rate	Rank	Rate	Rank	Rate	Rank
Atlanta	48	18	100	12	292	12	898	1
Baltimore	56	11	79	19	251	17	713	5
Boston	67	4	119	7	322	7	608	10
Buffalo	49	17	74	20	219	22	375	22
Chicago	56	11	87	17	231	20	394	20
Cincinnati	63	6	111	8	271	14	638	7
Cleveland	54	13	71	22	280	13	444	14
Dallas	43	21	97	13	318	9	403	18
Denver	67	4	134	2	370	2	497	13
Detroit	68	3	95	14	329	6	794	2
Houston	53	14	122	5	363	3	658	6
Los Angeles	53	14	105	9	321	8	358	25
Miami	22	26	44	26	169	24	396	19
Milwaukee	61	8	103	10	309	11	370	23
Minneapolis	70	2	120	6	382	1	527	11
Newark	42	22	50	25	204	23	729	4
New Orleans	46	20	94	16	260	15	621	9
New York	36	24	51	24	127	26	431	15
Oakland	59	9	102	11	318	9	774	3
Philadelphia	63	6	95	14	238	18	506	12
Pittsburgh	47	19	83	18	226	21	370	23
Portland, Ore.	59	9	123	4	334	5	394	20
St. Louis	42	22	73	21	253	16	625	8
San Diego	53	14	141	1	353	4	407	17
San Francisco	71	1	129	3	238	18	333	26
Washington	31	25	65	23	141	25	418	16

* Rates per 1,000 potential victims. For personal crimes these potential victims are all persons 12 years of age or older; for household victimization, they are all separate households; and for commercial victimization they are all separate business establishments.

SOURCES: LEAA, 1974b, 1975a, 1975c.

San Francisco and Oakland are part of a single SMA for which the UCR publishes only one total crime rate, whereas they are separate cities in NCP surveys. In UCR tabulations for the 25 SMAs, the San Francisco–Oakland SMA has the highest total index-crime rate. In the NCP victim surveys for 26 cities, San Francisco has the highest rate of personal crimes of violence and the third highest of personal crimes of theft. Nevertheless, this leading city in personal predations has the

**TABLE 4-2   Rates and Ranks of Index Crimes for 25 Standard
Metropolitan Areas per UCR 1973***
(Plus SMA population in millions and percentage of
central city in SMA)

STANDARD METRO- POLITAN AREA	VIOLENT INDEX CRIMES		PROPERTY INDEX CRIMES		TOTAL INDEX CRIMES		POPU- LA- TION	PERCENT- AGE OF CENTRAL CITY IN SMA
	Rate	Rank	Rate	Rank	Rate	Rank		
Atlanta	6.2	10	47	11	53	13	1.7	29
Baltimore	9.2	2	46	12	55	9	2.1	42
Boston	4.1	18	43	16	47	19	3.4	19
Buffalo	3.0	21	32	24	35	25	1.3	35
Chicago	7.3	5	43	15	51	15	7.1	47
Cincinnati	2.8	24	37	21	40	21	1.4	33
Cleveland	4.5	16	33	23	38	23	2.1	37
Dallas	5.0	14	48	10	53	12	2.6	33
Denver	5.2	13	61	3	66	5	1.4	38
Detroit	8.2	4	53	7	61	7	4.5	34
Houston	5.0	15	43	17	48	18	2.2	57
Los Angeles	8.4	3	58	4	66	4	6.9	41
Miami	9.5	1	58	5	67	3	1.4	24
Milwaukee	1.7	25	36	22	38	22	1.4	50
Minneapolis	3.0	22	46	13	49	16	2.0	21
Newark	5.5	12	39	20	44	20	2.1	18
New Orleans	6.6	8	41	19	48	17	1.1	55
New York	1.2	26	43	18	55	10	10.0	79
Oakland**							3.1	12
Philadelphia	4.4	17	30	25	35	24	4.9	40
Pittsburgh	2.8	23	21	26	24	26	2.4	22
Portland, Ore.	4.0	19	58	6	62	6	1.1	36
St. Louis	6.0	11	51	9	57	8	2.4	26
San Diego	3.1	20	51	8	54	11	1.5	47
San Francisco	6.8	6	66	1	73	1	3.1	23
Washington	6.4	9	46	14	52	14	3.0	25

* Rates per 1,000 population.
** Same SMA as San Francisco.

SOURCES: FBI, 1974; U.S. Census. Estimates, 1973.

lowest rate of commercial crime of the 26 cities covered by NCP and is
eighteenth in household victimization. Oakland is more intermediate
in all of these rates.

Miami affords the most striking contrast in a comparison of
Tables 4–1 and 4–2. By NCP data it is the lowest of the 26 cities in
personal-crime rates, twenty-fourth in household, and nineteenth in

commercial victimizations; yet by FBI figures it is highest in rates of violent crime and fifth highest in property crime. One probable explanation for these discrepancies is that Miami is a resort city. Crimes known to the police and counted in FBI figures include those reported by both transients and residents, but in calculating SMA crime rates, all known offenses—including those against transients, many of whom are especially victimized—are divided only by the number of permanent residents that the U.S. Census reports. NCP victim surveys, on the other hand, count only the victimizations experienced by residents—transients are not included in its samples—and calculate rates by the same Census totals for residents used by the FBI. (Incidentally, both use the annual Census estimates for population totals, to correct for growth since the last decennial Census.)

This explanation for the discrepancy between UCR and NCP rates—the UCR count's crimes suffered by tourists, whereas the NCP omits them—is supported by the fact that the only SMAs for which the UCR reported higher rates of index crimes than the highest in Table 4–1 (San Francisco–Oakland's 73 per 1,000) were all tourist centers: Phoenix with a rate of 82 per 1,000; Daytona Beach, Florida, with 79; and both Las Vegas, Nevada, and Fort Lauderdale–Hollywood, Florida, with 75. Further evidence is the fact that the 30 metropolitan areas with the highest index-crime rates according to 1974 UCR figures include not only these and other resort cities, but also five cities with much seasonal migrant farm labor (Bakersfield, Fresno, Modesto, and Stockton in California, and Yakima in Washington). Other SMAs in the highest 30 have many of both tourist and farm-labor transients (e.g., Orlando).

Another striking feature of Tables 4–1 and 4–2 is their data on our largest city. Although crimes on the streets of New York are highly publicized, it ranks tenth among the 25 SMAs in the UCR index-crime rates, and is twenty-fourth among the NCP's 26 cities in personal-crime rates, as well as lowest in household and fifteenth in commercial victimization. It, too, has many transients who suffer some of the crimes known to the police, but these are fewer in proportion to the base of permanent residents than are the transients of resort cities. Also, as Table 4–2 shows, New York is highest of the 25 SMAs in percentage of population within the central city.

Despite the limitations of any comparisons and the advice in NCP publications against comparing their survey data with UCR statistics, LEAA newsletters and press releases repeatedly make such comparisons. Claiming that they first adjusted the figures from each source so that the offenses and populations covered are as nearly identical as possible, the LEAA announced in 1974 (as did the President's Commission earlier) that nearly half the victims of index crimes did not report these offenses to the police. In the five largest cities other than New York, omissions of crimes in police statistics were asserted to be even greater. Philadelphia, with a former police chief as mayor, submitted index-crime rates for UCR only one-fifth as high as those reported by victims to NCP interviewers, while UCR statistics for Chicago, Los Angeles, and Detroit reported only about one-third the rates given by victims. New York City had the national average of UCR rates —namely, half those of the NCP survey (*LEAA Newsletter,* June 1974, and *Los Angeles Times,* April 15, 1974).

According to the LEAA (*Newsletter,* March 1974), NCP surveys showed that UCR rates were 47 percent complete for rape, 64 percent for aggravated assault, 44 percent for robbery, 43 percent for larceny over $50, and 37 percent for burglary. Skogan (1977) reports that only in 28 percent of the index-crime victimizations mentioned by the 1973 NCP national sample could household interviewers recall someones' having notified the police. This low rate applied mostly to petty theft, the most frequent offense; police were called in 40 percent of assaults, 46 percent of burglaries, and 68 percent of auto thefts.

According to the NCP, the most frequently victimized age group is between 12 and 19. Personal and household victimization decreases with age, with those over 65 most immune, perhaps because they stay at home more. Among people under 35, males are victims of personal offenses more often than females, but after age 35 such victimization rates are about the same. Personal-victimization rates for blacks are 85 per 1,000, as compared with 74 per 1,000 for whites. People in families with annual incomes of less than $3,000 suffer crimes of violence more often than others, while people in families with incomes of $15,000 or over are most likely to be the victims of property crimes (LEAA, 1975b).

Some small-scale victim surveys have been done by university and other researchers. In a midwestern SMA "inner city" neighborhood and in a close-in suburb three miles away, local researchers found victim-reported index offenses 10 times as numerous as police-reported index offenses in the inner city, but only six times as frequent in the suburb. Among the factors in this discrepancy are: (1) the offender was unknown to the victim in 59 percent of the crimes in the suburb, but in only 42 percent of the crimes in the inner city; and (2) the victim called the police in 61 percent of the suburban crimes but in only 32 percent of those in the inner city. The researchers estimated that police statistics covered only one in four index crimes of the inner city, but three of five in the suburb (Reynolds & Blyth, 1975). This contrast suggests that inner city residents, have less confidence in the police, but it is interesting that the inner city victims more often report that they do not call the police because they think they know the offender. Such knowledge may prevail in the inner city because children and housewives leave their immediate neighborhood much less often than their suburban counterparts, and are therefore, more likely to suspect a neighborhood juvenile as the culprit.

The U.S. Department of Commerce, other government agencies, and business organizations often undertake special surveys of losses from crime in particular types of business (see U.S. Department of Commerce, 1974). One partial check on the relative validity of FBI and NCP statistics investigated the percentage of homeowner or renter policies on which claims of loss by burglary or theft were made. By this criterion, cities are closer to their NCP than their FBI ranking by property-crime rates, although not identical with either (*Society,* November/December 1974: 10). These rankings may also reflect variations among cities in insured housing. Theft- and burglary-insurance premiums for geographical areas are determined by the claims made against policies in each area, and thus should reflect victimization rates. However, the premiums have only moderate correlations with FBI property-crime rates for the areas (Price, 1966). Perhaps most important is that thefts from tourists and transients, which inflate FBI crime rates for cities that attract many visitors, are much less likely to be covered by insurance than thefts from households or businesses, on which the NCP concentrates.

Practical benefits that victim survey research can yield include: (1) an estimate of the degree of error in police statistics for various predatory crimes; (2) a better basis for assessing the performance of local police and their need for federal funds, by eliminating the possibility of a conflict of interest that exists when police performance or needs are evaluated only with police statistics; (3) better estimates of the risk of crime for different types of neighborhoods, housing, and categories of victims (e.g., by age, sex, and ethnicity), as a guide to efforts at crime prevention; (4) (after they are collected over a period of several years) *more dependable figures on crime trends than this or any other nation has ever had on many types of predatory offense.* This last benefit will be extremely valuable in assessing the effects of any large-scale program (such as guaranteed employment) or of any social or economic trend on crime rates, especially if these programs or trends occur in some cities or regions and not in others.

Nevertheless, victim surveys have distinct limitations. They are subject to error from faulty recall, especially for minor offenses. Interviewers must be carefully trained in probing to ascertain that their subjects fully understand the questions about different types of predatory crime. Memory-cue questions are needed to ensure that recollections go back to exactly the period covered, such as six months or one year. When queries are for a full year, more of the reported offenses are dated in the past six months than in the earlier six months, which suggests that there is some forgetting. Probing also reveals, however, that some major crimes suffered more than a year earlier are still reported (on this and other victim-interviewing problems, see Biderman, 1967; Panel for the Evaluation of Crime Surveys, 1976; Tuchfarber & Klecka, 1976).

Some underreporting always occurs. For example, when goods are taken by stealth the owners are often unaware that anything is missing or do not know that their loss is the result of crime rather than of accidental misplacement, so they do not report it to either the police or a victim survey. Victims who find an offense extremely humiliating often do not tell other people in their home about it, let alone tell it to someone taking a poll. Even persons in the household who know about it would not report it to a polltaker. Rape is, of course, the most humiliating of the index crimes. There is also evidence that when someone is assaulted by a relative or by any other acquaintance, these experiences are often not reported in victim surveys (even if the police were called at the time) (Williams, 1975). And then, there are always a few persons who refuse to answer such surveys, or answer only facetiously.

Another major limitation of victim surveys is that they do not indicate rates of victimless crime. For this purpose, and sometimes for others, one must question persons directly about the offenses they have committed.

COUNTING CRIMES BY ADMITTED OFFENSES

It usually is presumed that we cannot know the extent of nonpredatory crimes, such as using an illegal drug or patronizing a prostitute, from offenses reported to the police or from government-operated victim surveys. Those involved in these offenses might expect admission of lawbreaking to bring arrest. Yet, to a remarkable extent, people will admit crimes to researchers whom they "size up" as impartial and trustworthy.

In most admitted-offense research, students—the favorite guinea pig of professors—are asked to check a list of delinquent and criminal acts to indicate which they have done, but to do so anonymously. However, at least two researchers did request names from high-school students and then searched local police records to determine which students had been arrested. In one of these studies nearly half the students who indicated that they had stolen items worth between $2 and $50 also had arrest records (Hirschi, 1969: 57). The other study developed a scoring system for weighting delinquency records by the number and seriousness of offenses. The researchers found a close association between the score of the delinquency that students admitted and the score for their court-recorded delinquency (Erickson, 1972).

Diverse research suggests that most responses in admitted-offense surveys are valid. Experiments show that a group's crime rates are about the same whether measured with anonymous or nonanonymous questionnaires (Kulik et al., 1966), or nonanonymous interviews (Krohn et al., 1974); but validity declines if interviewer and respondent differ in ethnicity or gender (Teilmann, 1976). The Gallup, Harris, and other polls have repeatedly asked national samples about their use of marijuana and other illegal drugs; yet even at the time that mere possession of these substances was a felony, over half the college youth and many in other groups admitted such drug use. Gold (1970), when interviewing members of juvenile groups about their crimes, also asked those with whom he had close rapport what crimes the others had committed. He concluded from the accounts by his informants that 72 percent of the other members were complete revealers, 11 percent partial concealers, and 17 percent outright concealers.

Clark and Tifft (1966) asked each of 45 male students at the University of Illinois to choose but conceal a number and then to enter it—rather than his name—on a form on which he would indicate how many of 35 types of delinquent or criminal act he had committed since leaving high school. Each student was later called for a private session at which he was asked to select his questionnaire from a file by using the identifying number, and to correct any entries that seemed erroneous. (The original entries had already been recorded.) He was then given a polygraph (lie-detector) test on his responses. At the time the students filled in the questionnaires, they did not know that these later inquiries would occur. The 40 available for these end-of-semester sessions all made some changes on their questionnaires, but they altered only eight percent of their original responses on whether they had ever committed a delinquent act and revised the reported frequency for only $10^{1}/_{2}$ percent of their offenses. About 75 percent of these revisions raised, and 25 percent lowered, the frequency of an admitted act. Of the changes, slightly over half were made in checking the questionnaire before the polygraph examination and the rest during the examination. Most changes appeared to be due to careless recall rather than falsification, and to have been corrected because the later sessions prodded memories.

The first major contribution of admitted-offense surveys is to shatter a popular conception of criminals and noncriminals as two completely contrasting kinds of people, with the criminals a small minority. In a still-unparalleled study, Wallerstein and Wyle (1947) had 1,020 male and 678 female adults, of diverse ages and with a wide range of conventional occupations, anonymously complete questionnaires that listed 49 offenses. Ninety-nine percent of the respondents admitted committing one or more of the offenses after the age of 16;

men reported an average of 18 separate types of crime and women 11, as follows:

TYPE OF CRIME	PERCENTAGE FOR MEN	PERCENTAGE FOR WOMEN
Petty theft	89	83
Disorderly conduct	85	76
Malicious mischief	84	81
Assault	49	05
Tax evasion	57	40
Robbery	11	01
Falsification and fraud	46	34
Criminal libel	36	29
Concealed weapons	35	03
Auto theft	26	08
Other grand theft	13	11
Burglary	17	04

Admitted-offense studies have been conducted with high-school and college students for decades. They generally yield lower percentages than Wallerstein and Wyle obtained, but most of these young subjects admit some shoplifting, and large proportions admit vandalism (see, for example, Short & Nye, 1958; Clark & Wenninger, 1962; Clark & Tifft, 1966; Institute for Juvenile Research, undated). Kinsey (1948) startled many Americans by his report that 37 percent of his sample of adult males admitted to some homosexual acts that were then criminal in every state. More recent surveys (e.g., Hunt, 1974) suggest that the current percentage is not over 18, and that Kinsey's figure is spuriously high due to poor sampling and vague definition. Also shocking to many older people in recent years are surveys in which two-thirds of seniors in many colleges have admitted using marijuana, as have a majority of high-school seniors in some cities, even in states where this could be prosecuted as a felony.

A second important contribution of admitted-offense surveys is to challenge some presumptions about the correlation of delinquency and crime to other factors that are fostered by arrest statistics. Although arrests and convictions, as well as reports of crime to the police, have almost always been much more extensive from poor and low-status individuals and slum neighborhoods than from the middle and upper classes, admitted delinquency by junior-high and high-school youths has repeatedly been found unrelated to the occupational status of their parents, and less closely related than police figures suggest to the predominant occupational status or wealth of their neighborhood (for details, see Chapter 8). Chambliss and Nagasawa (1969), for a school district in a West Coast city, also challenged official statistics that Japanese-American youth have negligible delinquency rates and that rates for blacks are much higher than for whites; on their questionnaire the admissions of delinquency were very similar for blacks and whites and not much lower for those of Japanese ancestry.

Some contend that official statistics on crime and criminals are so defective as measures of the prevalence of offenses as to be useful only for describing the activities and concerns of the police and other government officials (Kitsuse & Cicourel, 1963). Yet in some circumstances one may still justify estimating rates of crime and characteristics of criminals from statistics on the actions of criminal-justice agencies.

ARRESTS AND CONVICTIONS AS CLUES TO CRIME RATES

Early statisticians insisted on estimating offense rates only by using data on convicted offenders, because information on arrestess would be discredited if some were found not guilty. Later scholars concluded that the most complete total crime rates for a community come from offenses known and recorded by its police, since statistics on arrested or convicted persons omit the "dark figure" of crimes that police do not solve; some also claimed that arrests omit fewer offenders than do convictions (Biderman & Reiss, 1967). It was noted, further, that plea bargaining often distorts the labeling of an offense between arrest and conviction (Newman, 1962). Eventually, concern with another "dark figure," the crimes unreported to the police or unrecorded by them, prompted victim and admitted-offense surveys that presumably yield from individually imperfect memories more accurate total crime estimates than any police or court data. Nevertheless, to know the characteristics of some types of criminal today, as well as the history of crime in periods when neither UCR nor relevant survey research existed, we must rely upon statistics of arrests or convictions.

Admitted-offense surveys do yield quite reliable data on many offenders by asking people about both their background and the crimes they have committed. Yet for serious crimes, and for offenses mainly by people not readily available for interviews or questionnaires, we can only identify the attributes of offenders by tabulating the characteristics of that fraction who are arrested or convicted. Granted, those caught are only part of the total who commit offenses, but one might assume that this captured segment has about the same percentage of all ages, races, or other attributes as the unidentified offenders. When this assumption is accepted or when qualifications are stated to take it into account, the percentage of all offenders with any particular description —young or old, black or white, educated or uneducated—can be estimated from the percentage of arrestees or prisoners fitting that description. Admitted-offense surveys of high-school students in which names are requested and arrest records are checked indicate that those who admit crimes and the arrestees do not differ greatly in attributes and attitudes (Hirschi, 1969; Elliott & Voss, 1974).

For any offense in which the police are almost always called, and which they usually clear by an arrest, we can assume that the characteristics of arrestees are similar to those of all who commit the crime. Murder is the prominent crime that most nearly fits these conditions. For all other types of predation, the arrestees probably differ from those uncaught, not only because a small percentage are arrested, but also because the police search more diligently for some types of criminals than for others, and perhaps because they usually catch soonest those who are stupid or inexperienced. The extent to which such factors make arrestees for most predations different from those not caught cannot be precisely known, although sometimes the direction of the error they create can reasonably be inferred.

In nonpredatory offenses, police rarely are notified. They alone must decide where to concentrate their surveillance, entrapment, informants, or other efforts to catch these offenders. That one cannot know the attributes of all drug-law violators with much precision just from studying drug arrestees was graphically demonstrated by De-Fleur (1975), who showed that the number and neighborhood of these arrests in Chicago fluctuate with the size, legal procedures, and racial policies of the narcotics division involved. Since the police take the initiative in locating nonpredatory crimes, what they look for and where and how they look largely determine the type of offender they find.

There are essentially three ways of counting juvenile arrests—police contacts, bookings, and referrals to juvenile court—but police agencies are not explicit and uniform on which they use, particularly in juvenile-status offenses such as truancy and curfew violation, in which they simply call the parents or take the child home. Officers also differ on recording juvenile cases in which they make an arrest on serious charges but exonerate the arrestee before formal booking has occurred (Klein et al., 1975).

Table 4-3 indicates the age and sex distribution of arrestees by offense in the United States. These figures are computed from an FBI tabulation of reports from 13,000 law-enforcement offices, including some state-operated bureaus that collect local police statistics. They cover more than 84 percent of the American population, although some law-enforcement agencies do not submit this information. The fact that marked deviation from most of the statistics in the table is rare among police forces that do supply such data inspires confidence that the figures would be similar for arrestees in other areas. By far the most

TABLE 4-3 Age and Gender of Arrestees, by Offense, 1975
(Totals for the U.S.)

OFFENSE	PERCENT-AGE OF ALL ARRESTS	PERCENT-AGE OF ARRESTEES UNDER 18	AGE OF MOST ARRESTS (MODAL AGE)	MEDIAN AGE	PERCENT-AGE OF ARRESTEES WHO ARE FEMALE
Murder and non-negligent manslaughter	0.2	10	20	26.4	16
Manslaughter by negligence	0.04	12	18	24.8	11
Forcible rape	0.3	18	19	23.3	1
Robbery	1.6	34	18	19.9	7
Aggravated assault	2.5	18	18	25.1	13
Violent Index crimes:	4.6	23	18	22.8	10
Burglary	5.6	53	16	17.7	5
Larceny (theft)	12.0	45	16	18.7	31
Motor-vehicle theft	1.5	55	16	17.5	7
Property Index crimes:	19.1	48	16	18.2	22
Other assault	4.4	20	18	24.5	14
Arson	0.2	53	15	17.4	11
Forgery and counterfeiting	0.7	13	19	23.9	29
Fraud	1.8	3	24	28.1	34
Embezzlement	0.1	7	22	27.6	31
Stolen property	1.3	33	18	20.3	11
Vandalism	2.2	65	15	16.2	8
Weapons offenses	1.6	16	18	24.7	8
Prostitution and commercial vice	0.6	5	21	22.8	74
Sex offenses except forcible rape and prostitution	0.6	21	18	24.7	8
Narcotics offenses	6.3	24	18	20.6	14
Gambling	0.6	4	27	37.8	9
Offenses against family and children	0.7	12	18	27.2	12
Driving under the influence	11.3	2	21	33.2	8
Liquor-law violations	3.3	40	17	18.7	14
Drunkenness	14.7	4	21	37.6	7
Disorderly conduct	7.9	19	19	23.3	18
Vagrancy	0.7	9	18	33.8	11
All other offenses (except traffic)	12.9	25	18	22.5	16
Suspicion	0.4	27	18	20.7	14
Curfew and loitering	1.4	100	16	16.1	20
Runaways	2.4	100	15	15.4	57
All Arrests	**100.0**	**26**	**16**	**22.9**	**16**

SOURCES: Compiled and calculated from FBI, 1976:188–89,190,191

ARRESTS AND CONVICTIONS AS CLUES TO CRIME RATES

serious unknown is how closely those who commit these crimes but are not arrested resemble those who are arrested.

These statistics of arrestee attributes are certainly valuable as evidence of the dimensions of the activities and concerns of the criminal-justice system (Kitsuse & Cicourel, 1963). Inferences could also be made on the number and attributes of offenders not arrested, for both predatory and nonpredatory crimes, if more admitted-offense statistics were carefully collected by polls of *representative* samples of the population.

Perhaps the most striking feature of Table 4-3 is the low age of those charged with property crimes, especially burglary and theft. Most are teenagers. There is a somewhat older age distribution for crimes of violence, but for them, too, the peak age is under 20. The fraud and embezzlement arrestees are distinctly older, for one usually must have some maturity and business experience to perpetrate most of these types of crime. The oldest arrestees are those charged with drunkenness, driving under the influence, and gambling. As already noted, arrests reflect not only the attributes of those who commit crimes, but also the areas and groups on which police decide to concentrate their investigations, especially for nonpredatory offenses such as gambling and drunkenness.

One in three arrestees for theft is now female, as compared with one in five only 10 years earlier. According to the UCR the percentage of forgery and counterfeiting arrestees who were women increased from 18 to 29 in the decade between 1965 and 1975, and from 20 to 31 for fraud. Liberation trends apparently expand female opportunities in both legal and illegal economic pursuits. As Chapter 9 details, however, arrests of males for violent offenses increased even more than arrests of females during most of the 1960s and 1970s.

Arrest data not only suggest the attributes of offenders, but also are virtually our only clues to total crime rates and their correlates in periods when no other types of offense statistics were maintained. Even if imperfect for this purpose, they are often of considerable interest, especially if it seems reasonable that no sharp fluctuations occurred in police clearance rates. For example Hobbs (1943), comparing criminal cases before the Philadelphia courts for the period between 1771 and 1810 with cases there in 1937, concluded that rates of crime had not changed appreciably if one eliminated offenses, such as auto theft, not existing in the earlier period. Powell (1966), using police statistics for Buffalo between 1854 and 1964, noted temporary increases in arrest rates for murder and assault following the Civil War and World War II, but contrastingly *during* World War I; yet he found no overall increase in arrest rates for this total 110-year span. One could speculate that during the Civil War and World War II, too many men in high-crime-rate ages were in the armed forces for arrest rates to increase until the men were demobilized, whereas in our much briefer participation in World War I, not so many entered the armed forces. Ferdinand (1967) showed that Boston's murder, larceny, and assault arrest rates declined from 1849 to 1951, with some fluctuations comparable to those that Powell found in Buffalo. Only for assault does Ferdinand note evidence of change in police arrest policies that may account for much of the fluctuation in arrest rates.

Larceny is far from fully reported or cleared by arrest, but if its reporting and clearance rates do not fluctuate sharply, we can assume that the arrest trends are proportional to actual offense trends. This was what Glaser and Rice (1959) assumed when they found strong positive correlations in Boston, Cincinnati, and Chicago between unemployment rates for the male labor force between 1930 and 1956 and property-theft arrest rates of persons 21 through 45 years old, but somewhat negative correlations for the younger ages.

In summary, arrest rates for major predatory crimes may be useful data for estimating the correlations between actual offense rates and other variables over long periods of time for which other data are not available, and for evidence on the attributes of offenders. They are much less useful in studying nonpredatory offenses. In any usage, however, evidence of fluctuation or bias in arrest practices should be sought, for they may be clues to the invalidity of arrest rates as indices of crime trends and correlates.

COUNTING CRIMES OF THE ELITE AND THE POWERFUL

Perhaps the major limitation of victim and admitted-offense surveys, of crimes known to the police, and of arrest statistics is their inapplicability to the crimes that probably victimize more people for larger amounts of money than any other predations: the crimes of corporations in violation of antitrust laws, of laws against misrepresentation in advertising, and of antipollution and other laws. Also important but not easily counted are crimes of fraud and corruption in politics, and most of the offenses by organized crime.

The offenses listed above are revealed mainly by intrepid journalists, by investigative congressional, legislative, or aldermanic committees and commissions, by special or "runaway" grand juries, and by unusually daring regular or special prosecutors. America has had a long history of journalistic leadership in exposing political corruption. Especially noteworthy is Lincoln Steffens, best known for *Shame of the Cities* (1904) and *Autobiography* (1931). More recently, Carl Bernstein and Bob Woodward, in *All The President's Men* (1974), relate how they "blew the lid" on the Watergate scandals that resulted in the resignation of President Nixon to avoid trial for impeachment. Prominent in the exposure of much predation by corporations and wealthy individuals or their organizations during the second half of the twentieth century have been lawyer Ralph Nader, historian Ferdinand Lundberg, and sociologist G. William Domhoff. The Senate Committee headed by the late Estes Kefauver during the 1950s was probably the most influential of many congressional committees investigating organized crime (but see Moore, 1976). Numerous analogous committees investigated corruption on state and municipal levels, some headed by political officeholders and others by presumably neutral appointees—for example, the Knapp Commission investigations of the New York Police Department during the 1970s. Frequently, unions have exposed criminal violation of safety laws in mines and factories.

In some respects it may be inappropriate to speak of these investigators as providing us with a "count" of crimes in high or powerful places. What they produce is a more accurate impression of the prevalence of these offenses, rather than a precise enumeration. Indeed, many of the crimes on this upper level of power could not readily be counted even if we had access to all the facts. How many cases of pollution are represented by a large factory or mining complex that has illegally been pouring dangerous effluents into a river for decades? How is this added to the monthly payments by a gambling syndicate to many police and government officials over a period of years? Or is each of these counted as just one crime when added to a single false advertisement?

More influential than traditional statistics gathering, these investigations, particularly those by congressional or state legislative committees, produce new laws that further the inclusion process whereby the interests of the less powerful are gradually becoming more protected. Yet such legislation is often blocked or weakened by loopholes inserted through the influence of lobbyists before it is enacted, or it is evaded after it becomes law. Nevertheless, through such laws there has been a cumulative expansion in the definition of crime in the United States in recent years. Some of the new legislation has encouraged greater monitoring and surveillance, and penalties are slowly becoming severer for pollution, political corruption, and misrepresentation in selling or lending. It has also required better record keeping and more public airing of potentially illegal transactions by corporations and government officials. There has been evidence that publicity deters offenses by some of these organizations and individuals, since they depend on public goodwill for most of their income or power. Therefore, a fuller exposure of crimes by the elite and the powerful may reduce the number of such offenses, although notoriety without prosecution does not always suffice as a deterrent.

SUMMARY AND CONCLUSION

"Anyone who tries to uncover facts and figures about crime and criminals learns quickly that there are many figures but very few facts," Wilkins (1972: 1) observes: "Whether [crime] data exist that are adequate for any particular purpose depends on . . . that purpose." As Hindelang (1974a: 2) points out, however: "If *adequate* measurement of phenomena were a prerequisite for even the cautious use of such measurements, few measurement techniques would improve through evolution . . . ."

Crime may be counted in many ways, all of them imperfect. The optimum measures differ for various types of offense, but alternative sources of data are available for some crimes. To assess the validity of a statistic, we must always know how it is procured.

One of the major risks in reading or listening to pronouncements on crime is what Singer (1971) calls "the vitality of mythical numbers." Many commentators make wild guesses about the prevalence or cost of a given offense, such as asserting that heroin addicts in New York City steal $2 to $5 billion worth of property a year; then others quote the dramatic figures as though they had been calculated from factual data. This indicates the importance of knowing the sources of all figures, and of testing their validity by calculating their implications. For example, Singer notes that $2 to $5 billion is several times the total value of goods or money lost annually to the types of crimes that addicts commit in New York City (although he may not really know the total lost to shoplifting, unreported thefts from trucks and cars, and unreported burglaries).

Table 4-4 summarizes the major ways of counting crime, where the results are published, what they measure, and their limitations. Crimes known to the police are the most widely used data, but victim surveys show police figures to be accurate only for murder and auto theft and for some highly specialized predations, such as bank robberies. These surveys are still not fully appreciated as a major advance in crime statistics, although they have obvious limitations·for nonpredatory crimes (such as drug abuse and prostitution) in which all participants willingly engage. Fortunately for public-policy guidance, admitted-offense surveys indicate the prevalence and correlates of nonpredatory offenses and augment our knowledge of predatory behavior.

Arrest and conviction statistics are our only resource for esti-

TABLE 4-4   Major Ways of Counting Crimes: Their Contributions and Limitations

SOURCE OF INFORMATION	PRINCIPAL PUBLICATIONS	INFORMATION PROVIDED	PRINCIPAL DEFICIENCIES
Crimes known to the police	FBI's *Crime in the U.S.: Uniform Crime Reports* (UCR); similar state and local publications	Rates on seven index crimes by metropolitan areas, states, and regions, plus other details on some predations.	Trends go back only to 1933 and are not very comparable before 1958; victim surveys indicate crimes known to police are very incomplete; diminishing error rate probably impairs validity of conclusions from its overall trends.
Victim surveys	LEAA–Census *National Crime Panel* (NCP) reports; U.S. Dept. of Commerce and other special reports	Volume of predatory crime by geographic area and victim attributes; rates of report to the police; reasons for not reporting; victims' views	Inadequate on homicide and nonpredatory offenses; only begun on regular basis in 1970s, so limited in trend data and in detailed geographic rates.
Admitted-offense surveys	Gallup, Harris, and other polls, and various special studies	Rates of committing nonpredatory and predatory crimes, plus characteristics of offenders and their accounts.	Less adequate on murder and other very serious or professional predations; not available on long-term basis.
Arrests	FBI's *Crime in the U.S.; Uniform Crime Reports* (UCR); similar state and local publications	Relative proportions of age, sex, race, and other traits of offenders; historical-trend data back to periods before other types of crime statistics were available.	Nonpredatory and petty-predation arrest rates fluctuate mainly with investigation and arrest policies and number of police personnel; these also somewhat affect other offense rates.
Special investigations	Exposés, books, reports of investigative committees and commissions; records of major trials	Accounts of predations by corporations, of political corruption, of organized crime activities.	Not routinely available; data often imprecise and incomplete; not readily quantifiable for trend analysis or other comparisons.

mating trends of offenses in periods for which no other type of statistic is available. Arrest data may also be useful for knowledge of the traits of offenders, but only for predatory crimes. To assess the validity of these figures, one should also investigate fluctuations and bias in law-enforcement practices and resources.

Special investigations by journalists and others, though often too limited, provide our best clues to the dimensions of large-scale crimes in business and politics. When exposure of these offenses evokes more press and government surveillance of corporations, candidates, and officials, or requires a public accounting of their financial transactions, the volume of their crimes should decrease, and our knowledge of such crimes should increase.

FIVE

DOES CRIME PAY?

Whether crime pays depends on what is gained and what is lost. Important to the offender is the income or other satisfaction it provides, but just as crucial is the risk of being caught. Of equal relevance is the price if caught: punishment by government, psychological stress, social stigma, and what economists call "opportunity costs"—the jobs or other benefits forfeited by engaging in crime or by being arrested. Clearly, all these factors vary with the crime and the criminal.

THE RISK OF BEING CAUGHT

Comparison of the FBI's *Uniform Crime Report* statistics with those of victim surveys, as in the preceding chapter, shows that no more than half the index offenses are reported to the police. Other tabulations by the FBI (1975:166) indicate that the police clear only one-fifth of the index crimes known to them. Clearance means that the police are certain that the reported crimes did occur, and that the culprits are all either arrested or not arrestable (e.g., dead or already in custody for other crimes). (Also, in some cases the crime is cleared by showing that the alleged offense did not occur.) If the police know of only half the index crimes and clear but one-fifth of them, then about one-tenth of the index crimes are cleared; this figure will be called the "net clearance rate."

The correct net clearance rate for index crimes is probably even smaller than 10 percent. Although crimes reported to victim surveys are twice as numerous as those reported to the police, these still do not include all offenses. Frequently omitted are crimes by friends or relatives that the victim does not mention when interviewed; deliberately excluded as a matter of policy are shoplifting and employees' pilfering, most of which is never known by the victim and, even when known, is often not reported to the police. Thus the percentage of offenses known to police is probably even lower than Table 5–1 indicates, especially for assault, rape, and theft. Furthermore, police may err in assuming that an arrested person will be found guilty, and thus show clearance rates that are too high. The fact that some arrestees are later proved innocent may be offset in the long run by crimes solved *after* nonclearance statistics are submitted, usually because the guilty person is arrested for new crimes and is found to have committed the earlier offenses as well. Allegedly, however, police achieve some later clearances by telling an arrestee who has admitted some crimes that if he also confesses to other offenses (thus "clearing the books" of several unsolved cases), they will not press charges so severely and will report his cooperation to the judge.

Despite these limitations in its accuracy, Table 5–1 is surely correct in its evidence that the proportion of crimes known to the police varies by offense, as do their clearance rates and hence their net clearance rate. Only in the seven index crimes, which are listed in this table, are both the percentage of crimes known to the police and the clearance rates available.

Property crimes are less likely to result in arrest than violent crimes because most property crimes are committed dispassionately, against strangers (including impersonal corporations), and by stealth (the victim does not see the offender). Violent offenses are done when emotionally confronting the victim and, except in robbery, usually by someone known personally to the victim; thus in most cases it is easier to catch assaulters than thieves. Furthermore, because injuring or killing people is so much more serious than taking their possessions, police usually put their greatest effort and resources into solving crimes of severe violence.

A high percentage of fraud is unreported to the police because many victims never know they were cheated, or think they were bilked while themselves engaged in illegal transactions, or for other reasons. Thus the net clearance rate may be under five percent.

It is unlikely that the police are aware of more than a fraction of one percent of *separate* nonpredatory criminal acts—such as taking or selling illegal drugs and engaging in a sexual offense with a consenting partner—even though they have impressions of where this behavior is most prevalent. Therefore, regardless of clearance rates on the nonpredatory acts that the police investigate, the net clearance rate is probably minute. If we assume, for the moment, that all those who commit a crime may be called unsuccessful if it is cleared by the police, then it follows that their failure rate per offense varies from a high of 80 percent for murder to much less than one percent for many nonpredatory acts. Table 5–1 indicates that the index property crimes are between 85 and 93 percent successful for the perpetrators.

CRIME AS A GAMBLE

It should be noted that the figures above refer to the percentage of attempted offenses that are successful, not to the percentage of *criminal careers* that are *always* successful. If all careers include *many* crimes by one person, the percentage of careers that *never* experience a failure may be very small, despite success in a great number of separate crimes. "Getting away with" crime is often only a lure, drawing people into a game with a "stacked deck" in which failure is certain.

TABLE 5-1 Index Crimes Cleared by Arrest, 1974

CRIME	PERCENTAGE REPORTED TO POLICE* (A)	PERCENTAGE POLICE CLEAR BY ARREST** (B)	NET CLEARANCE RATE (A) x (B)	"SUCCESS" RATE IN AVOIDING ARREST
Theft	40%	20%	8%	92%
Burglary	37	18	7	93
Robbery	44	27	12	88
Motor-vehicle theft	100	15	15	85
Aggravated assault	64	63	40	60
Forcible rape	47	51	24	76
Murder and nonnegligent manslaughter	100	80	80	20

* Uniform Crime Report totals as percentage of National Crime Panel totals for comparable offenses and populations, as calculated from data in *LEAA Newsletter*, March 1974.
** From FBI, 1974: 166.

This conclusion is based on the multiplicative rule for the probability of several independent events. The chance of all of a group of such events occurring is the product of the probabilities of each separate event occurring. The reader who does not remember this from an algebra or elementary statistics course can test this rule by tossing two coins many times, keeping a record of whether they turn up heads or tails. The chances of a normal coin turning up heads when tossed is 0.5—it will be heads half the time. The probability of two coins both being heads, however, is 0.5 multiplied by 0.5, or 0.25; only in a quarter of the tosses will both coins be heads (another quarter of the tosses will yield two tails and half will have one head and one tail). Similarly for three coins, the probability of all three being heads is 0.5 times 0.5 times 0.5, or 0.125—once in eight times.

Applying this multiplicative rule to crimes, suppose that one person commits many offenses and is successful in avoiding arrest 90 percent of the time. For any *pairs* of such crimes, the chances of success in *both* of the pair is not 90 percent of all pairs of crimes, but 0.9 for the first one multiplied by 0.9 for the second one, hence 0.81. Thus only in 81 percent *of all pairs* of crimes will the 90-percent-successful criminals succeed in *both* crimes. For any sets of three such crimes, the chance of success *in all three* is 0.9 times 0.9 times 0.9, or 0.729. Thus only in 72.9 percent *of sets of three crimes* will the 90-percent-successful criminals succeed *in all three crimes*. If N represents the number of separate criminal acts that a person commits and S represents the proportion of such acts in which the person is successful, then the probability of success *in all N acts* is S^N. Pocket or desk calculators make it simple to compute these odds for N up to about 10, but tables of logarithms make it fairly easy for N of any size.

Table 5–2 shows that even with such high success rates as 80 to 95 percent on any separate crime, the chances of committing these offenses several times per week without ever being caught for months or years are negligible. Nevertheless, with theft, burglary, and robbery —the offenses that, according to Table 5–1, are about 90 percent successful—the odds are that perpetrators frequently have several consecutive successes. If these crimes "pay" on some occasions, one should expect many offenders to return repeatedly to committing them despite their almost inevitable eventual failure, and even though this failure is just as probable on the first offense in a new series as on any subsequent one. Their recidivism could be produced by the same psychological principle that explains why periodic winnings lead many people to gamble continually at cards or horses or with Nevada's "one-armed bandits," despite their almost inevitable long-run net losses.

A source of persistence in often-rewarded but ultimately costly conduct by offenders or gamblers is what psychologists call the "variable-reinforcement schedule." It has repeatedly been demonstrated, both with humans and animals, that when behavior becomes habitual because it was always followed by a reward, it usually ceases soon if the reward is terminated; but when the behavior was rewarded only at an intermittent and variable rate, it continues with impressive perseverance after all rewards cease. B. F. Skinner, who pioneered research on this principle by showing that pigeons would mechanically and montonously repeat any act of which they were capable if they previously received a variable-reward schedule for it, observes:

> The efficacy of such schedules in generating high rates [of behavior repetition] is well-known to the proprietors of gambling establishments. Slot machines, roulette wheels, dice cages, horse races, and so on pay off on a schedule of variable-ratio reinforcement. . . . The pathological gambler exemplifies the result. Like the pigeon [after variable-reinforcement experiments] with its five responses per second for many hours, he is the victim of an unpredictable . . . reinforcement. The long-term net gain or loss is almost irrelevant in accounting for the effectiveness of this schedule (1953: 104).

The behavior of humans is affected by factors different from those of pigeons, mainly because humans can verbally explain and evaluate their experience. Also, if people gamble at crime instead of with mechanical devices, their risks vary with the way they behave; most of those who repeatedly "get away with" offenses become more careless about the risks they take. After several successive easy and rewarding crimes, they are likely to become cocksure and foolhardy, as

TABLE 5-2 The Probability of Success (S^N) in All N Crimes with a Given Percentage of Success (100S) in Separate Crimes

(Probabilities are given to the nearest 10,000th)

N	PERCENTAGE OF SUCCESS IN SEPARATE CRIMES (100S)					
	50%	80%	90%	95%	99%	99.9%
1	.5000	.8000	.9000	.9500	.9900	.9990
2	.2500	.6400	.8100	.9025	.9801	.9980
3	.1250	.5120	.7290	.8574	.9703	.9970
4	.0625	.4096	.6561	.8145	.9606	.9960
5	.0313	.3277	.5905	.7738	.9510	.9950
6	.0156	.2621	.5314	.7351	.9415	.9940
7	.0078	.2097	.4783	.6983	.9321	.9930
8	.0039	.1678	.4305	.6634	.9227	.9920
9	.0020	.1342	.3874	.6302	.9135	.9910
10	.0010	.1074	.3487	.5987	.9044	.9900
15	.0000*	.0352	.2059	.4633	.8601	.9851
20	.0000	.0115	.1216	.3585	.8179	.9802
25	.0000	.0038	.0718	.2774	.7778	.9753
30	.0000	.0012	.0424	.2146	.7397	.9704
40	.0000	.0001	.0148	.1285	.6690	.9608
50	.0000	.0000*	.0052	.0769	.6050	.9512
75	.0000	.0000	.0004	.0213	.4706	.9277
100	.0000	.0000	.0000*	.0059	.3660	.9048
500	.0000	.0000	.0000	.0001	.0066	.6064
1,000	.0000	.0000	.0000	.0000*	.0000*	.3677
5,000	.0000	.0000	.0000	.0000	.0000	.0067
10,000	.0000	.0000	.0000	.0000	.0000	.0000*

* Entries of .0000 are used wherever the proportion is less than .00005 (5 in 100,000).

well as to acquire the successful gamblers' delusion that they are endowed with "luck." An arrest or a "close call" may make an offender more cautious, and some gain skills in avoiding arrest simply from experience in committing crimes. But a long "streak" of success usually fosters both carelessness and superstitious repetition of a specific *modus operandi,* thus increasing vulnerability to arrest.

The probabilities of success at specific types of crime are averages around which there may be considerable variation from one criminal to the next. Furthermore, the odds presented in Table 5-1 are based on arrests, but as Letkemann observes: "The amateur criminal's central concern is to avoid *detection;* the experienced criminal is concerned that he avoid *conviction*" (1973: 30). As chapter 13 elaborates, many who are professionals or in organized crime are able to "beat the rap" because of their skills and resources for eliminating evidence, intimidating or bribing witnesses, securing astute counsel, and refraining from pleading guilty unless the charges are markedly reduced.

Professional criminals may thus have not only much better chances of success in avoiding arrest than those indicated in Table 5–1, but also high prospects of avoiding severe penalties when caught. Possibly some small fraction of burglars achieve a 99 percent nonpunishment rate; yet Table 5–2 shows that little more than a third of those with this rare ability will be able to commit 100 crimes without penalty in order to average four burglaries a week for six months without much "trouble." Less than one percent will successfully commit 500 crimes in a row without a severe setback from the law, and thus perhaps steal with relative impunity for several years. A very minute group of safecrackers and jewelry thieves gain enough in each offense to live well from crime without stealing often (see Mack, 1972; Letkemann, 1973).

Those with a 99.9 percent success rate at crime probably commit nonpredatory offenses, such as prostitution or moderate drug use only in private settings with people they know, or engage in routine but illegal business crimes rather than the index-crime type of predation; yet not much over a third of them can take this risk a thousand times—for example, five times a week for about four years—without being caught. These probabilities bring us to the question of how much risk one can afford, which is the ultimate issue in determining whether crime pays.

BENEFITS AND COSTS OF CRIME

Whether crime pays can be examined objectively, from the standpoint of an outside observer, or subjectively, from the perspective of the offender. Objective assessment is especially feasible on the economics of property crime, which can be evaluated in dollars. In either case, as indicated at the beginning of this chapter, whether crime pays depends upon:

1. the risks of arrest or conviction
2. the benefits from the crime if not caught
3. the costs of being caught; what one loses by it.

Obviously, these three items vary with the offense and with the offender. Let us look briefly at four of the most common of the immense number of combinations of crime and criminal:

1. Index Crimes by Teenagers

Table 4-3 shows that the peak ages of arrest for index crimes range from 15 for theft, by far the most frequent of these offenses, to 19 for murder and for rape. Table 5–1 shows that the prospect of these offenses not being cleared by arrest ranges from 20 percent for murder to 93 percent for burglary, with theft uncleared in 92 percent of the reported cases. We also noted that certain types of theft are largely unreported, particularly shoplifting and pilfering by employees, and these probably have a much higher prospect of not resulting in arrest than do the reported varieties.

Presumably the average teenager is more brash, inexperienced, and impulsive in committing offenses than older criminals, and therefore, has much less chance of avoiding arrest than these percentages suggest. Even with average success rates, however, the prospects of repeating these crimes one or more times per week for several months without being arrested are quite poor, as shown in Table 5-2.

According to *Uniform Crime Reports* for 1974, the average value of money or property gained was $321 in a robbery, $391 in a burglary, and $156 in a theft (FBI, 1975: 178). These figures probably greatly overstate the usual net value of the loot to the criminal, for in most burglaries and thefts the principal items taken are merchandise rather than money. Criminals are likely to sell stolen goods for about 20 percent of their retail value (Preble & Casey, 1969: 19; Cobb, 1973: 25; Krohm, 1973: 32). Furthermore, the evaluations on which FBI figures are based are usually made by the victims, who tend to exaggerate when they report the worth of stolen goods to the police. This is done either deliberately to cheat the insurance company or inadvertently by neglecting to consider depreciation from age and use. The income of criminals depends greatly on the proportion of their loot that is cash (typically high in robberies) rather than merchandise (more common in burglary and theft) that they must sell cheaply. A liberal estimate of their average net gain is $300 per robbery, $80 per burglary, and $40 per theft. Teenage criminals probably average even less, for these figures include all offenses in each category; robberies include bank robberies (which are usually by adults) and all crimes by professionals, as well as impulsive street robberies by amateurs. Not counted here is auto theft. Teenagers often steal autos worth very large sums, using them primarily for temporary transportation, and more for "joyriding" than to reach a particular destination or for resale.

Objectively, if teenagers seek to support themselves completely from crime, they will probably be unsuccessful. They are almost certain to be caught before many months, for they must repeat most crimes often to attain even a low income, and their cost of living tends to escalate rapidly whenever they have easily gotten money. Many have expensive appetites for liquor, drugs, sex, and are inclined to conspicuous consumption in clothing and vehicles. They enjoy displaying any sudden wealth by generosity to others and high-priced partying—a pattern they often call "highrolling." Furthermore, unlike older professional criminals, they are especially prone to imprudence and carelessness in their offenses whenever they are successful at several in a row. Thus the high teenage arrest rate probably reflects, in part, the tendency for crime not to pay for them.

There is a subjective view that makes crime seem rational for many teenage delinquents, as they perceive their alternative opportunities. First of all, they tend to be somewhat unrealistically optimistic in assessing their prospects of avoiding arrest (see Claster, 1967; Jensen, 1969). Second, youth are often in situations with an audience of peers or others in which the probability of immediate damage to their reputation for toughness, sophistication, or courage if they decline to commit an illegal act is much greater than their chance of arrest (see Short & Strodtbeck, 1965: Chapters 8 and 9). Third, those teenagers who engage in serious delinquent and criminal conduct generally have little stake in school, home, or employment, and have no great expectations from these areas (Hirschi, 1969). From their vantage point, they often have little to lose but much to gain from crime; they are achieving a sense of self-worth, especially during exhilarating escapades while their offenses succeed, even if this leads to arrest and detention.

Because there is often 80 or 90 percent success in separate offenses, many youth get some experience in committing crimes with impunity or hear of others who have done so. Therefore, when social or economic pressures develop that an offense could solve, lawbreaking may seem to many of them a "practical gamble." In some adolescent-group settings, crime may be not only a solution to money problems but also an opportunity to demonstrate courage to oneself and to others by successful risk taking. Because of the risks, it is considered an act of bravery (see Goffman, 1967: 170–74; Werthman, 1967).

The prospect of arrest for adolescents who persist in crime is nevertheless so high that they usually end their crime sprees before many weeks or months. They are either caught, nearly caught, or know someone who has been caught. Also, their lawbreaking may cease because of a change in their social and economic circumstances, giving them more to lose from a reputation as criminal. They may fall in love, get a job, have a happier school situation, or start a new type of recreation, perhaps with different companions—any of which might be jeopardized if they "got in trouble." Although teenagers have by far the highest rate of arrest for theft, burglary, and robbery, involvement in crime, as Matza (1964: 28) observes, is casual, intermittent, and transient. This will change for many when they must support themselves entirely and when engaging in crime conflicts with trying to hold a job, and perhaps with raising a family. For many others, however, their job or job prospects are such that they still have little to lose by crime.

2. Index Property Crimes by Adult Exdelinquents

Teenage delinquents are predominantly unspecialized in their offenses, even when they are repeatedly arrested (Wolfgang et al., 1972: Chapter 9). As they become older and can no longer so readily assume that room and board are freely available at home, those who persist in crime increasingly specialize in property offenses, to provide income for the pleasures of drink, drugs, and sex. (For necessities alone, work or welfare assistance usually suffices.) These persistent index-crime offenders are mostly young adults who cannot support themselves regularly or well at legitimate jobs. Their deficient education, arrest or conviction record, lack of work experience or vocational skills, and— too frequently—minority-group status bring unattractive, unremunerative, and insecure types of employment, or none at all (for a good description, see Liebow, 1967).

Adolescent groups commit diverse offenses impulsively as collective adventures, but adult exdelinquents more often undertake property crimes of many types alone or with the minimum number of partners expedient for the task. They seek *income* rather than "kicks." Those with appropriate talents and contacts become quite specialized and professional in their offenses, especially if an expensive drug habit increases their need for funds; others remain versatile "flat-footed hustlers," epitomized by one who told Preble and Casey (1969: 18): "I'm capable of doing most things—jostling [picking pockets], boosting [shoplifting], con games, burglary, mugging, or stickups; whenever I see the opportunity, that's where I'm at."

Occasionally the illegal pursuits of the property offenders described here are interrupted by periods of employment, but temporary, unskilled jobs are usually all they can procure. Some stay on unemployment compensation or welfare allotments much of the time, but have appetites for alcohol, drugs, or other pleasures for which these payments do not suffice. Whenever their money runs low, opportunities for property crime become especially attractive to them. If in young adulthood they have expensive cravings that they can support only by crime, 40 percent of their time is likely to be spent in incarceration (Preble & Casey, 1969: 20). However, since there is much variation in this proportion, and since over 90 percent of the offenses do not result in arrest, they often have numerous consecutive successes and thus are readily tempted to gamble.

Krohm (1973) estimated the net cash income from the average burglary in Chicago as $36.70 and the average daily pay for unskilled labor as $26.80 (but as even less if the laborer is a former convict). Krohm assumes that one burglary can be committed per day, computes average confinement time of burglars as their days of unemployment, and allows for the average time lost by unskilled laborers due to unemployment. He then estimates that the net annual earnings of adults would average somewhat less from burglary than from unskilled labor. The scale is tipped in favor of burglary only if one goes to the rather ridiculous extreme of counting as income the $17.50 per day that Krohm claims is the value of room and board in prison. He finds, on the other hand, that juvenile burglars clearly gain more money from crime than from labor. Their incarceration when caught is briefer than that of adults, but they lose more time from joblessness and earn less than adults if they try to support themselves by work.

Even if such exact figures are questionable, it is evident that when an adult's prospective legal income is at or below the poverty level and if a jail term adds relatively little to the stigma and insecurity experienced when free, the risk of confinement may not be a strong deterrent to seizing a good chance to increase income several-fold by crime. This uncertain advantage of work over crime for unskilled ex-convicts may explain, for example, why at least 95 percent of federal-prison recidivists seem to follow a "zig-zag" postrelease path—seeking work rather than returning to crime immediately, but eventually taking the risks that lead to their reimprisonment (Glaser, 1969: Chapters 9 and 17). The competition between crime and work for these people suggests that adequate economic assistance in postrelease emergencies, combined with secure employment, might greatly reduce their rates of recidivism. This conclusion is supported by several studies showing that this type of offender has recidivism reduced by: (1) the widely applicable types of vocational training in prison, such as welding, machine-shop skills, and auto repair (McKee, 1972); (2) initial release with room and board, in halfway houses (Hall et al., 1966; Jeffery & Woolpert, 1974; LeClair, 1975); (3) postrelease financial aid through cash payments in emergencies (Lenihan, 1974; Reinarman & Miller, 1975; U.S. Dept. of Labor, 1977).

Perhaps the evidence that index property crimes less clearly "pay" (both subjectively and objectively) for the average adult offender than for juveniles explains why most criminals in both age groups eventually either "grow out of" illegal pursuits or change from index offenses to safer types of crime.

3. Illegal Services by Organized Criminals

Whenever large segments of the public compulsively pursue an illegal activity that requires the purchase of goods or services, a valuable business opportunity is available exclusively to those willing to operate outside the law and is eschewed by investors who value their respectability. Because of the cravings of customers—for example, their desires for drugs, gambling, or prostitutes—the demand in these marketplaces is inelastic; customers will pay high prices, if necessary, for what they want.

Since this type of business is illegal, the police and courts cannot be called upon to guarantee fair competition and honest services. Instead, it is *caveat emptor*—let the buyer beware—and the illegal businessman must beware, too, for ruthless competitors will try to push him out of business. Only strong organizations—not individual entrepreneurs—can operate securely. Out of warfare among criminal organizations, a set of territorial monopolies develops, occasionally challenged by new organizations or by shifting coalitions and factions fighting for power within the old ones.

To supply certain illegal goods and services, such as imported narcotics or large-scale gambling, inherently requires a large organization with many specialized roles and functions at scattered locations, apart from the personnel needed to suppress competitors. This is one type of employment in which a record of delinquency or crime may be an asset rather than a liability. In addition, because of the large investments in fixed locations that enterprises such as gambling require for maximum attraction of customers, they are often safe commercial risks only if police and politicians can be bribed before the establishments are opened. "Payoffs" must also be made regularly thereafter. This corruption amounts to official licensing of the businesses, and it thereby augments their security, especially when *all* competing local politicians are also paid.

Crime in these organizations really pays. It is especially profitable and secure for the top echelon, but there is also a large hierarchy of well-rewarded subordinates. Most employees have no direct contact with persons in more than one or two of the numerous levels above them, thus reducing the risks that many will be exposed to prosecution if a few are caught. Occasionally there are murders of leaders by rivals for power, or of low-ranking personnel for insubordination or disloyalty, but there can be long periods of peace and profit in most of these establishments. Indeed, the leaders often gain respectability by investing in legitimate businesses, frequently making these more profitable by the tactics of corruption or coercion used in their criminal organizations. (For a fuller description, see Chapter 13.)

Even when law enforcement poses some threat to members of these criminal establishments, the closing of one source of supply simply expands the market available to others as long as the demand for their goods and services is extensive and inelastic. Therefore, new criminal syndicates are formed or old ones restructured whenever any segment of organized crime is successfully prosecuted. Since prosecution rarely jeopardizes a large percentage of such an organization's staff or capital, however, the resulting losses in income are usually only temporary.

The main threat to profit from these crimes is the decriminalization of the activities they service. If customers can legally purchase what they crave, legitimate business can compete with the criminal organizations in meeting the demand. Of course, because criminal organizations have more experience, established customers, connections, expertise, and inclination to ruthlessness in competition, they often have initial advantages and dominance in newly decriminalized commerce. This was evident in the liquor business for many years after the Prohibition Amendment was repealed, but it is much less prevalent now. A similar gradual rather than abrupt reduction of opportunities for criminals will probably occur in most other types of criminal business—such as gambling, marijuana sale, and prostitution—if these are increasingly decriminalized.

4. Avocational Crimes by Respected Business Persons

As the late Edwin H. Sutherland (1949) pointed out when he coined the term "white-collar crime," every type of business and occupation has some practices, generally labeled "crooked" or "rackets" by others in the trade, that violate criminal law but seldom lead to prosecution and punishment. Illegal fee-splitting and unnecessary surgery in medicine, collusion in price fixing when only a few firms dominate a market, misrepresentation in advertising and selling, bribery of union officials by employers, bribery of corporation purchasing agents by representatives of their suppliers, improper government favors to campaign contributors, padding of business expense accounts and time sheets, tax evasion, and pilfering of company supplies by employees are among many examples. The cost of these predations is paid by the public, since prices in business and taxes in government must be raised to offset budget deficits. Probably their total cost in the United States exceeds that of all other types of offense, even the immense sales and plunder of organized crime.

Because most of these offenses seldom are prosecuted, they usually "pay" for those who perpetrate them, although employee crimes may sometimes be noted by superiors and lead to blocked promotions or to dismissal and poor references. A distinctive feature of these crimes, however, is that they are not the primary source of income for the culprits; hence they are avocational. Furthermore, the offenders do not regard themselves and generally are not regarded by others as criminals. Consequently, formal prosecution, conviction, and punishment can be highly deterrent—both to those caught and to others made fearful of being caught—but thus far such law enforcement and adjudication are rare. The deterrent effect often requires a stigmatizing conviction followed by impressive penalties, not simply a plea of *nolo contendre* followed by nominal fines. Effective punishments include any periods of jailing or imprisonment, major fines, and requirements of large-scale restitution and public apology (for fuller discussion, see Chapter 12).

Such prosecution and penalty, if more frequent, may render these crimes unprofitable. The inclusion and value-generalization processes in social evolution, discussed in Chapter 2, are gradually expanding the laws and prosecution resources directed against avocational crime in business and government. New varieties of these offenses continually emerge, however, as our ever-changing technology creates new occupations, businesses, and procedures in which employers, customers, and the government may be bilked.

SUMMARY AND CONCLUSION

The risks, costs, and benefits of crime depend on both the crime and the criminal.

To assess risks, we must determine: (1) the rates of clearance by arrest, which are imperfectly known but are estimated for index offenses in Table 5-1; (2) the consequences of arrest in terms of prosecution, detention, and other punishment, which vary greatly from one jurisdiction to the next and pose a research problem not yet widely or well addressed.

In general, the risk of apprehension and punishment is much greater for crimes of violence than for crimes against property. The index property offenses have an 85 to 93 percent prospect of success, if this prospect is defined as 100 percent minus the net clearance rate by arrest. This net rate takes into account both the probability of the victim's notifying the police and the effectiveness of police responses.

Although their high success rates mean that property offenders "get away with" most of their crimes, the notion that this permits most of them to support themselves for years with impunity is an illusion. Table 5-2 shows that the probability of continuous success with repetition of a crime that has a 90 to 99 percent success rate is negligible for any appreciable number of repetitions. The small net income to criminals from most separate index offenses, however, makes much repetition essential for self-support, especially if living standards expand whenever crime is successful. Thus, those who expect to live by *these* crimes are usually not long free. An exception may be the relatively small number of professional criminals who are unusually resourceful not only at avoiding arrest, but also at using threats, bribes, and bargaining to diminish their rates of conviction and the severity of their penalties.

The risks of arrest or conviction, the benefits if not caught, and the losses if caught—hence the net gain or loss in crime—not only vary tremendously, but also can be assessed both objectively, in economic terms, and subjectively. They are discussed here for four typical combinations of offense and offender:

1. *Index crimes by teenagers* tend to be unspecialized and committed not only to gain money (even when they are property crimes), but also to demonstrate abilities and character traits to themselves and to peers or other audiences. Although objectively risky, crime may subjectively "pay" for any youths who are alienated from school, home, and work; who greatly value their reputations for sophistication, daring, and toughness, and for whom the deprivations of juvenile correctional confinement are not extremely severe compared with life in the community.

2. *Index property crimes by adult exdelinquents* reflect their very limited employment opportunities, as well as the prospect of their having appetites too expensive to be satisfied by welfare payments. Since the advantage of legitimate over illegitimate economic pursuits is not clear for them, they tend to mix or alternate these types of endeavors, but eventually either "outgrow" crime or turn to safer offenses. Employment aid for the jobless and assistance to released offenders in economic crises can markedly reduce the appeal to them of index property crimes.

3. *Illegal services by organized criminals* are sold profitably and relatively safely because these organizations use force and bribery to achieve a monopoly in supplying large and inelastic public demands. These businesses provide occupations in which a criminal record can be an asset rather than a liability, and in which job security is strengthened by corrupting the criminal-justice system. The main threat to their profitability is not the prospect that laws against them may be effectively enforced, but that their monopoly will be reduced or eliminated through decriminalization of the goods or services they sell.

4. *Avocational crimes by respected business persons* flourish in all types of occupations and organizations in which "crooked practices" and "rackets" may be committed with impunity. Because the perpetrators do not depend upon these predations as their primary source of income, and do not regard themselves as criminal, they are usually markedly deterred if stigmatizing prosecution and significant penalties occur. Thus far, however, prosecution is rare. Although these offenses probably cost the public more than any other type of crime, only when the inclusion and value-generalization processes (discussed in Chapter 2) make the public and its government less tolerant of such predations will they diminish.

Understanding how behavior becomes defined as crime, and knowing its dimensions and consequences—the main thrust of these first five chapters—are useful foundations for more intensive study of offenses, offenders, and the criminal-justice system. Indeed, whether crime "pays" depends on the wisdom of our reactions to it, and, thus, on how well we apply both scientific knowledge and humane values to controlling crime and achieving justice.

PART TWO
EXPLANATIONS

SIX

GENERAL THEORIES OF CRIMINAL CONDUCT

People always search for simple explanations to make sense of the puzzling array of facts and impressions encountered in life. The study of crime is no exception. It has had one "grand theory" after another, although the influence of each has waxed or waned in various periods. Since few of these theories have completely disappeared, many viewpoints now coexist. Usually, different people employ alternative theories to interpret the same events, and often one person uses several theories to explain diverse aspects or types of lawbreaking.

FROM MEDIEVAL TO MODERN THOUGHT

Interpretations of crime in the Western world since the fall of the Roman Empire (around A. D. 476) can be identified with three epochs. Each was distinguished by ways of thinking about offenses that remain influential even today.

The Middle Ages

From the sixth through the sixteenth centuries (embracing the medieval, Renaissance, and early Reformation periods), Europeans conceived of the universe as relatively small, confined to earth, heaven, and hell. Humanity was viewed as having fallen from grace in the Garden of Eden and capable of perfection only after death. The basis for argument on abstract questions was reference to authority, especially the Scriptures, as interpreted by the early Church Fathers. Beginning in the twelfth century, these were supplemented by the works of the Scholastics at the medieval universities. During the thirteenth century St. Thomas Aquinas was particularly influential. He revived reliance on the works of Aristotle for guidance in secular issues.

Throughout these eras there was a strong tendency to divide the world into Good and Evil, manifested by sacred and profane influences, and to see a heirarchy of superiority and inferiority in the class structure and in all of nature. The nobility, and the clergy recruited from it, were deemed much more intelligent than the commoners and serfs. These rankings were considered immutable, either by God's design or as a consequence of the fall from grace. All misfortunes—whether crime, war, famine, flood, or infertility of women and of soil—were traced to mankind's evil nature, to Satan, or to Divine Wrath.

Felonies, considered mortal sins because they violated Divine Law and jeopardized the offender's soul, included heresy, witchcraft, and deliberate murder of one's superiors. The felon, it was thought, had yielded to the Devil's temptations, which play on our evil passions. Not just death, but death by torture, such as burning at the stake or boiling in oil, was imposed for heresy and witchcraft, as well as for murder committed by a low-status person against a high-status victim (Hibbert, 1963: Chapter 2).

Lesser offenses—the misdemeanors—were deemed violations only of human law. Aquinas ascribed them to the "irascible" rather than evil angers and appetites. Failure to curb these passions required only that one ask the Lord's forgiveness and be willing to do penance. In this period,

> criminal law played an unimportant role as a means of preserving the social heirarchy. Tradition, a well-balanced system of social dependence, and the religious acknowledgement of the established order were sufficient and efficient safeguards. The main emphasis of criminal law lay on the maintenance of public order between equals in status and wealth. If, in the heat of the moment or in a state of intoxication, someone committed an offense against decency, accepted morality, or religion, or severely injured or killed his neighbor —violation of property rights did not count much in this society of landowners—a solemn gathering of free men would be held to pronounce judgement and make the culprit pay . . . or do penance so that the vengeance of the injured parties would not develop into blood feud or anarchy. . . . Crime was looked upon as an act of war. In the absence of a strong central power the public peace was endangered by the smallest quarrels between neighbors, as these quarrels automatically involved relatives and servants. The preservation of peace was, therefore, the primary preoccupation of the criminal law. As a result of its method of private arbitration, it performed this task almost entirely by imposition of fines.
>
> Class distinctions were manifested by differences in the extent of penance . . . carefully graded according to the social status of the evildoer and of the wronged party. . . . The inability of lower-class evildoers to pay fines led to the substitution of corporal punishment in their case (Rusche & Kirchheimer, 1939: 9).

A wave of crime, disease, or other misfortune was usually ascribed either to Divine Wrath or to witchcraft. Some offenders were deemed innocent when their crimes were blamed on the influence of a witch or a wizard, a person described in English law as having had "conference with the Devil, to consult with him to do some act" (Murray, 1960). This perspective, of course, encouraged lawbreakers or their friends and relatives to blame their misdeeds on satanic machination. King James I wrote a widely respected *Daemonology* on how to cope with witches. Pope Innocent VIII recommended that inquisitors

Salem, Massachusetts witchcraft trial, 1692 (see Erikson, 1966—137-55).

of the canonical courts refer to *Malleus Malificarum* (*Hammer of Witches*), a fifteenth-century manual by the clerics Kramer and Sprenger (1484/1971) when investigating and punishing witchcraft.

Some of the explanations for crime in this period are still upheld literally by adherents of certain religious sects. But such ancient ideas persevere more often—even among some social scientists—in the notion that evil conduct is caused only by evil persons. The muckraking approach to prostitution, gambling, and drug use expresses a witchhunting mentality. It is countered by the contention that crime rates will not change unless the social conditions causing them are altered. The norms of showing repentance and paying for one's sins still prevail, but this emphasis may be justified by psychological as well as religious precepts.

The Enlightenment

During the seventeenth and eighteenth centuries, merchants, bankers, and independent craftsmen—the middle classes—challenged the power of the nobility and the clergy. Philosophers of this era called for an "Age of Reason." They stressed values derived from the Reformation and the Counter-Reformation, which encouraged individual effort to better one's status on earth as a means of preparing for the afterlife. Growth of science enlarged conceptions of the universe, making society seem humanly perfectible in a world governed by natural laws in which God no longer intervenes. The mind, however, was deemed separate from the body and not subject to natural laws. The leading thinkers of the Enlightenment—for example, Voltaire, Rousseau, Locke, and Hume—conceived of all persons (regardless of status) as endowed by their Creator with reason and, therefore, with natural rights.

As indicated in Chapter 3, the foremost extension of the Enlightenment's deification of reason to explain crime was the work of Cesare Beccaria. Stress on human rationality was soon reflected in the criminal law, especially in Britain, where the Utilitarian philosophy was enthusiastically endorsed. Jeremy Bentham, its principal exponent, portrayed people as calculators. He advocated achieving the greatest good for the greatest number by imposing punishments on offenders just sufficient in painfulness to offset the pleasures that might be expected from lawbreaking. But he neglected the arbitrary values and the irrational emotions often involved in crime, and he dealt inadequately with the fact that a criminal also calculates the probability of evading all penalty by not getting caught.

Enlightenment principles are evident in conceptions of crime control as primarily a matter of deterrence and, hence, the notion that people refrain from crime only when government punishment is sufficient. After more than a century of diminished influence, these ideas are being revived. Some advocates of a determinate sentence for each crime and the abolition of parole argue partly from eighteenth-century writings (see von Hirsch, 1976: 6).

The Modern Era

The theory of evolution prompted a search for natural laws governing both thought and emotion, applicable not only to humans but also to all animals. These developments weakened the earlier dualistic view of the intellect as independent of biology. The behavioral sciences of psychology, sociology, and anthropology emerged as autonomous disciplines, at first with a strong biological grounding from instinct theories. Chapter 7 elaborates on: (1) how this led to quasi-scientific explanations for crime that were eventually discredited, for they posited genetic determinants of offenses, closely linked to human physiques; (2) contrastingly, how new research and theory show that some bodily conditions may indeed facilitate or impede the learning of legal conduct or the expression of urges to commit criminal acts.

During the nineteenth century, both Social Darwinism and

Marxism emerged, offering very different explanations for lawbreaking with contrasting policy implications. The perspective of the theory of evolution, exemplified by Spencer in Britain and by Sumner in America, ascribed crime to deficient diligence, temperance, and thrift, due either to low intelligence or to indulgence of the poor. Its views were compatible with both a harsh eugenics approach emphasizing castration or execution to prevent survival of the "unfit," and a deterrence philosophy of mandatory and severe punishment. Although Marx did not discuss crime extensively, Wilhelm Bonger in Holland and Enrico Ferri in Italy were prominent among many Continental criminologists in the early twentieth century who blamed crime mainly on poverty. They contended that replacement of the capitalist system by socialism is the only way to end predation.

In the 1970s both political conservatism and Marxism are prominent in polemical works on the causes and prevention of crime. These will be touched on in Chapter 14. From about 1925 to the present, however, a tremendous body of nonpolemical social-science theory and research on the causes and correlates of lawbreaking has also accumulated; this will be summarized and assessed in the rest of this chapter and in those that follow, through Chapter 13.

Those Marxists who call themselves "critical criminologists" (see, for example, Taylor et al., 1975) assert or imply that even the nonpolemical social scientists who claim to be "value-free" have a "hidden agenda" of "establishment values" that shape their thought and bias their findings. This book's assumption is that values determine our choice of problems for research and may affect the variables we consider and the data we accept as valid, but that our errors of prediction will be minimized if we still strive to be as value-free as possible in the collection and assessment of empirical evidence. This requires that we endeavor to be aware of our possible bias in theory formulation and research methods. One way of pursuing this goal is to try to consider the widest range of approaches to explaining crime, and the evidence marshaled in support of each.

PSYCHOANALYTIC STUDIES OF DELINQUENCY

Sigmund Freud (1856–1939), though not the first, was probably the most influential proponent of the idea that one's basic character is largely determined in the early years of one's childhood. This theme became the central tenet of the overlapping disciplines of psychoanalysis, psychiatry, clinical psychology, and psychiatric social work, whose case studies of offenders ascribe crime to personality.

Defining delinquency as all "thoughts, actions, desires and strivings which deviate from moral and ethical principles" (Eissler, 1949: 3), psychoanalysts describe humans as completely "delinquent" at birth, grasping for gratifications without considering others. Accordingly, they view much later delinquency and crime as fixation at or regression to an infantile stage of psychological development. The Freudians ascribe this initial dominance of behavior by the "pleasure principle" primarily to instinctual cravings, which they label collectively as the *id*. Such urges, in which sexual desires are prominent, Freud (1940) saw as gradually controlled in normal development by the "reality principle"—an awareness of which types of pleasure pursuit are successful and which are not—but only if the conscious personality, the *ego*, is capable of controlling the *id*.

Freudians also regard behavior as regulated by the ethical norms learned from others, and these are expressed in an aspect of the personality called the *superego*. If these moral standards yield an unfavorable assessment when applied to one's own conduct, they evoke guilt feelings, conscious or unconscious. Such feelings are a major focus of psychoanalytic diagnosis and treatment of personality disorders, especially in adults. The superego is ordinarily called the conscience, and sometimes its various aspects are referred to as the "censor" and the "ego ideal."

The classic work on delinquency in the psychoanalytic tradition is *Wayward Youth* by August Aichhorn (1925), a Viennese educator who became a friend and follower of Freud. Finding that the young children with behavior problems who were sent to his private school would not lie on a couch and free-associate as adults did, he established a very permissive residence for them where their spontaneous behavior could be observed and interpreted by the staff, who could also gradually gain rapport with them. Aichhorn's "milieu approach" to both diagnostic examination and therapy was furthered later by medically trained psychoanalysts, notably Bruno Bettelheim (1950) and Fritz Redl (Redl & Wineman, 1951), who operated residences in the United States for emotionally disturbed and predominantly delinquent children. They were successful writers, conveying vividly and persuasively the dynamics of interaction of their young clients. Their accounts are impressive whether or not one accepts all of their often quite speculative interpretations.

One basic assumption in their approach, perhaps most clearly set forth by Aichhorn, is that the *manifest* delinquent behavior of a child is not as important for understanding and treating misconduct as the *latent delinquency,* the unconscious thought, desires, and fears that motivate overt acts. Analysts rely on their inferences about the covert symbolic meaning of visible conduct. For example, they ascribe much delinquency to failure to cope adequately with the Oedipus Complex —a boy's normal, though repressed, sexual desire for his mother and, hence, jealousy of his father—and with the Electra Complex—a girl's repressed sexual orientation to her father and consequent jealousy of her mother.

Psychoanalysts attribute much crime to the failure of adolescents and adults to resolve their infantile and early-childhood problems. Unconscious fixation on early complexes and fears, or regression to them, is considered the basic cause for what Aichhorn calls "neurotic" delinquency—characterized by weak ego control of the id and much repressed guilt—as opposed to "dissocial" delinquency—characterized by a superego with criminal values learned from parents or others. These therapists strive to provide their clients with insight into unconscious feelings and to facilitate development of strong egos and socially acceptable superegos. They are especially difficult to refute by empirical evidence when they postulate that offenders who recidivate have unconscious desires to punish themselves for guilt in early childhood relationships with parents; these self-destructive wishes, they claim, cause criminals to commit offenses in order to be caught, drug addicts to try to kill themselves by chemical torture, and gamblers to try to lose. Occasionally a recidivist claims to have had such desires, but for most there is no means of proving or disproving these theories on the unconscious.

OTHER CLINICAL APPROACHES

A view of the criminal as "young beyond his years," as failing to develop the normal adult's control over delinquent impulses and, thus, as mentally ill is a pervasive heritage from Freud in many psychological approaches to offenders. Nevertheless, there are alternatives to Freud's conception of the mechanisms by which childhood maladjustments are later manifested in crime-prone personalities.

Erik Erikson (1963, 1968), a psychoanalyst much influenced by anthropology and sociology, stresses the problems of developing an *ego identity* during and after childhood. He sees this needed, gratifying, and guiding self-conception as achievable only by resolution of eight kinds of conflict that persons of all cultures encounter sequentially from the cradle to the grave: (1) trust versus mistrust, a dilemma that begins in infancy as the dependability of nurture from the mother; (2) autonomy versus shame and doubt, originating as the problem of anal control in toilet training; (3) initiative versus guilt, arising in early-childhood awareness of physical abilities and social-manipulation capacities for helping or hurting others; (4) industry versus inferiority, the concern with mastering assigned tasks during what Freud called the "latency" period in sexual development (approximately the decade that precedes puberty); (5) identity from role performance versus confusion about one's role, a peak concern during puberty and adolescence; (6) achieving satisfying intimacy with others—both sexually and in friendships of mutual trust—versus isolation, a central problem in young adulthood; (7) a sense of productivity and creativity versus feelings of stagnation, a recurrent issue in adulthood; (8) ego integrity—a sense of satisfaction with the past and present and a lack of anxiety about the future—versus self-disgust and despair, a source of tension in maturity and old age. The implication of this theory is that a variety of deviant conduct, including violation of the criminal law and diffuse boredom and unhappiness, is made more probable by failure to resolve any of these conflicts of the "Eight Ages of Man."

The belief that childhood difficulties underlie adult misconduct has many other interpretations in modern clinical psychology. Thus in Eric Berne's (1964) influential "transactional analysis" of "games people play," the "child" in us appears whenever we react with petulance or rage to the "parent" in others. Berne conceives the parent as a domineering role adopted by everyone at times, from childhood on, in trying to cope with others as our parents have coped with us. Some psychologists give little attention to identifying the causes of adolescent or adult misconduct, for they simply assume maldevelopment in childhood and then focus on helping the offender to achieve better relationships with others and to behave responsibly. This approach is most explicit in William Glasser's "reality therapy" (1965), which decries a conception of delinquency or crime as the product of mental illness, and views preoccupation with the past as a device by which both patients and clinicians avoid moral responsibility for the present and the future.

Since the services of psychiatrists and psychoanalysts with medical degrees are costly, criminal-justice agencies generally consult them only in atypical cases, such as notorious or bizarre crimes involving unusual behavior. This preoccupation with people whose conduct is puzzling fosters speculation, including the guess that manifest behavior symbolizes something quite different in the subject's unconscious thought. These theories must be accepted largely on faith. Research on their validity can rely only on individual case illustrations (rather than on statistical evidence from representative samples of all offenders of a specified category) and on interpretations that rarely include predictions definite enough to be disproven. Accordingly, criminologists who are committed to more objective research tend to ignore psychoanalytic theories as not rigorously testable and, hence, as unscientific.

PERSONALITY RESEARCH AND TYPOLOGIES OF DELINQUENCY

There have been extensive efforts to identify law violators by personality tests, some of which are described in the next chapter when discussing research on psychopathy and on extroversion. In general, the most marked and consistent differentiation between convicted criminals and those without a known record of offenses is achieved by tests such as the Pd (Psychopathy) scale of the Minnesota Multiphasic Personality Inventory or the So (Socialization) scale of the California Personality Inventory, which ask subjects about acts and values either comprising or highly correlated with delinquency. Other scales on these inventories, as well as performance and projective tests, claim to measure personality disorders believed to have their origin in early child development; but they have proved relatively unsuccessful in distinguishing offenders from nonoffenders (Waldo & Dinitz, 1967; Hindelang, 1972). Apparently whatever disorders they may measure are about as common in law-abiding as in law-violating persons.

Probably the most useful statistical studies of crime causation begin or end with differentiation of offenders by type. This approach has yielded much convergence of psychologically and sociologically derived explanations, although each is often applied primarily to its own kinds of offenders and phase of the life cycle. As already indicated, Aichhorn distinguished neurotic delinquency, which he ascribed primarily to early relationships with parents, from dissocial delinquency, which he blamed on societally unacceptable standards of morality taught to children of various ages by unethical parents or others. Much subsequent research oriented to identifying types uses somewhat similar categories.

The psychiatrist Richard L. Jenkins, a specialist in examining delinquents for juvenile courts, reported in 1943 that they were of three main types: quiet but deceitful, aggressive, and the loyal member of a street gang (Jenkins, in Reckless, 1943). This typology, still used in the 1970s by some psychiatrists in several countries, was tested with ratings of 500 delinquents from case files of the Michigan Child Guidance Clinic on 45 traits. Children were designated "overinhibited" if the file reported three or more of six traits ascribed to this type (seclusiveness, shyness, apathy, worrying, sensitivity, submissiveness), "unsocialized aggressive" if they had three or more of six traits deemed indicative of this category (assaultive tendencies, initiatory fighting, cruelty, defiance of authority, malicious mischief, inadequate guilt feelings), and "socialized delinquents" if they had three or more of seven traits of the gang member (bad companions, gang activities, cooperative stealing, furtive stealing, habitual school truancy, leaving home, staying out late). By this procedure only 195 of the 500 juveniles, or 39 percent, could be classified into one of these categories, including 13 who fit the criteria for two types. During the one to five years of contact that the clinic had with these youth before the research, only the overinhibited showed marked rates of improvement (Hewitt & Jenkins, 1946).

Inability to classify 61 percent of the delinquents by the Hewitt and Jenkins procedure probably indicates both deficiencies of clinical case records and the fact that most persons do not fall readily into distinct behavioral categories. Types distinguished impressionistically tend to be idealizations of reality (Wood, 1969; Lopreato & Alston, 1970) because typologists usually conceive of their categories by thinking only of the extreme cases on conduct or attitude dimensions. Actually, most persons are near the middle of a bell-shaped curve of intensity on these dimensions. Furthermore, human behavior and feelings are less consistent and stable and, consequently, less reliably classifiable than personality or delinquency typologies imply (Toch, 1970). (For fuller discussion of these themes, see Glaser, 1974: Chapter 2.)

Subsequent research over three decades has yielded classifications roughly paralleling those of Hewitt and Jenkins; for example:

1. Analysis by Albert J. Reiss, Jr. (1952) of juvenile-court records in Chicago on 1,110 male probationers applied a typology of partly Freudian and partly sociological derivation. A rubric had to be assigned for each case, and there was appreciable consistency in independent ratings of the same cases. The 22 percent categorized as "weak-ego" type resembled Aichhorn's "neurotics" and the Hewitt and Jenkins "overinhibited"; the 12 percent labeled "defective superego" were much like the "unsocialized aggressive"; the remaining 66 percent, called "relatively integrated," were predominantly street-gang delinquents.

2. During the 1960s, Herbert C. Quay and his associates procured adjectival ratings by staff and personality-test results on hundreds of inmates of juvenile correctional institutions. Using the statistical technique of factor analysis, which identifies clusters of traits that are correlated with each other, they demonstrated that most of these juvenile delinquents were differentiated by three fairly distinct sets of traits: a "neurotic disturbed" group, an aggressive group called "unsocialized psychopathic," and the "subcultural socialized," who were predominantly gang delinquents (Peterson et al., 1961; Quay, 1965).

3. California's Community Treatment Program, the longest con-

trolled experiment in American correctional history, studied 1,014 offenders. It began in 1961 with nine categories of delinquents, but concluded in 1974 that only three were reliably and usefully distinguished: "neurotics" comprised 53 percent of the total cases and were the group for whom community treatment rather than incarceration resulted in lower recidivism rates both before and after the supervision period; 21 percent were classified "power oriented," as manipulative or aggressive youth, many of them gang members, and they were less recidivistic after incarceration than after community treatment; "passive conformists" comprised but 14 percent and showed no clear advantage with any treatment alternative. Several infrequently used categories absorbed the remaining 12 percent (Palmer, 1974).

All of these studies, and others that could be cited, differentiate (1) a neurotic or conflicted group, apparently not highly committed to crime; (2) self-centered, often cruel and deceptive offenders, resembling so-called psychopaths; (3) those with close ties to other offenders, often members or former members of gangs. The percentages in these three categories vary from one inquiry to the next, of course, for the definitions were not identical and the source of cases in each study was unique (e.g., one investigated only probationers, another surveyed institutional inmates, and still another researched parolees, each in a different locale). In every study, many subjects had some characteristics resembling more than one of the three types, suggesting the possible utility of a general theory to explain much criminality.

DRIFTS IN THE REINFORCEMENT AND DETERRENCE OF CRIME

All behavior not controlled by biological factors is presumably learned. A large variety of theory has been developed and tested to account for the rate of learning and the behavior or knowledge learned (see, for example, Hilgard & Bower, 1975). The most useful principles of learning theory, in simple form, are:

1. Behavior that is gratifying tends to be repeated in the types of circumstance in which it was gratifying.

2. Behavior that is not gratifying eventually tends to be terminated.

3. Behavior tends not to occur while punished in the circumstan-

ces in which it previously was gratifying, but to reappear after the punishment ceases or is evaded or endured, unless alternative behavior becomes as gratifying in these circumstances.

A more complex and technical wording might be appropriate in psychology, but for our discussion the above formulation suffices.

Surely nobody is reared through childhood and adolescence without being taught some conventional anticriminal values, but few if any refrain from committing and rationalizing some acts that could be called criminal. Therefore, a vast majority who drift into clearly illegal conduct in this period or later must be conflicted about it at times, despite most people's impressive ability to rationalize their offenses and to compartmentalize their criminal life so it does not affect their legitimate activities. Whether juveniles who engage in crime subsequently become more devoted to it or complete the transition to adulthood without further offenses may depend greatly on the consequences of their initial criminal activity. These consequences may be divided into two broad categories: (1) relatively direct psychological reinforcements and (2) more indirect reinforcements that can be called social-polarization pressures, such as labeling. Only the first will be discussed here; the second will be examined in the two sections that follow.

The first principle of learning set forth above—gratifying behavior tends to be repeated—has been well established by an immense variety of psychological experiments. Nevertheless, rewards and punishments for criminal acts are much more subtle and diverse in the complex social world than the positive and negative reinforcements that a psychologist can manipulate in a laboratory. Thus even people successful in crimes do not always repeat them until caught. Some do persist in this fashion, of course, like gamblers who stay with the roulette wheel, slot machine, or poker game until "cleaned out." Most people whose experience in crime starts with ordinary types of property predation, however, seem to begin in adolescence; but they "quit while they're ahead" not long after they start, and before the consequences become severe. This is evident in the tapering off of such offense rates with age.

Table 4-3 showed that adolescents predominate among arrestees in property felonies—burglary, grand theft, and auto theft. The rewards in these acts, of course, are money or goods, but they often also include much that is less tangible, such as a sense of competence from success and the mutual admiration and support of confederates. These intangible rewards frequently prove more important than the stolen property. On the other hand, the subjective penalties may be harsher than the physical or psychological pain of arrest, adjudication, and legal punishment, and can counterbalance the rewards. The subtle negative consequences include second thoughts on the morality of the act (especially if the victim is a person rather than a corporation), but especially fear of what people to whom the offender feels attached might think, say, and do if they knew of the offense.

Not nearly enough is known about the illegal acts of unapprehended adolescent offenders. Nevertheless, there is strong reason to believe that typically, their crimes do not continuously increase in frequency or severity until they are caught (or afterwards), although some do have such a linear progression. In undergraduate criminology classes, for example, the author found at several universities that about three-fourths of the students will admit on an anonymous questionnaire that they have engaged in shoplifting, although 90 percent say this was never for anything worth over $50. When asked to indicate the age when their shoplifting was at a peak, the most frequent answer is 12; when asked at what age they last did it, the most frequent response is 15. Yet there are also responses of stopping at later ages, and about a fifth of those college students who report having shoplifted admit that that they have not stopped the practice.

When those who say that they did stop shoplifting are asked the reasons for this termination, 45 percent indicate "became afraid of being caught," one-third "decided it was morally wrong," a quarter report being caught, about one-tenth "felt I was too old for this," and still fewer "stopped going with people who did this sort of thing" or "felt it would now threaten my reputation." (Multiple reasons were acceptable. These precoded "check off" categories were derived from the most frequent responses to earlier questionnaires, on which students were asked to put their reasons for stopping entirely in their own words. Even in the above, however, an "other reason" category remained, but it was seldom used.)

Being students who presumably expected to finish college, most who completed these questionnaires had what Toby (1957a) aptly calls "stakes in conformity." Arrests or convictions could bar them from jobs or professions to which they aspire, interrupt their college attendance, and create great strains on their reputations and relationships.

A lower stake in conformity more typically characterizes younger adolescents, persons who already have criminal records, and those with advanced alcoholism or opiate addiction—the three groups most frequently arrested for burglary or grand theft. As indicated, the reason most often given by college students for stopping their shoplifting is fear of being caught, rather than actually having been caught; even though they "get away with" their thefts, they become increasingly apprehensive of the risk of humiliation, stigma, or other negative consequences of being caught. Similar responses would presumably be given if these polls were of persons who did not go to college, since statistics on age and crime rates indicate that most of them also terminate the stealing they commit earlier in adolescence.

Chapter 5 explained why few of those who engage in ordinary theft and burglary can long pursue it as a livelihood without being arrested. The odds it presented may account for the fact that rates of committing crime are sporadic and episodic for most persons. On the one hand, each separate crime may seem a fairly safe risk and be especially attractive when stake in conformity is low and the perceived opportunities or social pressures to commit it are great. Also, people can "neutralize" their beliefs that stealing, cheating, and assault are evil by rationalizing as "different" their reasons for doing these things (Sykes & Matza, 1957). Such rationalization seems to occur most readily when a mood of alienation from parents, friends, school, or job reduces their sense of stake in conformity. Furthermore, if people are in a time and place in which companions dare them to commit a crime and in which it seems evident that success will be admired, a stake in nonconformity develops. Taking what appears to be "a practical gamble" permits one to show off one's "character," Goffman (1967: 170–74) points out, and the greater the risk the more favorable the reputation gained if one performs well. Similarly, situational anticipations of "losing face" if timid often foster illegal acts even where an objective view would deem it foolhardy (Short & Strodtbeck, 1965: Chapter 11).

On the other hand, the rates of arrest for those with persistence at most types of crime are high enough to make prospects of nearly getting caught or of knowing someone who is caught a frequent experience to anyone who commits offenses or knows others involved in them. These events may increase perception of the risk in illegal behavior, regardless of success at it thus far. A sense of stake in conformity, a concern with "what people will say" or do, varies somewhat with conflict and mood from day to day, fluctuating with "the way things go" at home, at school and at jobs. Thus many variables may explain why, as Matza (1964: 28) says, much involvement in crime is casual, intermittent, and transient. Nevertheless, one general proposition on criminal careers that follows from discussion thus far in this chapter is: *The recidivism rates of those apprehended for crimes depend greatly upon the prior stakes in conformity and nonconformity of these persons, and hence on their anticipations from crime and on whether these anticipations are changed by their experiences of being caught.*

LABELING

A recurrent theme in sociological writings on crime and delinquency is the theory of secondary deviance (Lemert, 1967), often called *labeling theory.* In its testable formulation, this is the idea that labeling persons as delinquent or criminal causes others to react to them in a manner that fosters further law-violating behavior, through making them think of themselves as offenders and through limiting their opportunities in legitimate pursuits. This view overlooks people—including many who break the law—whose prior self-conceptions as law-abiding and whose stake in their reputation as conforming cause them to be deterred if they are labeled law violators (Glaser, 1971: Chapter 4; Thorsell & Klemke, 1972). Most persons who are not known as criminals, if caught for violating laws that they do not oppose (e.g., laws against theft), make great efforts to redeem their reputation. They offer excuses, apologies, and regrets: they try to say or do things to salvage their good names with persons who may now have a lesser respect for them, and they are likely to be more careful to avoid crime in the future.

Often it is not until persons are charged with an offense that their difficulties become urgent concerns to their family and friends. Indeed, close kin may come to the assistance of an accused mainly out of fear of stigma to themselves from their relative's misdeed. All these patterns of reaction to labeling help explain the dramatic decline in crime by most persons after a first arrest, especially when they are progressing in school, on the job, or in a stable marriage. Official intervention usually reduces recidivism, Fisher and Erickson (1973) show.

This deterrent effect of labeling is described vividly in Mary O. Cameron's (1964) account of middle-class housewives and adolescents who, when apprehended for shoplifting, abruptly terminate what has often been a fairly extensive practice. This effect of labeling is also documented statistically and interpreted in Ralph England's (1957) analysis of the high success rate of first offenders on probation.

Unfortunately, the most conspicuous clientele of the criminal-justice system are the failures of prior action by the police, courts, and correctional agencies, the people these agencies have dealt with longest and most repeatedly. The visibility of such recidivist offenders makes the public and even the criminal justice officials overlook the majority of lawbreakers whose first arrest, regardless of its disposition, is either the last one or the last one for a long time.

In some contexts negative labels even deter addicted offenders, as when they are used deliberately by self-help groups such as Alcoholics Anonymous and Gamblers Anonymous, to conventionalize their own behavior (Warren, 1974a). They call themselves alcoholics or gamblers to help each other belie these labels by changing their conduct.

Perhaps the most frequent disproof of the implication in some sociological literature that negative labels always criminalize occurs when these tags are completely unwarranted, as when based on false information or deliberate effort to malign. Such accusations are almost certain to be resisted and to evoke conduct clearly contradicting the allegations. This branding may have a stigmatizing effect, however, if others consider it warranted. Certainly there are instances in which it has driven people to behave in a manner that makes the originally erroneous designation become fitting. Yet whether negative labels are based on truth or falsity, there are many ways of "fighting back"—from direct repudiation to flight, from evasion to modification of the label—so that it is not so unfavorable (Rogers & Buffalo, 1974).

One may hypothesize (paraphrasing Thorsell & Klemke, 1972) that being labeled delinquent or criminal is most likely to deter rather than foster further offenses, if:

1. the labeled persons are not yet committed to crime as a career.

2. the labeling occurs in a private setting, but with the prospect that future deviance will be publicized.

3. the labeling is done by esteemed persons not similarly labeled.

4. the label is easily removable when the offenses cease.

5. the labeling evokes an effort by others to reintegrate the offenders into the community.

Schur (1971, 1973) points out that stereotyping is a major aspect of the criminalization of individuals by the labels that others give them. People acquire fixed ideas of what a delinquent or criminal is like, and as soon as they hear that someone has committed a crime they assume that this person has all the traits they associate with such offenders. Indeed, the convenient terminology used here—"delinquents," "offenders," and "criminals"—as well as the identification of persons by their specific crime—such as "burglar," "thief," and "rapist"— unavoidably increases the tendency to categorize large and very diverse groups of persons as if they were identical. Although Thorsell and Klemke point out that labels are less criminalizing if easily removable, there are no time limits on criminal labels. Once persons have stolen things, there are no rules on when to stop calling them thieves; the same applies to all other terms for those who have committed crimes.

Being labeled criminal decreases stake in conformity when it becomes the basis for prejudice and discrimination against those who, regardless of their prior conduct, are now trying to pursue a legitimate course of behavior, perhaps in a job, at school, or in law-abiding social groups or organizations. Often the tag, such as exconvict, becomes the reason for scapegoating them, and suspecting them of crimes they did not commit. The labeled persons, when aware of such prejudice, frequently become uncomfortable and self-conscious, and therefore quit school or jobs, or leave conventional social groups, finding more acceptance in criminal social circles.

Being called criminal, of course, especially when the label is deserved, can create a stake in nonconformity if it fosters pride in one's offenses, acclaim from others, and a reputation "to live up to" in delinquent or criminal cliques and gangs. This is the essence of the theory of secondary deviation, as applied to criminology. If a reputation for offenses is perceived favorably or is deemed unavoidable, if it evokes social support in lawbreaking, or if it results in acquiring criminal techniques, opportunities, or rationalizations, the label can indeed foster new crime or secondary deviance. Thus, any appreciable consequences of a label on an offender's anticipations for the future are likely to have a feedback effect on behavior, whether it is (1) what Wilkins (1965: 85ff.) calls "deviance amplification" through generating secondary deviance, or (2) deterrence of further offenses by jeopardizing but not destroying the stake in conformity.

STRAIN, POLARIZATION, AND CRIMINALITY

When persons are frustrated in conventional pursuits, Talcott Parsons (1951: Chapter 7) observes, they become ambivalent toward those in authority or toward rules and laws that give them trouble; but interaction with others commits them to more definite pro or con attitudes. The behavior reflecting these attitudes, however, may be passive or active.

Parsons uses these three dichotomies—pro or con, persons or rules and laws, and active or passive—to identify eight patterns of polarization in attitude and conduct. Four patterns support and four resist criminal-justice officials or the criminal law. These categories and their relationships to the three dichotomous variables are summarized in Figure 6–1.

Let us consider first the persons who become polarized in anticriminality and who express this attitude actively. When focusing on those they perceive as offenders, they try to dominate; when focusing on rules and laws, they are rigid enforcers. These are the persons who insist that everyone "go by the book" and tolerate no "stretching" of regulations or statutes.

Contrastingly, those who actively express a polarization in procriminal attitudes are rebellious toward authority figures or toward rules and laws. By being defiant they frustrate officials, and by being incorrigible they flout rules. When compulsive suppressors interact with compulsively rebellious persons, their opposition is likely to escalate into bitter conflict. If this occurs, the commitment of each side to its own perspective usually intensifies. When customary efforts at suppression fail, extremely cruel and rigid methods are used. But these only polarize the rebels into more destructive acts that take the form of disobedience for its own sake, unless complete domination is achieved by the enforcers or full independence by those who defy them. Such polarization of attitudes and their expression in extreme acts or utterances is frequently evident with the escalation of quarrels in families, correctional institutions, or law-enforcement activities that are headed by very authoritarian individuals, especially if the rebels are sufficiently numerous or resourceful to avoid being dominated.

Four passive modes of behavior are also indicated in Figure 6–1. The passively anticriminal person is extremely acquiescent to government leadership or directives and thus completely submissive to persons or organizations in authority and compulsively perfectionist in observing forms and procedures. This is the "bureaucratic personality" (Merton, 1968), never "putting his neck out" to deviate from official regulations, even from those that clearly have no function. Contrastingly, the passively procriminal person withdraws from conflict, but is compulsively independent of authoritative persons or organizations. This reaction is exemplified by those who are law violators in conjunction with adopting so-called hippie or hobo lifestyles (although these modes of living need not include criminality). If such a passive offender's hostility is focused on laws, it is by evasion and habitual but quiet deception and disobedience, as constrasted with the incorrigible's conspicuous disregard for the law.

Both anticriminal-acquiescent and procriminal-withdrawn persons avoid antagonists and therefore do not escalate their hostility by conflict, but both irritate their more active opposites. Thus those who withdraw to remain stubbornly insubordinate and those who persistently evade efforts to enforce the law frustrate anyone who is domineering or a compulsive enforcer. Such frustration strengthens the hostility of actively anticriminal persons toward all offenders. The actively rebellious, on the other hand, are especially scornful of anyone highly submissive to authority or perfectionistically obedient to laws, and their expression of this disdain makes them even more polarized in procriminal attitudes.

It follows that reactions to delinquent or criminal behavior vary with the dynamics of interaction. When anticriminal people treat lawbreakers as completely and irrevocably evil, and forever label the offenders negatively, they may foster increased commitment to delinquency or crime by "blocking the road back." When those alleged to be delinquent or criminal are dealt with collectively by teachers, police, or others in a hostile manner, they become socially acceptable only to each other, and more polarized in their prodelinquent or criminal attitudes. It is by such collective conflict that juvenile play groups become delinquent gangs, as Thrasher (1927) observed in his classic work on this subject.

Polarization of delinquent or criminal attitudes is avoided or

Figure 6–1 Eight Patterns of Polarization in Procriminal or Anticriminal Attitude and Conduct

Attitudinal Direction	Mode of Expressing Attitude in Conduct			
	Active		Passive	
	Supression		Acquiescence	
Anticriminal	(1) If focused on persons: Compulsive dominance	(2) If focused on laws: Compulsive enforcement	(3) If focused on persons: Unquestioning submission to authority	(4) If focused on laws: Compulsive perfectionism
	Rebellion		Withdrawal	
Procriminal	(5) If focused on persons: Defiance	(6) If focused on laws: Incorrigibility	(7) If focused on persons: Compulsive Independence	(8) If focused on laws: Evasion

Source: Based on Parsons, 1951:258.

reduced by several alternatives to the escalation described above. Sometimes, favorable anticipations in lawbreaking are "nipped in the bud" by clearly negative consequences, but this is unlikely. Processes by which anticriminal people can reform offenders and reintegrate them into anticriminal social circles, Parsons (1951) and Pitts (1968) suggest, include:

1. preventing buildup of tensions by treating the offender as capable of reforming, and not as an outcast

2. tolerating some minor infractions (without approving or endorsing them) as a means of "letting off steam," but reinforcing the desire to conform when the offender is "really trying" to "straighten out"

3. not responding in a hostile manner, although not reacting postively, to unenthusiastic or negative communications from the offender

4. providing rewards, especially increased esteem, for clearly successful performance by the offender in alternatives to crime.

This can be called the "social-learning" theory of rehabilitation. It is compatible with the approaches of the less doctrinaire followers of many "schools" of psychotherapy and behavioral modification, from Freudians to Skinnerians.

The escalation and rehabilitation processes described in the foregoing can be readily illustrated by personal observation, but the reliability with which the eight types in Figure 6-1 can be applied to a cross section of the populace has yet to be demonstrated. Like most typologies, it is an idealization of reality that portrays the extremes of dimensions on which all people vary. Although a few individuals usually epitomize one of the eight "pure" types, most persons resemble several of these types, but in different social relationships. They change over time as their attitudes polarize or depolarize, but rarely are they extreme in any type. Focus on persons or on laws—for example, on police officers or on the criminal code—probably varies with the circumstances an individual finds frustrating. Furthermore, attitudes may be directed only toward statutes on a specific offense (such as marijuana use) and as it affects particular persons, rather than toward the criminal law as a whole.

As Cohen (1959) pointed out, this Parsonian analysis (which has been somewhat reformulated here) is conceptually superior to the forms of "strain theory" that simply assert that those who are frustrated in legitimate endeavors try alternative illegitimate pursuits. Parsons indicates how commitments for and against criminal deviance fluctuate with interaction among persons of contrasting attitudes; he provides a sociological theory of effective rehabilitation; and he indicates how most criminality reflects a longer period of interaction than that which immediately precedes the offense. Yet the validity and utility of this Parsonian analysis can at present more readily be illustrated than rigorously demonstrated. Accounts of collective behavior in delinquency and crime, such as those presented by Short (1974), provide a rich source of such illustrations. Most persons long involved in law enforcement, corrections, or delinquency prevention will find that the conceptual distinctions in Figure 6-1, as interpreted here, illuminate much that they frequently observe at first hand.

OTHER BROAD THEORIES

A valid abstract theory, if concise, is a quick guide to the most probable explanation for specific events. Although such theories are necessarily given in very broad terms, they provide an initial perspective on what to look for in understanding the specifics of individual offenses. A good abstract theory, therefore, is informative on a wide variety of problems for which valid explanation and guidance are needed (Zetterberg, 1963).

Multiple-Causation Theory

Many general theories claim to explain most criminal conduct; yet some authors (for example, the Gluecks, 1950) contend that "multi-causality"—the assertion that crime has many causes—is the only tenable criminological theory. However, if this statement results only in a list of alleged causes or correlates of crime, without indicating when and how they interact, it adds nothing to the understanding of specific crimes. Therefore, the thesis that crime has many causes is not a "theory" in the sense that this term usually has in the philosophy of science. A theory explains a particular phenomenon by showing that its relationship to other events or conditions is a consequence of more widely applicable general principles.

Differential-Association Theory

Sutherland's "differential-association" theory was originally expressed as an awkward series of propositions, but can be summarized as follows: *Criminal behavior is primarily a product of the learning that* (1) *occurs in intimate interpersonal relations, and that* (2) *is either supportive of or antagonistic to lawbreaking.* He stressed the priority, intensity, frequency, and duration of these relationships as determining their influence on conduct. Other factors, such as poverty or physique, were seen as affecting criminality only by how they determine social ties relevant to conformity to or violation of the law. Sutherland concluded that offenses are caused by learning "an excess of definitions favorable . . . over definitions unfavorable" to engaging in crime (Sutherland & Cressey, 1970: 75).

The research reported in Chapter 8 indicates that the relationships of youth to their peers, parents, and teachers are indeed correlated with adolescent criminality. Subsequent chapters suggest the influence of these and other social relationships on some types of adult offenses. Sutherland's "excess of definitions" concept, however, does not evoke a clear notion of what one should look for in applying and testing his theory. One reasonable inference is that he accounted for crime primarily by trying to determine the extent to which offenders identify themselves with criminal rather than with anticriminal persons or reference groups (Glaser, 1956; Clark, 1972).

Control Theory

Several theories attribute crime simply to the *breakdown of controls* over urges to commit offenses, but give little or no explanation for these urges. As already indicated in this chapter, psychoanalysis provides the oldest still influential theory of this type; it stresses as the cause of delinquency or crime the inability of the offender's ego and superego to control the frequently antisocial instincts that comprise the id. Reiss (1951) drops the instinct postulation, as have neo-Freudians, when he explains delinquency as a failure of personal and social controls to force individuals into conformity with the norms of their society. Nye (1958) distinguishes direct control by the individual's personality from indirect control by outside forces, particularly social relationships. Gold (1963: 26) equates control primarily with favorable attitudes toward persons opposed to crime, and thus calls Sutherland's differential association a form of control theory.

Hirschi (1969) has the fullest and most sophisticated formulation of control theory. He postulates that all people have occasional desires to commit offenses and would do so if they "dared." But he ascribes their usual control over these urges to their bonds with conventional society. He distinguishes four elements in such bonds: *attachment* to conventional persons, *commitment* to conventional pursuits (i.e., investment of time, effort, and funds in academic or other legitimate endeavors that crime would jeopardize), *involvement* in conventional activities (i.e., being too preoccupied to have time for criminal pursuits), and *belief* in conventional values (i.e., moral objection to crime). One necessary supplement to Hirschi's postulation of delinquent urges in everyone is the observation that these urges may be strengthened if people develop bonds to criminal or other *unconventional* society, with elements analogous to the four above. This omission was not serious in his research, however, because it was with nontruant junior high-school and high-school students rather than with career offenders.

Differential-Anticipation Theory

As a concise summary explanation for criminal conduct, we prefer a differential-anticipation theory, which combines and supplements elements of differential-association and control theory, and is compatible with biological and personality factors as additional influences. It asserts: *A person's crime or restraint from crime is determined by the consequences he anticipates from it; and these expectations are the result of:*

1. *social bonds*, both anticriminal and procriminal, that each individual develops in life: these create stakes in conforming to the conduct standards of others so as to please rather than alienate them
2. *differential learning*, by which we acquire tastes, skills, and rationalizations that determine whether gratification is achieved in criminal or in alternative activities

3. perceived opportunities, reflecting a person's observations of circumstances and assessments of prospects and risks in law-violating or conforming behavior.

Differential-anticipation theory assumes that a person will try to commit a crime wherever and whenever the expectations of gratification from it—as a result of social bonds, differential learning, and perceptions of opportunity—exceed the unfavorable anticipations from these sources. This perspective, foreshadowed in Chapter 5 and in essence identical with that developed independently by Briar and Piliavin (1965) on "situational inducements to delinquency," will be further elaborated in this book. The perspective will direct the search for more specific explanations of particular crime patterns; it will thereby integrate many other theories by showing how they direct us to different influences on a person's expectations from various types of conduct.

According to differential-anticipation theory, crime is only indirectly affected by (1) biologically inherited or subsequently developed physical abilities or deficiencies, (2) mental or emotional capacities, and (3) good or bad fortune in early or later life. However, these conditions influence conduct, in both legitimate and illegitimate pursuits, by affecting a person's learning, social relationships, and prospects for gratification. This theory is thus a reinforcement and a drift explanation for criminal behavior, expressed in general terms. Neurotic, egocentric, and enculturated offender types can be contrasted, from the standpoint of this theory, by their probable expectations from crime. Furthermore, differential anticipation is compatible with a theory of labeling as (1) in some cases increasing offenses by enhancing the offenders' social bonds with other law violators or their alienation from crime opponents, but as (2) in other cases deterring crime by causing the labeled persons to fear that further misconduct would jeopardize valued conventional social bonds and opportunities. Even the dynamics of polarization, in the Parsonian analysis presented in this chapter, can be conceived of as a theory on how anticipations of self-esteem from upholding or violating the criminal law are altered by interaction among persons of diverse orientations.

The basic assumption of differential-anticipation theory is that expectations determine conduct. This assumption is compatible with learning theory in psychology, which ascribes behavior to differential reinforcement, which presumably shapes expectations. It is also consistent with symbolic interaction theory in sociology, which conceives of lines of conduct as emergent from a person's mental rehearsal of possible acts of self and others. Accordingly, whenever deliberation guides activity, the consequences of alternative behavior are covertly anticipated before any act is overtly performed (Blumer, 1960; Hulett, 1966; Morrione, 1975).

SUMMARY AND CONCLUSION

Contrasting patterns of thought in past epochs were found still evident in current reactions to offenses. The theories of the modern era discussed in this chapter are concisely summarized in Table 6-1.

Clinical psychotherapists of most prevailing viewpoints ascribe crime to defects of personality, which they trace to inadequate resolution of childhood emotional problems. But these specialists offer diverse theories of the particular kinds of early experience that cause later misconduct. These theories are especially relied upon to diagnose the most notorious and enigmatic offenders. Objectively scored personality tests, however, markedly and consistently differentiate offenders from nonoffenders only if they ask about attitudes and activities associated with law violations. Tests of other personality variables or of psychological disorders apparently measure traits that are as common in law-abiding as in law-violating careers.

Efforts of psychodiagnosticians to classify offenders, especially juveniles, repeatedly point to: (1) a so-called neurotic group that seems conflicted and anxious about their involvement in law violations; (2) a group of more self-centered individuals resembling many portrayals of the psychopath; (3) those who have been extensively socialized by other offenders, such as youth highly committed to delinquent gangs. The proportions of these three types vary with the population sampled and with the definitions employed, but all typologies reflect only the extremes of dimensions. Most offenders are less than extreme on any type-identifying variables and often fit more than one category. Thus, such typologies supplement and challenge but do not clearly contradict more abstract theories of criminality.

The reinforcements of and deterrents to crime are often subtle, shifting, and inconsistent, thus limiting the precise prediction of an offender's conduct. Therefore, labeling someone a criminal does not necessarily foster that person's criminality. There are innumerable examples of persons who drift into illegal behavior but who, because they have a strong stake in a reputation as law-abiding, are dramatically deterred from further offenses merely by being caught and thereby labeled. Labels can be criminalizing, however, when they reinforce an existing stake in a reputation as delinquent or criminal (as occurs sometimes with gang membership) or when they seriously impede the possibility of achieving or maintaining a stake in conformity (as when they impair employment opportunities or social acceptance). These criminogenic effects of labeling are especially critical for persons still between childhood and adulthood—the adolescents. As Chapter 8 shows, it is in this group that polarization of procriminal or anticriminal attitudes seems to occur most dramatically, in response to strains and control efforts in the school, the home, and the neighborhood.

Two prominent abstract theories of criminal conduct are differential association and control. We adopt here a differential-anticipation theory that combines features of both of these. It emphasizes anticriminal and procriminal social bonds and learning, but also focuses on perceived opportunities as determinants of behavior in specific situations. Although this abstract perspective is informative for explaining the widest range of criminal conduct, it is not always incompatible with the other theories. Each theory may augment our understanding of some law violation in particular circumstances. This will become evident in the ensuing chapters, devoted to explaining more specific patterns and correlates of criminality in the light of both theory and research.

TABLE 6-1   General Theories to Explain Criminal Conduct

THEORIES	CENTRAL PRINCIPLES	SELECTED REFERENCES
Psychoana-lytic	1. Delinquency and crime result from failure of the ego and superego to control the immoral impulses of the id. 2. In understanding and controlling delinquency, the manifest delinquent conduct is not as important as the latent delinquency, its unconscious motivation. 3. Failure to resolve psychosexual complexes of childhood fosters latent delinquency by creating unconscious fixation at or regression to early states of psychological development.	Aichhorn, 1925; Eissler, 1949; Redl and Wineman, 1951
Neo- and non-Freudian clinical psychology	Delinquency and crime represent failure to solve one or more of life's sequential problems of developing an adequate ego identity and controlling impulses from an earlier age.	Erikson, 1963, 1968; Berne, 1964
Reality therapy	Delinquency and crime reflect failure to take responsibility for one's conduct, and blaming it instead on others or on past or present events.	Glasser, 1965
Personality	Delinquent and criminal conduct expresses abnormal personality patterns of three main types: (1) neurotic, (2) egocentric, (3) criminally enculturated.	Hewitt and Jenkins, 1946; Reiss, 1952; Quay, 1965; Palmer, 1974
Reinforcement and deterrence drift	1. Anticriminal or procriminal behavior or thought that is gratifying tends to be repeated, and that which is not is terminated. 2. Behavior that was once gratifying but is punished tends to recur whenever punishment can be endured or avoided—unless alternative behavior has become more gratifying or stake in avoiding penalty has developed sufficiently to be a deterrent. 3. Rewards and penalties are subtle and shifting—largely verbal meanings that emerge in the character games and rationalizations that determine which gambles seem practical.	Toby, 1957a; Matza, 1964; Goffman, 1967: 149–270
Labeling	1. *Secondary deviation theory:* Being labeled delinquent or criminal fosters self-concepts and social consequences conducive to more crime. 2. *Deterrence alternative:* Being labeled delinquent or criminal fosters defense against such labels by avoiding further offenses and trying to regain a reputation as law-abiding.	Lemert, 1967; Schur, 1971; 1973 Glaser, 1971; Thorsell and Klemke, 1972;

Table 6-1 (cont.)

THEORIES	CENTRAL PRINCIPLES	SELECTED REFERENCES
Labeling (cont.)	3. The labelee's stakes in conformity or nonconformity with the criminal law determine which alternative is pursued.	Rogers and Buffalo, 1974
Strain and polarization	1. When frustration creates ambivalence toward persons in authority or to rules, interaction fosters pro- or anticriminal polarization, expressed either actively or passively. 2. Eight patterns of attitude and conduct thus created can escalate polarization if opposites interact. 3. Depolarization of the procriminal requires their acceptance as reformable, initial tolerance of some deviance but without reinforcing it, and rewarding conformity.	Parsons, 1951: Ch. 7; Pitts, 1968
Differential association	1. Criminal and anticriminal techniques, motives, drives, attitudes, and rationalizations are learned mainly in interaction with others in intimate groups. 2. The influence of such learning experiences varies with the frequency, priority, and intensity of these associations. 3. Whether the net direction of this influence is pro- or anticriminal depends on whether one learns an excess of definitions favorable or unfavorable to law violation.	Sutherland and Cressey, all eds.
Differential identification or reference	Criminality is determined by the extent to which a person identifies with pro- or anticriminal persons or reference groups.	Glaser, 1956; Clark, 1972
Control	All people commit delinquency or crime when they dare, unless their conduct is controlled by their attachment to conventional persons, their commitment to conventional pursuits, their involvement in conventional activities, or their belief in conventional values.	Hirschi, 1969
Differential anticipation	1. Social bonds with anti- or procriminal persons create stakes in conformity or nonconformity with the criminal law. 2. These bonds, as well as differentially learned tastes, skills, and rationalizations, and perceptions of opportunities and risks determine anticipations of the outcome of criminal or alternative activities. 3. Anticipations guide conduct.	Glaser, 1962, 1969, and this book; Briar and Piliavin, 1965

SUMMARY AND CONCLUSION

SEVEN

BIOLOGICAL FACTORS IN CRIME

A journalist of the late nineteenth century is said to have coined the term "criminology" as an abbreviation for "criminal anthropology" (Geis, 1959), the study of skeletons, physiognomies, and other bodily features of convicted offenders. These investigations reflected the impact of the theory of evolution. It produced a regression from Enlightenment philosophies of equality among all people at birth (discussed in Chapters 3 and 6) to an elitist assumption that the economic leaders of Western civilization (and the theorists who support them) are the highest biological stage in human development (see Hofstadter, 1955).

This Social Darwinist perspective was patently unsound. It ignored: (1) the dynamics of cultural diffusion and change, which brought different ethnic groups—e.g., the Chinese, the Egyptians, the Bantu, the Mayans—to the forefront of technological development in different historical eras; and (2) the wide distribution of mental capacity throughout the human species, which makes people of every ethnic descent capable of mastering the civilization of any other if reared in it. The Social Darwinist viewpoint included a conception of the lower classes as inherently inferior and of criminals as altogether a group apart, a subhuman species, an atavism. Since then, the biological orientation to crime has had a series of quite different formulations, but the implication of hereditary deficiency is still frequently evident.

THE POSITIVE SCHOOL

Cesare Lombroso (1836–1909), an Italian prison physician and leader of criminal–anthropological inquiry, founded the "positive school" of criminology. Its designation was derived from the French philosopher August Comte, who saw human thought as evolving from theological to metaphysical to positive—or scientific—perspectives and procedures. Imitating and borrowing from the language and ideas of the more firmly established natural sciences, Lombroso held that crime expressed an evolutionary throwback to the brute mentality of a more apelike human. The primitiveness of this "criminal type" was presumed evident in its physical anomalies, especially in the skull and facial bones.

Lombroso's findings were discredited because he did not *demonstrate* statistically the percentage of anomalous bones in criminals compared with the percentage in noncriminal control groups; instead he only *illustrated* his theory by describing individual criminals who had what he presumed were unusual physical features. In later writings he repeatedly reduced the proportion of offenses that he ascribed to biology (Wolfgang, 1968), accepting for some offenders the views of socialist associates in the positive school, who blamed poverty for much crime. The most dramatic negation of his atavism explanations came in 1913 from Charles Goring, a British scientist who compared skull features of convicts, soldiers, university students, and hospital patients and found no significant statistical differences. In the twentieth century, Lombrosian concepts of "born-criminal types" reappeared in efforts to link crime to physique or to chromosomes (discussed later), but these endeavors were also largely discredited despite lavish claims made by their initial proponents.

Lombroso's positive school made an important lasting contribution, however, although his studies did not. His praise of the scientific method fostered systematic and objective empirical inquiry by his followers not only on physical anthropology but also on the correlation of social and economic conditions to crime.

INTELLIGENCE

In the early twentieth century, a "neo-Lombrosian" or "neopositive" approach developed in criminology. It still stressed biological inheritance as the main cause of crime, but claimed that this was evident in intelligence, regardless of physique. The mental-testing movement of this period produced the concept of Intelligence Quotient (IQ), along with innumerable studies that showed the average intelligence measurements of lawbreakers to be appreciably lower than those of noncriminals. Yet a number of considerations led to rejection of intelligence as sole or primary explanation for crime.

First among the grounds for criticizing these studies is the wide variation in IQ among both criminals and noncriminals. Some lawbreakers are clearly of higher mental capacity than many who conform to the law. Second, when tested offenders are compared, not with a cross section of the general population but with people of similar economic, linguistic, and educational background, the deficiencies in their performance on intelligence tests are not so great. Third, test questions often assume familiarity with the dominant culture and middle-class lifestyles, an erroneous assumption for those reared, for example, in urban ghettos. Fourth, there is much evidence that low scores on intelligence tests may be improved by good schooling; they are not purely the products of biological inheritance, as the neo-Lombrosians assumed. Fifth, low motivation to do well on an intelligence test impedes performance. Prisoners tested shortly after incarceration often have less interest in achieving their best possible scores than many people tested in other circumstances. Retesting low scorers who become seriously involved in the better prison-school programs frequently produces higher scores. Sixth, prenatal and childhood nutritional deficiencies, as well as stimulus deprivation in the early years, have been shown to impair intelligence (Broman et al., 1975; Lewis, 1976).

As the next chapter indicates, if low intelligence has any effects on crime rates, they are probably indirect. Mental retardation can conceivably foster delinquency, by causing poor grades and frustration in school work, and thus making many types of law violation more appealing than studying. Of course, stupidity can also lead to poor judgment in crime, thus increasing the chances of being caught and being in a sample of prisoners who are tested. Chapter 5 suggested, however, that it is not true that "only the dumb ones get caught"; in crime as in other gambling, even bright persons become addicted to taking repeated risks, and they, too, lose, often sooner than later. An adequate study of the relationship of intelligence to crime still is lacking, but it is evident that its findings would indicate a complex interaction among test scores, life histories, and specific types of offense.

BRAIN DISORDERS

Much former and some recent literature implies that biological inheritance is a complete explanation for criminal acts. Critics readily discredit such extreme claims, but in doing so they often disregard evidence of interaction between specific biological conditions and other factors in crime. Thus a physical or mental handicap may, in some cases, foster social rejection or impede schoolwork, and thus differentially affect a person's anticipations from criminal or conventional conduct.

People do not inherit particular forms of behavior other than the simplest reflexes—certainly not the thought and conduct involved in any willful offense. Instead they possess biologically acquired capacities to learn and tendencies to emotional arousal and muscular reaction that vary partly with heredity and partly with health and upbringing. The biological factors independent of learning in these generalized propensities include not only innate conditions of the nervous and endocrinal systems, but also modifications resulting from nutrition, strain, or disease, which can begin in the womb or occur at any other stage of life. Finally, we should note that both criminal and noncriminal conduct may employ or be evoked by any of these biological capacities or tendencies.

The arousal of emotions in all mammals is linked to parts of the brain in a manner that recent research shows is much more complex than had long been assumed (there had previously been references to a specific "visceral," or "emotional" brain). Damage to segments of the nervous system may elicit conduct expressive of intense feelings. In nonhuman subjects this can be demonstrated very rigorously, because researchers can perform brain surgery on an animal, or stimulate its nervous tissue electrically or chemically, to see what change in behavior follows. In this fashion aggressive conduct suggesting intense rage, and hyperactivity suggesting fear, sexual arousal, and other emotions, have been elicited in rats, dogs, monkeys, and other creatures. It is interesting, however, that even with animals the reaction to a certain deliberate physical disturbance to the brain is not completely uniform, but varies somewhat with the social setting of the animals, such as their position in a heirarchy of initiating aggression within their group, and other aspects of their learning experience and ancestry (Shah & Roth, 1974: 111–15; Garth J. Thomas, correspondence).

For people, the evidence of relationship between deviant emotions or conduct and nervous-system damage is less rigorous than for other animals. Since researchers cannot experiment surgically on humans to demonstrate the effects of brain damage, they must look for persons with physical injury to the nervous system from an accident or a tumor, or infer brain impairment from evidence of nervous-system disease. Only then do they inquire whether the subjects act oddly. Alternatively, when unusual behavior is seen, clues are sought on the possibility of brain damage, such as a history of nervous-system diseases, endocrinal disturbances, or severe blows to the head. Yet because classification of conduct as deviant is imprecise, anyone looking for deviant behavior can usually "find" it in most people, even in those for whom the inference of physical brain damage is in error.

Epilepsy and related diseases of the central nervous system—now identified by electroencephalogram (EEG), which records fluctuations of electrical currents in the brain—have historically been linked to unusual conduct and occasionally to crime. In *grand mal*, a person periodically suffers a seizure or "fit" of convulsions, loses consciousness, has no memory afterward of this experience, and then has a period of drowsiness and confusion in which the behavior may strike others as erratic or irrational. In *petit mal* and lesser forms of epilepsy-related disturbance, there is often only a brief period of automatic repetition of whatever acts are being done at the moment, without awareness afterward that this automatic behavior occurred. Aggressive acts are unusual during automatism (Knox, 1968), for these "fugue states" are subtle and resemble ordinary daydreaming or semi-consciousness.

A tremendous variety of deviant behavior—including repeated arson, assault, sexual deviation, and theft—have in exceptional cases been ascribed entirely or primarily to epilepsy or other brain-rhythm disorders. Most such claims can be challenged because of the diversity and complexity of the offenses, which could not be the mechanically repetitive behavior distinctive of seizure and postseizure activity; nevertheless, temporary dyscontrol related to epileptoid disorders may underlie some episodic bursts of violence. Such crimes, however, are committed by only a minute fraction of epileptics, and by many more with normal brain waves. In addition, there is not perfect reliability in distinguishing minor abnormalities in EEG recordings from normal fluctuations.

The cause of epilepsy is not determined with confidence in most cases, but the frequency and intensity of seizures can usually be controlled with drugs, it often declines or disappears, and treating epileptics as normal generally elicits conduct patterns within the usual range of those without this ailment. Yet the fact that seizures are often stigmatizing and that they usually begin in early childhood, could make them foster deviant conduct social-psychologically rather than biologically. Commonly 30 to 60 percent, but as high as 84 percent of delinquents, as compared with about 15 percent of nondelinquents, have been found to have EEG patterns outside the normal range. It has been suggested that such deviant EEGs—not all of which imply epilepsy—are a consequence of deviant life and delayed social maturation rather than their cause, and that many EEGs will not be explicable unless we develop what Hodge and associates (1953) call a "physiological sociology" (see also Hare, 1970: 30–36).

More adequate data are needed on the frequency of criminality in those of the general population who are identified as epileptic as compared with those who are not, rather than just data on epilepsy among criminals. Current impressions may be biased by the lesser forms of this ailment being often discovered only when the subjects are incarcerated.

CHROMOSOMAL ABNORMALITIES

As readers will recall from elementary biology, each cell of the human body normally has in its nucleus 46 microscopic filaments called chromosomes, which carry the determinants of heredity. Each chromosome transmits a set of related traits, but the chromosomes are in pairs, one coming from each parent when an ovum is fertilized by a sperm. The pair that governs sex-linked characteristics in females are both of a type known as "X," whereas males have one "X" and one "Y" chromosome. Occasionally individuals have three or more of these sex-linked chromosomes, either in various X and Y combinations or all X.

The ascription of crime to extra chromosomes has an interesting history. The surplus-chromosome anomaly first discovered is the 47, XXY pattern, double female chromosomes found in some males who typically are late in developing sexual characteristics, have small testes, and sometimes femininelike breasts. This cluster of traits, known as Klinefelter's Syndrome, is disproportionately but by no means exclusively associated with mental retardation and deviant conduct. It is far from clear, however, that the deviant behavior is a direct consequence of biological abnormality or of mental retardation, rather than of social reactions to the unusual sexual anatomy.

In 1961 the first report of a male having an extra Y chromosome occurred, the 47, XYY pattern. This condition was prominently linked to crime in worldwide journalistic accounts in 1968, when the defense in a Paris murder case entered a plea of not guilty by reason of insanity because the accused had XYY chromosomes. A panel of experts appointed to advise the court on this plea recommended reduction of sentence. Soon thereafter an Australian was acquitted of murder on grounds of insanity, which the press reported as due to an XYY condition, although the judge evidently was responding to other, more typical psychiatric evidence. About that time Richard Speck was convicted in Chicago for the sexual abuse and murder of eight nurses. When his defense lawyer was asked whether he would appeal, he told a reporter that he certainly would, and that perhaps his client had XYY chromosomes since he had the physical features of above-average height and poor complexion associated with this condition. For several years thereafter newspaper, magazine, and television accounts of the XYY syndrome alleged that an extra male chromosome made such people unusually aggressive and that this was exemplified by Richard Speck; they ignored the fact that his lawyer's proposed appeal prompted a microscopic examination of Speck's cells that revealed a normal 46, XY pattern (NIMH, 1970).

Faced with the prospect that the courts would be flooded with appeals for reversals of murder, rape, and assault convictions of men who might be found to have XYY chromosomes, and given the confusion and uncertainty about this genetic condition, the National Institute of Mental Health in the United States and similar agencies in several other countries sponsored extensive investigations of this phenomenon and its behavioral correlates. Since classifying cells by chromosome type is expensive and the researchers were eager to find the relatively rare XYY cases, most earlier studies were biased by sampling only populations presumed to have unusual concentrations of such cases, notably the tall inmates of prisons or of hospitals for the criminally insane. Not until the 1970s when such research expanded and became somewhat cheaper were there many reports of systematic search for this pattern in large representative samples of all males.

The findings from these studies are inconclusive. In the general population, the prevalence of the 47, XYY anomaly has been estimated to range from one in 1,500 to one in 3,000 males, on the basis of various samples of a few thousand persons in different parts of the world. In some penal institutions the frequency appears to be no different from this, while in others it is up to 20 times as high, especially in security hospitals for mentally-disturbed criminals. The condition is so infrequent, however, that larger samples would be necessary for more precise estimates of rates. Its only persistent physical correlate is that of being taller than the average height in one's family (Borgaonkar & Shah, 1974).

Despite their presumed extra "maleness," the XYY prisoners have less frequently been charged with violent offenses—including rape—and more frequently with theft and unaggressive sexual deviance than other inmates of their institutions, but these differences are neither pronounced nor consistent in all studies. Similar offenses are found in both XXYs and XYYs, and both genotypes seem to average below normal in intelligence (though with much variation around their average IQ). Both may thus have higher-than-average criminal records because of handicaps in schooling, a factor in crime discussed in Chapter 8 (Borgaonkar & Shah, 1974; Witkin et al., 1976). In the single known case of XYY identical twins, at age 17 one was distinctly more stable and well-adjusted than his brother, suggesting that the many nongenetic factors in behavior include complementary roles in family dynamics (Rainer et al., 1972). From all research to date, one clearly established conclusion is that chromosomal abnormalities are not a major source of crime; another is that any relationship they do have with offenses involves interaction with other factors.

PHYSIQUE

Recurrent in the past century have been neo-Lombrosian efforts to link crime to body structure (see Vold, 1958: Chapter 4). Perhaps most influential in the United States is William H. Sheldon's (1949) system of measuring the three body proportions that he assumes reflect the relative growth of the inner, middle, and outer layers of the early embryo into their respective segments of the final anatomy. Endomorphy, one such ratio of measurements, is determined by the size of the abdominal organs; endomorphs are high on this "gut" dimension, tending to be fat, rounded, and, Sheldon claims, relaxed but extroverted. Mesomorphy reflects muscular growth; mesomorphs tend to be husky, and Sheldon ascribes to them an aggressive and extroverted personality. Since ectomorphy is a function of skin, hair, and nervous-system development, ectomorphs have little body mass in relation to body surface. Thus they weigh little for their height and, Sheldon asserts, tend to be introverted and anxious.

Sheldon's efforts to demonstrate an association of these dimensions with delinquency were severely criticized because he classified both personalities and delinquency mainly by his subjective impressions. He could have estimated body proportions at first glance before he measured them, and thus could have prejudged the character of his subjects by their shapes. Yet his finding that delinquents average distinctly more mesomorphy, slightly more endomorphy, and less ectomorphy than nonoffenders is supported by the more rigorous investigations of the Gluecks (1950, 1956) and others (see Shah & Roth, 1974: 141–42). Nevertheless, much diversity in type of physique occurs among both offenders and nonoffenders; so the difference in their average proportions is not very useful in identifying criminals.

Sociologists suggest that social selection may account for whatever differences in general physique may exist, on the average, between offenders and others. They point out that husky youths are likely to be more successful in fighting and physical sports and thus more acceptable in delinquent groups and more neglectful of studies. It is even alleged that when police suspect a group of boys of some offense, they more often stop and question the husky ones than the slight or the fat ones.

The British psychologist H. J. Eysenck (1964) contends, however, that mesomorphy's connection with delinquency stems from the correlation of this type of physique with extroversion, a personality trait that he claims makes people less readily conditioned by pain than introverts. Therefore, extroversion would impede learning from punishment. He and others report that convicted offenders score higher than nonoffenders on extroversion tests, and Hindelang (1971a) found a correlation between extroversion scores and delinquency admitted in questionnaires by high-school students. The reaction of offenders to punishment, alleged to be affected by extroversion and mesomorphy, has also been studied more directly, with a rationale derived from theories of psychopathy.

PSYCHOPATHY AND AROUSAL

The concept of psychopathy was developed in psychiatry to designate persons who seem to lack a conscience. Case studies described psychopaths as often charming and ingratiating, but as lying, cheating, and inflicting severe physical or mental anguish on those who trust them, without feeling remorse. Allegedly also identifying psychopathy are impulsivity, inability to profit from experience (especially, incapacity to learn from punishment), inability to love, irresponsibility, and lack of emotion in situations in which it would be normal. During the 1930s some psychiatrists diagnosed well over 90 percent of prisoners as psychopaths (Sutherland & Cressey, 1970: 159). In the hasty procedures of prison psychiatry in this period—one psychiatrist would perfunctorily diagnose dozens of inmates daily—the label "constitutional psychopathic inferior" (CPI) was often used to imply the neo-Lombrosian notion that these were hereditarily inferior creatures.

Critics of this perspective, from many disciplines, contend that the diagnosis of psychopathy reflects the middle- and upper-class background of the prison psychiatrists, and it merely means that crime is relabeled psychopathy. Some claim that only a small percentage of prisoners, if any, really fits the classic descriptions of a psychopath as lacking a conscience, and that most simply share a subculture with language and conduct norms that shock traditional psychiatrists. It is asserted, furthermore, that most offenders who condone crime against outsiders maintain moral values in their relationships with friends and relatives (see "Conscience on Second Boulevard," in Redl & Wineman, 1951: 200–208).

Psychiatry maintains an image of the psychopath, drawn especially from Cleckley's (1941) early case-study portrayals, as persons who combine quite diverse traits. Implicit in this image is an assumption, unsupported by evidence, that there must be a close statistical association among these traits, which include: recidivistic lawbreaking, other antisocial aggression, lack of conscience, impulsiveness, lying, inability to learn from experience, irresponsibility, unstable moods, and still other attributes (some of which contradict each other) (see Hare, 1970: 11). Many offenders have some but not all of these qualities. Two examples are confidence men who swindle elderly widows and pensioners, and professional killers. These contrasting types of recidivistic criminals seem to lack a conscience; but they certainly are deliberate and patient rather than impulsive, and they learn skills from experience. During World War II the major psychiatric grounds for rejecting men from military service were diagnoses of psychoneurotic, psychotic, or psychopathic. But at induction stations with 50 or more psychiatric rejections, the percentage diagnosed as psychopathic ranged from zero to 81.3 percent (Stouffer et al., 1950: 475).

In reaction to these diverse grounds for questioning the psychopathy label, and because of contentions that deficiencies of conscience are due to repeated social rejection or to shortcomings in role-taking ability rather than to constitutional defects, the American Psychiatric Association's 1952 manual on diagnosis replaced this term with *sociopath,* which has gained common use. *Psychopath* has never disappeared, however, and seemed to regain popularity in psychiatry and psychology during the 1960s because of research suggesting that this condition does indeed have a biological basis.

The second half of the twentieth century has produced more frequently successful efforts to find physiological correlates of psychopathy. In this research, which will be summarized here, clinicians usually select the prisoners most clearly fitting traditional descriptions of the psychopath, who are then compared physiologically with other inmates or with nonoffenders. Sometimes comparisons are made between any persons with felony convictions and others without criminal records. Frequently students with high scores on a psychopathy test are compared neurologically with those with low scores.

David T. Lykken (1957), who pioneered the physiological-psychology approach in the study of psychopathy, developed a scale in which subjects are asked which they would choose if forced to select from various pairs of unpleasant tasks or experiences—one normally arousing guilt or anxiety, such as having an accident while driving a borrowed car, and one that is merely distasteful or tedious, such as cleaning a cesspool. Prisoners clinically designated as psychopaths reject more often than others the merely distasteful circumstances in favor of situations that in others arouse guilt or anxiety. Much less theoretically focused but more commonly used is the "Psychopathic Deviate Scale" ("Pd") of the Minnesota Multiphasic Personality Inventory (MMPI), which was developed by determining empirically which questions most clearly differentiate adjudicated delinquents from other youth. It includes such diverse items as "I am sure to get a raw deal from life" and "I have used alcohol excessively."

The rationale underlying searches for biological variables that differentiate alleged psychopaths from others is based on neural physiology. The autonomic nervous system, which largely controls the predominantly involuntary body functions, is located mainly outside the brain, for it is diffused to all major segments of our anatomy. It has two components: the sympathetic system increases blood flow to the muscles during emotional arousal, while decreasing blood flow to the abdominal organs; the parasympathetic system has an opposite effect on blood flow and thereby relaxes a person. The sympathetic system is supplemented by the hormone epinephrine (adrenaline), which increases the heartbeat and the use of blood sugar in the muscles; norepinephrine (noradrenaline) supplements the parasympathetic system. Presumably arousal, also called the activation syndrome, is a reflexive set of bodily changes that mobilizes energy for fight or flight in danger, and is found in one form or another in virtually all animals. A sensitive index of the physiological alterations in the human body experiencing this arousal is the galvanic skin response (GSR), a decrease in the skin's resistance to electricity due to increased perspiration and to minute changes in the electrical charges of the skin cells themselves.

Experiments reveal that those designated as psychopaths generally have (1) less increase in GSR following "noxious stimulants" (for example, a high-pitched tone or an electric shock), and (2) slower rate of returning to their normal GSR state after experiencing such arousal. Furthermore, they are slower in becoming conditioned to avoid shocks if given without warning whenever they make errors in solving puzzles developed by psychologists. This slowness in avoidance conditioning was the basis for Lykken's (1957) inference that psychopaths are deficient in ability to learn to avoid punishment, and that this explains their difficulties in noncriminal pursuits and their persistence in crime. Contrastingly, psychopaths have not been found markedly or consistently inferior to others in improving their rate of learning when given positive rewards for correct behavior.

Mednick (1974) asserts that an important basis for learning law-abiding behavior lies in the interaction of physiological factors with early life experiences. The following is a paraphrase (with his permission) of a letter summarizing his views:

> Normally a child who thinks about doing something antisocial, such as stealing or hitting someone, has some fear if his family has regularly punished him for this act. If he inhibits this antisocial behavior, the anticipatory fear will dissipate. If it dissipates *quickly,* the large reduction in fear will be a reward for inhibiting the antisocial behavior, and the child will learn to inhibit such impulses in the future. However, if the child's fear responses are very limited or if fear dissipation is *very slow* because of a slow-recovery autonomic nervous system, there will not be much experience of reward for inhibiting punished antisocial responses.

> By this reasoning, one can hypothesize that the psychopathic criminal has a relatively unresponsive, slow-recovering autonomic nervous system. If socializing agents (e.g., family and school) never punish a child for antisocial behavior, however, failure to learn expected standards of conduct might be the consequence even if the nervous-system condition were more favorable.

> Speed of return to normal GSR after arousal—called the "electrodermal recovery rate"—is a highly hereditary attribute, since it is much more similar in identical than in fraternal twins. Therefore, persons born with a slow rate, which is conducive to psychopathy, will less readily learn to inhibit delinquent or criminal urges even if they are punished for misconduct.

Complementing the above research have been experiments demonstrating that alleged psychopaths show a much greater increase than others in heartbeat, GSR, and learning to avoid shock when injected with epinephrine, suggesting a deficiency of this hormone in the psychopaths or an excess of its antagonist, norepinephrine (Allen et al., 1969; Schachter, 1971: Chapter 13). But there is evidence that only such prisoners who have been relatively nonaggressive have these distinctive responses to epinephrine (Lindner et al., 1970). Findings of slower learning are less consistent than these data on physiological differences (Allen et al., 1969; Hare, 1970).

Also pertinent here is Schachter's (1971: Chapter 12) experiment in which injection of chlorpromazine, which depresses the sympathetic system and hence reduces anxiety, was associated with more cheating than was injection with a placebo. The subjects were introductory psychology students seated in booths from which they could not see their neighbors while marking their answer sheets. The experimenter then sneaked these sheets out of the room and photocopied them, while their instructor occupied the students with other matters. The instructor told them he would be too busy to grade the papers, and returned them for grading from the correct answers written on the board. The students were also not informed that some of the supposedly correct answers were deliberately made incorrect, so that even those who actually had perfect papers would have some incentive to cheat. This experiment suggests that lesser anxiety, such as that associated with the GSR response pattern of psychopaths, reduces discomfort from any fear of punishment or from anticipation of guilt feelings that might otherwise inhibit cheating.

Performance on a wide assortment of tests of abilities has been found to vary somewhat with ratings of the psychopathy of the persons tested, and also to be affected by drugs that stimulate or depress the sympathetic or parasympathetic system. Persons considered psychopathic generally have lower scores on tests requiring routine repetitive tasks (they don't persist in dull activity), but they are equal or superior to others on cognitive tasks (Wheeler, 1974). They have not been clearly or consistently differentiated from other offenders by extroversion scales (Hare, 1970: 63).

Schachter (1971: 183) reasoned that because of their low emotional arousal, psychopaths would commit dispassionate rather than passionate offenses. He observes that prisoners whom psychologists deem psychopathic have records of much more burglary, theft, and fraud and of fewer assaultive offenses than other prisoners. This finding may partly reflect the selection criteria, since repetition of offenses is one of the bases for making a diagnosis of psychopathy. Offenders usually repeat property crimes of stealth much more than assaultive crimes, probably because the former are more regularly rewarding and less risky than the violent acts. Yet his observation is consistent with the cited finding that only nonaggressive alleged psychopaths have GSRs distinctly affected by epinephrine.

Abnormalities in EEG wave pattern, mentioned in discussing brain ailments, do not very clearly differentiate offenders classified as psychopaths from other convicted persons. Yet several studies show that the wave's slowness, apart from its shape, statistically characterizes groups with records of crimes of stealth and deceit, while abnormal wave shapes are more common in persons with records of criminal violence. There is also some evidence that the wave speed is hereditary. Slightly lower and less variable heartbeat, on the average, has also been found to differentiate alleged psychopaths from other offenders (Hare, 1970: 46–47).

There have been various interpretations of these data on the correlates of psychopathy. Some of the first writers on this subject, such as Lykken and Eysenck, stressed the psychopath's inherent nervous-system deficiencies in arousal. Quay (1965) interpreted the criminality of psychopaths as a search for stimuli because of stimulus deprivation in their lives; it is noteworthy that animals exhibit restlessness and aggressiveness when deprived of stimuli. Hare (1970) suggested that both failure to be conditioned by pain and a search for stimuli may be due to a deprivation in early-learning experiences rather than simply to constitutional defects.

A social-learning-deficiency explanation for the psychopath's lack of emotional arousal is consistent with Schachter's (1971: Part I) demonstration that the arousal of specific emotions occurs only when humans learn to attach a particular verbal label and meaning to vaguely experienced physiological changes. Psychopaths do not score lower than others in tests of verbal thinking ability, but they may be less socialized than most persons in the verbal interpretation of feelings.

The diversity, complexity, and vagueness of the criteria by which people are designated psychopaths, and the consequent wide range of variation among such persons, must often create a large overlap between groups when large samples of alleged psychopaths are compared with presumed normals. Nevertheless, much more conclusive evidence for a genetic influence has been produced by the recent research summarized here than was ever before available. The possibility of reducing recidivism by supplying arousal-inducing drugs to offenders with slow GSR recovery rates should be experimentally or quasi-experimentally investigated. A pioneer experiment of this type (Goldman et al., 1974) was terminated not long after it began, for there were legal objections to its manipulation of human subjects; but procedures might be designed to be compatible with both legal concerns and scientific rigor.

ANCESTRY

Long cited in support of hereditary interpretations of crime have been dramatic case illustrations, as well as statistics, that criminal records tend to run in families: children of convicted criminals are more likely to have criminal records than children of noncriminals. Obviously, this finding can be explained quite plausibly by the inference that parents with criminal records are less often able or willing to instill anticriminal values in their children. The contention that such environmental influences do not account for all association of crime with criminal ancestry, however, is supported by studies of twins and of adoptions, conducted mostly in Europe, where both criminal and biological (health) records are more centralized, uniform, and complete than they are in the United States.

Identical twins have identical heredity. Careful studies indicate that they are at least twice as likely to be concordant in criminality (meaning that if one had a record the other did also) as fraternal twins, who are no more similar in heredity than any pair of siblings (Christiansen, 1974). It may be argued, on the other hand, that, since identical twins are more alike than fraternal twins, they more often do things together and are more similarly responded to by others. Thus environment could be a factor in the findings on concordance. Yet a case for some genetic influence can also be made from studies showing that acquisition of a criminal record by adopted males is somewhat related to whether their biological fathers had a criminal record, even when there was little or no contact between them (see Mednick, 1974: 216–27). Table 7-1 suggests, however, that the influence of the adoptive father is as strong or stronger than that of the biological father.

To further investigate the relative influence of heredity and environment, a Copenhagen sample was developed of families with all possible combinations of serious criminality in father and son, but none in the mother. The sons were given a variety of physiological and psychological tests as well as psychiatric interviews (Mednick, 1977). Noncriminal sons of criminal fathers had a mean IQ of 113 and the fastest GSR recovery rate, significantly higher than the other groups. Presumably their intelligence helped them achieve good school records that compensated for any criminogenic inheritance, and their GSR recovery rate suggests that they did not inherit what may be the principal biological factor in criminogenesis. Average IQs of 105 were found in criminal sons of criminal or noncriminal fathers, and of 100 for the noncriminal sons of noncriminal fathers. The slowest average GSR recovery rate of all four groups was found in the criminal sons of noncriminal fathers. This highly hereditary characteristic of the autonomic nervous system seemed very closely related to crime in this four-group comparison. It may foster criminality by impeding ability to learn from a noncriminal environment the inhibitions necessary for a crime-free life.

A member of the Danish research group, Sarnoff A. Mednick, suggested in an April 1976 lecture at the University of Southern California that the relationship between heredity and criminality should be clearest in settings in which the environment is not highly criminogenic, as in homes with noncriminal fathers, or in Copenhagen, which has no real slums or large concentrations of recently urbanized poor families, as contrasted with most large American cities. Supporting this inference, he found that the greater concordance of criminality in identical twins than in fraternal twins was more pronounced in rural than in urban areas within Denmark, as well as in middle- or upper-class homes. The Danish researchers are further investigating these relationships by a long-run study on the island of Mauritius, in the Indian Ocean, to reexamine children who at age three showed great variation in electrodermal recovery rate. While their focus is on inher-

TABLE 7-1   Criminality of Adopted Danish Males Aged 30–44 and of Nonadopted Controls, by Criminality of Biological and Adoptive Fathers*

CRIMINAL RECORD OF FATHER	NONE REGIS- TERED	MINOR OFFENSES ONLY	CRIM- INAL OFFENSE	NO. OF CASES	INDICES OF RELATIONSHIP AND SIGNIFICANCE
For adopted sons:					
Noncriminal					
adopted father	51.6%	33.9%	14.5%	(975)	Gamma = .31
Criminal					
adopted father	35.4	37.5	27.1	(44)	
No. of cases	(554)	(385)	(180)	(1119)	Chi Sq. = 19.5, p < .001
Noncriminal					
Biological					
father	52.8	33.7	13.6	(618)	Gamma = .22
Criminal					
biological					
father	41.6	35.7	22.7	(353)	
No. of cases	(473)	(334)	(164)	(971)**	Chi Sq. = 16.9, p < .001
*For nonadopted controls:****					
Noncriminal					
Father	64.4	27.7	8.0	(993)	Gamma = .24
Criminal					
father	52.7	30.7	16.5	(127)	
No. of cases	(706)	(314)	(100)	(1120)	Chi Sq. = 12.0, p < .01

* Calculated from Mednick, et al., 1974:219, which provides percentages by the independent instead of the dependent variable and provides no measure of relationship.

** For 148 of the adopted sons, the biological father was unknown.

*** Control cases matched to adopted sons by age, occupational status of father, and residential area.

ited autonomic-nervous-system indices, American research on effects of epinephrine injections in altering these indices suggests the possibility that biochemical differences underlie genetic factors in crime.

HORMONES

Hormones, the chemicals released into the bloodstream by endocrine glands in various parts of the body, control and are themselves affected by the body's growth, activity, and patterns of emotional reaction. The influence of epinephrine from the adrenal glands has already been discussed; we indicated that a deficiency in its secretion by these glands appears to be a correlate and possibly a basic cause of the behavior traits by which people are classified as psychopaths. Even more definite is evidence on the influence of sex hormones. These include: (1) androgens, which must be present in children for male sexual characteristics to develop and which elicit aggression if injected into adult male animals; and (2) estrogens, which elicit female sex characteristics in growth and estrus or "heat" in adult female animals.

Influence of androgens on aggression in human males has not been established. Indeed there is evidence that learned attitudes on sexual pursuits may affect the body's secretion of the androgen testosterone, rather than the hormone affecting the attitudes. However, female secretion of estrogens and of progesterone, a hormone related to some androgens, varies cyclically with both menstruation and pregnancy and seems to have definite relationships to mood changes in many women (Shah & Roth, 1974: 122–24).

About 25 to 40 percent of women suffer moderate to severe discomfort during approximately four days preceding and four days of menstruation, with a large variety of symptoms, including cramps, dizziness, fatigue, and irritability. There is growing evidence that about half the assaultive behavior committed by women occurs during these eight days of the month, which are characterized by exceptionally low levels of progesterone in the bloodstream (Shah & Roth, 1974: 124–25; Ellis & Austin, 1971: 338–95). A disproportionate amount of other deviant conduct by women also occurs during this brief period. This is perhaps the highest correlation of crime with a physiological condition that has been established. Yet we should note that most women do not commit criminally aggressive acts when they have premenstrual or menstrual disturbances, and some commit such acts at other times. Furthermore, all evidence suggests higher rates of violence by males than by females. As will be indicated in Chapter 9, when discussing assaults, cultural values and social settings have an especially strong bearing on the likelihood of a person's committing a violent act, and only when these factors are conducive to aggression does a physiological state of irritability greatly augment the probability of physical violence.

Not only the sex hormones, but also a wide variety of hormonal and other chemical imbalances produce irritability, including high levels of epinephrine (adrenaline), low blood sugar (hypoglycemia), and various stimulants. There have been claims of disproportionate amounts of violence being committed during each of these states of body chemistry, but the data on them consist mainly of illustrative separate cases, rather than systematic statistical comparisons of violence rates with and without these conditions.

SUMMARY AND CONCLUSION

Biological factors in crime have been both grossly overstated and totally dismissed in the literature of criminology, particularly by those who made the ascription of offenses to heredity a polemical issue. After all the evidence is sifted, the three conclusions that seem most well established are these: (1) boys and young men incarcerated for crime include a larger proportion with husky (mesomorphic) physique than are found in the general population, but social selection of this type of youth by delinquent groups may be the primary cause of such statistical findings; (2) persons classified as "psychopaths" by clinical judgments that stress their repetition of offenses and lack of remorse, or by psychological tests indicating that they do not anticipate anxiety or guilt, generally have nervous-system characteristics different from those of most other persons, as measured by galvanic skin response—notably, much slower rates of recovery from whatever autonomic arousal they do experience; (3) various correlates of physical irritability, such as the premenstrual and menstrual periods in women, are disproportionately associated with the perpetration of violent offenses. Details of these conclusions are summarized in Table 7-2.

Since none of these three biological conditions is either necessary or sufficient for occurrence of crime, these factors must interact with other influences on behavior. Just as ascription of psychopathy to poor socialization in the home is rejected by pointing out "that most of the persons who come from what appear to be similarly disturbed backgrounds do not become psychopaths" (Hare, 1970: 97), so one can also say that most people who are husky, slow in arousal recovery, or irritable from their body's chemical imbalance do not commit serious or repeated crime. Indeed, each of these biological conditions may facilitate either law-abiding or illegal behavior, and will never completely block any conduct.

It is no more logical to believe that hereditary traits make "a born criminal" than to assert that genetics determines employment in a particular occupation. Indeed, no inherited attributes are nearly so closely associated with crime as some biologically transmitted qualities are with certain types of employment, such as good eyesight with airplane piloting or height with professional basketball playing. The skills these pursuits require are not inherited, but must be learned; even more important, a motivation to learn them must be acquired, or else the biological qualities that facilitate success in one job will be used in another, even in one for which they are not especially advantageous.

From the standpoint of differential-anticipation theory, genetically or nutritionally derived intelligence deficiencies are related to offenses as they affect success in schooling, employment, and other legitimate alternatives to law violations. A slow arousal-recovery rate is criminogenic because it impedes learning of favorable anticipations from the avoidance of censure and punishment. Nevertheless, the weakness of statistical correlations between these conditions and crime rates makes it evident that there are other potent influences on offenses. Especially needed is more knowledge of the interaction between biologically acquired characteristics and social factors in fostering or impeding various types of crime.

TABLE 7-2   Biological Factors in Crime

FACTOR	PREDOMINANT RESEARCH CONCLUSIONS	SELECTED REFERENCES
Physique	Atavistic anomalies of physique are not directly related to crime. Mesomorphic (husky) physique is somewhat correlated with crime, but this may reflect social selection by offenders and police, as well as its correlation with an autonomic-nervous-system arousal pattern conducive to crime.	Vold, 1958; Eysenck, 1964.
Brain disorders	Epilepsy-related disorders identified by abnormal EEG wave shapes are more frequent in offenders than in nonoffenders, but may be related to the social stigma of epilepsy; still, a small percentage of violent-outburst offenses suggest some brief breakdown in neural control.	Hodge, 1953; Shah & Roth, 1974.
Chromosomal anomalies	47,XXY and 47,XYY chromosome patterns are too rare to account for more than a fraction of one percent of crime and, though found more in offenders than in others, are more frequent in property offenders than in violent or sex criminals.	Borgaonkar & Shah, 1974.
Abnormal autonomic-nervous-system arousal and recovery patterns	The extent and rate of autonomic-nervous-system arousal and recovery from any sudden disturbance, as measured by GSR pattern or EEG speed, are somewhat correlated with being classified psychopathic by clinicians or by certain tests, and with slowness in avoidance conditioning. Those classified as psychopaths improve more than others in GSR recovery and in avoidance conditioning when injected with epinephrine, a hormone that increases arousal. Also, cheating on tests increases with injection of chlorpromazine, a drug that reduces arousal.	Allen et al., 1969; Hare, 1970; Schachter, 1971.
Ancestry	Identical twins are more similar in criminal record than fraternal twins, especially in noncriminogenic environments. Also, there is some correlation of criminality in adopted sons with criminality in biological father.	Christiansen, 1968; Mednick, 1974.
Hormones	Deficient epinephrine (adrenaline) levels have been found in psychopaths. Also, about half of the violence committed by females occurs in the menstrual and premenstrual eight days of the month, when progesterone is low.	Shah & Roth, 1974.
Intelligence	Learning deficiencies from heredity, brain damage, prenatal-or-childhood malnutrition, and disease, impede learning noncriminal roles and adjusting in school (see Chapter 8).	Broman et al., 1975; Lewis, 1976.

SUMMARY AND CONCLUSION

EIGHT

EXPLAINING THE CRIME PEAK IN ADOLESCENCE

Any effective effort to understand and control crime in our society must give special attention to adolescence, for two main reasons. First, it is during this stage of life that arrest and adjudication for serious crimes occur most frequently; the ages of peak arrest rate are 16 for theft and burglary, 18 for robbery and assault, 19 for rape, and 20 for murder (as shown in Table 4–3). Second, although capacities and experiences acquired earlier are important, it is during adolescence that adulthood is most directly shaped. Therefore, preventing the crime and recidivism of adolescents can greatly change their entire lives and also be of tremendous benefit to society.

SOCIAL DEFINITIONS OF ADOLESCENCE

Most simply defined, adolescence is the period between childhood and adulthood, and thus an age of transition. Biologically, it begins with emergence of those physical features that distinguish adults from children, such as pubic hair, growth of breasts, menses, change of voice; it ends with termination of growth in height. Sociologically, its onset roughly coincides with these biological changes, when juveniles are physically capable of performing as adults at work or play, but it ends at various ages—whenever a person assumes the social roles characteristic of an adult, especially full-time employment. Becoming an adult is often a gradual and even an intermittent process.

In the United States, biological and sociological entry into adolescence usually occurs between the ages of 12 and 14, but this range is not uniform (see Gold & Douvan, 1969: Part II). Most relevant to this chapter's concern with crime rates is that both the usual termination age of sociological adolescence and its ambiguity have increased rapidly in recent American history.

Prevailing standards for adolescent conduct are usually clearest and most uniform in the least urbanized and industrialized societies. When, for example, Samoa had little modern technology, even young children worked side-by-side with the grownups, doing what their strength and skill permitted and gradually shifting to adult work roles (Mead, 1928). In colonial America over two centuries ago, collaborative work by people of all ages prevailed, and only a minority of the children had much formal schooling (U.S. President's Science Advisory Panel on Youth, 1974: 12–13). In general, without technological development, adolescence is not the prolonged period of ambiguity it is in the more complex "advanced" nations, where young persons may for a decade be neither viewed as children nor treated fully as adults. Adolescence in industrialized societies is an increasingly protracted and confused period, a time of much concern about identity, as indicated in the summary of Erikson's eight ages of man (Chapter 6).

Another noteworthy anthropological observation on adolescence is that in those simpler societies where some marked discontinuity of conduct between childhood and adulthood is preserved—such as in rights to do dangerous hunting or other specialized adult tasks—the changes authorizing these adult roles are often made dramatic and unambiguous by "age-grading" ceremonies, frequently called "rites of passage" since van Gennep's (1908) classic work of that title. Any stage of life that such societies discern tends to be heralded by rites that clearly mark its beginning and end. These ceremonies eliminate doubt and disagreement over how a person should be treated at a particular age. With elaborate ritual, youths may be deliberately marked by scars, tattoos, removal of a tooth, or change of hairstyle, so that all can easily see that they are now adults. After these formalities, the young adults often acquire new names and are differently addressed. In societies with such formal age-grading, juveniles are less inclined to seek more rights or fewer responsibilities than adults allot. Consequently, in these societies there is not the great uncertainty and argument that American adolescents usually experience regarding how independent they should be or what obligations they have. (For fuller discussion, see Eisenstadt, 1956; Gluckman, 1962.)

Our society is not completely without age-grading rituals; religious-confirmation and school-graduation ceremonies are our rites of passage. The contrast between how youths are treated and what is expected of them before and after such ceremonies, however, is not as great now as it was formerly, nor nearly as great as with age-grading rites in some technologically less-developed countries.

As societies grow more differentiated, adolescence typically becomes not only a more extended period of status ambiguity and economic dependence on parents, but also, one of increasing divergence from adult lifestyles. Youth has always been characterized by high rates of crime, but this pattern becomes even more pronounced in rapidly changing societies.

SOCIAL EVOLUTION, ADOLESCENT SEGREGATION, AND CRIME

As a consequence of social differentiation and adaptive upgrading (discussed in Chapter 2), life becomes increasingly age-segregated. Children and adolescents in the United States formerly prepared for adulthood by sharing more of adult life than they do today. Since the family performed more of all major societal functions—including economic production, education, and recreation—a child's daily life was spent in closer collaboration with parents or other adults (see Gillis, 1974). There were more tasks to share in the household or, more often than now, in a family farm or other business. Most youth, when still in their early teenage years, left school for full-time jobs to work with adults at unskilled or semiskilled labor. Those who had prospects of becoming skilled workers were apprenticed to craftsmen—bakers, butchers, masons, carpenters, printers, and others.

In former times, girls, especially those of the middle class, had limited employment choices, and most were oriented to being house-wives. Any other occupation that they could anticipate would be termi-nated by marriage. They were not often encouraged or even permitted to finish either high school or, especially, college. Women who com-pleted higher education most often prepared for public-school teach-ing, for which spinsterhood was a job requirement.

The median school years completed by the total population age 25 or older has risen an average of almost one grade per decade, from 8.6 in 1940 to 12.1 in 1970 (Bureau of the Census 1970a: Table 75; 1970b: Table 2). By the 1970s a majority of adults had gone beyond high school, whereas 30 years earlier not many more than half had finished elementary school. The number of days in school per year has also increased by more than a third in the past half-century (U.S. Presi-dent's Scientific Advisory Panel on Youth, 1974: 80).

Because of technological change and the processes of social evolution described in Chapter 2—which create a great reduction in family businesses, easing of household chores, increase in full-time employment of both parents away from home, reliance on schools for a larger variety of educational functions for a longer period and more recreational activities in specialized centers (both public and commer-cial) that appeal to distinct age groups—children and adolescents spend less and less time with adults. More than ever before, preadults have their closest personal relationships with others of their own age.

In some respects, juveniles now have greater autonomy. Hav-ing become more socially separated, they operate without as much adult supervision and control. Girls, especially, are much less chaper-oned. The consequent worldliness of today's teenagers has led some writers to lament the "vanishing adolescent" (Friedenberg, 1959; Gil-lis, 1974: Chapter 5), implying that youth "grow-up" too soon. Yet it seems unlikely that todays's high-schoolers acquire adult values as frequently from the "school of experience." They formerly began work at adult jobs while still in the early teenage years, and from earliest childhood were in close contact with the adults whose roles they emu-lated. Fewer of today's youth can predict what occupations they will have, and most of those who aspire to a specialized profession have little early contact with it.

Adolescents are now financially dependent for a longer time

because they remain students longer. Our more extended obligatory or expected school attendance means a longer period in which adolescents are physically mature but not self-supporting or spouse-supported. The difference between most adolescents and adults in work roles is perhaps the most fundamental source of the other contrasts between them.

Being a student usually means being in a separate social world of one's age peers. This is especially true when the school is large. The longer one is a student—from nursery to elementary to high school, and on to college or university—the larger usually is the institution one attends, and the more impersonal the relationship of students to faculty.

Added to a 20- to 30-hour week in school are the many hours youths devote to extracurricular activities. Such purely voluntary time at school appeals to them partly because it provides more personal relationships to teachers than the typical classroom, and for some this may compensate for limited contacts with or estrangement from parents. Students who are unhappy in school, however, view it as a prison from which they seek as much escape as possible. They are likely to be more separated from adults, especially much more so than those in extracurricular activities. As will be elaborated in the next section of this chapter, the segregation of adolescents in their own social world and a failure of many to see the relevance of schooling to their present or future lives have had profound consequences and are directly related to crime. These trends accompany industrialization in most countries (for analysis in Britain, see Musgrove, 1964).

A basic law of sociology and anthropology is that social separation produces cultural differentiation. Therefore, the more time that adolescents spend in isolation from adults, the more likely they are to develop subcultures with unique forms of language, clothing styles, music, and other shared customs and preferences, including values—their ideas of what is morally good and bad (see Schwartz & Merten, 1967).

Some difference in taste among age groups has always existed, but youth today appear to have become more innovative and to have subcultures that contrast more drastically than ever with those of older people. Thus long hair, unisex clothing, and especially an unprecedented tolerance of diversity in personal appearance and of drug use and other conduct became widespread among adolescents during the 1960s and 1970s. Also distinctive of youth, perhaps now more than ever, is involvement in crime. But juveniles who commit numerous offenses usually engage in many types of crimes (Hindelang, 1971b), and the most recidivistic are the least specialized (Wolfgang et al., 1972: 160–61, 188–89). This suggests that much of their delinquency is expressive, using whatever chance arises to feel independent or show daring and defiance of authority, especially when with peers. Therefore, this chapter discusses theory and research on the causation of all types of delinquency and adolescent crime viewed collectively; later chapters deal with more specialized offense patterns and, thereby, with persons of different age groups.

For crime-causation theory, the differentiation of some young offenders from other adolescents by an arbitrary legal age is irrelevant. This chapter's concern is with adolescence as a criminogenic status rather than as a specific age span or as the legal category of "juvenile delinquency" in a particular jurisdiction. Since little research has focused on adolescence as it is defined here, our empirical data are derived mainly from populations legally called "juvenile," but defined somewhat differently from one state to the next. Although almost all fall into our category of "adolescent," they do not include the somewhat older persons we also regard as adolescents because they are not yet in adult occupational roles. *The unspecialized adolescent offender is the criminal type of most concern to American society.*

The school and the family, reinforced by various organizations and individuals (e.g., employers, preachers, scoutmasters), are generally presumed to instill in adolescents those attitudes, skills, and beliefs that foster avoidance of crime. Other types of persons or organizations, such as adolescent peer groups, gangs, and even the majority of adults in lower-class neighborhoods have traditionally been viewed by theorists as the main promoters of youth crimes. Recent research, however, repeatedly indicates that most adolescent offenders are more markedly and consistently differentiated from nonoffenders by their conflict with the school, the family, and other presumably anticriminal influences, than by rapport with the allegedly crime-promoting persons or groups in their neighborhoods. These recent findings suggest some need for modification of traditional sociological explanations for delinquency. How drastic the reformulation need be depends upon how one interprets the old theories and the new data.

SCHOOLS AND CRIME PREVENTION

In a classic study, the Gluecks (1950) compared 500 boys in a state training school for delinquents with 500 youths without delinquency records who were similar to the inmates in age, ethnicity, intelligence, and home neighborhood. Of more than 400 features of these two groups on which statistics were tabulated, delinquency of their companions in the community most differentiated the inmates from the nondelinquents. But the second greatest contrast was the percentage with a history of school truancy, and the third, the proportion with a record of misbehavior in public school. In this and many other studies (notably Robins & Hill, 1966), conflict with school authorities appeared to be one of the best predictors of a juvenile's subsequent conflict with police and courts for more serious offenses. This predictive relationship ostensibly justifies juvenile-court concern with such noncriminal misconduct as truancy and incorrigibility in school. But whether such court intervention increases or diminishes the prospect of further crime is often debatable.

Much recent research has assessed delinquency, not by police and court records, but by admitted-offense questionnaires (discussed in Chapter 4). Criminologists have thereby studied representative samples of adolescents rather than simply those with records in juvenile court. In one of the most sophisticated research projects, Hirschi (1969) asked a large sample of students from metropolitan high schools and junior high schools whether they had committed assault, vandalism, or any of four types of theft. From the school records he found their aptitude scores and grades, and from the police he procured records on juvenile delinquents to check for names in his sample. All information on individuals was, of course, kept confidential, but statistical findings were published on the male students.

Hirschi found that among the items most correlated with both police- and self-reported delinquency were poor performance on aptitude tests, poor grades, dislike of school, a low number of hours devoted to homework, indifference to teachers' opinions of them, belief that the teachers pick on them, and belief that a student's smoking (except in the classroom) is "none of the school's business." Many other studies have similar findings (Gold, 1963: 121; Rhodes & Reiss, 1969; Empey & Lubeck, 1971: 82; Polk & Schafer, 1972; Frease, 1973). Some multivariate analyses conclude that a poor school record is more closely related to delinquency than belonging to a lower socioeconomic class or a minority group (Polk & Halferty, 1966; Jensen, 1976). Elliott and Voss infer from their data (1974: 135) that delinquency causes academic failure more often than failure causes delinquency. Yet unpleasant experience in school and pleasure in delinquency may continually foster each other, so that none can say which comes first.

The apparently growing extent to which school difficulties foster delinquency may make any learning impediments, including low IQ, now more closely correlated with offenses than they were a half-century ago. Also, with increased evidence that prenatal and childhood nutritional deficiencies impair the development of intelligence, as does stimulus deprivation during infancy, it follows that food supplementation for pregnant women, infants, and young children, as well as good nursery schools, might reduce later lawbreaking.

In an earlier study of male and female high-school students, Stinchcombe (1964) classified them not by crime but by "rebelliousness" toward school, as measured by their reporting that they had "skipped school with a gang of kids," received a failure notice in a course that was not college-preparatory, or been sent out of the classroom by the teacher. Those classified as rebels most frequently called half or more of their classes "pretty boring," thought their work unrewarded, considered grades unimportant, and the teachers unfair, and claimed the right to smoke. On these and many other questionnaire items, Stinchcombe's rebels responded similarly to Hirschi's delinquents.

Stinchcombe found rebelliousness closely linked with failure to perceive the high school's relevance to future job prospects. Girls expecting to marry by age 18, students not expecting to enter college or to use their high-school education occupationally, and those not in college-preparatory curricula were especially rebellious. Other researchers (Hargreaves, 1967; Schafer & Olexa, 1971; Kelly, 1974) found noncollege "tracks" in public schools highly correlated with delinquency. Blake and Johnson (undated) argue that this occurs because "tracking" perpetuates family inequality. Hirschi (1969: 170–83) also demonstrated that expectations of a college education are associated with lower delinquency rates. In a high-delinquency area of Chicago, Caplan (1974) found that not expecting to finish high school was the best predictor of delinquency of 120 factors investigated.

When Hirschi (1969: 131–32, 156) made statistical analyses of the independent effects of different factors (technically called the assessment of each variable while "holding the others constant"), he found that a low number of delinquent friends proved most correlated with nondelinquency; but *liking school* was not far behind and was closer than either communication with father or liking teachers. Such findings create the impression that as the average duration of school attendance has become protracted for American youth, crime rates have become more distinctive of those adolescents who fail to find gratification in schoolwork. Revision of delinquency-causation theory may now be warranted, for differentiation of society has made schooling affect the late adolescent and early adult life of much more of the population than ever before.

It is noteworthy that arrest rates for the leading property felonies drop off rapidly after age 16, the most prevalent upper limit of compulsory school in the United States, and even more after 17 and 18, also frequent ages of school termination (see Glaser, 1975: Tables 3-2, 3-3, and 3-4). McKissack (1967) reports that in England conviction rates diminish after the fifteenth birthday, when compulsory education ends and most youth enter the work force. Elliott and Voss (1974) report that delinquency in the United States declines during school vacations.

Following up for four years on all ninth graders in eight California high schools, Elliott and Voss (1974) found circumstances at school much more closely related to delinquency, especially for boys, than those of the home or community. The most dramatic finding in this and in Elliott's earlier study (1966), however, was that both police-recorded and self-admitted delinquency declined markedly after the students dropped out of school, especially if they were married or employed or both. In short, when these young people terminated sociological adolescence by acquiring adult roles, their criminality usually ceased. Delinquency was predictive of dropping out of school, but dropping out was predictive of a decline in delinquency (Elliott & Voss, 1974: 124).

Elliott's earlier study (1966), a three-year followup on police and school records of all tenth-grade boys in San Diego's two largest high schools, found that those from lower socioeconomic neighborhoods who dropped out of school had police-referral rates thereafter that were less than one-third their predropout rates; meanwhile, boys from higher-status neighborhoods who were dropouts had only slightly lower delinquency rates after than before they left school. One may infer from these data that for lower-class boys, dropping out of school meant satisfactory termination of adolescence as we have defined it, since they could now go to work at low-skilled jobs and be autonomous at a status level comparable to that of adults in their neighborhood, or comparable to that which these adults had when they first left school.

One may speculate that official delinquency rates for youth from higher-status neighborhoods are similar before and in the first few years after dropout because: (1) most such youth, even if they break the law (e.g., with drugs), never have an official delinquency record; (2) dropping out of school in these neighborhoods creates more relative deprivation than in the lower-status areas, for those who remain in school can usually expect to acquire college diplomas and much higher-status jobs than the dropouts. Total arrest rates of *all* who quit school in upper-class areas, most of whom never are arrested, do not decline after dropout, for more are first arrested after they leave school than before. Yet in *every* neighborhood and *every* socioeconomic class, most of those who are first arrested *while still in school* are less frequently arrested after they drop out.

At the turn of the century, Zeller (1966: 5) estimates, many youth did not even enter high school, but of those who did, 85 to 95 percent did not complete it. Indeed, not until 1950 did the rate of graduation exceed the dropout rate. The decline in delinquency rates after juveniles leave high school (regardless of why or when they leave), and the lower scholastic-achievement-test scores at many schools since the reduction in dropout rates, have stimulated some rethinking of the policies of courts, schools, and social agencies of trying to keep youth enrolled as full-time students as long as possible.

It could be highly informative to investigate social-psychologically the lives of delinquents before and after leaving school, to try to trace the changes in experience and self-perception that might explain why postschool life proves less criminogenic. Such findings might usefully supplement the objective data on delinquency and dropping out to justify reconsidering arbitrary ages for compulsory education, eliminating involuntary school after around age 15, but facilitating and providing incentives for voluntary return to part- or full-time school at any age thereafter. The Schwendingers (1976a, 1976b) assert that capitalism generates a marginal class of chronically unemployed and underemployed people whose children do poorly in school, become delinquent, and replenish this marginal class. Chapter 14 contends that this vicious cycle is now diminishing in the United States and is avoidable in advanced industrial societies with democratically regulated mixed economies and with government job subsidies if needed.

THE FAMILY AND CRIME PREVENTION

Emphasis on the family as a key factor in crime causation and prevention has had several distinctly contrasting sources. During the first third of the twentieth century, those who studied juveniles in correctional institutions proclaimed the broken home the main cause of delinquency, since 70 to 80 percent of these inmates lacked the presence of one or both natural parents, and many had parents disabled by alcoholism or other handicaps. This interpretation was somewhat modified after studies of high-delinquency areas found that broken or impaired homes were frequent for all their youth, and that absence of an adequate parental figure in the home often strongly influences the juvenile court's decision to institutionalize a child. Thus the broken homes of juveniles, somewhat independently of the seriousness of their alleged behavior, may cause a judge to adjudicate them delinquent in order to legitimate their placement in foster homes or institutions.

During the middle third of this century, Freudian theory (described in Chapter 6) directed attention to strains in the family as the primary causes of delinquency. A recurrent theme in psychoanalytic writings—that separation from a mother figure or other deprivation of maternal affection during the first five years of life is a major cause of delinquency—is contradicted by statistical evidence from Hirschi's large sample of male students. Hirschi found that there is no more prospect of delinquency in boys from homes broken by loss of one or both parents before their child is five years of age than in homes broken when the child is older (1969: 86–87).

Research on the Broken Home

The broken home has many statistical relationships to official delinquency rates that are hard to ascribe simply to the juvenile court's concern with assuring adult supervision for children. From statistics for Cook County, Illinois, in 1929 and for several New Jersey counties between 1952 and 1953, Toby (1957b) concluded that broken homes and other evidence of family disorganization are associated with delinquency, especially for girls (at any age) and for younger boys. Datesman and Scarpitti (1976) point out, with data gathered in Delaware, that the stronger correlation of broken homes with delinquency for girls occurs almost exclusively with the juvenile-status offenses of ungovernability and running away from home. Differences between the genders did not exist in the correlation of broken homes with property offenses. *Parent-initiated* complaints to the police or the juvenile court about juvenile-status offenses, such as being away from home at night without permission, are quite frequent for girls, and may be more probable with only one parent in the home.

Robins and Hill (1966), following up on 296 black males 20 years after their first-grade entry into ghetto schools in St. Louis, had findings exactly opposite to Toby's. In this group they found 17 percent delinquent before age 15 in homes with the father present, and only nine percent with the father absent. However, for boys with no delinquency record before their fifteenth birthday, 18 percent of those from broken homes and only 10 percent from unbroken homes had a subsequent delinquent record. Hardt (1968) reports that in one metropolitan area, both self-admitted and police-reported delinquency rates of junior-high-school boys were greatest in female-headed households. For police data this situation was more pronounced in white neighborhoods of lower offense rates than in a black neighborhood with the highest rates. These findings suggest that police are more often called for juvenile offenses of boys from broken homes in white areas. At any rate, regardless of how protective the mother can be in a slum when her children are young, both of these studies in such areas imply that she will have an especially difficult time keeping older teenage boys out of delinquent activities if the home is fatherless.

Willie (1967) found that the broken-home rate of neighborhoods in Washington, D.C. is associated with their delinquency rate independently of their degree of poverty, but that this rate is greatest where both poverty and broken-home rates are high. Chilton and Markle (1972) found that far more of Florida youngsters charged with delinquency live in disrupted families than do children in the general population. They also found that juveniles charged with serious offenses were more often from broken homes than those accused of only minor infractions, except that the seriousness of crimes was about the same in broken and unbroken homes among the poorest families. Clearly, broken homes somewhat increase the probability of delinquency, but by no means make it a certainty, since other factors may offset the family's impact on a juvenile's experience.

Family Attitudes and Delinquency

Although research on broken homes focuses on the objective question of whether children reside with their natural parents, this may be less relevant to adolescent crime than the subjective bonds in a child's family. The Gluecks (1950) concluded that the institutionalized delinquents they studied were more differentiated from nondelinquents by having parental figures (parents or stepparents) in conflict with each other and by having conflict with their parental figures than by not having both natural parents at home. They implied that one parent with whom a child has affection and rapport generally provides more protection against delinquency than two with whom relationships are severely strained. Elliott and Voss (1974) conclude from their data that troubled parent–child relationships are more often reflected in female than in male delinquency, but that school factors are more directly linked than parental rejection to adolescent law violation.

Hirschi (1969: Chapter 6) found that self-reported delinquency rates were appreciably associated with a boy's stating: (1) that his mother seldom knew where he was; (2) that he seldom discussed personal matters with either parent; (3) that his parents seldom explained their rules or feelings to him; (4) that there were few if any ways in which he would want to be like his father. There was little difference between the parents in their apparent impact on male delinquency rates. Jensen (1972), in a reanalysis of Hirschi's data, found that these indices of weak bonds between parents and son retained almost the same implication of high delinquency regardless of neighborhood conditions and of whether or not the juvenile's friends were delinquent. Linden and Hackler's (1973) Seattle study showed ties to law-abiding parents or peers about equally associated with nondelinquency.

The Gluecks (1950) and others found that a larger percentage of juveniles adjudicated delinquent than of other children had parents with criminal records. This parental record, of course, could have prejudiced the court in deciding which juveniles are delinquent. In an important study that used an admitted-delinquency questionnaire, Nye (1958) asked high-school students in three small cities in Washington how often they felt each parent was not telling the truth. The number of youth who said they never felt that way about either parent was three times higher a proportion of those reporting least delinquency as of those reporting the most. Similar results were yielded by the question of "how honest" they considered their parents.

Nye's questionnaire also revealed marked association between delinquency and perception of home discipline as unfair, nagging, or showing partiality (1958: Chapter 9). There seemed to be a U-shaped curve for the impact of control, with either extreme rigidity and severity or extreme permissiveness associated with delinquency, but an intermediate level associated with nondelinquency. Apparently extreme regulation impinges so much on an adolescent's sense of autonomy that it evokes rebelliousness. On the other hand, extreme permissiveness may make the child unaware of parental preferences and deficient in attachment to parents, since there is not clearly more reinforcement when showing affection and being "good" than when "bad" and hostile.

In a long-run followup of boys designated at an early age as likely to become delinquent, Stanfield (1966) found that consistency of the father's discipline was more closely associated with a low conviction rate than the father's occupational status or the frequency of the boy's contacts with delinquent gang members; this disciplinary consistency was especially associated with low conviction rates in homes with fathers of low occupational status.

When Gold (1963: Chapter 6) interviewed boys with and without police records of delinquency, the offenders less often reported sharing family activities and taking problems to their fathers, and more frequently said that their fathers used corporal punishment. Empey and Lubeck (1971: 77–81) in Provo, Utah, and in Los Angeles found both conflict between a boy's parents and his conflict with them were more frequent among adjudicated delinquents than among presumed nonoffenders. One might reasonably assume, however, that family punishment, quarrels, and alienation may be consequences rather than causes of delinquency; the misconduct of children not only creates parent–child conflicts but it also often evokes discord between spouses, when each blames the other for their offspring's problems.

It is obvious that family relationships should have a strong bearing on delinquency, for despite the growing functions of the school, parents or other adults in the home still provide much of a child's moral instruction, especially when the child is young. Psychoanalytic theory suggests that a person's conscience is inculcated mainly by parents, and is relatively fixed in early childhood. But Hirschi (1969: 87) asks how we can then explain the increase of delinquency during early adolescence and its later decline. He accounts for the impact of parents on delinquency rates by asserting:

> The more strongly a child is attached to his parents, the more strongly he is bound to their expectations, and therefore the more strongly he is bound to conformity with the legal norms of the larger system (Hirschi, 1969: 94).

If the attachment to parents is the primary reason for a child's obedience of the criminal law, perhaps (1) attachments to other persons may also have such influence, and (2) this influence might be either for or against conformity with the law.

ADOLESCENT FRIENDSHIPS AND CRIME

Much of the early sociological literature on delinquency stressed the causal impact of companions, especially youth gangs, but some writers from other disciplines, particularly the Gluecks (1950), challenged this view. Although the factor that most clearly differentiated delinquents from nondelinquents in their study was whether most of the subject's companions were offenders, the Gluecks argued that this finding actually proves that "birds of a feather flock together," that bad companions are a consequence rather than a cause of delinquency. This argument was also used by many psychoanalytically oriented writers.

ANTICRIMINAL AND PROCRIMINAL FRIENDS

The traditional sociological view of peer influence as a main cause of delinquency received its first strong opposition from the sociological research of Hirschi (1969: Tables 44, 46–48, 50), who found:

1. Boys who reported the *least* number of delinquent acts or who *least* often thought of themselves as delinquent would most often assert that:
    a) they want to be like their best friends
    b) they respect their best friends' opinions about the important things in life
    c) "the worst thing about getting caught stealing" would be the reactions of their friends (as compared with the reaction of parents or treatment by the police).

2. The percentage reporting *little or no* respect for the opinions of their close friends was:
    a) greatest among those who said that they and their close friends had committed delinquent acts
    b) least among those who said that neither they nor their friends had committed delinquent acts.

Thus, on the whole, "good boys" appear to be more deeply attached to their buddies than "bad boys."

Consistent with this conclusion, Linden and Hackler (1973) in Seattle found that nondelinquency was much more strongly related to closeness of ties with conventional peers than delinquency was to ties with other offenders. Yet for those boys with no strong bonds to any conventional persons—parents or peers—offense rates were highly correlated to ties with delinquents. Similarly, when Hirschi analyzed the relative impact of each factor he investigated (holding all others constant) the highest correlation was between number of offenses reported and number of delinquent friends (1969: 156). Also highly correlated with law violations were the number of close friends who had been picked up by the police and of friends whom most teachers would not like. As implied by the view that delinquent friends became substitutes for family ties, boys who indicated least communication with their father (or stepfather) had both the highest rates of delinquency and the largest number of friends picked up by the police (1969: Tables 24, 25, 40 & 49).

Delinquents much more often than nondelinquents said they would hide their friends in case of trouble (the "ace-in-the-hole" scale), participate with them in illegal activites, or regularly join them for purely social activities (Empey & Lubeck, 1971: 14, 59–63), as well as "still run around" with friends who are "leading them into trouble" (Elliott & Voss, 1974). These studies suggest that nondelinquents are autonomous, abandoning friends who become lawbreakers; but Hirschi's data show that they have greater respect and feelings of closeness than delinquents to the friends they retain.

Empey and Lubeck found no appreciable relationship between delinquency and whether boys would inform on their friends to teachers, parents, or the police (the "ratfink" scale). Apparently, norms against informing are shared by most American youth.

Suggestive of conflicted feelings in most young offenders is Short and Strodtbeck's (1965: Chapter 3) finding that while delinquent gang members differ from nondelinquents in their approval of criminal methods for gaining wealth or status, they share with them a positive valuation of legitimate pursuits—such as getting and holding a job—that are alternatives to crime. Such conflict especially characterizes the "neurotics," noted in Chapter 6 as a category evident in all psychological typologies of offenders; they have or readily develop attachments to anticriminals as well as to criminals and they have had the greatest reduction in delinquency rates from programs stressing individual counseling (Adams, 1961; Palmer, 1974). It appears that youth labeled "delinquent" usually have more mixed rather than contrasting norms and values when compared with youth dubbed "nondelinquent."

Causal Priority

Which comes first, bad conduct or bad companions? Are the Gluecks correct in saying that boys, like birds, flock together because they are similar, or do they become similar by flocking together? Such questions may be sterile because friendships and delinquent attitudes develop concomitantly; yet sometimes one precedes the other. Research indicates that committing delinquent acts alone varies with the type of offense, but that most adolescent predations are committed by two or more youths, acting together (Shaw & McKay, 1931; Eynon & Reckless, 1961; Hindelang, 1971c; Erickson, 1971, 1973), and in small friendship pairs or cliques rather than in gangs (Lerman, 1967). Some lawbreaking, such as shoplifting and passing forged checks, is most readily done alone, but such lone offenders may nevertheless be encouraged and assisted by others before and afterward (see Jackson, 1969).

Rather complex statistical methods have been developed for inferring the predominant sequence, hence the probable causal relationships, among intercorrelated variables (Blalock, 1971). In perhaps the most adequate application of such methods to data on delinquency, Liska (1973) concludes that the most frequent sequence in vandalism and assault is to have attitudes favorable to such acts, then to acquire friends with similar views, and then to engage in the activity. Contrastingly, he finds that the predominant sequence for theft is first to have attitudes conducive to stealing, then to steal, and then to acquire similarly inclined friends. This is compatible with Hindelang's (1971c) conclusion that adolescent theft of goods (or money) worth less than $10 is most often committed alone, while theft of larger amounts of money or more valued goods is most often done in groups. Perhaps petty stealing leads to acquiring friends inclined to steal, and this fosters larger thefts.

Delinquent pursuits may appeal mainly as a second choice to many youth, as an alternative to the three major goals and sources of prestige that Coleman (1961) found predominant among American high-school students: good grades, popularity (primarily among girls), and athletic distinction (primarily among boys). Turner (1964) reduced these goals to two objectives—in teenage vocabulary, being a "brain" or a "wheel." Hirschi's data on the weak ties of delinquents to parents and teachers suggest that their bonds to other adolescents may be the strongest they have to anyone and, therefore, the most influential on their values. Apparently nondelinquents, on the whole, have stronger attachments to both adults and peers. Indeed, the paucity of the friendships and commitments of delinquents to others of any age appears to be the principal source of their amenability to gang socialization, as Karacki and Toby (1962) persuasively argue. Extreme lack of attachments or perceived obligations may make anyone more amenable not only to all types of available socialization, but also to anomic individual expression of impulses to commit crimes or to engage in other behavior that psychologists and judges label mental illness because its motivation is unclear.

Peer Pressures for Crime

Hirschi's "control theory" of delinquency, expressed in the quotation at the close of this chapter's section on families, implies that the more closely a boy is attached to his parents or to nondelinquent friends, the more he is bound by their expectations. This theory explains delinquency as resulting from a breakdown of such anticriminal social controls. Yet, by the same principle, if juveniles are attached primarily to persons of their own age or older who *favor* criminal conduct, surely the expectations of such persons may have considerable influence on how the youngsters behave.

Adolescents frequently claim that their offenses are peer fostered, in the sense that they had misgivings about joining in the criminal acts but felt obliged to go along with the others. This would seem to be an unacceptable excuse in many if not most cases, since no group can consist entirely of followers any more than entirely of initiators of collective action. Nevertheless, numerous social-psychological experiments since the classic work of Asch (1956) show that persons will accept deviant beliefs and commit deviant acts more readily when these are endorsed by others who are present. Such tendencies to conformity by both group leaders and followers, especially if the members are friends, are predicted by the well-validated balance and cognitive-dissonance theories in social psychology (for synopses, see Brown, 1965: 573–90 and Schrag, 1971: 53–55). Psychologists have also found a "risky-shift" phenomenon—people take more chances in groups than alone, although under some conditions of group leadership they will also forego previously planned risk taking and become cautious (Pruitt, 1971; Cartwright, 1971). This and other types of compulsion to conformity must be important aspects of group criminality among adolescents.

Extremely relevant to an understanding of adolescent crimes is the observation that much of life with others is what Goffman (1967: 149–270) calls a "character game." This is exemplified by challenging, teasing, flirting, showing off, debating, kidding, bluffing, and other interaction in which the response elicited in front of others is meant to suggest the character or ability of the actor. For persons insecure in status—as are most adolescents when their claims to adulthood are placed in doubt by peers who challenge them to do something risky— these "games" can be extremely decisive. They cannot back out without being humiliated either as "chicken" (timid), as being less sophisticated in adult behavior than they had pretended, or as being dependent on or subservient to parents or teachers. Furthermore, for those adolescents who crave more prestige, delinquent "acting out" with or in view of companions represents an easy way to gain favorable attention; many, therefore, will actually goad others to challenge them (well illustrated in Werthman, 1967). As indicated in Chapter 5, the risk-taking pressure can be a major factor in the gambles of teenagers with serious crime.

Studies repeatedly confirm that an intensity of concern with expressing their maturity by having cars, smoking, and dating especially distinguishes delinquents from other adolescents. The very fact that such interests require money makes pressure to steal greater for youth maladjusted in school than for those absorbed in school activities. Stinchcombe (1964: 42–45, 119, 122) found that rebellious students of both sexes most often claimed the right to smoke, thought cars a necessity, owned cars, dated, and said that "being accepted and liked" is more important than "pleasing parents." Hirschi (1969: 194–95) shows that delinquents spend more time "riding around in a car" and "talking to friends" than nondelinquents, yet more often complained of having "nothing to do"; as already indicated, they spend much less time on homework. These types of differences, Stinchcombe argues, mainly reflect contrasting expectations of the future:

> For those students who form an image of their future in the bureaucratic and professional labor market, the tests, grade averages, and respect of teachers are meaningful. . . .
>
> The working-classs and future-housewife subcommunities in the high school find other . . . symbols of identity . . . dating, smoking, car ownership, masculinity and aggression, athletic achievement, all can be transformed into symbols of the kind of person one is, or is becoming (1964: 106-7).

The law has evolved beyond some former puritanical statutes that defined smoking per se as delinquency if done by a juvenile. Driving around in cars, smoking, and petting confer a sense of adulthood desired by all adolescents. What distinguishes the more delinquent among them is their engaging in these acts more avidly, at an earlier age, more readily in lieu of homework or other obligations, and with greater hostility to adult opposition.

The importance that some adolescents attach to asserting a sense of adulthood and getting a favorable response from companions by teen-culture achievements or delinquency, even at the expense of schooling or of a reputation as "respectable," often ensnares them into what Wiley (1967) has called a "mobility trap." They get immediate respect in a segment of the adolescent community from doing things that will impede their subsequent chances for status as law-abiding adults, in contrast with youths who attain distinction through studies or in extracurricular activities that also enhance their later achievement abilities. Turner (1964) documents the great concern of many adolescents of all class backgrounds with becoming eminent or successful in some pursuit. This often extends shortsightedly to various avocational activities that impede realistic vocational preparation. Being a "big shot" in delinquent circles often makes them less satisfied later with mediocre roles, yet gives them a poor school record and perhaps a police record that block chances for attractive legitimate roles as adults.

ADOLESCENT GANGS, CLUBS, AND DELINQUENCY

Informal clubs and gangs have long been part of juvenile life. Also extensive are formal youth groups, such as Boy and Girl Scouts, the many clubs in high schools and churches, and teams of various sorts, both in the schools and in the neighborhoods, from Little League to "pickup teams." How are these related to adolescent crime?

Gangs

Juvenile gangs are especially associated with delinquency in deteriorated city neighborhoods; these are generally older residential areas penetrated by commercial and industrial developments. They are settled predominantly by poor newcomers, mostly from ethnic minorities, because only the least attractive areas are available to them. Such slums have a concentration of social problems—disease, broken families, alcoholism, gambling, prostitution, and other adult crime—concomitant with poverty. Because housing is crowded and private yards minimal, the streets and any other publicly-accessible space become the main social and recreational centers for children and for some adults (see Suttles, 1968).

Many of the parents in these neighborhoods are of rural or foreign background and do not know the slum street world as well as their children do. This parental ignorance, along with the home problems and its crowdedness, often leaves slums youngsters "on their own" in the street to a greater extent than children elsewhere. Also, since most of these parents have little formal education and there is little reading in the homes, and because so many speak mainly a foreign language or a dialect of English with grammar and pronunciation different from that dominant in our society, their offspring are handicapped in school. In such settings, juvenile play groups can successfully compete with the school and the home in giving children opportunities for achievement as well as friendship, recreation, affection, and protection. The streets also supply many models and traditions of criminal activity. As Tannenbaum (1938: 14–15) described it:

> The family may live in such crowded quarters as to force the child into the street to such an extent that street life takes the place of family life. . . . The family may be living in a neighborhood where . . . street pilfering is a local custom; where there is hostility to the police; where there is race friction and warfare; where the children, without the knowledge of their parents, may find means of employment in illicit ways, . . . where they can hear all sorts of tales and observe practices or be invited to participate in practices, or become conscious of habits, attitudes, morals, which are entirely in conflict with the teaching, habits, and points of view of the family in which they live. And because the family under these conditions may be an inadequate instrument for the purpose of supervising and coordinating all the child's activities, the family may lose the battle for the imposition of its own standards. . . .

The concentration of delinquent gangs and subcultures in the slums was attributed by early sociologists to the social disorganization of these neighborhoods and to the continuity of youth gangs and criminal adults who transmit these subcultures. Disorganization was ascribed to the repeated settlement of these locales by newly arrived poor migrants to the city, who were powerless to keep the areas from being sanctuaries for crime and political corruption. Yet youth and adult groups gave traditional slums much hidden organization. Indeed, organized crime and political machines, as well as ethnic associations and churches, provided much of the welfare assistance in the slums during the 1920s and 1930s, which antedates the extensive development of government welfare services.

Juvenile gangs vary greatly in size and formality. Some are loose-knit and others tightly organized, some have fewer than ten and some claim thousands of members, some are preoccupied with fighting or crime and others are primarily social and athletic. Their patterns of leadership and ratio of core to fringe members also vary. (For description of these variations, see Klein, 1971: Chapter 3; Cartwright et al., 1975: Chapter 1). Perhaps most distinctive of these groups are the names—for example, Vicelords, Crips, Stones, Dukes, Caballeros— that give members an exciting identity and a source of pride (Suttles, 1968: Chapter 9). Most gangs are exclusively male, but there are some affiliated girls' groups, and autonomous gangs of girls are occasionally reported.

Gangs are dynamic, modifying greatly both during short-run mobilizations to cope with momentary crises and over a period of years in reaction to changes in their social, cultural, political, and economic circumstances (Yablonsky, 1962; Jansyn, 1966; Miller, 1976; Short,

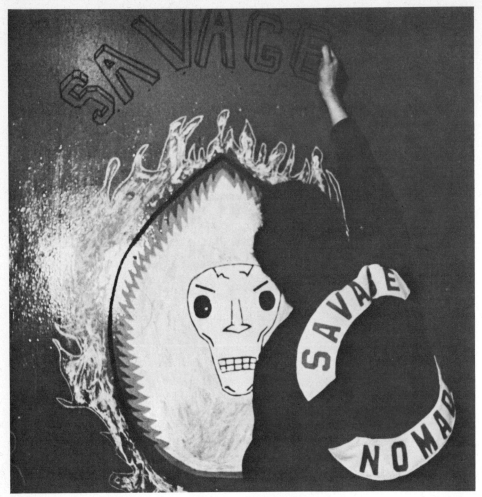

What's in a name? A more gratifying identity.

1974, 1976: Chapter 5). Toby (1968) suggests that delinquent gangs develop wherever there exists a combination of (1) some adolescents who feel relatively deprived and (2) lack of close supervision by adults. He points out that gangs develop even in countries, such as Sweden, that have no slums, no large and poor minorities, and a liberal welfare system.

Any major change that occurs in the predominant access of juveniles in an area to adult roles will alter the subculture of values and lore and possibly even the existence of their gangs. This important principle, of wide applicability, is a major contribution of Cloward and Ohlin's *Delinquency and Opportunity* (1960), though it is insufficiently appreciated by most commentators on this book. The trends in the late 1950s that they explained are ongoing, and their interpretation remains relevant. They attribute the emergence of distinctive new types of delinquent subculture among youth from very poor homes in American cities to such changes in numerous slums as: (1) a decline of central-city political machines that once tightly organized most slums and dispensed much patronage in the form of city jobs and services; (2) partly because of this, residence of more of the professional and organized crime leaders in other parts of the city and its suburbs; (3) outside management and massive size of the public-housing projects that replaced some traditional slums, as well as expulsion of project residents whenever their income rises slightly above the poverty level; (4) absence not only in these projects, but also in many old and new slum areas, of the traditional slum's local businesses and well-known politicians, clergy, and even racketeers, all of whom helped control youth and socialize them for adult-role opportunities.

When delinquents become less integrated with adult offenders, Cloward and Ohlin contend, they are more "creative" in their offenses. More juvenile lawbreaking becomes purely expressive, as an end in itself, such as fighting and drug use. Since World War II, American slums and housing projects have repeatedly created "conflict" delinquent subcultures, exemplified by the large-scale, quasi-military juvenile gangs of major cities (notably Chicago and Los Angeles) that periodically escalate their levels of violence. During the 1970s much of the fighting has been with handguns. Gang members usually only talk about fighting other gangs, but a conspicuous minority among them shoot people, sometimes killing or wounding those who are only casually in opposition to them, or who are just bystanders.

Youth who outgrow involvement in such conflict subcultures, but cannot accept the much lesser excitement of the unskilled jobs to which their poor school records limit them, comprise what Cloward and Ohlin call the "double failures," those who have been unsuccessful in both criminal and noncriminal pathways to adult prestige and autonomy. It is this group, they claim, that is most attracted to the "retreatist" delinquent subcultures devoted to drug use (and, as Chapter 10 shows, they often become nonretreatist professional criminals if addicted). The general principle that juvenile subcultures vary with the types of adult role to which they have access is suggested by many in-depth accounts of specific gangs (e.g., Spergel, 1964; Keiser, 1969; Klein, 1971; Dawley, 1973).

Two major government undertakings that were expected to reduce slum delinquency failed because they did not successfully address the basic problem of the inaccessibility of legitimate adult roles to adolescents. One effort has already been discussed—rebuilding slums physically by massive public-housing construction. The policy of concentrating problem families in these "projects" only isolates the resident juveniles from adult life to a greater extent than they ever were in traditional slums. Therefore, if they cannot obtain a sense of achievement in school or in jobs, they are readily attracted to violent gangs or to the drug culture.

The second government effort assigned "street workers" to gangs. These young adults were to provide juvenile gang members with recreational aid and counseling. As Klein (1971) shows, having such street workers gave the gangs more "fun" and made them more cohesive, so that the members remained removed from adult ties and work roles, and as delinquent as before.

Formal Adolescent Groups

Because of changes in the nature of adult life, the type of group in which adolescents participate greatly affects their later careers (Loeb, 1973; Kahane, 1975). As industrialization and urbanization differentiate society, more of adult life is spent in formal organizations—at work, shopping, dealing with government, and even at recreation—in contrast to the informal and personal life in the family and in small shops and offices. With these changes come more decision making by formal negotiation, written contract, orderly discussion and voting, rather than by (1) informal cajoling, shouting, or nagging to reach consensus, or (2) authoritarian process wherein some people give orders and others simply obey or fight or leave. Because industrialization thus increases the discontinuity between the informality of childhood and the formality of adult life, it widens the gap that an adolescent must bridge to become a successful adult. The school and the groups that adolescents join are the major agencies for bridging this gap.

The severity of this discontinuity, Loeb (1973) stresses, is greatly affected by the nature of childhood and adolescent group experience. To begin with, children's chances of being culturally prepared in the home for participation in formal social relationships will probably be greater if their parents have white-collar rather than manual occupations, work in large organizations, belong to a formal (nonemotional) church congregation or other religious organization, have had extensive schooling, and are members of an ethnic group that has long been in the middle rather than the lower strata of American society. Such factors influence an adolescent's sense of ease in formal groups.

The following is an enumeration of features that contrast purely formal with purely informal adolescent groups (based on Loeb, 1973); but we should note that (1) most adolescent groups are between these extremes, though closer to one or the other, and (2) there is always some informal group life, even within formal groups:

Some groups give prestige in adolescence while also preparing for eminence as adults.

Informal groups are:

1. *uninstitutionalized* (e.g., a group of friends); hence, they change or are terminated readily except, of course, if based on marriage or kinship.

2. *without clear purpose* other than the members' attraction to each other.

3. *free-flowing and face-to-face in communication,* usually without intermediaries.

4. *ambiguous or indefinite in roles* allocated to various members.

Formal groups are:

1. *institutionalized* (e.g., the Boy Scouts, or a high school club); hence, they have continuity as organizations despite turnover of membership, especially when adults are involved in them.

2. *organized for particular goals or purposes,* and engaged mainly in activities instrumental to their attainment

3. *deliberate and orderly communication, often through representatives,* much of it in writing as memos and minutes that are later cited as official.

4. *definite about positions or offices* assigned to various members

<table>
<tr><td>

5. *governed by the personal influence* of some members over others, reflecting whatever respect, fear, sense of obligation, or other subjective sentiment leaders arouse in followers or rivals

</td><td>

5. *governed by rules* that prescribe rights and duties for each position or office, and for the membership as a whole

</td></tr>
<tr><td>

6. *differentiated in roles and responsibilities only through spontaneous personal alignments and preferences*

</td><td>

6. *differentiated in roles and responsibilities by formal procedures* (e.g., elections) for filling specific offices, committees, etc.

</td></tr>
<tr><td>

7. *selective in admitting new members only by the subjective assessment* of whether old members will "like" them

</td><td>

7. *selective in admitting new members by formal requirements and application procedures*

</td></tr>
<tr><td>

8. *spontaneous, impulsive and arbitrary in collective decision making*

</td><td>

8. *deliberate, rational, and explanatory in collective decision making*

</td></tr>
<tr><td>

9. *ignorant, unconcerned, or defiant about effect of many laws* or social norms on their preferred activities

</td><td>

9. *informed and concerned about effect of laws* or other explicit social norms on their preferred activities

</td></tr>
<tr><td>

10. *promotive of discontinuity between adolescent habits or skills and adult-role requirements* in advanced industrial and postindustrial societies

</td><td>

10. *promotive of continuity between adolescent habits or skills and adult-role requirements* in advanced industrial and postindustrial societies

</td></tr>
</table>

One can also differentiate democratic from authoritarian adolescent groups (what Loeb calls "open" and "closed" groups) by their membership's participation in decision making, independently of their formalism. For example, a teacher-dominated classroom or a coach-dominated athletic team is an authoritarian formal group; however, a youth organization operating with elected officers and parliamentary procedure and with minimum interference from adult supervisors is a democratic formal group. A fairly equalitarian friendship pair or clique is a democratic informal group, but an individually dominated friendship group or clique is an authoritarian informal group. Adolescent participation in formal groups prepares them for adult employment in large organizations, but participation in democratic formal groups prepares many for managerial staff roles in such organizations.

Classic sociological literature (e.g., Thrasher, 1927, and Cohen, 1955) portrays gangs as close-knit and mutually loyal groups rendered cohesive by their conflict with other gangs. More systematic research shows that this unity is highly variable, and that the interaction skills or deficiencies that adolescents develop for adult life depend greatly upon the formality and democracy of their groups. Yet the social groups available or attractive to adolescents may largely reflect the socioeconomic class of their parents.

ADOLESCENT CRIME AND SOCIOECONOMIC CONDITIONS

The practice of explaining crime by blaming it on poverty has had a long and meandering history. Perhaps the only identifiable group of writers fairly consistent from one era to the next on this issue have been the followers of Karl Marx, who regularly attribute crime to the deprivations of the working class, for which they blame capitalism.

Crime and the Business Cycle

A review of studies on the correlation of crime to unemployment rates could at one time assert that "assumptions involving either positive or negative relationships . . . may be supported with some show of statistical significance. The obvious inference is that the general relations of economic conditions and criminality are so indefinite that no clear . . . conclusion can be drawn" (Vold, 1958: 181). Such a complete discrediting of poverty as an explanation for crime collapses, however, when other variables, particularly age of offenders, are taken into account.

Arrests of adults consistently increase when joblessness rises (Glaser & Rice, 1959), but arrests of teenagers of compulsory school age actually decrease when adults are unemployed and increase during prosperity. Similar findings have been reported for England and Wales (Fleisher, 1966: 74). This contrast for different age groups is most pronounced in war periods, when both adult unemployment and crime drop but juvenile delinquency rises. The reversal for youngsters of the adult correlations between economic fluctuations and crime (verified mainly in the first half of the twentieth century) may be due to school-age children being more independent when business booms or the nation is at war. In addition to the wartime departure of many adult males, there is in any period of prosperity a rise in the employment of mothers outside the home, and in the use of commercial recreational facilities in which adults and juveniles separate. On the other hand, when work is scarce parents are at home more and the family does more things together, thus briefly offsetting the long-run trend of increased age segregation.

Crime, Socioeconomic Class, and Neighborhood

That poverty does not fully account for adolescent crime is suggested by this chapter's earlier discussion of the impact on these offense rates of school, peers, and family. We have already cited Willie's (1967) demonstration in Washington, D.C., that poverty and broken homes have both independent and joint effects on increasing delinquency rates. Gordon (1967), in a sophisticated review of all major studies, concluded that the poverty of a city neighborhood has the most persistent and unambiguous relationship to its official crime rate of any statistical factor investigated. Discrimination against the poor by law enforcement and by the courts, however, is often alleged to account for the high arrest and conviction rates in poor neighborhoods.

Ostensibly, the most devastating blows to all theories on the relationship of socioeconomic class to delinquency rates were delivered by a series of studies that used questionnaires asking junior-high and high-school students about their delinquency, instead of relying on official arrest or adjudication data for their school district. The economic statuses of the students, as estimated from the occupations that they reported for their parents, had no marked or consistent relationship to the extent of delinquency that the students admitted (Nye et al., 1958; Dentler & Monroe, 1961; Akers, 1964; Erickson & Empey, 1965; Hirschi, 1969). The implication was that these findings disprove traditional assumptions that "poor kids" are the most delinquent. The fact that official rates of arrest and adjudication for delinquency are highest in low-income neighborhoods could then be ascribed purely to police and court bias against poor juveniles.

Whether such survey data fully refute theories ascribing delinquency to slum conditions and subcultures can be questioned. First, all correlations between admitted delinquency and parental occupations in the major studies cited above were within a single school or a single set of school districts, mainly in small cities. They did not compare delinquency rates of urban neighborhoods of contrasting socioeconomic levels, as the earlier studies had done. It is conceivable that children within a single school district tend to share its prevailing youth culture regardless of their parents' occupations, since the school is their common meeting ground and it segregates them from children of other neighborhoods.

Second, there is much variation of income and status within each of the major occupational designations used in these questionnaire studies. The income and socioeconomic levels of persons with the same broad category of employment (e.g., skilled worker or professional) are quite diverse, and usually vary with the predominant income level of their neighborhood. Accordingly, it is often misleading to classify children as sharing the same socioeconomic class simply because the researcher uses the same broad label for the occupations of their parents. Thus persons with a job title such as "manager" or "salesman" who live in a wealthy suburb probably have much higher income and education, on the average, than people with the same job titles living in a slum. One may manage a giant corporation and the other a two-employee shop, one may sell skyscrapers and the other hot dogs. Most children probably share the predominant juvenile subculture of their neighborhood and school, regardless of the jobs their parents hold. Furthermore, as indicated in discussing gangs, this subculture varies with the extent and nature of relationships between adolescents and adults. Therefore, one can hypothesize that among school districts of marked contrast in adult occupations and socioeconomic class, there are differences in frequency and type of delinquency, even if within these areas one finds little or no correlation between parental occupations and admitted delinquency.

The first strong evidence for the validity of this hunch came from a survey by Clark and Wenninger (1962). They gave admitted-delinquency questionnaires to students from sixth through twelfth grade in four communities: a poor rural, consolidated school district, and three contrasting neighborhoods within one of our largest metropolitan areas—an extremely wealthy residential suburb, an inner-city black ghetto, and a small industrial suburb. In the wealthy suburb about 80 percent of the students had parents with jobs in the upper half of the Duncan index for classifying occupations by their average socioeconomic status; in the slum only 17 percent were in this upper range. The rural area had only about six percent of its fathers in the upper half of the Duncan scale, while the industrial suburb had 33 percent.

Clark and Wenninger found no relationship, within any neighborhood, between admitted delinquency and the status of the father's occupation, but much difference in quantity and type of admitted offense among the four communities. On the whole, delinquency was least often reported by the rural students and most often by those in the slums. More theft, violence, truancy from school, vandalism, and deliberately trying to disrupt church or school activities were admitted in the slums than in other communities. Because Clark and Wenninger (as well as Hirschi, Dentler, and many other delinquency researchers) gave questionnaires only in the schools, we can infer that these contrasts for various neighborhoods understate actual differences. It seems probable, as McDonald (1969: 77–78) shows in Britain, that slum schools in the United States have a higher percentage of students absent, that absentees are above average in delinquency rate, and that they are not present to fill out the questionnaires.

Clark and Wenninger found that different kinds of neighborhoods have different kinds of juvenile offenses, for reasons that often are readily inferred. For example, the far greater number of buildings per person in rural and suburban areas may account for the fact that juveniles from these areas more frequently reported going into other people's houses or sheds without permission. Perhaps slum children have less delinquency involving pornographic literature than juveniles in the other areas because the poor have least access to any reading matter and possibly more observation of explicit sexual conduct in their own crowded housing.

Youth from affluent areas report infractions that reflect their wealth. Vaz (1971) found that middle-class youth have "institutionalized" such nonpredatory delinquency as gambling for money, drag-racing, and moderate amounts of drinking or truancy; for these activities have become so customary among them that those who decline to participate may become less popular among their peers. The answers from Clark and Wenninger's prosperous suburb most resembled the responses from the rural school district, while industrial-suburb students, on the whole, were most similar in delinquency to the slum students. We should emphasize in conclusion, however, that the differences in admitted-delinquency rates that Clark and Wenninger found among areas of diverse socioeconomic class were not nearly as great as the contrasts among these areas in arrest and adjudication rates.

Hardt (1968) supplemented questionnaires from male junior-high-school students of an Eastern metropolitan area by a check on police records. Both sources showed offense rates of 14- and 15-year-old boys distinctly higher in poor than in the middle-class areas. But for 12- and 13-year-old boys this contrast appeared only in the police records, whereas for the older boys it was greater with the police information. Hardt accounts for these differences with evidence from the questionnaires that the police stop and ticket juveniles more freely in poor than in more prosperous neighborhoods.

Consistent with the Clark and Wenninger (1962) data on questionnaire-admitted infractions, Reiss and Rhodes (1961) found in a slightly earlier study that the rate of court-recorded and unofficial delinquency in a large city was much more closely related to the predominant occupational status of a neighborhood's adults than to the variations of parental status among individual youths within any neighborhood. They also found, in an interview inquiry on self-reported offenses among 156 white males with juvenile-court records, that virtually all "career delinquents"—those who seemed oriented to crime as a lifetime occupation—came from neighborhoods lowest in the average occupational status of fathers. But they were only a minute fraction of all delinquents even in these areas. Reiss (1976) also notes that lower-socioeconomic-class areas report distinctly more felonies by juveniles. The similarities of delinquency rates across class lines are mainly in petty infractions.

Probably the most thorough questionnaire study on social class and delinquency was done in Britain by Canadian sociologist Lynn McDonald (1969). She found (1) that the working-class children significantly exceeded those of the middle class in rates of admitted truancy, school misconduct, theft of things not even wanted, borrowing without returning, sneaking into the cinema, fruit theft, stealing from building sites, and receiving stolen property; (2) that class differences were in the same direction but smaller for petty shoplifting; and (3) that both groups were about the same in theft from school desks or lockers and not paying on buses or trains. The middle-class children more often reported stealing from family members or friends, but McDonald remarks: "It could simply be that working-class children, with less precise concepts of property ownership, did not regard as theft the taking of things from family and friends that middle-class children did. Working-class children could be more prone to see their action as borrowing" (1969: 91). Within each school district the working-class children admitted theft more often than students from the middle class; but in predominantly middle-class areas, both groups were much lower in reporting this offense than in predominantly lower-class areas.

In a distinctive study by Gold (1970), a representative sample of 13- to 17-year-olds in Flint, Michigan (whether in or out of school), were individually interviewed and asked to select from a set of descriptive cards those offenses that they had committed. They were then questioned on these and other experiences and on their personal background and beliefs. When the socioeconomic status of the youths was determined from the occupations they reported for their parents, it was found that the lowest-status boys had admitted distinctly more serious crimes than those of higher status. But there was no appreciable difference in the delinquency admitted by girls of different status. Police records in Flint show eight times as high a serious-delinquency rate in the lower class as in the middle class; but according to Gold, the correct ratio should be about three to two—50 percent higher in the lower class (1970: 116).

Quite different evidence of higher adolescent property-crime rates among the poor is provided by the victimization surveys of the 1970s, described in Chapter 4. The poor report suffering household burglaries, assaults, and personal robberies much more often than the rest of the population (LEAA, 1975b: 18, 22), and these offenses are usually perpetrated by neighborhood youth. Therefore, it seems probable that actual rates of committing such crime are also appreciably higher among the poor, especially in urban slum areas. This does not deny, of course, that neighborhood differences in arrest and conviction rates also reflect handicaps of the poor in dealing with the criminal-justice system.

In summary, the traditional impression (based on arrest and conviction records)—that poor youth and poor neighborhood have crime and delinquency rates several times higher than the more affluent—undoubtedly exaggerates the facts. Also invalid, however, is the contention that all socioeconomic classes have exactly the same delinquency rates. This claim is based on the results of questionnaires to high-school students in which the researcher determined social class from the reported parental occupations. Higher rates of admitted serious delinquency are revealed for children of the urban working class than for those of the middle class—50 percent higher in one study—when researchers try to include truants as well as those present in school in their questionnaire distribution, or when they classify the social class of their subjects by the predominant economic level of the school district. More precise estimates of the variation in adolescent-crime rates by socioeconomic class require not only more rigorous research methods, however, but also different generalizations on different types of offense.

Theories on Class Aspects of Delinquency

Landmark sociological studies (Shaw, 1929; Shaw and McKay, 1931, 1942; Thrasher, 1927) demonstrated that high rates of adolescent arrest and adjudication were concentrated in urban slum neighborhoods with the highest poverty rates, and that these areas also had high rates for many other social problems, from physical and mental diseases to overcrowded housing and illegitimate births. These researchers contended, however, that urban social and cultural conditions rather than poverty explain this concentration of problems in the slums. They pointed out that some rural populations are as poor as the slum residents or poorer, but have low delinquency rates. They supplemented their statistical maps on the distribution of crime in the city with case studies of urban delinquents; and they interpreted the life stories of these offenders as showing that the social disorganization of slum life, and the adolescent gangs and subcultures described in the preceding section of this chapter, account for the high delinquency rates there. They claimed that virtually all youth reared in these areas would be enculturated with delinquent values, just as children reared in Paris learn French and those reared in Omaha learn English; this, then, was an *enculturation theory* of neighborhood delinquency rates.

During the 1950s and early 1960s the influence of *functionalism* in sociological theory led to new explanations for delinquency, pioneered by Cohen's (1955) influential revision of the enculturation theory. Cohen did not focus on the ecological data of poor urban

Here is evidence for Cohen's theory of delinquency as negativistic, nonutilitarian expressive reactions to school difficulties.

neighborhoods having high juvenile arrest and adjudication rates, which was the concern of Shaw and McKay. He sought instead to explain why these delinquency rates are higher for young male offspring of the lower class than for children of the middle class. His interpretation, a variety of what Hirschi (1969) calls "strain theory," was that lower-class delinquency is a "function" or consequence of those middle-class standards for school achievement and conduct that the lower-class homes cannot as readily prepare their children to meet. Therefore, according to Cohen's theory, the boys who find school most frustrating collaborate in development and support of an alternative set of behavior standards that they can meet. Cohen saw this alternative delinquent subculture as a "reaction formation"—a deliberate pursuit of the opposite of conventional norms—and as an expression of defiance toward the persons or institutions advocating endeavors at which these youth are unsuccessful.

Cohen saw as expressions of such reaction the many delinquent acts that are not utilitarian but only negativistic by ordinary views of the offenders' self-interest. These are exemplified by vandalism of school property, stealing for the fun of it, and other deliberate acts of rebellion against adult authority. Just how large this proportion is—whether a vast majority of delinquent acts, as he suggests, or a small minority, as some have implied—is difficult to establish because of measurement problems, but it is easily demonstrated that an appreciable amount of adolescent crime does have these expressive features.

Cohen's theory that delinquency expresses the reactions of lower-class youth to frustration from middle-class standards was challenged by Reiss and Rhodes (1961) and Clark and Wenninger (1962). They argued that the theory was contradicted by their findings that delinquency rates tend to be lower for poor youth in affluent than in predominantly poor neighborhoods. If Cohen's theory were valid, they said, the poor would be more frustrated, and hence more delinquent, living among the middle class, where the disadvantages of being poor are more evident than in areas where all are poor. Indeed, Reiss and Rhodes found that "a low status boy in a predominantly high status area with a low rate of delinquency has almost no chance of being classified a juvenile court delinquent. . . . The more the lower class boy is in a minority in the school and residential community, the less likely he is to become delinquent." Yet Eberts and Schwirian (1968) found that total crime rates for metropolitan areas are greatest in those cities where the poor are a distinct local minority and contrast most in income with the more affluent; this merits further study by type of offense and age of offender rather than simply by total crime.

Two conclusions emerge from the research cited above, and from similar findings in other studies:

1. An individual adolescent's conduct is generally more influenced by enculturation in the home neighborhood, by internalizing its predominant norms and values in the course of interaction with peers and neighbors, than by the family's poverty or affluence compared with others there.

2. The greater the contrast between an entire neighborhood's poverty and the wealth of the rest of the metropolitan area, the more crime there is likely to be in the poor sector.

This second finding may reflect, in part, a tendency of the police to be more severe with youth in poor neighborhoods than elsewhere (Hardt, 1968). But contrasts between city areas in reported-victimization and admitted-delinquency rates indicate that crime concentrations in the most deprived sectors usually exceed those accounted for by variations in police practice.

The evidence from many studies (summarized earlier in this chapter) that there is an extremely close relationship between dissatisfaction with school and delinquency makes plausible Cohen's contention that much vandalism in schools and other adolescent expressive offenses are indeed ways of symbolizing reaction against the behavior demands that frustrate these youth. Vandalism occurs in all schools, at every social class and age level, but particularly among 10-to-12-year-old males (Martin, 1959; Hardt & Peterson, 1968; Ward, 1973). It is an important and insufficiently researched social problem.

Anthropologist Walter B. Miller (1959; Kvaraceus & Miller, 1959: Chapter 9) proposes still another explanation for the higher delinquency rates of juveniles (particularly males) of the lowest socioeconomic class. He argues that their offenses simply express a subculture distinguishing both adolescents and adults of their stratum from persons of higher socioeconomic status. Especially characteristic of all age groups in the poorest segments of our city populations—including most of those who are not arrested, as well as those arrested—are, according to Miller, the following "focal concerns":

1. *Trouble.* Being arrested, having an illegitimate pregnancy, injuries, illness, and being unemployed are all viewed as varieties of "trouble," and trouble preoccupies the very poor. Criminal behavior tends to be assessed among them not so much by moral absolutes as by whether it gets people into or out of trouble. One can infer that from the lower-class juvenile's perceptions of the alternative actions feasible to get out of trouble, delinquent behavior is often much more rational than it would be to those of another class with different perceived options.

2. *Toughness.* Physical strength, endurance, insensitivity to pain, and courage are much more highly valued in the lower class as proof of masculinity and of adulthood. This valuation of toughness justifies greater tolerance of assault and fosters greater stoicism toward physical punishment or discomfort in police or correctional experience.

3. *Smartness.* Skill in gaining advantages by deception is admired more in the lower socioeconomic class, thus encouraging a manipulative orientation to teachers, police, therapists, and each other, as well as in crimes of fraud.

4. *Excitement.* The monotony of work and of affordable legal forms of recreation for the lower class make its people more attracted to the excitement in delinquency and crime than others would be.

5. *Fate.* The unpredictability of earnings in the lower class makes the idea of "luck" more appealing to them than to those of more secure and adequate income, hence their greater participation in long-shot gambling, such as the "numbers" racket or other lotteries, and their greater risk taking in crime.

6. *Autonomy.* Similar to the emphasis on toughness is pride in being "in charge" of one's own behavior, rather than having other people "tell me what to do"; this accounts for the greater rate of insubordination reported for lower-class males in schools, the armed forces, and elsewhere.

The delinquency-fostering values implicit in some of these focal concerns, Miller claims, are adaptive to lower-class life. They enhance gratification for the majority of this class, especially those with little chance of leaving the slum who must cope with it as best they can. These values may make people more suspicious, stimulated, and self-satisfied in the slum setting, which should minimize frustration there.

Many have contended that if the focal concerns and values delineated by Miller and others alleging a "culture of poverty" (e.g., Lewis, 1959, 1961, 1966) make the thinking of all age groups in the lower class differ from that in the middle class, it is (1) a difference of degree and emphasis rather than an utter contrast, and (2) a result of economic deprivation and social exclusion rather than of contrasting class subcultures (Valentine, 1968; Rainwater, 1970; Leacock, 1971). Rodman (1968) observes that with American social classes defined by arbitrary cutting points in scales of income or classifications of occupation, we should not expect them to have subcultures as distinct and uniform as they would be if they were groups completely isolated from each other or, at least, not sharing common mass media, schools, and other sources of values. Of course, people in all classes are usually indoctrinated from childhood on to give at least lip service to the so-called middle-class virtues of hard work, honesty, thrift, cleanliness, moderation in pleasures, and use of violence only defensively and minimally. Yet most persons feel pressured to "stretch" one or another of these values at times. The data cited in this chapter on both official and admitted delinquency support the findings on adult conduct and attitude (Rodman, 1963) to suggest that stretching occurs most frequently among the poor in slum neighborhoods, for here the pressures are greatest.

Miller's six focal concerns, implying some perspectives opposite to those ascribed to the middle class, certainly develop at every status level, especially among youth. Since they refer to experiences most common in lower-class slum life, however, it is there that the judgments they imply are probably most often praised and become shared belief systems, or subcultures, at least among delinquents. Nevertheless, contrast in values among diverse types of neighborhoods appear from research to be: (1) mostly in range of conduct and belief *tolerated* rather than *preferred* (Della Fave, 1974); (2) not a matter of homogeneity in any neighborhood (Kobrin, 1951); (3) not nearly as contrasting as stereotypes of the lower class suggest (see also discussion of subculture-of-poverty theories in Chapter 9).

Miller's theory and the above observations are compatible with the Shaw–McKay, the Reiss–Rhodes and the Clark–Wenninger evidence that the predominant class in a neighborhood determines its subculture. Hirschi (1969: 212–23), whose study covered many school districts in different towns, found Miller's themes unrelated to the social class of students as defined by the occupations of their parents. This finding does not clearly discredit Miller, however, since one would not expect a common subculture among students from scattered locales, but only among those who interact with each other or are, at least, in the same or similar school districts. Furthermore, Miller does not contend that the focal concerns are homogeneous in all slum residents. Like many typologies discussed in this book, these categories provide at best an idealized description, helping us bear in mind the dimensions of thought and conduct found to some extent everywhere, but probably more frequently and markedly in lower-class neighborhoods.

Considerable psychological research has been done on habits of thought presumed to differentiate socioeconomic classes, but with largely inconclusive findings when all studies are reviewed collectively (Allen, 1970: Chapter 13). Even when differences in average trait scores are found between lower- and middle-class subjects, the difference is usually relatively small and there is a large overlap between the range of scores in one class and in the other. While some researchers ascribe to the poor (compared with the middle class) a shorter time-goal orientation, more negative self-concepts, greater responsiveness to material than to verbal rewards, less motivation to achievement, and more crediting of their success or failure to external forces (e.g., "luck"), the most rigorous investigations find little correlation of these traits with indices of socioeconomic status.

Innumerable illustrative cases of extremely law-abiding youth and adults in slums support the view that close attachment to anticriminal persons or institutions can strongly counteract procriminal subcultures, even in areas of high crime rate and low socioeconomic status. Some evidence of an insulating effect of family and other relationships in high-crime-rate neighborhoods was provided in the study by Glaser, Lander, and Abbott (1971), which found that the greatest difference between addicted and nonaddicted siblings in a slum area (beginning in early childhood) is the nonaddict's greater attachment to home, work, and school, and lesser participation in adolescent street life. The slums appear to be more mixed than other areas in the prevalence of values supporting adolescent crime, rather than in complete contrast to other areas. Indeed, as Kobrin (1951) pointed out in a classic article, there is continuous conflict of values in high-delinquency areas.

In summary, the predominant thrust of available evidence seems to be that socioeconomic conditions affect adolescent-crime rates mainly when youth from the most deprived status levels are concentrated in separated residential areas or school districts. Apparently it is not so much the strain suffered by poor youth from their perceived contrast with middle-class youngsters as their segregation in urban slums that results in their developing the most criminally oriented adolescent subcultures. Nevertheless, even the poorest juveniles who are highly isolated by residence and school district from youth of a different background develop some attachments to anticriminal persons or institutions that effectively reduce the likelihood of their involvement in serious crime.

ADOLESCENT CRIME AND ETHNICITY

Periodically throughout American history, a different set of ethnic groups has been overly represented among adolescents arrested, adjudicated, and incarcerated. In the late nineteenth and early twentieth centuries the Irish were predominant; later they were replaced by Poles and Italians; and since the 1940s blacks, Mexican-Americans, and Puerto Ricans have been conspicuous. Always these delinquent adolescents were disproportionately the children of recent poor migrants to urban slums.

Some of the distinctive features of slums that account for the extensive conflict of their juveniles with the law were indicated in preceding sections, in discussing gangs, socioeconomic class, and adolescent crime. These slum conditions are independent of race and nationality, since with few exceptions high arrest rates have characterized whatever ethnic group happened to be settled there. But the crime rates of their adolescents gradually diminish as the group moves out of the slums and is assimilated into more mixed and affluent areas. Only ethnic communities that greatly emphasize cohesive family life, family businesses, and educational pursuits manage to have relatively low official delinquency rates in the slums. The insulation by cohesive ethnic institutions has kept crime rates low among the Jews, the Chinese, the Japanese, and more recently the Cuban refugees (of predominantly middle-class background) in slum areas, especially when their children were least assimilated into the larger slum society. Blacks, on the other hand, found it especially difficult to move out of the slums and to rise from a very low economic status because of their history of slavery and of white resistance to granting them full equality after slavery was abolished. They were denied housing outside their ghettos even when they could afford it, and they received discriminatory treatment from the police and other white-dominated governmental agencies—conditions that produced generations of poor schooling, poverty, broken families, limited political power, and segregation.

Highly interrelated historically in determining whether an ethnic group stays in the slum or leaves it, and whether it has a high or a low official crime rate, are its *political power, economic status, educational attainment,* and *degree of segregation.* A change in any one of these four aspects of ethnic-group relations in the direction of greater equality and greater participation in activities with the rest of society tends to change the remaining three in the same direction.

Blacks began to move relatively rapidly in the direction of equality on these four dimensions only in the late 1960s, and then mainly the younger generation in the North and the West who had completed high school or college. By the 1970 census it could be reported for the first time that, outside the South, there was no appreciable difference of income between white and black husband–wife families in which the head of the family was under 35; and that for those under 25 with both husband and wife working, the black family's earnings were 113 percent of such white families (Bureau of the Census, 1971). As pointed out by Andrew F. Brimmer, the first black to become a governor of the Federal Reserve Board, the major schism in income within the black community is between its high-school or college-educated members and those who are less educated (quoted in Moynihan, 1972). Despite the recession of the early 1970s, the reduction of inequalities that began in the 1960s continued (Farley, 1977).

As this educational schism is lessened in black, Mexican-American, and other poor minority youth, many sources of high adolescent-crime rates will diminish for these ethnic groups. The main factors in their offenses, indicated by this chapter's evidence, remain: (1) problems of schooling and of its relationship to employment; (2) problems of insufficient involvement of adolescents with family or with other anticriminal adults and peers; (3) problems of segregation in the slums.

SUMMARY AND CONCLUSION

The basic explanation for today's peaking of offense rates during the teenage years is that technological changes have altered home and community life, creating a longer, more ambiguous, and more age-segregated adolescence than has ever existed before. The social separation of youngsters has produced adolescent subcultures that may divert them from the schooling needed in our complex industrialized world to prepare for adult roles.

The number of years that Americans spend as students has increased by about one year per decade for half a century, and now exceeds 12 years for most. With this trend, the crime peak in adolescence seems to have become more than ever related to maladjustment in school. Those who find education a pathway to adulthood are least delinquent, but those who find it frustrating more often seek distinction and autonomy in law-violating conduct. Research shows that their offense records decline if they then drop out of school, especially if they find jobs or marry. This suggests a need to reconsider our system -of compulsory education, making departure for employment possible at an earlier age but also facilitating and motivating full-time or part-time schooling whenever people desire it.

Strong bonds to parents and nondelinquent peers are closely associated with avoidance of serious law violations; conversely, alienation of youth from conventional adults and ties with delinquents are highly correlated with offense rates. Lone stealing usually precedes having companions supportive of theft, but having violence-oriented associates precedes committing assaultive offenses. Those adolescents most alienated from school attach more than the usual importance to involvement with peers in behavior expressive of adult status, and their group situations often create considerable pressure on everyone to engage in delinquency. Juvenile gangs seem to be substitutes for family ties, especially in slums, but the relationships of the gang members to adults largely determine the type of delinquent subcultures they develop. Formal groups, especially democratic ones, prepare youth best for a crime-free adulthood.

Adolescent-crime rates seem to be fostered by poverty, but this relationship is complex. Although crime rates of adults and older teenagers increase with unemployment and decline with prosperity, delinquency by children of compulsory school age increases in periods of full employment, especially in wartime. Some data suggest no relationship of admitted delinquency to social class, but the most rigorous studies indicate that the poor do admit the highest offense rates. However, these do not exceed the rates of middle- and upper-class juveniles by nearly as much as arrest and conviction rates suggest, for there is clear evidence that the affluent have advantages over the poor in dealing with the criminal-justice system. The strain and enculturation theories exaggerate when they imply homogeneity of occupational classes or neighborhoods in attitudes and behavior. Statistically, adolescent conduct appears to be more influenced by enculturation in the norms and values predominant in a residential area than by contrasts in affluence among peers there. Those neighborhoods that contrast most in poverty with the rest of their metropolitan area have highest offense rates.

Although some poor ethnic minorities have been overly represented in official arrest and conviction statistics throughout the twentieth century, the particular groups have changed every few decades. High official crime rates are fostered by an ethnic groups's low cohesiveness, lack of political and economic power, below-average educational attainment, and segregation. Alleviating any of these factors improves the others. When a minority overcomes all of these problems or when it is assimilated into the dominant segments of the society, its adolescent-offense rate declines.

An overview of this chapter, provided by Table 8.1, shows that causal factors in the crime peak during adolescence are interrelated, and that the crime rates of young people closely reflect differential anticipations. When involvement with law-abiding adults is extensive, when school is gratifying, when bonds with anticriminal parents and peers are close, and when poverty is not oppressive, youth will tend to be predominantly law abiding in attitudes and behavior. As this chapter has shown, the unspecialized adolescent offenders—the main source of FBI index crime rates, which peak in the teenage years and early twenties—are disproportionately cut off from conventional adults, find school humiliating and irrelevant to their perceptions of the future, are painfully poor, and are in informal cliques or gangs with other youth sharing the same perspectives. In the chapters on specific types of offense and offender that follow, some of the relationships of adolescent to adult criminal careers will be discussed.

TABLE 8-1   Interrelated Causal Factors in the Crime Peak During Adolescence

CAUSE	EVIDENCE	SELECTED REFERENCES
Duration, role ambiguity, and segregation of the adolescent experience make it, for many, a poor preparation for adult roles	Prolongation and segregation of student life; reduction of children's work in household chores, family farms, or other businesses, or at jobs; divergence of adolescent from adult subcultures (e.g., in drug use)—all linked to trends of adolescent deviance.	Eisenstadt, 1956; U.S. President's Scientific Advisory Panel on Youth, 1974; Gillis, 1974
Many children, as their age advances, find schoolwork frustrating and irrelevant	High correlation of delinquency with low grades, little time spent on schoolwork, and dislike of school; decline in delinquency following dropout from school.	Stinchcombe, 1964; Hirschi, 1969; Polk & Schafer, 1972; Elliott & Voss, 1974
Weak bonds in the family reduce anticriminal influence of parents and increase the appeal of delinquent groups	Correlation of some delinquency with broken homes, and of all delinquency to conflict with and unfavorable attitudes toward parents.	Glueck & Glueck, 1950; Nye, 1958; Willie, 1967; Hirschi, 1969; Empey & Lubeck, 1971; Jensen, 1972; Linden & Hackler, 1973
Segregation of children of recent migrants in urban slums impedes their school success and their identification with law-abiding adults, and fosters delinquent subcultures	High rates of admitted and official serious delinquency in urban slums; flourishing there of violent delinquent gangs and of drug addiction supported by predatory crime.	Thrasher, 1927; Shaw & McKay, 1942; Kobrin, 1951; Cloward & Ohlin, 1960; Reiss & Rhodes, 1961; Clark & Wenninger, 1962; Short & Strodtbeck, 1965; Hardt, 1968; Suttles, 1968; Klein, 1971

TABLE 8-1 (cont'd.)

CAUSE	EVIDENCE	SELECTED REFERENCES
Inexperience in formal groups, especially formal democratic groups, impedes adolescents in holding jobs and dealing with bureaucracies in modern society	Delinquents are primarily in casual, small groups; extracurricular activities at school are highly correlated with nondelinquency.	Hirschi, 1969; Polk & Schafer, 1972; Loeb, 1973; Kahane, 1975

NINE

VIOLENT OFFENSES

Crimes that coerce, injure, or kill—the "show of violence"—terrify the public beyond all measure and seem impossible for the government to control. Although systematic study makes them no less shocking, it can yield clues to their causes and prevention. A first step is to recognize how deeprooted they are in the background of our society.

VIOLENCE IN AMERICAN HISTORY

The United States began as a land of immigrants, many fleeing strife in Europe, yet in conflict with each other and with the native Americans, the Indians. There were coerced immigrants, too—people shipped here by force: British criminals and debtors as indentured servants, and blacks as slaves. Fugitive white bondsmen wandered in the wilderness, becoming rugged backwoods dwellers and Indian fighters in the Appalachian Mountains. Blacks had a bloody history of suppressed revolts, and those who escaped could not so easily hide their slave identity. "Southern fears of black insurrection . . . as well as life in the wilderness, contributed to . . . widespread familiarity with firearms. . . . The United States was, in fact, born a 'gun culture' . . . which associated freedom with armed self-defense" (Lane, 1976).

Gun ownership, a monopoly of the aristocracy in Europe, was a right of all classes except slaves in the American colonies. Hunting in the mainly untilled wilderness was the chief source of meat, and tanned animal skins were a leading export. Firearms soon spread to the Indians, who traded for them avidly, especially with the French. Starting in early adolescence, all colonial males hunted with rifles, and thus most became marksmen for conflicts among people (Kennett & Anderson, 1975: Chapters 1 & 2).

From colonial days until well into the twentieth century, the ubiquity of arms frequently prompted Americans to take the law into their own hands. Vigilante groups and mobs committed crimes, not only against alleged offenders but also as robbers and killers of minorities—often new immigrants—whom they envied or feared (Brown, 1969; Hofstadter & Wallace, 1970: 11–24). The European custom of dueling with pistols, cultivated especially in the South, spread to the West, where it evolved into the quick-draw gunfights dramatized in our motion-picture and television "horse operas" (Frantz, 1969; Lane, 1976).

Traditionally, violent crime was associated with the frontier, where alleged opportunities and sparse population made the slogan "Go West" especially attractive to failures and criminal outcasts from the older Eastern communities. The consequent predominance of rootless, unmarried men in the newly settled territories, and the absence of strong community institutions or policing agencies, fostered lawlessness. Yet, as indicated in Chapter 8, many of our larger cities had an internal frontier, the slum areas where new poor migrants found the only housing they could afford and the only neighborhoods in which residents would not reject them as different and inferior. Unemployed single men without strong family ties drifted into the slums as well as to the West, and some turned to crime, especially during economic depressions. In the first half of the nineteenth century there were few police and there were sections of our major cities that neither police nor mayors (or other officials) dared enter except in large groups to put down riots. Violent urban-crime rates appear to have been at their highest level in American history during this period and to have declined since then (Lane, 1969, 1976), but the reduction has not been continuous.

Quite different from most criminal violence is the systematically organized use of force for political or economic purposes. "The United States has had the bloodiest and most violent labor history of any industrial nation in the world" (Taft & Ross, 1969: 270). This strife first peaked in the 1880s with the start of a half-century struggle for an eight-hour day and for the right to collective bargaining. These issues aroused much more intense hostility than simply differences over wages. Such conflicts were often deadly, mainly because National Guard units had been expanded, armories constructed for them in areas with frequent labor disputes, and the first state police established (in Pennsylvania) primarily to suppress strikes. After the National Labor Relations Act of 1935 created agencies for enforcing the right of workers and the obligation of employers to engage in collective bargaining, labor violence declined markedly, but certainly did not disappear. These principles have not yet been extended to farmworkers except by some state law, notably in California.

During the second half of the twentieth century, there have been many explosions of racial or political violence in the United States and, frequently, rising murder rates. Does our culture, more than the customs and beliefs of other countries, now foster use of physical force in disputes? Statistics on the causes of death, almost identically compiled in many nations under procedures and definitions made uniform by international agreement, once included "homicide" but in recent years subsumed these in an "all other" category. The last available homicide figures, in Table 9-1, indicate:

1. The homicide rate is several times higher in the United States

TABLE 9-1 Annual Deaths Due to Homicide per 100,000 Population by Country

(Year for which rates apply in parentheses)

COUNTRY	RATE	COUNTRY	RATE
United States	12.1 (1973)	Austria	2.4 (1973)
Canada	3.9 (1973)	Belgium	2.7 (1971)
		Czechoslovakia	2.1 (1972)
Chile	47.7 (1971)	Denmark	3.7 (1972)
Colombia	21.2 (1970)	Finland	5.9 (1973)
Costa Rica	6.2 (1973)	France	2.5 (1970)
Cuba	7.8 (1970)	West Germany	3.1 (1972)
Ecuador	8.1 (1972)	East Germany	0.7 (1970)
Guatemala	20.8 (1971)	Greece	2.3 (1973)
Mexico	31.0 (1973)	Northern Ireland	25.3 (1973)
Venezuela	9.7 (1971)	Ireland	3.0 (1972)
		Italy	1.6 (1972)
Israel	6.0 (1973)	Netherlands	1.0 (1972)
Japan	2.4 (1973)	Norway	1.1 (1972)
Philippines	27.7 (1972)	Poland	4.6 (1973)
		Spain	0.2 (1972)
Australia	3.4 (1973)	Sweden	7.4 (1972)
New Zealand	1.7 (1972)	United Kingdom	3.3 (1973)

SOURCE: United Nations, *Demographic Yearbook, 1974*, 1975. This information was dropped in the *Yearbook* for 1975 (published in 1976) because of the adoption of a different set of categories for classifying the causes of death.

than in other technologically advanced nations for which statistics are available.

2. Mexico and a few other Latin American countries (generally intermediate in technological development) have homicide rates several times that of the United States.

3. Countries with much internal strife (e.g., Northern Ireland, the Philippines), of course, have exceptionally high homicide rates.

Two important observations should be made on data unavailable for Table 9-1:

4. National homicide rates have never been published by many less-developed countries, including such populous ones as India, Indonesia, and Brazil, as well as most governments in Africa.

5. Communist-dominated countries of Eastern Europe publish homicide rates, but the Soviet Union and China do not.

Violent crimes include murder, assault, robbery, rape, child battering, and—least frequent, but often sensational—kidnapping. The diverse crimes called "hijacking" usually involve kidnapping or robbery or both. But most of the data in this chapter will be on homicide because, as Chapter 4 indicated, it is not only the most serious of these offenses but also the most accurately counted. Physical attacks that are not fatal are called assaults, but whether they have painful, injurious, or lethal consequences often depends not so much on the intentions of those involved as on their weapons, skill, and luck, as well as on the speed and quality of medical aid. Assault is a felony—often called "aggravated assault," "assault and battery," "assault to kill," or, in Britain, "wounding"—when it results in serious injury or when there is evidence that death or great harm was intended. Yet most assaults are classified as misdemeanors, either at arrest or when the accused agrees later to plead guilty in exchange for a reduction of the charge.

Because arbitrary factors determine the outcome of a physical attack, it is appropriate to explain homicide and assault together. Indeed, almost all broad statements on homicide in the section that follows also apply to assault. The fact that these legally distinct crimes have highly similar statistical correlates suggests that they have the same causes (Pittman & Handy, 1964). Homicide statistics, however, are much more complete than figures on assault. Child battering, robbery, and rape are somewhat different in origin and in correlates from assault and homicide, and will be considered separately; rape, although it entails assault, will be dealt with mainly in Chapter 11, on sex and crime. Robbery will be discussed in some detail in this chapter and also (along with kidnapping and hijacking) in Chapters 12 and 13, on avocational and vocational crime.

VARIATIONS IN HOMICIDE IN THE UNITED STATES

To understand why homicide rates are higher in the United States than in other industrialized nations, but are even greater in some less-developed countries, we will first identify statistical correlates of murder within this country. Seven factors are especially relevant: historical period, region, gender, ethnicity, urbanization, age, and victim–offender relationship. After we briefly describe the dimensions of killing, explanations for homicide in the United States and elsewhere can be tested by how well they fit these and other statistical facts.

1. Murder Trends

The FBI's homicide statistics for the United States are based on murder and nonnegligent manslaughter cases known to the police. Though published since 1933, they only gradually became quite complete, and not until the 1950s did the jurisdictions they cover include over 90 percent of the nation's population. Independently, statistics on homicide defined as nonaccidental killings have been reported for a much longer period by the United States Office of Vital Statistics, as part of their tabulation of all causes of death in this country. These are based on local health-board information from physicians and coroners, who must record an official explanation whenever anyone dies. The international comparisons of homicide in Table 9-1 come from this type of compilation, rather than from police reports. But police and public-health definitions of homicide differ slightly.

FBI statistics on murder reflect the legal definition of this offense as either (1) deliberate killing with premeditation and malice, or (2) under the "felony murder rule" in most state laws, any death that results from another "dangerous" or "forcible" felony—usually defined to include robbery, rape, burglary, and kidnapping—even if the demise is accidental rather than an intended part of that crime and, indeed, even if the felon does not do the killing. Thus, if three men collaborate in a store holdup, with one inside pointing a gun at the manager, a second in the doorway as lookout, and a third at the wheel of their getaway car, all three can be charged with murder if the man inside accidentally shoots the manager dead while trying to tie him up, or if the police fire at them but kill an innocent bystander instead. Vital Statistics may define both of these types of death as accidental rather than as homicides. The FBI (1976: 19) reports that *almost a third of homicides in 1975 were known or believed to be consequences of other felonies, and not from actual intent to kill.* This was a new high, up from 21 percent a decade earlier.

Vital Statistics on homicide include deaths that police and courts excuse, such as killing in self-defense. Public-health data on homicide appear to have been rather incomplete until 1920, but as Table 9-2 indicates, rates of killings reported by the FBI and Vital Statistics have usually been under 10 percent apart since 1950. Such convergence creates confidence that they now cover predominantly the same cases and that both are fairly accurate.

Homicide rates peaked during the Depression, declined until about 1960, then increased until the mid-1970s. What caused the decade of rapidly rising murder rates that began in the late 1960s? A search for answers, believed to be multiple, will be a recurrent concern of this chapter when it shifts from measuring to explaining homicide.

2. Regional Differences

Homicide in both urban and rural areas has been tabulated by region in FBI reports only since 1957. Table 9-3 presents the earliest and latest data available, which show that *the Southeastern states have the*

TABLE 9-2   U.S. Homicide Rates per 100,000 Persons per Year, 1900–75
(At five-year intervals, per FBI and Vital Statistics Reports)

YEAR	DEATHS ASCRIBED TO HOMICIDE, PER PHYSICIANS' AND CORONERS' REPORTS TO U.S. VITAL STATISTICS*	MURDER AND NONNEGLIGENT MANSLAUGHTER KNOWN TO POLICE AND REPORTED TO FBI**
1975	10.2	9.6
1970	8.3	7.8
1965	5.5	5.1
1960	4.7	5.1
1955	4.5	4.8
1950	5.3	5.1
1945	5.7	5.1
1940	6.3	5.4
1935	8.3	6.0
1930	8.8	
1925	8.3	
1920	6.8	
1915	5.9	
1910	4.6	
1905	2.1	
1900	1.2	

* From *Historical Statistics of the United States, Colonial Times to 1970*. Washington: U.S. Bureau of the Census, 1976; 1975 figure by correspondence with National Center for Health Statistics, as several years lag in their official publication.
** From FBI, *Crime in the United States: Uniform Crime Reports* for the year indicated (not available before 1933).

highest rates, but that their contrast with other regions was greater formerly than now. In 1975, Alabama led the nation with 16 homicides per 100,000 population, while North Dakota was lowest with 0.8.

Between 1957 and 1975 differences among states and regions were shrinking, for most of the non-Southern areas doubled and tripled their rates of killings while increases in the South averaged about 50 percent. Incidentally, the South has almost always been lower than all or most of the rest of the country in rates of nonviolent crime, such as theft and burglary. Regional differences, it will be shown, are highly relevant to some explanations for use of force within the United States.

3. The Violent Gender

In traditional stereotypes, women are weak and gentle while men are strong and violent. Crime statistics also show a contrast between the

TABLE 9-3 Murder and Nonnegligent Manslaughter Known to the Police, per 100,000 Persons by U.S. Regions: 1957 and 1975

REGION	1957	1975
New England Conn., Me., Mass., N.H., R.I., Vt.	1.4	3.7
Middle Atlantic N.J., N.Y., Pa.	2.4	8.9
East North Central Ill., Ind., Mich., Ohio, Wis.	3.5	9.1
West North Central Iowa, Kans., Minn., Mo., Nebr., S.D., N.D.	2.5	5.5
South Atlantic Del., Fla., Ga., Md., N.C., Va., S.C., W.Va.	9.1	12.9
East South Central Ala., Miss., Ky., Tenn.	9.9	12.7
West South Central Ark., La., Okla., Texas	7.6	12.4
Mountain Ariz., Colo., Ida., Mont., Nev., N.M., Utah, Wyo.	3.7	7.9
Pacific Alaska, Calif., Hawaii, Ore., Wash.	3.2	9.4
Total U.S.	**4.7**	**9.6**

SOURCE: FBI, *Crime in the United States: Uniform Crime Reports,* 1957, 1975.

genders. Although *the proportion of homicide arrestees who were female almost doubled between 1935 and 1965, it remained low*—the increase was from about 10 percent up to nearly 20 percent. *After 1965, killings by females rose, but murders by males increased even more,* so that the percentage by women declined. Liberation may have made the genders more nearly equal in illegal as well as legal opportunities, but homicide was an especially masculine crime in the 1960s and early 1970s, when its protagonists were younger, more urban, and more lethally armed than ever, as later sections will detail.

Table 9-4 summarizes data on which these conclusions are based. As indicated in Chapter 4, our knowledge of offenders is limited to persons arrested or convicted. In generalizing about all who commit a particular crime, we must assume that those never caught are either not numerous or not sufficiently different from those we know about to cause great errors. We can be more confident in our accuracy for homicide than for other offenses, because police rates of clearance by arrest are highest for lethal crimes; but this clearance rate declined from over 90 percent before 1966 to a new low of 78 percent in 1975. Much of this drop is believed due to the growing number of killings that occur in conjunction with other felonies, especially robbery, and mainly by

TABLE 9-4 Homicide Arrestees and Victims Reported to the FBI by Gender

(By five-year intervals, 1935–75)

YEAR	ARRESTEES			VICTIMS		
	Males	Females	Percent Female	Males	Females	Percent Female
1975	13.912	2,573	15.6	14,193	4,449	23.9
1970	10,857	1,979	15.4	10,681	2,968	21.7
1965	6,055	1,293	17.6	6,539	2,234	25.5
1960	3,687	820	18.2	6,269	2,195	25.9**
1955*	1,698	375	18.1	5,630	1,788	24.1**
1950*	5,482	854	13.5	6,089	1,853	23.3**
1945*	4,732	649	12.1	5,969	1,578	20.9**
1940*	5,671	680	10.7	6,647	1,682	20.2**
1935*	6,170	679	9.9	8,367	2,029	19.5**

* Before 1952 these figures were based on individual fingerprint reports submitted to the FBI. Thereafter, the tabulations were prepared by separate police departments; but until the 1960s many did not send in such reports. Those submitted in 1955 were from cities whose total populations were only about one-fourth that of the nation as a whole.

** Data on victims were not published by the FBI in 1960 or earlier; so figures from U.S. Vital Statistics on deaths from homicide are presented to fill these gaps. From *Statistical Abstract of the U.S.: 1975*, p.154.

SOURCE: FBI, *Crime in the United States: Uniform Crime Reports* for the years indicated.

men. These are usually committed by strangers who plan in advance to avoid being identified and to escape quickly, whereas most other murders are done in anger by spouses, kin, or acquaintances of the victims, often where they can be seen, and usually with little or no planning.

There has been an increase in female victims of homicide in recent years, according to FBI data in Table 9-4, but an even more rapid rise in male victims; so nationally the proportion of females among those killed has declined slightly from its peak of more than 25 percent in the mid-1960s. In Chicago, "intersexual killings" dropped from 37 percent in 1965 to 24 percent in 1973 (Block, 1975). A California tabulation found that females were the victims in 14 percent of killings by women, but in 27 percent by men (Bureau of Criminal Statistics, 1974).

The FBI reports that in 1975 females were 13.1 percent of arrestees for aggravated assault, 13.8 for other assault, and 15.6 for murder and nonnegligent manslaughter. Women commit more assaults than these figures indicate (especially if we can assume that they generally do less damage than men when they use force), because unless death or very serious injury results, there is great reluctance to notify the police of violence by women and police reluctance to arrest them. The stereotype of men dominating the "weaker sex" makes it humiliating for males attacked by women to report this offense, and possibly female victims of some assault by women are reluctant to complain to a predominantly male police force. Therefore, arrest figures cannot provide much certainty about the differences between the genders in non-fatal attacks; yet most people share the impression that males are by far the more physically assaultive, and that distinctly male factors affect violence in our society.

4. Ethnicity and Killing

FBI classification of arrestees by ethnic descent is limited to "White, Negro, Indian, Chinese, Japanese, All Others." By these crude categories, Table 9-5 shows that blacks reached a peak of 62.2 percent of homicide arrestees in 1971, then declined slightly. The census reported that blacks were 12.7 percent of the population in 1970, 10.5 in 1960, 10.0 in 1950, and 9.8 in 1940. *For more than three decades the proportion of blacks among arrestees for homicide has been from four to six times their percentage of the total population.* These figures somewhat exaggerate ethnic differences, if one can assume that blacks are more often arrested unjustly than whites; however, since the killer

TABLE 9-5   Homicide Arrestees and Victims Reported to the FBI by Percentages in Racial Categories
(By five-year intervals, 1935–75)

Year	ARRESTEES			VICTIMS		
	Whites	Blacks	Other**	Whites	Blacks	Other**
1975	43	54	2	51	47	2
1970	38	60	2	44	55	1
1965	41	57	2	45	53	1
1960	37	61	2	47	53	——***
1955*	39	60	1	45	55	——***
1950*	53	45	2	45	55	——***
1945*	54	45	1	47	53	——***
1940*	56	40	4	45	55	——***
1935*	62	34	4	51	49	——***

NOTE: Percentages are rounded to the nearest whole percent and therefore do not always equal exactly 100.
  * Before 1952 these figures were based on individual fingerprint reports submitted to the FBI. Thereafter, the tabulations were prepared by separate police departments; but until the 1960s many did not send in such reports. Those submitted in 1955 were from cities whose total populations were only about one-fourth that of the nation as a whole. See Table 9-4 for actual numbers reported.
 ** This is the total from columns in the FBI reports headed "Indian," "Chinese," "Japanese," and "All others (including race unknown)."
*** Data on victims were not published by the FBI in 1960 or earlier; so figures from U.S. Vital Statistics on deaths from homicide are presented to fill these gaps. They combine black with "other" ethnic groups. From *Statistical Abstract of the U.S.: 1975*, p.154.
SOURCE: FBI, *Crime in the United States: Uniform Crime Reports* for the years indicated.

and the killed are usually of the same race, and only in a small number of cases is there persistent disagreement about who did it, the errors of arrest statistics are probably minimal for this offense.

Analysis of a random sample of homicides from 17 major American cities in 1967 found: in 66 percent, nonwhites killed nonwhites; in 24 percent, whites killed whites; in seven percent, nonwhites killed whites; in four percent, whites killed nonwhites (Curtis, 1974: 21). A California study of homicides, classifying ethnicity differently, found that Anglos were 90 percent of the victims of other Anglos, blacks 80 percent the victims of other blacks, Mexican-Americans 74 percent of the victims of other Mexican-Americans, and "others" (e.g., Indian, Oriental) 53 percent of those slain by offenders also called "others." Mexican-Americans, the largest ethnic minority in the Southwest, had a homicide rate in California about twice that of Anglos but only one-fifth that of blacks (Bureau of Criminal Statistics, 1974: 19).

5. Murder and the Metropolis

Only since the 1960s have urban-homicide rates reported to the FBI consistently exceeded rural rates, and (as Table 9.6 shows) *the increase in the United States after 1965 occurred especially in the largest cities.* Rates have become about six times as high in cities of over a million as in those under 10,000; the contrast would be greater if suburbs of this small size were omitted in such a comparison.

Almost three-fourths of the American population now lives in metropolitan areas, and the rise to this figure during recent decades was undoubtedly a factor in the growing national homicide rate. During the decade between 1963 and 1972, the fifty largest cities in the United States doubled their homicide rates, on the average, with two (Detroit and Honolulu) more than tripling; this led to an estimate that between two and four percent of persons born in and spending their lives in these cities will be murdered (Barnett et al., 1975).

Theories on homicide causation should certainly try to explain why cities, particularly large ones, have so recently become so much more deadly than rural areas.

6. The Homicidal Stage of Life

Murders have been committed by persons of every age level, but there has been some shift in the ages when they are most frequent. The median age of arrest for homicide, according to the FBI, was just above 30 for three decades before 1965, then gradually dropped to 26.4 in the decade that followed. While the homicide rate was going up, the median age of killers was going down. Ages 25 through 29 had the peak

**TABLE 9-6 Murder and Nonnegligent Manslaughter Known to the
Police per 100,000 Persons**

(By population unit, at five-year intervals, 1950–75)

SIZE OF POPULATION UNIT	1975	1970	1965	1960	1955	1950
Cities:						
Over 1 Million	24.6	18.4	9.6	6.1		
500,000–1 Million	20.1	18.2	10.4	7.4		
250,000–500,000	17.6	14.7	7.2	7.0		
Over 250,000	21.4	17.5	9.2	6.8	6.2	6.8
100,000–250,000	10.9	10.0	6.4	5.6	5.9	6.0
50,000–100,000	7.2	5.2	3.5	3.3	3.9	4.4
25,000–50,000	5.7	4.2	3.1	2.9	3.3	3.3
10,000–25,000	4.4	3.3	2.3	2.4	2.4	3.5
Under 10,000	3.9	2.6	2.0	2.7	2.4	2.8
Total Cities	11.1	9.3	5.5	4.6	4.7	5.1
Suburban in Above	5.4	3.8	2.7			
Total Rural	8.4	5.5	4.2	6.4	5.0	5.1
Total U.S.	9.6	7.8	5.1	5.1	4.8	5.1

SOURCE: FBI, *Crime in the United States: Uniform Crime Reports* for the years indicated. Gaps are due to earlier reports not having all of the detailed tabulations present in later reports.

rates of arrest for homicides in the early 1960s, but by the mid-1970s they were exceeded by the 18-through-24-year-olds.

A juvenilization of urban murder has occurred, for the greatest growth in city homicide-arrest rates between the 1960 and 1970 censuses was among 15-through-19-year-olds (Glaser, 1975: 132). Today, *the probability of being charged with murder is higher for adolescents and young adults of central cities than for those in any other stage of life there.* But such violence is confined to only a few in this age range. Of nearly 10,000 boys born in Philadelphia in 1945 and traced there from their tenth through their eighteenth birthdays, six percent had records of five or more offenses, and this six percent was charged with over two-thirds of the violent crimes and over half the total number of offenses ascribed to the entire 10,000 (Wolfgang et al., 1972).

Most of the post–World War II burgeoning of central-city murder rates seems to have been between 1965 and 1970. Block and Zimring (1973) demonstrate for Chicago what may also have been true in other metropolises, that in this brief period rates of homicide arrests and victims for black males 15 through 24 virtually tripled. There were also great increases in killings by gun and in robbery-related slayings. These trends continued in the 1970s, but less dramatically (Block, 1975). Thus all dimensions of homicides in the United States discussed thus far, and still other features, seem to converge in the big cities.

7. The Killers and the Killed

Although "crime in the streets" has long been a dependable theme for politicians seeking to blame incumbents for a problem that worries the public, violent crime most often occurs in the home. The FBI (1976: 19) described 22 percent of 1975 murders as within kinship groups, down from 31 percent a decade earlier; and in about half these cases, in both periods, murderer and victim were married to each other. In 45 percent of 1975 killings, victim and accused were not kin, but were in an argument or quarrel suggesting that they were at least acquaintances, and many were former friends or lovers. It was known or suspected in about 32 percent of the 1975 murders that interest in committing another felony, such as robbery or rape, triggered the slaying. Yet as we observed in earlier sections, felony involvement, though more frequent than formerly, still does not occur in most homicides; a majority are simply personal quarrels that become lethal.

The arbitrariness of events that determines whether assaultive conduct becomes homicidal is highlighted by findings that *about a third of murders are victim-precipitated*—the person killed strikes the first blow in the exchange that culminates in death. Estimates of this proportion vary in different studies, from a low of 22 percent for 17 major American cities in 1967 (Curtis, 1974: 82), to a high of 38 percent in Chicago in 1965 (Voss & Hepburn, 1968: 506). But in the lower estimate, 44 percent of the cases were classified as "victim-precipitation unknown," whereas only 21 percent were unknown in the Chicago study. If all behavior leading to death were known in every case, the proportion of murders that are victim-precipitated might well be as high as 40 percent of those that involve no other felony; but a blow that is more psychologically than physically damaging may start an exchange that ultimately proves lethal. In most murders not connected with another felony, both offender and victim had been drinking, a condition encouraging violence that is discussed more fully in Chapter 10. Certainly both the relationship between the killer and the killed and the processes whereby quarrels escalate to homicide must be considered in explanations for this crime, but most important in making such quarrels deadly may simply be the weapons available.

GUNS IN THE UNITED STATES

Whether an effort by one person to express hostility against another becomes simple assault, aggravated assault, or murder often depends almost exclusively on what kind of weapon, if any, is both acceptable and at hand to an attacker. Although it is possible to kill with many objects, or with none at all, the gun is the most quickly lethal of widely available devices for attacking people. Although knives can also be fatal, analysis of Chicago police records shows that the percentage of attacks resulting in death is over five times as high for guns as for knives (Zimring, 1968). The handgun, because it is readily concealed, is the most effective firearm for short-range killing or for robbery.

The production and import of handguns in the United States rose from less than a quarter million annually before 1947 to one million in 1965; it then accelerated to over three million in 1969, and declined to about two million per year by the mid-1970s (Newton & Zimring, 1969: 174; U.S. Department of Commerce, 1976: 156). These trends closely paralleled the trends of urban violence, but had diverse causes. The increase began with sales in the United States of cheap surplus military arms from Europe after World War II. Target-shooting clubs, hunting, and gun collecting boomed during this period of growing affluence (Bakal, 1966: Chapter 5). Arming the home also became more widespread when our "cold war" with communism intensified, and fantasies of survivors of atomic holocaust preying on each other prompted construction of residential air-raid shelters stocked with water, food, and weapons. Similarly, after each advance of the civil-rights movement in the South, lines of frightened white citizens formed at gun shops, and this scene was repeated in the North and West with the urban riots of the late 1960s (Kennett & Anderson, 1975: Chapter 9).

Despite this rise in sales, polls show that between 1959 and 1973, home ownership of handguns increased only from 32 to 42 percent, while possession of any type of firearm—rifles, shotguns, or handguns—dropped slightly, from 49 to 47 percent (Wright & Marston, 1975). This is a decline from colonial days, when there were as many guns as settlers in Jamestown (Kennett & Anderson, 1975: 249). The mechanization of agriculture in huge corporate landholdings has sharply reduced the number of farm families, for whom hunting guns had long been standard (Erskine, 1972). Estimates of the total number of weapons among the American civilian population range from a conservative 90 million (indicated by the polls) to a high of 200 million, a figure that allows for those who have several guns, owners who deny having a gun (perhaps because they did not acquire it by licensed purchase or because they fear gun control), and those whom the pollsters probably miss, such as delinquents and criminals. The high estimate brings us close to the colonial one-gun-per-person ratio, but with a much less uniform distribution among households. The actual number can never be known with precision.

According to the polls, handguns are owned disproportionately by people of middle-level occupations and income. Protestants have a rate of ownership twice that of Catholics and five times that of Jews. Somewhat more whites than blacks report pistol possession, and the rate is over twice as high in the South as in other regions. Nationally, and combining all ethnic groups, distribution of these weapons has little relationship to education, although it is somewhat more prevalent among people who have not completed eighth grade and among high-school graduates .than among those between these levels of schooling, or among college graduates. In the *urban and suburban white* population, however, handguns are: (1) by far most prevalent among high-school graduates with no college; (2) twice as common among those who say "too much" is spent on welfare than among those who say "too little"; (3) three times as prevalent among persons who find the courts "not harsh enough" as among those opining "too harsh"; (4) over twice as frequent if they describe their "financial situation" as "above average"; (5) unrelated to being burglarized in the past year or having blacks in their neighborhood (Wright & Marston, 1975). These poll findings imply that the most heavily armed in our society are so-called upper-working-class and lower-middle-class whites who feel that they "have made it" by American success values, despite limited education. They strongly resent both government aid to people who have been less successful and "leniency" to lawbreakers, and they are ready to protect their gains by gunfire.

These "house guns" that people keep on hand for defense of their possessions are six times likelier to kill someone by accident or by being convenient when a quarrel intensifies or suicide is contemplated than to be used against an intruder (Hirsch et al., 1973; Rushforth et al., 1975). Yet it is estimated that about 100,000 firearms are stolen each year, primarily during household burglaries committed when no one is at home (Alviani & Drake, 1975: 6). Since juveniles and young adults commit most burglaries, it is probable that house guns are a major source of "street guns," the weapons most used in youth crime. Certainly the distribution of such lethal devices must be considered in explaining the dimensions and locations of violent crime, in addition to beliefs conducive to violence.

CULTURES AND SUBCULTURES OF VIOLENCE

In the classic definition of "culture" as "that complex whole which includes knowledge, belief, art, morals, law, custom and other capabilities and habits acquired by man as a member of society," anthropologist Tyler (1871: 1) identifies primarily the learning that humans transmit from one generation to the next, and thereby accumulate as their view of the world. Herbert Spencer (1885: 4) was the first of many to describe culture as "superorganic," to distinguish it as our social rather than biological inheritance. We should remember that culture includes customs in the use of words—a language—and the socially shared ideas they express, as well as nonverbal customs, but not the people who learn and transmit them. Distinguishing culture from people permits us to recognize how social separation fosters cultural differentiation, but many writers confuse the two by referring to groups as cultures (Schneider & Bonjean, 1973: 118–23).

Marked and persistent differences in rates of violence from one society to another are often presumed to reflect contrasts in cultural norms on assaultive conduct. What in some cultures is viewed as moral or obligatory killing, in defense of one's honor, is condemned in others as that most heinous crime, murder. In her classic work, Benedict (1934) counterposed the serenity of the Zuni with the discord of the Dobu. Bohannon (1960) and other anthropologists report cultures with even greater differences than these in norms on killing.

The high homicide rate in Mexico is often ascribed to an emphasis in their culture on *machismo,* a "manliness" ideal of toughness, physical strength, adventurousness, courage, and dominance over females, as well as to the stress on "honor," which implies "extreme sensitivity to insult" (Heller, 1966: 35–36). Wolfgang and Ferracuti (1967: 262–63, 279–80) point to a "fatalistic acceptance of death" to explain the readiness with which murder is committed and the risk of being killed is taken in Mexico, but, they assert, both this resignation to presumed destiny and a high murder rate characterize only the lower socioeconomic classes in that country.

Contrasting behavior in different classes implies a theme also developed in Chapter 8, on the crime peak in adolescence, that when any segment of a society is appreciably separated socially, it becomes different culturally. Members of such a segment retain most of their traditional language, technology, customs, and beliefs, but develop some distinctive verbal expressions, tastes, and values (e.g., ideas of good and bad), thus sharing expectations of how members of their group should and will behave in particular circumstances. Relatively stable sets of ideas and habits that differentiate segments of a society are called "subcultures." Groups that view use of physical force more favorably than others—as described above in the lower classes of Mexico—are said to have a "subculture of violence."

It is relatively easy to show which people have the highest rates of murder or assault, but more difficult to prove that such frequent crime is due to a distinctive subculture rather than to conditions that foster violence. As Ball-Rokeach (1975: 838) observes, ". . . violence correlations do not a subculture of violence make." Examination of the segments of American society that we showed to have high homicide rates yields somewhat conflicting evidence on their subcultures. Belief and customs pertinent to use of force in these groups and in their various social categories—such as poor people—should be considered in trying to assess subcultural explanations for their rates of violent crime.

A much-cited article (Ball-Rokeach, 1973) challenges the validity of a subcultural explanation for violent behavior by pointing to the weak association (Gamma = .20) between a national sample's "Attitude Toward Violence" scores (derived from three questions— whether they approve of teenage boys punching or beating each other, public-school teachers hitting students, and judges imposing the death penalty) and "Violent Behavior" scores (from four questions on whether they had ever punched, beaten, or cut anyone or been victims of such conduct, with no exclusions of violence at play or at an early age). Such a weak relationship should not be surprising, however, considering: (1) the crudity of these three queries as an index of attitudes on interpersonal violence; (2) the probable variety of interpretations that adults gave to the questions, since only 40 percent said they had ever punched or beaten anyone and 46 percent that they had been punched or beaten. Could the other 54 and 60 percent, respectively, have experienced childhood? With such questionable clues to violent behavior, the article's most-stressed findings are likewise not surprising—that these scores had little relationship to responses on questions about abstract values (e.g., freedom, mature love, obedience), or on education or income.

In the same article Ball-Rokeach also submits as evidence against subcultural explanations for violence the finding that the abstract-value questions, when given to a group of prisoners, failed to elicit responses from murderers different from those of other prisoners, or to show a contrast in values between men sentenced for violence and those "doing time" for nonviolent offenses. That classifications of convicts by last offense does not separate them by measures of their abstract values is not so phenomenal, since most inmates now sentenced for one type of crime have previously committed diverse other types (Hindelang, 1971b; Wolfgang et al., 1972: 160–61, 188–89), and because such value inquiries are of doubtful validity in a prison setting (Magura, 1975). Furthermore, Ball-Rokeach classified unarmed robbers as nonviolent; yet these "muggers" more frequently use physical force in their crimes than the armed robbers appropriately called violent (Conklin, 1972: 116).

Quite different evidence for questioning subcultural explanations for violence is provided by Erlanger (1974a). In a survey of Milwaukee males aged 21 through 64, blacks more than whites—and, within these ethnic groups, the poor more than the affluent—reported having "angry fistfights with other men." In no groups, however, were fistfighters a majority; and *especially* among the black and the poor, more nonfighters than fighters claimed to feel "happy," "respected and listened to by others," or "well liked by other people and having lots of friends." Since fistfighters felt little social support from their group, Erlanger infers that their conduct does not reflect group culture. But even when aggressiveness against insult is expected and encouraged, the most readily violent individuals may seldom receive wide approval. Such conflict within groups creates strains and widespread tension, as is repeatedly made clear in accounts of violent societies, from Benedict (1934) on Dobu to depictions of fighting street gangs in our ghettos (Keiser, 1969; Dawley, 1973). Furthermore, research on the subcultures of delinquents indicates that even where toughness and "not being pushed around" are most admired, still more respect is given to those who can "play it cool" and avoid physical combat without being dominated (Finestone, 1957b; Short & Strodtbeck, 1965: 60). It is probable that the fistfighters in Erlanger's sample are aware of being derogated by many people, and may be ambivalent about their use of violence but unskilled at other subculturally acceptable tactics. In most groups with subcultures of violence, there is much more talk of fighting than actual fighting, and great prestige for dominating by bluff or wit, but greatest loss of face for submission to insult without countering vigorously, either verbally or physically.

The fact that in most homicide in the United States both the killer and victim usually come from the same high-violence-rate group, and that so many of their murders are victim-precipitated, strongly suggests that: (1) almost everyone in these groups shares the same beliefs about using physical force when insulted or challenged, and (2) such beliefs comprise a subculture of violence. The dialogue, including exchange of insults and challenges, that precedes or accompanies fatal fights often suggests a subcultural basis for these quarrels. Critics of this interpretation contend, however, that identical conditions cause identical beliefs; for example, that conflict-generating values may result from sharing the same frustrating poverty, unemployment, limited experience in formal organizations, and congested housing or neighborhoods, and thus, be found among all people with similar problems. The implication of this "structural" type of explanation is that there are life circumstances that would evoke such violence from anyone, and that previously acquired beliefs make no difference in conduct in stressful situations—a view that hardly seems plausible when stated in this "pure" formulation.

There are three important rebuttals of the structural explanations. The first points out the quite *imperfect correlation* between conditions and conduct; for example, there are many people with low violence rates despite terrible conditions, while some highly violent groups are not greatly deprived. The second stresses *persistence*: people said to have a subculture of violence maintain high rates of assaultive conduct long after they move to new settings with better opportunities, and they still transmit beliefs justifying ready use of force to their children. The third is *interpretative*: the dialogue reported as distinctive of groups with high violence rates suggests that they have unusually strong beliefs in the importance of not being "put down" and need to show their dominance physically if demeaned or insulted.

To resolve these disputes between structural and subcultural explanations for violence, a *cultural-adaptation* theory is useful (Della Fave, 1974). It grants that certain types of social and economic conditions foster particular ways of thinking and behaving, but notes that after such customs prevail and are socially approved, they become part of a subculture that has a "functional autonomy," in that it can persist after the conditions that create it disappear. Thus, for a full explanation one should blend the structural with subcultural perspectives. As social theorists from Marx to Parsons have observed, cultures tend to be adaptive to circumstances, but they also frequently have inertia and do not change as quickly as the conditions that shape them.

These views will be assessed when we discuss supposed locations and sources of subcultures of violence, checking how well the evidence supports them as explanations for the dimensions of homicide in the United States.

1. Is There a Southern Regional Subculture of Violence?

That the Southern states have higher homicide rates than the rest of the country was clear from Table 9-3, which also showed this regional contrast to be diminishing. A parallel pattern for aggravated-assault rates can be demonstrated from FBI figures (Glaser, 1975: 125). Regional American subcultures are revealed by unique terms and pronunciations of the English language, food specialties, and patterns of relationships between ethnic groups, but probably nowhere more clearly than in the South. These contrasts among regions, however, were once much greater than they are today. Nevertheless, such customs in the South do not demonstrate a regional subculture of violence.

Support for a subcultural explanation of Southern homicide rates comes mainly from accounts of the region's history, buttressed by a variety of official statistics, whereas challenging evidence comes from reanalysis of the statistics and recent survey research. Hackney (1969) observes: "In various guises, the image of the violent South confronts the historian at every turn: dueling gentlemen and masters whipping slaves, flatboatman . . . in a rough-and-tumble fight, lynching mobs, country folk at a bear baiting or a gander pulling . . ., panic-stricken communities harshly suppressing real and imagined slave revolts, robed night riders engaged in systematic terrorism, unknown assassins, church burners. . . . The image is so pervasive that it compels the attention of anyone interested in understanding the South."

When contrasted with the Northeast and North Central states, the South retained well into mid-twentieth century more of a frontier environment of small, isolated settlements. Travel between them and to the larger cities was impeded by a wilderness of mountains, swamps, and forests. Its poverty slowed the building of roads through these areas, especially before the interstate highway system and government programs to develop the Southern Appalachians boomed in the 1950s and 1960s.

Perhaps the major reason for the tenacity of a distinct regional subculture in the South was that, until mid-twentieth century, it had relatively little population influx. After the Civil War, the South became the poorest part of the country, with the highest birth rates; so it received relatively few European immigrants, and many of its residents moved to other regions without being replaced by people from the North or the West. This is especially true if one excludes Florida and defines "South" as the rest of the Confederacy.

Although some Southern whites blamed their high violence rates on the black population, Hackney (1969) shows that, for the years in which data are available, Southern whites always had rates of homicide exceeding those of whites in other regions, in addition to Southern blacks surpassing blacks elsewhere in this offense. When rural homicide rates were higher than city rates (before 1956), the South's lead in murder was sometimes ascribed to low urbanization, but Hackney demonstrates that rates in the South far exceeded those in equally rural states of other regions. Statistically, he shows by partial correlation that its Southern location (defined by him as in the Confederacy) is more predictive of a state's homicide rate than its percentage of urban population, median schooling, per capita income, unemployment, and median age. Finally, he cites survey data indicating that the proportion of families owning firearms is much higher in the South than in the nation as a whole (see also, Reed, 1972: Chapter 5).

Gastil (1971) bolsters the regional-subculture thesis with evidence that the homicide rate was higher in the South than in other regions throughout the nineteenth century, and that murder was not punished as certainly or as severely there as elsewhere. In 1952, 1953, and 1960—the only years for which data on length of imprisonment (before parole or sentence expiration) are available nationally—confinement for murder was briefest in the Southern states (National Prisoner Statistics, 1953: 22; 1960: 5). Between 1965 and 1971, when state parole statistics were first compiled nationally, the Southern agencies were shown to be more lenient to murderers (Glaser & Zeigler, 1974). Of course, the average term of incarceration for murder in the South was slightly reduced by their using capital punishment more than other regions, but those executed in the years cited were a small percentage of convicted murderers, often less than one percent. Yet duration of imprisonment for homicide was only about half as long as in the North Central and Northeastern states, and appreciably less than in the West. Thus the South seems to have been less outraged at killings and quicker to forgive and forget the murderers it did not execute— which means almost all of them—than the rest of the country. Also, a higher percentage of murders in the South result from interpersonal quarrels—arguments among spouses, kin, lovers or their rivals, or other persons—rather than from efforts to commit another crime, such as robbery (FBI, 1976: 19).

Support for a subcultural explanation of Southern homicide rates also comes from evidence of their persistence among Southerners who move elsewhere. Thus Pettigrew and Spier (1962) show that state rates of death from homicide for blacks in the Midwest during the 1950s could be predicted quite well by these rates for whites in the states in which the blacks were born. Since at that time killer and killed were of the same race in over 90 percent of murders, these correlations indicate that the high rates among blacks in Michigan and Ohio could be ascribed largely to a "homicidal" subculture that blacks shared with whites in the Southern states from which the blacks had moved. To support this view, one may also cite Wolfgang's (1958: 331) finding that the highest murder rates in Philadelphia were among its newest settlers from the South; being newest, they would be least assimilated into social circles with Northern values. Thus reduction of interregional differences in homicide in the post–World War II decades appears to have come largely from the migration to stressful Northern slums of persons with the Southern subculture of violence, including many poor whites.

Gastil (1971) assigned a somewhat arbitrary index of "Southernness" to all states, based mainly on the proportion of their population that was of Southern origin. In his series of multiple correlations, this index accounts for more of the variance in state homicide rates than income, education, percentage of urban population, and age. His theme and Hackney's, that Southernness accounts for murder rates, became less impressive when Loftin and Hill (1974) showed that a state's murder rate is as closely related to its rate of *extreme poverty* as to its Southernness. Thus a state's homicide rates are much more correlated with the percentage of its people having an annual income of less than $1,000, than with its median income, and are about as correlated with an index of income inequality and with a "Structural Poverty Index" as with Gastil's Southernness index or with whether the state was in the Confederacy. These findings reflect, of course, the high concentration of extreme poverty in the Southern states, particularly in the 1960s when the data were procured. The relationship of extreme poverty to violence will be discussed further.

Erlanger (1975) has compiled diverse evidence countering claims that the South's high homicide rates reflect subcultural beliefs generally more conducive to violence than those elsewhere:

1. Milwaukee male blacks born in the South have fewer hostile fistfights as adults than those born elsewhere.

2. Both black and white men in rural North Carolina report less of such combat than men in Milwaukee.

3. A 1966 survey found that Northern-born men more often have hostile fistfights than those from the South with the same amount of education.

4. The President's Commission victim survey (described in Chapter 4) found that people in the Southern states less often reported that a member of their household had been assaulted seriously than those questioned in other regions. (Erlanger neglects to discuss the puzzling contradiction between this victim survey and FBI statistics from police departments that regularly show higher rates of assault in the South than elsewhere.)

5. A Violence Commission national survey of men between 21 and 65 found that the same or smaller percentages in the South said that they could imagine situations in which they would approve six types of interpersonal violence (e.g., a teenage boy punching another, a husband slapping his wife's face, a husband shooting his wife).

It is possible, of course, that the subculture of the South fosters courtesy—hence more avoidance of fistfights over minor difficulties—than prevails elsewhere, but also more approval of lethal violence for what are perceived as gross wrongs or insults. Such a set of regional subcultural contrasts would account for both the survey and the police and prison statistics presented here, and would fit common subjective impressions as well. In addition, Northern-born blacks in the North are likely to be younger than Southern-born blacks there, and more often reared in urban slums.

Interestingly, Erlanger (1975) also presents findings that support the notion that the South has a subculture of violence:

1. The National Commission on the Causes and Prevention of Violence found that Southern males between 21 and 65 more often said that, as adults, they had been threatened or cut with a knife.

2. Other polls showed the South higher than the rest of the country in approval of spanking, corporal punishment in the schools, and gun ownership.

Several further explanations for the various discrepancies on the South are probably valid. One is simply that the South has been changing, so that historical data indicate a regional subculture of violence more clearly and consistently than recent surveys. As Table 9-3 showed, interregional differences in homicide rates are diminishing. This trend may be partly because the South exported its subculture of homicidal violence to the rest of the country when many of its less successful citizens moved elsewhere (as several cited studies suggest), and partly because the South is becoming more like the North in urbanization, industrialization, occupation, income, and education, as McKinney and Bourque (1971) demonstrate.

Another explanation for the diverse data on Southern violence may spring from what Robinson's (1950) classic article pointed out is a frequent pitfall of ecological correlation: linking attributes of an entire population to their rates of something relatively rare (such as homicide) that are based on the conduct of very few of them. Thus Loftin and Hill (1974), in their study already summarized here, show that state homicide rates are more closely correlated with the size of the small minority of each state who are extremely poor than with many attributes of their total population. This finding suggests that poverty is a prime cause of violence, but the conduct of the very poor can also be interpreted subculturally.

2. "Culture of Poverty" as an Explanation of Violence

The idea that the poor everywhere share a distinctive subculture was popularized by anthropologist Oscar Lewis in introductions to his best-selling accounts of family life in Mexican and Puerto Rican slums (1959, 1961, 1966). He "tried to understand poverty and its associated traits . . . as a subculture with its own structure and rationale, as a way of life which is passed down from generation to generation . . . that transcends regional, rural–urban, and national differences" (1966: xliii). To this subculture he ascribes fatalism, authoritarianism, and violence, as well as a sharp contrast between advocated and actual sexual conduct. He sees it as fostering female-dominated childrearing and believes, as do many, that boys for whom the controlling adult world is entirely female develop a need to flaunt their masculinity.

Lewis also asserts: "People with a culture of poverty are aware of middle-class values . . . and even claim some of them as their own, but on the whole . . . do not live by them" (1966: xlvi). Valentine (1968) argues that Lewis actually ascribes the customs and beliefs of the poor not to a transmitted subculture but to their circumstances, such as absence of savings or even of food reserves, and lack of collective political power. Yet case studies and comments by Lewis and others—

as well as the author's many conversations with slum residents—suggest that both learned ideas and living conditions may encourage violence and that these two types of influence can have *additive* effects.

Sharply challenging both the subculture-of-poverty explanation for lawbreaking and the thesis that indigence itself evokes offenses are the many cases in which the very poor are law abiding and the affluent are not. Alternative perspectives on the imperfect relationships of crime to poverty are of three types. The simplest is the principle of *relative deprivation:* people deviate from prescribed behavior only if they compare themselves with others more fortunate, but they are content when their reference groups consist of persons in like circumstances (Merton, 1957: Chapter 8). Indeed, crime rates are highest in those metropolitan areas in which the disparity of income between rich and poor is greatest, whether measuring this contrast by the ratio of persons with over $10,000 annual earnings to those under $3,000, or by the percentage of whites and blacks in white-collar jobs compared with national averages for these racial groups (Eberts & Schwirian, 1968).

Closely related to the theory of relative deprivation is the idea that crime is more often associated with poverty in societies emphasizing *achievement* than in those that stress *ascription* of unchangeable status to each person, from birth to death. Thus, if all people are told that they can rise socially and thereby greatly enhance their living standards and their prestige, they more strongly resent lack of opportunity to progress than when the prevailing belief is that each person is born to a lifelong status. Ascription implies the dogma that it is immoral for people not to "know their place," to aspire to or achieve a status to which they were not born, and even to be deprived of inherited higher rank. This belief remains widespread, despite many changes since its peak under feudalism.

It follows that in a feudal or caste society one would expect less discontent among the poor than in a more open-class society in which people generally try to improve their social status. Thus in the developing countries, law violation among the poor increases with technological modernization, since new jobs from mechanization of agriculture, mining, and industry expand the hope of economic advancement much more rapidly than they materialize for most people. But even if national crime rates are high when traditional social orders are changing, they are uneven, since these countries have concomitantly: (1) many stable, small, old rural communities with little crime despite a low living standard; (2) urban slums that crowd together the displaced, alienated, and socially isolated poor where crime is rampant; (3) roving bands of desperados in the wilderness sections, robbing travelers and raiding settlements, with much accompanying homicide; (4) often deadly feuds between some families or clans. This was the pattern in nineteenth-century America, as well as in Europe during the Renaissance and Reformation (Inciardi, 1974, 1975), persisting in many developing countries today. Of course, it is difficult to test these impressions rigorously because of the lack of statistics on homicide or other crime for earlier periods of modern industrial societies or for the currently less-developed nations.

In the United States—especially in the South, as the civil-rights movement grew in the 1950s and 1960s—blacks rapidly became less accepting of the long-standing "Jim Crowism" that tabooed their trying to enter occupations from which they had been barred. Thus the economic aspirations of their youth rose much more than their actual access to better jobs. Therefore, their shift from the ascriptive "Jim Crow" outlook to an emphasis on achievement increased their sense of frustration from too little progress, both in the South, where discrimination had been officially endorsed by the white-controlled local and state governments, and in the North, where it was disavowed but existed in fact. These developments could account for much of the burgeoning black support for the civil-rights movement in the South and for the Northern ghetto upheavals in the late 1960s. The dissatisfaction of black youth grew especially when their actual or prospective jobs, if any, were still mainly blind alleys leading nowhere, their housing as substandard as ever, and their communities as disorganized. *Both violent and nonviolent crimes surge when events increase expectations much more than opportunities.*

The third perspective on the imperfect correlation of crime with poverty is of longest standing in sociological literature and is repeatedly confirmed to this day: *Crime is more closely related to weak anticriminal social bonds and informal controls within a community than to economic deprivation.* This implies that willingness to engage in offenses is associated with any prolonged separation or alienation from the groups and institutions that instill anticriminal norms and that alleviate what Miller calls the "focal concerns" of the poor. This explanation in terms of social bonds and informal controls was standard for the fact that arrests were much fewer in Chinatowns and in the Jewish ghettos of New York's East Side or Chicago's Maxwell Street before World War II than in adjacent slums that were not poorer; for these close-knit ethnic communities were informally regulated by strong family ties, and by religious, business, and fraternal organizations. These were also sources of mutual aid. Most of their residents were employed in or near their homes, and they maintained ethnic-cultural schools for their youth to attend after public-school hours, thus keeping them close to adults. They also dealt with many of their offenders themselves.

The data presented in the 1930s by the late Professor E. W. Burgess to his classes at the University of Chicago, supporting the thesis that community organization rather than ethnic virtue accounts for lower crime rates in some ethnic enclaves, included a description of the Italian-Americans in Chicago's then-outlying suburb of Blue Island. They worked primarily in the nearby Rock Island Railroad yards, had a cohesive social life built around their church and other community institutions, and had very low delinquency and crime rates; yet they were just as poor, and came from the same part of Italy at the same time, as the residents of Chicago's notoriously crime-ridden Near West Side slums, where Al Capone reigned.

In the 1960s in Kampala, Uganda, a few years before the Amin regime, Clinard and Abbott (1973, 1976) found that people in a low-crime-rate slum area were much more predominantly from the same tribe, had fewer incomplete families, and engaged in more visiting among neighbors than the dwellers in another slum in which crime was rampant. They refer to the difference in these equally poor areas as one of "communicative integration," because instilling and maintaining a culture requires both continual communication among those who share it and their separation or insulation from the influence of those with countercultural values.

The three factors just discussed as closely related to crime—relative deprivation, achievement orientation, and weak social bonds—may well have additive effects in reducing support for norms of the dominant society and in fostering emergence of new subcultures, especially among the poor. Furthermore, individuals who are least successful in a society—those who do poorly in school or are chronically unemployed—have little reputation to lose with teachers or employers from attacking others physically; and those who use force get a quick sense of power (if they are judicious in whom they attack). Readiness to be assaultive, however, is most rewarding in the company of others (particularly males) who assess it positively, thereby fostering their collective cultivation of a subculture of violence by much talk and gesture about achievement in fighting, apart from actual combat. Such interaction is typical in "conflict gangs" of delinquents and in "outlaw" motorcycle gangs, which include some not-so-young adults.

3. Do Homicide Rates Reflect a Subculture of Masculinity?

Our society's chauvinistic stereotype that boys and men are less gentle than girls and women was cited in presenting the evidence that males commit much more of our murders and probably of most other assault. Interpreting the findings on fistfighting by Milwaukee men summarized above, Erlanger (1974a) speculates: "It is possible that rather than a 'subculture of violence,' something like a 'subculture of masculinity' exists, with violence being only one of many possible . . . outlets and not necessarily the preferred one." Which males commit most violence, and is their conduct structurally or subculturally determined, or both?

The fact that adolescent gangs in black ghettos of our major cities emphasize use of violence and are disproportionately from households without fathers has led to conjecture that such homes create an exceptional need to demonstrate masculinity. Yet accent on manliness and on using violence against rebuffs to "honor" (Horowitz & Schwartz, 1974) also characterizes Mexican-American boys, among whom fatherless homes are less frequent. Presumably their *machismo* is quite independent of family structure, and perhaps the masculinity cult in black and Anglo youth communities also exists as strongly in boys from unbroken homes as in others. Chapter 8 presented evidence that weakness of bonds to parents is a factor in delinquency that may exist with or without both parents at home, although perhaps more probable with one absent. But even maternal domination of young males because the father works far from home is alleged to generate a "compulsive masculinity" that persists in adulthood (Toby, 1966). These hypotheses on maternal domination have not been rigorously tested; for example, by comparing the impact of motherless, fatherless, and complete homes on violence rates in similar economic and neighborhood circumstances, or the relationship of fathers' hours away from home to the delinquency rate of sons.

Every male experiences the social and psychological pressures to express masculinity, at all stages of life and in diverse settings. The dominant culture provides such varied "solutions" for this problem as athletics, fighting, drinking, bossing females, and showing responsibility and strength in male work and family roles. There are great variations, for many reasons, in an individual male's need to impress himself and others with his masculinity, and in the available means for accomplishing this. Violence probably flourishes most in predominantly male settings, for these heighten competition in expressing manliness and frequently offer the fewest alternative ways of doing so. Thus the structural influence of all-boy or all-men settings augments gender subcultures in causing preoccupation with masculinity in boarding schools, the armed forces, aboard ships, and among underemployed black men on slum streetcorners described in widely read anthropological studies (Liebow, 1967; Hannerz, 1969). This may be changing, as all-male settings diminish. Since women's liberation is reducing traditional pressures to conform to gender stereotypes, it may lead men to become less violent.

The data summarized thus far suggest that the more rapid increase in homicides by males in the late 1960s and early 1970s resulted especially from a surge of violence by minority-group boys and young men in our urban slums. This boom in murder appears to have been caused by: (1) increased concentration in these areas of adolescents with school problems and young adults without jobs, discussed in Chapter 8; (2) their greater access to lethal weapons, on which details have already been presented in this chapter; (3) some unique historical events in this period that may have altered subcultures.

4. Emotional Escalation of Conflicts and Cultural Change

Most violence prosecuted as crime is not planned far in advance, but develops rather quickly when customary personal control of conduct is broken down by what has been called a "circular reaction" (Blumer, 1969). This process can be illustrated by a quarrel between two persons. The anger conveyed by the words, tone, or gestures of one arouses similar emotion in the other's response, which then evokes still greater intensity of this feeling in the initiator; but this feedback further infuriates the second, and if their mutual provocation is not interrupted they rapidly reach an extreme pitch of rage.

In such agitated states, people tend not to contemplate consequences before speaking or acting, and they are highly suggestible. Because each person's gesture tends to arouse a similar but more emotional response, so many homicides are victim-precipitated. Most murders are neither well planned nor incidental to other felonies, but are instead committed by temporarily enraged persons who have been intimately involved with each other as spouses, kin, or friends. Even affectionate relationships usually have ambivalent features, as Freud and Simmel noted independently, with love–hate mixtures and alternations (see quotations and discussion in Coser, 1956: 60–65). "We confront the stranger, with whom we share neither characteristics nor broad interests, objectively; we hold our personalities in reserve and thus a particular difference does not involve us. . . . The more we have in common with another *as whole persons,* however, the more easily will our totality be involved in every single relation to him. Hence the wholly disproportionate violence to which normally well-controlled people can be moved within their relations to those closest to them" (Simmel, 1955: 44).

When a very close relationship is threatened or destroyed, the disillusion that often follows can replace the love–hate ambivalence by deep hostility: " . . . the deepest hatred grows out of broken love. . . . To have to recognize that a deep love—and not only a sexual love—was an error, a failure of intuition, so compromises us before ourselves . . . that we unavoidably make the object of this intolerable feeling pay for it. We cover our secret awareness of our own responsibility for it by hatred, which makes it easy for us to pass all responsibility on to the other" (Simmel, 1955: 46).

"Love triangles" cause many homicides. Another's affection, once it develops, tends to be perceived by the one who reciprocates it as a proprietary right, with or without marriage (Simmel, 1955: 50–55). When such a person feels discarded, the wish to destroy the lover or the rival, or both, may become the deed. Perhaps the growing independence of women, a possible factor in our high divorce rates, will bring a decline in "triangle" murders, just as it reduced former tendencies of judges and juries to excuse homicides as "affairs of honor" when adultery was involved and the accused killed the lover of his or her spouse. Now that the autonomy of each partner is more recognized by both, a dead relationship may increasingly be viewed as neither worth preserving nor cause for murder.

In many residential neighborhoods, the most frequent basis of calls for police assistance is domestic discord. If circular reactions of the disputants have swelled to a crescendo, however, one or both are likely to assault an officer for interfering. The family fight is actually one of the most dangerous assignments for the police. Special training programs pioneered by psychologist Morton Bard (1970) in the New York Police Department, and copied with variations throughout the country, instruct officers in distracting quarrelers from preoccupation with their conflict, so that the circular-reaction process can be interrupted and calm may be achieved.

A circular-reaction sequence, like that of feuding couples, occurs in the contagion and heightening of any mood in a crowd. Examples include grief at a funeral, fervor at a religious revival, elation at a teen idol's concert, panic in a burning theater, and anger in a mob. The expression of emotion by some arouses a similar feeling in others, whose responses intensify the emotions of the initiators. The subsequent interchanges evoke a still-greater agitation in all, to the point of frenzy, if the circular process is not interrupted by distracting events.

Mob riots are especially likely to develop in this fashion when much irritation is already prevalent. They occur most often on weekends, holidays, or other periods of idleness, when people are not diverted by their routines from involvement in emotional exchanges. When crowds share a high pitch of anger, they are particularly responsive to suggestions that they express their hostility by attacking a convenient target. This is how lynch mobs and antiminority riots begin, and it is also how minority groups were moved to counterrioting, most conspicuously in the late 1960s.

In our modern age, the circular process of emotion arousal can spread through vast populations exposed to the same mass media, which may shape and augment interpersonal communications in millions of separated social settings, intensifying everyone's feelings as though all were assembled in a single place. The grief and anger that followed the assassinations of John F. Kennedy in 1963 and Robert F.

Kennedy and Martin Luther King in 1968 was heightened because their supporters throughout the nation were exposed to identical emotion-arousing media communications and were in personal contact with others who received the same stimuli.

These assassinations occurred during the years of recurrent emotion arousal by the civil-rights movement, which often gave its scattered millions of supporters uniform feelings because of mass communications (and, of course, provoked different feelings in antagonists). Blacks, potentially the movement's most direct beneficiaries, alternately had high expectations from its successes and anger about the mass arrests, beatings, bombings, and killings perpetrated by its opposition. Yet each such heinous act, publicized immediately by the mass media, so evoked sympathy from many people of all racial groups and created so much more fervor in the movement's adherents as to accelerate civil-rights legislation.

From 1965 to the end of the decade, as indicated in discussing the subculture of poverty, the main effect of the civil-rights movement was probably to intensify in blacks a feeling of relative deprivation, even among many whose social and economic conditions were improving more rapidly than in preceding years. The talk of equality made the persisting inequality more glaring, and also (particularly in youth) broke down the traditional ascription mentality whereby it had long been taken for granted that everyone is born to a specific station in life with little prospect of much change.

What most stirred mass emotions during this period, apart from the two 1968 assassinations, was a series of large-scale riots in black ghettos of major cities. Beginning in the Watts area of Los Angeles in 1965, they erupted at scattered intervals over the next five years in Detroit, Gary, Cleveland, Newark, Philadelphia, Washington, Oakland, and many more metropolises, primarily outside the South. The large riots and subsequent debates on their causes were nationally reported in great detail, and tended to polarize both riot support and opposition.

Each of the publicized riots became a focus of attention to residents of other ghettos, for whom it provided a model of possible conduct, and to public officials, for whom it meant a need to appear to be eradicating the alleged causes. Leaders of the black community finally gained media audiences and access to heads of governments to voice their grievances. During this period, polls showed that ghetto residents shifted rapidly from disapproval of to support for much of the mob violence; persons from a wide range of ages felt that it had been "helpful" in evoking government action on their problems. A growing percentage expressed attitudes of militance, although a majority insisted they themselves were not willing to participate in riots (Caplan, 1970).

The Savage Skulls do battle in the Bronx.

A variety of clues suggests that a subculture of violence grew during this period, particularly among ghetto youth. Block and Zimring (1973) provide much detail on Chicago homicides during this span that none have compiled for other cities. Relevant conditions were similar in all ghettos in the North and West, however, and the prevalence of trends in similar metropolitan areas could account for the surge in these years (detailed earlier in this chapter) of national homicide rates for males, blacks, and youth, especially in the largest cities. These researchers show for the period 1965 to 1970: (1) near tripling of Chicago homicide arrest rates for black males 15 through 24; (2) more than tripling victimization by homicide in this group; (3) rapid proliferation of guns among them (and among whites).

During these years black young adults were experiencing the continuing social bifurcation (described in Chapter 8) between those entering white-collar jobs after completing high school or college and those blocked in mobility by their delinquency and rebellion against schooling in the earlier grades. The hypothesis offered here is that mass communication about successful riot violence, especially in the late 1960s, intensified both: (1) political activism by the educated and employed blacks, for they identified with the civil-rights leaders who were gaining prestige and power by nonviolent means, and later, with blacks who were winning elections; (2) personal violence by delinquent black youth, who were becoming more relatively deprived as education became more crucial for mobility, and who identified with the rioters shown in the media as successful in law violations, such as assault and looting. It has been observed about riots that once publicity occurs, delinquents of the same ethnicity as the rioters travel many miles, if necessary, to join the upheaval. Miller (1976) notes that the rioting appealed to the delinquents' focal concerns with toughness and excitement; they joined in the disturbances with more elation than hostility, and these developments contributed to the renaissance of violent gangs.

The theory that the notoriety given to violent events evokes their *contagion* has had diverse types of factual support:

1. The John F. Kennedy assassination in 1963 and, to a lesser extent, the highly publicized mass killings by Speck and Whitman in 1966, were followed, within a month, by a surge of violent offenses (Berkowitz & Macaulay, 1971). Many crimes copied features of these slayings, and the murderers ascribed their acts to these examples.
2. In many nations and for many years, there have been greater increases in homicide rates after wars, particularly in countries suffering many combat deaths (Archer & Gartner, 1976).
3. An increase in homicides in the days on which executions occur has been demonstrated (Graves, 1956).
4. Children seeing aggressive acts on television will play more aggressively (discussed further in the next section of this chapter) (Bandura, 1973a, 1973b).
5. The crimes of kidnapping, airplane hijacking, and political terrorism seem to occur in waves, spurred by highly publicized successes, and deterred by conspicuous failures.

More varied and rigorous research is needed for any of these assertions to be conclusively tested or, if valid, made more precise.

Two independent ethnographic studies in Chicago document the experimentation by black slum youth during the mid-1960s with a variety of subculturally standardized roles emphasizing violence (Suttles, 1968: 125–29; Ellis & Newman, 1971). Spilerman (1971), noting the increasing national uniformity of riot correlates in the 1960s, ascribes it to the mass media's making black disappointments anywhere salient to blacks everywhere within the United States.

Changing any firmly established beliefs is an emotional experience, if the issues to which they apply are considered important. Frequently, a positive function of violence in political controversies is to increase the probability of open discussion and concession in matters of prejudice and discrimination on which the parties in power would otherwise not budge (Coser, 1967: Chapter 5; Gamson, 1975: Chapter 6). This, of course, was the theme of the American Declaration of Independence.

These positive consequences of violence are especially probable if further mass violence is made unnecessary because its leaders gain legitimacy and can express their views with prospects of influence proportional to their popular support. Contrastingly, long-term violence by some terrorists often changes eventually to banditry if they and their supporters are barred from political activity. Such a shift by terrorists from bona fide political objectives to professional robbery and extortion has occurred repeatedly in countries where their efforts do not create or restore institutionalized free elections or do not bring them to power, as in the early history of the Mafia (Hobsbawm, 1959) and in much of Latin America, notably Argentina and Brazil. It occurs even in democratic countries among followers of terrorist groups that long persist in declining any offers to share power in the existing government (for example, in Northern Ireland).

In the United States, the civil-rights struggle of the 1950s and 1960s and the wave of ghetto riots in the latter period were followed by some reduction of inequality—social, political, and economic—sufficient to facilitate further change by nonviolent political processes. They especially altered social customs in race relations, conspicuously in the South. Meanwhile, however, a negative result of the riots appears to have been to intensify temporarily a subculture of criminal violence among black male delinquents within the ghettos. Although their upward trend in violence has now been reversed, descent from a high plateau may take some time and require better youth-employment opportunities. A decline requires anticipations from nonviolence and stakes in conformity that compete successfully with their expectations of eminence or loot from aggression.

These observations have stressed the effects of a specific type of news in a particular period. But what is the impact of all the other portrayals of violence in news and fiction?

5. Do Tales of Violence Create a Culture of Violence?

The preceding section answered this question positively; it inferred that vivid communication by television of the violent events of the 1960s, particularly the ghetto riots, fostered not only a contagion of rioting but also a long-lasting elevation of homicide rates among black youth, as well as political changes that ended that riot era. But what of the very old issue: *Does violence portrayed in the mass media cause crimes by some members of its audience?* This question has been raised for decades, addressed to the theater, movies, newspapers, radio, and comic books even before television existed, and is now targeted mainly on TV. If the answer is either moot or negative, as many claim, is this compatible with the thesis that media publicity on violent news events in the 1960s contributed to further violence?

As we stated in the opening paragraph of this book, tales of violent crime have permeated folklore, literature, and news messages since time immemorial. Americans may be shocked by statistics on their television's content: about eight of 10 fictional programs contain violence; they average about seven violent incidents per hour; about six of 10 of these incidents involve use of weapons; only about two of 10 major incidents of violence result in lawful punishment of the offender; violence is especially concentrated in children's cartoons, averaging 20 violent incidents per hour (National Commission on Violence, 1969: 191–93). Furthermore, motion pictures (compared with printed tales) usually greatly augment the vividness and realism—and, with home television, the accessibility—of portrayals of violence. But were Grimm's *Fairy Tales* milder? And would violence be less widespread in a society if none were depicted in any of its communication media?

Psychologists offer contradictory theories and research results. One view is that all people have a certain amount of aggressive impulse, but by avid attention to violent tales or events (such as sports) they aggress vicariously, and thus are drained of urges to engage in such conduct overtly. Exponents of this *catharsis* theory of media effects cite research in which seeing violent films changed neither the responses of college students to questionnaires on aggressive attitudes or word associations, nor the amount of aggression displayed by children in their homes (Feshbach, 1961; Feshbach & Singer, 1971). One study even claimed that violence seen in films is followed by less hostile content in dreams (Foulks, 1967).

Critics question the measurement procedures in these studies, and some have found opposite results, especially for lower-class boys (Liebert et al., 1975). The most consistent evidence indicates that if media portrayals of violence have any effect, it is that they are *modeled*, particularly by children. Modeling is most likely, research suggests, if the aggressor in the film procures attractive things by taking them away from someone, gains power rather than punishment by using force, or seems justified in aggressing. Such theories are supported by findings of increased vehemence by children in attacking a large inflated "punching doll" after viewing violence in films. This aggression is increased when irritating experiences or provocative remarks are introduced by the experimenter, for all of these have separate but additive effects (Bandura, 1973a: Chapter 2). In other studies, college students showed more punitive attitudes in their responses to questionnaires after seeing aggressive films (especially if under aggravating conditions) (Berkowitz, 1962: Chapter 9). In a controlled experiment, inmates housed in cottages of a youth correctional institution who were shown only violent films were distinctly more aggressive than those in other cottages shown only neutral films (Leyens et al., 1975).

A variant of the modeling principle has sometimes been called the *cue* or *triggering* theory. Essentially, it holds that stimuli from media presentations of violence evoke aggressive behavior only from persons who already have inclinations to commit such acts and need only prompting. This view is supported by innumerable cases of persons who have deliberately imitated unusual crimes soon after seeing them portrayed, for few other viewers mimic the depicted lawbreaking. Prison inmates avidly study and discuss both the criminal and the police techniques shown in the media. When specific practices—such as making a zip-gun from a radio aerial broken off a car or taping a window before breaking it to make a burglary more silent—were presented on popular programs, they were widely copied by delinquents. Some television producers claim to have adopted a policy of avoiding such portrayals.

All of the foregoing refers to short-term effects on individuals rather than to long-term effects on groups, and hence does not seem so relevant to cultural change. Yet throughout their lives, many persons consume a daily diet of film violence. A psychological theory, on *desensitization* from seeing so much aggression, alleges that such experience has a long-term effect on both individuals and groups. It has been demonstrated that the galvanic skin response (GSR), indicative of physiological arousal (discussed in Chapter 7), often becomes quite elevated when people observe violent scenes on television, but that after prolonged viewing of such material, the arousal it evokes declines (Howitt & Cumberbatch, 1975: 80). It has been speculated that we become inured to violence by others and to committing it ourselves when it becomes commonplace in news or experience, and that television may be producing a culture of violence toleration.

Desensitization may explain the predominantly positive correlations between habitually viewing violent television dramas and aggressive conduct by adolescents (Comstock & Rubinstein, 1972). Unfortunately, whether they commit violence because they view it or prefer to view it because they are aggressive cannot be determined from these correlations. Controlled experiments show that after children see violence in films, they are slower to call on adults to intervene when they observe aggression by other children (Thomas & Drabman, 1975).

One comforting set of conclusions from an early British study of children's reactions to violence on television was that they are less disturbed if: (1) the violence is so stylized that it is done in a manner unfamiliar in real life, but conventional in certain types of drama (e.g., in westerns or cartoons); (2) the settings are unfamiliar, provided they are not eerie or spooky; (3) the victim is clearly a "baddie" rather than a "goodie" or, at least, is not distinctly good; (4) the events are presented as make-believe rather than real; (5) the children do not identify with or worry about the characters (Himmelweit et al., 1958). These findings imply few effects on children from cartoons and fairy tales, but they can be interpreted as suggesting that young children and adolescents too often model their behavior after:

1. crime depicted in ordinary urban settings with familiar-looking people

2. dramas in which both the "good" and "bad" are struck from behind, tortured, or brutally beaten in a manner that can be imitated by anyone who has superior strength or numbers, or merely the advantage of surprise

3. stories in which destruction, control, or robbery of others is accomplished very easily with a gun.

The $30 billion spent annually in the United States on advertising—about $5 billion of it on television—suggests that many people have faith in the impact of mass communications on conduct. Sales statistics prove this confidence warranted, and much systematic research shows how effects are achieved by marketing and election campaigns, and by efforts to get the public to adopt new agricultural or public-health practices. These diverse inquiries agree on the conclusion that a change in the beliefs and habits of many persons usually requires a two-step process. The first is becoming aware of and taking an interest in a possible mode of behavior. Mass media can produce this step. The second, however, is deliberation and decision on whether to embrace it. This second step is usually taken only after conferring with others, generally family or friends. Practices become widespread only after a few "opinion leaders" or influential members of a group or community become the vanguard (Katz, 1957, 1960; DeFleur, 1970: 124-29).

The relevance to this chapter of the two-step principle in mass communication is that media messages that stir the national audience —or an identifiable segment of it—to talk about something among themselves, and thus to be collectively aroused or more aware of its implications, can alter a culture or subculture. Apparently this is how news of the ghetto riots, so salient to the residents of other ghettos, had the effects that the preceding section indicates. Sometimes specific programs of violence appeal so strongly to particular groups of juveniles, such as members of a delinquent clique or gang, that they adopt a group name, apparel, talk, and conduct modeled on the program.

An indirect but pertinent effect of the mass media on our culture is its impact on beliefs about the prevalence of violence and the risks of being a victim. An older study, which should be widely replicated, showed little or no relationship between the amount of space devoted to crime in the newspapers and the local crime rate, and that this space varies greatly from one paper to the next (Davis, 1952). An analogous conclusion probably applies to television and radio stations, for in all media a few dramatic offenses get much more attention than the thousands of other more routine ones; yet station policy dictates the extent and nature of crime reports.

If a prominent person is a victim or perpetrator of serious law-breaking, if a crime is shocking or daring, and especially if an assaulter or killer is a stranger to the victim, the offense will usually be much more newsworthy than the typical homicides and assaults that metropolises expereince every day. As a result, one notorious killer or a group, such as the Manson "family" or the "Boston Strangler," can create a contagion of fear that causes millions to live in continual anxiety. The public is not comforted by the fact that these few offenders have only a negligible effect on the statistical crime rate.

To a large extent the newspaper space and television time devoted to crime depend upon what else is newsworthy at the moment. When there are no international wars, major calamities, or elections in progress, many offenses gain a prominence that they promptly lose when other events have primary attention.

Polls show that most of the public not only objects to the amount of violence on television, but also will usually exclude from its "Top Ten" of most-viewed programs those that portray violence (Gallup Poll reported in *Los Angeles Times,* February 17, 1977; compilation of Top Ten from *Weekly Variety,* 1955–1975, prepared for me by Ferriss Kaplan, May 1977). Our media, with few exceptions, are operated for profit and, therefore, prefer to present whatever commands the biggest audience (Brown, 1971); this suggests that violent shows will be reduced if they are more completely boycotted. However, broadcasters allegedly exert pressure against federal sponsorship of rigorous research on the impact of television violence, and for suppression of reports on research already undertaken (Cater & Strickland, 1975). Perhaps they fear that the research results would foster boycotts.

A large number of studies have compared the reading and viewing habits of offenders and nonoffenders. Attendance at movies and reading comic books are associated with delinquency, though not consistently and markedly, while time spent watching television is not (Howitt & Cumberbatch, 1975: Chapter 5). Such findings, however, may reflect the social settings and functions of these activities and of those with which they compete. Thus movie theaters and drive-ins provide adolescents with a rendezvous away from home and school, as well as a dark place for sexual explorations; and comic books are a diversion when school is boring. Contrastingly, television often can be watched only at home, with other members of the family; so it competes with peer activities away from home and sometimes even adds to

Memorial Day parade.

the familiarity of adolescents with legitimate modes of speech, conduct, and work for which they are poorly prepared in their homes.

These media functions make it very difficult to assess their net effect on violence and to recommend policies that would reduce crime. The research cited indicates that television would be less conducive to assaultive conduct if it diminished its violence-triggering content and still kept its young audience. Such editing, if imaginative, need not make it so bland as to repel juvenile viewers and send them into the streets. On the other hand, excess staring at the tube can impede a child's schoolwork, thus perhaps indirectly fostering delinquency. One can infer that a policy of optimum media fare for juveniles would prescribe programs that are both attractive and educational, yet have no realistic depictions of assaultive conduct. But if this were the basis for editorial or censorship policy, there would still be many disagreements over the types of programs that are appropriate.

The risks, for a free society, of endangering freedom of the media certainly offset prospects of reducing violent crime by imposing censorship. Yet some government control is unavoidable, since broadcasting channels are limited in number and television or radio stations must be licensed to ensure that there is only one per channel in each broadcasting region. Thus far, educational television programs abjuring violence have generally not had access to the prime channels, and government regulations of commercial broadcasters have not greatly affected their shows of violence.

When mass boycotts of objectionable programs are advocated to protect children, opponents argued that scientific knowledge of media effects is still too inconclusive to warrant such measures. An assertion in rebuttal is that the best judgment now possible is preferable to the risks of inaction on such a serious problem. At present, the only influential public impact on programming comes not from organized boycotts but from the decisions of millions of parents to discourage certain types of viewing or listening, to encourage others, and to support public television when they find it fills a need.

When Sweden's leading national newspaper adopted a policy in 1970 of markedly reducing the reporting of violence, there followed in 1971 the first drop in that country's violent crimes since 1962, and a decline in all of its large cities except Malmo, which had a major local newspaper notorious for its emphasis on crime (Lenke, 1974: 96). If there were more such inadvertent experiments through policy changes by various media, followup research on subsequent violence rates might yield more certain knowledge than we can procure from either laboratory and questionnaire research or the many correlational studies that compare reading or viewing habits of offenders and nonoffenders.

The research on explaining violence that we have discussed thus far in this chapter has been primarily on collective rates of violence; yet most assaultive crimes are individual acts. This suggests they are a problem for students of psychology rather than of cultures and subcultures. Nonetheless, our focus on the group led to analysis of such individual phenomena as catharsis and modeling, while the study of alleged individual psychopathology may bring new perspectives on groups and subcultures.

PSYCHOLOGICAL ASPECTS OF VIOLENCE

Inherited biological characteristics allegedly fostering crime were explored in Chapter 7, which indicated that aggressive conduct is more probable with any conditions that increase irritability, including some brain ailments and endocrine imbalances. The correlations are imperfect because humans can learn to be nonviolent despite irritation. A few writers, notably the biologist Konrad Lorenz and the playwright Robert Ardrey, popularized the ascription of human violence to aggressive instincts derived from lower animal ancestry, but these authors have been quite conclusively shown to be in error (Montagu, 1973; Skinner, 1974: Chapter 3). The distinctive feature of human conduct is the small extent to which it is specifically determined by heredity; except for simple reflexes, we have no behavior that is not learned— this is why our conduct is so much more diverse than that of any other species. Also, no other animal accumulates learning from one generation to the next, over scores of centuries as a culture, for no other animal has a language nearly as adequate as those of humans for storage and transfer of learning.

A historically very influential explanation for violence is the frustration–aggression theory. It posits drives in all of us that, when blocked, are pent up and build a pressure that, if not released gradually by more passive acts, ultimately erupts as aggressive conduct. According to this theory, all aggression comes from frustration and all frustration causes aggression. The implication that each person has a certain amount of drive that must come out in one way or another is analogous to the law of the conservation of energy in classical physics, or of pressure in fluids and gases. It is sometimes called a "hydraulic" conception of emotion and conduct. Research suggests that this early formulation is too simple, but psychologists vary in the thoroughness with which they replace it (Megargee, 1972; Bandura, 1973a: Chapter 1).

All of us at times have a surge of anger at frustration. Any unexpected sudden blockage of conduct creates an activation syndrome of increased alertness, muscle tone, and available energy. As Chapter 7 indicated, these reactions are due largely to epinephrine released reflexively from the adrenal glands, an inherited pattern in animals that helps them flee or fight in emergencies. What we call our physiological arousal in such situations and how we interpret it, Schachter (1971) shows, is largely a result of verbal communication and learning. Indeed, whether, when frustrated, the resulting activation is expressed by panic, striking someone, breaking something, joking, resuming the blocked activity, or doing something else, is mainly a consequence of learning experience in such circumstances, most of which is acquired socially.

The catharsis principle (discussed in the preceding section) and the "ventilative therapies" imply that each person has a certain amount of aggression energy that must be "let out." The fact that the initiation of assault increases if it is rewarded, however, suggests that people need not be frustrated to be aggressive. It has also been demonstrated that nonviolent ways of coping with frustration are learned when they are positively reinforced and will effectively reduce aggressive conduct (Bandura, 1973a; 1973b; Patterson et al., 1974), while ventilative therapies of encouraging displays of hostility by violence increase subsequent use of force (Straus, 1974). Of course, if violence facilitates disclosure of a previously hidden hostility, and this revelation produces more open and fair discussion and resolution of disagreements, the initial violence may lead to conflict reduction (Bach & Wyden, 1968).

Behavior is learned most readily when it reduces unrest and anxiety, for "drive reduction" (as some psychologists label this experience) seems to be the most influential reinforcement shaping our conduct. Therefore, any activity by a person who is physiologically aroused following frustration will probably become habitual in such circumstances if it reduces unrest. Aggression, of course, provides immediate activity, but it may start circular interaction in conflict with others that creates more arousal. Alternative behavior when frustrated can use energy more constructively and not create subsequent unrest.

Often cited as proof of the validity of frustration–aggression theory is the fact that people frequently experience an urge to strike someone who impedes their doing what they wish, and at times need a conscious effort to control such urges. Also common in everyday life is *displacement,* a person's tendency when frustrated to aggress against anything that is easily accessible (for example, banging on a piece of furniture) or "taking it out on" someone if fear or inability prevents aggression against the source of frustration (for example, being churlish to subordinates, spouse, or children after being "chewed out" by the boss). Again, however, the reinforcements received in prior social learning, from early childhood on, shape both displacement and inhibition of the urge to be active when aroused. To repeat, any kind of behavior that reduces the activation syndrome aroused by frustration will probably follow again in similar circumstances (Bandura, 1973a: 34–36).

A distinction between "undercontrolled" and "overcontrolled" personality types was made by Megargee (1966) to account for some striking contrasts in persons convicted of criminal violence. His main focus is on the overcontrolled, whom personality tests show to be stable, calm, submissive, conscientious, responsible, adaptable, conforming, considerate, and naive (White et al., 1971). Some persons convicted of extremely violent crimes have no prior criminal record and are highly controlled by all evidence except their one major offense. They were model citizens before their only serious deviation, and model prisoners and parolees afterward. The usual theoretical interpretation of their violence is based on the hydraulic metaphor of frustration–aggression: they repress their hostility so much that it is released only as an explosive outburst. An equally plausible explanation would point out that most people who are highly controlled never commit violence, but that the few murderers among them may never have learned any moderate ways of coping with people or situations that persistently "bug" them. Such ignorance might exist if, beginning at an early age, their annoyances were diminished when they reacted unaggressively, but were ill-received when they were mildly or moderately aggressive. Some of these offenders seem to be so timid and inept with people they perceive as persistently blocking them, that they react only when so frustrated as to be indifferent to the personal consequences of their aggression. Thus they are often quite deliberately suicidal in their homicides, in some cases shooting others and then themselves, or killing others when they obviously will be killed too. Murder followed by suicide is a common pattern, and comprises a much higher percentage of suicides in countries with a low homicide rate, such as Britain. It may be the most characteristic crime of the "overcontrolled" aggressive.

Some have suggested that the prevalence of overcontrolled aggressors is exaggerated, because closer investigation often reveals that their prior aggression simply was not known to those who considered them overcontrolled (Bandura, 1973: 179–81). More typical in violent offenders, at any rate, is the undercontrolled pattern, the person who readily "flies off the handle." Toch (1969) found that both prisoners with records of much fighting and police officers more frequently in fights than their fellow officers had fairly standard patterns of using violence to promote or defend their self-image. These "undercontrolled," bullying, exploitative, or emotionally explosive men seemed to seek out or manufacture situations to assault others physically. Each of them had a characteristic way of manipulating his victim into making remarks or gestures that could be interpreted as a threat, then used this mild act to justify a response by extreme force. Their flimsy rationalizations resembled those of more notorious offenders considered dangerously insane.

PARANOID VIOLENCE BY INDIVIDUALS AND GROUPS

A few ostensibly overcontrolled persons commit seemingly senseless aggressions against persons who have not annoyed them and from whom they want nothing. Usually, if questioned, the assaulters have some rationalization; they say that they were threatened or persecuted by their victims, that their victims represent an evil type, that their crimes were to help others, perhaps the entire nation. When psychologists or psychiatrists classify such excuses as delusions, the defendants are called paranoid and their sanity is questioned (see Chapter 3).

Sometimes the so-called delusions are shared by several persons instead of being purely private. This is illustrated by the Manson "family," charged with several murders, conspiracies, and an attempted assassination of an American president—all of which they ascribed to their interest in correcting social or governmental faults. Paranoid traits are extremely diverse, ranging from clearly psychotic delusions to the normal inclinations to exaggerate one's own virtues and blame others for one's difficulties. These traits may express the personality defense mechanism that Freud called *projection*—seeing one's faults in others—or they may be based upon realistic perceptions of others, without great exaggeration. Their intense forms develop gradually and their manifestation usually varies with the situation.

Because of the ubiquity and diversity of paranoid symptoms, their association with a variety of other traits, and their subtle graduation from ordinary to exceptional intensity, pyschiatrists decades ago ceased to regard paranoia as a separate mental ailment. Instead they use *paranoid* as an adjective to describe conditions in which symptoms of paranoia are present (e.g., paranoid schizophrenia). It is a term descriptive of a variety of behavior in both criminal-justice and mental-health clientele, and of behavior by persons not likely to be formally designated criminal or mentally ill.

A readily evident feature of paranoid complaints about others is that they enhance one's view of oneself. A second important feature is that, like other beliefs, an individual's commitment to them is strengthened by group support. People who share an ideology that exaggerates their own virtues and nurtures delusions about the faults of others can be called, collectively, a paranoid group.

Psychiatrists have frequently observed complete illusions or hallucinations in bizarre forms shared among small or even large groups of schizophrenic patients; this pattern acquired the French designation *folie a deux, folie a trois,* and so on. It appears to be a consequence of mutual suggestion in circular reactions among them. Paranoid delusions in less extreme forms, often appropriately called myths, have since earliest known times been developed by innumerable groups to rationalize their failures or frustrations. Examples include the defeated and bankrupt Germans in the 1920s and 1930s, who cultivated Nazi myths of Aryan superiority and of victimization by Jews to justify their genocidal policies and efforts at world conquest. Many other nationalistic groups cultivate hateful stereotypes of the people of another country that once conquered them. Quite similar at times, with as much paranoia, a fighting youth gang claims superiority to and mistreatment by a rival gang. The isolation of these groups, often self-induced because of their "state of war" and their consequent suspicion of disloyalty or betrayal whenever their members communicate with outsiders, intensifies their delusions. Thus, myths of group superiority or persecution are widespread; they are buttressed by self-serving rationalizations and distorted accounts that reinforce the paranoid ideologies that motivate violence.

At times it was no delusion that persons in some American prisons were incarcerated mainly for civil-rights activity or opposition to the Vietnam War, and thus confined mainly for their political beliefs rather than for their alleged crimes of obstructing the police, inciting to riot, or other charges. During the same period, and since then, more typical convicts, sentenced for predations, have also adopted the label "political prisoner"; but they have used somewhat delusionary justifications for doing so, rather than admit that it is certainly less stigmatizing than the labels they usually receive for their crimes, such as "murderer" or "crook." By thus redefining themselves as "victims of the system," they justify predations that are self-aggrandizing and not compatible with any political or social ideal.

Perhaps because of the attractiveness of the "political prisoner" label as a badge of honor rather than of disgrace, many persons convicted of clearly criminal predations cultivate an identification with political movements, both those that advocate violence and others. In this way these convicts regard themselves as imprisoned on political rather than traditionally criminal grounds and gain friendships in some outside organizations that welcome them. Some also ascribe their confinement to their membership in an ethnic minority, conveniently forgetting that they pleaded guilty to thefts and assaults against people of their own group. More sophisticated offenders attribute their crimes to "institutionalized racism," the economic and political deprivations of their entire ethnic group.

Both in correctional institutions and in the outside community, predatory offenders often rationalize their victimizing acts by political slogans and ideologies. The offenders thus attract both real and imagined support for their predations, and some develop collective paranoid patterns that make them among the most difficult groups for the criminal-justice system. During the 1970s these groups ranged from the highly personalized Manson "family" to the apparently more for-malized Symbionese Liberation Army. More identified with ethnic movements in correctional institutions, especially in California, are the Mexican Mafia and the Aryan Brotherhood, in which some inmates are organized for predations, for mutual-aid and for propagation of ethnic ideologies. These prison groups have ideologies that mix themes from the criminal world with such values as personal auton-omy and manliness from subcultures of violence—all rationalized with moralistic social-reform arguments. Street gangs also often make polit-ical assertions, Miller (1976) notes, claiming to work for some public benefit and, hence, to merit public support. An assaultive group's sub-culture of violence includes not only norms supporting assaults but also a credo to rationalize the choice of target or method of attack. But it is appropriately called paranoid only if its beliefs are at least partly based on delusions. Furthermore, as Lemert (1967: Chapter 15) bril-liantly shows, these delusions often result from the exclusion of the paranoids by other groups.

It is usually fruitless to argue about the veracity of ideological assertions when dealing with core members or leaders of a well-estab-lished paranoid group. Although fringe members or sympathizers can sometimes be persuaded to shift their support on the basis of evidence or logic, the dedicated group members derive conceptions of their moral worth from tenets that they mouth glibly, or shout in bombastic rhetoric. They have a personal stake in resisting change, and see those who challenge their views as threats. Therefore, they resort to arguing ad hominem, to ignoring evidence or logic that they cannot discredit, or to using other questionable debating devices. Even when their ide-ology contains some sound or at least not readily disproven allegations, these are mixed with delusions or distortions. Members harp on the themes that are not readily discredited, ignoring their errors in other assertions.

Public officials who deal with such a group collectively, segre-gating its members and labeling them all with the same terms, tend to unify them further. Making the leaders feel important by dealing with them as spokespersons intensifies their solidarity with their group. The alternative approach is to recognize the aptitudes of these leaders as individuals, and to attract them into legitimate pursuits that reward these talents and align them with nonoffenders. Persons with a sound idealism are sometimes attracted to groups with a paranoid ideology, but will find even more attractive any organization that more clearly has a constructive impact in the world, if they are welcomed by the membership. These include a large variety of political, religious, so-cial-reform, mutual-aid, and educational efforts that have already re-cruited potential delinquents, prisoners, and former offenders. Many other constructive groups also could appeal to such individuals, and thus give them more stake in conformity.

Quite in contrast to these paranoid offenders, however, are violent people who shock the public by being heartless in their choice of victim.

CHILD BATTERERS

Most of the men studied by Toch (1969) who seemed undercontrolled in their violence did, in fact, exert some control, for their blows were mainly against people who would not or could not effectively strike back. The safest target for an adult attacker is a child, and it is safest when the child's parent or guardian does the attacking (especially if no other parental figure is present), for no one else is likely to intervene in the youngster's behalf. Criminal assault against children, therefore, is mainly by their parents, although parental concern for the comfort and nurture of offspring is a strongly espoused value in our culture—and, with situational exceptions, in all others.

Infanticide was formerly a culturally approved practice in certain circumstances among many societies; but killing a child intentionally or by negligence is clearly murder or manslaughter in our criminal statutes and those of most other governments today. The law has been hazier, however, regarding serious though nonlethal assault against one's own children, for corporal punishment of offspring has long been deemed a parental prerogative. Beginning in the nineteenth century but much more frequently in recent years, *excessively severe* violence toward children by parents or anyone else has been adjudged criminal; but this is a very difficult legal principle to enforce if the accused has good defense counsel (Raffali, 1970). The number of complaints of such behavior brought to the courts has surged in the last few decades, observers agree, but statistics are blurred by the variety of charges under which it may be prosecuted and by the court's willingness to dismiss the case if the accusations are strongly contested and the child's care is improved.

A national survey estimated the annual rate of serious physical abuse of children under 18 as 9.3 per 100,000 (Gil, 1970), which would make it comparable to the homicide rate. This estimate has been criticized as quite crude by Light (1973), who, in recommending much more precise research methods, quotes the following American Medical Association opinion:

> It is likely that the battered-child syndrome will be found to be a more frequent cause of death than such . . . diseases as leukemia, cystic fibrosis, and muscular dystrophy, and . . . rank with automobile accidents and the . . . encephalides as causes of acquired disturbances of the central nervous system.

A New York City followup of 302 battered children reported by a group of hospitals in one year found that 35 had died and 55 had suffered permanent brain damage from their injuries (Raffali, 1970). California reports 55,000 cases of child maltreatment annually, including both assault and neglect (Younger, 1976).

The social movement responsible for the criminal law's increasing attention to violence toward children is worldwide and has many sources, but in the United States it is often traced to one dramatic event in 1866. Residents of a New York tenement told a public-health nurse that a child in one of the apartments was being maltreated. The nurse found this child, Mary Ellen, chained to a bed, severely bruised from beatings and malnourished from a diet of bread and water. The parents insisted that the law gave them the right to treat Mary Ellen as they chose, and the police confirmed this view. Thus, complainants seeking the child's removal had to arrange that this be done by the Society for Prevention of Cruelty to Animals, on grounds that she was a member of the animal kingdom, which the SPCA was authorized to protect. This case led to founding in 1871 of the Society for Prevention of Cruelty to Children, which—until its termination in 1940 and replacement by other organizations—spearheaded a struggle to extend humane-treatment laws from beasts to humans. The effort, however, did not make rapid progress until the 1960s, when its new leaders were pediatric radiologists. Being in hospital roles, they are less constrained than family physicians to protect abusive parents and therefore publicized their evidence of bone fractures caused by parental battering (Pfohl, 1977).

Although criminal courts could punish child batterers under the laws against assault, mayhem (physical injury), and homicide that are used when adults are victims of violent crimes, it is the juvenile or family courts that deal with parents or guardians who injure their children. This is done under statutes penalizing "willful cruelty toward child: endangering life, limb or health" or "infliction of traumatic injury on child"—parts of legislation on "Abandonment and Neglect of Children" (cited from the California Penal Code). Although such laws authorize imprisonment of the offenders, these courts are less concerned with imposing penalties than with assuring appropriate care for the young victims.

Typically it is a parent or stepparent who is charged. If the court finds the home unfit, it has legal grounds for placing the children elsewhere. But no other home may be available that has the positive concerns for the children that even periodically abusive parents usually have. A court's reluctance to punish parents may stem from viewing them as more ill or inept than evil, and from the fact that jailing them probably reduces the prospect of improving the child's care. When judges decide, after investigation by social workers, that the most feasible arrangement is release of the child to the home, they often place the parents on probation with requirements that they be visited by court staff and participate in a training or therapy program. Frequently these probationary conditions are informally initiated while the children are temporarily removed from the home during inquiry and hearings on the case, for the parents are instructed that compliance with suggestions made at their hearings is necessary to impress the judge that their home will be acceptable.

Paulsen (1968: 176) observes:

> Criminal sanctions are a poor means of preventing child abuse. Day-to-day family life, charged with the most intimate emotions, is not likely to be . . . easily ruled by the threat of fines or imprisonment. . . . The criminal law can destroy a child's family relationship; it cannot preserve or rebuild it.

But Raffali (1970) cautions:

> Warnings by police, judges, probation personnel, etc., have proven inadequate to prevent repetition of child battery. Therefore, the child must be considered to be in grave danger unless it can be proven otherwise.

The DeCourcys (1973) and others argue, therefore, that legal counsel should be appointed for the abused child, independent of the prosecutor and of the parents' attorney. Helfer and Kempe (1968:200) insist, however:

> In our experience more satisfactory dispositions are made when attorneys, parents, welfare personnel, and physicians meet together in the judge's chambers and, using proper legal formality, discuss all aspects of the case in question. The judge is then in a much better position to make an intelligent decision resulting in a more satisfactory disposition for all concerned.

The major problem in administering these laws is in detecting physical abuse of children. Parents or guardians usually inflict it in private, and other adults who suspect that harsh treatment occurs still regard this as a right of the parent. If the abusers are asked to explain their child's injuries, they blame them on accidents and either force the child not to contradict this story or discredit the child as lying. Nevertheless, physicians and nurses are increasingly alerted to look for evidence of physical abuse of children, and all 50 states have laws requiring that they report abuse to the police or other government agencies. One estimate is that between 30,000 and 37,500 children are "badly hurt" each year, and perhaps a quarter-million are seriously abused (Zalba, 1971). About half the victims are under seven; boys are injured more frequently until about age 12, and girls more frequently in the teenage years (Gil, 1971).

The symptoms of child abuse, which the medical literature calls the "battered child syndrome," include, particularly in infants, subdural hematoma (swellings, with blood, next to the skull or bones) and fractured limbs revealed by x-rays, usually with several injuries in different stages of healing, indicating that the battering has been going on for some time. Human bite marks are frequent, as well as extensive bruises and abrasions both recent and permanent, not readily accounted for by the explanations that the parent or guardian offers (Fontana, 1973: 25–29).

In the cases typically reported, the parents are provoked by fairly common types of aggravation from children: failure to use the toilet, persistent crying, aggression toward siblings, breaking something, or any type of disobedience—even refusal to eat. They simply do not comprehend the child's limitations, or how their anger upsets the youngster. With teenagers, parents object more to unauthorized absence from home, choice of peers, and, with girls, to alleged promiscuity. Instead of merely reprimanding or at most slapping, these parents strike in anger with full force—sometimes with any convenient hard object—or they shove the child about, so that injuries occur from bumping into furniture, door corners, or plumbing fixtures. Furthermore, ". . . they feel righteous about the punishments they have inflicted. . . . They avoid facing the degree of injury they have caused, but they justify their behavior because they feel their children have been 'bad'" (Goode, 1971: 633).

A theme pervading studies of such child batterers is that they themselves were treated in this fashion; they grew up in violent households with parents who readily used force to control them (Bakan, 1971: Chapter 5). Children may even accept derogation by the parents as proper, and thus have a poor self-image that they later project to their own progeny. As one of my students (Jacqui Hood) observes, "Hurt people hurt people." This perpetuation of childrearing patterns is explained by the "linkage" theory of socialization: children are brought up in a manner that creates a personality compatible with their family setting. Thus if people come from homes that emphasize obedience, they never develop much ability to reach consensus by discussion; and as parents they do not need such skill, for they demand strict compliance from their offspring (Straus, 1971). But such stress on discipline may mold them and their children primarily for either subordinate or rigidly authoritative occupations, since they are not used to innovating or negotiating. The permissive home, on the other hand, may produce more venturesome offspring with greater creativity, possibly in deviant as well as approved conduct.

One study found that parents who batter their children change residence more frequently than other families of similar status and background, which suggests that they probably have few close ties with others in the community (Lauer et al., 1974). Conflict between spouses is common. Frequently one is a stepparent to the child, and in about half the cases the child was conceived before marriage (Zalba, 1971). Often the child is resented as unwanted or, in any case, is in the way of other current interests.

Although surveys find these children disproportionately within poor families, this may be in whole or in part a consequence of their being identified mainly in the emergency rooms of public hospitals, where staff are trained to detect signs of battering. More affluent families have private physicians who not only are less alert to these symptoms but also are reluctant to obey the legal requirement that they report such cases, for they wish neither to alienate their clients nor to have to spend time testifying against them in court (Raffali, 1970; Zalba, 1971).

Studies of social-class differences in the use of corporal punishment quite consistently indicate that it is most common among the poor, although recent surveys find it almost as frequently in the middle class (Erlanger, 1974b). The figures are based either on parents describing their practices or on adults indicating how much they were spanked as children, rather than on more objective observations. One may speculate that the middle classes stress conformity so much that they first physically punish their children to get them to achieve, then lie about it to deny the nonconformity of such punishment! Steinmetz (1974) presents evidence that corporal punishment is linked not so much to whether a parent does manual work as to the following classification of jobs. The "persuasive" (executives, salesmen), who try to dominate others and the "motoric" (dentists, truck drivers), who control machines were, in this order, more physically punishing with their children than the "supportive" (teachers, social workers) or "conforming" (clerks, accountants). This is an unusual classification of occupations, but it appears to be correlated to behavior patterns beyond the job situation.

Once child abuse is reported, investigations usually begin immediately. These may involve a social worker, police juvenile officer, and court probation office, or only one or two of these. Before the child leaves the hospital, or within a few hours if hospitalization is not required, they usually make an initial decision, after consulting with physicians and perhaps the parents, about whether the case should be referred to court and, if referred, about whether the youngster should be given temporary shelter away from home. The decision to remove the child requires approval by a judge as soon as possible. Investigations may then take weeks or months, with tentative arrangements repeatedly made and reviewed at court hearings. Usually the child is sooner or later returned to the home, and the parents placed under probationary supervision. There are innumerable cases in which treatment and supervision of parents has been negligible and return of the child unwarranted, for battering continues, with serious—even fatal— consequences.

Psychiatric approaches to treatment of physically abusive parents address all aspects of their lives, especially the marital situation. Frequently the initial problem is that the parents regard battering the child as justified, court interference as unwarranted, and mandatory therapy as an imposition. Yet Steele and Pollock (1968: 139) report their experiences in treating such parents psychiatrically:

> We learn not to be dismayed by a patient's first negative, rejecting attitudes, particularly if he or she has been heckled and threatened by others. It is easy to say to the patient, "It sounds as if you have been having a perfectly dreadful time. Let's see what we can do about it." Such simple statements of sympathy give the patient at least a faint idea he has been listened to without being criticized. The therapist is then to some extent "on the side of the angels," offering asylum and protection from the threatening world.

A major objective of treatment is to reduce the parents' isolation by improving their relationships with others who can help them— not only with the therapists, but also with any friends, neighbors, and relatives, including their own parents, who may be available as a potential source of comfort and assistance. With most of these clients, this is extremely difficult to accomplish. Parents Anonymous is an organization, modeled partly on Alcoholics Anonymous (described in Chapter 10), for people with problems in childrearing. Attendance usually begins only because the court orders it; nevertheless, participation often continues partly because it reduces the stigma of having been haled into court for child abuse, since all members share this experience. New entrants meet people "in the same boat," who show that the burden is bearable and who perhaps have learned to be less violent with their children. The members do not give their last names and require that discussions be kept confidential, but friendships often develop among members outside the organization.

As might be expected, Parents Anonymous members also support each other in rationalizations for their offenses. Thus Conrad Nordquist (1973), a graduate student who gained admission as an observer for five months at an all-female group in Los Angeles, describes how a member complained that she left her children at home for about an hour while she went for a drink. When she returned, the apartment had been broken into by the police and the children removed from her custody for three months. Everyone at the meeting expressed sympathy, none questioning her story. But the official report was that neighbors complained that the children had been crying for hours, and that the police had found the children tied to their beds. Others similarly blamed unfair police or courts, or lying neighbors or babysitters, though also describing severe physical measures that they used on their children. There was a tendency to describe only success in getting the child to obey by these methods, and no one at the meetings criticized the narrators. One new arrival said that she came to the organization because she wanted to learn about being a better mother, but neglected to mention that the court had advised she enter it to regain custody of her children. It is possible, of course, that members might be alienated if they were immediately and harshly challenged on these tales of the past; yet as they gained rapport, they sometimes expressed relevant concerns, including fear of killing their children in their anger, but this was atypical. Contrastingly, in the generally more voluntary Alcoholics Anonymous meetings, emphasis is placed on admitting past wrongs, and members debunk each other's rationalizations.

Because of the parents' emotional stress in confronting their serious problems, Nordquist estimated that at least four-fifths of Parents Anonymous meeting time was spent in discussions completely unrelated to the presumed common interest of childrearing. Indeed, their favorite topic seemed to be means of "getting out" socially, for these are largely isolated and stigmatized women, predominantly living without men or with men not the fathers of their children. Hence, they frequently find their offspring "in the way" of the romance and partying they wish to pursue; when they feel thus trapped, this group may alleviate both their stigma and their isolation.

Gerald R. Patterson and his associates (1974) have been perhaps the most successful and influential of many Skinnerian psychologists in training parents to change the behavior of violent children, primarily by altering the conduct of violent parents. The trainees are first dealt with in small groups, which study programmed texts on the principles of operant conditioning with children. When a parent or couple achieves a near-perfect score in these studies, their supervisor and all the family confer on applying the principles. They must identify the kinds of behavior that please each parent and develop a program of reward points that the parents agree to give the child for this conduct. These points are redeemable in tangible items, such as extra desserts, money, a fishing trip, or deciding where the family will go on an evening or weekend. All family participants sign a contract specifying this agreement at the bottom of a form for recording occurrence of the desired behavior.

Also identified in Patterson's parental training are the sequences of offensive conduct by the child from which anger and violence most often escalate in a particular family. For the most provocative of these—from which a child-beating seems most predictable and unavoidable—it is stipulated that *each time* these acts occur, the parent will simply direct the child to take "time-out," for a specified number of minutes. This means nonviolent departure to the emptiest room available. No debating the action before or after is permitted, to avoid verbal provocations in which each has previously indulged. It is agreed in advance that if the child objects verbally or physically to the time-out, each act of resistance means an additional few minutes there. If the child dirties or disarrays the time-out room, departure from it is not permitted until the room is restored to order. The case supervisor is in daily contact with the family, at least by telephone, to see how the arrangements are followed. The most common problem is that parents forget to deliver the rewards for good behavior, which are to be granted independently of time-outs. Also, many still debate and escalate to physical punishment instead of dispassionately imposing the time-out. Compliance with the agreements, however, usually produces an increase in mutually desired behavior by all family members and a sharp reduction of violence (see also Kozloff, 1976).

Homicide and the battered-child syndrome may seem to be contrasts in criminal violence, but they converge too often, when battering proves fatal. These crimes frequently have in common an escalation of anger by circular reaction, culminating in a physical attack on the victim rather than nonviolent communication. More clearly contrasting, therefore, is the next concern of this chapter—force or threat of force, usually deliberate, to coerce transfer of property from victims to criminals.

ROBBERY

In ordinary speech people say they were "robbed" when they suffered any kind of actual or alleged property crime, from a burglary to a purchase that was not as good as the salesman led them to expect (or even when their team lost because of an umpire's controversial decision). In the criminal law, however, "to rob" is to take something by force or threat of force against a person. Robberies are predations against both persons and property, and are distinguished as "armed" or "unarmed" according to whether a weapon is displayed.

Paralleling the surge between 1965 and 1970 in homicide and guns already discussed, reported robberies soared from 72 per 100,000 people in 1965 to 172 in 1970. The rate was 60 in 1960, but reached 218

A holdup: Crime against persons or against property?

by 1975 (FBI, 1976: 49). Yet it is estimated from victim-survey data (discussed in Chapter 4) that these statistics include only about half the robberies committed (LEAA *Newsletter,* March 1974).

The police classified 65 percent of the robberies in 1975 as armed: 45 percent with firearms, 12 percent with knives or cutting instruments, and eight percent with other weapons. The remaining 35 percent, without weapons, are called "strongarmed" (FBI, 1976: 26) or "mugging." In one out of six robberies with firearms, force is used, but the victim is more often struck than shot with the weapon. Indeed, holdup men or women often carry unloaded guns, and many use toy guns or merely pretend to have a gun in a pocket or purse. Their main objective is usually to get money by intimidation. Contrastingly, in about three-eighths of robberies with knives and in more than three-fourths of unarmed robberies, the victim is physically attacked rather than merely threatened (Conklin, 1972: 112–16).

Attacks by muggers appear to have been the main source of the public's growing fear of crime during the 1960s and 1970s. More and more city people were afraid to go out at night, afraid to ride in their apartment-house elevators or use its basement laundry facilities alone, and afraid even to enter some neighborhoods at any time. These crimes fostered a wave of self-defense efforts: people increasingly began studying karate and other Oriental martial arts (which muggers also learned, of course), carrying whistles, and arming with mace, knives, and guns, whether legally or illegally (LeJeune & Alex, 1973).

The probability of force being used in an *armed* robbery triples if the victim resists, but violence is used in over 70 percent of unresisted muggings and in over 90 percent where opposition occurs. Surprise is the key weapon in unarmed robbery, and the victim is usually so quickly overwhelmed by the attack that resistance is negligible (Conklin, 1972). Resisting robbery increases the risk of being injured, but yelling and screaming does not, and it sometimes makes the robber flee without loot (Feeney & Weir, 1975). Physical injuries—sometimes permanently crippling or even fatal—are inflicted in about a third of personal robberies. Well over 90 percent of robberies reported to the police and six out of seven mentioned to household pollers by persons age 12 or older are committed by strangers (LEAA, 1976b). About half occur on the street (FBI, 1976: 26).

Between 1960 and 1975, arrests for robbery more than tripled for males. But they more than quadrupled for males under 18 and multiplied seven-and-a-half times for females under 18 (FBI, 1976: 183). Males were *victims* two-and-a-half times as often as females, and the victim rate for blacks was about two-and-a-half times that for whites (LEAA, 1976b). There are still seven boys to one girl arrested for robbery, mainly for robbing adults; but even more extensive is their predation on other children. Crimes among juveniles are least often reported to the police, least often recorded when reported, and least often result in arrests; so they are largely omitted in FBI statistics. The National Crime Panel's 1974 survey found recent robbery victims at twice as high a rate among 12-to-24-year-olds as among older people, with 12-to-15-year-olds the most preyed upon (LEAA, 1976b: 16). A Chicago study found robbery of newsboys by youth gangs a serious problem (Sagalyn, 1971: 12). In many areas it is risky to send children on errands to make purchases or even to give them lunch money and allowances.

Robberies by juveniles are predominantly unarmed, while older offenders more often use weapons. It is apparently because juveniles were the major source of the robbery increase between 1960 and 1970 that there was only a small rise in the percentage that was armed. Over half the juvenile robbery arrests are for purse snatching, especially from aged victims. Most of the remaining unarmed robberies are muggings, generally committed by two or more accomplices, while lone offenders are more common in purse snatchings (Conklin, 1972: Chapter 5).

The especially great surge between 1965 and 1970 in reported robbery rates appears to have been concentrated in the same groups for which a sharp rise in homicides in this period has been indicated; and it appears to have had the same causes. Both the robbers and the robbed were disproportionately young black males, according to FBI and NCP data. An Oakland, California, study of police cases probably omits most robberies with juvenile victims when it concludes that robberies, unlike homicides, were mainly interracial, with blacks snatching purses from whites around shopping areas by day and robbing tavern and nightclub patrons at late hours (Feeney & Weir, 1975).

Most robberies were discussed in Chapter 8, for they are part of the diversified delinquency and crime repertoires of sociological adolescents, regardless of age; the younger ones are maladjusted in school, and the older ones typically are unable to get or to hold jobs and thus learn legitimate adult roles. By the time they become adult robbery arrestees, they usually have a record of violent offenses, more often for assault than robbery; but if arrested for robbery while still juveniles, they are more likely to have a record of theft (Conklin, 1972: 102–4). This is consistent with the nonspecialization of juveniles in particular types of offense, indicated in Chapter 8. Normandeau (1968) concluded that most Philadelphia robbers come from a subculture of theft rather than violence, although he found some persons who were highly sadistic and seemed to be pursuing violence as a goal separate from desire for money.

Interviews with the Oakland robbers indicated that over half the adults did not plan their offenses at all, and many had not started out to commit robbery, but did so impulsively when they saw what appeared to be a good opportunity for success. Three-fourths of them were unemployed, and almost a fourth of these were drug addicts (Feeney & Weir, 1975). Adult strongarm robbers in Boston also include a high proportion of alcoholics in a subculture of violence who decide to rob their victims only after beating them in fights (Conklin, 1975: Chapter 4). Less numerous but more attention-getting are armed robbers of places where thousands of dollars in cash are kept, such as banks and savings-and-loan establishments. These offenders include both avocational criminals, discussed in Chapter 12, and especially the professional criminals dealt with in Chapter 13, who also rob jewelers, armored cars, and other highly lucrative but heavily guarded targets.

A separate NCP survey inquires about commercial robberies. For 1974 it estimated 39 robberies per 1,000 businesses, led by retail food stores with 132 per 1,000, followed by eating and drinking places with 94. All other types of business distinguished by NCP were much less frequently victimized, including under five per 1,000 in manufacturing. The rate of robbery was highest in firms with $50,000 or more in gross receipts, and was only about half as high in owner-operated firms with no paid employees as in all businesses hiring four or more persons. The proportion of robberies completed to those attempted was lowest in the owner-operated businesses, for people apparently resist more to protect their own property than that of an employer. Ninety percent of the victims of commercial robberies said that they reported the offenses to the police (LEAA, 1976b).

Aggravated assault and homicide among intimates or acquaintances arouse sympathy for the victims even if they provoked the quarrel, but the public especially pities those attacked by strangers. When such outrages increased with the rise in strongarm robberies, there was a demand that government do something for the injured.

COMPENSATION TO VICTIMS OF VIOLENT CRIMES

Primitive, ancient, and medieval law often required a person convicted of predatory crime to compensate the victim or the victim's family as though in a tort suit, by payments of wealth or services for the damage or loss inflicted (as Chapter 6 indicated, this was primarily applied when the disputants were of the same social class). In modern times this practice ceased to be routine, although restitution is frequently ordered in granting probation, primarily in property crimes. During the second half of the twentieth century, the idea of restitution by the offender has been somewhat revived and expanded, as an aspect of sentencing and correction. Simultaneous with this trend, but only for violent offenses, has been a movement for state compensation to felony victims, whether or not the offender is caught and can make restitution.

A victim has always had the legal right in Anglo-American law to sue the criminal for property stolen or destroyed or for bodily injury; but usually the offender has little wealth and, if imprisoned, will have even less (except for corporate offenders, discussed in Chapter 12). Furthermore, in United States civil law it generally takes years to complete a suit, and attorney fees may be great. Therefore, suits occur only in exceptional cases in which the criminal has wealth, but in most such instances restitutive payment will be made in advance of court hearings in an effort to influence the complainant (sometimes illegally), or upon conviction for the crime, to impress the judge that the offender is repentant and merits a mild sentence. In Continental European law, incidentally, civil claims by the victims can be made in a criminal trial and payment by the offender ordered by the judge. Indeed, the victim can initiate the criminal proceedings if the police fail to act or the prosecutor does not file charges; an incentive to accuse a criminal is the prospect of payment for damages (Bassiouni, 1974: 568).

The movement to have the state compensate victims of violent crimes appears to have been motivated primarily by compassion. Often the correctional system makes a great effort to help the criminal, providing free medical service, vocational training, and psychiatric services, if needed. Contrastingly, the victim of a mugging may be long hospitalized—even permanently crippled—and may suffer severe psychological stress that causes loss of employment; yet when private resources are exhausted, there is no government aid other than the minimal welfare benefits. Indeed, it has been pointed out that the police carry the attacker away but call an ambulance for the victim, for which the victim must pay. In addition, it is argued that because the state undertakes to safeguard the public from violence, it should be liable for damages whenever the protection is inadequate.

The first program of state compensation for victims of violent crime was established by New Zealand in 1963, followed by Great Britain in 1964. In the following year California initiated such an effort, and in 1967 New York began what was then the largest and most liberal compensation system. Nine other states established these services in subsequent years. At first, with little public awareness of state money for victims, few claims were made, but this situation is rapidly changing. Alaska, California, and Minnesota police are required to inform victims of their right to compensation; Alaska and California hospitals must also give this advice, and in Hawaii it must be done by the courts (Newton, 1976).

In practice, a variety of problems and limitations make the programs less than ideal. All states compensate for medical expenses and loss of earnings due to physical injuries inflicted by assailants, but none for property loss or damage, and only Hawaii and Delaware make payment for pain and suffering. Most states pay funeral expenses and a few for disfigurement or physical or mental disability (Newton, 1976).

Massachusetts is unique in having compensation claims assessed by the local criminal court rather than by a special state board, but the judge who rules on payments to the victim must not be the one who tries the offender. This program has been criticized for lack of central responsibility to ensure uniform and effective operation. Contrastingly, Washington administers compensation to victims of violent crime through its workman's compensation agency, thus using for any crime victim a staff accustomed to investigating and assessing injuries. Because most state programs are still relatively new and quite varied, their procedures are frequently revised on the basis of slowly cumulating experience (Edelhertz & Geis, 1974).

Persistent issues in public compensation to victims of violence include:

1. *Delay.* The time required for investigation and decision often takes the better part of a year or longer (Brooks, 1975), although several states permit some emergency payments, at an administrator's discretion, before the investigation is completed (Newton, 1976).

2. *Minimum payments.* To avoid the burden of investigating small claims, some systems require that losses be a certain

minimum, while others deduct $100 from all approved claims. Such policies can impose a hardship on the poorest victims, for though their loss of earnings may be low, a little income foregone may impair their procurement of necessities more than would large losses to the more affluent. New York, California, and Maryland require proof of financial need, which rests the principle of compensation purely on an ethic of compassion rather than on the idea of the state's responsibility for the protection of its people (Edelhertz & Geis, 1974).

3. *Maximum payments.* Most states have maximum payments, usually with separate limits for loss of earnings, medical costs, funerals, and retraining due to physical handicap. In some cases limits are questionable, for they do not meet actual losses. There is less sympathy when this inadequacy is due to a wealthy victim's unusually high loss of earnings if laid up briefly by injuries than when the state cannot nearly recompense a poor victim the lifelong losses from permanent injuries or from interruptions of career or study lasting several years.

4. *Victim and offender of the same household.* All states except California bar compensation in these cases, which eliminates a large proportion of homicide and aggravated-assault victims from eligibility, and is a major cost saving. It is alleged that investigation of such claims would elicit false statements by those involved, and that payment might benefit the offender. Counterarguments include the fact that the victim's account of the offense is accepted in paying for injuries ascribed to unwitnessed crimes by unapprehended strangers, and that medical costs and loss of earnings are objective consequences of a violent crime regardless of who does it (Brooks, 1975).

5. *Victims who contribute to their victimization.* Six levels of victim culpability in the offenses from which they suffer have been distinguished by Lamborn (1968):

   a) *Invitation:* the victim was "asking for trouble"; for example, by walking into a dangerous area alone at night or by flashing a large roll of bills in a public place of dubious reputation.

   b) *Facilitation:* making the offense easier, as by failure to close a hotel room door or to investigate people before employing them in positions of trust.

   c) *Provocation:* exemplified by the person who insults and challenges a potential assailant, or even gestures as though to attack.

   d) *Perpetration:* the usual definition of victim-precipitation in homicide, in which the person killed in a fracas actually starts the hitting; this also occurs when the legal victim of statutory rape seduces the offender.

e) *Cooperation:* typical in nonpredatory offenses, as in the sale of drugs or of a prostitute's services, but also exists in violent crimes, as when two persons undertake a bombing and one is killed by the blast.

f) *Instigation:* the victim wants to be victimized, as when a suicidal person threatens an armed person or police officer with a firearm in order to be shot.

Usually the last three categories are likely to be denied compensation and the first three are not, but this is quite variable in both law and practice. Some states have almost a no-fault approach in assessing a victim's claims, while others virtually impose a legal trial on the victim, with rights to an attorney, whenever there is suspicion of the victim's partial responsibility for the offense. Hawaii sometimes awards on the basis of the objective losses, then deducts a percentage because of the victim's culpability (Edelhertz & Geis, 1974: Chapter 5).

6. *Residence.* Several states pay only to their residents, while others pay anyone victimized within the state. A controversial case in Hawaii stressed the importance of its tourist trade in authorizing $10,000 to a victim who had been in the state for only two days. California and Delaware authorize compensation to residents who are victims of violent crimes when outside the state, but deny payments to nonresidents who suffer crimes within the state (Newton, 1976).

Somewhat related to the issue of compensating victims of violent crime is that of "Good Samaritans," persons who tried to protect someone from crime but were themselves injured or suffered other losses as a result. For example, a man chases a purse snatcher and trips, shattering his knee, or a citizen, in helping a police officer, is injured and becomes paraplegic. These are two examples of "Good Samaritans" paid under California's pioneer law for them, enacted in 1965 simultaneously with its victim-compensation statute. Several other states now have such measures, even some states that do not compensate victims. Most of these payments are for losses incurred in trying to capture an offender, sometimes taking up the chase while leaving the victim to bleed. Contrastingly, the Good Samaritan of the Bible helped a wounded victim whom others had passed by; he did not chase the robbers (Luke 10: 29–37). Vermont is the only state that (like several Continental European countries) makes it a misdemeanor for a person not to intervene, when possible, to assist people in danger of victimization from crime. Some doubt has been expressed, however, about the wisdom of citizen intervention by means other than calling the police, for nonprofessional actions may result in greater injury to more people (Geis et al., 1976).

The burgeoning of violence in the late 1960s and 1970s included not only the muggings that spurred compensation laws, but also a surge in shootings and holdups from that optimal device for murder and robbery, the handgun. How can its prevalence be diminished?

GUN CONTROL

Earlier, in reporting survey research on the correlates of handgun possession, we stated that these weapons were acquired by homeowners for protection. But do they protect? Rates of homicide and of aggravated assault, as well as the percentage of these offenses that involve guns, are highest in the regions where guns are most prevalent. The South leads in all these variables—guns, killings, attacks, and percentage of these offenses committed with firearms—while the Northeast is lowest and the Midwest and West intermediate. In 1975, 73 percent of murders in the South were by firearms, as contrasted with 51 percent in the Northeastern states (FBI, 1976: 18). Exactly the same regional distribution prevails in accidental deaths of civilians from firearms and in the slaying of law-enforcement officers, over 95 percent of which is done with guns (Alviani & Drake, 1975: 1–2). In the decade between 1965 and 1975, 402 law-enforcement officers were killed in the South, as contrasted with 149 in the Northeast (FBI, 1976: 224). In relation to population in 1970, the midpoint of this decade, the rates of these police deaths per million persons were 6.4 in the South, 5.1 in the West, 4.6 in the North Central states, and 3.0 in the Northeast. Thus all regional statistics suggest that the more readily guns are available, the more dangerous life becomes whenever anger or fear intensifies.

The counterargument, given to pollsters by two-thirds of handgun owners, is that guns are needed for self-defense and property protection. But the facts prove this to be a dangerous myth for most people. A Cleveland study found guns in the home killed occupants, guests, or other unintended victims six times as often as they killed criminal intruders. Similar findings come from Detroit, New York, Los Angeles, and other cities (Alviani & Drake, 1975). Thousands of children are killed or crippled annually when they find house guns and play with them. Furthermore, burglars generally enter when no one is at home and firearms are attractive loot, thus accounting for most of the estimated 100,000 weapons stolen each year. Stolen guns are a main source of criminal armament and a serious bar to immediate crime reduction from gun-control programs.

The Second Amendment to the Constitution reads: "A well-regulated Militia, being necessary to the security of a free State, the right of the people to keep and bear Arms shall not be infringed." This portion of the Bill of Rights was added to the Constitution in 1791 because state and local militia, organized mainly for protection against Indians, had often been disarmed by British troops just before and during the American Revolution. Whenever a wave of robbery or murder has disturbed the public or an American leader has been assassinated—including Presidents Lincoln, McKinley, and Kennedy—laws against owning or concealing guns have been proposed, only to be treated as heresy by people who cite only the last portion of the Second Amendment—"the right of the people to keep and bear Arms shall not be infringed." Yet courts have repeatedly affirmed that the Second Amendment's reference to a militia makes it clearly applicable only to today's National Guard units of the 50 states (Newton & Zimring, 1969: Appendix J).

The first firm foundation in a long effort to build controls over guns into law was New York's Sullivan Act of 1911, which banned many concealable deadly weapons—including daggers, stilettos, and even brass knuckles—and forbade sale of pistols to anyone who did not first procure a permit from the police. Penalties could be severe for its violation, including prison terms for former felons. Enacted when weapons already were widely owned and purchase in adjacent states was easy, this New York law has often been criticized for not eliminating gun crimes, and has repeatedly been challenged in the courts and amended in the legislature, but it still survives. Its mandatory prison terms allegedly reduce the carrying of pistols by criminals, and the much more severe penalties if an illegal gun is loaded may diminish accidental or impulsive shootings. Defenders of the law could once say that New York long had a distinctly lower murder rate than the national average, despite high rates for other types of crime and the largest slums (Bakal, 1966: 151–59; Kennett & Anderson, 1975: Chapter 7). Today New York no longer has less homicide than the rest of the country, perhaps because the cultural and economic conditions of its slums are worse, and its gun-control laws less effective with a more mobile populace. Some estimate that in New York City there are two illegal sales of handguns for every three with a permit (Sherrill, 1973: 94). This reflects the fact that over three-fourths of the states still have only minimal gun controls, and federal statutes are notoriously weak; so guns are easily purchased in Southern states and peddled in New York, allegedly at a rate of 100,000 per year (Brill, 1976). The absence of uniform strong controls may explain the lack of correlation between current state handgun laws and rates of violent crime (Seitz, 1972; Murray 1975).

Efforts to enact *federal* gun-control legislation have produced a half-century of blockage or mild compromise by various interest groups, despite the public's *clear majority support for strong registra-*

tion laws since 1938, according to Gallup polls. The 1927 Miller Act banned sending pistols by mail in retail sales or as gifts, with a few exceptions, but did not restrict this method of delivering rifles, such as the mail-order bargain that allegedly killed President Kennedy. The 1934 National Firearms Act was the first victim of massive lobbying by the National Rifle Association—an organization, headed by former generals, that grew rapidly by getting surplus weapons and ammunition from the Army for its members, and often collaborated with American gun manufacturers in pressuring Congress to forget gun controls. The 1934 law originally proposed strict regulations for transfer of handguns in interstate commerce, but ultimately restricted only machine guns, sawed-off shotguns, and silencers. Even this restriction was frequently evaded by selling presumably disabled machine guns that actually were not difficult to make operable (Sherrill, 1973: 57–63; Kennett & Anderson, 1975: Chapter 8).

The 1938 Federal Firearms Act proposed to keep handguns from felons by requiring that all importers and interstate shippers procure a federal license. As finally enacted, however, the fee was only one dollar, and a short form, available at the post office, had to be filled out. The regulations proved unenforceable, at least with the resources and practices of the Treasury Department's Alcohol, Tobacco and Firearms Bureau. Most people who procured a dealer's license did so only to buy guns by mail for their own use, since postal purchase was otherwise prohibited, although some actual dealers could sell weapons to criminals with impunity, or were themselves criminals (Sherrill, 1973: 64–66, 130–41; Zimring, 1975: 139–44).

The 1968 Gun Control Act reflects collaboration of American gun manufacturers seeking to reduce competition from imported weapons, and citizens aroused (without earlier legislative result) by President Kennedy's assassination and mobilized anew by the slayings of Robert Kennedy and Dr. Martin Luther King. Together, this unusual combination of interest groups overcame initial resistance by the National Rifle Association to get a compromise bill enacted that restricted imports of handguns and military-type weapons (e.g., hand grenades, antitank rifles). It did not ban the importing of gun parts to be assembled here; this was already done, for tariff rates were cheaper on parts than on completed weapons. Some have said that the strongest feature of the Act is its name (Sherrill, 1973: 136–38, 280–97, 302–4; Kennett & Anderson, 1975: 242–45; Zimring, 1975).

The continued sale in the United States of handguns made entirely or partly from foreign-made components led American gun manufacturers and the politicians they supported to campaign against "Saturday-night specials"—the allegedly cheap guns from imported parts, too short for accuracy, liable to explode in the shooter's hand, and used by the poor in drunken fights and robberies. Efforts to define these weapons by their physical features and to estimate the extent of their use in robberies produced no consistent results. During most of the 1970s politicians opposing gun controls said they wished to ban only Saturday-night specials, but none of a large variety of bills for this purpose passed Congress (Sherrill, 1973: 311–22; Alviani & Drake, 1975: 11–13).

Even if a strong gun-control law is passed, it is unlikely to result quickly in marked reduction of shootings and robberies. Most of these crimes, especially robberies, are done by delinquents and criminals with "street guns," rather than with "house guns" kept by law-abiding citizens for protection, target-shooting, or collection. Registration of currently owned guns and licensing their retention, plus strict controls on new sales, would identify many house guns but not street guns, for only the most law-abiding would cooperate. The main immediate advantage of these measures of gun control would be in tracing pistols found on criminals and produced by theft of a registered house gun or by misrepresentation in licensed purchasing. Registration of currently owned guns might be encouraged not only by a penalty for failing to do so, but also by offering to try to trace any gun that is reported stolen, and by providing free safety inspection of the gun. Passing an examination in safe gun operation, maintenance, and storage would be an appropriate requirement for licensing, comparable to license tests for that other highly dangerous activity, driving an automobile.

Certainly, the black market for handguns will continue as long as there is a demand for them, since they are easily concealable and no party to their illegal sale or transfer will normally report these transactions to the police. Yet the overall accessibility of these weapons can eventually be diminished by severely restricting their legal importation, manufacture, sale, or transfer. These policies will make handguns less readily available to emotional quarrelers, delinquents, and other unspecialized or infrequent offenders, who commit most of the violent offenses in the United States. Disarming professional criminals is also a desirable goal, of course, but is not readily feasible until they are caught in a crime. Gun-control laws may aid in catching them by imposing severe penalties on previously convicted felons found in possession of a firearm.

Gun-registration efforts and restriction of manufacture and import may be accompanied by "buy-back" programs to purchase and destroy handguns already in circulation. Trial efforts indicate a risk that these undertakings may overpay—for example, giving full price for defective weapons—but such shortcomings should be avoidable. Some street guns will be turned in and the black market reduced if the price is merely reasonable for their quality, it is paid in cash, and the sale place is accessible. Also, requiring that the old weapon be turned in for destruction whenever a new one is to be purchased would impede the black market. As guns become less prevalent, fewer will fall into the hands of burglars and other criminals as loot.

With these measures, progress toward greatly diminishing the availability of pistols will still be slow, and will affect mainly the avocational offenders. Other conditions are probably much more important than gun control in reducing violent or other crime. Such a conclusion is suggested by the experience of Switzerland, where every able-bodied male is required to keep one or more military firearms in his home; yet crimes with guns are rare. This, however, is in a country with no slums or extreme poverty, with relatively little stress on violence as an achievement, and with a high degree of integration of the populace, fostered in part by the universal military organization from which distribution of arms stems. The Swiss experience, and this book's discussion thus far, suggest that reduction of violence in the United States would come mostly through: (1) less social separation of scholastically maladjusted adolescents from law-abiding adults; (2) more socially integrated neighborhoods; (3) less relative deprivation of the poor; (4) more charismatic peaceful heroes, to compete successfully as models for youth with the notorious and glamorous figures from subcultures of violence. What is most clear is that when a problem's causes are deeprooted, effective policies are rarely simple.

SUMMARY AND CONCLUSION

The United States, since its inception as a set of colonies, has probably led the world in nonmilitary guns per capita and has usually exceeded almost all other countries of comparable technological development in its homicide rates. These dubious distinctions at first had fairly obvious origins. The land was a wilderness, filled with wild game and occasionally hostile natives; there were also cleavages among the settlers, and they had enslaved blacks. In the South and West, especially, both situational and subcultural developments made bullets the accepted arbiter in private quarrels. As Northeastern cities grew, their slums were internal frontiers where violence also flourished. Finally, with the burgeoning of a corporate economy in the late nineteenth and early twentieth centuries, the United States had the bloodiest labor strife the world has known. More recent decades brought interracial conflict.

Features of our homicide rates that require explanation include:

1. their decline from the Depression to the 1960s, then their rapid upsurge

2. the fact that most murder has always been among intimates or acquaintances and that perhaps a third is victim-precipitated, although the proportion of murders that springs from other felonies—notably robbery—reached a new peak of about one in three during the 1970s

3. their persistently higher levels in the Southern states but diminishing regional contrast in the 1960s and 1970s, since increases were greatest outside the South

4. their male predominance, despite rapidly rising female murder rates

5. their rapid increase among juveniles, so that murder is more than ever a teenage enterprise

6. their rapid urbanization since the mid-1960s, after being greatest in rural areas before then.

All these trends coalesced in the ghettos of Northern and Western cities between 1965 and 1970, when young black males appear to have tripled the rates of killing and being killed. The upsurge then slowed, but many slum adolescents in minority groups remain highly murderous in the 1970s. Probably related to this development is the fact that handguns were proliferating rapidly during this period, particularly house guns among the less educated who were "making it" financially, and street guns among burglars and their customers.

Since high murder rates distinctive of some *categories* of the population, such as poor or black persons, as well as any marked changes in these rates, are produced by less than one percent of the people in these categories, ecological-correlation fallacies readily develop in trying to explain homicide. This is evident when everyone is stereotyped as murderous who has a widespread attribute, such as being poor, simply because poverty is most prevalent in states that have higher rates of a relatively rare behavior such as homicide. The rare conduct could be a consequence of a not fully known combination of conditions—possibly also rare—and likewise correlated to the percentage of the population having the more frequent trait. The best way to assess whether correlations among state statistics reflect causal ties is to conceptualize and test in other ways a theory of the behavioral processes or events that connect the independent variables to their alleged effects. We have done this repeatedly, throughout the chapter. Confidence in a causal explanation grows if diverse types of tests, especially experiments and quasi-experiments but also interpretative case studies, consistently support either the original theory or its revision in the light of cumulative evidence.

Cultural and subcultural theories imply that group transmission of beliefs favorable to use of force accounts for the distribution of violent crime. Some have alleged that such theories are disproved by survey-research findings, but the reports of a lack of correlation between violent conduct and aggression-supporting values proves to be doubtful on methodological grounds. Evidence of a lack of social support for fighters in groups with high violence rates can be interpreted as indicating only that social strain and cultural ambivalence are generated by those who are physically aggressive, even in social circles where they are most numerous. That most homicides reflect subculturally shared beliefs about using physical force is inferred from the extent to which both the killer and the victim are in the same high-violence-rate groups, by the large proportion of murders that are victim-precipitated, and by the dialogue that precedes and accompanies their affrays.

An alternative to subcultural explanations is the thesis that high-violence-rate groups have structural conditions, such as extreme poverty, that evoke much use of physical force in every population that suffers these conditions. Nevertheless, when there is a distinctly imperfect correlation between these structural conditions and violence—when groups persist in aggression even after presumably causative conditions change, and fighters verbally express beliefs justifying violence more than is customary among other people—a subcultural explanation seems valid. Some social adapatation to stress may foster violence, which becomes part of a new subculture as the ideas supporting it are disseminated. Also, there is a functional autonomy in cultural components, whereby beliefs persist even after the circumstances for which they were adaptive vanish.

That the high homicide rates in the South reflect a regional subculture of violence is supported by an analysis of history, by persistence of these rates among Southerners who migrate, and by a large variety of statistical indicators, including the higher correlation of state homicide rates with "Southernness" than with any other attributes, such as median income. This view has been challenged by evidence that indices of extreme income inequality are as closely correlated with state homicide rates as is Southernness, for the Southern states have the greatest such inequality; and by evidence that some indicators of violence, such as fistfighting, are less prevalent in the South than elsewhere. It is pointed out that both structural and cultural contrasts between the South and other regions are diminishing, but that the distinctive Southern subculture may indeed foster less escalation of minor quarrels to fisticuffs and, simultaneously, more tolerance of homicidal shooting for what are viewed as gross personal wrongs. There are diverse data suggesting less outrage at murder in the South than elsewhere; for example, prison terms for killing are briefest in the South. The equivalence of extreme poverty and Southernness as correlates of homicide, however, bear on an issue with a separate literature.

The violence associated with "subcultures of poverty" is not an automatic consequence of indigence, as is evident in its linkage with: (1) relative rather than absolute deprivation; (2) achievement rather than ascriptive values; (3) lack of anticriminal social bonds or of informal social controls in poor communities. These three structural conditions seem to have additive effects, with subcultures a fourth factor in fostering violence. All four weaken satisfactions anticipated from nonviolence and make the risks in aggression more tolerable.

The theme that use of force expresses masculinity is associated with the contention that such an emphasis is a structural consequence, for males, of being reared in fatherless or other female-dominated homes. Evidence is much less adequate for this theory than for the idea that any high concentration of males increases competition among them. Possibly, the values that develop in one-gender groups persist as subcultures in their members when they move to "coed" settings, but women's liberation may diminish pressures to conform to gender stereotypes in any situation.

The circular-reaction process of emotion arousal, plus the ambivalent sentiments and deep commitment that characterize intimate relationships, account for the fact that love, kinship, or friendship are antecedent to most homicide. Circular interaction also accounts for the development of more intense feelings in gatherings that have a common stimulus of emotion, such as riot mobs, than in isolated individuals. Mass media, however, can cause widely scattered persons to share the same emotions at the same time. Through the two-step process the media can create similar feelings in small groups discussing the same broadcasted reports throughout the nation.

These social processes of media influence were especially evident in the impact of the assassinations, civil-rights struggles, and urban riots of the 1960s. A theory of contagion from these events, by the circular-reaction and two-step mechanisms, plausibly explains both the increase in political activity by educated and employed blacks in the late 1960s and early 1970s and the rise of violent crime in this period among those young blacks most unsuccessful in school and employment. Evidence of the mass media's effect on violence is not optimum, but it tends to confirm theories of modeling, triggering, and desensitization, rather than theories of catharsis. Modeling and triggering account for the contagion effects of highly publicized offenses; with the two-step theory of an intervening social-interaction process in media effects, they imply that violence tends to increase in any segment of an audience that readily identifies with characters in portrayals of physical aggression.

Relationships between irritation or frustration and violence are less adequately explained by "hydraulic theories" of pressure and release than by social-learning theory stressing that any activity, aggressive or nonaggressive, is gratifying if it reduces the arousal from frustration. Social learning explains especially well the undercontrolled pattern of violence, but may also fit allegedly overcontrolled violent individuals.

Another psychological process fostering violence is paranoid delusion. What is often insufficiently appreciated is that such delusions can be developed and reinforced collaboratively by several individuals, and thus become the ideologies of what can be called paranoid groups. Several of these organizations have been notorious for perpetrating criminal violence. They are most effectively controlled not by reaction to them as groups, but by involving their individual members in other more rewarding social relationships, thus reducing that exclusion by the rest of society that fosters paranoia, and thereby altering their differential anticipations.

Child battering is a widespread and serious form of criminal violence that has been increasingly recognized in recent decades, after centuries of indifference. Battering parents are often the product of an upbringing similar to the one they impose. They have unrealistic expectations of their children and a self-righteousness that blinds them to the damage they do. Prison sentences can be lawfully imposed on them, but may not be in the best interest of the child. Yet until the court has confidence that the parents, under probationary supervision, will improve their child's care, it must remove a severely-abused offspring from the parental home.

Robbery, a violent crime directed at economic gain, has displayed much the same trends and correlates as homicide in recent decades. It has been increasingly an act of adolescents and young adults maladjusted in school or unsuccessful in the job market. Some robbery of adults by other adults is related to the substance abuses discussed in Chapter 10, but the most dramatic forms are professional offenses described in Chapter 13.

Government compensation to victims of violent crime, initiated in several states in the 1960s, became a growing movement in the 1970s. Most such programs are still in flux, as experimentation occurs in methods of administering them and disputes persist on the adequacy and fairness of various payment policies. At issue are such matters as minimum and maximum compensation and the relevance to these claims of a victim's partial culpability in an offense.

Gun control has been favored by a majority of the American public since 1938, according to public-opinion polls, but efforts to pass significant control legislation and to procure adequate enforcement of existing statutes have been stymied by powerful interest groups. Although no legislation will eliminate all gun crimes, particularly of the professional variety, appropriate policies can slowly make firearms less readily accessible to nonprofessional assaulters and robbers, especially juveniles.

Perhaps the most frequently proposed method of preventing assaultive conduct is to lock up all violent people for as long as they are dangerous to others. But, practically speaking, this cannot be the hoped-for panacea, because the "show of violence" is not so readily predictable. The courts can now impose an indefinite term of confinement as mentally ill on anyone they deem dangerous. This is the basis for both maximum-security and less secure hospitalization of persons diagnosed as paranoid schizophrenic and of others adjudged criminally insane—some after demonstrating homicidal behavior, but often for not much more than verbal conduct that disturbed others. The frequent injustice and ineffectiveness in the administration of these laws was described in Chapter 3.

Attempts to predict which prisoners or parolees will be seriously violent have resulted in many more erroneous than correct forecasts (Molof, 1965; Wenk et al., 1972; Wenk & Emrich, 1972). Two major reasons for these errors appear to be the following:

1. Most offenders, particularly adolescents, are unspecialized in their crimes and share in subcultures fostering not only violence, but also other lawbreaking (e.g., theft, drugs). Therefore, many with official records for only nonviolent offenses may next be in physical conflict, while many held for assaultive acts may next be caught for theft.

2. Penalties seem to deter violence more effectively than they deter property or drug offenses, perhaps because the desire to use force is more temporary and because offender values also endorse "playing it cool" and avoiding fights without losing face. Furthermore, violent crimes are less often vocationally oriented than others, the one major exception being professional robbery. A three-year followup of male parolees from throughout the nation found that only four percent of those sentenced for willful homicide were charged with any type of new offense, and less than one percent with new homicide, while one percent of robbery and assault parolees were charged with homicide during this postrelease period (Uniform Parole Reports *Newsletter,* July 1976).

After someone confined for homicide or other violent conduct is released and commits new violence, it is easy to assert that the new offense would not have occurred had the confinement been prolonged; but this hindsight cannot be replaced with accurate forecasts at the time of release. If, in hopes of avoiding all error, we locked up everyone convicted of violent crimes and "threw away the key," confining them for life, the number of people incarcerated would become enormous in a few years, especially if nonhomicidal violence were included; costs and intolerable injustice would also result, while violence would probably continue, particularly among adolescents.

An optimum policy for reducing violence seems to require, first, all the measures for diminishing adolescent offenses suggested in Chapter 8; particularly, an effort to reduce the separation of the generations by providing youth with a combination of employment opportunities among adults with school work for those who prefer it, and a reduction of age-grading in other activities. Encouraging more participation of youths in formal organizations—in school, in work and recreation, in ecology, community-improvement, and other social movements, and in politics—will cultivate their skills at nonviolent resolution of differences, help bridge the generations, and improve their ability to cope with the bureaucracies of the modern world. Reducing the extremes of economic inequality, particularly chronic unemployment, is a prerequisite to much achievement of the foregoing goals. Diminishing the availability of handguns by the measures enumerated in this chapter should greatly reduce the proportion of assaults that prove lethal and the rate of nonprofessional armed robbery. Finally, charismatic leadership in antiviolence values and the reflection of such values in the mass media can reduce criminal use of physical force in our society. Closely related to much of the violence, however, are some of the forms of chemical ingestion—particularly the consumption of alcohol—with which our next chapter is concerned.

TEN

SUBSTANCE ABUSE AND CRIME

People take an incredible array of substances to alter moods or relieve discomforts. They swallow not only coffee, tea, and alcoholic beverages, but also pep pills, tranquilizers, antidepressants, muscle relaxers, pain killers, and hallucinogens. They inhale the smoke of tobacco, marijuana, and opium. They sniff glue, paint thinner, and gasoline. They inject heroin, cocaine, and a multitude of other drugs. Most survive this violence to their bodies, at least in the short run, but some are less fortunate.

Substance use considered harmful is called "abuse," as in "drug abuse." To discourage it, the production, sale, and even possession of some materials, such as marijuana and opiates, have been declared criminal. Other products, some more dangerous than those the law prohibits, are taken with impunity. By far the most used and abused mood-altering drug is alcohol, but bias and ideology determine what is called "abuse" or even "drug" (Goode, 1972: Chapter 1).

One relationship of substance abuse to crime, as already indicated, is that some of it is in itself criminal; another is that drugs are alleged at times to so alter the minds of users as to cause them to commit crimes. This raises questions of whether they are responsible for their acts if drugs prevented them from knowing right from wrong, or even what they were doing. The law usually holds that persons who voluntarily consume substances, knowing the probable effects, are accountable for the consequences. In some states, however (California, for one), they can be viewed legally as having diminished responsibility when "under the influence" (for fuller discussion, see Fingarette, 1975).

A third and more indirect relationship to crime occurs when people commit offenses to get money for a substance they urgently crave. *Addiction*, defined broadly as an extremely compulsive craving for and habitual use of a substance—whether it be tobacco, alcohol, or heroin—creates an inelastic demand, so that many addicts will go to surprising lengths and pay a phenomenal price for it. Heroin addicts allegedly commit 30 percent or more of the thefts and most of the prostitution in some major cities to procure funds for this drug. Alcoholics often engage in petty theft or forgery to buy drinks.

Whether addiction is a disease is a much-debated issue, resolved only by an arbitrary preference of definitions. To Webster's dictionary, "disease" is "an impairment of the normal state of the living animal . . . or any of its components that interrupts or modifies the performance of the vital functions." Addiction to some of the substances discussed in this chapter, such as alcohol, often "modifies or interrupts . . . vital functions" and impairs the performance of parts of the body. Indeed, it does this much more than many of the forms of conduct called "mental disease." Yet other compulsive behavior, such as overeating, can also severely impair vital functions, but is not called "disease."

Whether the term "disease" is used for addictive-substance abuse will be left to the reader's preference. Yet among our concerns will be government policies that define the consequences of addictions as crimes, rather than as the products of an ailment. Indeed, there are at times simultaneous programs of treating addiction to alcohol, opiates, or other drugs as a disease and legal reaction to it as though it were a willful offense. These and other relationships of various mood alterants to crime are so diverse, however, that for clarity it is best to discuss each substance separately in its relationship to crime.

ALCOHOL

The substance most widely abused, since earliest recorded history, is ethyl alcohol, consumed in beverages such as beer, wine, and whiskey. One survey (Cahalan et al., 1969) concludes:

> 32 percent of Americans 21 or older either never drink alcohol or take it, on the average, less than once a year.

> 15 percent imbibe less than once a month but more than once a year.

> 28 percent drink at least once a month, but usually in small quantities.

> 13 percent drink several times per month, but rarely more than three or four on each occasion.

> 12 percent drink almost every day, often consuming five or more drinks at each occasion, or have that much at least once a week.

Most of those who can be said to abuse alcohol are probably in the last category, although some people disrupt their lives by drinking heavily in brief sprees between long periods of teetotalling.

Alcoholism has been defined by one or more of four traits: drinking much more than is customary, drinking that seriously impairs important role obligations (e.g., as employee, student, spouse, parent), drinking that severely damages physical or emotional health, and, especially, drinking without power to quit even when suffering these deleterious effects (Trice, 1966: 28–30). Those who accept such definitions, however, interpret them differently, so that many people are called "alcoholic" by some but not by others. Therefore, specific rates of alcoholism provide only an illusion of precision, and as the National Institute of Mental Health (1967: 11) points out: "There is no support for such publicized assertions as 'one out of every ten drinkers'—or 'one out of every three'—is now fated to become an alcoholic." An even broader term than alcoholism is "problem drinking."

Instead of claiming to have precise rates of alcoholism, we can infer the relative prevalence of disruptive drinking in different groups through use of diverse, clearly specified indicators; for example, by compiling rates of sickness ascribed to alcohol, arrest rates for alcohol-related offenses, and the percentage of alcohol found in breath or blood tests, as well as by polling people on their drinking habits.

Drinking and Arrests

The criminal law in most of the world has been much involved in combatting excessive drinking. Indeed, in 1919 the United States tried to outlaw alcoholic beverages completely by the Eighteenth Amendment to the Constitution, while some states had their own prohibition statues before 1919 and remained "dry" for years or decades after 1933, when the Twenty-first Amendment repealed the Eighteenth.

It is generally agreed that our Prohibition experiment was a dismal failure. Because the consumption of alcoholic beverages is a voluntary act and because all involved—suppliers, sellers, drinkers— are collaborating, there usually were no victims complaining to the police when the law was violated. In most parts of the country, especially in our major cities, large segments of the population were accustomed to drinking and considered Prohibition an invasion of their rights. Because only persons willing to violate the law could sell alcoholic beverages, those already involved in crime had a tremendous business opportunity. In this commerce, however, they could not call on the police to protect their property or on government to regulate competitive sales practices. Accordingly, bootleggers formed private armies to war on rivals, preying on others as well, and accumulated immense wealth with which they corrupted local and state government and financed a variety of illegal and legal enterprises. (This "organized crime" is discussed in Chapter 13.)

The most frequent basis for arrest in the United States is drunkenness, any disturbance of behavior ascribed to alcohol. As indicated in Chapter 1, the crime is actually public intoxication; it is not illegal to be drunk in private. The second largest category of arrests is theft, but third is "driving under the influence," and fourth is "disorderly conduct" (FBI, 1975: 186), which usually includes drunken-Felonies in which a majority of arrestees were drinking at the time of their alleged offense include murder, forgery, and aggravated assault; most misdemeanor assaults are also associated with drinking, as are about half the rapes and a third of child-abuse cases. A Census survey of all state-prison inmates in 1974 concludes that 43 percent had been drinking at the time of the offense for which they were imprisoned (LEAA, 1976). Indeed, a conservative estimate is that about half the people arrested on any charge in the United States either are under the influence of alcohol when taken into custody, or are held for acts committed when drunk, or both. If they admit the alleged crime, they usually blame it on drink.

Both the actual number of arrests for public drunkenness and their percentage of total arrests have declined in recent years. In 1955, as Table 10-1 shows, 42 percent of arrests reported to the FBI were for drunkenness, five percent for driving "under the influence" and 10 percent for disorderly conduct; by 1975 drunkenness accounted for only about 13 percent of arrests, but drunk-driving arrests doubled, probably due largely to the increased numbers of automobiles and drivers and the intensification of law enforcement. The decline in arrests for drunkenness, however, results more from change in laws and in police policy than from decline in drunken behavior.

Increasingly, drunkenness in public—if not while driving or doing other dangerous things—is ignored by onlookers and police, or the inebriate is removed to a safe place by the police (without arrest, if removal is not resisted). Such flexibility is required in about half the states, since they have decriminalized public drunkenness. Their legislators recognized the traditional arrest–trial–incarceration cycle for drunks as costly and futile, a revolving door contributing little or nothing to reducing alcoholism. This change in the law, which shifts concern with drunkenness largely from the criminal-justice system to public-health and welfare agencies and makes the inebriate's participation voluntary, expresses an evolving value (discussed in Chapter 2) whereby people are increasingly allowed to "do their own thing" if they do not harm others. Further influencing this gradual change are charges that traditional law-enforcement procedures are often illegal— for example, when police have quotas for drunk arrests that they mechanically fill in skid-row areas; when courts do not offer drunks

TABLE 10-1 **Trends in Drunkenness and Related Arrests as Percentage of Total Arrests Reported to the FBI**
(By five-year intervals, 1955–75)

OFFENSE	1955	1960	1965	1970	1975
Drunkenness	42	38	31	22	13
Driving under the influence	5	4	5	7	10
Disorderly conduct	10	11	12	9	8

SOURCE: FBI, *Crime in the U.S.: Uniform Crime Reports*, for the years indicated.

representation by counsel; and when judges too quickly find all alleged drunks guilty. Packer (1968: 345) observes: "Drunkenness is the paradigm . . . illustration of the twofold evil that results from misusing the criminal sanction: we burden the operations of the criminal process to no avail, and we delude ourselves into believing that we have thereby solved a social problem." The relationship of alcohol to crime becomes clearer with an understanding of drinking, drunkenness, and alcoholism—three different phenomena that we will examine separately.

Drinking and Behavior Change

Alcohol intake varies tremendously from one country to another, as well as within each country. There is also much diversity in the behavior associated with and alleged to be caused by drinking. Indeed, that a single chemical—ethyl alcohol—seems to make one species act in so many different ways suggests that drunken comportment is not due to the chemical alone; culture, subculture, and personality must also be credited.

The influence of culture is evident in the widely shared assumptions about appropriate conduct while drinking. In the United States, as in many other countries, partaking of alcoholic beverages with others is usually a ritual in which conviviality and good wishes are expressed, even among people unacquainted or unfriendly before drinks are served. Thus a first function of imbibing in our culture, especially in gatherings of nonintimates, is to define the situation as one permitting an increase in informality and friendliness.

A drinking place simulates a primary group for those who are lonely or feel estranged even with their own families. The price of a drink in a barroom buys the right to "feel at home" there. Also, as Sherri Cavan observes in her insightful ethnography of San Francisco bars (1966), the public drinking place suspends many of the consequences one expects elsewhere for what one says and does (see also, Roebuck & Frese, 1976).

Biologically, the impact of alcohol is like that of fatigue: it impairs coordination and makes one sleepy. Such effects depend on the percentage of alcohol in the bloodstream; thus a given amount of drink influences a small person more than a large one, but the effect also varies with speed of intake. Contrary to some popular impressions, alcohol adds to the effects of fatigue or sedatives, rather than reversing them; it depresses the body's rate of physiological functioning, but creates the illusion of stimulation through at least four factors. First, it causes dilation of capillaries near the skin (hence flushing), which makes the drinker look and feel warm and excited, but actually lowers body temperature by increasing heat loss through the skin. Second, it depresses the "higher" centers of the nervous system, which impose voluntary control on conduct; and it is assumed to do this more rapidly than it depresses the "lower" system involved in emotional impulses, thus impairing the drinker's capacity to inhibit impulsive acts. This "disinhibition" effect also explains why "slaphappiness" or irritability frequently accompanies extreme fatigue without alcohol, but it does not account for all changes that occur in conduct when the percentage of alcohol in the blood rises.

A third factor in drunken comportment, sometimes creating an illusion of stimulation, is that drinkers share cultural expectations about appropriate conduct while "high" or drunk. MacAndrew and Edgerton (1969) vividly describe how diversely behavior changes with alcohol from one culture to another. In some societies drinkers withdraw to imbibe alone; in others they mingle but stifle expressions of emotion; in some they sit in a circle, exchanging pleasant gestures with each drink until all are highly inebriated; in still others they become boisterously merry, or bellicose, or sexually promiscuous. Furthermore, these authors show, a society's intoxicated behavior often changes if its people contact those of other cultures whose drunkenness customs differ from their own. Finally, they point out that even in societies where much assault, some of it deadly, accompanies drunkenness, the brawlers definitely select whom they attack, and will suddenly act very soberly if someone enters to whom they are expected to show deference.

Despite the widely held belief that American Indians crave liquor inordinately and go "hog wild" when intoxicated, there has been much variation in their use of liquor and comportment when drunk. Except for a few Southwest tribes, native Americans had no alcoholic beverages until they acquired them from European soldiers and fur traders, who were destructive, extremely violent with each other, and sexually promiscuous with native women when drunk. Many Indians adapted this behavior to their own cultures, some of which already had periods and circumstances when "time out" from customary morality was accepted, but previously without liquor. Native Americans, MacAndrew and Edgerton (1969) continue, learned from Europeans that misconduct would be excused when ascribed to drunkenness; so they feigned intoxication to "get away with" some acts and because they observed that whites feared drunken Indians. These natives could sober up quickly whenever the situation demanded, and set limits to their deviations from normal conduct when drunk. Today, some tribes that drink the most alcohol (e.g., the Hopi) have the lowest rates of public drunkenness, and Navajos living off the reservation ten or more years drink much more moderately than those on the reservation (Levy & Kunitz, 1974); this further illustrates that neither alcoholism nor drunkenness is inherent in descent.

Not only behavior when drunk, but also the prevalence of alcoholism, may be greatly influenced by culture. Thus among world nations, Italy and France rank very high in alcohol consumption per capita, but drunkenness and alcoholism are much more frequent in France. Survey research indicates that alcoholic beverages are regarded as foods in both countries; wine is offered to fairly young children with meals, especially in Italy. In France much more than in Italy, however, imbibing heavily is considered a sign of virility, particularly among youth, who engage in ritualistic drinking bouts from which none can refrain without appearing unmanly. In France, moreover, inebriety is viewed as an amusing condition, for which there are innumerable droll expressions, while in Italy it has an unfavorable connotation and is more often a family and personal disgrace (Sadoun et al., 1965).

Ullman (1958) points to much drinking and mild intoxication among Chinese-Americans and much drinking but little intoxication among Italian-Americans and Orthodox-Jewish Americans, but little alcoholism in any of these groups. This contrasts with much alcoholism but conflict over youth drinking among Irish-Americans and some Protestant groups. Ullman generalizes: "In any group or society in which the drinking customs, values, and sanctions—together with the attitudes of all segments of the group or society—are well established, known to and agreed upon by all, and are consistent with the rest of the culture, the rate of alcoholism will be low."

In the United States some drinking situations are relatively staid and formal—such as the cocktail hour preceding a business conference or an official banquet—during which some people consume much but all control their conduct, even when the alcohol in their bloodstream makes this difficult. In less-inhibited settings, however, as at "wild" parties, people are expected to abandon sober behavior once the drinking is well under way; so latecomers become as raucous as the rest even before imbibing much. There are many other variations in the sociocultural contexts of heavy drinking in the United States, and a few of these have distinct relationships to specific offenses.

Patterns in Drunkenness and Crime

For decades, according to FBI reports, the median age of arrest for drunkenness has been around 42, and for "driving under the influence" around 36 or 37. Age-specific urban arrest rates for drunkenness, calculated from 1970 census data and FBI statistics, were 3.8 times higher for those in their forties (2,775 per 100,000 persons) than for those 15 through 19 years of age (739 per 100,000); intermediate were people in their twenties (1,500 per 100,000) and those in their thirties (1,750 per 100,000) (Glaser, 1975: 174). It is estimated that around half the approximately 50,000 annual auto-accident deaths are due to driving under the influence.

A national survey found that problems from drinking reported by men between 21 and 60 are most concentrated among the 21-to-25-year-olds, become about half as frequent in age ranges above that, and diminish much further after 55 (Cahalan & Room, 1974: 50). The men cite family, job, accident, and police difficulties from alcohol. Apparently younger people, despite these problems, are less often liable to arrest for being publicly drunk than older alcoholics (such as those in skid-row areas, discussed later in this chapter). They probably also drive less after drinking than somewhat older people; or perhaps the older arrestees do not recognize such driving as their problem—it is just a problem to others on the road!

The comparative rates of alcoholism in different groups are commonly inferred from the distribution of cirrhosis of the liver, an ailment ascribed mainly to alcoholism. Among women, cirrhosis is most frequent in young singles and in older mothers. The latter have generally devoted themselves to the housewife role exclusively and find it of diminished importance when their children grow up.

Some generalizations will be made here on three patterns of drinking and crime. Each is somewhat age-linked, but we should stress that there are some of each type at every drinking age.

1. Autonomy-Expressive Drinking Throughout the United States it is illegal for persons under 18—and in many states for those under 21 —to purchase alcoholic beverages; but violation of these laws is far from rare. A national survey in 1975 found that 92 percent of male high-school seniors have had an alcoholic drink and 87 percent more than twice—an increase from the 1969 figures of 81 and 69 percent, respectively (Johnston, 1976). Some of this is legal, such as the family custom of beer or wine at meals; but as we noted in Chapter 8, adolescents value drinking on their own—like smoking and driving—as a means of expressing adulthood and autonomy, especially when alienated from school and family.

In the United States, as in France, Mexico, and many other countries, heavy drinking is often equated with manliness. Interestingly, in the regions of our country that had strong temperance movements and retained local prohibition or strong restrictions even after 1933—the formerly "dry" states of the Southeast, Southwest, Plains, and Mountains—drinking seems to be especially symbolic of youth's rebellion against their parents. This can be inferred from Cahalan and Room's national survey (1974), which found that these states had less drinking per capita but the highest proportions of young males who reported serious problems from drunken binges. Where drinking is most proscribed by the dominant population, Room (1975) suggests, the tipplers represent more of a counterculture than elsewhere; hence, their imbibing is more expressive and extreme. He cites a national sampling of breath alcohol in drivers, which more frequently found high levels of inebriation in the "dry" states. The Cahalan and Room survey also found exceptionally high percentages of problem drinkers among young urban males of Latin American and black ethnicity. This may be related to their concerns with expressing manhood, discussed in Chapter 9.

Although unmarried women alienated from their parents more often join men in heavy drinking and sometimes become involved in alcohol-related offenses, the vast majority of arrests for drunken assaults and for public drunkenness are of men. Most of them are young, but an adolescent-like assertion of masculinity is sometimes also an aspect of drinking by middle-aged or older men, especially when done in predominantly male settings. Bales (1942: 4) observes:

> In our culture there is a common belief that being able to drink a lot means virility, potency, and manhood. It is thus often possible to evade certain responsibilities of adult life by becoming irresponsible through intoxication, while at the same time "saving face" and preserving adult status because intoxication commonly signifies robust manhood. There is also the common idea that one proves he is a "good fellow," one of the group, by drinking. Intoxication may open the way to the expression of . . . anti-social tendencies (such as aggression, unpermissible sexuality, obstinacy, etc.) and at the same time protect the person from too much disapproval, since drinking provides the excuse for the behavior. Because drinking is socially approved in certain situations and thought of as "social drinking," the person who is actually an addict may take advantage of these situations to avoid becoming known and disapproved as a "solitary drinker." These ideas about alcohol provide protected channels, as it were, through which emotions and desire can be expressed, which if expressed in other ways would receive more social disapproval.

Among drinkers, norms dictate keeping pace with each other, taking turns buying new rounds for all whenever one or two glasses are empty, and staying with the group at least until one's turn to buy has come—all of which fosters heavier consumption than might otherwise occur (Cavan, 1966: 114–17; Room, 1975: 365). When drinking is done to prove manliness, there also is pressure to prove it in other ways, such as belligerency if affronted and fighting if sufficiently provoked. Except for forgery, drinking-related crime is most frequent in poor and uneducated groups. Yet the craving for drink within every age, status, and cultural group suggests a strong personality factor in alcoholism for both genders.

Psychologists refer to the "addiction-prone" personality of alcoholics and other chronic drug abusers as having high dependency on others. Indeed, many alcoholics seem to crave the social intimacy of the drinking group more than the drink itself, until they get to a very advanced alcoholism. Some psychoanalysts call the alcoholic's craving "oral dependency," a fixation at or regression to infantile reliance on the mother's breast for nourishment; but this view, made plausible by the alcoholic's desire to put liquids into his mouth, does not account for the choice of fluid. The alcoholic seems to have both a need to assert autonomy (independence from the family) and a fear of being without companionship, whether real or simulated.

From a long list of adjectives, eight were checked as self-descriptive by 70 percent or more of a large group of male alcoholics of various ages. All eight words denote primary-group qualities, welcomed in informal gatherings: affectionate, appreciative, cooperative, easygoing, forgiving, friendly, generous, and soft-hearted. Contrastingly, 27 words chosen by 70 percent or more of a nonalcoholic group to describe themselves, but passed over by the alcoholics, were all traits conducive to success in secondary or formal organizations, such as adaptable, ambitious, cautious, conscientious, considerate, dependable, independent, logical, loyal, peaceable, practical, responsible, sincere, steady, and tolerant. "Cooperative" and "friendly" were chosen as self-descriptions by 70 percent or more of both groups (Connor, 1962).

Some psychologists interpret all alcoholic traits, including preoccupation with masculinity, as expressing a need for personal power, since power themes on projective Thematic Apperception Tests (TATs) increase with the frequency of alcohol intake (McClelland et al., 1972). This implies that a repressed desire to dominate is disinhibited by drink; thus from this perspective, too, drinking is autonomy-expressive. Of course, any place where people drink together provides a stage on which to strut before an audience, and thus to feel the manipulative power of "having the floor." Whether through disinhibition or social setting, however, drinking supplies only a temporary sense of dominance, and so creates a need for more drinking.

Adult alcoholics, in their apparently desperate need for intimate social relations or for dominance, resemble insecure adolescents

struggling for satisfactory roles and status. Indeed, in sprees and escapades of heavy drinking, many older problem drinkers express quan-
daries of identity and role ambiguity, cry in self-pity, and rage against
family or authorities, much like the adolescent offenders described in
Chapter 8. Thus older-age drunkenness can be called a recapitulation
of adolescene. It is usually more continuous than the binge drinking of
youth, however, and it is differently related to crime.

2. The Skid-Row Alcoholic On the edges of central business districts
in American cities, generally near bus or railroad stations, there have
for decades been areas known as "skid row," where homeless men
congregate. Many older and some younger alcoholics reside there,
along with nonalcoholic pensioners. A few female habitués, most of
them alleged to be prostitutes or former prostitutes, share the scene.
Several studies of such neighborhoods in the last two decades have
successively provided a somewhat new and different perspective
(Pittman & Gordon, 1958; Bogue, 1963; Wallace, 1965; Spradley,
1970; Wiseman, 1970; Blumberg et al., 1973; Bahr & Caplow, 1973).

Originally skid rows were centers of employment agencies for
day laborers, especially railroad track crews, farmworkers, and lumber-
jacks. Usually these areas are identifiable by their low-rent rooming
houses and hotels ("flop houses"), cheap bars, pawn shops, and missions offering religious services along with food and temporary shelter.
Except in the worst weather, there is frequent "hanging out" on the
street by transients, beggars, and drunks (not necessarily mutually exclusive categories). As Rooney (1970: 18) summarizes: ". . . skid row
came to serve a number of major functions for single men separated
from the institutions of the stable, family-oriented community; it was
an employment center for migratory workers, a place of 'hibernation'
during the winter, a locale for recreation at any season, a supply and
outfitting center, a year-round residence for casual workers, and a re-
fuge for drop-outs from the working class." Also common in these
areas of large cities in recent years are offices that purchase blood
donations, an important source of income for residents (and often of
hepatitis or other illness for the blood recipients). Statistically analyzing skid-row men, Muedeking and Bahr (1976) find four distinct types:
(1) the transient, who stays there only between jobs or when on binges;
(2) the unattached poor man, usually a failure at marriage and unattached to kin; (3) the excessive drinker (often called the "police-case
inebriate" or the "wino") who imbibes heavily every day by whatever
means he can manage; (4) the welfare client, often not alcoholic but old
or in poor health.

Skid row was traditionally the target area for public-drunkenness arrests, and still is in some cities. At times, however, many on skid
row desire shelter and food at the police stations; law enforcement is

then dubbed "Golden Rule arrest," particularly during winters in the North when the men might otherwise freeze to death, or when they have passed out from drink in a location where they could be run over.

As decriminalization of public drunkenness grows, jailing is replaced by detoxification at public hospitals or in special centers for alcoholics, many operated with state aid by the same organizations that provide missions (notably the Salvation Army and Volunteers of America). People found publicly drunk but cooperative are transported to these centers by the police, and there receive showers, medical attention, temporary housing, food, and access to social-welfare and counseling services. The length of stay is usually limited to a week, but an effort is made to provide shelter and work for them before they leave. Many employees of the centers are rehabilitated former clients. This detoxification procedure costs less and is more efficient in reducing subsequent public drunkenness than the traditional cycle of arrest, adjudication, brief jailing, and rearrest (cf., LEAA, 1970).

Crimes other than public drunkenness also are common in skid row. Men with recently cashed welfare checks or any valuables (even a good pair of shoes), as well as the shops, are continually victimized by alcoholics seeking small sums for drink. Those who weaken or pass out from inebriation—especially at night or in sidestreets, alleys, or doorways—risk strongarm robbery not only from other alcoholics, but also from aggressive delinquents who "roll" drunks for quick and easy sums, however small. Skid row has an appreciable number of murders; and a smaller-than-usual percentage are solved by the police, for both the victims and the offenders are likely to be transients. There is also cheap prostitution and dealing in stolen goods.

Urban renewal razes many skid-row buildings, but in most cases the displaced people move close by. With growth of welfare services and less need for unskilled day labor, skid rows have become smaller, and some predict their disappearance with the demise of current residents, whose death rate is high (Siegal et al., 1975). Yet a major motivation for the unending drift to these areas appears to be the camaraderie of the "bottle gangs" (Rubington, 1968) and the ready conversation of "street people" with strangers (Wiseman, 1970: 38–41). Since many people sever social bonds, for whatever reason, it is probable that as old skid rows decline, analogous "escape" areas will take their place; indeed, there is already evidence of new neighborhoods for transients resembling old skid rows in ambience, if not in structure and locale (e.g., much of Venice and Manhattan Beach in Los Angeles, and of the East Village in New York).

3. The Drinking and Naive-Forgery Syndrome A standard type in city jails and state prisons are alcoholic forgers who used the checking or credit accounts of friends, kin, or others for relatively small sums simply to keep drinking. Older than most inmates (though some are young), they are generally also better educated and of middle-class background, with intermittent white-collar employment, particularly in sales. They are skilled at "talking their way out" of punishment—most easily if they make restitution—but they run short of funds at their next drinking spree and repeat the crime. Friends or relatives often make restitution for them and decline to press charges when victimized, but eventually they are "taken once too often." Jail or probation is imposed several times for these forgeries (rarely do they commit other types of offense), but repetition ultimately sends them to the penitentiary.

These are typical of what Lemert (1953) calls "naive forgers," and he illustrates the chain of events that culminates in their crime:

> A man . . . falls in with a small group of persons who have embarked upon a two- or three-day or even a week's period of drinking and carousing. The impetus to continue . . . gets mutually reinforced. . . . If . . . a participant runs out of money, the pressures immediately become critical to take such measures as are necessary to preserve the behavior sequence. (1953: 303)

As Lemert points out, the forgers are "naive" in their drifting with the flow of events into such shortsighted behavior, with little thought of consequences. This is in contrast to the more prudent pursuit of the professional, or "systematic," forgers described in Chapter 13 (Lemert, 1958). The tension caused by the naive offender's shortage of funds, Lemert suggests, is "closed" by the forgery, although this behavioral response is "more frequently impulsive and unverbalized than deliberative. . . ." (1953: 304)

The compulsiveness of this offense pattern is indicated by its high rate of recidivism, which reflects the chronic nature of alcoholism. Furthermore, in Nebraska, when the legislature made the penalties much severer on forged checks over $35 than for those under that amount, the ratio of forged checks below this figure to those above it did not change (Beutel, 1957). Apparently the penalties were irrelevant to the forgers. The fact that in procuring funds, reinforcement is immediate while the penalty is remote and uncertain doubtless has much to do with the persistence of this behavior syndrome.

Typically the primary-group traits of alcoholics make them facile at ingratiating themselves with those who can cash checks or honor credit cards, and it has been said that they can often employ a glib "line" to get unwarranted funds or credit when more "respectable" persons who are perfectly trustworthy cannot. Forgery is a growing crime among women, but in their case less clearly linked to alcoholism. These offenses are a lesser problem in some other countries because cashing checks and using credit cards are much more difficult; vulnerability to forgery is a price our merchants are willing to pay to get sales. Some even contend that we should let the check casher or credit card honorer beware, and reduce the maximum penalties for small-scale forgeries, making them misdemeanors rather than penitentiary offenses if the amount involved is under $1,000.

Termination of an alcoholic-forgery syndrome appears to require a "cure" for alcoholism, and as we will discuss shortly, this is a highly uncertain occurrence. Nebraska State Penitentiary inmates have established a Checkwriters Anonymous organization modeled on Alcoholics Anonymous, but its effectiveness is not yet clearly established.

Controlling Crime by Treating Alcoholism

Chronic alcoholism has always been difficult to terminate, especially by coerced treatment. Indeed, a free and sincere decision to cease heavy drinking or to abstain from alcohol completely is a necessary first step, and in some cases it appears to be all that is required. This kind of motivation, however, does not come until, as former alcoholics say, they "hit bottom." "Bottom," however, is not the same for all alcoholics. Some quit at the first trauma, when seeing their job or marriage in jeopardy; others do not stop until long after they have lost all jobs and status they may have had, are rejected by all kin, dwell homeless and mendicant on skid row, are repeatedly incarcerated, and suffer declining health, blackouts, and delirium tremens. Many never quit, and they die of cirrhosis of the liver or other alcohol-linked diseases.

A model for curing addictions that has since been copied by persons suffering from many other types of personal problems—to let those with the problem help each other—was begun in 1935 as Alcoholics Anonymous. Its principles include regular meetings of small groups of alcoholics wishing to stay sober, recognition and averment that they are alcoholics, confession of all wrongs they have done others, endeavor to make restitution for these wrongs, faith in a Higher Power, and constant availability to assist other alcoholics. They address each other only by first names and rather ritualistically exchange warm personal greetings when they meet. Although each AA unit is autonomous and has no paid officers, participants contribute to the support of offices in major world cities, which, among other functions, issue pocket-size directories of AA meeting places and schedules in their area, so that many of the more than half-million AA members frequently visit other chapters.

Robert Freed Bales, whose international leadership in small-group research and clinical social psychology evolved from his early study of AA, developed what is still a highly persuasive interpretation of its successful "cure" of alcoholism. Consistent with theories presented earlier in this chapter, he infers that the alcoholic male typically had a prolonged, emotionally intense interaction with a mother figure, combined in early childhood with domination by another person such as his father, or that the relationship to his mother alternated between dominance and subordination. Bales adds:

> We would expect the conflict . . . which took place between an over-dominant, over-protective mother and her child to become habitual in the personality of the child. . . . he . . . would tend to be over-dominant and over-protective towards her when possible and towards other suitable persons when she was away. . . .

> Once the alcoholic addiction becomes the specific means of adjustment to this conflict in interpersonal relations, we would expect it to remain a tenacious reaction so long as the type of situation remained the same. It seems to be true that pleading, preaching, reproaching, protecting, shaming and all the other techniques commonly resorted to by the family have no lasting effect in reforming the confirmed addict. . . .

> It is exactly here that the framework provided by an AA group becomes significant. The alcoholic integrated in such a group is enabled to behave in a morally ascendant, protective, mothering way toward another who in turn behaves as he once did. He is at the focal point of obligations he himself has initiated. . . . The dependency pattern is not eliminated, but his own behavior is no longer overtly the dependent one (1942: 12–13).

Two AA beliefs—(1) that only a person who has suffered from an addiction can understand and gain rapport with someone undergoing the same experience, and (2) that mental health for oneself is gained by helping others—have acquired many applications in efforts to alter conduct and change moods or attitudes. There are Narcotics Anonymous, Gamblers Anonymous, and analogous organizations often so "anonymous" that their names do not reveal their goals, such as Synanon or Daytop Village (both for drug addicts). These somewhat formal groups such as AA, especially attract those whose educational and class background makes them accustomed to highly deliberate verbalization; they are eschewed by many less-articulate persons and by those uncomfortable in gatherings with strangers. As Wiseman says:

> AA has never had much appeal for the lower-class alcholic. It is primarily a middle-class organization, focused on helping ex-alcoholics regain their lost status. Skid Row alcoholics dislike what they refer to as "drunkalogs," in which members tell with relish just how low they had sunk while drinking. They dislike what they call the

"snottiness" and "holier-than-thou" attitude of the reformed alcoholic (or "AA virgins" as they call them). The only reason Skid Row men go to AA is to convince another person (someone who would be impressed by such attendance) that they are really trying to lick the alcohol problem. . . .

Other Skid Row men tell of going to AA meetings out of desperation for *any* companionship and for the refreshments served. After the meeting, they feel a strong urge to drink so that life becomes a round of early evening AA sessions followed by late evening drinking, and morning hangovers (1970: 233).

As Trice (1957a, 1957b) found, AA affiliation is most likely to continue after initial contacts, if the problem drinker (1) is from a subcultural group that recognizes heavy drinking as a problem and is aware of its symptoms; (2) develops bonds with the small casual groups that form spontaneously before and after the formal meetings; (3) does not have spouse or close friends who compete with the AA experience; (4) has friends or kin who refuse aid. Class subcultural differences in conception of persistent heavy drinking as a disease may tend not only to make AA a predominantly middle-class organization, but also to explain why death rates from cirrhosis of the liver, generally considered an index of severe alcoholism, are higher among the very poor than among the more affluent.

A frequent complication in helping alcoholics to help themselves is that their spouses and children have learned not to trust or depend on them. A woman with an alcoholic husband learns to be both mother and father to their offspring; the child learns that no matter how affectionate the father is and how sincere his promises seem, he is not likely to be a dependable parent. Accordingly, an alcoholic who has begun to recover often cannot gain acceptance as a responsible member within the family, and this situation fosters relapse into alcoholism. Indeed, some persons seek to retain a sense of moral superiority over their alcoholic spouse and resist his or her effort to become less dependent on them. AA has organized auxiliary groups of spouses (Al Anon) and of teenage children of alcoholics (Al Teen) to prepare the family for normal relationships. Their association in these groups with kin of other alcoholics fosters mutual aid among them and reduces the stigma of having an alcoholic in the family. This aid is especially needed if the AA member relapses, a turn of events always probable with those once addicted to any substance; the longer the period of abstinence, however, the smaller the likelihood of relapse.

Many prisons and some jails encourage formation of AA units by their inmates, and facilitate frequent visits by AA volunteers from the community. In large penitentiaries the AA membership usually includes prisoners of middle-class background, and some of lower-class origin who have raised their educational level while incarcerated. Most inmates want contact with outsiders, and therefore some join AA who were not really alcoholics. Friendships between AA members in and out of prison often result, and sometimes produce a welcome and tangible assistance in the community for releasees.

An early claim of AA was that about half their voluntary participants cease drinking immediately and another quarter do so eventually (Bales, 1942). They lack very precise figures on such effectiveness, however, for they oppose periodic followup research on their members, since this would violate anonymity. Yet they have assisted in some anonymous surveys of their membership at a single time; one study sampled all American and Canadian units, one sampled only New York City, and one London. From 37 to 52 percent of these different groups said that they had been sober less than a year, 25 to 35 percent one to five years, and the rest for longer periods. One can infer from these data that perhaps half of those who remain in AA never relapse, but that most achieve enduring abstinence within five years (and many within one or two) (Leach, 1976); one cannot know dropout rates. AA members contend that they are always alcoholics, even if currently sober, living each day with hope but without absolute certainty that they will not relapse.

In a San Diego experiment, a judge sentenced all public-drunkenness offenders to a $25 fine and 30 days in jail, but suspended the jail term conditional on their remaining sober and law abiding for six months, with additional requirments randomly assigned, as follows: (1) participate in treatment in an alcoholism clinic; (2) attend five meetings of AA within 30 days; (3) no additional requirements (Ditman et al., 1967). The results, summarized in Table 10.2, clearly indicate no benefit and even suggest harm in both the clinics and AA, although the better outcome without any treatment was not statistically significant. The fact that participation was coerced may have contributed to the failure of this experiment, but it should be noted that much presumably voluntary attendance at AA or other programs actually is done only to please a spouse, parent, or others, on whom they often depend for material aid, or to impress favorably a probation officer who might otherwise incarcerate them for violating conditional-release rules by becoming drunk.

There are, of course, many modes of treating alcoholism. Typical of advertised commercial cures, but also used in highly respected and unadvertised medical programs, is aversive conditioning. The patients are given disulfiram (Antabuse) or citrated calcium carbimide (Temposil), and when such drugs are taken for some time, imbibing alcoholic beverages is followed by severe headaches and sometimes by nausea or other unpleasant feelings. In some aversion therapy the patient is simply given a nausea-producing drug simultaneously with an

TABLE 10-2   Percentage Results of San Diego Experiment with Randomly Assigned Alternative Conditions for Suspension of Sentence in Public-Drunkenness Offenses*

ALTERNATIVE TREATMENTS	6-MONTH FOLLOWUP RESULTS			
	No Rearrests	Rearrested within one month	Rearrested after first month	No. of cases (100%)
Alcoholism clinic	32%	21%	47%	82
Alcoholics Anonymous	31	22	47	86
No treatment	44	22	34	73

* Based on Ditman et al., 1967. The 241 cases omit 60 for whom both state and local arrest records for the followup period could not be obtained.

alcoholic beverage, in hopes that this will produce a mental association of drinking with vomiting. Individual and group psychotherapy programs are quite diverse, except in trying to persuade clients to think of themselves as alcoholics and as capable of conquering their ailment. AA and psychiatric alcoholic-treatment proponents were once highly critical of each other, but now have more rapport; many psychotherapists encourage clients to join AA, and some AA members see mental-health specialists for marital, parental, or other problems apart from the craving for alcohol.

The effectiveness of treatment services is probably most influenced by its selection of clients. From evaluation of alcoholism clinics, Gerard and Saenger (1966) concluded that the more integrated the roles of the clients with conventional society on entering treatment (i.e., the more conventional their employment and marital status), the more likely they are to persist in treatment; and the longer they remain in treatment, the more persistent their sobriety, regardless of the type of treatment. A Rand Corporation study (Armor et al., 1976) found severity of alcoholism symptoms and instability in marriage, job, and residence most predictive of treatment failure.

One tenet of AA and of many treatment specialists is that alcoholics differ biologically and psychologically from other persons because they cannot drink in moderation, that once an alcoholic begins to drink there is no letup. The Rand study, by concluding that alcoholics who drink moderately while in treatment stay sober at about the same rate as those who avoid all alcoholic beverages, evoked furious protests from those who advocate total abstinence (*Los Angeles Times,* June 10 and 12, August 8 and 19, 1976). Yet it also cites research findings at California's Patton State Hospital that 90 to 95 percent of alcoholic patients who drank moderately after their release were functioning well in society two years later, and in the controversy it aroused, there were many announcements of similar observations (*Los Angeles Times,* August 9 and 19, 1976). The Rand researchers speculate that perhaps only certain types of alcoholics can drink moderately, but they note that no one knows how to distinguish these types.

The Rand investigators find that about half the untreated and 70 percent of clinic-treated alcoholics reduce their rate of disabling heavy drinking, with progress contingent on the amount of treatment received. Improvement is about the same with various treatment alternatives, including Antabuse, hospitalization, and outpatient care; they believe it is about the same rate as is attained by AA. Emrick (1975) also finds no difference in outcome by type of treatment in 384 studies. When AA was combined with other programs that the Rand group studied, the success rate with low amounts of other treatment was considerably higher if AA attendance was regular; with high amounts of other treatment there was about the same high success rate with either regular or no AA attendance, but less success with irregular AA attendance.

It appears that every approach to alleviating alcoholism works successfully with some people, and thus generates devout adherents, but does not attract and may not succeed with other alcoholics. There will always be some problem drinkers not reached by any program, a large proportion who will moderate or end their drinking without treatment, and a few who will imbibe heavily until it causes their demise. There is reason to believe, however, that alcoholism was even more extensive 75 to 100 years ago; it should continue to diminish as adaptive upgrading, in raising the general educational level, spreads the idea that addictive drinking is a personal problem that can be alleviated rather than a weakness of character that should not be admitted.

Leading scholars conclude that the disruptive effects of drinking in the United States will diminish if: (1) children are exposed to alcohol in its diluted forms early in life, and they see it used moderately by their parents, primarily to accompany food; (2) no moral importance is attached to drinking—it is neither a virtue nor a sin—and it is not viewed as a sign of masculinity, stylishness, or wit; (3) abstinence is socially acceptable, so that it is no more rude or ungracious to decline a drink than to decline a piece of bread; (4) excessive drinking or drunkenness is not viewed as socially desirable (NIMH, 1967: 28). Yet from the generalization of values as society evolves (discussed in Chapter 2), drunkenness is less often deemed immoral, whether or not considered desirable, as long as the inebriates do not injure others. These trends could reduce the need for drinking to express rebellion against prohibitions, and thus diminish alcohol-related crimes of violence as well as drunken driving. Yet graver issues remain with other types of substance abuse that foster a staggering amount of predatory crime.

OPIATES

A beautiful poppy, its white blossoms four or five inches in diameter, has been cultivated in the Middle East and India since ancient times for the pain-killing and calming effects of the resin from its egg-sized, immature seed pods. When cut, the pods exude a white liquid that solidifies and browns, then is scraped off and sold as lumps, cakes, or bricks of raw opium. It has been grown in many parts of the world, but during the 1970s most of the illegal supply for the United States came from Mexico.

Raw opium was once eaten; after the spread of tobacco it was also smoked, but increasingly in modern times it has been consumed in chemically refined derivatives called "opiates." The first of these was laudanum, created by the sixteenth-century Swiss physician Paracelsus, who dissolved opium in alcohol. Often sherry wine was used as the solvent and a variety of other substances were added, from pearls to cinnamon. Coleridge, Poe, and Elizabeth Barrett Browning were among the prominent persons who took it regularly. In the nineteenth and early twentieth centuries American general stores sold laudanum as a folk remedy for rheumatic aches of old age, menstrual pain, toothache, diarrhea, and to quiet crying babies.

Morphine, the active chemical in these effects of opium, was isolated in 1806 and became the most widely used pain-killing drug in medical practice after the development of the hypodermic needle in 1856, which permitted its direct injection into the bloodstream. Both armies in our Civil War distributed needles and drugs for relief of their wounded, many of whom self-administered the morphine and became addicted. Usage spread after the war, when opiate addiction came to be known as "the soldier's disease" (Morgan, 1974).

In 1898 the same employee of the Bayer Company in Germany who coined the term "aspirin" gave the name "heroin" to a new morphine derivative hailed as a pain killer; it worked more quickly and with fewer side effects than morphine, and was erroneously thought to be less addictive, as it was taken orally and in very small doses (Judson, 1974: 4; Kramer, 1976: 405). Heroin is one of many opium derivatives—including codeine and paregoric—still used as medicine in most of the world. There also are synthetic opiates, such as methadone.

A feature of all opiates is that the human body develops a *tolerance* for a regular dosage, thus a greater amount is eventually needed to get the customary effect, and a long-term regular user may take a dose that would kill a novice. With tolerance the body is adjusted to a given concentration so that the person feels normal with it and sick without it. The individual is then said to be *physiologically dependent* on opiates, which is sometimes called "true addiction," or in popular parlance, being "hooked" or "strung out." When this condition develops, sudden cessation of opiate use causes *withdrawal effects,* also called *abstinence syndrome,* often likened to symptoms of a severe flu—running nose, chills, stomach cramps, nausea, trembling. These effects vanish quickly when opiates are taken again. Most opium derivatives and synthetics have "cross tolerance," meaning that any of them can prevent or alleviate an abstinence syndrome from any other.

It is perhaps a Puritan heritage that makes many Americans object on moral grounds to the desperation of addicts for more drugs (Duster, 1970). It was once common to assert or imply that opiates create "dope fiends," that they chemically cause users to develop "mad cravings" for drugs and to commit any crime to get them. In a pioneer empirical study with the approach to social psychology that his mentor Herbert Blumer later called "symbolic interactionism," Lindesmith (1937, 1938) rejected chemical explanations for addiction. He showed that patients receiving morphine do not develop cravings for more of it until they verbally interpret their withdrawal symptoms as caused by cessation of opiate use and learn that their discomfort can be terminated by again taking these drugs. Therefore, Lindesmith asserted, ". . . when the person is cut off from communication with his fellows he is immune to addiction" (1937: 213). Evidence cited to support this theory included the fact that patients who receive morphine but do not know that they are getting it do not become addicted. Indeed, physicians often make prescriptions incomprehensible to lay persons to reduce the risk of having the medication's effects foster drug abuse.

Initially, consistent with the symbolic-interactionist approach, Lindesmith contended that nonhuman animals could not become addicted to opiates "because it presupposes the higher cortical functions associated with language behavior and found only in man" (1968: 125, summarizing his earlier views). Wikler (1965, 1968) reported research in which (1) rats are offered an opiate solution but prefer water; (2) the rats are injected with opiates, allowed to suffer withdrawal symptoms while deprived of fluids, and then given the opiate solution. These rats thereafter always drink the opiate solution avidly; they seem to be addicted. Wikler's explanation for addiction in all animals, including man, is therefore one of classical conditioning by getting relief of distress with these drugs, supplemented in humans by operant conditioning from pleasant social circumstances in drug-taking. Lindesmith (1968: 127) grants that this research contradicts his earlier assertion that animals cannot be addicted, accepts Wikler's conditioning theory, but notes that there are still unique features in human addiction due to linguistic interpretations of drug effects.

Both Wikler (1965: 87) and Lindesmith (1968: 176–80) reject the idea, advanced especially by Ausubel (1958), that addict craving for opiates comes mainly from getting definite pleasure—euphoria—from them. They cite the fact that when people were given a variety of

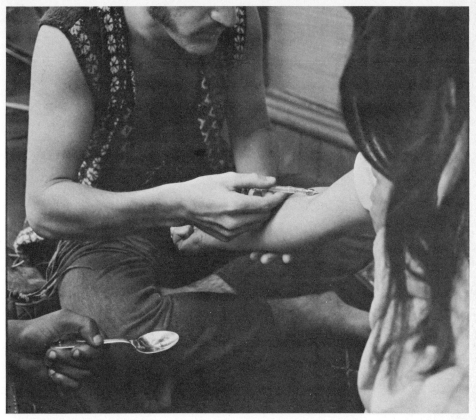

Insulting the body's chemistry.

unlabeled drugs and placebos, in random sequences, most subjects reported unpleasant sensations after opiates (Lasagna et al., 1955). McAuliffe (1975) points out, however, that in this and similar studies many subjects also described some pleasant experiences from opiates, usually mixed with the unpleasant, and that interviewed addicts also mention simultaneous exhilaration and nausea. It should be stressed that mood changes with drugs reflect not only sensations that the drugs cause, but also how humans learn to interpret these effects for themselves and others (Becker, 1973).

In an earlier article, McAuliffe and Gordon (1974) report that "street addicts" exhibit two patterns in frequency of euphoric sensations ("highs") from opiates: "hardcores" claim they get "highs" regularly, with or without some sickness, take a large dosage, and rely mainly on crime to pay for the drugs; "weekenders," most of whom hold jobs, use only enough opiates daily to relieve sickness but report having "highs" when they take larger doses on weekends or at other times. McAuliffe (1975) also points out the widespread evidence for the psychological principle that humans and animals tend to maintain for remarkably long periods, despite discomfort, any activities that receive intermittent reinforcement (consistent with the discussion in Chapter 5 of the relationship of intermittent reward to persistence in gambling by betting or by crime).

Whether or not they are physiologically dependent on opiates, regular users often acquire psychological habituation to their rituals of injection, beliefs from the drug subculture that their bodies need heroin, and a high valuation of their roles and statuses in drug-taking groups. Therefore, users of small dosages or of very dilute and adulterated street heroin, who are not getting enough actual opiate to have a clearly physiological withdrawal, nevertheless "climb the walls" in desperation and misery when they cannot get drugs. Some narcotics users, inspired by the social support of former addicts to "kick the habit" voluntarily and suddenly (to "go cold turkey"), instead of detoxifying gradually, do so without clear withdrawal symptoms. Although the groups of former addicts see this as a conquest of mind over body, these alleged addicts may not have had much opiate in their systems when they quit, since the objective features of abstinence syndrome, such as tremors and nausea, are universal in medical patients and even in laboratory animals given a regular and large dosage of these drugs and then denied them.

The foregoing impressions may be distorted because almost all studies of opiate use have been only of addicts or regular users. Yet many more people try opiates than use them continually or become addicted. In 1974 to 1975, six percent of a representative sample of American men 21 to 31 years old said they had used heroin, but only two percent reported taking it in the past year, and half of those who ever used it did so fewer than ten times (O'Donnell et al., 1976). A survey of American veterans of the Vietnam War eight to 12 months after their return to the United States found that 34 percent took opiates in Vietnam and 20 percent became addicted there, but only one percent reported resumption of opiate use in the United States (Robins, 1974). The persistence of their cravings—whether physiological, psychological, or sociocultural in origin—and the laws that try to control addicts determine the involvement of opiate users in crime.

The Opiate-Prohibition Movement and its Consequences

In 1909 the United States banned importation of raw opium, allegedly from prejudice against the Chinese immigrants who smoked it and in fear that this custom would spread. Yet opiates, the chemicals derived from opium, were imported and sold without prescription as home remedies, were in many patent medicines, and were recommended by virtually all physicians for a variety of ailments. There was, however, public awareness that large doses could impair work performance (as do many substances, from alcohol to tranquilizers) and that users could become addicted. Several states tried to restrict the distribution of these drugs, but had little success because they could be brought in from adjacent states. Meanwhile, a series of treaties were negotiated to regulate their international flow (Brecher, 1972: Chapters 1 and 6; Musto, 1973: Chapters 1, 2, and 5).

The Harrison Act of 1914 levied a federal tax of one cent per ounce on each sale of opiates. It was not designed for revenue, but to fulfill our obligations at a 1912 Hague Convention on international narcotics control, by requiring recordkeeping on all distribution of these drugs. Similar legislation was enacted in Britain and many other countries. The bill, a compromise between medical, pharmacist, and drug-manufacturing interests, specifically exempted commercial preparations with small percentages of opiates. It was not vigorously enforced until the wave of puritanical righteousness that enacted the Prohibition Amendment swept on in the 1920s against other deviations from the dominant lifestyles. During this period the laws against alcohol and opiates were both enforced by the Prohibition Bureau of the Treasury Department.

For forty years the nation's leader of drug-law enforcement was Harry J. Anslinger. Employed in the 1920s by the State Department to combat smuggling of alcoholic beverages into the United States, he became in 1929 the Treasury Department's Assistant Commissioner of Prohibition and, in 1930, the first head of its new Bureau of Narcotics. He remained there until retirement in 1962, selected his deputy as successor, and was America's representative in international narcotics control until 1970, while still influential at home. Anslinger was tremendously effective as a moral entrepreneur (see Chapter 2), in mobilizing bias against narcotics users in the United States and abroad, and as an enforcement bureaucrat in expanding the power of his agency and the drug-prohibition movement. His reflexive reaction to the spread of addiction, like that of most law-enforcement officials and prohibitionists, was almost always to demand severer penalties and more policing. In this process the Bureau of Narcotics repeatedly exaggerated the harmful effects of the substances it sought to control and impeded dissemination of opposing views (Lindesmith, 1965: 243–65; Dickson, 1968; Schaller, 1970: Musto, 1973: 210–12; Bruun et al., 1975: 124–26, 140–43, 234).

The Harrison Act authorized medical use of opiates, making no reference to addiction, and Supreme Court decisions as late as the 1926 Linder case let physicians determine when to prescribe these drugs. Nevertheless, federal enforcement officials in subsequent decades persistently gave most doctors the impression that they risked imprisonment and loss of license if they gave opiates to addicts to prevent withdrawal effects (Lindesmith, 1959, 1965: Chapter 1; Dickson, 1968: 150–51; Musto, 1973: Chapters 3, 6–8). Physicians continued to administer morphine to nonaddicts in acute pain (e.g., from cancer, burns, or fractures), but not to those cured of such ailments who thereby became addicted. A 1924 law banned the importation of heroin to the United States because it is the preferred drug of addicts, although it is used medically in other countries since it relieves pain more quickly than morphine.

Until World War II, American addicts were predominantly middle-aged and elderly morphine users, included more females than males, were more in the rural South than the urban North, and began their drug use for medical purposes (Pescor, 1943). Many people in medically related occupations—particularly physicians, nurses, and pharmacists—became addicted from taking opiates on their own to relieve pains. Most addicts obtained drugs by diverting morphine or other opiates from medical inventories with forged prescriptions, purchasing from pharmacists who juggled stock records, using then-uncontrolled codeine and paregoric medicines, or stealing from hospitals, physicians' offices, and drug stores. Yet doctors in the rural South who prescribed morphine for older addicts were not prosecuted for it (O'Donnell, 1969), and the law was rarely enforced anywhere against addicted physicians and upper-class addicts (Lindesmith, 1965: 90). In Europe, however, heroin was used in regular medical practice as well as by addicts. European pharmaceutical firms reportedly sold surplus stocks to smugglers in bulk (Bruun et al., 1975: 223ff.); so heroin was especially available around port cities in the United States.

During World War II our armed forces preempted medical supplies, and opiate stocks were also curtailed by German and Japanese attacks on shipping. The price that addicts had to pay for these drugs soared, as did the growing of opium poppies in the United States. This led to a 1942 law prohibiting such horticulture, which after the war expanded in other parts of the world. The smuggling of heroin, made in Europe from Turkish and Iranian opium, was especially profitable in the postwar years, and became a major enterprise of organized crime (see Chapter 13).

When the source of opiates for addicts shifted from medical supplies in the United States to smuggling by organized crime, the recruits to addiction also changed. By the early 1960s, Ball (1965) reported that the new addicts were mostly young male heroin users from minority ethnic groups in Northern urban slums, especially those of New York, far outnumbering and quite different from older morphine users. Also, although earlier addicts who acquired criminal records did so only after addiction, the new ones generally had a history of delinquency and crime before use of opiates (Finestone, 1957a;

O'Donnell, 1966). The concentration of both drug distribution and the new addicts in the minority-group urban ghettos suggests that when organized criminals smuggling heroin sought to expand their market, they did this close to their base by touting opiate use to youth who were already law violators. As Chapter 8 shows, such recruits were generally unemployed school failures, thus receptive to new ways of feeling independent and eminent. Indeed, there is evidence that the young addicts were more intelligent and ambitious than most nonaddicted youthful offenders of their ethnic and neighborhood background (Glaser et al., 1971).

Because our opiate-prohibition laws ultimately increased the number of customers for illegal narcotics so immensely, narcotics diverted from medical supplies did not begin to suffice. Smuggled heroin, however, is expensive. Although an addict's daily requirement could cost a dollar or less if legal, it is illegally sold for $25 to $100. Few addicts can get this income legitimately. For slum residents, especially youth, to have a drug habit is to have a "hustle"—any method of getting money in a hurry. Hustles include shoplifting, stealing from autos, prostitution, pandering confidence games, drug peddling, burglary, robbery, or combinations of these.

Opiates induce drowsiness—a half-wakeful nodding after an initial arousal or "rush" following injection—but the "nod" period reduces the time left for hustling. When wakeful, addicts must work frantically to get funds for the next drug purchase. As Lewis (1970) points out, hustling requires ingenuity, industry, and organizing skill, not only to steal goods but also to dispose of them; sales are usually made at about a fifth of retail value (Preble & Casey, 1969). This drug world, mislabeled "escapist" and "retreatist," is actually a busy and demanding way of life more aptly called "ripping and running" (Agar, 1973). It gives youth a chance to feel pride in their competence at hustling and as connoisseurs of drugs in a social world where these abilities are highly valued (Sutter, 1966; Finestone, 1967b; Abrams et al., 1968; Preble & Casey, 1969; Gould et al., 1974:Chapter 2; Smith & Stephens, 1976). In their desperation for opiates, they often neglect food, shelter, and health, with the least successful hustlers eventually ending up dirty, ill, and crowded into basements or abandoned buildings. In this condition they apply for welfare benefits and even seek treatment, but often more for respite than for cure.

Interview evidence suggests that about half the addicts sometimes engage in drug selling (McGlothlin, 1976: 65) and that nearly all drug dealers use or have used illicit drugs themselves (Blum, 1972a: 16–30). Selling (at the retail level) generally does not begin for profit, but for convenience; when drug users have funds for more of a substance than they need and can get a good buy on a larger quantity, they take it, then share with friends at cost, on credit, or as a favor. Expertise as a supplier confers prestige, nurturing pride in profits and in business acumen. People usually start opiate use with the sharing of drugs among friends, and make purchases later, often to reciprocate. If new to heroin, they urge it on the uninitiated by lauding it, but later their drug transactions are only with others already in the drug world (Hunt & Chambers, 1976). Blum concludes: "Most dealers have played a role in introducing novices to use, but only rarely can one speak of the seduction of the innocent" (1972: 57). On sellers of all types of abused drugs, he conjectures: "the dealer who initiates most believes he is doing a good thing for his clients. . . . We suspect he is like the driven missionary who must have converts lest he himself lose faith" (1972: 152).

Law enforcement could not stem the spread of the drug subculture. During the late 1960s and 1970s, whites were a growing proportion of narcotics arrestees and of admittees to treatment for addiction. Also, females were apparently becoming a larger percentage of addicts; after declining from a majority of patients in the 1930s to less than 10 percent in the 1950s, they were 20 to 25 percent in samplings during the 1970s (Sells, 1976).

Intensive interviews with Los Angeles-area addicts in federal custody or community supervision reveal that the post–World War II addict lifestyle of the black ghettos was now only one of five, from distinctly different segments of the American population (Lewis & Glaser, 1974):

1. "Expressive students," epitomized by so-called hippies or counterculture members, are a predominantly white group seeking new experiences from drugs, exotic religions, popular psychologies, vegetarianism, and other experiments (most are college dropouts or nonentrants).

2. "Low riders" are predominantly white, working-class members of motorcycle gangs stressing toughness, defiance of authority, violence, drinking, drug use, and sometimes conspicuous dirtiness—never bathing or washing their riding clothes.

3. "Barrio addicts" come from extremely impoverished rural Mexican and Mexican-American communities. Many of them regularly smuggle heroin over the border for pay and to get drugs for themselves from dealers, but have no further involvement in narcotics distribution within the United States. They inject heroin at social gatherings, usually only "chipping" small amounts at parties rather than using it routinely, yet periodically they take too much when celebrating, or when under stress or in pain, and continue to take more to relieve or prevent withdrawal symptoms.

4. "Ghetto hustlers," predominantly from the black community, are members of the slum "street culture" of drug use and hustling (described earlier), which developed soon after World War II and continues in the 1970s.

5. "Social-world alternators" are persons from middle- or upper-class background who drift into heroin-using subcultures, but after difficulties return to "straight society" and try to resume their former social roles. Often, after arrest and long incarceration, they attain high-level paraprofessional positions in treatment agencies. There they have an advantage over addicts of lower-status backgrounds, in being better able to communicate with the professionals—psychiatrists, psychologists, and social workers—and in being better than the professionals at communicating with addicts.

With the post–World War II diffusion of opiate addiction to the urban ghettos, the federal Bureau of Narcotics portrayed these drugs as creating violent "dope fiends" and demanded severer sentences (although most addicts typically commit nonviolent offenses). Since legislators were unfamiliar with the banned substances and there were no lobbies for the addicts, penalties were increased. The Harrison Act of 1914 left punishment for selling opiates to judicial discretion, but the maximum prison term was 10 years. It was amended by the Boggs Act of 1951, which made federal punishment for selling illegal drugs two to five years on first conviction, five to 10 on second, and 10 to 20 on third, plus large fines on each offense. A suspended sentence and probation were permitted only on the first conviction. Despite this measure and burgeoning enforcement staffs, addiction spread; so the law was amended by the Narcotics Control Act in 1956, which increased maximum federal imprisonment to 10 years on first offense, 20 on second, and 40 on third, with any sale to a minor counted as a third offense, and suspended sentence, probation, or parole prohibited on any conviction. (Identical penalties were also imposed under this law for sale of marijuana or cocaine, drugs discussed later in this chapter.)

After the Harrison Act, most state and local police viewed narcotics crimes as purely federal concerns, but as addiction spread the national Bureau of Narcotics increasingly solicited state collaboration. In the 1930s and again in the 1950s, it persuaded the states, Puerto Rico, and Congress legislating for the District of Columbia to adopt Uniform Narcotic Drug Acts drafted by the Bureau, but with penalties left to the discretion of each state. Most imposed punishments as severe as those of the federal statutes, as did almost all of those few states that drafted their own laws.

For several reasons these laws did not curtail addiction. First, few drug transactions result in arrest, since the substances involved are very compact and all participants share a common interest in keeping them secret. Second, when their cravings are intense, addicts focus on immediate gratification rather than on the usually low and unknowable risks. Third, they are usually caught only by entrapment with paid informers, and often with illegal searches, so that prosecutors are quite content to accept a plea of guilty to a lesser offense rather than engage in the time-consuming and uncertain pursuit of convictions under the severe laws (Gould et al., Chapters 5 and 6). Fourth, many apprehended addicts are granted immunity for aiding the prosecution, and often a large number of "small timers" are not even arrested in hopes of their leading undercover agents and informers to large-scale dealers. Yet one study found that 52 percent of advanced addicts applying for methadone treatment were unknown to the police (Weissman et al., 1973).

After increased penalties in the 1950s failed to alter a half-century record of ineffectiveness with the 1914 Harrison Act's principle of federal taxation to prevent misuse of opiates, the Comprehensive Drug Abuse Prevention and Control Act of 1970 shifted the legal grounds for control from tax collection to restricting interstate commerce of all potentially abused drugs. The Controlled Substances Act of 1970 gave the Food and Drug Administration authority to designate such drugs and to regulate their medical and research distribution. A parallel Uniform State Dangerous Substances Control Act was urged by the federal government, and 40 states adopted it. For the first time, however, Congress balked at the administration's request for severer minimum penalties, but established five-, 10-, and 15-year maximums for various types of first offense; these maximums are doubled with repetition and include a 25-year sentence for promoting a "continuous criminal enterprise." Large fines could supplement each of these penalties.

In conjunction with the 1970 legislative changes, the Bureau of Narcotics in the Treasury Department was replaced by the Bureau of Narcotics and Dangerous Drugs in the Justice Department, and in 1973 by a new Drug Enforcement Administration, with staff and budget for the "war on dope" expanded several times beyond their size a decade earlier. The DEA assumed international functions, providing money and training to narcotics-policing agencies of foreign countries, such as Turkey and Mexico, and even compensating foreign farmers for their reduction of opium growing. Domestically, it enforces the orders of the Food and Drug Administration under the Controlled Substances Act.

All these federal measures and the several hundred millions of dollars that they cost annually (Goldberg & DeLong, 1972) proved futile in reducing heroin use in the United States. In fact, like previous surges of prohibition fervor, they may only have increased the damage

A narcotics raid.

to American citizens from the predations of opiate addicts and the overload imposed on the criminal-justice system. Despite record numbers of arrests and drug seizures, the DEA was repeatedly forced to admit that imports of illegal drugs continued to rise (*Los Angeles Times,* May 21, 1975 and July 18, 1976). Their tremendous expenditures to interdict illegal opium growing and export from the Middle and Far East only expanded Latin American production, with Mexico becoming the principal source of supply during the 1970s. Frustrated in legal methods of law enforcement, some DEA units, as well as state and local narcotics police, were often charged with illegal raids and with mishandling suspects (including persons accused altogether erroneously), with actions stemming from reliance on informers, and with harassing alleged dealers and addicts whom they cannot convict.

Because there are many places where opium can grow and because relatively little land can produce all that the world uses, whenever one source is closed others expand or new ones develop. Also, its chemical processing into drugs can be done almost anywhere, especially for an illegal market that does not require highly pure products. Since the cravings of addicts persist, the price rises whenever the amount of available narcotics diminishes, and free enterprise in various places then responds to the incentive of higher profits by supplying more. The drug is compact and easily smuggled; hence any closure of one mode of delivery only increases the flow from others or motivates the opening of new ones. There are innumerable autonomous dealers at the retail, semiwholesale, and wholesale level, with addicts themselves moving in and out of these businesses as their funds and opportunities vary (Preble & Casey, 1969; Blum, 1972a, 1973). Also, as Goldstein points out (1976), if opium growing and heroin smuggling were ever effectively suppressed, synthetic opiates resembling heroin could be illicitly produced in many locations. Thus the basic cause of failure in suppression efforts is the inelastic demand for opiates. To understand how the market for these drugs might be curtailed, one should review searches for addiction "cures," some of which have frequently been shaped by both prohibition and treatment concerns.

Reducing Crime by Treating Opiate Addiction

One way to prevent predations by addicts, of course, would be to end their cravings for opiates. More diverse methods have probably been tried for this purpose than have been used in efforts to alter any other type of conduct. Attempts to change addicts range from the severe penalties reported in the preceding section to the varied modes of persuasion and chemical "insulation" (some blending punishment with treatment) described in the following summaries:

1. **Hospital and Clinical Programs**   Medical treatment of opiate addiction is perhaps as old as addiction itself. It often consists primarily of providing drugs to relieve withdrawal symptoms. When opiates are legally available to physicians, they are usually prescribed in amounts that do not seriously interfere with the addict's employment. Sometimes the dosage is tapered down to zero, but the failure of this method to create lasting abstinence is so frequent that physicians experienced with addicts do not attempt to force cessation of drug use on their patients. Several large clinics, which maintained most of their addict patients on controlled dosages of morphine, opened in the United States soon after World War I, but were closed a few years later because of the Prohibition Bureau's claim that the clinics were failures, a claim that still is disputed (Terry & Pellens, 1928; Lindesmith, 1965: Chapter 5; Musto, 1973: Chapter 7). With the growth of psychotherapy in the twentieth century, medically sponsored treatment was often directed at relieving anxieties and emotional conflicts to reduce cravings for drugs.

In 1935 the United States Public Health Service opened a prisonlike hospital at Lexington, Kentucky, to which addicts serving federal prison sentences were transferred and to which other addicts were encouraged to come voluntarily for treatment. So many came from the

South that a similar federal institution was opened in 1938 at Fort Worth, Texas. These hospitals ended the physiological dependence of addicts by giving them opiates in doses gradually diminished to zero; they used primarily morphine until methadone was pioneered in the United States for this purpose at Lexington after World War II. Physicians believe this "detoxification" requires three to six months to eliminate all physiological dependence, but the major medical symptoms disappear in seven to 10 days. Detoxification centers were later established in numerous public and private hospitals and clinics in the United States, especially in New York City. Many addicts apply for this service when their tolerance for heroin makes their addiction too expensive, but they depart early, against medical advice, when the dosage becomes somewhat lower or their welfare or pension checks are due.

Anslinger praised the federal-hospital detoxification program as 64 percent successful, since this was the percentage released from Lexington who did not return during a limited followup period. But this figure did not account for those reimprisoned or rehospitalized elsewhere, still addicted in the community, or dead. (Death rates are high among street addicts from contaminants in illegal heroin, unsanitary needles, and the strains of their lifestyle.) More thorough followup studies of former patients in these hospitals found higher failure rates, including over 90 percent readdiction for New York City releasees (Vaillant, 1966); but they also found less relapse by those from areas where addiction is relatively infrequent (O'Donnell, 1969). In a 20-year followup of 100 Lexington patients from New York City, Vaillant (1973) found that only 10 of 361 separate hospitalizations were followed by five or more years of abstinence. The growth of other types of treatment programs, to be described here, resulted in the 1970s in the conversion of both federal hospitals for addicts into federal prisons for diverse inmates. Similar closure or drastic change occurred in many state and local hospital programs for addicts.

2. Civil Commitment   States that imprison addicts for possession or sale of opiates also define opiate addiction as a mental disease warranting forced hospitalization. Although it necessitates the crime of opiate possession, addiction is not a ground for acquittal on such a criminal charge. Imprisonment and civil commitment, although the latter is alleged to be for psychotherapeutic treatment, are in practice merely alternative strategies for catching addicts, each getting some of those the other does not apprehend. Until 1962, California law had not only imprisonment for possession or sale of narcotics and mental-hospital confinement for addiction, but also a statute making addiction itself a misdemeanor. This last law was declared unconstitutional in that year by the United States Supreme Court in *Robinson* v. *California,* on the grounds that to penalize for an illness is to violate the Eighth Amendment's ban on "cruel and unusual punishments"; but the Court advised that the state might still confine addicts without their consent as mentally ill.

Anticipating the Robinson ruling, California in 1961 authorized mandatory civil commitment for treatment of any person whom a court found to be addicted to opiates. Even if an addict is convicted of a crime, this commitment can occur in lieu of imprisonment, provided the offense is not for assault, for large-scale drug trafficking, or part of a record of "excessive crime." A judge's order for such commitment must be based on testimony of two court-appointed psychiatrists that the person is addicted to narcotics. The alleged addict can have a trial and present witnesses to dispute this diagnosis.

The California program supervises addicts for seven years, with conditional release on aftercare permissible at any time, and early discharge if they spend three years in the community free of addiction. Upon discharge from civil commitment, those sent there as addicts when convicted for a crime are returned to court for a decision on whether they should still be punished for that offense. Further penalties are usually not imposed, because the law violation (even if for nondrug crimes) reflected an addiction for which the person has already been confined and treated. On the other hand, those still addicted at the end of seven years may be recommitted for another three years, though this rarely occurs.

California's civil-commitment program is administered by its Department of Corrections, and the addicts are confined in edifices much like modern prisons; so critics, from the outset, questioned whether this law did anything important other than making it easier to punish people for addiction. Nevertheless, the federal government and several states, notably New York, enacted similar legislation. Unless arrested for federal offenses and held in federal prisons, civilly committed addicts are placed in segregated sections of state prisons or prisonlike "treatment" facilities.

Many addicts charged with crime decide, often on advice of counsel, that confinement will be briefer or more pleasant if they petition the court for civil commitment. Police and prosecutors often refer criminal suspects to the courts as alleged addicts, for a civil-commitment hearing, when the prospects of obtaining a conviction on criminal charges are weak. Civil commitment has the effect of imprisonment, as far as law enforcement is concerned, and with less effort and uncertainty.

When civil commitment was begun, the public was encouraged to refer addicted children, spouses, other relatives, or friends for the promised therapy, and addicts were invited to turn themselves in for "cure." When it became apparent that, despite relatively large staffs of psychotherapists, the programs accomplished little and did not differ much from imprisonment, such referrals and self-commitments declined almost to the vanishing point. With loss of confidence in civil commitment as cure, its use to bypass criminal-justice procedures was severely criticized as an unjust infringement of liberties (see Aronowitz, 1967; Kittrie, 1971: 243–58; Dershowitz, 1975).

New York State, which in the 1960s allegedly had half the nation's addicts, began a modest civil-commitment program in its state hospitals in 1963. But in 1966 it enacted a statute modeled on California's, and by 1970 had well over 20,000 addicts in institutions, on aftercare, or in state-inspected private, city, or county treatment agencies. Its law differs from California's in having a commitment term of three years for most, and five for some, instead of seven. Also, it monitors very diverse local programs, many of which it also subsidizes, and an addict in one of the approved programs cannot involuntarily be sent to the state's civil-commitment facilities for addicts unless convicted of a crime. The state has also subsidized a large variety of antinarcotics education in schools, in storefront community centers, and elsewhere.

New York's programs were initiated with the claim that they would "get the addicts off the streets," but despite a billion dollars spent on them in about five years, illegal opiate use did not diminish. The state did not adequately tabulate and release followup data on clients in state and local programs, but it was clear that high failure rates prevailed in civil-commitment and most other types of treatment. Therefore, in 1973 the extensive treatment funding was supplemented by a severe law, imposing a maximum of life imprisonment and a minimum of 15 years for anyone selling over an ounce of opiates or possessing over two ounces; punishment was also increased for lesser amounts, limits were placed on plea bargaining, and greater penalties were imposed for second offenses. A $1,000 reward was offered for information leading to conviction of a drug pusher, additional judges were appointed to expedite prosecution, and a half-million dollars was spent in advertising the law, hoping thereby to deter drug use. At the same time, as a result of a tenfold increase of federal funding for treatment programs between 1968 and 1972, there were few waiting lists or other barriers to addicts requesting aid.

Under this 1973 law there was a continuation of the slight annual decline of new cases in treatment and in narcotics arrests since 1970, when the rates were at a peak. Thousands of tips on drug sellers were received from the public for the $1,000 reward, but less than one in a thousand led to conviction and payment. Property crimes associated with narcotics use did not decline, and drugs were reported to be as readily available as ever. The only noteworthy consequence of New York's severe penalties was an increase from seven to 17 percent in narcotics cases tried rather than plea bargained, but this did not diminish opiate use (Winick, 1975).

Followup studies indicate a high failure rate for early federal and California civil-commitment releasees, but greater success during the 1970s. This change, however, resulted primarily from redefining "failure," whereby release to aftercare in the community (comparable to parole supervision) is no longer revoked if a urine test indicates use of opiates. Relapse to drug use remains characteristic of most releasees, but if the addict is employed and otherwise cooperative, the authorities prefer counseling and warning or any direct assistance to the reconfinement that had previously been routine. Revocation of release occurs mainly for new offenses or for absconding, rather than simply for "dirty urine."

Interviews and investigations of records were undertaken between 1975 and 1976 for (1) persons admitted in 1962 and 1963 to civil commitment in California but soon released by writ when the initial commitment procedures were found to deny legal rights, and (2) those admitted in 1964 under revised procedures who had seven years of state supervision. In the seven years following their admission, those with civil commitment for a full term had significantly less daily narcotics use, more employment, and less crime when in the community than those released early. These differences also continued beyond the seven-year period. Preadmission rates on these variables had been about the same for these two groups, both of which had median ages of about 26 on admission. Five-year followups of 1964 admissions, when supervision in the community was tight, and of 1970 admissions, when it was more tolerant of rule violations, found that around a third of each group used drugs, sold drugs (mostly without profit), and was involved in crime on aftercare. Only about half had full- or part-time jobs. Assistance, particularly in the crucial area of employment, was far from adequate, but these findings suggest that a public-health approach to aiding people with addiction, emphasizing help and not punishment, is at least as effective as prohibition in changing conduct. The researchers conclude, however, that the 1970 group's record would have been worse than that for 1964 were it not that methadone maintenance (to be discussed shortly) was available in 1970 (McGlothlin et al., 1976).

There are apparently many similarities in the termination of opiate addiction and alcoholism. Voluntary abstinence, once someone is physiologically dependent on opiates ("strung out"), seems to require a sense of having "hit bottom" and some confidence in one's capacity to "kick the habit." For some, a long incarceration, especially with close postrelease supervision, seems to produce not only involuntary abstinence, but also disillusion with drugs and recognition of their ability to continue drug-free. Vaillant's (1973) 20-year study of 100 New York addicts released from Lexington federal hospital in 1952 and 1953 found that well over 90 percent soon returned to drugs; but two decades later 23 were dead and only 25 were still using opiates. In this long followup period the 100 had many separate penal confinements, but abstinence for five or more years followed 70 percent of their 34 releases from prison and parole, 14 percent of their 50 releases from nine months or more of incarceration without parole, and only three percent of their 363 releases from jailings for less than nine months.

New York State statistics also suggest that prison and parole had higher success with addicts than civil commitment and aftercare. Actually, these programs resembled each other and had many of the same facilities and personnel, but the enterprises exclusively for drug addicts generally exposed them to more continuous talk of the drug world than prevails in prisons. Indeed, there is much smuggling of drugs into most state and federal civil-commitment facilities, as well as into some prisons. Since their release is often dependent on the belief of psychologists or other experts that their ailment has been treated successfully, inmates in group therapy may hypocritically recite antinarcotics testimonials and show "insight" into their addiction simultaneously with using opiates.

Certainly, some type of conversion to and resocialization in a drug-free culture seems necessary for abstinence. It must often be initially bolstered through close supervision and aid in the community by what Brill (1972: 144–45) calls "rational authority"—whether by probation, parole or aftercare officers, or groups of former addicts—to ensure their becoming accustomed to drug-free lifestyles. However, there may well be objections on civil-rights grounds to much of this supervision, especially if the addict is not charged with a predation.

3. Mutual-Treatment Groups of Former Addicts   In 1958 Synanon was established for heroin addicts in the Los Angeles area. This organization is modeled partly on Alcoholics Anonymous but has many widely imitated distinctive features. These include the following:

1. Members reside in an organization building from which they cannot depart at will if they wish to remain members.
2. There is an initial waiting period followed by humiliating assignments, such as cleaning latrines, to be certain that new members are motivated to persevere in the program.
3. Members attend frequent group discussions on the AA model of confession, but these are often more intellectual and less polite. Experienced members vehemently debunk excuses of new members for their past misconduct or for their claims to current insight and improvement; yet they also express affection and group cohesion.
4. There is an absolute prohibition of any nonmedical drug use, including alcohol and (more recently) tobacco; even a wariness

of alleged medical use exists, so that aspirin and other pills are forbidden on the premises.

5. Members may experience a gradation of assignments, offices, and privileges—to permit advancement from menial tasks to those of increased responsibility—or a demotion for misconduct, decreed either by collective judgment of all residents or by top office holders who may also impose other penalties, even expulsion.

6. Excursions from the residence are permitted only after a long period of good conduct, often more than a year, and then only when accompanied by more tested and trusted members until another extensive trial period elapses (Volkman & Cressey, 1963; Yablonsky, 1965; Karen & Bower, 1968).

These cohesive social worlds may compete in attractiveness with drug-using circles for addicts who cannot comfortably enter and feel at ease in "straight" society. Synanon gained much favorable publicity in the early 1960s when it was aided by many celebrities and intellectuals in the Los Angeles area. Part of its appeal and that of similar groups seems to be their continuation of the "hustling spirit" of the drug world, with members working avidly to gain public support and contributions by: (1) being cordial hosts to outsiders, who are invited to drug-free and alcohol-free parties; (2) providing speakers to schools, churches, and clubs; (3) soliciting donations or grants. A few of these groups, notably Synanon and San Francisco's Delancey Street Foundation, operate businesses, ranging from gas stations to plastics manufacturing, some of which are quite successful. Synanon, now a multi-million-dollar organization with several branches, offers its services not only to addicts but also to nonaddict "lifestylers" who join because they like the environment and to those with emotional problems other than drugs. It solicits financial compensation from any practicants or their parents who can afford it.

All members in organizations of former addicts are encouraged to show personal responsibility and to strive for higher status within the group, but the ceiling on advancement in those groups that have entrenched top directors causes many near the top to leave and start independent establishments. Thus Daytop Village in New York was organized by a former deputy director of Synanon; Exodus House and several other groups split from Daytop; still others were started by departees from Exodus, and so forth through a long series of splinterings. There have also been some independent beginnings modeled on the old groups, but differing from most by special features, such as the Teen Challenge link with fundamentalist religion, Narcanon with Scientology, Odyssey House with a nonaddict psychiatrist-lawyer as leader, and "The Family" with government sponsorship in California mental hospitals and Youth Authority correctional institutions. Some are not very retentive, encouraging members to move from the house soon after admission; others maintain close custody, to prevent extensive involvement with outsiders. A few, notably Synanon, seem to be trying to establish a separate subsociety within the United States, permanently apart from the larger society. Many addiction-treatment programs in prisons and hospitals have Synanon-model "therapeutic communities" and recruit members of outside ex-addict groups to lead them.

It is difficult to assess the effectiveness of organizations of former addicts. They do not count as members those who leave or are expelled, and thus point primarily to current members when boasting of their successes (although some admit people never addicted to opiates). Older organizations, especially Synanon, have had some participants for a decade or more, a number of whom have married and reared families in group-owned homes. Senior members often claim that everyone who leaves the group relapses to addiction, but usually they only hear about departees who are rearrested or are seen with addicts, and not of those who, by abstaining, disappear into conventional society. It is clear that each ex-addict organization creates a quasi-family of members, offering opportunities to achieve a sense of self-worth in a law-abiding life, which many who join them were previously unable to acquire outside the drug-using world.

Since 1969, narcotic-addiction treatment programs receiving federal funding have been required to submit a report for each patient on admission, on alternate months during treatment, and on departure. These reports are sent to the Institute of Behavioral Research at Texas Christian University (TCU) at Fort Worth, where the information is recorded on computer tapes. The research center also follows up large samples of these patients in the community. Its data indicate that therapeutic community programs, which are predominantly former-addict groups, retain only about 30 percent of their patients for a year after admission; the mean length of stay is six-and-a-half months (Sells et al., 1976: 9). Followup interviews and investigation of a sample admitted to these programs between 1969 and 1972, as compared with a sample admitted to detoxification outpatient centers, suggest that about 80 percent in both groups that had previously used opiates took them again within the approximately five-year followup period. Forty-eight percent of the therapeutic-community patients spent some time in jail during these five years, as compared with 63 percent of those in the detoxification programs; 55 percent of the therapeutic-community participants were employed part- or full-time when interviewed, as compared with 46 percent of the clientele of the detoxification center. These small differences, of course, could well have been due to the lesser restriction of admission to the detoxification centers, rather than to benefits from the therapeutic community (Brown & Carroll, 1976). Quite in contrast to treatment methods discussed thus far, however, are efforts at chemical "insulation."

4. Opiate Antagonists   Some programs give their clients chemicals to neutralize opiates. Addicts who ingest these substances when they have heroin in their bodies, or who take an opiate afterwards, suffer withdrawal effects. Opiates constrict the pupils, but the antagonist Nalline (nallomorphine) expands them if there are opiates in the bloodstream; a test for opiate use consists of measuring the pupils, in constant light, before and half an hour after Nalline injection. Another antagonist, cyclazocine, taken orally, reduces the effects of all morphinelike drugs for about 24 hours, but has no appreciable impact on persons who do not take opiates. A new drug, Naltrexone, seems to be adequate as an antagonist for two or three days.

A few programs administer cyclazocine to addicts, and great claims were once made for it. Because it offers the addict no particularly attractive experience and sometimes causes unpleasant symptoms, it is difficult to coerce its use. Patients usually continue on this drug only because it is required for probation, parole, or employment, or because spouses or parents insist, but often this pressure is not long effective. Cyclazocine and other antagonists appear to be least attractive to people living in areas of high drug use, and these are the vast majority of addicts in the United States today (Brill & Laskowitz, 1972).

5. Methadone Maintenance   Methadone, a synthetic opiate, was developed in Germany during World War II as a substitute for morphine in medical practice, and was introduced by the United States Public Health Service shortly after the war to detoxify addicts at Lexington. In the mid-1960s Dr. Vincent P. Dole and his wife, Dr. Marie E. Nyswander, both of Rockefeller University developed an alternative to detoxification. They increased the daily methadone given to addicts until additional increments seemed to produce no further effect. When maintained at this peak dosage, addicts do not feel much, if anything, from additional opiates. Since it takes about 24 hours for the body to metabolize half the methadone, and since it can be consumed orally, it is possible to "insulate" addicts from heroin by giving them this drug daily, usually dissolved in a synthetic fruit juice. This program, of course, keeps the subjects addicted, and they suffer acute withdrawal symptoms if abruptly denied the high dosage to which the body becomes adjusted.

Because it metabolizes slowly (whereas the body uses up half a shot of heroin in two to four hours), methadone does not interfere with work performance if the dosage is optimum (Gordon, 1973). Too much causes drowsiness and too little some restlessness and greater sensation from heroin. The drug itself is relatively inexpensive, generally costing less than 25 cents per day. The main costs in its distribution to addicts are administrative staff, facilities and perhaps accompanying social- and occupational-rehabilitation services. At first the maintenance programs, denounced by many as legalizing addiction, were licensed only for small-scale research. Methadone's severest critics were former addicts in Synanon-type therapeutic communities, who had pride in achieving abstinence and a vested interest in the government support their programs received. They spread pure myths that methadone threatened health, so that some addicts terribly ill from contaminated heroin and unsanitary needles still say "methadone would rot my bones." Actually, over a decade of methadone maintenance has shown it to be remarkably free of harmful effects (Dole & Nyswander, 1976).

In the initial programs, methadone was used only for maintenance of adult addicts who had used opiates four or more years and were unsuccessful in at least two prior efforts at treatment. When the number of agencies authorized to provide maintenance was greatly expanded in the late 1960s and thereafter, the prior-treatment requirement was dropped and the period of addiction cut to two years. During most of the 1970s there may have been as many as 100,000 Americans receiving methadone maintenance daily, from public or private medical sources, or illegally. Nevertheless, it is estimated that no more than one in three opiate addicts sought maintenance when it was most readily available, and some used heroin thereafter, presumably in search of euphoria or social support.

The results of methadone maintenance have been somewhat uneven. In the pioneer Dole–Nyswander program, 80 percent were retained for over two years and had marked reduction in crime and increase in employment. The best predictor of failure was prior abuse of nonopiate drugs, such as alcohol, which often continues when they are on methadone (Methadone Maintenance Evaluation Committee, 1968; Babst et al., 1971; Cushman, 1974; Nash, 1976). To receive their methadone, clients had to leave a urine sample. Urinalysis revealed that at first an appreciable number still used heroin, but almost all ceased soon. Such reversion to heroin resulted in warning and counseling, but not expulsion from the maintenance program; the few who left did so mainly through arrest and long confinement. It has been observed that patients had to be "weaned away from the needle, which appears to be associated with their addict lifestyle" (Chambers & Brill, 1975: 151). All persons on maintenance first had to come daily to receive and consume methadone at the distribution center, but after they had established a record of "clean" urine and good performance in legitimate major roles—typically, as employee, housewife, or student —they were trusted with several days' supply to take home.

The original methadone-maintenance patients were on a waiting list, for the admission procedure then was to keep them in a small hospital ward for several weeks of observation while the dosage was gradually increased. Some waited for over a year before they could enter the program. Such a long wait created a very effective screening of applicants, for anyone still available in the community when their turn came to be admitted must have been exceptionally stable and highly motivated to join. By the 1970s this and other programs were less selective and operated almost entirely on an outpatient basis. Their success in increasing employment and reducing crime by addicts declined, but is still impressive. Thus a comparison between paroled addicts in a California methadone-maintenance program and those on a waiting list to enter maintenance shows a significant drop in arrests and increase in employment rates as soon as the subjects begin maintenance (Jones & Berecochea, 1973).

Noteworthy causes of the declining success rate of methadone programs in the 1970s include the three following broad factors:

1. *Lowered selectivity.* When waiting periods were eliminated, many were admitted who probably would have been arrested or would have lost interest if they had to wait. Under federal regulations any adult and some adolescents who are both dependent on opiates when they apply for methadone maintenance and are shown by official records to have been addicted for at least two years can be admitted. This time reckoning can include an intervening period of incarceration, during which addicts presumably could not obtain drugs (LEAA, 1973: Appendix A); thus, some new clients are not long out of prison. Since the illegality and cost of heroin drives most addicts to procure a high income from professional crime, it should not be surprising (1) if many receiving maintenance still find crime an easier source of income than any legitimate occupation available to them (Vorenberg & Lukoff, 1973), or (2) if some enter the maintenance programs for temporary relief and reduction of their habitual dosage when entrance is easy, but still crave euphoria from heroin and remain in drug-using social circles.

2. *Decline in aid and encouragement.* Overcrowding at many distribution centers reduces counseling and assistance as well as personal rapport between clients and staff, making participation less attractive to addicts. In California, where state support for methadone maintenance has been quite limited, the few programs are located at a considerable distance from many of their clients. Some centers also have inconvenient hours for employed persons, and many are purely medical programs,

operating what Nash (1976) calls "filling stations" for methadone with no other services. Since a large part of the appeal of drug use is that it conveys a sense of competence and acceptance in an esoteric social world, and since most of the addicts have had little comparable success in other settings, it should not be expected that merely supplying them with a chemical will keep them from returning to the company of addicts and from conforming to the expectations of such associates.

3. *Client expulsion.* A prohibitionist mentality exists at many methadone-maintenance centers, and has become almost mandatory under federal regulations. Some centers impose strict rules on clients, readily suspend or expel rule violators, and require that addicts who become well adjusted in legitimate roles gradually reduce their methadone dosage to zero, whether or not they wish to cease maintenance. Some New York City programs in the early 1970s were staffed by abstinent former addicts who were vociferously against methadone. Although persuading patients to become completely drug-free is called for in very general terms by federal regulations (LEAA, 1973: 60), these rules in practice are tightened (allegedly in response to pressure from an influential congressman) by the requirement that program administrators justify in writing, to the satisfaction of federal inspectors, their keeping any addict on maintenance for over two years (Dole, 1974: 688).

An additional feature of the tightening of controls, begun in 1973 under joint action of the Food and Drug Administration and the Drug Enforcement Administration, is a close check by federal inspectors on the storage, dosage, and recordkeeping in distribution of methadone. This surveillance is explained as an effort to combat a black market in methadone among addicts, who could illegally purchase a day's supply for about five dollars. The regulations and inspections reportedly discourage physicians from operating methadone programs, and lead many addicts to buy black-market methadone and to self-administer detoxification or maintenance. Of course, since they spend less for this than they would for heroin, they may not have to commit crimes to support this practice; thus the public may benefit, even though the black marketeers may be stealing the methadone and diluting it.

The followup of addicts from reports submitted to Texas Christian University (already described in the section on former-addict groups) revealed that methadone-maintenance programs retained their male patients for an average of 14 months, compared with six-and-a-half months for therapeutic communities and two months for outpatient detoxification and drug-free treatment programs (Sells et al., 1976: 9). Earlier tabulations indicate similar rates for females (Joe et al., 1972). There is some evidence that addicts who leave treatment programs are more likely to remain abstinent than those who never enter them; many leave one program to go to another, including some who resume methadone maintenance elsewhere (Nash, 1976). During treatment, methadone-maintenance patients have more drug-free days, at much lower treatment cost, than those in any other type of program (Demaree et al., 1975: 30). A five-year followup of a sample of the cases in the 1972 TCU retention study found that methadone-maintenance and therapeutic-community clients, after leaving treatment had about the same rates of opiate use, employment, and incarceration (Brown & Carroll, 1976; Sells, 1976).

Apparently the major problem in reducing crime by treatment of opiate addiction, as was shown with alcoholism, is to enhance the programs' appeal to clients. Such improvement in methadone-maintenance programs should occur if the problems of selectivity, aid, encouragement, and control (discussed above) are diminished. Use of acetylmethadol or LAAM—synthetic opiates with maintenance effects lasting about three days after each ingestion (Jaffe et al., 1970; Jaffe & Senay., 1971)—received strong federal encouragement in the 1970s in hopes that it would permit maintenance without addicts having to take methadone home. This extreme concern with avoiding any diversion of methadone to the black market or to abuse may restrict the potential appeal of these programs to addicts. The evidence that many addicts, rather than accept maintenance with any of these drugs, would still commit crime if necessary to obtain heroin or morphine has evoked increasing support for legalizing the medically supervised maintenance of addicts on any safe drug that they crave. This practice has long existed in Britain and other Western European countries.

6. Multiopiate Maintenance   As indicated at the outset of this discussion of preventing crime by treating addicts, approved practice in the United States before the Harrison Act was to supply the addicts with opiates, under the supervision of a physician. The British retained this policy after they joined us in carrying out the Hague Treaty by restricting the distribution of these drugs to medical channels and keeping records on them. But in Britian, as in many other countries, mild solutions of heroin are still widely used as medicine, since they are more effective than other remedies for certain ailments and since such use practically never results in addiction (Judson, 1974: Chapter 1).

Until 1968 the British permitted every physician to prescribe opiates to addicts for prevention or relief of withdrawal symptoms. A small drug-enforcement unit of the Home Office regularly checks prescriptions and keeps a record of persons receiving opiates for longer than six months, consulting discreetly with the physician to determine whether the drug is used for maintaining addiction or for other medical purposes, such as relief of pain in terminal cancer. This permits the British to comply more accurately than the United States to the Hague Treaty's requirement that the number of addicts in each country be reported to an international agency, now part of the United Nations. The British reported 616 in 1936, only 306 in 1950, and 437 in 1960. But the number rose to 1,729 by 1967, due largely to: (1) a few indiscriminately prescribing physicians who gave some patients excessive amounts; (2) a fad of drug use among some young popular-music enthusiasts; (3) small-scale smuggling by migrants from the British colony of Hong Kong. In 1968 the British restricted the prescribing of opiates for addicts to designated treatment clinics. These clinics have persuaded a majority of their patients to switch to full or partial maintenance on injected methadone, and they view this as a "stepping stone to coming off heroin" (Chambers & Brill, 1973: 335, 339). Yet the British medical profession never abandoned the conclusion reached in a report of the 1920s, that "morphine and presumably heroin could not in all cases be totally withdrawn from a person addicted to these drugs. . . . Such an addict required a certain amount of the drug in order to keep him normal" (Judson, 1974: 19).

The London clinics also have a staff of social workers, who assist clients in housing, employment, or other needs; foster social mixing of addicts with nonaddicts; and counsel the families of clients. At these very practical clinics, improving the addict's employment opportunities and social relationships have higher priority than achieving abstinence, but in the long run this policy probably minimizes opiate use more effectively than a more puritanical or prohibitionist approach. The total number of addicts in Britain in the 1970s stabilized at fewer than 3,000 (Hawks, 1974; Judson, 1974). With a population of about one-quarter that of the United States, the British have only about one percent of our number of addicts, and they suffer much less predatory crime per addict.

Recently many have claimed that the British tabulations cover only about half of their actual total of addicted persons, since opium is smuggled in from the Orient and the West Indies. Yet even if this is true, most of those not now known to the officials will register for legally supplied drugs if they persist in opiate use, and will thus be counted. Furthermore, the highest estimates give Britain a rate of addiction only a few percent of that in the United States, and with not nearly as much of a related crime problem.

Stimson (1973) differentiates four patterns of drug use in a sample of male clients of London clinics. "Stables" are regularly employed adults who generally inject themselves at home, are rarely involved in crime or other deviant conduct, seldom use extra drugs, and keep their addiction a secret as much as they can. "Junkies" are youth who use drugs socially, away from home; and partly because they often use up their weekly opiate prescription before their next one is due, they also use other substances. They are unstable in residence and employment, are often infected from sharing unsterile syringes, and are involved in much delinquency and crime. "Loners" resemble the "stables" in being older and injecting their drugs alone at home; but like the "junkies," they are unsteady in employment and use extra opiates obtained illegally. "Two-worlders" are mostly younger men with stable employment who, on weekends or during other free time, join the "junkies" in using drugs socially and engaging in crime or other deviant conduct. In a smaller English town, however, Plant (1975) found diverse but predominantly stable and nondeviant life-styles among users of opiates.

It is evident that within both the United States and Britain, opiate addiction is differently integrated into the various total living arrangements and customs. Therefore, in neither country can a single formula for dealing with every addict minimize either drug use or crime. American policies keep the addicted automatically guilty both of the crime of drug possession and of other crime to pay for the drugs. By avoiding such social costs, Britain maintains contact with its addicts and progresses rationally toward optimum individual programs to prevent their engaging in crime or posing other serious problems. When reducing drug use is compatible with these objectives, the British also encourage addicts to try smaller dosages, with a goal of abstinence. However, acceptance of this goal is purely voluntary. A 1977 Scotland Yard press release indicates that only five percent of registered addicts in Britain still use heroin rather than synthetics (*Los Angeles Times*, March 24, 1977).

Mainly as a result of our decades of futile emphasis on prohibition, we have, compared with the British, larger concentrations of addicts in our population, an exorbitant price for heroin on an illegal market, a larger and more versatile illicit-distribution system, and addicts who, on the average, are more professional at procuring income criminally. Therefore, unlike the British, we cannot now give our opiate users a week's supply of heroin without the prospect that many will get more than they use and sell the surplus, perhaps fostering new addicts. Nevertheless, it seems desirable to experiment with a variety of methods for working toward the model of rationality that the British offer in this field, rather than persist in the amplification of our drug problem by a prohibitionist approach. For example, we could adopt a combination of public-health and welfare-oriented policies, such as the following:

1. Encourage former-addict and other drug-free programs to attract as many addicts as they can, and aid them in providing

whatever services and facilities prove cost-effective for their goal of fostering abstinence.

2. Keep methadone and related drugs readily available to addicts who desire them, by:

   a) providing detoxification with methadone, consumed at a clinic, immediately to anyone who requests it and is found by Nalline or other tests to be using opiates

   b) providing methadone, acetylmethadol, or LAAM maintenance to anyone requesting it who is known to have been long addicted, and offering it without restrictions on the duration of its availability

   c) offering social services to all detoxification and maintenance clients by helping them to qualify for, procure, and hold legitimate jobs, to improve their family relationships, and to find gratification in law-abiding social circles

   d) encouraging voluntary dosage-reduction experiments by those on maintenance, with the goal of abstinence, and permitting medically supervised reversal of this process (toward renewed maintenance) should they insist later that they desire it

   e) permitting those who achieve a stable and law-abiding life to purchase a gradually increased supply of their maintenance drug to use at home, but checking by urine test to ascertain the probability that they alone are using all that they are given

3. Make small experiments in offering other opiates, such as morphine and heroin, to some of those who have long been addicted and do not enter other maintenance programs, perhaps testing policies such as the following:

   a) Offer the drug only during hours when clients are not working or job-seeking; also require that the heroin or morphine recipient remain at the addiction-treatment center for long enough after an injection for its effects to be experienced mainly there, and that methadone or other long-acting maintenance drugs be taken before departure from the center.

   b) Require that the addict participate satisfactorily in a law-abiding lifestyle—by work, study, training, or some combination of these—in order to receive the heroin or morphine.

   c) Try "STEPS"—the "Sequential Transitions Employing Pharmacologic Support" proposed by Goldstein (1975, 1976) and diagrammed in Figure 10-1. It begins with morphine received at a clinic three or four times daily, the first month intravenously and the second subcutaneously

Figure 10–1

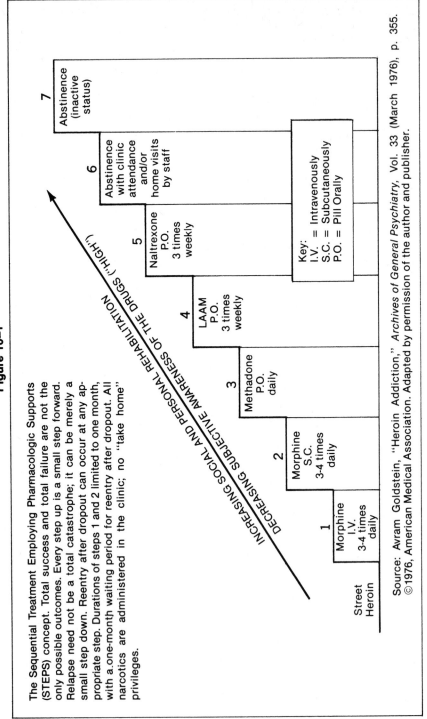

The Sequential Treatment Employing Pharmacologic Supports (STEPS) concept. Total success and total failure are not the only possible outcomes. Every step up is a small step forward. Relapse need not be a total catastrophe; it can be merely a small step down. Reentry after dropout can occur at any appropriate step. Durations of steps 1 and 2 limited to one month, with a one-month waiting period for reentry after dropout. All narcotics are administered in the clinic; no "take home" privileges.

INCREASING SOCIAL AND PERSONAL REHABILITATION ("HIGH")

DECREASING SUBJECTIVE AWARENESS OF THE DRUGS

| 1 | 2 | 3 | 4 | 5 | 6 | 7 |

Street Heroin

Morphine I.V. 3-4 times daily

Morphine S.C. 3-4 times daily

Methadone P.O. daily

LAAM P.O. 3 times weekly

Naltrexone P.O. 3 times weekly

Abstinence with clinic attendance and/or home visits by staff

Abstinence (inactive status)

Key:
I.V. = Intravenously
S.C. = Subcutaneously
P.O. = Pill Orally

Source: Avram Goldstein, "Heroin Addiction," *Archives of General Psychiatry,* Vol. 33 (March 1976), p. 355. ©1976, American Medical Association. Adapted by permission of the author and publisher.

(under the skin), thus decreasing the speed of absorption in the second month. It then changes to methadone once a day, to LAAM thrice each week, to Naltrexone opiate antagonist thrice each week, to abstinence. The rate of transition from one step to the next, once methadone is begun, may vary from one case to another, with some possible regression in steps if relapse to heroin occurs; reentry at the highest appropriate step is permitted within a month after any dropout. How many addicts this will attract and their rate of progress through these stages is worth investigating.

All these programs, and others that seem promising, should be closely monitored and their cases followed up for evaluation with a view to learning what combination of methods does most, per dollar invested, to minimize predatory crime by addicts and new cases of addiction.

In each program of drug-free and multiopiate maintenance treatment, staff should probably include those who have successfully completed that type of treatment, along with specialists in medicine, social work, and other diverse backgrounds, if needed. It is presumed that such a mixed staff will enhance the appeal of these programs to addicts, although experience in addiction and in the type of treatment offered by no means guarantees that an individual will be a satisfactory employee.

As addicts grow older they usually have a "maturing out" of their drug habit (Winick, 1962) with or without treatment, but a flexible program permits us to reduce its cost to society before abstinence is achieved, and perhaps to aid and hasten this maturation. The fact that this maturing occurs suggests an implication of Cloward and Ohlin's (1960) "double failure" theory, that most of today's drug abuse is part of the meandering adolescent search for a sense of adultlike autonomy, for some eminence that is respected by others, for a sense of personal success. The ultimate abstinence of most addicts indicates that despite their self-images as connoisseurs of exotic "kicks" and as "smart hustlers," drug addiction eventually proves to be only another detour—whether short or long, single or recurrent—in their path to a fairly stable and conventional adulthood. Yet, to some, the camaraderie and excitement of their drug use remains a lure at any age, whenever setbacks or loneliness become intense in their legitimate occupations or social worlds.

Perhaps this adolescent experimentation with drugs would, on the average, be briefer and less costly to society if we dealt with it as we do with alcohol, as more a public-health than a criminal-justice problem. Several economists have presented evidence and argument that one of the main sources of social damage from the prohibitionist approach to opiate addiction has been that every time the police are even temporarily successful in making heroin somewhat scarce, it simply: (1) increases the price of illegal heroin to addicts so that they steal more; and (2) increases the profits to illegal drug importers and peddlers, so that more people enter these pursuits and encourage other people to try their wares (Holahan, 1972; Votey & Phillips, 1976; Fujii, 1974, 1975). It seems probable that a program of liberally expanding multiopiate maintenance would be the quickest and most cost-effective method of reducing predatory crime in many American cities where addiction is concentrated. As Peter F. Drucker (1972), the prominent advisor to the American business world, obverves, a policy of making illegal opiate selling unprofitable by expanding the supply of legally available drugs to addicts is needed not so much to help the addicts as to make our cities safer for the victims of addict predations, the nonaddicts.

MARIJUANA

Few plants have been as useful to so many societies as *Cannabis sativa,* the Indian hemp plant, also known as marijuana (often spelled "marihuana" and popularly called "pot" or "grass"). It grows, wild or cultivated, in almost all soils and climates. Since ancient times and in many lands, it has been a source of fiber for rope and cloth, of seeds for birdfood and paint oil, of medication, and of smoking material. Sailing ships depended on it for rope, for which it was grown extensively in the United States from colonial days—when it gave George Washington a money crop at Mount Vernon—until the early twentieth century.

Most parts of cannabis, but especially the flowers of the female plant, contain resins with a family of chemicals called tetrahydrocannabinols (THC), which are the active agents in its limited physiological effects. The amount of this component varies greatly with horticultural conditions; it is highest when the plant is widely spaced and with initial irrigation in a dry, hot climate, but least when growing wild in dense weeds in the North (for example, in Illinois and Iowa). THC is most concentrated in the resin itself, which is extracted from the flowers and sold separately as *hashish;* it is even stronger in hashish oil and in laboratories, as synthesized pure THC. For some little-understood reason, a given amount of THC has a greater effect when smoked than when swallowed (Isbell et al., 1967); but it also has some impact when eaten (even when baked in cookies or used as tea); and more can be consumed in a given time if it is eaten rather than smoked.

THC is a very mild hallucinogen, causing slight alterations in visual and sensory perceptions and in sense of time. If the consequences of smoking a certain number of marijuana cigarettes are compared with those of the same number of shots of whiskey, the alcohol is found to impair cognition, reaction time, work performance, and automobile driving much more than the marijuana (Weil et al., 1968; Crancer et al., 1969; Mendelson et al., 1974). Indeed, in laboratory situations marijuana heightened work tempo somewhat (Mendelson et al., 1974), a finding consistent with folk belief in the West Indies, where it is given to laborers who are under pressure to harvest sugar cane rapidly (Comitas, 1975). Marijuana users inhale deeply, retaining the smoke as long as they can for maximum effect. Tobacco smoked that way is much more toxic, quickly making one ill (Goode, 1972: 129–31).

The psychological impact of smoking marijuana depends greatly on how the smoker interprets its mild sensory effects. Expectations learned and encouragement received for various aesthetic or mood reactions largely determine one's experience with it. Most typical among American users when they consider themselves "intoxicated" or "stoned" from marijuana are silliness and what Goode (1970: 168) calls "a sense of wonderment" at ordinary perceptions (see also, Becker, 1953, 1955, 1967, 1973).

There are no demonstrable withdrawal effects from cessation of marijuana use, and thus no physiological dependence on the drug. In this sense it is not addictive, and it does not seem to be as habituating as many more clearly abused substances in the United States (e.g., alcohol and tobacco) since few users smoke it regularly for years. Despite publicized scaremongering in the debates over whether it should be legalized, marijuana has not been proved dangerous to physical or mental health in long-run ordinary usage (as is alcohol). Some claims that heavy use of hashish in India and Africa causes physical and mental deterioration refer to dosages of THC much greater than are used in the United States, cite conditions relatively rare even there, and do not prove them due to the drug. Many long-term heavy users in Jamaica were found unharmed by it. There has been much variation in the United States in who smokes marijuana, where, and with what consequences, if any.

THE RISE AND DECLINE OF THE MARIJUANA-PROHIBITION MOVEMENT

Marijuana was not widely used in this country during the first half of this century, but it is alleged to have spread slightly as a substitute for alcohol after the Prohibition Amendment was enacted. Indeed, in some technologically underdeveloped countries it has long been used by those too poor to afford alcoholic beverages, and derogated by the middle and upper classes who drink (Comitas, 1975; Partridge, 1975; Rubin, 1975: 257–66). In the United States it was smoked mainly by poor blacks in the Southeast and in the Northern slums to which they migrated, as well as by Mexican-Americans in the Southwest. It was then adopted as an exotic practice by some jazz musicians and bohemian artists (McGlothlin, 1975).

The prohibition movement was extended to marijuana quite gradually, beginning with a 1915 law in Utah, which was followed during the 1920s by about a dozen other states in the Southeast and Southwest, where its use by lower-class groups was viewed as a problem by the elite. The 1931 annual report of the Bureau of Narcotics stated that marijuana use was not a serious problem, and the 1932 report suggested that its regulation should be a state rather than federal responsibility (Becker, 1963: 138–39).

When the Bureau of Narcotics budget was sharply cut after 1932 by a Depression-burdened Congress, Anslinger changed his views on marijuana, apparently because he saw it as a means of rebuilding his empire (Dickson, 1968). Repeating the "mad fiend" themes in the alcohol- and opiate-prohibition propaganda of decades earlier, the Bureau started in 1935 to circulate through the mass media fantastic stories as "proof" for its scientifically preposterous claims that marijuana makes people homicidally and suicidally insane. By 1936 it had persuaded all states to prohibit this substance, most adopting the Bureau's Uniform Narcotic Drug Act, which penalized marijuana and opiate use identically. In 1937 it got Congress to enact the Marijuana Tax Act, which levied what was thought would be a prohibitive charge, one dollar per ounce or fraction thereof, on all transactions with this substance. The law imposed a penalty of up to five years in prison and $2,000 fine for violation, and gave the Bureau wide latitude in enforcement. In 1938 one-fourth of the Bureau's narcotics arrests were for marijuana, and this new burden was thereafter stressed in Director Anslinger's budget requests (Lindesmith, 1965: Chapter 8; Solomon, 1966: Appendix 2; Schaller, 1970; Bonnie & Whitebread, 1970, 1974).

The Boggs Act of 1951, the Narcotics Control Act of 1956, and most state laws grouped marijuana with opiates and subjected their possession to identical penalties, whose maximums were much more severe than that of the original tax act. State and federal laws before the Controlled Substances Act of 1970 designated both drugs "narcotics." This misleading terminology, encouraged by the Bureau of Narcotics, is still used in some statutes and much common speech, but was abandoned by the Bureau's successor, the Drug Enforcement Administration. Its "Drugs of Abuse" pamphlet designates only opiates and some opiatelike synthetic drugs as "narcotics" (pointing out that federal law also applies this term to one stimulant, cocaine).

The Bureau of Narcotics justified uniformity of penalties for very diverse substances by claiming that one led to another, that smoking marijuana led to heroin use. Although there is nothing inherent in marijuana (any more than in tobacco, coffee, or tea) to cause a user to seek heroin, such a progression was once more frequent than now simply because both substances were sold primarily in minority slum areas, often by the same dealers, and most readily to those who had already been in conflict with the law. Johnson (1972) showed that having heroin-using friends, not the level of marijuana use, predicts shift from "pot" to opiates. Such correlation as existed between the two types of drug use, and between marijuana use and other crime, largely vanished in the 1970s when: (1) marijuana use became, more than ever before, far more prevalent than opiate use; (2) the two types of drugs were taken by different segments of the population. Marijuana is much cheaper than illegal heroin, often less costly than whiskey, and its use is not very compulsive; therefore property crimes to purchase it are certainly less probable than for opiates, and even alcohol cravings are more likely to inspire theft or forgery than yearnings for "pot."

As McGlothlin (1975) points out, marijuana became distinctly a drug for middle-class youth in the 1960s, largely because of earlier publicity about LSD and other hallucinogens that were licensed in the 1950s for psychological research. Hallucinogenic drugs received special notoriety with the controversial discharge of Timothy Leary from the Harvard University faculty in 1963 for violating an agreement to cease giving them to students. They were widely adopted by students and "counterculture" groups. In 1965 California passed the first statute prohibiting LSD, quickly followed by other states; but these laws were openly flouted at large "be-in" and "love-in" gatherings. Mass-media attention to LSD reached a peak around 1967 and 1968, but thereafter it focused instead on marijuana, which it had completely overlooked just a few years earlier (McGlothlin, 1975: 535). Because the cannabis product was more readily available, and much more controllable and less frightening in its effects, it soon replaced the stronger hallucinogens as a symbol of togetherness and of disdain for "straight" society, and as an alternative to alcohol for social and recreational purposes (described well in Partridge, 1973).

Opposition to the Vietnam War in the 1970s increasingly unified students of diverse background in criticizing dominant norms, so that marijuana on campus spread from the "radical fringe" to fraternity and sorority row. The Gallup Poll reported that the percentage of college students who had smoked it increased from five percent in the fall of 1967 to 51 percent in December 1971 (Gallup Opinion Index, April 1972: 16). The Gallup Poll found that in the general population in 1977, 59 percent of those between 18 and 25 but only five percent of those over 50, had tried it (*Los Angeles Times*, May 15, 1977). The percentage of male high-school seniors who had used illegal drugs increased from 19 percent in 1969 to 54 percent in 1975, with most of these smoking marijuana (Institute for Social Research *Newsletter,* Summer 1976). Studies of university alumni a few years after graduation indicate that about a third of those who smoke "pot" in college stop thereafter, primarily because of job or childrearing constraints; about the same proportion or more of those who do not use it in college, however, try it as alumni, usually in the social world of young-adult "singles" (Henly & Adams, 1973; Brown et al., 1974).

As people of older generations belatedly shared youth's opposition to the Vietnam War, and as the offspring of conventional and higher-status families joined those of lower prestige or greater delinquency in using marijuana, the horror over this custom diminished, though few but youth smoked "grass." Of course, current or former student "pot" users were a growing portion of the adult electorate, especially after the vote was extended to 18-year-olds in 1973. The first strong political resistance to penalizing marijuana possession or sale as severely as opiate crimes surfaced in the late 1960s, and under the Controlled Substances Act of 1970 criminal trafficking in opiates receives a maximum penalty of 15 years, while five years is the limit for marijuana, plus fines.

Arrests for marijuana possession or sale often climbed by about 100 percent per year during the 1960s, but penalties plummetted (Grupp, 1970, 1971). The number of possession cases overlooked by police or dismissed with a warning (hence not recorded as arrest) undoubtedly grew, too, although in most states imprisonment could be imposed for having even minute amounts. During the 1970s, however, state laws were revised to differentiate marijuana penalties markedly according to the quantity involved. Oregon, in 1973, was the first of many states to make a moderate fine the maximum punishment for possessing a small amount, and even this law was seldom applied. Polls indicated that no surge in popularity of marijuana followed a drop in the penalty; adjacent states that differed by several years in the dates when they made their laws more lenient had about the same trends in use of this substance (*Los Angeles Times*, March 9, 1977).

With only a small fraction of teenage marijuana smokers arrested for this officially felonious offense, sporadic police actions against typical users, no matter whether warranted by the statutes, appeared to youth and their parents and friends as blatantly and flagrantly violating American concepts of equal and uniform justice under law. Blind to how unenforceability led to the demise of the Eighteenth Amendment on alcohol, some law-enforcement officials unintentionally accelerated the downfall of marijuana prohibition by evoking publicity for its ineffectiveness. Thus the Los Angeles Police Department in 1974 announced that a poll it commissioned found that 48 percent of the city's high-school students and 20 percent of its junior-high students had used marijuana. Then it heavily invested federal grants in undercover investigations at those schools where the figures were well above these averages, and a few months later made dragnet arrests of hundreds of students. Some of the schools were in middle- and upper-class areas, and the remonstrances this sudden law enforcement aroused were sufficient to liberate the youths and squelch such police practice. Although a ballot initiative for the decriminalization of marijuana had been soundly defeated in the 1972 elections, there was by 1975 no effective opposition to passage of a state law like Oregon's, reducing penalties to a fine for possession of small amounts.

More characteristic in enforcement of marijuana laws was arrest and prosecution of youth for possession or transfer of small amounts only when the police encountered what they considered hostility, or when the arrestees were suspected of other offenses that could not be proved in court. The frequent manipulation, harassment, and exploitation of young drug-law arrestees by police, prosecution, and even defense attorneys generated a vast disrespect for the criminal-justice system in many youth and in much of the legal profession (Kaplan, 1970; Hellman, 1975; Sanders, 1975).

Polls in the second half of the 1970s show a clear majority of high-school seniors and college students favoring legalization of marijuana; indeed, the high-school students were more approving of use of this substance than of smoking one or more packs of tobacco cigarettes per day (Institute for Social Research *Newsletter*, Summer 1976). It seems probable that the policy of decriminalizing marijuana possession and use will continue to spread more rapidly than legitimation of its sale and distribution. Because it can be grown everywhere in the United States (even though with less potency in some areas) and because large numbers of people are now involved in its illegal import and distribution, its increased acceptance will undoubtedly foster tolerance for its local production for use rather than sale; eventually, there may well be some type of licensed cultivation and sale. Kaplan (1973) offers a model licensing law with a high tax rate, especially on the higher-THC variety of the two controlled-strength grades that would be permitted. If legal marijuana smoking partially replaces alcohol use in the United States, available evidence suggests that this will reduce property crime due to diminished capacity to work, drunken driving, and criminal violence now associated with male subcultures of drinking.

OTHER SUBSTANCE ABUSE

There are more products to be discussed, for people take innumerable substances not for nutrition, but for stimulation, sleep, or fantasy. To achieve these and other mental effects, they sniff, inject, or swallow

glue, ether, cocaine, LSD, and a tremendous variety of other "psychotropic" material—chemicals "acting on the mind." Included also are
drugs prescribed legitimately by physicians, mainly for adults, but
very frequently taken by juveniles with neither medical nor parental
approval, and sometimes used or sold illegally by adults.

A national survey of 18-to-55 year-olds found that 28 percent of
women and 17 percent of men take tranquilizers, antidepressants, sedatives, and other psychotropic drugs (Borgatta, 1974). A survey of
18-to-74-year-olds found that 38 percent of women and 22 percent of
men use "psychotherapeutic" drugs (Mellinger et al., 1974). In a Los
Angeles suburban area, 82 percent of the women said they had used
psychotropic drugs, 53 percent during the preceding year (Prather &
Fidell, 1975). How much of this activity was medically prescribed we
cannot know, but an immense amount was not, and there are federal
and state penalties for illegal trafficking in most of these substances.
There are millions of juvenile and adult "polydrug abusers" in our
country, people taking two or more types of drug nonmedically; many
dabble with a large variety of licit and illicit pills and capsules.

Most of the products still to be considered are not as consistently linked to lawbreaking in the United States as the three already
discussed—alcohol, opiates, and marijuana; yet their "improper" use
may be punished as delinquency or crime. Several are alleged to contribute to predatory offenses, although this is disputable. For each
major category of substance abuse, however, the relationship to crime
is unique, so each must be described separately:

1. Inhaling Glue or Other Vapors

Many anaesthetics that patients are made to inhale to render them
unconscious during surgery will, if breathed in a lesser concentration,
create a sense of intoxication much like that from alcohol, but briefer
and without hangover. Nitrous oxide (laughing gas), ether, and chloroform have been taken by many people for this recreational purpose at
various times and places; such use is still reported occasionally, although sniffing chloroform involves great risk of lethal overdose, and
ether vapor is highly flammable. Britain and Northern Ireland had
widespread use of ether by working people in the late nineteenth and
twentieth centuries when prohibitionists tried to deter them from using whiskey by taxing it heavily, and "ether jags" were held in the
United States during Prohibition (Brecher, 1972: Chapter 43).

In modern times, more mundane substances are sniffed for
their intoxicating effects, but primarily by juveniles. Starting in the late
1950s and continuing to the present, inducing dizziness and hallucinations by sniffing toluol glues, gasoline, paint thinner, and even the
freon in aerosol spray cans has been surprisingly popular among American children from around age 12 to 15; they shift to other substance

abuse thereafter (Preble & Laury, 1967; Rubin & Babbs, 1970; Sokol, 1973). There is no physiological dependence on these substances, but some children are extremely persistent at it, ignoring punishments or threats.

The usual age range for this type of mood-changing effort links it to delinquency rather than crime, but it has at least three relationships to law violation. In the first place, glue sniffing is especially popular among those already in conflict with the police, school, or home, although it is also done by some otherwise-exemplary juveniles. It is often a group activity, with children trying to have identical hallucinations or fantasies through mutual suggestion, and considering such visions a collective achievement (Preble & Laury, 1967). It thus provides an opportunity for a sense of eminence especially attractive to children unsuccessful in school, sports, or other activities.

Second, in a wave of hysteria over juvenile sniffing during the 1960s, state and local laws of questionable constitutionality were passed prohibiting deliberate smelling of glue or selling it for this use, even though these offenses cannot be very precisely defined. Yet the more adults try to frighten children by alleging dangers from glue sniffing, the more popular it becomes, especially among already-delinquent juveniles, some of whom first hear of it when warned against it. As with scare tactics in many other types of antidrug education, the teachers are soon discredited when it becomes clear that the pupils are the only ones experienced in the derogated activity, that they find it harmless, and that contrary evidence is not convincing (Brecher, 1972: Chapter 44).

Finally, this practice may foster some other types of crime, not simply shoplifting and burglary to get glue from model airplane kits (though not the horrible "glue fiend" atrocities ascribed to it by some scaremongers). Glue sniffing probably contributes to other types of law violation, not in itself, but through juvenile-court orders that confine very young glue sniffers in detention homes and training schools with older predatory delinquents, who provide most of the "training" at these establishments. Arrest for glue sniffing often stigmatizes juveniles in the eyes of teachers and other adults, who cannot comprehend such activity, and thus makes the glue sniffers value each other's company and that of older offenders more, since they are denied alternative associates. Thus the labeling process, discussed in Chapter 7, may more often be criminalizing than deterrent for glue-sniffing young juveniles, and may account for what is alleged to be their high recidivism rate in the same offense and for their other delinquency. In a small-scale controlled experiment with different treatment methods, marked success was achieved in programs that emphasized getting these children involved and interested in other types of group activity, and helping them be more successful in schoolwork (Rubin & Babbs, 1970).

Most allegations that glue or other substances inhaled by these children would injure them physically have proved unfounded, but there is a grave risk of these substances being taken in a manner that cuts off oxygen. This occurs primarily when, in order to get a more concentrated dose and a quicker effect, some of the substance is placed in a bag, usually of plastic, into which the user puts his head. There is great danger of irreversible brain damage, if not death, from even brief oxygen deficiency (hypoxia) through this practice (Julien, 1975: 62).

Some prevention of this abuse has been achieved by replacing toluol glues with other types of adhesive, by placing irritants such as oil of horseradish into toluol glues, and by eliminating freon-spray cans (for other reasons). It appears that with inhalant sniffing, as with so many types of nonpredatory offense, considering the behavior a problem for the criminal-justice system rather than for public-health agencies has increased rather than diminished its prevalence and its linkage with other types of crime.

2. Cocaine

When the Spanish conquistadors scaled the Andes in what is now Peru, Bolivia, and adjacent countries, they found the natives chewing the leaves of a coca bush to give endurance in that rugged terrain. These leaves are still chewed and used for tea there, but their active ingredient, cocaine, was extracted in pure form in Germany in 1844 and by the beginning of the twentieth century had become quite widely used as a stimulant. It was sold in wines in Europe and in the original version of Coca-Cola when first marketed in Atlanta in 1904, as well as in numerous tonics and other patent medicines.

Cocaine is a stimulant, quite contrasting in its effects to all the other mood-changing substances discussed so far in this chapter. It "produces excitement, restlessness, and an increase in body temperature . . . also . . . a decreased sense of fatigue which permits continuation of muscular effort" (Helms et al., 1975: 208). It is described as quickly uplifting the spirits of persons who are depressed and giving them an exaggerated conception of their own strength. It depresses the appetite, so that regular users lose weight. Only a small amount is absorbed by the body if taken orally, but if injected the effects are quicker and more pronounced, although they last for only about half an hour. Compensatory fatigue follows repeated use.

There are no serious effects from small doses of cocaine, but some people start taking larger and larger amounts more and more frequently, which can lead to hallucinations of skin sensations often described as insects or reptiles running all over one's body. Continuous hyperexcitation from stimulants can be dangerous to health, especially when accompanied by little eating. In rare cases lethal cocaine poisoning occurs.

When sniffed, cocaine powder is not only absorbed into the body as a stimulant but also has a local anaesthetic effect at the place of entry and can injure nasal tissue. (Novocaine, the local anaesthetic used in dentistry, is a cocaine derivative.) It does not create withdrawal effects and physiological dependence, but some people become very habituated to its use, craving more of the excitation soon after the effect of each dose wears off. Opiate addicts sometimes take "speedballs" a mixture of cocaine and heroin said to intensify the initial "rush" from the heroin.

A cocaine-prohibition movement started in the United States around the turn of the century as a reflection of antiblack prejudice. This drug was then widely used in the South, by whites more than blacks, but prejudiced prohibitionists called it the "Negro drug" and claimed that it made black men rape white women (Musto, 1973: 6–8; Helms et al., 1975). It was equated with the opiates and made subject to the same punishments as heroin in all federal narcotics legislation from the Harrison Act of 1914 to the Controlled Substances Act of 1970.

From the late 1960s to the present, the popularity of cocaine in the United States has surged, attracting a wide spectrum of the population, from the poor to the affluent. Of a representative sample of men 20 to 30 years old in 1974, 14 percent had used it, seven percent in the year preceding the interview (O'Donnell et al., 1976). Nine percent of high-school seniors had used it in 1975 (Johnston, 1976). It is related to crime only because possession or sale is felonious, with severe penalties possible but rarely imposed in the fraction of one percent of law violations that result in arrest. Its classification as a narcotic under the Controlled Substance Act has been challenged in the courts (Helms et al., 1975), but thus far unsuccessfully.

3. Amphetamines

Amphetamines are chemicals similar to the hormone epinephrine (adrenaline), discussed in Chapter 7, which stimulates the body to mobilize energy for flight or fight in emergency. Developed in the first quarter of the twentieth century and extensively used in the second, they were prohibited in the third quarter and thereafter. Their principal legitimate use is to counter fatigue during long work periods, such as long-distance truck driving or staying up all night to finish a term paper. Athletes are tested to make sure they do not use them, for they provide a temporary competitive advantage. Popularly called "pep pills," their commercial names include Benzedrine and Dexadrine. Formerly Benzedrine was available not only in pills, but also in plastic inhalers to reduce constriction of nasal passages from colds or allergies. Amphetamines were also standard in diet pills, for they curb the appetite. Today they are prescribed primarily in treatment of hyperactivity in children, for whom they have a little-understood effect that diminishes restlessness and improves attention span.

These chemicals work well for all such purposes, but not without limits. Their appetite-reducing quality wears off in a few weeks unless the dosage is increased to a level that produces harmful side effects. They prevent falling asleep on the job, but the rate of error when long awake because of them is higher than in normal wakeful periods. Finally, when the drug wears off, the body compensates by extreme fatigue and sometimes by depression. Amphetamines may be dangerous for persons with high blood pressure or certain heart ailments.

Abuse of amphetamines occurs when people continue taking larger doses of these so-called uppers or whites, to defer the inevitable letdown. Large quantities of such pills are "popped" orally by young teenagers, but are dissolved by older youth for injection, which accelerates the drug's effects and brings an immediate "flash" or "rush." Some youngsters, called "needle freaks," seem psychologically addicted to hypodermics, allegedly even injecting ice water into their veins when they have no drugs. The term "speed" is sometimes used for all the amphetamines, but especially for metamphetamine, a particularly potent variety preferred for injection.

"Speed freaks" often take metamphetamine every few hours for a "run" of several days of excitation, then "crash" for several days of sleep. These are the "spree" or "escapist" users, as contrasted to "adaptive" users, who take it, when necessary, to facilitate their work (Chambers et al., 1972a). "Speed freaks" often live communally in dilapidated housing called "crash pads" or in vans. Paranoid delusions and memory lapses are common near the end of a "run," while acute depression and a high suicide rate follow awakening from a "crash," until a new "run" is begun. Their living standard and appearance characteristically deteriorate. They typically seek transient labor when destitute, but sometimes engage in petty theft, begging, and salvaging food and salable junk from trash cans.

A worldwide prohibition movement against amphetamines developed in the 1950s and 1960s. Japan had a post–World War II surge in their use when surplus stocks from its army were placed on sale. Being a tightly policed nation of islands with a tradition of strict obedience to government, however, Japan achieved perhaps the only successful suppression of a drug by law enforcement ever recorded. By the 1950s it had an estimated two million abusers, but after arrests peaked above 55,000 in 1955, the practice diminished, and only 271 arrests were made in 1958. This experience is presented as justification for a prohibitionist approach to drug abuse in other countries (Brill & Hirose, 1969), but we should note that use of amphetamines and other drugs, as well as law-enforcement efforts, increased again in Japan in the 1960s and subsequently; arrests were made disproportionately among students and in the Korean minority population, which may reflect police prejudices. We should also note that in Japan as in other countries, youth conduct today often influences adults and foreshadows later trends in society as a whole. These trends include value generalization (discussed in Chapter 2)—the greater tolerance for deviant acts, such as drug-taking, that do not injure others. Also, because participants in such nonpredatory behavior are not complainants who notify the police, laws prohibiting it are increasingly difficult to enforce, even in Japan.

Also cited in prohibitionist arguments is the allegation that Swedish socialized medicine, by distributing amphetamines freely, created a problem of abuse. Actually, sales of these drugs without medical prescription were permitted in Sweden only between 1939 and 1943, but the problem of their abuse did not develop until around 1960, when youth gangs were dabbling in these and other drugs smuggled in from other European countries. After a crackdown by several nations in the 1960s reduced supplies of smuggled amphetamines and after controls on prescriptions were tightened, they were made in numerous small, illegal laboratories for sale on the black market, and were thereby introduced to many new customers. Realizing that the prohibition effort had only compounded their problem, Sweden in the late 1960s began small-scale experiments in prescribing amphetamines, in conjunction with therapeutic programs, for those who had misused these drugs (Brecher, 1972: Chapter 39)

In congressional hearings on the Controlled Substances Act of 1970, testimony of numerous experts indicated that the amount of amphetamines made in the United States was many times that required for medical needs, and that health problems from abuse of these drugs were much more severe than those from marijuana. Drug-manufacturers' lobbyists, however, succeeded in keeping amphetamines off the most severely restricted categories under this law (Pekannen, 1973; Chambliss, 1974: 18–20) until 1972, when pressure from another congressional committee investigating youth crime caused the Food and Drug Administration to reclassify the most abused forms of amphetamine so that their sale is subject to the same range of federal penalties as marijuana. The increased price of amphetamines as a result of greater prohibition efforts is allegedly responsible for the rise in popularity of cocaine during the 1970s, for the two drugs are similar in effect and many users consider them interchangeable, although cocaine is more costly.

Interviews with a representative sample of American men 20 to 30 years old in 1974 grouped together all stimulants other than cocaine (this meant primarily amphetamines). Twenty-seven percent reported having used them, 12 percent in the preceding year (O'Donnell et al., 1976). Amphetamines had been used by 22 percent of high-school seniors in 1975 (Johnston, 1976). They are sometimes part of a poly-drug habit that includes heroin and must be supported by crime, but this is exceptional; generally amphetamines are not linked with professional predation. Prohibition efforts do not seem to work in suppressing their use, and making them a concern of public health rather than criminal justice may reduce their social and personal damage. Thus some small colleges permit students to get amphetamine "pep pills" from the school dispensary when they feel they have to stay up all night to cram for an exam or finish a term paper, and they encourage them to come to the dispensary to rest afterward. In this way the dosage taken and the quality of the drugs can be known, the effects can be monitored by a nurse or physician, and the market for criminal dealers is reduced or eliminated. Probably more such medical control of the administration of these drugs would lessen their relationship to crime.

4. Barbiturates and Other Sedatives and Tranquilizers

Products derived from barbituric acid were first used in medical practice in 1903 and soon were widely taken as sleeping pills, sedatives, and tranquilizers. Since World War II they have been supplemented but not replaced by a variety of new tranquilizers and analgesics. The most commonly used and abused barbiturates are Nembutal and Seconal, lasting only a few hours, as well as the longer-acting Amytal and the longest-lasting, phenobarbital (Luminal), which may cause drowsiness for 24 hours.

Adults are usually introduced to barbiturates through medical prescription; but whether or not legitimately procured, they are then widely overused. Of men 20 to 30 years old in 1974, 20 percent had taken sedatives, almost always barbiturates, nine percent in the preceding year (O'Donnell et al., 1976). A New York State survey found that salespersons were the occupational group most often using these drugs, with over 12 percent of both men and women in this work taking them regularly (Chambers et al., 1972b). One national survey of youth and adults, however, found that the highest rate of *first* use of sedatives or stimulants in the year preceding the interview was by the 14-to-15-year-old group, with four percent being initiated to each of these types of drugs in that year (Abelson & Atkinson, 1975). Juveniles almost always procure these substances illegally.

Many abusers, from teenagers to the middle aged, alternate between barbiturate "downers" to relax and amphetamine "uppers" to wake up and become alert. Some take these opposite-acting substances simultaneously. These are sold in combination pills with an outer layer of amphetamine around a core of barbiturate; the mixture provides an immediate lift followed by relaxation. About a third of opiate addicts also use barbiturates; these persons and "speed freaks" are about the only ones who inject these drugs, for these substances are fully absorbed into the system if taken orally. Little crime is associated with use of barbiturates alone.

Barbiturates are the most lethal of commonly abused drugs. They are the most frequent cause of death by poisoning, through accidental or intentional overdose. Alcohol and barbiturates have similar influences on behavior and on vital processes, with the impact of one adding to that of the other. Therefore, irritability is sometimes a first effect, as with fatigue. Driving after taking sedatives resembles driving under the influence of alcohol, and taking both barbiturates and alcohol is especially likely to be fatal. The body develops a tolerance to only a slightly larger dose of barbiturates than a novice can stand, but once this adjustment occurs, sudden withdrawal can produce symptoms like the abstinence syndrome of opiates, only more severe and lasting for days, somtimes culminating in fatal convulsions.

As with amphetamines, experts at congressional hearings testified that many times more barbiturates are sold in the United States than are required for medical needs, that they are certainly more dangerous than marijuana, and that they are in several respects more dangerous than heroin. Nevertheless, the drug industry lobby prevented a classification of barbiturates under this law that would subject them to the most-restricted distribution and most-severe penalties for illegal sales (Pekannen, 1973). Different types of this drug are now in three separate categories of control, although logically all merit regulation as close as that given the most-prohibited drugs (Chambliss, 1974: 18–20). Efforts at public health and education probably do more to reduce personal damage from taking these or other abused drugs than the little-used state and federal penalties. When people, especially juveniles, are physiologically dependent on barbiturates, it is much less rational to subject them to confinement as delinquent or criminal than to provide care in a medical setting that includes a gradually reduced dosage (to prevent dangerous withdrawal effects), plus counseling and assistance in altering the life circumstances that led to this abuse.

In the second half of the twentieth century, barbiturates have been supplemented or replaced by tranquilizers, strong analgesics, and nonbarbiturate sedatives of very diverse types. Although usually supplied by prescription, an appreciable quantity is misused. Valium, a muscle-relaxing tranquilizer, is the most widely prescribed drug in the United States. According to a news release of the National Institute on Drug Abuse in July 1976, it is associated with 10 percent of drug-abuse crises (e.g., coma, convulsions, or delirium tremens) and four percent of drug deaths. Opiates account for 15 percent of these deaths, and

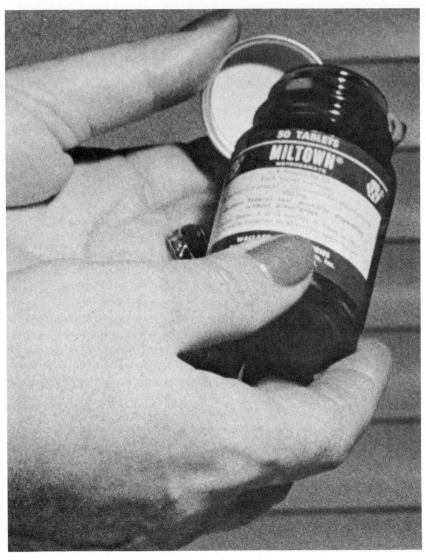

One of many often-abused but legal psychoactive drugs.

alcohol in combination with other drugs (usually barbiturates) is linked with 13 percent. Addictive use is reported for the analgesics Darvon (Chambers, Moffet & Cuskey, 1971) and Pentazocine (Chambers, Inciardi & Stephens, 1971), most tranquilizers, and such nonbarbiturate sedatives as glutethimide (sold as Doriden) and methaqualone (Julien, 1975).

Many of these abused substances are far more dangerous than

marijuana, but because their introduction has had a different history, people are not jailed or imprisoned and branded criminal for possessing them. Perhaps most influential in their protected status has been their prescription by respected physicians to predominantly middle-class users before they were misused by some persons in this group as well as by others of lower statuts. Thus, control of these drugs is centered in the public-health rather than the criminal-justice system, although the Controlled Substances Act permits the Food and Drug Administration to make their illegal sale a penitentiary offense by classifying them as warranting control. Thus far the tranquilizers Equanil, Librium, Miltown, Serax, Tranxene, and Valium have been designated as in Schedule IV under this Act, for which "readily retrievable" records must be kept, with criminal trafficking in them subject to a maximum federal sentence of one year's confinement and a $5,000 fine on first offense. Somewhat greater restriction and severer penalties are imposed on glutethimide and methaqualone sales, but the abuse of both of these is reported to be increasing.

5. LSD and Other Hallucinogens or Psychedelics

LSD is the common abbreviation for a complex lysergic acid (also called LSD-25), which in 1943 was found to have tremendous power to evoke hallucinations in anyone taking even a minute quantity. As indicated in discussing the spread of marijuana in the United States, the predecessor of "pot" among American college youth was an LSD fad in the early 1960s; many of those frightened by LSD then switched to "grass," but by no means all.

LSD and other substances with similar effects, called "hallucinogens" or "psychedelics," are still common. A survey of American men 20 to 30 years old in 1974 found that 22 percent had used these drugs, seven percent in the preceding year (O'Donnell, 1976). In a national sample of juveniles and adults, the age group with the highest percentage that had tried these drugs *for the first time* within the past year, four percent, were 16 to 17 years old, while 3.4 percent of the 14-to-15-year-olds and 2.4 percent of the 18-to-21-year-olds reported this initiation in the past year. For no other age group was the figure as high as one percent, and no such experience was reported by any of 1,340 people age 35 or older (Abelson & Atkinson, 1975). Thus LSD use, even more than smoking marijuana, provides an index of age segregation in our society and disproves the shallow claim that adolescent subcultures are a myth.

The psychedelic drugs are sometimes called "psychomimetic," for their effects seem to mimic the hallucinations in schizophrenic psychoses. Until prohibited by an amendment to federal drug laws in 1965, they were widely used in psychiatric treatment in the United

States, and still are in other countries. Actually, the visions from these drugs differ from those of psychotic persons because the drug taker is always aware that what is seen is an effect of the drug, while the psychotic perceives hallucinations as reality.

In the dreams of psychedelic "trips," as in ordinary slumber, the content is determined by individual experiences, wishes, fears, and expectations, and are not highly predictable. Sometimes they are pleasant, usually they are startling, and occasionally they are horrible nightmares, or "bummers." The visions are so dramatic that few people wish to repeat them soon; thus, the frequency of such "tripping" is rarely more than once per week, usually much less often than that. On the atypical occasions when people do rash things after taking these drugs, the cause is usually their panic at the effects; they feel they are losing their minds. This is prevented if they are well briefed about what to expect and have a previous user nearby to assure them that what they see is normal and temporary. Especially frightening, though rare in use of psychedelics, are "flashbacks," the recurrence of a drug-induced vision at some unexpected moment in the midst of everyday life weeks, months, or even years later.

Psychedelic chemicals are found in a variety of plants, and long before LSD was discovered, various peoples used these substances and attached religious significance to their effects, incorporating them into rituals. In the arid parts of Mexico and the Southwestern United States, peyote, a spineless cactus, is topped by a small crown containing *mescaline,* a natural psychedelic. The Aztecs are believed to have started the practice of slicing and drying this crown to produce "mescal buttons," which are sucked, chewed, and swallowed, to produce visions. The Native American Church of North America continues rituals with peyote and claims a quarter-million members among American Indians. It has been estimated that half the current adult Indian population has used mescal buttons, which are also sold to some youths of other ethnicity (Brecher, 1972: Chapter 45). *Psilocybin* is another natural hallucinogenic drug from Mexico, originally derived from a wild mushroom. More common in recent years have been a variety of new synthetic psychedelics with various chemical abbreviations, such as DOM (also called STP), DMT, and PCP.

It is estimated that an amount of LSD equal in size to an aspirin tablet can suffice for 3,000 "trips." A drop within a solution, absorbed in a cube of sugar or a small square of blotting paper and then dried, provides the usual dose, which is taken orally. The body develops an immediate tolerance for LSD, in that an additional amount will have no effect, and taking it on two successive days will make it ineffective on the third. There are no clear withdrawal effects except from the psychological disturbance, and any regularity of usage is a psychological rather than a physiological dependence. There are allegations that some persons, if already severely disturbed mentally, become psychotic, at least temporarily, when they use LSD or other psychedelics, but these psychoses are rare and of uncertain cause. Claims of other physical harm, including injury to chromosomes that would affect heredity, have been discredited by subsequent researchers (Julien, 1975: 159). Heroin addicts tend to be frightened by the unpredictable emotional upset from psychedelics, and use of these drugs is seldom associated with predatory crime.

As already indicated, California legislation barring LSD was enacted in 1965 and soon copied by other states. The Controlled Substances Act of 1970 classifies it with marijuana for federal restrictions and penalties. In many states the punishment is more severe; furthermore, there has not been a movement toward greater leniency like that of marijuana laws in the 1970s, perhaps because psychedelic users are not as numerous, are rarely arrested, and even more rarely receive the maximum penalty now applicable to them. Occasionally police close an illicit psychedelic-manufacturing plant or arrest a dealer, but since the demand for LSD remains unchanged, it is soon met by a supply from another source.

SUMMARY AND CONCLUSION

Prohibition laws, making it criminal to possess or sell a particular substance, have been applied in the United States to many mood-altering substances. Usually prejudice against the alleged users of the banned material, erroneous ideas about the effects of the substance, or special interests of enforcement bureaucracies have been major influences in the enactment of such laws, quite apart from the actual dangerousness of the substances (Kramer, 1976). Furthermore, these laws do not work. Not only has no prohibition eliminated the abuse it was intended to suppress, even when extremly severe penalties were imposed, but many of these statutes seem to increase the behavior that they outlaw and to foster other types of crime, in addition to reducing public respect for the criminal-justice system as a whole.

Important aspects of each form of substance abuse for which there are criminal penalties or other relationships to crime are summarized in Table 10-3. Some noteworthy additional features that this chapter elaborated include the following:

1. Three distinct drinking patterns were usefully distinguished, identifiable by the population they attract and the crimes they engender:
    a) *Autonomy-expressive drinking* is particularly characteristic of adolescence, but is continued by some for decades

TABLE 10-3 Abused Substances: Their Effects, Prohibition, Prevalence, and Bearing on Crime

SUBSTANCES	PHYSICAL AND BEHAVIORAL EFFECTS	PROHIBITION HISTORY AND CURRENT PREVALENCE	BEARING ON CRIME
Alcoholic beverages	Pseudostimulant, actual depressant. Culturally in U.S., it fosters conviviality, but also violence. Physical and mental abilities decline as alcohol in blood rises; lethal if too much is drunk too quickly. Chronic excess use damages liver and nervous system.	Eighteenth Amendment (1919-33) prohibits; longer in some states. This fails to stop abuse, fosters organized crime, corrupts criminal-justice system. About 2/3 of adults in U.S. drink several times per year; 1/8 almost daily.	Public drunkenness still the most frequent arrest in U.S., though increasingly decriminalized. Drinking fosters most criminal negligence (e.g., in driving) and violence, plus much petty theft and forgery.
Opiates (e.g., heroin, morphine)	Deadens pain, may cause both nausea, and euphoria, then drowsiness. Culturally in U.S., it gives a sense of distinctive experience. Causes tolerance and withdrawal effects; hence physiological dependence. Long-run effects unclear except from infected needles and contaminants. Hard to stop, but most eventually do, sooner or later.	Control by 1914 Harrison Act; penalties much raised in 1950s, but prohibition helps spread its use to larger populations and its closer links to criminal income, until the slow rise of public-health approach in 1970s. Probably a few million have tried it; a half-million persist as addicts or regular users.	Fosters much predation and prostitution, especially in metropolitan areas. Enforcement frustration evokes illegal police methods, but these are still in vain.
Marijuana and hashish	Mild hallucinogen. Culturally in U.S., it adds silliness and sense of wonderment at mundane things. No clear physiological dependence; most use intermittent. No clear damage from dosages used in U.S.; alleged damage from heavier use elsewhere disputed.	Scattered state prohibitions made national by Marijuana Tax Act of 1937. Penalties made same as for opiates in 1950s, then reduced in 1970s. Most between 17 and 30 have tried it; few over 50 years old have.	No clear relationship to crimes other than that of its illegal possession or sale.

TABLE 10-3 (cont'd)

SUBSTANCES	PHYSICAL AND BEHAVIORAL EFFECTS	PROHIBITION HISTORY AND CURRENT PREVALENCE	BEARING ON CRIME
Inhalants (e.g., toluol glues, paint thinners, gasoline, freon)	Mild hallucinogens. Culturally linked with group fantasies and sense of distinction. Very dangerous when used in bags that cut off oxygen. Other risks not proved.	Scattered state and local penalties for sniffing or selling to sniff. Used mostly by 12-to-15-year-olds, especially those in conflict with home and school.	Arrestees for sniffing made more criminal by detention with older predators and by stigma with parents and teachers.
Cocaine	Strong stimulant; cuts fatigue and appetite. Not clearly addictive, but habituating to some. Heavy dosage causes tactile hallucinations; overdose can be fatal.	Prohibited by Harrison Act of 1914 and most later antinarcotic laws with same penalty as heroin. About 1/7 of males between 20 and 30 in U.S. have used it.	No clear relationship to crimes other than its illegal possession or sale.
Amphetamines (e.g., Benzedrine, Dexedrine, Methedrine)	Strong stimulants; cut fatigue and appetite. Chronic heavy use debilitates, fosters paranoid delusions, then heavy sleep followed by depression.	Prohibition against nonmedical traffic developed slowly in 1960s and 1970s. About 1/4 of males between 20 and 30 in U.S. have used it.	Petty thefts by "speed freaks" and illegal traffic, plus criminalizing effects of detention and stigma on young "pill-poppers."
Barbiturates (e.g., Nembutal, Seconal); other sedatives (e.g., Doriden, Methaqualone); tranquilizers (e.g., Valium)	Sedatives; induce sleep. Various types differ in speed and duration of effects. Dangerous in driving. Overdose often fatal, especially if alcohol is also used. Highly addictive, and severe withdrawal effects may be fatal.	Prohibition against nonmedical traffic developed slowly in 1960s and 1970s. Frequently abused at all age levels.	Fosters some criminal negligence (in driving) and illegal traffic, plus criminalizing effects of detention and stigma on young "pill-poppers."
LSD and other strong hallucinogens (e.g., Psilocybin, STP, DMT)	Small amount gives vivid hallucinations; little added effect from larger amounts. Panics from unexpected effects, flashbacks, and "bummers."	First prohibited by state law in 1965; highly restricted by 1970 Controlled Substances Act. About 1/5 of males between 20 and 30 in U.S. have used it.	No clear relationship to crime, except the felony of trafficking.

longer. It emphasizes assertion of independence from authority figures, efforts to dominate in primary-group types of interaction, and, in males, expressions of manliness, including violence.

b) *Skid-row alcoholism* involves chronic excessive drinking, especially concentrated in areas of cheap shelter for homeless men. Most arrests for public drunkenness still occur there, although this condition is increasingly decriminalized.

c) *Compulsive drinking and naive forgery* is a highly recidivistic offense pattern found especially among alcoholics of middle-class background.

2. Because of society's adaptive upgrading, treatment of alcoholism is increasingly accepted and offers growing promise, and hence may help to control crime. Diverse modes of treatment have comparable impact, but attract different types of clientele.

3. Involuntary-treatment methods of opiate addiction by confinement, whether under criminal or civil law, seem similar in consequences. Followup research by Vaillant and McGlothlin suggest that either method of interruption in the lives of addicts, along with long-term supervision and assistance in the community, have some effect in moving people toward abstinence, although justification of such controls on legal grounds is debatable when no crime is proven. Mutual-aid organizations of former addicts point to more dramatic successes, but these appear to be from a small percentage of the addict population that they can attract and indefinitely retain. Opiate antagonists offer chemical insulation against readdiction, but few accept it voluntarily. Alternatively, methadone and even slower-metabolizing synthetic opiates permit maintenance of addiction more cheaply and compatibly with employment than is possible with heroin; about one in three addicts seeks it, and perhaps more would if it were offered more conveniently, with less restriction on duration, and with supplementary aid. Ultimately, however, multiopiate-maintenance programs, flexibly administered but with some controls to prevent abuse, offer the greatest promise for markedly reducing predation by opiate addicts.

Education to Combat Substance Abuse

Education is often advocated as a means of reducing substance abuse, and special programs for this purpose—in schools, youth organizations, and the mass media—have received federal, state, and foundation subsidies. Yet there is much evidence that most of this effort is ineffective, and some actually increases interest in trying drugs (Du-Pont, 1974). There seem to be several reasons for the failure of these endeavors.

First, the credibility of opponents of drug use has been weakened by their obvious exaggerations of the harmful effects of abused substances, especially marijuana. Second, the targets of such education —adolescents and young adults—are frequently much more familiar with the substances discussed, especially the nonopiates, than the instructors, and this readily becomes evident in discussions. Indeed, it has been observed that the same antidrug motion pictures that impress parents and teachers as very convincing are considered ridiculous by younger audiences. Research indicates that high-school students attach most credibility to reports on drugs from a peer or neighbor who has used them (Dembo et al., 1977); college students also rely mainly on personal informants for their decisions on whether or not to try drugs (Hanneman, 1973).

A third factor in adolescent rejection of antidrug education is that taking an allegedly dangerous substance provides an opportunity to show fearlessness before one's peers. Particularly for youth lacking eminence in adult-approved activities, an educator's description of a drug as risky may create an incentive to try it.

Remedies for these failures in antidrug education seem to lie mainly in collaboration between students and teachers in determining the truth. Frankness in teaching is now stressed. Former addicts are often used as speakers and counselors on drugs, since many of their organizations offer this service. Students have also been involved in designing, conducting, and reporting scientific surveys of substance abuse in their school and community, as a means of antidrug education (Wenk, 1975). The effectiveness of these methods is not yet well demonstrated, and their impact is likely to vary greatly with the individuals directing them; they impress many adults as quite convincing to the juveniles, but this was also true of lectures, movies, and other more traditional pedagogical methods that proved counterproductive.

Three Criminological Principles on Prohibiting Addictive, Nonpredatory Conduct

This chapter highlights the importance of the dichotomy developed in the first two chapters, between *predatory* offenses, in which someone is deliberately victimized (as in murder, robbery, and burglary) so that people are likely to call the police, and *nonpredatory* crime, in which all participants engage voluntarily, so that none has an interest in prosecuting the other and, in fact, all are guilty under the law. Since taking illegal substances is nonpredatory conduct, is rarely done in public, and is widespread, the police can only be aware of a fraction of one percent of it.

If the substance taking is compulsive, either because of psychophysiological effects or subcultural support or both, there will be an extremely inelastic demand for the forbidden material, and users will pay high prices and risk severe penalties to obtain it. Therefore, we can set forth a principle of criminology that history repeatedly validates:

1. **Enforcement of prohibition laws against possessing, taking, or selling a substance to which people are addicted or strongly habituated will diminish the visibility but will not greatly lessen the occurrence of law violations.**

This dictum appears to be true regardless of how severe the punishment for the few who are caught. When, in the 1950s, federal and state penalties against recurrent sale to minors of so-called narcotics (types as diverse as marijuana, cocaine, and opiates) included sentences up to life imprisonment, law violations did not abate—they rose. An established tenet is that after sufficient penalty is imposed to make an act distinctly not worthwhile, increases in certainty and speed of government reactions are more deterrent than additional severity. The fact that drug taking and dealing are readily hidden makes it impossible to raise the certainty of apprehension, except on a very local and temporary basis. When there are many sources of supply, closing one only expands the others and stimulates the opening of new ones.

Those who regard substance abuse as evil argue that making it risky to pursue in public achieves its reduction, even if not its elimination. Thus some proposals for marijuana decriminalization include bans on advertising it. Similarly, restrictions were placed on advertising and sales locations of alcoholic beverages after their commerce was legalized, and many contend that these limitations should be greater. Most drugs legally available but readily abused are sold only by prescription. Certainly such regulation has not prevented their illicit distribution, but if it somewhat reduces their misuse, it can be justified from a public-health standpoint (although "libertarians" object on moral grounds even to these restrictions; e.g., Szasz, 1974).

If any effort to prohibit possession or sale of a substance is even partially successful, and thus increases the work required and risks taken in its production and distribution, it raises the price that must be charged. If it is a drug to which people become very compulsively addicted, they are then more likely to have to get funds illegally to purchase what they crave. This demand justifies treatment programs that supply such drugs legally, under controls, to their addicted patients. Thus, we have established a second principle on addiction and crime:

2. **The higher the financial cost of gratifying an addiction, the more often addicted persons engage in predatory crime or other illegal-income pursuits, such as prostitution and pimping.**

The validity of this generalization was dramatically demonstrated with opiates. Before World War II most people addicted to these substances could afford to purchase them from their legitimate income, even if their illegal purchases sometimes cost more than the standard price for prescribed opiates. When access to such drugs from medical supplies was diminished (first by wartime conditions and then by postwar restrictions) while the number of addicts burgeoned, the cost of maintaining addiction boomed, and it became much more closely associated with professional crime and commercial sex. The fact that people are not permitted to receive methadone maintenance until they have been heavily addicted for so long that most have become much more adept at criminal livelihoods than at legitimate employment, diminishes the extent to which such maintenance can decrease criminality.

When the use of an illegal substance spreads widely in any group, inability to enforce the law becomes very evident, and thus the police and courts become less awe-inspiring. Whenever substance taking is popular, it is also quite justified to most people. Thus, laws prohibiting it seem unethical, especially when their enforcement must be quite selective, or be done by procedures of questionable morality and legality, such as entrapment or violation of privacy. This is the basis of a third principle:

3. **Widespread tolerance of the use of illegal substances fosters corruption in enforcement and adjudication of the law as well as disrespect for the criminal-justice system.**

The truth of this proposition was dramatized when the 1933 "Wickersham Report"—the findings of the National Commission on Law Observance and Enforcement—described the extreme corruption of police and courts in their enforcement of the Eighteenth Amendment. Although the Commission itself recommended only more rigorous enforcement, its revelations were an important factor in hastening repeal of the Amendment, for many people who did not wish to drink were shocked by the immoral consequences of unenforceable prohibition legislation. Although professionalization of police forces and judges has made them much less readily corruptible than during the Prohibition Era, their often high-handed, inconsistent, but futile efforts to enforce laws against "soft drugs"—the nonopiates—similarly alienate our youthful generation. This has probably contributed to a large variety of law violation by young people.

The three principles set forth here, supplemented in Chapter 13 by additional propositions on organized crime, apply with little modification to other compulsively pursued nonpredatory behavior, including illegal gambling and one of our next chapter's concerns, illicit sexual conduct.

ELEVEN
SEX CRIMES

One person's passion can be another's revulsion. Controversies over standards of sexual behavior have occurred throughout history, with governments defining as criminal whatever outrages the most influential moral entrepreneurs.

Sex crimes, like other offenses, may be dichotomized as: (1) predations—the deliberate injuries to others, such as rape or other physical molestation—that are virtually never redefined as legal, as well as sexual peeping and indecent exposure, although the damage from these is less tangible; (2) nonpredatory acts, in which all participants collaborate willingly, as in prostitution and homosexuality, and which at times have been noncriminal. Somewhat marginal to this division are pornography, incest, and bigamy; the last two may involve deliberate deception or coercion, but are sometimes by mutual and informed consent.

ACQUISITION OF SEX NORMS

Sexual behavior varies tremendously from one stage of life to another for any person, from one person to another within any society, and from one society to another. It is a product of continual interplay among biological conditions, sociocultural norms, and individual experiences. Criminal law is an additional influence, partly dependent on the norms, but more rigid and hence often ineffective, especially against nonpredatory offenses, since they are not readily policed.

This chapter deals with crimes that reflect beliefs in the morality of a large variety of behavior related to sexual activity and to gender differences, beliefs acquired at different stages of life, from childhood to old age (Gagnon, 1974). Although more diverse and flexible today than a few decades ago, these moral teachings still strongly influence what people regard as criminal. Probably the first such belief learned about sex, beginning quite early in childhood, is that it is shameful to expose one's genitals to persons of the opposite gender. Thus, underlying public attitudes on crimes of self-display are deeply rooted feelings on nudity, and although these taboos have weakened in the 1970s, they still predominate. Perhaps the second acquired belief in this field is that certain words or pictures about sex are shameful or "dirty"; so ideas on pornography may also go back to childhood.

Adolescence brings increasingly great preoccupation with sexuality. The adolescent dreams of adult erotic life, especially during the fantasies that accompany a usually very private and guilt-ridden practice, masturbation. Since imagination is unfettered, both legitimate and criminal sexual conduct is intensively contemplated, and thus experienced vicariously, during this activity. For some, this behavior continues for years or decades, even after marriage and late in life. National surveys, more likely to underestimate, find that well over 90 percent of males and a growing majority of females in the United States have masturbated. Whether the fantasies of illegal sex that sometimes accompany masturbation stimulate overt behavior or are a substitute that prevents it, no one knows (they probably have both types of effects, at different times and with different people) (Hunt, 1974: Chapter 2).

During the late· teenage years, social life with the opposite gender usually expands, as does concern about competence and popularity in it. Courtship and sexual intimacy are more frequent, with parental control in these activities typically low. From then through early adulthood, particularly in the twenties, love becomes a primary value, with physical passion viewed as a crucial part of it. Yet for a variety of reasons that will be indicated, many in this period seek illegal sex acts as supplements or alternatives to other erotic experience (Stoll, 1974).

There is generally less preoccupation with sexual matters in middle and old age, as jobs, childcare, and avocations become demanding while biological vigor often declines. Yet an unsatisfactory love life and the exploration of illegal alternatives occur in these years among many of both the married and the unmarried. In addition, although divorce is most common among couples in their twenties, it happens at every age with increasing frequency; when it does, both parties usually return to the courting behavior of early adulthood, but some become involved in law-violating erotic acts. Finally, certain types of sex offense are committed by a few men in reaction to the relative impotence of old age.

Apart from the changes related to the life cycle, we should note that ours is a rather pluralistic society, with diverse preferences in sexual activity as in almost everything else. People who share some sexual interests that conflict with predominant customs tend to associate together and develop a subculture that supports their way of love. Yet all genital sex acts except masturbation and coitus between husband and wife are criminal in many or most states, though some are rarely prosecuted. As we will elaborate, only a small fraction of any type of sex crime is reported to the police. Indeed, some of the nonpredatory sex offenses have been committed by a majority of at least one gender of the population, even when few wished to have them declared noncriminal.

The principal sex offenses will be discussed separately, but all are somewhat similar in their causes. Each reflects a person's social bonds, learning, and perceived opportunities—hence varying anticipations in legal and illegal behavior—during one or more of the life-stage changes outlined here. The most prevalent of these law violations is the sale and purchase of sexual intercourse.

PROSTITUTION AND PANDERING

Two double standards on sexual morality are traditional in Western society and in much of the rest of the world. One is closely related to the other, and both distinctly apply to prostitution. They have greatly diminished in recent years, but have by no means disappeared.

By the first double standard, promiscuity is approved for males —an achievement to brag about—but is immoral for females. Where this view prevails, a man is expected to "sow his wild oats" before marriage; and even adultery after marriage does not discredit him. On the other hand, feminine virtue, by this standard, means virginity at marriage and fidelity afterward.

Pressure for men to be sexually active but women chaste implies a second double standard: the existence in the same society of some women who conform to this requirement and of others who give men premarital sex. The dichotomy of "good" and "bad" women is a mathematical necessity for a double standard of male promiscuity and female "purity." Thus when societies stress female chastity—especially traditional in Catholic countries and in much of Africa and the Orient—there is both careful chaperoning of "good" girls until marriage and open prostitution, often licensed. American soldiers in World War II were surprised by this combination of practices in France, Italy, and North Africa and, for decades later, in Latin America also, where it is part of the "machismo" subculture discussed in Chapter 9. These double standards have existed since ancient times (see the tales of harlots in Joshua, Luke, and other books of the Bible), and it persists, with variations, in many cultures (e.g., the geishas in Japan). Yet these standards have diminished almost everywhere and, with this trend, prostitution has also changed.

For at least a half-century before World War II, most American men were initiated into sex by prostitutes while still teenagers, and they often repeated these transactions until marriage. As late as 1972, according to Hunt's (1974: 144) *Playboy*-sponsored national survey, *Sexual Behavior in the 1970s,* a majority of American men over 35 had had sex with prostitutes, but fewer than 30 percent of those 18 to 35. By the 1970s, more convergence in sexual experience had developed between the genders; males probably had premarital sex somewhat less often than their fathers and grandfathers who had used prostitutes, but women were virgins at marriage less frequently than their mothers and grandmothers.

Girls now apparently have earlier sexual experience than boys, on the average. An Illinois survey of 16- and 17-year-olds in 1971 found that 21 percent of the boys and 22 percent of the girls already had coitus (Miller & Simon, 1974). A Colorado study in 1972 and 1973 found that 55 percent of female high-school seniors and only 33 percent of the males were not virgins, but these rates converged in college to 85 percent of female students and 82 percent of' males (Jessor & Jessor, 1975). A 1976 national survey directed by Zelnik and Kanter found that 35 percent of girls between 15 and 20 had had coitus, and of these, over 60 percent had had it with more than one partner (*Los Angeles Times,* April 8, 1977). Ira Reiss's thorough study, *The Social Context of Premarital Sexual Permissiveness* (1967), concluded that social-class differences in age of sexual intimacy are much smaller than was suggested earlier by Alfred C. Kinsey's pioneer scientific surveys of sexual conduct—the famous "Kinsey Reports"—*Sexual Behavior in the Human Male* (1948) and *Sexual Behavior in the Human Female* (1953).

Apparently, increased access to contraception, legal abortion, greater adolescent autonomy, and gender equality all foster more sexual intimacy in early youth. A 1972 national study of married women found that four-fifths of those under 25 had premarital coitus, compared with only about a third of those over 54 (Hunt, 1974: 150). Thus, the current generation has much less of a double standard on sexual relations. Today's prostitution caters to a smaller percentage of men under 30, but still finds many customers between 30 and the 50s, according to Winick and Kinsie's (1971: 186) study of this occupation, *The Lively Commerce.* The prostitutes are likely to be in their early 20s, as far as we can infer from arrest data (see Table 4-3).

Before World War II, prostitutes generally worked in brothels. These "houses of ill fame" were usually managed by a "madam," a former prostitute who often owned it, although some organized criminal syndicates operated chains of houses and moved both girls and madams from one to another. For a bordello to be known to many customers, it had to be at one address for a long time; thus the police would also be readily aware of it, especially since it often operated in conjunction with a bar or dance hall where the women contacted customers and then took them upstairs (see B. Jackson, 1972: Chapter 4). Therefore, before such a place even opened, and regularly thereafter, graft was paid to police and politicians to keep it from being closed; essentially these officials licensed such businesses, though illegally. The decline of houses of prostitution was due partly to increased difficulty in maintaining the necessary corruption of local government as patronage appointments of police and machine politics diminished, but mostly to reduced demand for prostitutes and to competition for the remaining market from streetwalkers, bar hustlers, call girls, and massage parlors.

Prostitutes are disproportionately, but by no means exclusively from poverty-stricken homes. Typically promiscuous at first, especially with "big spenders" who buy them entertainment or gifts, they later join the "oldest profession" when its income prospects are suggested by more experienced women or by pimps. Such advisors coach them on pleasing customers quickly, defending themselves against the client's possible violence and robbery (or on cheating or robbing him, especially if he is a transient), providing fellatio and other deviant sexual stimulation that some customers desire, recognizing veneral diseases, being wary of the police, realizing obligations to others in the business, and rationalizing their activity (Bryan, 1965, 1966; Winick & Kinsie, 1971).

The primary motivation of prostitutes is economic; they anticipate more financial reward from this than from other feasible employment. Accordingly, those of middle-class background, or experienced in legitimate occupations in which jobs are available, are typically attracted only by the more lucrative forms of prostitution, such as call girls for business executives, often recruited in groups for sales conventions. A growing number are only part-time prostitutes, also spending time in other jobs, as students or even as housewives. As they make contacts or learn skills for procuring customers, however, they are attracted to it full time. Compared with alternatively available occupations, it often appeals not only as more remunerative, but sometimes as providing more interesting companions and colleagues (particularly for call girls) and (especially if not with a pimp) as offering greater independence and flexible hours. Exploiting the occupation fully requires a callous attitude toward the customers, or "johns"; but some report sympathy and even affection for them, and many develop long-term friendships with a few (Bryan, 1965, 1966).

Pimps are men who live from the earnings of prostitutes; *panderers* are those who recruit, encourage, or coerce women to become prostitutes. In practice, however, the words are used interchangeably, perhaps because the same persons perform both functions. They usually are called "pimps," and if convicted for these acts they can be more severely punished than the women who work for them. A pimp generally trains, protects, and manages the careers of several prostitutes. Most recruit by offering aid to women in crises; for example, bailing them out of jail, providing clothes and cosmetics for "hustling," or offering drugs to those addicted and suffering from withdrawal. Others court promiscuous or drug-dabbling women, and promise a mutually rewarding business. Frequently there is an amorous relationship between the pimp and several prostitutes simultaneously, the male often having a "Don Juan" or *macho* pride in conquest and a contempt for his quasi-slaves, yet sometimes misleading each to think she is his favorite. The loyalty of women to these men under such conditions has been attributed psychologically to a socially devalued person's appreciating anyone who shows regard for her or who simply offers unjudging friendship when she is lonely from a life of feigned pleasure and affection. Usually there is also a sense of obligation to the pimp for gifts, professional advice that enhances income, intervention with the police and courts, and protection when customers become violent. However, some pimps assault and terrorize prostitutes and foster their addiction. Some psychoanalysts speculate that such women masochistically desire abuse to alleviate unconscious guilt feelings.

Many prostitutes regularly divide earnings with their pimps as they formerly did with madams, often 50–50, but instances are reported of pimps who take all income from several women and dole back only minimal spending money. Police find it much more difficult to entrap and convict for pandering than for prostitution; so they get at pimps mainly by harassment, often of questionable legality. A growing number of prostitutes are now reported to be "outlaws"—operating independently or in a loose partnership with other prostitutes rather than with pimps. These arrangements vary greatly from one region to another (Benjamin & Masters, 1964: Chapter 7; Bryan, 1965; Winick & Kinsie, 1971: Chapter 4). Taxi drivers, bellboys, and bartenders also often direct men to prostitutes, for which they receive tips from the customers and "kickbacks" from the women.

A change in recent decades is the large percentage of prostitutes and pimps who are drug addicts. They comprise a majority in many cities, with pimps frequently the drug suppliers. Especially desperate for drugs when feeling sick from withdrawal effects, "strung-out" women are often aggressive streetwalkers and even muggers, notorious around some hotels and bus terminals in New York but probably found in other cities as well. Certainly, when prostitution reflects desperation for drugs, its effective reduction requires that prostitutes be helped either to end their drug habit or to get drugs legally (by methods discussed in Chapter 10).

There are little systematic data on the termination of careers as prostitutes, but Kingsley Davis says: "Movement in and out of prostitution is relatively easy. For most women the occupation is pursued at the age when it is most lucrative, and then abandoned" (1976: 252). Being out of the conventional job market, however, may make it difficult for a woman to turn from prostitution to legitimate employment. Gagnon and Simon report that performing the sexual act for a fee is legal in Denmark as long as the woman also has another job. The purpose of this policy, they assert, is to ensure that "sufficient ties will be maintained to the conventional community so that the woman will have a past other than one of prostitution when she chooses to leave this career" (1973: 233).

Massage parlors proliferated in American cities in the 1970s, so that there are now hundreds, identified by prominent signs, scattered in many commercial zones and shopping centers of almost every major metropolitan area. They have become a significant field of female employment. The official service offered is only massage, but this routinely extends to the customer's fondling the masseuse and to her masturbating him. The customer may desire more, however, and since the service is provided in private rooms, may also receive fellatio and coitus if he is trusted and pays sufficiently for such "extras." Masseuses vary greatly in background, but some are college-educated women attracted by the high income this job can offer (Rasmussen & Kuhn, 1976).

The rapid growth of these establishments will probably have a tremendous impact on traditional forms of prostitution and possibly on rates of male sex offenses. Many of these places may now actually be—de facto but not officially—houses of prostitution, more open and more widely distributed than such businesses in the United States have ever been. "The traditional brothel has largely vanished from the American scene, but in its place one may find 'massage parlors'. . . . Out of deference to social sensibilities, the names have been changed to protect the identity of the vices" (Adler, 1975: 56).

In the United States prostitution is officially legal only in Nevada, where it is authorized in all but the two most populous counties, those containing Las Vegas and Reno. There is a regular flow from these recreational centers to the thinly populated locales that welcome tourist trade and tax income from licensed brothels. Opinion polls in the 1970s indicate that a majority of the country favors licensed prostitution.

Support for legalization doubtless reflects the cost, corruption, and predominant failure of efforts to suppress prostituion. Several European countries have laws only against public soliciting, but they tolerate or license prostitutes. Usually their controls over soliciting are effective only against the more brazen hawking in areas that are continuously policed, but this restriction of visibility may be all that is accomplished or desired in most American law enforcement. Indeed, it is alleged that although downtown business interests in most American cities encourage policing against any prostitution that annoys the public, they want no interference with the discreet sale of sexual services to tourists and conventioneers in their hotels. Furthermore, they have regularly blocked efforts to enforce laws that punish patrons of prostitutes (Roby, 1969). A woman judge in San Francisco upset police and court officials in the mid-1970s by refusing to convict prostitutes unless their customers were also prosecuted.

In many cities of Continental Europe, notably those of Germany and the Netherlands, prostitution is licensed only in limited areas; for example, the Eros Hotel in Hamburg has over a hundred rooms for a similar number of female employees. This practice harks back to the "red-light districts" of many American cities in the nineteenth and early twentieth centuries, when prostitution was "wide

Some of Nevada's legal prostitutes and their pimp.

ELEVEN SEX CRIMES

open" in certain areas through its tolerance by corrupted police. For massage parlors and for pornographic book stores and movies, American cities are increasingly adopting the "Detroit Plan," approved by the Supreme Court, which requires a distance of at least 1,000 feet between any two such establishments, along with the approval of at least 51 percent of residents or businesses within 500 feet of its site.

An argument for prostitution that dates back to St. Augustine is that it reduces the molestation or assault of women by sexually frustrated men. This long-untested claim received some support from an Australian finding that after the 1959 closing of brothels in Queensland, rapes rose 149 percent in a period during which other physical assaults increased 49 percent (Geis, 1972: 211).

There has been much growth in group psychotherapy programs stressing physical touching and nudity. Such practices, culminating in sexual intercourse with volunteer or paid partners called "sexual surrogates," have been used to treat sexual inadequacy, following the influential research with these methods by Masters and Johnson (1966, 1970; see also Brecher & Brecher, 1966). Criminologist Freda Adler (1975: 82) has suggested that many prostitutes who develop rapport with their clients now serve as psychiatric social workers, and in a period of greater sexual freedom, they might do it more effectively.

Leading criminal-justice issues in the administration of antiprostitution laws are well summarized in the following statement by columnist George F. Will:

> The harmful public consequences associated with prostitution are either unaffected by attempts to proscribe it, or are produced by those attempts.
>
> Prostitution is immoral, but it is not a threat to the fabric of society. Disrespect for the law is such a threat, and antiprostitution laws foster such disrespect. The laws do not work, and they usually involve violations of three provisions of the Constitution.
>
> Antiprostitution laws invariably violate the right to privacy, a right implicit in First Amendment values and given explicit constitutional rank in a Supreme Court decision a decade ago dealing with private sexual activity.
>
> Antiprostitution laws, usually in their words and invariably in their applications, violate the equal protection provision of the Constitution by discriminating againt women. In five states the laws apply only to women, not to their customers. Even where the laws are cast in sexually neutral language or where "patronizing a prostitute" also is a crime, the pattern of enforcement is discriminatory.

Prostitutes' customers rarely are arrested, and when they are arrested it usually is only to induce them to testify against prostitutes. . . .

Because neither prostitutes nor their customers complain to the police about prostitution, it is not easy for the police to make prostitution arrests. So male police officers frequently pose as customers or female officers pose as prostitutes, in order to lure prostitutes into soliciting, or to lure men into propositioning. These police practices should be considered illegal entrapment, and violations of constitutional guarantee of due process.

Such behavior degrades the dignity of the police profession. And it is expensive. In 1971 San Francisco spent $375,000 processing 2,000 prostituion arrests. It costs Seattle about $1 million annually for prostitution arrests and trials.

It is estimated that only five percent of the nation's more than a quarter of a million prostitutes have venereal diseases. The rate for high school students between the ages of 15 and 19 is estimated to be at least three times that high. The VD rate is low among prostitutes because they know a lot about the problem. Of course, even a rate of five percent is a public health problem, but as long as prostitutes are liable to criminal sanctions, they will be reluctant to risk seeking regular treatment.

Criminalizing prostitution tends to make criminals out of policemen as well as prostitutes.

Prostitution, banned nearly everywhere, exists nearly everywhere, and often pays for its existence with graft that corrupts the law enforcement machinery. Seventy percent of all women in prison today were first arrested for prostitution, and many say they've learned about "real crime" while in prison. Indeed, many turned to "real crime" because prostitution arrest records made it difficult for them to find more respectable employment.

To the extent that solicitation by prostitutes is a public nuisance, it can be regulated by statutes concerning street solicitation for commercial purposes (© 1974, The Washington Post Company. Reprinted with permission).

One objection to legalizing prostitution is that it would demean and exploit women, but these have been even more clearly the effects of illegal prostitution, which has persisted since ancient times, even where outlawed. One study found unlicensed prostitutes on the American side of a Mexican border city younger and more aggressive in initiating sexual jostling with men in bars and on the streets than the registered prostitutes on the Mexican side, who were older, more stable, more affectionate and cheerful, and had regular health checkups (Roebuck & McNamara, 1973).

ELEVEN   SEX CRIMES

Paid male partners, offering sexual services for females desiring it, are available to some extent as gigolos, hired escorts with degree of intimacy unspecified. There is little published research on gigolos. They are believed to be much less numerous than female prostitutes, but men are virtually never prosecuted for selling sexual services to women. If some commercial dating and escort services provide sexual as well as social partners, the fee is officially charged only for the social aspect, and it alone is obligatory.

Another recent development in the United States is the increase in homosexual prostitutes, primarily male. Laws in several states have been revised to eliminate sexist definitions of prostitution, so that it now denotes any person engaging in, offering, or agreeing to coitus or other sexual acts with any other person for a fee. Male prostitutes have allegedly been particularly responsible for the spread of veneral disease; females, guarding against pregnancy, often require that clients use condoms, frequently providing and putting them on their customers, and these devices also protect against infection. Many female prostitutes also see physicians regularly or take prophylactic doses of penicillin even when no symptoms are present.

Male prostitutes are typically young and were introduced to homosexuality at an early age, often as "kept boys" of older men. They solicit in gay bars, on the streets where such bars are concentrated, and in all-night movie houses. Also, many heterosexual delinquents "play the queers" for extra income—even for a few dollars to spend on a girl later in the evening—and do not consider their activities with a male as sexual (Reiss, 1961; Benjamin & Masters, 1964: Chapter 10; Esselstyn, 1968). The Los Angeles Police Department claims that, in this city alone, "more than 25,000 juveniles from 14 to 17 years of age are used sexually by approximately 15,000 adult males" (*Los Angeles Times,* November 19, 1976), although others say that these figures are too high. Most of these youth are allegedly runaways (called "chickens") whose services are often managed by adults ("chicken hawks") who rent them out for deviant sex and for making pornographic films, which are distributed privately and often shown before sexual acts to arouse the participants. The runaways gather around bus stations, teenage discotheques, and amusement arcades, where recruiters entice them with money, gifts, and, above all, friendship, which is especially welcomed by boys estranged from their parents and communities. Rossman (1973) claims that a "sexual underground" of young boys recruited for service to adult homosexuals exists in all major cities of the world, much of it run by cruel and exploitative international organizations.

Many changing sex norms—for example, increased contacts between men and women in school, work, and recreation as gender barriers diminish, and through computer dating, singles clubs, and gay community centers—reduce the market for various types of prostitution. More persons than ever get and prefer sex from affection rather than commerce, including much more living together as though married, when legally single. Yet there remain, and probably will always be, some who are willing to buy and others to sell sex that is available immediately or by appointment, and without emotional involvement or continuing obligation.

Trends in the generalization of values (discussed in Chapter 2) suggest that adults selling sex to other adults in private will probably be a diminishing concern of the criminal law, but will be investigated and controlled more by public-health offices. The focus will be on combatting venereal disease and, for heterosexual women, unwanted pregnancies; but these are consequences of all promiscuity, perhaps least frequent in that which is professional. Municipal and county agencies will doubtless restrict the advertising and location of sexual-service businesses, just as they zone and regulate other commerce. Sex acts not based on informed and mature mutual consent, however—those that are assaultive offenses—will probably always be dealt with by the criminal-justice system.

RAPE

The dictionary defines rape as "illicit sexual intercourse without the consent of the woman and effected by force, duress, intimidation or deception as to the nature of the act" (Webster's 3rd International Unabridged). The law often says that such an act is rape only if done to "a female [who is] not the wife of the perpetrator" (California Penal Code). Feminists contend that the law views rape as a form of robbery and a wife as her husband's property, so he cannot be charged with raping her because he cannot rob himself. This notion is especially detestable to the growing proportion of women who consider themselves autonomous persons, each belonging only to herself regardless of marital status. Part of a current movement to aid and protect the victims of wife beaters is an effort to change rape laws so that forcing a spouse into coitus is also a crime. Indeed, the battered wife is a frequent but little-studied victim of predation, for whose protection criminal law will probably be enacted (Gelles, 1972; Miller, 1975; Martin, 1976).

The FBI (1976: 6) counts rape and attempted rape as the same crime, and finds that about one-fourth of those reported to the police are only attempts (1976: 22). In most states, however, a man is guilty of rape, rather than the less severely punished crime of attempted rape, only if his sex organ penetrates the female. Except for the participants there are usually no witnesses, but should someone else see it, that

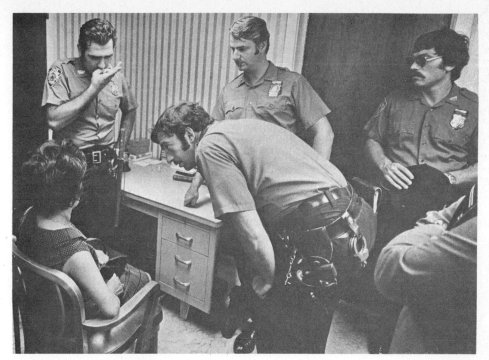

A traditional rape investigation.

person is unlikely to be near enough to discern penetration. Therefore, proof of rape depends mainly on the credibility of the victim's allegations. It is often asserted that the disparity of strength between women and men is not so great as to permit penetration if there is vigorous resistance. Indeed, a woman's claim that she was raped is often not accepted by police and courts unless she (or the accused, if known) has bruises, scratches, or other evidence of struggle or of the use of a weapon. Gagnon points out that, by this traditional police perspective, if "the woman is known to the man, has had sex with him before, has a bad reputation, seems nonhysterical and uninjured, she ceases to be a victim and becomes a woman who . . . was a tease and deserved what she got" (1974: 262).

Although many attempts at rape are successfully repelled despite determined male efforts, most women in our society are not conditioned to be violent, even in self-defense. Some, when attacked roughly, submit in terror, too frightened to muster their physical potential for effective resistance, or habituated just to plead verbally (for case examples, see Burgess & Holmstrom, 1974: Chapter 1; Schultz, 1975: Section I). The increased prevalence of handguns (discussed in Chapter 9) results in their more frequent use to bully women into sexual submission. Other weapons, such as knives or clubs—and sometimes merely verbal threats to injure the victim or her children—can also coerce some cooperation. Intimidation purely by verbal threats can be legally prosecuted as rape in many states, but it is difficult to prove and probably few of its occurrences are reported to the police.

Further discouraging a woman from pressing charges is the fact that she usually encounters only male police and prosecution officials. If the accused is tried, she is badgered by a defense attorney who probes intensively into whether she knew the defendant and had slept with him or with other men previously. No such prior history of the woman justifies rape, but it often persuades a judge or jury to discredit her claim of unwilling coitus with the accused. If this probing is unrestrained by the prosecutor's objections and by the judge, it can be a vicious public destruction of the woman's reputation and self-respect.

The victim usually feels soiled by the rape, more so if it is known at home, by neighbors, or at work or school. She is frequently prey to skeptical queries or snide remarks, and her relationships with friends and relatives, particularly males, may be permanently scarred. Self-consciousness and shame from these experiences often lead a victim to leave her home, job, or school (Burgess & Holmstrom, 1974). Because communicating about being raped can be so humiliating, only a fraction of these crimes is reported to the police. What is the size of this fraction?

The victim survey of the President's Commission in 1967 estimated that about one-fourth of all rapes were known to the police, whereas the National Crime Panel's survey (described in Chapter 4) concluded in 1974 that half were known. Other studies suggest that police underestimate the prevalence of this offense much more than these statistics imply. In the 1950s, on questionnaires distributed in university classes from which male students were dismissed, 11 percent of the 291 female respondents said that in the preceding year they had suffered forceful attempts at sexual intercourse, including six percent that were accompanied by menacing threats or painful physical coercion. However, none of the women reported these episodes to parents or other authorities, half told no one, and most of the remainder confided only in close friends (Kirkpatrick & Kanin, 1957). A replication of this study queried 262 first-year college women about their senior year in high school and found that 21 percent experienced attempts to coerce intercourse, including nine percent with violence. Here, too, only 10 percent of the total reported the episodes to parents or other authorities (Kanin, 1957). Regardless of the precise percentages that a representative sample might give today if responding validly to such an inquiry, one can infer from these studies that many persons speaking for all members of their household to victim-survey researchers do not know about the rapes or attempted rapes of young females in their own families. If they do know, or if they themselves were the victims, how many would talk about it to a stranger, even one who is a government pollster?

Another reason for nonreporting indicated by these college studies is that most of the offenses are committed by men with whom the women are fairly well acquainted; a majority of these attempts to force intercourse were by men who were "steady dates" or to whom the women were "pinned" or "engaged," while less than a third were by new acquaintances. It thus appears that most attempts at rape, and probably most actual rapes occur when a woman shows a man some affection but does not wish this to develop into sexual intercourse. Contrastingly, in Amir's (1971) sample of Philadelphia police cases, the offender was a stranger in 52 percent of the rapes, an acquaintance in 14 percent, a close neighbor in 19 percent, a family friend or relative in eight percent, and a close friend in only six percent (see Reiss, 1974, on limitations of these data). The college findings suggest that rapes by strangers are probably a small minority of total rapes, but Amir's study indicates that they constitute about half of those reported to the police.

Amir judged that 19 percent of these reported rapes were victim-precipitated, for this was the percentage of cases in which he inferred from police files that the woman had agreed to and then refused coitus, did not make a strong enough objection when the act was suggested, or used "what could be interpreted as indecency in language and gestures, or . . . what could be taken as an invitation to sexual relations" (1971: 266). He did not check the reliability of his percentage estimation by comparing interpretations of these records made independently by two or more other persons; the validity of the entries in these records is also uncertain. Estimates of victim-precipitation rates in other studies vary greatly with the case information available and its interpretation (Curtis, 1974: 87–92).

Unwarranted accusations of rape have occasionally gained notoriety, an ancient one being the Biblical tale of Joseph and Potiphar's wife (Genesis 39). Among the most prominent in this century was Alabama's Scottsboro Case of the 1930s, in which one of two white accusers of nine black youth later admitted that she had lied to avoid prosecution for vagrancy; however, the last surviving prisoner was not pardoned until 1976 (for other examples, see Sagarin, 1975). Also, some women spurned by their lovers, wives caught in infidelity by their husbands, and daughters discovered in compromising circumstances by their parents have falsely charged rape. On the average, police classify 15 percent of the rape complaints they receive as unfounded (FBI, 1976: 24); but this probably results not so much from the accusations being false as from the victim ceasing to press charges because she finds the humiliation, time and strain involved in trips to police station and court too great, or because the offender or his family threatens reprisal if she testifies. It seems unlikely that unwarranted accusations are so numerous as to justify the police and prosecution acting from the outset as though the charges are false; it is more appropriate for them to encourage the complainant to persist in her testimony to the conclusion of prosecution (as they often do). They should prepare her for the stress of the defense counsel's probable attempts to discredit and demean her and to delay proceedings (Burgess & Holmstrom, 1974: Chapter 5).

From the victim's perspective, there are two kinds of rape. In the "blitz" variety, a stranger attacks without warning, often without ever being clearly seen; for example, by sneaking up on a woman in the dark or entering her home at night without her awareness. In the "confidence" type, the woman is misled so that she can be raped; for example, by a man pretending to provide safe transportation, to be a repairman, or to be a "nice" date (Burgess & Holmstrom, 1974: Chapter 1).

The trauma of being raped has two phases. Initially there is disorganization and incredulity, the terrorized woman not quite believing it is really happening or has occurred. Anger, fear, and shame soon follow. The intensity of physical pain depends on the wounds, bruises, or sprains inflicted, but the mental anguish in the first few days produces nausea, tremors, sobbing, insomnia or nightmares, loss of appetite, inability to concentrate, and irritability. Women report overreacting to minor misconduct by their children, spouses, or associates, then weeping and feeling guilty about losing their tempers. The long-term consequences may entail changes in lifestyle, such as the flight from home, job, school, and friends already mentioned, lack of ease in any relations with men, and extreme anxiety about being anywhere alone. Sometimes a husband will reject his wife because she was raped by another man. Recurrent nightmares, even upsetting daydreams and flashback memories, plague many raped women for years. Some develop morbid fears of any man with features that remind them of the rapist (Burgess & Holmstrom, 1974: Chapter 3). Physical and psychological impairments of sexual response in lovemaking are sometimes long lasting and can damage subsequent marital relationships (Masters & Johnson, 1970: 257, 276, 280–81). Despite Britain's hardpressed economy, its Criminal Injuries Compensation Board decided that a victim of rape is entitled to a thousand pounds if it leaves her with "no significant physical injuries and average psychological reaction," and up to twice as much for greater damage, plus free medical and psychotherapeutic services (*Los Angeles Times,* November 27, 1976).

During the late 1960s and especially in the 1970s, the women's liberation movement concentrated on hitherto largely overlooked problems in the handling of rape cases by police, judicial, and medical personnel. Because of the vigorous and persistent efforts of feminists, most large cities endeavored to make all police staff sympathetic, not skeptical, to women who report being raped, and required use of female officers in interrogating rape victims. Rape-victim advocates were appointed in Portland, Oregon's prosecution office, and this innovation was copied elsewhere. Women's organizations or local governments in many cities established counseling centers to aid and advise rape victims, to educate all women on how to discourage or resist this offense, and to encourage them to report it and preserve evidence if it does occur. Hospital emergency staff and other medical personnel were instructed to give rape victims priority and sympathy when examining them, to identify and preserve evidence (particularly semen and blood), and to note scratches, bruises, and torn clothing. Several widely distributed publications give details on how to operate a Rape Investigation Unit within a police force, how to prosecute rape cases more effectively, and how medical centers, counseling agencies, and political-action organizations can develop special programs for rape victims (perhaps the best of these books are: Burgess & Holmstrom, 1974; Brodyaga et al., 1975). Finally, evaluation and coordination of these efforts were furthered when, despite a presidential veto two years earlier, Congress in 1975 founded the Center for the Prevention and Control of Rape within the National Institute of Mental Health.

The many developments described above may have produced a marked increase in percentage of rapes reported to the police, and thus an illusion of greater rates of this offense. An even greater upsurge in reporting might result from the British proposal that names of rape complainants never be publicized (Geis, 1977). Another effect of the liberation movement on women is a more militant attitude toward fighting back—both legally, by reporting and prosecuting male aggression, and literally, by learning karate, jiu-jitsu, and other arts of physical self-defense.

In a majority of states, laws on rape were revised in the past decade, for example: to reduce requirements for corroboratory evidence (*Yale Law Journal*, 1972); to bar questioning about the victim's sex life not bearing directly on the alleged crime; to extend the time period following the offense in which charges may be filed. In response to feminist lobbying, several states also changed their legal definition of rape to apply to either gender, oral and anal sexual contact, degrees of criminality when penetration does not occur, and coercion of the victim by threats against a third person. Michigan allows a woman to charge her spouse with sexual assault if they are living apart and one has filed for separate maintenance or divorce (Brodyaga et al., 1975: 271).

As indicated in Chapter 1, often included in the definition of rape is any intercourse engaged in willingly by a girl who is below the

Figure 11–1 Types of Rapists and Nonrapists Classified by Their Attitudes toward their Actual or Potential Victims

Desire for Affection from Her	Respect for Her Personal Autonomy		
	Low	Fluctuating	High
High	1.Naive grasper	2. Meaning stretcher	Nonrapist wooer or lover
Low	3. Sex looter	4. Group conformer	Other nonrapist

age of consent (usually 16, but sometimes 18). Many states distinguish this collaborative offense from forcible rape, calling it "statutory rape" or simply "unlawful sexual intercourse," and punishing it less severely than rape. Data presented in the preceding section on loss of virginity during adolescence as a factor in the declining market for prostitution indicates that statutory rape may now be experienced by at least 20 percent of 16- and 17-year-old girls and five to 10 percent of girls 14 to 17. The National Organization for Women advocates lowering the age of consent to 12 (Brodyaga et al., 1975: 272). When two children (e.g., age 14 or 15) have coitus by mutual consent, it is not classifiable in most states as statutory rape, but may be adjudicated as delinquency. In defining unlawful sexual intercourse, emphasis is increasingly placed on age disparity. When both are juvenile, there is no criminal prosecution, although counseling may be provided; but definite penalties are imposed on appreciably older persons who seduce youngsters. All of these offenses may overlap the crime of sexual molestation of a child, which is discussed separately in the next section of this chapter.

There are numerous classifications of rapists, but typologies depend for their justification on their purpose, on the source of cases (e.g., arrestees, clinic patients, prisons, or admitted-offense questionnaires), and on tests of their reliability and validity. Gebhard and associates completed the massive study *Sex Offenders,* begun by the late Alfred C. Kinsey. From interviews with 140 rapists, they distinguished seven types: assaultive, amoral, drunken, explosive, double-standard, mental defective, and psychotic (1965: 197–205). Although they present a case or two illustrative of each type, the attributes that identify these seven varieties are not mutually exclusive; therefore, many rapists have features from several of these categories (on such problems in all classification, see Glaser, 1974: Chapter 2).

To explain the conduct of rapists, we may find it useful to

separate them into four broad rubrics reflecting two main dimensions of attitude during the crime, as indicated in Figure 11-1. Since intensity in these two dimensions are matters of degree and may change with time, any cross-section of these criminals will include some near the dividing point of a dimension who are not reliably classifiable by only one type. Yet because rapists differ somewhat in their respect for the autonomy of a victim and clearly differ in desire for affection from her, many are quite unambiguously classifiable on this scheme. Since each of the four numbered rubrics in Figure 11-1 is defined by a unique combination of roughly measurable highness or lowness on variables relevant to understanding rape, the typology can have both theoretical and practical value. Let us consider its four categories of rapists:

1. *Naive graspers* are youth with little of the adolescent dating experience of their peers, often with no information on sex other than that gleaned from smutty jokes, pornography, and perhaps some braggarts who claim many seductions. Such youths develop intense feelings of inferiority, cravings for the alleged euphoria of these boasters, and unrealistic ideas about the ease of feminine sexual arousal. Self-conscious and socially awkward with women, they often follow them and imagine that their sexual advances would be accepted affectionately. Their sexual fantasies become the nightmares of their victims. They use romantic language when coercing women, and afterward suggest future meetings, especially with women who cease physical resistance or never begin it because they are threatened with guns or knives. If humiliated when crude approaches are rebuffed or when physical resistance is vigorous, some naive graspers escalate violence to even lethal extremes (e.g., Martin, 1953). The family and friends of these offenders are shocked when they learn of such sex mania in a presumed "good boy." One youth I knew in an Illinois prison had his first nonviolent coitus while free on bail pending trial for rape, when his father took him to a prostitute. Sometimes, however, these naive graspers are married, but dissatisfied because their sex life is not what they imagine it should be.

2. *Meaning stretchers* are probably the least prosecuted but most numerous rapists. The tradition that couples not yet intimate should not explicitly voice their sexual desires, and that a woman should slow a man's ardor even when she hopes it continues, often transforms amiability between a man and a woman to conflict. Confusion is frequent about a woman's "no," for it means just that when said by those who want romance without premarital sex, whereas it could mean "maybe" to women who use it only to defer sex until a more appropriate mood develops. The meaning stretcher tries to force coitus because he misconstrues a woman's friendliness or even affection as implying that she will acquiesce, although she has no such inclination

and is offended by his use of force or threat. When mutual respect and sensitivity exist, discord over the pace of lovemaking does not escalate to violence or threat; but when a man ignores a woman's autonomy and stretches the meaning she wishes to convey, what starts as amiable interaction can end as trauma for her.

The previously cited studies of college students suggest that when men try to coerce sex with women whom they have been steadily dating, it is least likely to be reported to authorities. Perhaps this is because some mutual affection has developed which in some cases permits reconciliation later, because their mixing in the same social circles makes them both anxious to avoid the humiliation of a rape prosecution, and because these rape efforts seldom escalate to extreme violence or threat if the women are persistent in their opposition. Indeed, women who resist successfully are then more "respected" by these men, for such rapes from fluctuating acceptance of female autonomy are related to the vestiges of our society's double standards (described in the preceding section) whereby a man is expected to try to make "conquests" of women to prove his masculinity.

To men with these double standards, women who, in contrast to "straight" girls, are easy "pickups," who are reputed to be promiscuous, who seem readily persuaded into sex play, or who reciprocate banter with explicit reference to copulation, are considered "fair game" for coerced seduction. When regarding some women as sex objects rather than as autonomous persons, the meaning stretcher becomes similar to the third type.

3. *Sex looters* are robbers, using women callously and without compassion. Such coldblooded predation is carried out by highly egocentric individuals in the "blitz" rapes already described or in sexual assaults made after gaining the victim's confidence by deliberate misrepresentation, with no interest in courting affection. Their crimes are the heinous sexual assaults by strangers, the rapes most often reported to the police. These looters usually have a history of aggression and property crime suggesting a blatant disrespect for the rights of others, especially those whom they do not know or do not consider one of their group. Some allegedly are sadists who psychiatrists suggest are more interested in aggression than in sex (see descriptions in Gebhard et al., 1965: 197–201; Burgess & Holmstrom, 1974: 22–32). About five percent of a sample of adult American males report occasionally gaining sexual pleasure from inflicting pain (Hunt, 1974: 333). Possibly such persons are disproportionately sex looters.

Sex looters are also exemplified by the leaders of mass subjugations of women, such as the alleged rapes of 200,000 women by West Pakistani soldiers after temporarily defeating the Bangladesh independence movement in 1971 (Roy, 1975), other reported rapes in military conquests by every nation throughout history, and many group rapes by youth cliques and gangs today. Although the leaders are sex looters, the followers may be less consistently contemptuous of female autonomy.

4. *Group conformers* are those who join the initiators of successive rapes, when several males collaborate in subjugating their victim. In group rapes among delinquents, known as "gang bangs" and "shags," several boys place one or more girls whom they consider promiscuous—or towards whose group they are prejudiced—in a situation in which intercourse can be coerced. These rapes are usually initiated by sex looters, the leaders or core members in cliques or gangs who are verbally and physically the most aggressive and brutal, but others perform sex acts with the victim after the first few have done so, and few refrain. Among such young males, the competition to prove masculinity makes abstention humiliating, while group-supported derogations of the girls and collective excitation often overcome individual scruples.

All participants in a group rape are subject to prosecution for rape if they collaborated in the coercion, and in many states they can receive the same penalties (Amir, 1971: Chapter 11). Relevant to both sex looters and group conformers is that the highest correlation of rape rates for cities and neighborhoods are the other index-crime rates (Geis, 1977): those who steal property also frequently take sex, and those who assault to injure also are likely to rape. This conclusion may be less valid for naive graspers, who confine their offenses more to sexual assault, or to meaning stretchers, whose rapes are largely unreported.

The typology in Figure 11-1 classifies offenders by their attitudes toward the victim in a specific rape. It is conceivable that some men may each commit several such assaults in their lifetimes, particularly if never punished for it, but have different attitudes at different times. Thus some may start as naive graspers, then become sufficiently socialized with women to show more respect for their autonomy; others may usually be meaning stretchers, but in certain circumstances, as when members of a conquering army, be sex looters or group conformers.

Drinking preceded one-third to one-half the rapes investigated in various studies (Amir, 1971: Chapter 8), and it can be associated with any of the four types distinguished here, just as it also precedes much legitimate sexual activity. As indicated in Chapter 10, the cultural connotations of imbibing alcohol include permitting familiarity between strangers, defining situations as more intimate than they would otherwise be, displaying masculinity by heavy consumption, and giving persons labeled "drunk" a license to aggression and to lewd or promiscuous sexuality. In addition, of course, the disinhibition interpretation of alcohol's effects in the bloodstream holds that it weakens cognitive controls over impulse expression before it weakens the impulses themselves. In the case of sexuality, however, heavy intoxication, like fatigue or sedation, also sharply reduces masculine sexual potency; thus, increased desire but weakened capacity for rape are common when men become highly inebriated.

Rapists are usually of the same race and neighborhood as their victims, although most public attention is given to interracial offenses. In 1975, 52 percent of rape arrestees were white, 45 percent were black, and the remainder of other ethnic categories (FBI, 1976: 24). According to police records of 17 major American cities in 1967, six of seven rapes by blacks were of blacks, and 99 percent by whites were of whites (Curtis, 1974: 21). In an old Chicago study of sex offenses cleared by the arrest of a male (mainly rapes), the offender and the victim came from the same police district in 64 percent of the cases and from adjacent city districts in 18 percent (Erlanson, 1941). As shown in Table 4-3, the median age of arrest for forcible rape in 1975 was 23.3, and the peak age 19. The 1967 police-record survey cited above found that 47 percent of rape victims were age 17 or under, 29 percent were between 18 and 25, and 24 percent were over 25. Apparently, young girls are the most vulnerable, but the percentage of rapes not reported to the police may be higher for adults of all ages. Although rapes occur with offenders and victims in almost every possible combination of ages, over two-thirds of juveniles arrested for this crime were accused of assaulting adults; those between 18 and 25 usually raped women in the same age range; and rapists over 25 most often attacked women under that age (Curtis, 1974: 35).

Imprisonment is almost always mandatory for an adult convicted of rape, but plea bargaining often reduces the charges to attempted rape, assault, or even trespassing, to permit lesser penalties. In 1966 an unusually brutal sex crime in Philadelphia led to quick passage of a state law raising the maximum penalty for rape with injury from 15 years to life in prison, and the minimum from zero to 15 years. Officials voiced the expectation that this would make "the criminal element . . . think twice" about committing this offense, but the statute had no discernible effect on rape rates (Schwartz, 1968).

Rape, this suggests, is not deterred by proclaimed penalties. Apparently it is committed without the expectation of being caught or even the thought of punishment. Nevertheless, once arrest and imprisonment occur they seem to be deterrent. A three-year followup of a national sample of men paroled in 1971 found that 76 percent of forcible-rape and 80 percent of statutory-rape offenders had no postrelease difficulty with the law, or only minor (rarely sexual) infractions resulting in less than 60-day penalties. This rate compared with 61 percent for auto theft, 63 percent for forgery and fraud, and 67 percent for burglary and armed robbery. Indeed, only eight percent of the forcible-rape parolees were charged with a new penitentiary offense during this three-year period, and only one percent was charged again with rape; this suggests that rape is one of the least recidivistic crimes (*Uniform Parole Reports Newsletter,* July 1976).

There is evidence, though now somewhat dated, that recidivism is very low for youthful offenders charged only with a sex offense, but is high for those with a record of several types of crime (Doshay, 1943). The "mixed" offenders seem to have the commitment to criminality typical of unspecialized delinquents and youthful convicts; they are mostly "sex looters" and "group conformers." The rapists without prior criminal record are more often "meaning stretchers" and "naive graspers," who have a stake in conformity and are strongly deterred if caught and convicted; regardless of the official penalty, their main punishment is in being publicly labeled. They are, in terms of the trichotomy described in Chapter 6, predominantly the neurotic or conflicted type of delinquent, while the sex looters are self-centered, and the group conformers are enculturated (see also the discussion of labeling in that chapter). The treatment of rapists by methods other than punishment is usually part of special treatment programs for all sex offenders (considered later in this chapter).

Rape rates might noticeably decline if more men adequately comprehended feminine sexual psychology. Therefore, sexual aggression should diminish with more realistic sex education as well as, at all ages, increased collaboration and companionship of males and females as equals at work, recreation, and other activities. The growth of clubs and programs for singles, dating and escort services, and free or moderately priced marital and sexual counseling should also help to reduce rapes, especially those of the naive grasper.

What would be the effect of legalized prostitution on the rape rate? As cited in the preceding section, Australian data suggest that when brothels were closed, rape increased markedly; and many feminists advocate decriminalization of prostitution on grounds that women have the right to decide what to do with their bodies as long as they do not injure others. Brownmiller (1975), however, argues vehemently for the suppression of prostitution and pornography because they foster the same male conception of women as objects that, she contends, causes rape. History suggests that efforts to suppress prostitution and pornography affect their public visibility much more than their prevalence and accessibility to potential patrons, and thus do not greatly change many demeaning views of women. Greater liberation and equality of both genders, fostering mutual respect and openness in their relationships, would probably reduce prostitution, pornography (to be discussed later in this chapter), and rape.

SEXUAL MOLESTATION OF CHILDREN

The older a male is when committing a sex felony, the younger his victim is likely to be. Rape can be carried out by or against persons of almost any adult age, although it is usually not done by old men or to children under 10. However, youngsters of fragile age are targets of what some state laws call "indecent liberties" or "carnal abuse." This most often consists of sexual fondling, such as stroking breasts or genitals, but sometimes the child is persuaded or coerced to masturbate the adult or to engage in or submit to oral-genital contact, and sometimes rape is attempted. Perpetrators of these crimes are of a wide age range, but what is distinctive is the proportion over 55—as high as 20 percent in some prison admissions, which is greater than any other felony. They are one source of the "dirty old man" stereotype.

Adults who prefer children as sexual objects are known in clinical psychology as "pedophiles." Their interest can be hetero- or homosexual, but the public is especially outraged by the advances of older men to very young girls. A study of New York City cases reported to the police found 10 girls to one boy among victims, and 97 percent of the offenders male; these contrasts between the genders may be somewhat inflated, however, through more complete reporting on male offenders and on girl rather than boy victims (De Francis, 1971).

A sense of inadequacy or disappointment in dealing with adult women seems most often to explain a man's search for affection or sexual arousal from persons so young that he anticipates dominating them more readily. In some cases, however, it is alleged that chance sexual arousal and orgasm in playing as a child with another child, or later, as an adult playing with a child, creates a lifelong fixation on children as sex objects (Bagley, 1969: 513). Pedophilia is persistently committed by a few teenage boys who seek out prepubertal girls, even four-to-seven-year-olds; it also is done by a startling number of young or middle-aged fathers against their own offspring or other children, particularly when their wives are in advanced pregnancy (Hartman & Nicolay, 1966); initiation of child molestation by a man only when he reaches middle or old age is commonly a reaction to impotence (Gebhard et al., 1965; Frisbie, 1969). In a New York City compilation, offenders ranged from 17 to 68 years old, with the median 31 (De Francis, 1971).

The late Alfred C. Kinsey (1953) estimated from his midcentury sampling that before they are 13 years old, about a quarter of American women have sexual experience with an adult. Further analyzing Kinsey's data, Gagnon (1965) shows: about one-eighth of the total sample recalled being confronted by a male exhibitionist, or "flasher," displaying his genitals (in most cases such an encounter occurred only once); about one-sixteenth had their genitals fondled by an adult; with about one-thirty-second coitus was attempted; another thirty-second had coitus; and a very few had oral-genital contacts. All of these acts by adults were crimes, but only six percent were reported to the police; and of these, most were misdemeanors by exhibitionists, who were generally strangers to the child. The genital contacts—all are felonies—were mainly by acquaintances or relatives and were not reported, perhaps partly because the child's cooperation in them was usually persuaded rather than forced. Thus offenders known to authorities must be only a small and unrepresentative fraction of the total in our society.

Forced sex acts sometimes accompany parental battering of their children or stepchildren (described in Chapter 9). Freud was surprised at the high proportion of his patients who had childhood sexual experience with adults, and in his early papers he considered it a basic cause of adult neuroses, though he later modified his views on its prevalence (Gagnon, 1965). Convicted child molesters are a standard part of state prison populations, although in several states some are sent to mental hospitals under special civil-commitment laws for all sex crimes (discussed later in this chapter). In most state parole systems, child molesters and alcoholic forgers vie for the highest rates of recidivism by the same offense, although a few states claim appreciable success with molesters in special sex-offender treatment programs (Frisbie, 1969) (also discussed later in this chapter). Gebhard and associates (1965: 133–54) found heterosexual aggressors against children the most recidivistic category of sex criminal.

A comprehensive sample of convicted child molesters in Wisconsin were mostly from working-class backgrounds, and about two-thirds were at least casually acquainted with the child before the offense (McCaghy, 1967). In 75 percent of the cases there was no evidence of coercion, but four percent used verbal threats and 20 percent used force, including the three percent who were highly violent. In about half the specific offenses for which they were convicted, molestation occurred in the course of nonsexual interaction with the child; in about a quarter of them the youngster was first enticed into a situation in which the sexual acts could be committed; and in the remaining quarter this activity was commenced immediately when the adult contacted the child. Offenses involving only fondling occurred most often with strangers; sexual perversions and extensive genital contacts initiated promptly were more commonly by a member of the child's family, a neighbor, or someone else of long acquaintance, and frequently this offense was discovered by others and reported to authorities only after it had been done repeatedly for months or years. A New York City study found that only a quarter of the felonies reported to police were by strangers, and the most persistent and extensive deviant sexual activity was within the family (De Francis, 1971). Such domestic crime is spotlighted in the Nabokov novel *Lolita*.

Distinctive of many convicted child molesters is their persistence and vehemence in denying the crime. Many, particularly those accused only of fondling a child, insist that their actions were all normal and nonsexual, and in some instances this claim may be valid (see "Hands," Sherwood Anderson's poignant short story of such a case in his *Winesburg, Ohio*). Nevertheless, so many of these men are repeatedly charged with the same offense with other children in new locations that the vast majority of arrests are probably not the result of prejudice against them or of police error as some claim. Indeed, when there is no clear evidence of genital touching, they are often allowed to plead guilty to disorderly conduct or to "loitering around a schoolyard" (Sudnow, 1965); the latter has been made a misdemeanor in many areas, partly to anticipate and prevent sexual molestation of children. Offenders frequently say that child witnesses against them were coached to distort the truth. Alternatively, they assert that the child initiated the sex act and that they misjudged the child's age. As McCaghy (1968) summarizes, they blame "frigid wives and torrid children" for their offenses, or if they cannot deny responsibility in any other way, they claim they were drunk at the time and that alcohol destroyed their self-control (see also Gebhard et al., 1965: 73; Frisbie, 1969: Chapter 8). It is a standard assumption in psychotherapeutic treatment of child molesters that a prerequisite to reducing their recidivism is to get them to assume responsibility for their crimes (Brecher, 1977).

Persons who are looked down upon seem to need someone to despise. Thus in prison, thieves and forgers rationalize, "At least I didn't hit anybody over the head or threaten anybody with a gun," while robbers and assaulters say, "At least I wasn't sneaky in getting somebody's money away from them." But all despise sex offenders, especially child molesters. Indeed, few offenses arouse more disgust in most adults than sexual abuse of children, and the awareness of how repulsive their crime makes them to others may be one factor in the vehemence with which they deny their offense. Perhaps in compensation for this low regard by others, pedophiliac prisoners seem very actively and overtly religious. Thus prisoners always seen carrying a Bible are stereotyped by other inmates and by staff as "probably sex offenders," implying child molesters more than rapists. Possibly acceptance by the chaplains and in inmate worship groups is especially appealing to them because they are so rejected elsewhere; they have the lowest status in the prison community of any convicts classified by offense.

In the Kinsey sample of women, almost all who recalled childhood sexual experience with adults described their immediate feelings about it as unpleasant when their participation was accidental (as in being exposed to an exhibitionist); about half who collaborated with the adult described their reaction in positive terms; but all who were coerced were distinctly negative. Only the small coerced group had predominantly unfavorable adult sexual adjustment. For those who married, however, the rate of reported orgasm in coitus was about the same for all groups and similar to that of women without such childhood experience (Gagnon, 1965). Personality tests reveal no clear defects of psychological development in sexually assaulted school-age children (Burton, 1968).

The emotional reactions of other adults are sometimes more traumatic or guilt producing to a molested child than the criminal acts of the offender. Sometimes the parents feel a need to show outrage to the community, to prove that they are good parents and not responsible for their offspring's misfortune. If the child's participation was purely involuntary, it is especially important that adults avoid giving the youngster a sense of shame and, in all cases, that they try to minimize publicity of the event to prevent stigmatizing the child.

Shielding the child from emotional injury and stigma becomes difficult if this youngster or another juvenile witness must be interrogated by the police or by attorneys, possibly in court, in order to prosecute the offender. De Francis (1971) observes:

> The initial shock of the crime is heightened and tensions are increased and compounded under questioning by police in their search for evidence. A sensitive child may be subjected to an excruciating experience during efforts to elicit the sordid facts of the crime. Emphasis on the minutest details of the offense serve to magnify the act out of proportion and add to the child's sense of guilt and shame.
>
> If the culprit is arrested, to the ordeal of police interrogation is added the nightmare of testifying at the arraignment or preliminary hearing. If the crime is a felony, the child will appear before the grand jury to give more testimony. After indictment comes the trial. In most jurisdictions this . . . is in the adult criminal court, and . . . frequently before a jury. The experience of testifying and of being subjected to cross-examination may be considerably more traumatizing than the crime itself. Efforts by defense counsel to discredit or confuse the child, even when held to a minimum, make this a nerve-wracking and terrifying ordeal.
>
> In all but a few communities the child faces these harrowing experiences with little help or preparation. . . . In too many cases the parents themselves also are victims of the emotionally damaging experience. They feel threatened by the occurrence. They may feel shame and guilt. Their self-esteem is lowered. They are anxious and fearful about what friends and neighbors may say. Their inexperience with problems of this kind frightens them. . . . Sometimes parental frustration is turned in angry blame toward the child, adding to the child's confusion and feelings of guilt.

The judge, and usually law-enforcement and prosecution officials beforehand, must assess the competence of the child to be a witness. This requires interrogation to reveal the child's understanding and character, preferably beginning with unrelated topics, such as the names and ages of other children in the home and the school attended, to develop rapport and assess maturity. The child's awareness of the difference between truth and falsehood must be established, and in view of the frequently high suggestibility of children, it is especially important to avoid leading questions. Close rapport of police and court personnel with the parents is necessary, and parents are usually asked not to continue the questioning or disturb the child's attitude toward officials if the child goes home after interrogation but is expected to return for further testimony (Flammang, 1975).

Since 1955, Israel has had special procedures for child witnesses. All questioning is conducted by an official youth interrogator, in an office away from the courtroom. He sends a summary of the questions and answers to the police and presents them in court. Further questions for the child may be submitted by the police or by defense or prosecution attorneys to the interrogator, with court approval. In exceptional cases the judge can also permit the child's examination in court (Reifen, 1958, 1975). In Denmark and Sweden, questioning of children is done only by trained policewomen, who give tape recordings of their interrogation sessions to other police officers and to the court (Libai, 1969). The problems of child testimony and their resolution by special procedures apply, of course, to any type of criminal or civil case in which a child may be a crucial witness.

As indicated, a large proportion of the sexual abuse of children is by close relatives. Thus, it frequently overlaps incest, offenses defined by kinship rather than age and almost universally outlawed in all human societies throughout history, though quite diversely defined.

INCEST

Every culture today has some taboos against sex or marriage between close relatives, as have nearly all those known to history and anthropology. Kin who violate these restrictions commit the crime of incest.

Although sex between siblings or between parents and their children or grandchildren is almost universally forbidden, rules for relatives more removed than these vary greatly. Prohibitions against uncle–niece, aunt–nephew and first-cousin marriage or even coitus are common but not ubiquitous; in some societies the acceptability of mating by such couples depends on whether kinship is by maternal or paternal ancestry. Usually half-relatives are barred from wedlock or sexual intercourse as though related by full descent, but in some jurisdictions even steprelatives and those acquired through adoptions also have legal barriers to physical intimacy while minors or sometimes permanently, as though they were "blood" kin. Taboos enacted into criminal laws penalizing incest in the United States differ slightly from one state to another, with first cousins allowed to marry in only about half the states (Hughes, 1964).

There are many speculations (summarized in Mead, 1968) on why incest is so universally regarded as a horrendous transgression. An incest taboo perhaps protects statuses and authority in the family, since sexual love between one parent and a child or between two siblings, especially with pregnancies, could conflict with the traditional childtraining or household responsibilities of one or both parents, with the parental marriage, and with the operation of family farms or businesses. Young (1967) argues that incest taboos in families are but a special case of prohibitions against romantic intimacies or alliances between pairs of individuals within many types of close-knit and highly interdependent groups; disapproval of such pairing develops because it tends to divide these groups. Thus he points to the restriction of sexual relations in small bands of zealots struggling to establish religious or farming settlements when the total project is insecure; cohesiveness and the equal claims of each to all in the total group are jeopardized if any two members develop much greater affection, loyalty, and obligation to one another than to the rest.

Incest comprises only a small fraction of one percent of all crimes reported to the police or resulting in arrest in any jurisdiction. But in a national survey in the 1930s in which many small groups of adults were given anonymous questionnaires, 1.5 percent of males indicated that they had had coitus with their sister and 3.9 percent with a first cousin, while 0.8 percent of females admitted having had it with a brother and 0.5 percent with a cousin (Hunt, 1974: 346). There were no accounts of copulation with a parent, but as shown in Table 11:1, some women admitted noncoital incestuous contacts with their fathers. Yet the few available compilations on persons arrested for incest indicate that at least 80 percent involve father–daughter coitus, less than 20 percent brother–sister, and at most one percent mother–son (Weinberg, 1955: 41; Gebhard et al., 1965: 38).

If any incest becomes known to others in the household, the strong wish to avoid disgrace to the entire family generally keeps it a secret. Brother–sister coitus is probably the incest least often reported to the police because the siblings, usually adolescents, do it willingly and secretly. Some coerced father–daughter incest is prosecuted as child molestation, and some that is voluntary is reported to the police by an enraged wife or her relatives; yet many an abusive and incestuous father is not legally charged because even those in the family who loathe his tabooed sexuality do not wish imprisonment for their

**TABLE 11-1   Incest Experience of a National Sample of U.S.
Population in the 1970s**

HAD INCESTUOUS CONTACTS OR COITUS WITH:	PERCENTAGE HAVING SEXUAL CONTACTS		PERCENTAGE HAVING COITUS	
	Males	Females	Males	Females
Father	0	0.5	0	0
Mother	0	0	0	0
Son	0	*	0	0
Daughter	*	0	0	0
Brother	*	3.6	0	0.8
Sister	3.8	0.7	1.5	0
Uncle	*	0.6	0	*
Aunt	*	0	*	0
Nephew	0	0	0	0
Niece	*	0	*	0
Grandfather	0	*	0	0
Grandmother	0	0	0	0
Male Cousin	*	3.2	0	0.5
Female Cousin	9.2	*	3.9	0
Brother-in-Law	0	*	0	0
Sister-in-Law	*	0	*	0
Stepfather	0	*	0	*
Stepmother	0	0	0	0

* less than 0.5
SOURCE: Morton Hunt, *Sexual Behavior in the 1970s*. N.Y.: Dell Publishing Co., 1974: 344, 346. © 1974 by Morton Hunt. Reprinted with permission of Playboy Press.

breadwinner, may still love him, and especially fear the stigma that exposure would bring to them all. Nevertheless, fathers comprise most of imprisoned incest offenders. Being thus identified and accessible, they are the principal subjects of research on this crime. There has been little study of the consequences of incest on the lives of all those involved, but a few women who as children were coerced into coitus by their fathers are included in Gagnon's (1965) inquiry (discussed in the preceding section), which found them to be the only type of child victims of sex offenses who were maladjusted sexually as adults.

Typically the father who commits incest dominates the home, and his eldest daughter becomes the housekeeper when the mother becomes ill, dies, or departs. Eventually the father procures from his child all the services previously provided by his wife. Frequently these households have little contact with outsiders, either because of a rural location or a preference for isolation, or both. In some instances, however, a drunken father beats both wife and child into submission, while in others a promiscuous daughter allegedly seduces her brother, father, or both. One farm laborer imprisoned for incest in Illinois told me he did it to keep his daughter from getting diseased or pregnant from the boys with whom she wanted to run around. Fathers who have seduced their very young or teenage daughters tend to become extremely jealous when these girls are later attractive to or interested in other males; acts of rage by the fathers at this time frequently lead their daughters or others to report the incest to the police. The development of a special treatment program for incest by the juvenile-probation office of Santa Clara County, California, resulted in an increase in the number of cases annually referred to the authorities in three years, from 36 to 180 within an area of 1.1 million people. With this increase, incest cases known to the court included, for the first time, many highly educated middle- and upper-class families; yet most cases were probably still unreported (Brecher, 1977).

It is clear that: (1) there is considerable diversity in causal factors underlying incest (Weinberg, 1955; Gebhard et al., 1965: Chapters 10–12; Bagley, 1969); (2) voluntary participation tends to be by persons isolated from conventional social circles and in circumstances in which they anticipate readier gratification from incestuous than from legitimate sexual activity; (3) any generalization based on prosecuted cases is quite biased, since only family controversy or chance discovery by authorities sends cases to court, whereas most incest is collaborative and unreported.

ADULTERY AND BIGAMY

Although most cultures known to anthropologists are polygamous, those in the Judeo-Christian tradition and many others now have norms of monogamy. The Ten Commandments proscribe adultery; the Catholic Church has always called it a mortal sin; Hawthorne's *The Scarlet Letter* dramatizes how Protestants have condemned it; and most of our states declare it criminal, with maximum punishment varying from a $10 fine in Maryland to five years imprisonment in several states. Nevertheless, infidelity is widespread and often not well hidden. In many countries of Latin America and Southern Europe, numerous practicing Catholics who can afford to keep mistresses do so openly. In the United States hundreds of thousands of couples are divorced on grounds of adultery, admitted or proven in public court hearings, but practically no one is arrested for it, despite laws against it.

In the United States there has been some growth of mate swapping, or "swinging," as well as of communal group marriages, but such practices attract a very small percentage of wedded people, and participation is usually short lived (DeLora & Warren, 1977: 248–66). Public-opinion surveys since World War II have consistently found that over 80 percent of married couples strongly condemn infidelity; yet around midcentury Kinsey shocked Americans by his estimate that about 45 percent of American husbands and about 18 percent of wives have some extramarital coitus. Despite a rising divorce rate and more frequent premarital sex since then, there is no clear evidence that the overall percentages have changed. But rates of extramarital coitus by both husbands and wives when still in their 20s have now converged, with about 20 to 25 percent of each violating marriage vows (Hunt, 1974: 253–91).

Every 50 to 100 years in most states, so many criminal laws and amendments have accumulated from separate legislative sessions that a commission is appointed to redraft the criminal code more concisely and to replace the old statutes completely. Because laws punishing adultery have for decades seldom been enforced, some new codes omit this offense, thus decriminalizing it. Rarely does a legislature directly challenge the norms by specifically repealing laws punishing infidelity, for no one wishes to be portrayed by a political opponent as favoring adultery. On the other hand, no lawmaker would dare alienate constituents by seeking rigorous enforcement of such laws. Indeed, many states still have laws penalizing "fornication"—coitus by any man and woman not married to each other—but no one is arrested and prosecuted on this charge.

The marriage rate in the United States has remained between 8.5 and 12.2 per thousand throughout the twentieth century, but divorces increased from less than one per thousand in 1910 to about five in the 1970s, close to half the marriage rate. The many people today who have two or more spouses sequentially may be said to practice "serial polygamy." Anyone requesting a legal marriage must swear to have no other spouse at that time; it is *bigamy*, a felony, to knowingly falsify this avowal by marrying when a prior espousal is not legally dissolved.

Bigamy is a type of fraud, usually by a man who loves and feels responsible for two women and tries to keep both happy, but occasionally by someone who finds he cannot divorce his wife when he desires another. The latter circumstance is now rare, since divorce has become much easier to obtain. Bigamy may follow adultery when a married man makes his "other woman" pregnant but has never told her of his existing marriage. It is sometimes maintained for many years without being exposed, especially by men who travel frequently and keep wives in different cities. Although all large municipalities and states regularly prosecute bigamy, it has never been a common offense and appears to be diminishing, perhaps because of greater acceptance of illegitimate birth and of cohabitation without marriage.

EXHIBITIONISTS AND PEEPERS

Many a woman—probably a majority in our society—has had a very startling, upsetting, though not directly injurious experience: a male stranger suddenly and deliberately exposes his genitals to her, usually when he has an erection and often while masturbating. There are reports that as many as 35 percent of sex-offense arrests are for genital exposure (DeLora & Warren, 1977: 353), almost always committed by men; yet one sampling of female victims found that only a quarter had notified the police (Davis & Davis, 1976). Unsystematic inquiries among female graduate students (by S. K. Davis) indicate that most have had one or more encounters with such "flashers."

Exhibitionism, the designation of this syndrome in clinical psychology and psychiatry, is quite different from the behavior of nudism cultists; either of these types of conduct in a public place, however, is punishable in almost all parts of the country under the same criminal statutes, which brand it "public indecency" or "lewd conduct" (usually a misdemeanor, but sometimes a felony). Nudists (in camps, though not so much at the few "clothing-optional" public beaches) are generally prudish in avoidance and disapproval of behavior that is sexually suggestive or calls attention to the genitals (Weinberg, 1970). Exhibitionists, on the other hand, are usually not naked, but primarily intend that women see their sexual organs and, sometimes, their emotional agitation. Goffman observes that "exhibitionists . . . spectacularly subvert the protective social control that keeps individuals interpersonally distant" and thus entrap others into social encounters that they can "neither immediately escape from nor properly sustain" (1963: 143).

The completion of Kinsey's study of sex offenders by Gebhard and associates (1975) included analysis of interviews with 135 arrested exhibitionists, perhaps the largest sample in the limited research on this type of lawbreaker. Some interesting features of their life histories, when compared with those of other types of sex offenders, are that they were the only group in which none had early coitus, that they masturbated extensively, and that those who were married had coitus much less frequently than most husbands in Kinsey's national sample.

Although a smaller Canadian study found two peak periods for exhibitionism, midpuberty (about 15) and the early 20s (Gigeroff et al., 1968), the Kinsey sample averaged nearly 30 years of age. Most were repeaters, however, for this is a highly recidivistic crime. Sixty percent of the Kinsey group had been married, but only 25 percent were still wed and had wives at home at the time of the crimes. Over 90 percent displayed their genitals to total strangers. Many did this in fairly public places, so that 24 percent were seen and reported by persons other

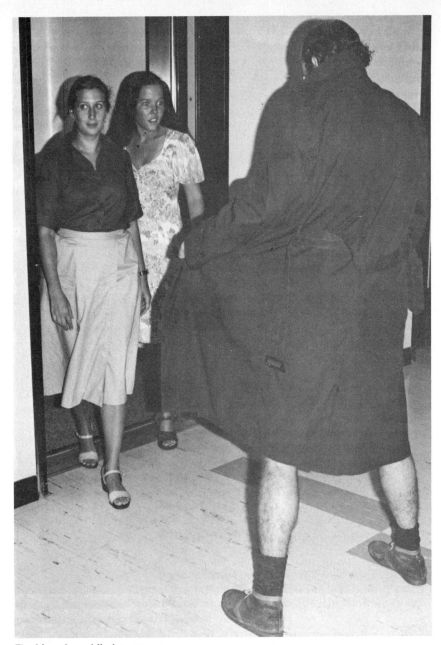

Flashing: A muddled message.

than the immediate victim. Indeed, 20 percent made the display from their automobiles, and some from their residences. Thus they took hardly any precautions to avoid being traced if reported to the police. By usual criteria for measuring intelligence, they generally are in a normal range, although in popular speech they are called "sex morons." About 20 percent blamed intoxication for their lawbreaking (Gebhard et al., 1965: Chapter 17). Apparently the typical "flasher" commits this offense rather impulsively when sexually aroused and frustrated by inability to have coitus as he fantasizes it would be with a strange woman.

Like the "naive graspers" among rapists, exhibitionists appear to have misconceptions about possible sexual gratifications. Both types of offenders are extremely awkward about approaching women and developing rapport and gradual intimacy, but exhibitionists—unlike the rapists—virtually never use physical force. Many admit that their display was not only a ploy for attention, but also an invitation to the women to touch them. It seems to be a crude plea for recognition of their sexual potential and of their craving for help. Women startled by being the object of such inept communication are usually terrified, often angered, sometimes amused (Davis & Davis, 1976). Gebhard and associates conclude that "on the whole the exhibitionists are to be pitied rather than feared" (1965: 399).

Ostensibly more passive, but actually more often dangerous, are the "peepers." They practice what clinical psychologists and psychiatrists call "voyeurism," although this term denotes anyone who gets sexual gratification by looking at erotically arousing objects or situations. The sexual-peeping forms of "invasion of privacy" crimes usually involve surreptitiously looking at someone who is not fully-clothed, not in a public place, unaware of being observed, and likely to be embarrassed if aware. Such offenders are usually called "Peeping Toms," from the legend about the only man who looked at Lady Godiva when she rode naked through Coventry. An arrestee for this crime is often a young man who has also committed the crimes of trespassing or breaking and entering to get a better view.

The average age of peepers in the Kinsey sample of sex offenders was 26.5, and 45 percent were married. They were disproportionately the youngest in families with mostly male children and, as youth, they lacked female friends. Beginning at an early age, however, they were involved in considerable delinquency of all types, and much of their peeping was apparently done in conjunction with burglary; they stole whatever they could, whether property or a view or both, and about 10 percent have records of attempted or completed rape. Possibly some are caught for peeping while also seeking to burglarize or rape, but others masturbate while peeping and most are apparently not aggressive. One was described as a "virgin college freshman who had never seen a nude woman and who stopped to peep into a room where a woman was undressing." Over 95 percent are arrested for peeping at strangers (Gebhard et al., 1965: Chapter 16).

During the late 1960s and throughout the 1970s, prevailing

conceptions of indecent bodily exposure have changed in the United States. A wide variety of clothing styles have become acceptable for women, including some swimwear and other apparel much more revealing than those customary a few decades before; popular magazines for men ceased hiding the sex organs in their photographs of nude women, and some women's magazines have similar pictures of men; bars and restaurants with "topless" or "bottomless" waitresses are licensed in several cities; demands for "clothing-optional" public beaches have grown in some areas, and are successful in at least two (San Diego and Santa Barbara); and "streaking"—dashing naked through a public place—was a fad for about a year, but died out perhaps because bareness no longer was so shocking. As a result of these trends, will the gravity with which people view sexual "flashing" and peeping decline? Will the penalties, now highly variable, become less severe?

No one can answer these questions with certainty, but we should note that the harm done by these offenses is genuine, even if not nearly of the same magnitude as rape. Exhibitionists and voyeurs are predators because they deny their victims a valued civil right, the right to privacy. People have a right not to be deliberately startled and confronted by a sight that often frightens them. They have a right to be free of unwanted observers when they are not in a public place and are taking reasonable precautions against being visible to strangers. With the generalization of values and inclusion trends in society (see Chapter 2), concern with the right of privacy persists, perhaps grows. Therefore, it seems improbable that "flashing" and peeping will be completely decriminalized, even if punished less severely.

SODOMY: HOMOSEXUALITY AND OTHER PENALIZED SEX ACTS

Traditionally in the United States, coitus in marriage has been the only lawful type of collaborative sex act. Moral entrepreneurs persuaded state governments throughout the country to call all other forms of cooperative genital stimulation crimes, declaring them offensive because they are "unnatural."

Typically, the law labels all noncoital forms of sex other than masturbation as "sodomy," or "crimes against nature." These proscribed acts include (1) oral-genital contacts, (2) anal intercourse, (3) attempted coitus with an animal, or bestiality. All such behavior is punishable under the laws of most states, even if the first two are done heterosexually by a married couple, but arrest and punishment has been primarily for oral-genital contact between males. Obviously, that which occurs in the marital chamber is the least likely to be reported.

An Illinois criminal code revision in 1961, however, made a homosexual act unlawful only if coerced, done in public, or with a minor. Illinois thereby became the first of more than a dozen states to decriminalize this conduct when done privately by consenting adults.

It can be argued that mutual noncoital and same-gender sex acts are not "unnatural," since they occur in many animal species and have been accepted in numerous human societies (Opler, 1965; Churchill, 1967). It should be noted that where such conduct is outlawed, only the sex acts themselves are crimes; it is legal to call oneself "homosexual," "gay," or—for a woman—"lesbian," even where this implies preference for sex acts that are criminal. Kinsey concluded from his sample that about half our married couples had some oral-genital contacts with their mates, although this was a felony in most states; it was reported much more often by the college educated. A survey in the 1970s found that acceptance of these acts had increased; about two-thirds of married people reported it, and this proportion did not vary much with their schooling (Hunt, 1974: 198).

Kinsey shocked many by his figures that at least 37 percent of American males and 20 percent of females have some experience in homosexual activity. His definitions and sampling were criticized by other scholars (e.g., Hunt, 1974: 303–27; Gagnon, 1974: 258) as exaggerating the actual prevalence; they estimate that in the 1970s about 10 to 12 percent of each gender engage in homosexual acts at some time, while two to five percent of males and about half that many females pursue it exclusively. It may well be, however, that there has been: (1) a decrease in homosexuality since midcentury, because intergender social and sexual intimacy is now more widely available to juveniles and young adults; and (2) an increase in the visibility of the existing homosexuality, creating the widely popular but erroneous impression that it is more prevalent than decades earlier.

Most people are exclusively heterosexual, some are homosexual, but many are bisexual—they have the same and the opposite gender as sexual partners, at different times. A small number are transsexuals, persons who think they are of the gender opposite to their biological bodies; they often have themselves transformed surgically and hormonally to make their bodies resemble what they believe is their gender (DeLora & Warren, 1977: Chapter 11). In questionnaires completed by over 3,500 members of male homosexual organizations and male patrons at "gay bars" in the United States, 51 percent described themselves as "exclusively homosexual," 30 percent as "predominantly homosexual, insignificantly heterosexual," 13 percent as "predominantly homosexual but significantly heterosexual," four percent as "equally homo- and heterosexual," and two percent as "predominantly heterosexual but significantly homosexual" (Weinberg & Williams, 1975: 144).

There has been much speculation on the causes of such variety in sexual taste. Advocates of punishment for deviants presume that anyone seeking erotic arousal from others of their own gender chooses to do something "unnatural," but homosexuals and transsexuals insist that their preference is their "nature." Freud postulated that we are all originally of dual gender, noting that in its very early stage the fetus seems hermaphroditic. Therefore, he inferred, everyone goes through an unconscious homosexual stage but, with normal psychological development, becomes heterosexual; from this standpoint, widely held for decades in psychoanalysis and psychiatry, homosexuality is a mental ailment resulting from fixation at or regression to an early stage of libidinal growth. In recent years, the idea of early hermaphrodism has been rejected because: (1) chromosome differences between the genders begin at conception (see Chapter 7, on chromosomal abnormalities); (2) humans demonstrably learn their modes of sexual expression from cultural, social, and uniquely individual experiences, and thus differ from those animals that develop sexual cravings and the ability to perform sex acts by instinct alone (Marmor, 1965: Chapter 1). The American Psychiatric Association in 1973 dropped "homosexuality" from its classification of mental diseases, but some of its members disagree with this decision.

Initiation into homosexuality is especially frequent in one-gender settings, such as boarding schools, many college dormitories, correctional institutions, mental hospitals, merchant ships, and the armed forces. Even when there are a few of the opposite gender in these places, heterosexual intimacy is usually unavailable for most persons. Kinsey pointed out that these circumstances are especially conducive to experimentation in sodomy by youth without much heterosexual experience:

> Since younger boys have not acquired all of the social traditions and taboos on sex, they are more impressionable. . . . If these adolescent years are spent . . . where there is little . . . opportunity . . . to develop . . . individuality, . . . no privacy . . . and . . . all . . . companions are males, his sexual life is very likely to be permanently stamped. . . . (1949: 224)

Similar reports are frequent on all-girl schools and correctional institutions. As we indicated in discussing male prostitution, many boys who are heterosexual but poor engage in sex acts with homosexual men for pay, but their erotic cravings are not thereby diverted from girls (Reiss, 1961; Gagnon, 1974: 258).

As Warren (1974b: 4) observes, the gay world is "almost universally stigmatized, and no one is socialized within or toward it as a child." Accordingly, homosexuals traditionally kept their erotic interests secret, both to avoid being discredited at their jobs and in other social situations and to avoid arrest and prosecution. They maintain their own "sphere" within the larger community, for an active social life without exposure and stigma. This territory includes "gay bars" and various other "hangouts," such as certain bus terminals, theaters, street corners, sections or parks, and, particularly for the affluent, their own homes. They have styles of approach with each other and with strangers so that those not homosexual do not recognize them as such, but those who are can infer their erotic interests accurately (Mileski & Black, 1972; Warren, 1974b). As in secret lodges, part of the appeal of the gay world is its sense of exclusiveness. Emphasis on partying also attracts many people, even some of the opposite gender—in male groups, the so-called fag hags—who share the sociability but not the sexual intimacies (Warren, 1976).

Police vice-squad detectives entrap homosexuals as they do prostitutes, by pretending to want sex with them. Detectives also check public toilets and park areas where men meet to perform fellatio (Humphreys, 1970). Still, only a small fraction of one percent of homosexual acts results in arrest. Abuses of actual and alleged homosexuals by police who extort money for not arresting them, and by delinquents who beat and rob them, are frequently reported. Because of their stigma, homosexuals are vulnerable to the threat of discrediting exposure should they press charges, and thus those who victimize them are seldom prosecuted (Donnelly et al., 1962: 178–85; Schur, 1965: 79–85; Geis, 1972: 31–34). Gagnon (1974: 258–59) points out that destigmatization of homosexuals, not decriminalization, is prerequisite to their obtaining equal justice under the law.

Despite continuing prejudices, harassment of homosexuals in many cities is less extensive in the 1970s because it has been fought by the Gay Liberation Movement. Many homosexuals have "come out of the closets" (Humphreys, 1972) to organize for mutual aid and to mobilize public support for their rights. They have opened social-service and legal-aid centers for gays, and have been diligent campaigners for politicians who have aided them. Their social contacts with heterosexuals often increase greatly as a consequence of this movement, since many "straights" are now attracted to gay parties and reciprocate the hospitality. Whether these activities recruit more people to homosexuality or more homosexuals to bi- or heterosexuality is unknown, but they probably reduce the stigma attached to homosexuals in the United States.

Some homosexual acts are criminal in all states. One, mentioned briefly in this chapter's section on rape, is coercion to commit these acts. This is a major problem in most large jails and other correctional institutions. A second is seduction of children to homosexual conduct, an aspect of child molestation. A desire to keep children

Gay liberation comes out of the closets.

uninformed about sodomy or even about all sex, and unattracted to it, motivates much effort to define as criminal some types of publications, motion pictures, and other public entertainment.

OBSCENITY AND PORNOGRAPHY

The First Amendment to the Constitution bars Congress from "abridging the freedom of speech, or of the press," but numerous federal, state, and local laws make it a crime to publish, distribute, display, perform, or otherwise communicate messages or images deemed pornographic or obscene. "Pornography" is a general term for all publications, presentations, or products that are intended to be and are in fact sexually arousing. "Obscenity," Webster's Dictionary informs us, refers to matters "grossly repugnant to the generally accepted notions of what is appropriate," and to matters "stressing or reveling in the lewd or lustful."

Interpretation of these key terms and their reconciliation with the First Amendment have always been difficult and controversial. Restrictions are now less rigid, but they remain unclear and often inconsistent. Thus publisher Ralph Ginzberg, after delaying by several years of court appeals a jail term for mailing his magazine *Eros*, complained that the government was by then tolerating publications much more blatantly pornographic. One of the arguments the Supreme Court weighed against him, however, was that he showed a clearly obscene intent in trying to mail his journal from the Pennsylvania towns of Intercourse and Blue Ball, although it was printed elsewhere.

The Supreme Court, especially in *Roth* v. *U.S.* (1957), upheld the right of the federal government to forbid mailing of items that are "prurient," which it defined as "having a tendency to excite lustful thoughts." This is a very imprecise concept, but it has been the basis for federal controls over international imports, interstate shipment, and broadcasting of allegedly obscene material, as well as for state and local bans on sale and display of pornography. In a series of split decisions in 1966, notably in Memoirs of a Woman of Pleasure v. *Attorney General of Massachusetts* (the "Fanny Hill" case), it extended these controls to works that offend "contemporary community standards" or that "lack redeeming social value." These guidelines received a conservative revision by Chief Justice Burger in *Miller* v. *California* (1973), which authorizes the banning of works that, "taken as a whole, do not have serious literary, artistic, political or scientific value," or of anything that "depicts or describes in a patently offensive way, sexual conduct specifically defined by the applicable state law." Thus it permits each state to have unique conceptions of what is obscene (McGeady, 1974). The serious value of a work of art and its possible pruriency are often controversial questions for which there are no conclusively "correct" answers.

One of the major concerns of Congress when it established the Commission on Obscenity and Pornography was to determine the effects of these materials on sexual conduct. The Commission's report (1970) estimated, from the surveys it sponsored, that 85 percent of adult men and 70 percent of adult women in the United States are exposed at some time in their lives to explicitly sexual publications or pictures (i.e., depicting coitus or sodomy); but fewer than half of these had seen them in the preceding two years, and only about 20 percent of these men see them fairly regularly. Customers of so-called adult bookstores and movies, the Commission's researchers found, were "predominantly white, middle-class, middle-aged, married males, dressed in business suits or neat casual attire," who come to these establishments alone. The average patron reported less adolescent sexual experience than most males in our society, but about an average amount as an adult.

From both survey research and laboratory experiments, the Commission found that women can as frequently have genital arousal from seeing sex films as men, but that males are the predominant customers in commercial establishments. Youth are more aroused than older people, but all become satiated with prolonged and repeated exposure, so that these presentations are then no longer sexually stimulating (Howard et al., 1973). Most people reported no change in coital or masturbatory behavior after viewing erotic films, but some—particularly married people—increased the frequency and variety of their coitus, and a few decreased it (Mann et al., 1973). Rapists, child molesters, homosexuals, and transsexuals reported less exposure to sexually explicit materials in their formative years than other males (Goldstein et al., 1973).

In July 1969, Denmark abolished all restrictions on the sale or display of pornographic material. No change in rape rates followed, but exhibitionism, peeping, and male prostitution declined, and total sex crimes in 1969 were 31 percent lower than those in 1968 (*New York Times*, January 5, 1970). After an initial upsurge of sales of pornographic publications, especially to tourists, this market collapsed and many "sex stores" were forced to close. Although part of the decrease in exhibitionism, peeping, and male prostitution may have been due to less complete reporting, a Danish study claims that the drop in child molestation did not result from a change in complaint rates but clearly followed the end of pornography restrictions (Kutchinsky, 1973). The importation of full-length "hard-core" pornographic motion pictures from the United States and the banning in 1975 of live sex-act shows

A paradise of prurience.

were said to have reduced sales of other types of pornography (*Los Angeles Times*, November 14, 1976).

When a British psychologist interspersed pictures of women's boots and of nude females in sexually stimulating positions, males aroused by this combination could subsequently be aroused by the boots alone (Cline, 1974: 208). Possibly, arousal by pornography is similarly conditioned. Becoming sexually aroused by an inanimate object is a type of deviant behavior known as *fetishism,* and this experiment suggests how it may develop. Fetishism does not violate criminal law, but mental-health specialists serving the courts sometimes classify as sex offenders persons convicted for stealing fetish objects, often women's soiled underwear. A tremendous variety of other deviant sexual practices, many prosecuted as sodomy, may similarly result from a conditioned arousal.

Gagnon and Simon pinpoint perhaps pornography's greatest potential for triggering offenses, when they conclude that it may "reaffirm the myth of a breed of women who are lusty and free in both surrender and enjoyment" (1973: 267). Although neither the naive-grasper type of rapist nor the exhibitionist may have seen more pornography than nonoffenders, what they did see could have been a larger factor in their thoughts about sex; for, as indicated, most of them have less early experience in coitus than the majority of other men. Thus, pornography might have fostered their delusions that their startling overtures could inspire females to respond with erotic passion.

Local antipornography "crusades" are regular reactions to the increased tolerance for adult movies and bookshops, as well as to conspicuous massage parlors. Intensive study of two such campaigns in small metropolitan areas indicates their disproportionate recruitment of the older, female, churchgoing, long-married, and politically conservative population (Zurcher et al, 1971). This support base is similar to that of the temperance movement and many other moral-entrepreneurial movements to prohibit nonpredatory conduct that challenges their lifestyle. Such campaigns are often part of a conservative "backlash" that typically follows—in reaction to the stresses of rapid change—a period of dominance by liberalism (see Chapter 2). The usual impact of such a crusade is to slow the growth of tolerance; it generates a compromise between the crusaders' objective of a rigid suppression of alleged pornography as criminal and the complete anarchy to which they claim we are drifting. Increasingly, an outcome of such conflict has been pornography regulation by municipal-zoning and public-health agencies, which is gradually replacing control by police and criminal courts.

The conclusion that pornography seriously deludes some youth about sex, and thereby stimulates sexual predation, is sufficient, to many, to justify efforts to reduce the visibility of pornographic presentations. For example, they urge that "adults only" motion pictures not be shown on television at hours when many children may watch them, and that adult book stores be prohibited near schools. However, the most influential factor in reducing the market for pornography would probably be improvement in the quality and availability of legitimate sex education. This is a far cry from demanding routine government censorship of the press, motion pictures, or other media. Such censorship could jeopardize freedom to present what most regard as nonpornographic communications, since definitions of pornography are vague and past censors have often been overzealous. Marvin E. Wolfgang and Otto N. Larsen, the two sociologists who were members of the Commission on Obscenity and Pornography, dissented from the majority recommendations for partial bans, by calling for no statutory barriers whatsoever. They asserted that "the First Amendment to the Constitution is abrogated by restrictions on textual and visual material that may be deemed by some 'obscene' or 'pornographic.'" In calling for repeal of all such statutes, they asserted:

> Advocating repeal is not advocating anarchy, for we believe that informal social controls will work better without the confusion of ambiguous and arbitrarily administered laws. With improvements in sex education and better understanding of human sexual behavior, society can more effectively handle, without legislation, the distribution of material deemed by some to be offensive to juveniles or adults (1970: xi).

In practice, the difficulties of winning a prosecution for pornography today make its restriction by censorship much less extensive than formerly, but there is a growing regulaton of the location of its sales places under Supreme Court-upheld zoning laws. Noteworthy is the Detroit Plan, mentioned in discussing prostitution, which requires establishments catering to sexual interests to be at least 1,000 feet apart and be approved by a majority of residents or businesses within 500 feet.

CIVIL-COMMITMENT LAWS FOR SEX OFFENDERS

About 30 of our states have laws whereby sex offenders can be held for an indefinite period in a mental hospital or in a section of a prison assigned to the mentally ill. This confinement may either replace or be in addition to a criminal-court penalty for each crime. No two "sexual psychopath" statutes are exactly alike, but all permit holding a sex criminal for "treatment" until a designated board or a court finds him or her (though rarely is it a "her") no longer dangerous.

In many states sex offenders first serve the prison terms for their crimes, but before they can be released by parole or discharge, a board must decide whether to recommit them for civil confinement under the sexual psychopath laws. In some states, however, people may be confined indefinitely under these laws as soon as they are convicted, so that they do not get prison terms, whereas others may later be returned to court as "not amenable to treatment" and then either be released outright or given a prison or probation term. An outright release reflects skepticism about the judgment on amenability to treatment or simply the belief that the person has been confined long enough for the gravity of his offense. In a few states the prosecutor may request civil-commitment hearings for alleged sex offenders at any time after they are accused, without even convicting them (Gebhard et al., 1965: Chapter 36; Craig, 1967; Kittrie, 1971: Chapter 4).

In ruling on civil commitment for sexual psychopathy, as in other hearings on mental hospitalization, the board or judge is permitted to decide on the basis of a "preponderance of the evidence" rather than following the criminal court's directive that there be proof of guilt "beyond a reasonable doubt." Legal counsel is not always provided for the accused in these deliberations, and he has little or no chance to challenge or appeal his designation as a psychopath. The court or board decisions are based mainly on reports of one, two, or three physicians—not always psychiatrists—who interview the subject, peruse prosecution documents, and, in some states, observe him during a temporary diagnostic confinement. A few states, notably Maryland, can apply this civil-commitment process to anyone convicted of a crime and deemed a "defective delinquent" (sometimes regardless of age) or a "psychopath," although they use these laws mainly for sex offenders (Craig, 1967; Kittrie, 1971: Chapter 4).

The standard sequence of events and set of assumptions for enactment of such laws usually begins with a campaign of fear that violent sex crimes are increasing and endanger all women and children (Sutherland, 1950). Intense anxiety is often triggered by one or two highly publicized assaults on which moral entrepreneurs focus attention while they go about inciting alarm. Actually, there seldom are sudden spurts in overall rates for any type of sex crime, but there often are sharp surges in media attention to them when unusually heinous ones occur or when the victims are from prominent families. The alarmists describe those who commit such offenses as "degenerate" and "depraved," or more clearly imply that they are biologically different from others by calling them "sexual psychopaths" or "defectives." This concept goes back to the German medical text *Psychopathia Sexualis* by Baron Richard von Krafft-Ebing, first published in 1886 and frequently reissued ever since in numerous editions and many translations. It is a collection of lurid descriptions of deviant sex acts, which this nineteenth-century physician ascribed to a "sex fiend" psychopathy caused by heredity or by mental deterioration.

Proponents of civil commitment assume that the most dangerous sex offenders can be identified with precision; so they urge that a search be made for them among all sex-crime arrestees, and that any who are found be confined indefinitely rather than given a sentence of specified duration. This is considered preventive, for it is implied that even arrestees for sex misdemeanors (e.g., exhibitionism or sodomy) will commit more serious sex crimes later, and thus should not be released as quickly as is customary when their penalty reflects mainly the presumed harm already done by their offense. The civil-commitment approach to sex offenders logically applies this type of reasoning, but it is based on deductions from erroneous postulates.

The main error is in assuming that sexual psychopaths can be reliably and validly identified by the procedures that the statutes prescribe. As this chapter has shown, the various sex crimes are not only extremely diverse, but also, the perpetrators of each of them are far from uniform and predictable. Furthermore, there is little consensus among psychiatrists or other specialists in identifying the most dangerous sex offenders, except when a prior record of repeated sex offenses exists that laymen would also presume is indicative of risk. The concept of psychopathy used in clinical practice by mental-health specialists, especially when applied to sex offenders, is much more subjective and vague than that developed in physiological psychology in recent years (described in Chapter 7) for which some objective measurements are feasible, such as the GSR arousal-recovery rate. (The relevance of these psychophysiological measurements to sex offense or other crime prediction has thus far been little investigated, but it is probable that they are useful only in conjunction with data on the past behavior and experience of the persons investigated.)

Second, the diagnosis of a confined sex offender as successfully treated and thus not dangerus to society if released is not impressively accurate. A followup of California cases civilly committed as "Mentally Disordered Sex Offenders," confined for an average of over a year of treatment and returned to court as "cured," found that this group had a higher recidivism rate than those returned to court as not amenable to treatment (Dix, 1976). The Maryland programs claim satisfactory clinical assessment of dangerousness, primarily in sex offenders, by pointing out that of those diagnosed by treatment staff as not dangerous and released by the court, eight percent later committed serious assaultive crime, while of those diagnosed as dangerous but released 35 percent committed such crimes (Kozol et al., 1972). Although this is impressive, we should note that had the court followed psychiatric advice on dangerousness, 65 percent would have been confined who in fact did not recidivate, and there are no data on the reliability of the diagnoses (Monahan, 1973).

In a New Jersey experiment, one of the nation's most experienced specialists in psychiatric work with sex offenders diagnosed 50 cases that were also assessed independently by two of his staff psychiatrists, each seeing 25 of them. In 92 percent of these cases there was agreement that the subject was a sexually deviant offender warranting commitment under the New Jersey law, and in 84 percent that he was dangerous (Brancale et al., 1972: 338). How much agreement would there be with psychiatrists less experienced in working together, and not collaborating in making diagnostic-decision rules? Also, if about 90 percent of the subjects are presumed to merit a particular diagnosis, two persons would agree by chance alone about 80 percent of the time in identifying this 90 percent. How much agreement would there be in diagnosing a group of subjects only about half of whom are presumed dangerous? Agreements by chance alone would then occur in only about a quarter of the cases.

In many states, the difficulties in applying these laws result in their disuse or in their unexpected interpretation. Where people imprisoned for sex crimes cannot be paroled or discharged without a hearing to determine whether they should be civilly committed as "psychopaths" or "sexually dangerous," hardly any are so designated. On the other hand, in California, where it had been anticipated that the civil-commitment law would send the most dangerous sex offenders to a maximum-security mental hospital for treatment instead of to prison, the convicted persons whom psychiatrists selected for hospitalization were those of above-average intelligence and education, young, and disproportionately of middle-class background, and thus deemed more amenable to psychotherapy rather than more dangerous than the others (Gebhard et al., 1965: 848–67).

Perhaps the strongest arguments against civil commitment as a substitute for the traditional criminal punishment for sex offenders are from the civil-liberties perspective, namely: (1) involuntary confinement is a penalty whether in a hospital or a prison; (2) it may be longer and less predictable in a hospital; (3) it is not demonstrated that hospital "treatment" reduces recidivism by these offenders more than imprisonment; (4) confinement and release decisions are not necessarily based on more precise and valid criteria if imposed by psychiatrists rather than by judges; (5) checks that all relevant evidence is fairly heard are presumed to occur more often in criminal proceedings than in civil-commitment hearings. Kittrie remarks:

> The psychopath . . . suffers from a disputed mental disorder. He is indefinitely committed for an offense, often unproved, that would impose only a mild sentence on others. To secure release, he must be cured of a condition that is not clearly definable and that some say is not treatable (1971: 191).

On the other hand, as Pitts (1968) points out, the view of deviant conduct as a medical problem may permit more flexibile and innovative treatment than occurs where it is seen as purely a criminal-justice concern of making the punishment fit the crime. Optimally, limiting the maximum penalty to what is appropriate from the standpoint of justice might be combined with trying to determine which treatment works best and why. Here and there, such innovative policies can be found, in very diverse settings.

SPECIAL-TREATMENT PROGRAMS FOR SEX OFFENDERS

During the 1950s, several states established centers for civilly commit-ted sex offenders, each headed by a psychiatrist in a maximum-security prison or mental hospital, but doing more diagnosis (for courts or parole boards) than psychotherapy. Expanded during the 1960s, some of these centers became especially innovative in treatments during the 1970s.

A significant advance in knowledge about these developments occurred in 1977, with the Department of Justice report by prize-win-ning medical writer Edward M. Brecher on his two years of visits to all programs he could locate (23 in 12 states). In some institutions he lived with the inmates for a few days, in addition to interviewing staff and others, and studying relevant documents. His LEAA "Prescriptive Package" is the primary source of program descriptions condensed here in analyzing four extremely important features of recent treatment efforts: (1) pressure for candor; (2) female personnel to train male het-erosexual offenders; (3) extension of treatment into the community; (4) mutual aid. Brecher's survey also describes three additional develop-ments of more-debated value: (5) castration; (6) sex-hormone medica-tion; (7) behavior modification.

1. Pressure for Candor

Modeled on Alcoholics Anonymous and Synanon (discussed in Chap-ter 10), treatment centers frequently divide offenders into small groups in which clients really confront their sexual problems for the first time when they clearly admit their crimes. Thus at Fort Steilacoom, Wash-ington, where Western State Hospital has one of the most outstanding programs, a typical therapy group consists of about 10 men who ritual-istically begin their meetings seated in a circle, with each stating his name and offenses; for example:

> I'm John. I raped three women and tried to rape five more.
>
> I'm Gene. I'm a flasher—hundreds of times.
>
> I'm Charlie. I had sex with my daughter from the time she was 11 until she blew the whistle (per Brecher, 1977).

A new member has difficulty admitting his crime to himself or to others. By the time he reaches the institution, he has usually spent months in jails and courts, or perhaps free on bail, reciting a denial that becomes automatic:

I'm here by mistake. This chick consented and then screamed rape.

I don't know what happened. I was dead drunk at the time.

I'm an alcoholic, not a sex fiend (Brecher, 1977).

The others, who had previously behaved in the same manner, now deride such talk. A newcomer is asked to write a brief autobiography for group discussion, and the "old timers" may devastatingly criticize its evasions or rationalizations. They may ask that it be rewritten more candidly, and sometimes several rewritings are required. Complete frankness, it is felt, is needed if they are to probe realistically into why the offenses were committed and what can be done to prevent their recurrence (Denenberg, 1974).

Insistence that he keep others honest—not just himself—especially disturbs anyone previously incarcerated for other delinquency or crime, for it means that he must publicly violate the convict code against being a "stool pigeon." He is expected to "snitch" when others make false statements and to report to the group any serious rule violation that occurs outside the meetings; if prevarication or misconduct by others that he must have known about and did not mention is exposed, he is questioned on why he was silent. It is implied that if he cannot report on others, he also cannot be completely frank in discussing himself and will not further the group's self-reformation (Brecher, 1977).

Increasingly these therapeutically oriented programs are free to select their clientele. Courts send them offenders for 30 to 90 days of observation, requesting advice on the amenability to treatment and the dangerousness of each case. As the preceding section indicated for California, the treatment centers thereby tend to receive what Chapter 6 called the neurotic, rather than the egocentric or subculturally criminal types of sex-law violators. In some states the centers can also return to the court civilly committed offenders who adjust poorly, and these persons may then be given prison terms. Thus, whenever it is probable that civil commitment will be easier or briefer than imprisonment, there is much incentive for the inmate to conform to therapy-group expectations. But candor that is forced may only be feigned; some inmates can "play the treatment game" well but not sincerely and thus not be changed by it. Staff and some participants often expose this deception but they, too, may be fooled.

An additional concern is that the courts can err: occasionally an innocent person is commited for a sex offense. Unfortunately, treatment programs are seldom prepared to accept this possibility; the easiest way for an innocent man to gain release may be to confess an act he did not commit. In rare instances treatment personnel develop doubts that a client is really maladjusted or even guilty, and try to get him out soon; however, this is exceptional. Often the process of judicial appeal is longer than the wait for parole. Our courts are certainly better designed, staffed, and located than treatment settings for accurately resolving questions of guilt; but they are slow and, being human, they, too, are fallible.

Another limitation in a therapeutic residential setting is that pressure to criticize each other's character often results in preoccupation with how housekeeping tasks were done and whether they are getting along together. This may do more for adjusting to institutional life than for revealing and changing the thought patterns and relationships of their crimes in the community. Also, strangers institutionalized for therapy usually cannot check the validity of each participant's account of his personal experiences. All members of these incarcerated groups are failures at the conduct they seek to achieve; therefore, expecting mutual insight and sexual change from them may be asking the blind to lead the blind. None of these sex offenders may have very realistic conceptions and adequate skill for legitimate and gratifying relationships. The other three program features discussed here attempt to correct these deficiencies of traditional programs.

Treatment in the community diminishes these problems, as in the distinctive program for incestuous families established by psychologist Henry Giarretto at the juvenile-probation office of Santa Clara County, California. All family members involved in this offense or aware of it when it was occurring may be asked to participate in the program, and a first requirement is that they admit their complicity. Typically this crime consists of father–daughter sex play that gradually increased in intimacy, without significant interference from the mother. In treatment, the father may ascribe his incest to an uncontrollable mental ailment, alcohol, or the devil, and the mother blame herself for their marriage going awry. However, to relieve the daughter of guilt feelings and of a sense of rejection conducive to delinquency when she is placed in a foster home upon the father's arrest, Giarretto insists that both parents tell their child she was the victim of poor parenting that allowed her to engage in this wrongdoing (Brecher, 1977).

In the Santa Clara program, the father (and sometimes others in the household) must take psychiatric treatment as a condition of his probation. It is claimed that for incest offenders, such an arrangement, with close monitoring, results in less recidivism than prison, or than referral to psychiatry without the threat probation will be revoked if attendance declines. All persons in this program, and often other members of their families, are also encouraged or even required to participate in Parents United (discussed later in this section), a group of persons from incestuous families that also stresses honesty about the offense and mutual aid (Brecher, 1977).

2. Female and Gay Personnel

Each therapy group at the Fort Steilacoom center has a staff supervisor, several of whom are women. About half the inmates are married and many have children. Although the marital relationships of offenders are often strained at the time of their crime (divorce frequently follows their arrest), most wives try to help their spouses reform. They are encouraged to visit the center and to bring their children. When a therapy group and staff agree that an inmate has progressed sufficiently, he is permitted to spend an evening with his wife in a cottage that was decorated by offenders' wives and community volunteers. A larger cottage just outside hospital grounds is available for a man near release to spend a weekend with his wife and family. Groups of married couples also meet weekly to discuss their problems (Denenberg, 1974; Brecher, 1977).

A major contribution of female volunteers at Fort Steilacoom is to engage in psychodrama and role playing with the inmates. By portraying a rape victim or the parent of a molested child, and then by having the inmates play such roles, they foster a view of the victims as people rather than as objects to be used. Most volunteers are attractive and personable mothers who participate regularly for years and are trained by staff. Often a crucial problem of the offenders, especially the unmarried ones, is lack of social skill and ease with women. The volunteers teach them how to greet, as well as to start and carry on a conversation. These activities seem most effective with heterosexuals; homosexual offenders have resisted efforts to change their gender preference and have also encountered hostility or stigma from the heterosexual majority in the program (Denenberg, 1974; Brecher, 1977).

California's "Mentally Disordered Sex Offender" program at Atascadero State Hospital, after much unsuccessful effort to change homosexuals into heterosexuals, anticipated this state's 1976 decriminalization of private homosexual acts among consenting adults by simply teaching homosexuals how to avoid arrest. They learn to make liaisons with adults rather than with children and to so do discreetly. For such instruction, volunteers from the outside gay community are role models in psychodramas of encounters in gay bars or other gathering places, and the inmates are informed of locations and organizations for such activities in their home areas. In addition, a lesbian paraprofessional conducts "consciousness-raising" sessions on problems of being gay in a predominantly "straight" society, such as dealing with family, finding and keeping jobs, and maintaining social life with both gay and straight friends or associates (Brecher, 1977).

The distinctive Treatment Program for Sex Offenders in South Florida State Hospital, founded and directed by psychologist Geraldine Boozer, has no volunteers but assigns clients to jobs with staff and patients of both genders in all parts of this mental institution. The offenders also invite relatives or friends to special gatherings of therapy groups. Women active in antirape efforts in the community (as is Dr. Boozer), judges, prosecutors, police officers, and social workers visit with the sex criminals in "rap sessions." Inmates see themselves as public-relations spokesmen for their groups and avidly contribute to discussions on preventing rape and child molestation; they have even suggested to the police possible ways of clearing unsolved rape cases (Brecher, 1977).

In a sex-education program at Minnesota Security Hospital, groups mainly of rapists and child molesters are joined by volunteers, mostly female, to discuss audiovisual material and lectures on sexual behavior. Tape recordings by four rape victims report: their feelings before, during, and after the crime; their subsequent experiences with police, attorneys, family, and friends; and their perception of the rapist's motivation, including the aggression and anger rather than sexuality underlying his conduct. The offenders' profound reactions to this were tape recorded and played to the rape victims, who in turn taped their reactions. Several rounds of such exchanges followed. Similarly, at the New Jersey State Prison in Trenton a therapy group of rapists has been visited by a nearby Women Against Rape organization to discuss this offense (Brecher, 1977). Presumably these types of communication give rapists a more realistic and sympathetic view of the thoughts and feelings of women, that may make them less likely to commit their assaults.

Many other programs also emphasize training male heterosexuals in social skills and comfortable ambience with women. At the University of Tennessee's Psychiatric Institute in Memphis, the rapists and child molesters in a special program make viodeotapes of their efforts to start and maintain conversation with women. The heterosexual social skills or deficiencies evident in the tapes are assessed independently by two or more observers of both genders, who use a rating scale developed by the program's director, Dr. Gene Abel. The tapes are then played and the scores discussed in training groups, so that the clients may improve in subsequent videotaped practice (Brecher, 1977).

Many sex-offender programs endeavor to educate clients in the physiology and psychology of sex, the mechanisms and processes of male and female arousal, and normal sexual changes with age. Charts and photographs of genital anatomy, films of normal lovemaking, and even demonstrations of foreplay have occasionally been presented. Resnik and Wolfgang (1972: Chapter 20) provocatively recommend going further, for example, that: (1) exhibitionists be required to masturbate before a paid female health worker, who would then present her reactions so that some sense of reality would replace their fantasy about its impact; (2) peepers and exhibitionists be encouraged to join nudist camps or participate in mixed-gender sauna baths, in conjunction with therapy sessions, to end their associating genital exposure exclusively with sexuality; (3) wives of married offenders participate in their husbands' reeducation, in hopes that such sharing may improve the sexual aspects of these marriages; (4) all sex offenders, and spouses of the married ones, receive the treatments for sexual inadequacy developed by Masters and Johnson (1970), aided by sexual surrogates if needed.

3. Extension of Treatment into the Community

During the last three months of civil commitment at Fort Steilacoom, an inmate is on "work release." He leaves the institution daily to seek a job, or to work at one. He returns each evening and on weekends to live with his therapy group and participate in its sessions. Following the work-release period, he is an outpatient for up to 18 months, during which he returns to the group only one evening a week (Brecher, 1977).

Extension of the institutional programs into the community through the work release and outpatient treatment has enormous value both to those who leave and return and to those not yet released. The man in the community who develops sexual desires that he has trouble satisfying legitimately and who feels tempted to renew his former criminal acts can discuss these urges immediately with the therapy supervisor, women volunteers, and other inmates with whom he had already gained close rapport while confined. The men not yet released can replace their fantasies with more realistic expectations of what it will be like outside. Successful releasees become role models for those not yet out, especially for newcomers who may be despondent and resistant to the program. Ties between those inside and outside are strengthened by the custom in which each therapy group member contributes according to his means to a small "grubstake" of pocket money for any member who is beginning work release. (Those confined may earn small wages for the work they do in other parts of the hospital by serving more traditional mental patients, and many get spending money from their families.) (Denenberg, 1974; Brecher, 1977).

A distinctive feature of the South Florida program is its attempt to get each offender to recognize his "prodromal syndrome," the circumstances, feelings, and thoughts that preceded his sex crimes. Thus some child molesters recognize that they began by watching children play at a park or school ground. One was aroused by the bell of Good Humor ice cream vendors, from whom he would buy refreshments for children and thus befriend them in order to fondle them sexually. Some rapists had vaguer types of restless feelings, sometimes beginning when they awoke in the morning and not culminating in an offense until evening or even the next day. When inmates depart, they are urged to phone the institution's "hot line" whenever they recognize their prodromal symptoms. The "hot line" is in this program's area within the institution, with a sign directing that it be answered only by sex offenders (reflecting institutional policy of maximizing inmate responsibility). Near the phone are names and phone numbers of program alumni who are "doing well" and have offered to help others. Those who call will be put in touch with one of these successful alumni if they request it or, if they wish, with the center's director or one of the staff. The Patton State Hospital program in California likewise stresses detection of "early warning signals" and awareness that help is available through the nearest telephone (Brecher, 1977).

At South Florida, the program's successful alumni volunteer as chaperones and hosts of inmates on weekend furloughs, calling for them at the institution and reporting how the weekend went when returning them. The director and program staff also meet regularly with volunteer groups of former sex offenders in the community (Brecher, 1977).

4. Mutual Aid

In these descriptions of treatments, we have repeatedly pointed out ways that sex offenders are encouraged to help each other, to help victims or potential victims, and even to help the criminal-justice system. This aid is intended not so much to benefit its recipients as to help those who extend it.

Brecher (1977: 56) asserts:

> All sex offender treatment programs agree that a feeling of inner worthlessness is the single most common attribute shared by convicted sex offenders—even those who put up a blustering front. They are already at the bottom of the barrel—so what do they have to lose? The lack of self-control arises in considerable part out of this lack of a *stake* in society. . . .

It is contended that most offenders have internalized the very values they violate, and thus have low self-respect. This applies especially to the neurotic types usually found most amenable to treatment. Almost all also consider themselves failures because they were unsuccessful in legitimate sexual pursuits, were caught in unlawful acts, and were unsatisfied by the offense itself. Some psychologists and psychiatrists believe that guilt feelings from a person's awareness of having done something wrong produce compulsive repetitions of discrediting behavior as a form of self-punishment. Doing good deeds dramatically breaks this process and, if one has confessed the wrongs to others, gives one a sense of community with good people and a more favorable view of oneself (Mowrer, 1964, 1975).

These principles obviously express much of the philosophy of Alcoholics Anonymous and Synanon (discussed in Chapter 10) and of the sex-offender therapy groups (already described) at Fort Steilacoom and South Florida. We noted that their programs extend into the community, where successful alumni help those still confined. In addition, therapy groups at these two institutions are held responsible for their members; they are expected to prevent escapes and to decide collectively on recommending members for release (Brecher, 1977). In trying to help another refrain from objectionable behavior, presumably one binds oneself to do likewise, but this self-constraint needs frequent support by more mutual aid.

Parents United, the offshoot organization within the incest program of the Santa Clara County juvenile-probation office, is notified whenever a new case is reported. A member, previously convicted of the same crime, contacts the newly exposed father, who may be free on bond pending trial; the mother hears from a woman whose spouse committed this offense. Everyone in the newly exposed incestuous family is usually sufficiently distraught by the arrest to welcome friendliness from someone who had the same trauma. They are further motivated when they learn that their cooperation will probably get the father not the long prison sentence that California law permits, but several years of probation after a few months of confinement in a county correctional facility during all hours not needed for his job or for meetings of Parents United. Giarretto, the psychologist founder-director of this program, finds low self-esteem and defensiveness an especially acute problem of incestuous families. He and Parents United help these people—individually at first, and later collectively—to recognize their potential as a family and to achieve this in part by helping others. Daughters United has also been established, in which victims of incest aid each other and especially help those newly exposed in this crime (Brecher, 1977).

New Jersey's pioneer program for sex offenders, with the acronym ROARE (Reeducation of Attitudes and Repressed Emotions), provides psychoanalytically oriented mutual aid. Participants help each other reenact childhood sexual memories, usually traumatic victimizations by adults, to which they trace their current attitudes. This recall is often deeply emotional, sometimes compared with religious conversion, and all sessions are videotaped so that selected portions can be played back for discussion. Clients are responsible for organizing therapeutic activities, such as videotaped soliloquies or psychodrama (Brancale et al., 1972; Serrill, 1974; Brecher, 1977).

A former sex offender, Richard Bryan, and his wife, Rosemary, organized a unique group in Los Angeles called SOANON—Sex Offenders Anonymous. Like its model among alcoholics, it is purely voluntary, and members do not reveal their last names. They are distinctive for helping each other develop physical restraints that impede repetition of their offenses. Thus a person who regularly picked up hitchhikers for sexual exploitation welds shut the doors on the right side of his car, and exhibitionists wear a special undergarment not easily opened in front (Brecher, 1977). No data were obtainable on their effectiveness, but it is noteworthy that these constraints are self-imposed.

5. Castration

This presumed absolute control over male sexuality is advocated whenever an especially heinous sex crime is reported. It has been used for centuries, most famously to prevent offenses by the guards of Middle-East harems, who were made eunuchs. By removing the testes, both sperm and hormone-creating glands are eliminated, as contrasted with sterilization by vasectomy, which severs the sperm tubes, or demasculinization of transsexuals, which removes all distinctly male organs. Vasectomy does not affect sexual arousal, and castration does not make it impossible, since male hormones can be procured from medical sources and, even without them, earlier interests can remain in the mind. In Europe, where sex offenders of many types have for years been castrated, especially in Scandinavia and Germany, from 1.1 to 7.3 percent recidivism has been reported in various followup studies (Stürup, 1972). Child molestation, exhibitionism, peeping, and sexual assault without consummated rape can certainly be done by castrated males.

In California, anyone civilly committed to the Department of Mental Hygiene as a "mentally disordered sex offender" may undergo involuntary surgery "for the prevention of procreation." Jackson (1972) reports that about 20,000 such operations have been ordered by judges, but that there are no data on whether vasectomies or castrations were performed or on the consequences for recidivism. In 1973, two sex-offense repeaters were sent to court from the civil-commitment program with the diagnosis that they were dangerous and nonamenable to treatment. Fearing that otherwise the judge would feel obliged to sentence them to 50-year maximum terms from which parole had almost always been denied to sex-law violators, they requested probation with castration. They filed waivers exempting the judge, their attorney, and the surgeon from any possible civil liability for this operation, but the doctor withdrew when the medical association advised he could be criminally prosecuted for inflicting bodily injury—mayhem—if he performed it (Brecher, 1977).

For years, castration has often been ordered for sex offenders in several other states, particularly in the South, but statistics have not been compiled on its use and effectiveness. Many object to this treatment on civil-rights grounds, as irreversible should error in conviction be discovered or rehabilitation be feasible, or as "cruel and unusual punishment," proscribed by the Eighth Amendment to the Constitution and offensive to human dignity. Its past frequency and consequences in the United States remain almost as unknown as its prospects for future use.

6. Sex-Hormone Medication

"Chemical castration" can be achieved with certain substances that neutralize a male's sex hormone or inhibit its production. This has been done in Europe and the United States with a few sex offenders of diverse types. This procedure can eliminate a man's physical capacity for genital arousal, though not necessarily his interest in his erotic stimuli, whether fetishes, children, or his wife. These drugs permit, however, a period of "psychic realignment" (Money, 1972: 355), during which the person who wishes to change his sexual behavior can work with his family, counselors, and, most of all, himself, to rearrange his life and alter his thinking.

An exhibitionist who "flashed" as often as 10 times daily reduced this frequency to zero while receiving injections of a chemical to deplete the supply of his male sex hormones. A married man who had periods of transvestism (wearing women's clothes) and of incest abstained for several months while on this drug, then returned to heterosexuality with his wife after the treatment was terminated. In such treatment, interest in unlawful sex acts sometimes recurs after the drug taking ceases, but the drugs are then renewed for a period of further "psychic realignment" (Money, 1972).

7. Behavior Modification

In modern psychology, this expression refers mainly to the deliberate use of positive reinforcements—rewards—to foster desired behavior, but also includes modeling conduct to foster its imitation, eliminating undesired behavior by never rewarding it, and desensitizing people to stimuli that disturb them by satiating them with such stimuli. These and related techniques, often with complex refinements, have been highly successful in many kinds of remedial training (Bandura, 1969).

Those ignorant of the enormous body of research literature on behavior modification mistakenly identify it with its most-publicized but actually least-used methods, aversive conditioning (the shaping of conduct by punishing what is not desired), and psychosurgery. Unfortunately, some use of excessively painful electric shock in attempts to produce behavior change, and some irresponsible but rare efforts to reform offenders by brain surgery, gave all behavior modification a bad press. The term "behavior therapy" is sometimes preferred because of the unfavorable connotation that "modification" has acquired. It emphasizes modeling and positive reinforcement, exemplified in the role-playing and mutual-aid programs for sex offenders described in preceding sections. Aversive conditioning occurs, whether intended or not, wherever sex offenders are involuntarily confined for their crimes, even if confinement is called "hospitalization."

Behavior therapy of male sex offenders who request treatment often begins by measuring what arouses them sexually. This is done by fitting a "penile transducer" on the sex organ, to record its expansions. Those exhibitionists or child molesters who are aroused by seductive pictures of attractive women are assumed to have normal sex desires that they cannot satisfy and so to need training in social and sexual skills with females. If instead of or in addition to normal desires, however, they are aroused by pictures of unlawful sex objects, such as young children, they are given unpleasant experiences—for example, mild electric shock or noxious odors—when shown the forbidden stimuli. Later they are asked merely to think of the odor or the shock when shown the disapproved sex objects. Offenders are also instructed on what to imagine while masturbating. At the Center for Behavior Modification in Minneapolis, a recidivist rapist who had habitually masturbated while handling women's undergarments was given electric shocks while he did this (Serber & Wolpe, 1972; Brecher, 1977). The effects of aversive conditioning are temporary, however, unless there are rewards for alternative behavior. The modification method most clearly proven effective is still positive reinforcement, primarily by successful experience and approval from others in legitimate sexual conduct, and unless this occurs little benefit can be expected from aversive experience.

Unfortunately, the effectiveness of these programs has never been well measured. Objective statistical data on the consequences of different treatment methods for specific types of sex offenders do not exist. The new programs sometimes report recidivism rates much lower than those of prison and parole systems, especially for child molesters, but how much of the difference is due to the innovative treatment and how much to their having only the most promising cases cannot be known without more adequate studies, preferably of experimental or quasi-experimental design.

SUMMARY AND CONCLUSION

Sexual interests, activities, and satisfactions change repeatedly in most lifetimes, and vary greatly from one person to another in our pluralistic society. The study of sex crimes in the United States is complicated by the rapid changes in norms on erotic activity, especially in recent decades, and by shifting definitions of what is unlawful; but acts that clearly victimize others sexually remain criminal and are of increasing public concern.

Prostitution was once patronized by a much larger proportion of our male populace than it serves today, for this "oldest profession" was made necessary by two once-explicit double standards of morality. The first standard approved promiscuity in men but not in women, and its consequence was the second, which divided women into the "good," who had no sex outside of marriage and the "bad" or "fallen," who made the first standard possible by being available to many men. These dualities have nearly vanished among our younger adults, for whom rates of premarital coitus do not differ by gender; indeed, surveys indicate that the average girl today is initiated into sexual intercourse at a younger age than the average boy, so that at certain age levels more girls have experienced it than boys.

Prostitution was formerly concentrated in brothels, but has increasingly been dispersed and diversified. These trends reflect changes in local politics and in the supply and demand for commercial sex, as well as the spread of addiction among women who can only earn the cost of the drugs they crave by selling the use of their bodies. Pimps have some service and some parasitic roles, but are probably diminishing with the growth of female entrepreneurial autonomy and new modes of selling sexual services. Homosexual prostitution is becoming more prominent, allegedly involving thousands of boys in every major metropolis. Paid male companions for women may be a consequence of progress toward gender equality in our society. There is predominant support for decriminalization of prostitution in the United States, according to national polls. But the burgeoning of massage parlors and singles clubs in the 1970s, plus changes in prevailing sex norms, may be sharply reducing the total demand for it, yet making it more accessible to its remaining clientele.

Women's liberation has highlighted problems of rape victims and has secured some relief for them from the criminal-justice system's traditional masculine bias, if not from their assailants. These developments may have increased reporting of this crime to the police, but there are clues that rapes occur much more frequently than either police or victim-survey figures reveal. The least-reported but most-numerous rapes and rape attempts are probably those by "meaning stretchers," typically a "date" rather than a stranger, who uses physical force or threat in seeking more sexual intimacy than she desires. Half the rapes reported to the police, however, are by strangers, mainly those differentiated here as sex looters, naive graspers, and group conformers. Most rapists are of the same ethnic background as their victims, and many rapes are attempted after drinking, but statistics on this aspect have serious limitations of definition and sampling.

Rapists do not seem deterred by announcements of increased penalties; but once imprisoned, they have low recidivism rates, especially those who do not have records of other types of delinquency or crime. More adequate sex education, particularly on the psychophysiology of sexual arousal in women, more contacts between the genders as equals, and perhaps legalized prostitution would probably reduce rape rates.

Sexual molestation of children is committed by a few males of every stage in life, from childhood to old age. About 90 percent of it is heterosexual. The offenders share an attraction to sex objects they can control. Once convicted they are highly stigmatized, especially in prison, and this may explain their vehemence and persistence in denying their offense; yet once released, they have higher rates of repeating the same crime than most other categories of prisoner.

Kinsey's data suggest that about one-eighth of females in the United States experience before age 13 felonious genital acts by an adult, that only a small percentage of these events are reported to the police, and that they seldom impair the later sexual adjustment of the victim. Indeed, the emotional reactions of parents or others on learning of the offense, and sometimes the questioning in police investigations and court hearings, are often more disturbing to the child than the offense itself. Israel and Scandinavian countries have introduced procedures to reduce these strains on children from testifying about this crime.

Incest has almost always and everywhere been tabooed, but has been somewhat variously defined. In the United States, a small percentage admit it on questionnaires, most often with siblings and cousins, but about 80 percent of the arrests are for father–daughter coitus. These cases are quite diverse, but appear most often to involve socially isolated families with an absent or very unassertive mother and a domineering father, who increasingly assigns spouse roles to his oldest daughter.

Statutes proscribing adultery are violated by tens of millions in the United States but are hardly ever enforced or repealed, for politicians presume that the public wishes them to honor fidelity by word, if not by deed. Trying to legalize adultery by being married to more than one spouse is illegal; bigamy is an infrequent type of felony, but new cases are regularly exposed in all large populations.

Much more frequently than most people realize, American

women are startled by male strangers exposing their genitals to them. These exhibitionists are of various ages, often married, and they seem to commit their crime with little thought about the risk of arrest. Although the experience is usually frightening to a woman, this little-studied type of sex criminal is almost always very timid about seducing females, let alone raping them; he fantasizes instead that women will be attracted to him by his display.

"Peeping Toms" commit a crime that appears to be even more passive than the exhibitionist's "flashing," but they much more frequently have a history of diverse juvenile delinquency and adult burglary or even rape. Although the average person today sees more publically displayed nudity than was customary in former decades and although they may therefore be less shocked by flashing or peeping, the right of privacy that these crimes violate are becoming, if anything, more valued. Therefore, such behavior will probably continue to be regarded as criminal, even if punished less severely.

"Sodomy," defined in criminal law as all "unnatural" sexual conduct, is a catch-all for many types of behavior, but has been used almost exclusively against homosexuals. Beginning in 1961, however, a growing number of states decriminalized uncoerced private sex acts between adults of the same gender. Homosexuals have long been stigmatized and exploited, but in recent years the Gay Liberation Movement brought them much more "out of the closets" socially and politically. This creates the impression that they are more numerous than previously, but it is possible that a decrease in one-sex institutions and more widely available heterosexual intimacy are reducing the number who engage in sex acts only with their own gender.

Freedom of speech and press in the United States has never been absolute, one limit being on presentations deemed obscene or pornographic. Yet the meanings of these restrictive concepts have been neither precise nor stable, despite Supreme Court efforts to specify them. Research has challenged the allegation that obscene movies or publications foster sex crimes, and when Denmark eliminated all controls over pornography its sex-offense rates declined, particularly child molesting. Possibly the studies have not adequately investigated subtleties in the effects of obscene works—especially their misrepresentation of female sexual psychology, which may foster the delusions of exhibitionists and of "naive grasper" rapists. Nevertheless, concern for civil liberties leads to preference for zoning and perhaps to limits on advertising and hours, rather than to absolute censorship.

Enactment of sexual psychopath laws in most states resulted from waves of intense public fear of sex criminals, combined with erroneous ideas about causation, identifiability, and potential treatment. The constitutionality of many of these laws remains controversial, but some of the treatment programs resulting from them became highly innovative during the 1970s. Their distinctive features include unusual emphasis on candor regarding the offense, use of females to train male heterosexual offenders in social skills with the opposite sex, extension of the programs from institutions into the community, as well as mutual aid by offenders with each other, former offenders, potential or actual victims, and the police.

One of the oldest and most drastic treatments for male sex criminals is castration. It has been much used and scientifically evaluated in Europe, where it has proved not as absolute a preventive as is often presumed, but nevertheless highly effective. Although debated on civil-rights grounds in the United States, it has been used extensively in California and some other states, but its effectiveness has not been assessed by followup studies here. The same effects as castration but more easily reversed can be achieved by injection of chemicals that neutralize male sex hormones. Such elimination of the capacity for genital arousal, temporarily, may create a respite from sexual urges that facilitates social and psychological reorientation toward more legitimate sexuality.

Unfortunately, research on the effectiveness of treatments and policies in coping with predatory sex crimes remains woefully deficient. The main impact on offense rates, however, may come from trends in society that alter the thinking of people about gender differences and sexual activity. This is implied in Diana Russell's assertion:

> If males and females were . . . liberated from their sex roles, the rape situation would change dramatically. . . . Male sexuality would become more like female sexuality, in that males would value sex within relationships more than sex for its own sake, and would respond to women more as people than as sexual objects. And female sexuality would become more similar to male sexuality, . . . as women would become more in touch with their sexual needs and less apt to obscure the real person and the true nature of the relationship with sexual fantasies. In short, . . . sex-role liberation would result in a mix of the male sexual and the female romantic elements in both males and females (1975:274). (© 1975 by Diana Russell. Reprinted with permission of Stein and Day Publishers.)

Russell's inferences seem to be supported by the very low rates of rape in Scandinavia, where there is reported to be more equality, friendliness, and frankness in heterosexual relationships than occur in most other countries (Linner, 1972). According to Christensen: (1) premarital pregnancy was less associated with a rush to get married or with a subsequent high probability of divorce in Denmark than in the United States (1960); (2) among Danish college students there was more frequent approval than practice of premarital coitus, while among American students the reverse was true, and Americans experienced more guilt feelings when they had sexual intercourse (1962). In many respects the social-evolutionary processes of generalization of values and inclusion have advanced further in Scandinavia than in the United States, and they may represent a future pattern that we are rapidly approaching. If that is the case, our sex predations may decline while our nonpredatory sex acts are increasingly being decriminalized.

TWELVE

AVOCATIONAL CRIME

Although delinquency and crime are deviant sources of autonomy that many try during adolescence, most—sooner or later—reach legitimate occupations. Yet many drift at a later age, either intermittently interrupting their law-abiding careers or supplementing them part time. These are the avocational offenders, adults who break the law but do not consider themselves criminal; illegal pursuits are not their major sources of income or status and they are usually deterred if publicly labeled as lawbreakers (Geis, 1974).

Postadolescents commit property offenses when relapsing to youthful moods, in seeking supplements to their legitimate earnings, or as a standard aspect of their business or job subculture. Yet by far the costliest crimes to society, more serious both in dollars and in human lives than all other offenses combined, are predations by widely respected organizations that are seldom branded criminal or severely penalized for this lawbreaking.

RECURRENCE OF ADOLESCENT-CRIME PATTERNS

The years of schooling required for entrance into adult occupations have increased for most of the population, as Chapter 8 detailed when pointing out that adolescents unsuccessful in this educational process are especially likely to drift into unspecialized delinquency and crime. But a sense of failure may develop even after one has "made it" in work, marriage, or other adult roles; strain may intensify for many reasons, at any time, to make anticipations from crime less unfavorable, especially for former offenders but even for a few who hardly ever violated laws when they were younger.

Frustration in legitimate endeavors tends to reduce stake in conformity, as Chapter 6 elaborated, alienating people from the laws or from persons in authority. Extreme or prolonged dissatisfaction especially fosters willingness to experiment with criminal conduct. Thus an appreciable amount of the violence and sex crime described in Chapters 9 and 11 is initiated in adulthood or even at an advanced age, and some property offenses also begin late. For example, persons plagued with debts or confronting failure after much investment of time and savings in business may commit arson to collect insurance, embezzle funds entrusted to their care, forge documents to gain money, or even take a gun and attempt to hold up a bank. Most such late beginnings in property crime are atypical, as Table 4-3 on the age distribution of arrests indicated, but they do occur. Some standard patterns in older-age avocational property offenses, notably embezzlement, will be described later in this chapter.

Ordinary property felonies, such as burglary or robbery, are not often committed by adults with legitimate employment or even by those who have worked long and been briefly unemployed; the probability of such crime later in life is greatest among those who engaged in it during adolescence. As Chapter 5 showed, although arrest and punishment come sooner or later to almost all in such offenses, they are successful in "getting away with" most of the separate crimes of these types that they attempt. Therefore, the memory of their successes and near successes leads many to gamble with the law anew. Gaining a legitimate income and a "respectable" community status increases their stake in conformity, for they then have more to lose if arrested. Yet a few revert to crime because they feel financially pressed; they have purchasing aspirations beyond their earnings, or they become so committed to a lifestyle and standard of living when they are "doing well" that they cannot accept an unexpected setback.

Such returns to crime are demonstrated by long-run recidivism studies. Of federal prisoners released in 1956, about a third were reimprisoned within two years, half in five years, and an additional eighth by the end of 18 years. Although over a third never recidivated, another third did so quite soon, and the remaining nearly one-third that concerns us here reverted to crime during the two-to-18-year postrelease period, even though apparently law abiding most of the time (Kitchener et al., 1977). Many of these late recidivists repeat the unspecialized-offense pattern typical of adolescence, often in conjunction with drinking. Frequently they receive emergency aid from parents, spouses, or other kin, but this often rearouses their adolescent pattern of resenting such dependence and recklessly committing crimes to express their autonomy, especially when the assisting persons are also domineering (Glaser, 1969: 331ff.; Petersilia et al., 1977).

Some avocational offenders never commit major property crimes; they are part-time lawbreakers who usually lead conventional lives. This description applies especially to adult nonprofessional shoplifters and price-tag switchers.

THEFT AND FRAUD BY SHOPPERS

About half the apprehended shoplifters are juveniles, more in some types of store, less in others. Few are professional "boosters," although these are common where opiate addiction is widespread. Most adult arrestees for this offense are avocational thieves, usually young single persons of both genders but also housewives, quite diverse in age and social class (Cameron, 1964; Won & Yamamoto, 1968).

Self-service stores facilitate shoplifting and price-tag switching, by having all wares readily accessible to customers and few clerks for the volume sold. Because such an arrangement requires less labor than selling over a counter, merchants prefer it even if it is a boon to crime; they also find that open shelves and counters foster not only impulse theft but also impulse purchasing. Where the volume of stealing makes self-service unprofitable, as with expensive cosmetics, perfumes, and jewelry, display-case selling is retained.

Recurrence of this typically juvenile crime in adult life may well reflect successful experience at it in childhood. In the author's university classes in several locales, and in published surveys, 60 to 75 percent of college students admit that they have done it, and 20 to 25 percent that they still do. Kraut (1976) found that the more frequently students shoplift, the more they assume that most others do and approve of it, and the more they describe the "typical shoplifter" by the same adjectives that they use for themselves. About a sixth of the student shoplifters he studied had been apprehended, and most repeated this offense after they were caught, even though they then saw the risk as greater. Cameron (1964), on the other hand, reports that shoplifting housewives were very much deterred by arrest.

Most shoplifters who are caught are not prosecuted, for a variety of reasons, including the fact that the victim does not want to lose the time required for courtroom testimony. The offenders become very contrite if arrested, and especially anxious that their parents or spouses not be notified. Juvenile and old-age offenders are least often prosecuted, and the value of goods stolen (rather than race or gender) usually determines the decision of whether to involve the police in a shoplifting case detected by store employees (Robin, 1963; Hindelang, 1974b). Since only the merchants, their employees, or hired guards apprehend shoplifters, the threats they use and the conditions they impose for not calling the police or not pressing charges may differ markedly from penalties that would be made by a court of law. Allegedly a common inducement to dropping charges in small businesses is that the offenders or their families make appreciable purchases, in addition to restitution.

Experiments staging shoplifting in front of customers or employees find that it is usually ignored. People do not wish to be involved. The young and the old are least likely to report this offense to others. The gender of the shoplifter and the observer does not seem to be closely related to the response evoked, but a thief with a "hippie" appearance or from a minority ethnic group is much more likely to be reported than one who looks "straight" (Gelfand et al., 1973; Steffensmeier & Terry, 1973; Blankenburg, 1976). The impression of security guards and other staff of the "typical" shoplifter can determine which customers are watched most closely as potential offenders, and thereby which thieves are caught and which are overlooked. Expecting conventional-looking people not to shoplift may increase the probability of their committing this crime successfully and thus persisting in it.

Informal inquiry with students and merchants indicates that price-tag switching is a common avocational offense, especially in large stores. Returning used or stolen goods as damaged or unsatisfactory, for cash or credit refund, is another ruse. Various studies suggest that both shoplifters and the general public are particularly indifferent to victimization of major companies, as contrasted to defrauding small

The five-finger discount.

shopkeepers, because a firm is considered impersonal and so rich that the loss will not be felt (Smigel, 1956; Kraut, 1976).

Gould (1969) marshals evidence and argument to suggest that as societies become more affluent, a sense of relative deprivation becomes more prevalent in the population, goods are less closely guarded, and the proportion of property crimes committed by "amateur" offenders increases. As social differentiation grows, more transactions pit an individual against a bureaucracy; since the latter is represented mainly by computer printouts, it is considered incapable of being hurt. Furthermore, complex organizations increase the possibility of employees committing crimes because they are entrusted with the property of others; and these others are perceived not as humans but as indifferent corporations.

EMBEZZLEMENT AND OTHER CRIMES
AGAINST EMPLOYERS

In virtually every type of job there are ways of cheating the employer, whether by taking company property, misrepresenting the amount of work done, padding expense accounts, or falsifying sick-leave claims. All these acts are crimes if done with intent to steal or defraud, but most are perpetrated regularly by some employees in every large firm, and sometimes by most. Prosecution for these offenses is relatively infrequent, although collectively, and sometimes individually, such predations total extremely large sums.

Embezzlement is the "fraudulent appropriation of property by a person to whom it has been entrusted" (California Penal Code). Examples include a bookkeeper manipulating records to take cash from someone's account, a lawyer illegally siphoning funds from an estate, a salesperson selling samples and keeping the proceeds, an organization treasurer pocketing money from dues or collections, and a cashier keeping some receipts by not ringing them up. Embezzlement of and frauds against federally insured and regulated banks and other financial institutions are twice as frequent as robberies, burglaries, and larcenies combined and involve seven times as much money. They are also increasing the most rapidly (Federal Home Loan Bank Board, 1977).

Large-scale embezzlement is usually committed by persons who have become established in a respected occupation and have no prior criminal record, for they must have good reputations to be entrusted with many valuables, or to control the records of extensive transactions. Deliberate misrepresentation to appear trustworthy in order to gain access to valuables that one intends to steal is the crime of "confidence game," described in the next chapter; "embezzlement" will be used here (as in Cressey, 1953) to designate violations of trust by persons who had no intent to embezzle when they first acquired the employment that enabled them to commit their crime. The legal charges on which these offenders may be convicted, however, are many; sometimes only one aspect of the total criminal act, such as theft or forgery, is designated.

In his classic study *Other People's Money,* Cressey concluded from interviewing 133 convicted embezzlers and examining records on many more that every such violation of financial trust begins with what seems an unshareable problem (1953: Chapter 2; 1965). For some offenders this problem is gambling losses or business reversal, perhaps from a foolish investment that they fear is incompatible with the reputation for sound financial judgment necessary for their employment (e.g., as banker or realtor). For others it reflects giving their family, political supporters, or friends a false impression of their income; they "keep up a front" that they cannot afford. People who mix socially in groups of higher income than their own often develop "false pride" in a wealth that they lack, and panic at the thought of losing face by revealing their financial straits to those who regard them as status peers. Occasionally the unshareable problem is simply the precedent of helping those less fortunate, altruistically making others dependent on them and thereby creating expectations on which they feel they cannot renege.

Robin (1970a) checked the records of 1,681 employees apprehended for dishonesty in three large department stores between 1949 and 1964 and concluded that almost all were in positions of trust taken "in good faith," and thus were embezzlers rather than confidence gamesters. Only in 72 cases did the files on these mainly unprosecuted individuals include the reasons for the offense, but all seemed to focus on an unshareable problem.

Banks and savings-and-loan institutions are estimated to lose over five times as much money by embezzlement as by robbery, but only the robberies are publicized, as a rule. Many firms bond their employees as insurance against such loss, and analysis of bonding-company files could yield more adequate data on this offense than is available from criminal-justice agencies, since so much of the exposed defalcation is not reported to the police. An old study of such fidelity-insurance records covering the years 1926 to 1933 found that over 90 percent of embezzlements are cumulative, sometimes done systematically for years, rather than "grab and run." It was also shown to be one of the few crimes committed more by married than by single employees, and traveling salesmen had the highest offense rates (Redden, 1942).

The embezzler's employment often requires expertise at detecting fraud—for example, as accountant, lawyer, or realtor—that can also be used in committing offenses. Part of the lore of many occupations consists of tales of how certain frauds were perpetrated, often related so frequently as to suggest that they are standard practices. Thus most of these offenders know how to appropriate someone's property long before they do it, and many refrain from crime for a long time after developing their unshareable problem. But Cressey states that in all cases he studied, the offense itself was never committed until the offender developed a verbal justification, which made it seem compatible with the offender's self-conception as a morally righteous person. As Smigel and Ross (1970: vi) observe, ". . . to violate the commandment 'Thou shalt not steal,' the violator must have recourse to other commandments which deflect that original rule or provide exceptions."

One of the most frequent rationales of embezzlers is that the money is only "borrowed." People often do spend for their personal needs funds they are holding for others, then replace the amount spent before their "borrowing" is detected. A common sequence in embezzlement is that such unofficial and illegal loans are made and then cannot be paid back in time; then, what was taken from one account is replaced with money from another, and this must be repaid with funds from still others, until "juggling of the records" becomes fantastically intricate and the total amount embezzled is far beyond the offender's capacity to repay legitimately (e.g., Parker, 1976: Chapter 16).

Firms victimized by embezzlement are usually more concerned with recovering losses than with punishing employees. Some realistically fear that customers will be reluctant to deal with them if the predation by their staff is publicized; so much discovered embezzlement never results in filing of criminal charges. Indeed, businesses handling savings or investments depend upon a reputation for honest employees with good judgment. Frequently, however, such companies expect their staff to dress and to participate in civic organizations as though more affluent than their salaries permit; they may thus generate the financial straits that become unshareable problems leading to embezzlement. Also, personnel handling financial records or valuables who are pressured to work long after the rest of the office is closed, or to come in early to keep up with their assignments, or to take work home —all without overtime pay—are given both special opportunities and rationales for embezzlement; they acquire privacy for altering records, as well as the idea that they are being exploited and are only taking what is owed them.

In many firms a certain amount of employee pilfering of the wares they handle is so extensive and routine that it is assumed all are helping themselves. For example, thefts of small tools and supplies for do-it-yourself home projects are common among maintenance and construction workers and in many types of factories. Horning (1970) found employee support for taking goods when the loss would not clearly jeopardize company operations or invite a "crackdown" on everyone working there. Gouldner (1954) found that norms on the amount or type of goods that may be taken become part of an established but unofficial company "indulgency pattern," so that any sudden change in policy that sharply reduces the pilfering one can "get away with" is strongly resented and contributes to wildcat strikes. Zeitlin (1971) reports that it is more profitable for some firms to accept moderate theft by employees than to control it, since stealing adds interest to otherwise dull jobs and reduces staff turnover.

Many stores reportedly lose more merchandise to employees than to shoplifters, but usually deal with this only by termination of employment rather than by prosecution. Robin (1970b) found that in this private administration of justice in three large department stores, the amount stolen was the major determinant of the decision to prosecute (as with shoplifting); however, lower-status workers were more likely to be prosecuted than higher-level staff, whenever both had stolen the same amounts. All those caught are asked to sign a confession, which 85 percent do, thereby protecting the company from possible lawsuit but also providing some thieves with a means of bargaining for leniency in exchange for signing.

Today bookkeeping is done primarily by computers. This creates both new ways of checking for possible embezzlements, and new ways of perpetrating them. Some multiple-access computers may be instructed by outsiders to alter the records of a firm, even to make a delivery or issue a check, provided the appropriate code is known. Expert Donn B. Parker told a United States Senate committee that all of the 430 cases of such fraud he had studied were discovered by accident, and that a conservative estimate of such losses nationally was $100 million per year (*Los Angeles Times*, September 20, 1976). Parker (1976) reports, however, that the first instance of such fraud he can find recorded occurred in 1966. Because the field is so new and rapidly changing, many of the people with skills for this crime (e.g., programmers) are relatively young, are not carefully screened, are given ready access to key records or equipment, and cannot be supervised by many other employees.

The Equity Funding scandal, a $2 billion fraud exposed in 1973 after developing for about a decade, is considered the largest swindle in American history. It depended heavily on abuse of computerized accounting to create an illusion that this was the fastest-growing and most profitable conglomerate in the world (Soble & Dallos, 1975; Parker, 1976: Chapter 13). It was one of many major scandals of the 1970s (Moffitt, 1976) in which stockholders were misled by corporation officials, and large segments of the general public were cheated by the firm, a type of crime somewhat different from embezzlement.

CRIMES BY OSTENSIBLY LEGITIMATE ORGANIZATIONS

In all fields of commerce and industry, there are ways of illegally victimizing customers, competitors, the government, or the general public. Most common is deliberate and gross misrepresentation in selling. It happens, at times, with virtually every product or service; for example, the quality or quantity of goods or work offered is exaggerated, especially its durability, its efficiency, or the speed and dependability of repairs.

Perhaps the most vehemently made claim for a free-enterprise economy since Adam Smith's (1776) has been that competition rewards and expands those businesses that give the public the most and the best for the least money. But this achievement requires (among other things) that public pressures and criminal law make all entrepreneurs compete fairly. Unfortunately, such morality is far from universal, and when purchasers can be duped, the deceptive dealer may have competitive advantages over the more honest. Furthermore, the most effective way to compete may be either to sabotage rivals, to buy them all out, to collaborate with them in price and quality fixing, or to form an organization of those well-established in an occupation (whether law, medicine, plumbing, or barbering) that illegally restricts training or licensing of new practitioners. Besides, even when competition leads to cost reductions that are passed on to customers, these savings may be gained by victimizing the rest of the public; for example, by evading corporation taxes or by disposing of waste in the cheapest way —spewing it into the air or water.

Criminologist Edwin H. Sutherland seems to have been referring to all the business predations suggested in the preceding two paragraphs, and perhaps to others as well, when he coined the phrase "white collar crime" to designate any offense "committed by a person of respectability and high social status in the course of his occupation" (1949: 9). He indicates that the offenders are primarily "business managers and executives," but that the white collar crimes do not include assaults, embezzlements, or other very personal predations, since such law violations are not the normal expectation in their jobs. He also excludes predations by predominantly criminal organizations that invest in some legitimate businesses (such as those described in Chapter 13), since these groups are not led by persons of "respectability." His definition is vague and his phrase does not provide a very apt label, but he seems to have had in mind primarily the offenses that are the topic of this section, *crimes by ostensibly legitimate organizations.* These "crimes in the suites" (of corporate offices) are much more costly to society than the crime in the streets with which the public is more concerned.

The criminal law was originally designed to punish only law violation by intelligent individuals who have rational minds (see Chapter 3); it has always had some difficulty dealing with crimes perpetrated in the name of an organization. The problem is especially evident when these offenses are long-standing and large-scale, involving many persons, with no one knowing when the illegal practices became customary. Such problems confronted the law even in medieval times, when guilds or merchants' associations were deemed guilty of crime; but they have become acute in our modern day of huge corporations and international conglomerates, as well as unions, professional associations, and political parties acting in behalf of tens or hundreds of thousands of individuals, and even for millions.

As Christopher Stone (1975: xi-xii) observes, "aside from governments and governmental agencies, more and more it is corporations that are effectively the *actors* in our society. . . . they . . . are our most evident producers, distributors, land managers, taxpayers, polluters, investors, investments, service providers, and . . . farmers . . . the most effective 'private' forces to do widespread good and . . . harm." Thurman Arnold pointed out in his classic, *The Folklore of Capitalism* (1937), that we tend to personify huge corporations as individuals when their executives claim that laws regulating these firms stifle "rugged individualism" and the "entrepreneurial spirit." Yet these organizations are like governments, only even more complex; they are controlled by pyramids of parent firms, holding companies, and investment blocs far removed from actual plant or store management. Their executives and bureaucracies may perhaps be inefficient or corrupt as often as those of government; for example, they tolerate conflicts of interest, and gifts to their executives to gain favors, long outlawed in federal and most state and local civil-service and elective offices.

Laws imposing government penalties for predations against private individuals evolved from tort legislation on the collection of payments for damage or injury (as Chapter 2 indicated). Only in the middle of the nineteenth century were corporations, rather than individuals, made subject to tort suits for damages caused by their employees when acting in behalf of the firm. With these changes, for example, if a railroad bridge collapsed from faulty construction and killed or injured people, the victims or their estates could sue a construction corporation or the railroad rather than the less-wealthy engineer or job supervisor. Only at the beginning of the twentieth century, with the antitrust laws, could entire corporations be convicted of crimes (C. Stone, 1975: Chapter 3), but the enforcement of these laws has not been nearly as vigorous as many deem warranted.

Regulation of most corporate crime begins not with the courts, but with inspection and regulatory agencies, such as the Federal Trade Commission (FTC), established in 1914 in conjunction with the Clayton Anti-Trust Act. Although this commission investigates complaints about restraint of trade and can issue "cease and desist" orders that have the force of law, it cannot impose punishment for noncompliance, for that requires prosecution by the Anti-Trust Division of the Justice Department and conviction of the accused (usually a corporation) in a federal court. A guilty company that anticipates eventual conviction can still delay obeying an FTC order for years of court hearings, thereby possibly making many millions more than its expenses from the litigation and penalties. It can then plead *nolo contendere* —do not contest the charges but do not admit guilt—to avoid being stigmatized as criminal.

Since 1962 the FTC has had additional functions for consumer protection, including control over accuracy of advertising, expanded especially by the Fair Packaging and Labeling Act of 1966. In these tasks it must collaborate with the Secretaries of Commerce and of Health, Education and Welfare to develop standards and negotiate agreements, not all of which are mandatory. Additional agencies with quasi-judicial powers to punish those who victimize the public include the Federal Communications Commission, the National Traffic Safety Bureau, the Civil Aeronautics Board, the Food and Drug Administration, and others, all subject to periodic administrative reorganization, redistribution of functions, and renaming. Also relevant are enforcement of such laws as the Occupational Safety and Health Act of 1970 by the Department of Labor—to penalize employers who endanger the health of their workers—and the many government offices and bureaus with authority to police and punish those who waste or spoil our natural resources—from forests to ocean beaches and from the air we breathe to the water we drink.

All these quasi-criminal-justice agencies, as well as the groups of government attorneys in the Department of Justice who are authorized to back them up in court, have been severely criticized for their limited effectiveness, and even for siding with the predators rather than the victims. Reform efforts have often accomplished little, Liebhafsky points out, because

> in every government agency staffed at lower levels by career employees, there . . . exist hardened attitudes and lines of policy. Political appointees . . . must rely upon the . . . experience and knowledge of the . . . civil servants . . . with access to the files who . . . are in a position to shape the views of . . . newcomers (1971: 225–26).

In addition, a congressional committee that drafts the legislation a regulatory agency enforces or that appropriates funds for its operations can exert pressure on the agency and will be catered to by it. Committee members may be influenced by spokespersons for the regulated organizations, who contribute to campaign funds and can do other political favors or injuries. There has also been a circulation of personnel between the regulating bodies and the firms they are supposed to monitor and control.

Despite repeated compromise or even surrender of regulatory agencies to corporation resistance, the record shows that there has been more growth in government control over business predation since the mid-1960s than in any prior period of comparable length. One factor in this trend has been the inclusion process in social evolution, prodded by Common Cause and the "open government" movement but especially by reactions to the Watergate scandal. As a result of these developments, contributions by business and professional organizations to political funds are now more restricted and publicized than ever before, and are increasingly being replaced by government payments to candidates for campaign costs. A second important factor has been called the "Nader phenomenon" (Geis, 1974).

A consumer's movement developed slowly in the United States in the twentieth century, stimulated during the Depression by the popular writings of Stuart Chase that led to product-testing organizations, particularly Consumers Union. Yet Ralph Nader and his associates, an economic historian asserts, "have, undoubtedly, done more than anything else in recent times to . . . give momentum . . . to efforts in behalf of consumers" (Creighton, 1976: 51). Nader's first book, *Unsafe at Any Speed* (1965), criticizing the design and assembly of automobiles as indifferent to safety, gained fame and influence primarily because of the publicity given to General Motors' use of detectives and telephone tapping in an unsuccessful attempt to find something in his private life that would discredit him. The exposure of these efforts gave his congressional testimony unusual attention, and was a major factor in passage of the National Traffic and Vehicle Safety Act of 1966 (Buckhorn, 1972; McCarry, 1972; Whiteside, 1972).

With the half-million-dollar out-of-court settlement of his suit against General Motors for invasion of privacy, income from book sales, public-speaking fees, and, later, tens of thousands of small annual contributions to his organization, Public Citizen, Nader recruited bright and dedicated young lawyers, scientists, and others—"Nader's Raiders"—to his Center for Study of Responsive Law. Aided by volunteers, many still students, they prepared a long series of "Nader Reports" on a large variety of crimes by organizations. They covered evasion of antitrust laws (Green et al., 1972), flouting of regulatory agencies and evading of competitive bidding for government contracts (Green, 1973), food contamination and worthless or dangerous medication (Turner, 1970), air pollution (Esposito & Silverman, 1970), crippling or killing employment conditions (Page & O'Brien, 1973), and other law violations or immoralities. In many cases when they charged firms with specific crimes, such as false advertising or short-weight packaging, they filed formal complaints that resulted in government action; but they claim that the agencies responsible for preventing corporate crime generally perform only half-heartedly or not at all, for they are subservient to the predators they are supposed to control.

For crime prevention, Nader urges employees of corporations to expose law violations by the firms that hire them, stockholders to be militant in the public interest, and all citizens to be more active in seeking vigorous enforcement of laws assuring business competition, safe products, healthy workplaces, and an unpolluted environment. He encourages local class-action suits, but his main target is national government, and he calls for federal chartering of all corporations with interstate business (Nader, 1973; Nader et al., 1976). Nader's critics include some industry staff who challenge the factuality of scattered details of the Nader Reports (although not the bulk of charges in these documents) and some right-wing journalists who, instead of addressing the issues he raises, claim that he is power hungry. Conservative economists question whether the government controls he advocates would increase or decrease competition and would improve products and the automatic workings of the marketplace. They trust the ability of consumers to avoid being duped more than the government's prospects of protecting them, and in advocating deregulation they present horror stories of the red tape, cost increases and ineffectiveness in some federal intervention (Peterson, 1971). Much extensive national and international organization is inevitable in modern industry because of the size and cost of some devices (e.g., jet transports, oil pipelines, and oil tankers); but to suggest that the consequent conglomerates will themselves be in perfect competition or will have much more than a perfunctory pubic-relations concern with preventing serious damage to nature is to ignore pressures for profits.

Former corporation lawyer and now law professor Christopher Stone (1975) contends that we must evolve more effective penalties and preventives for dealing with corporations as criminals. He points out that even when companies are fined enough to more than offset their profits from restraint of trade or pollution, the executives or directors responsible for the violations lose neither income nor tenure, but receive promotions and increases for expanding profits. Therefore, they have nothing to lose in disobeying laws on environmental protection and on product or employee safety, especially if they have some prospects of thereby gaining delays or altogether avoiding punishment. He reports that requirements that businesses present environmental-impact reports or data on their finances have resulted in the preparation of mountainous documents filled with undigested raw information. These are intentionally made so intimidating that no one will assess them well or even examine them closely; yet they will greatly delay or completely prevent conformity with court or agency requirements. He proposes, instead, that government bodies require convicted firms to pay for officials and staff independent of company authority to check on the corporation's quality control, pollution prevention, or other area of law violation. These investigators would report in writing to both the board of directors of the firms and the government agencies, and there would be time limits on company action to correct the reported deficiencies. Although some of these specific measures have already been imposed by courts as conditions of probation, they, too, are resisted or avoided and may never become customary. Nevertheless, they exemplify the proliferation of new procedures for government control of corporate crime that will undoubtedly continue and evolve into a new criminal law and correctional policy for organizations.

Much clearer and more effective than policing and prosecuting crimes by enormous firms is action against small businesspersons who cheat consumers. An old study (Lane, 1951) showed that the number of violations of government regulations varies inversely with the size of the firm. Stimulated by the consumer movement and by LEAA publications (e.g., Edelhertz, 1970; LEAA, 1975d), local agencies have expanded their staffs and streamlined procedures for combating fraudulent automobile, television, and other repair services, short-weighting, and other misrepresentation in retail selling. News programs find consumer advocates popular, and they refer complaints to appropriate agencies and publicize results. Elected officials, particularly district attorneys, find it politically expedient to take this mass audience into account as a potential source of votes; thus consumer-fraud prosecution has become more active. Sometimes, however, these government actions are directed only against lesser offenders or the lowest-level employees, while major corporations and top executives are not charged or are more successful in avoiding conviction than others of no greater guilt; they remain free to continue any profitable contamination or pollution (for an example, see Schuck, 1972).

GOVERNMENT CORRUPTION AND POLITICAL CRIMES

There have always been crimes in political office, and they were formerly much more widespread than they are today. An ancient document from India observes that one can no more determine whether government workers are taking money for themselves than one can decide whether a fish is drinking water while swimming in it. "In medieval Europe public offices, including that of tax collector, were commonly sold to the highest bidder. The successful buyer was able to recoup his expenses and more. . . . This remained a common practice in Great Britain until the early nineteenth century" (Douglas & Johnson, 1977: 5).

Except when carried to unusual excess, what is now decried as "spoils politics" (the holders of government positions take whatever they can for themselves) was generally acceptable under the system of authority that Max Weber (1922/1947: 343-58) called "traditional." This source of personal power had one of its purest forms in the patrimonial system of feudalism, in which a hereditary ruler gave his offspring—especially the sons—and other noblemen who supported him, large gifts of land (often the modern equivalent of townships or counties). They, in turn, bestowed estates within their lands to their offspring and other supporters. Each estate included the peasants and houseservants who lived on it. Subsequent transfers of holdings were made by inheritance and intermarriage within each status level.

Similarly, many government positions within each realm—for example, those of tax collector and customs inspector—were acquired as gifts from superiors or as a family right by inheritance, along with a landholding. Each office had a customary income from some combination of fees, fines, seizures, or bribes, shared with the office bestower. Land- or officeholders in the feudal hierarchies of wealth and power were obligated to give gifts and payments to their benefactors, and received them from subordinates, especially shares in the harvests. There were parallel obligations of military support or other services. Such systems, accepted as legitimate and regulated by custom, were reinforced by everyone's eagerness to please those who could help or hurt them.

Such systems of patrimony, with many local variations, have been the basis for most of the political and economic order until modern times. They were only gradually replaced by legal-authority systems (Weber, 1922/1947: 329-41) of "government of laws, not men." In the resulting bureaucracies, salaries—not monies or property collected by the office—are the only legitimate payments for government jobs, even those with power.

Bribery has not disappeared, even in the most technologically advanced and legalistic nations, but it strikingly pervades less-developed countries that are dominated by quasi-feudal families with large landholdings. Thus Americans and Western Europeans are shocked at the side payments to government functionaries in nonsocialist nations of Latin America, Asia, and Africa, and sometimes in socialist ones as well. Even in the universities this system prevails. Professors receive lavish gifts from students' families, and favoritism is expected in return, with objective examinations abhorred. Such practices also prevailed a century or two ago in much of Europe and the United States, but rarely now survive. Indeed, one can argue that socialism gained power not where capitalism created what Marx called "the seeds of its own destruction," but only: (1) where the growth of legal-authority systems, of a large middle class, and of competitive capitalist entrepreneurs was impeded by a corrupt and quasi-feudal landholding elite (e.g., Russia, China, Cuba, Vietnam), or (2) by conquest (e.g., Eastern Europe, North Korea).

As the next chapter emphasizes in discussing organized crime, corruption of officials still flourishes wherever there is much public demand for illegal services, such as off-track betting, prostitution, or drugs (see Manning & Redlinger, 1976). Indeed, sociological research has demonstrated that if formal rules and bureaucratic organization create strains, an informal set of understandings and practices is likely to develop to circumvent them (Blau, 1963; Homans, 1974). More decriminalization of popular nonpredatory behavior should further reduce the already-declining power of political machines.

With the Watergate scandal so recent, it may seem inappropriate to speak of a decline in political corruption. But the consequences of technological development (discussed in Chapter 2), which raise the population's average level of education and increase employment in formal organizations, have made more business and government activity subject to rules. These trends create both more possibility of rule evasion and more public outrage at any rule violation that occurs (Douglas, 1977: 401ff.). The apparently smaller proportion of corrupt government services, however, may reflect not so much a decline in total corruption as its more scattered distribution, for governments have greatly expanded, and most growth has been at local and state levels.

Watergate highlighted the increased danger of any corruption at the top level of national government, now that power is more concentrated in the Presidency. As historian Henry Steele Commager summarizes: "By countenancing burglary, wiretapping, *agents provocateurs*, the use of the Federal Bureau of Investigation, the Central Intelligence Agency and even the Internal Revenue Service to punish 'enemies,' by endorsing resort to secrecy, duplicity and deception in . . . government, Mr. Nixon sought to substitute his own fiat for the law" (1974: 155). In addition, by ordering the invasion of Cambodia, Nixon usurped congressional power to declare war. By suppression of news and by threats of not relicensing dissident television stations, his appointees weakened the First Amendment (Wise, 1973).

Fortunately, our system of checks and balances—of congressional and judicial curbs on the executive branch, and of regular elections—proved equal to the task of overcoming the Watergate threat. Since then, the regulation of political contributions and the reduction of government secrecy may make less probable the recurrence of such jeopardy to the democratic process, but only if there is constant vigilance against abuse of power.

Vigilance is sometimes attained through openly flouting the law by civil disobedience, but political protesters are often arrested primarily because they hold dissident views. Francis A. Allen understates this in asserting that "the identification and punishment of political offenders tends strongly to excess" (1974: 50). He adds:

> The "political" defendant . . . often seeks to test the values and motives of the official agencies against his own and thereby to subject justice to trial. His efforts in this connection may be carefully deliberated. "In court," wrote Father Philip Berrigan, "one puts values against legality according to legal rules and with slight chance of legal success. One does not look for justice; one hopes for a forum from which to communicate ideals, convictions and anguish" (1974: 60).

The tolerance that should be given to nonviolent political disobedience cannot be safely extended to the political terrorism that takes or threatens lives. However, during recent decades in the United States, there has repeatedly been a much more real and present danger to everyone from government actions against nonviolent dissidents than from these dissidents. Again, Allen is insightful:

> The fanaticism of the terrorist is sometimes matched by the fanaticism of the government agent. A kind of religious warfare results, with neither side revealing any disposition to doubt the virtue of its cause or to subject the efficacy of its means and measures to critical examination. The Watergate incident provided a glimpse of this fanaticism and its implications. If there is anything more deplorable than the acts committed in that and related incidents, it is the reasons publicly stated to explain and justify them (1974: 68).

The best justification for restraint in the prosecution or punishment of political criminals was well stated by the late Justice Learned Hand—"the spirit of liberty is the spirit which is not too sure that it is right" (quoted in Mondale, 1975: 263).

SUMMARY AND CONCLUSION

The fact that people appear to be committed to law-abiding lives and consider themselves noncriminal does not guarantee that they will not engage in felonious property offenses. Five types of avocational property crime in adult life were discussed here.

The nonspecialized offense patterns distinctive of adolescents groping for a sense of adult autonomy, especially when frustrated in school or work, can recur at any later age. Of course, the greater and more persistent their success in legitimate adult roles and the stronger their bonds with law-abiding persons, the lesser the probability of such recurrence. Yet among those once imprisoned, the prospect of reimprisonment for a new offense remains appreciable for a few years after each release, although diminishing greatly thereafter.

Part-time theft by shoplifting or price-tag switching is committed at one time or another by most juveniles and by a surprisingly large proportion of adults who live otherwise law-abiding lives. These include an appreciable number of housewives, of all social and economic levels. They generally appear to be strongly deterred when caught, although most are not prosecuted but merely threatened with having their deed exposed to their families.

Crimes against employers, such as pilfering supplies, are often routine, and sometimes it is expedient for the firm to ignore lesser thefts—they become an unofficial fringe benefit fostering job stability. Embezzlement is a recurrent, serious problem among employees who have access to much money or valuable goods. Those hired in such positions typically have a long record of trustworthiness, but a few nevertheless steal when plagued by what they perceive as an unshareable problem. Usually they do not consider themselves criminal and refrain from this offense until they not only have the problem and the opportunity for embezzlement, but also have convinced themselves of a rationalization for this offense. Employee frauds appear to be acquiring new characteristics as a result of computerized accounting.

Most large-scale crime, in terms of both economic impact on society and destruction of life, is committed by or in behalf of ostensibly legitimate corporations. Such offenses include misrepresentation in selling, restraint of competition, polluting the environment, and endangering the health of customers or employees. Punishment of these acts as crimes is mainly a twentieth-century development accelerated in recent years by the inclusion process and the consumer movement, particularly the "Nader phenomenon."

Government corruption expresses the survival of traditional systems of authority in which officeholders routinely collected bribes for normal government services and in which they, in turn, compensated those who appointed them. Although such practices have prevailed in most societies throughout history, they have been extensively replaced in technologically developed nations by legalistic bureaucracies with rules that foster a government of laws, not men. Much corruption continues, however, especially in agencies for the suppression of popular nonpredatory offenses. Yet the proportion of corrupt government activity has diminished, although the size of government has increased so much that the total volume of corruption may be as great as ever. In any case, when corruption is exposed, the public is more outraged by it.

Watergate dramatized the special dangers to our democracy that can result from corruption at the highest level of federal power. Prevention of its recurrence calls not only for legislation, but also for (1) persistent vigilance to expose and denounce abuses, and (2) restraints on the suppression of protest, even when it flouts the law, provided it is nonviolent.

THIRTEEN

CRIME AS PROFESSION OR BUSINESS

"Nothing succeeds like success"; so those with a run of luck at property offenses and scant prospect of comparable legitimate earnings almost invariably dream of an enduring livelihood from lawbreaking. Such expectations stimulate not only rationalization of the illegal acts, but also bonds with accomplices and pride in illicit exploits as evidence of personal superiority. Since ancient times, some people have pursued crime as a career, usually in collaboration with others. From the Commercial Revolution of rising world exploration in the fifteenth and sixteenth centuries to the present "postindustrial" age, each major series of economic changes displaced people from rural areas into urban slums, deprived many of their once-secure incomes while making others wealthy, increased the amount of transportable goods, and dispatched more of it on highways and seas. Every extensive economic development thus created both pressures and opportunities for professional predation.

Both legal and criminal lines of work are professional to the extent that they have: (1) subcultures with standards of competence and ethics; (2) distinctive terminology; (3) ideologies about the virtues of their calling and the faults of its critics or enemies; (4) traditional ways of gaining entry, acceptance, and prestige among colleagues; (5) gatherings of practitioners at which lore is exchanged and subcultures are nurtured; (6) pride in reputation and ability at one's craft that are major motivations to work hard and carefully, especially in projects that colleagues observe or hear about, for others in the same occupation become the principal reference group.

In law-violating trades, subcultures are spread and contacts grow by leisurely and intensive discourse in jails and prisons, as well as in bars and restaurants that are "hangouts" for criminals. When strangers meet in these places, mutual acquaintances, sophistication in use of esoteric terms, and evidence of professional judgment are clues to membership and rank in illegal vocations (just as they are in legitimate fields). In criminal specialties, city, state, regional, and even national networks of practitioners know each other personally or by reputation.

Most careers in crime evolve by gradual professionalization of initially unspecialized, adolescent illegal behavior, although occasionally an avocational "moonlighter" finds it profitable enough to pursue full time. Nevertheless, the lawbreaking finesse distinctive of a career criminal does not characterize everyone who persists in serious offenses. Interviews with robbers serving second or subsequent prison terms reveal two contrasting types. *Intensives* are supported only by crime when free, are sophisticated in their illegal activities, and are arrested or convicted for only a small percentage of their offenses. *Intermittents* alternate from legal employment to repetition of unspecialized, adolescent varities of impulsive lawbreaking, at which they are soon caught (Petersilia et al., 1977).

Professionals contrast most with recidivist amateurs in maintaining more ties with others who facilitate their crime and in dealing skillfully with the criminal-justice system. Their tactics include "fixing" police or prosecution if possible, bribing or intimidating victims or witnesses, and, for such contingencies, retaining astute lawyers, underworld contacts, and funds or credit. They cooperate with police or prosecution only if assured of benefits in exchange.

The professional criminal has a "warrior's psychosis," Tannenbaum (1938: Chapter 7) asserted, in "ruthlessness towards enemies and traitors" and "loyalties towards companions"; "bitterness against the 'squealer' is but a . . . defense . . . against annihilation," for "an all-pervading suspicion is a natural protective covering." Thus a burglar who beats up a partner for holding out some loot from him, or who years later shoots the "stool pigeon" who sent him to prison, becomes a hero in criminal circles. For offenders committed to careers in crime, these values are usually first acquired as juvenile delinquents, especially in gangs fearful of the police or of other gangs, and are continually reinforced thereafter, particularly in jails, training schools, and prisons. Although such subcultural ideas form a consistent philosophy habitually verbalized, their deeds do not always match their words; in practice, cheating and betrayal of companions in crime is not rare. Detectives depend upon informers and often hire a thief to catch a thief (Maurer, 1955: 33–34).

The typical rationalization of professional criminals is that all their lives they were deprived, wrongly and unfairly, while others no better were more fortunate. Everyone is seen as corrupt, as having "a price," as being as evil as they but unpunished and, indeed, gaining wealth and social prominence. Therefore, anyone preaching justice and morality is regarded as a hypocrite. These views are part of a subculture that, as Chapter 6 indicated, develops through intimate association among criminals and their social separation from adherents of the dominant culture.

The professional offenders' deeply ingrained subculture, Maurer (1955: 16–17) points out, makes it as futile to employ psychiatry or counseling to try to bring them into the dominant culture as it would have been to use these methods to convert Sioux Indians from their beliefs and give them guilt feelings for the Custer massacre. In terms of the typology presented in Chapter 6, most professional criminals are enculturated, but their frequent betrayal of confederates suggests that many are also egocentric (and perhaps, in the sense of low rates of psychophysiological response, explained in Chapter 7, psychopathic); of all offenders, they are least likely to be neurotic or conflicted about their lawbreaking. Experiments suggest that trying to reform people long enculturated in crime will probably be counterproductive if it relies on psychotherapy without facilitating their acquisition of a legitimate trade and their employment at it (Palmer, 1974); for the criminal social world teaches pride in manipulation and exploitation of anyone who tries to change offenders by primarily verbal methods.

The main themes of professional crime subcultures have changed little since ancient times and are similar in many parts of the world, but the skills they foster change somewhat when technological developments in commerce and industry create new opportunities for illegal income or reduce old ones (Inciardi, 1974, 1975; Mack & Kerner, 1975). The credos of vocational offenders, aptly called "parasitic subcultures" (Maurer, 1955), depend on the dominant society; yet like biological parasites, each criminal occupation (with a few exceptions, which will be indicated) has "organic unity" in Durkheim's (1893) sense, since it comprises a subsociety of differentiated but interdependent roles. Nevertheless, the involvement of individual offenders in criminal social worlds varies, for commitment to crime as a career has always been a matter of degree, and not all of it occurs in groups.

Vocational crime includes theft, swindling, robbery, and, especially in the twentieth century, organized illegal selling, often combined with coercion. There are several specialties within each of these broad categories, however, and many career offenders engage in more than one of them.

PROFESSIONAL THEFT AND BURGLARY

Pickpockets, swindlers, and burglars have long been concentrated in cities, for this is where their opportunities are greatest and where they most readily fade into the mass of strangers.

Pickpockets, or "cannons," have always tried to prey on persons intently watching some public event, especially at night, whether parades, demonstrations, athletics, or steamship arrivals (and, formerly, even hangings). Like sleight-of-hand magicians, these offenders also profit by creating a diversion and by developing quick and precise movements that require small, strong, and well-practiced hands, unencumbered by rings or watches. They usually dress well but not conspicuously. Some professionals work in teams of at least one *stall* to distract the victim, or *mark*, by jostling, quarreling, or pointing out something while his partner, the *tool*, locates and removes the wallet. Sometimes the loot is passed to a third colleague so that he can disappear with it, leaving the others "clean"; but they are most vulnerable at the moment when the tool is actually removing the wallet (von Hentig, 1943; Maurer, 1955). These methods have not changed for centuries, but allegedly it has become a diminishing and less-rewarding occupation. Home television reduces public assemblies, private automobiles are used more than crowded mass transport in all but a few American cities (e.g., New York), people in big cities fear going out at night, and credit cards or traveler's checks replace cash (although these, too, are often stolen and either used by the thief or sold to forgers).

Many other varieties of sneak theft are perfected for a livelihood, including professional shoplifting, or "boosting," which is also often done in teams; one or more accomplices distract store personnel or act as lookouts, while another steals. Clothing with large inside pockets and "booster-bloomer" underwear are sometimes worn to facilitate removal of loot. A related group crime is *till tapping*, taking cash from store registers, usually by having a confederate distract the cashier. *Car clouting*, theft from parked automobiles, is a modern specialty, with skilled practitioners able to break open or unlock a vehicle and quickly remove not only loose items but also built-in tape decks (Nelson & Smith, 1958) and, most recently, citizen band (CB) radio transceivers. These crimes usually begin as juvenile adventures, but become vocational for some who never gain comparable legitimate income or who become addicted to drugs, and many adults are versatile at these "hustles."

Burglary is also primarily a juvenile avocation, with most residential breakins committed by "kids in the neighborhood." However, some highly professional burglars commit large-scale thefts from offices, stores, museums, wealthy homes, and even banks. The professional burglar, Tannenbaum (1938: 182) observed, automatically "cases" dwellings and stores for probable loot and ease of entry, just as an architect views buildings for construction and design. Crucial to professional burglary are several types of social contact.

Professional burglars often use tipsters, or "fingers," rather than rely on their own ability to find "good scores" (valuable loot obtained safely), but the tipster can be another burglar who recruits collaborators for a "job" he plans. They may seek: (1) lookouts, often one in a nearby car listening to police radio calls; (2) an expert at neutralizing the alarm or opening the safe; (3) cohorts to help cut through walls and, if the loot is bulky, to carry it out to vehicles and drive off. These loose-knit teams change with the needs of each project, or "caper," as well as with the availability and reputation of potential partners. Tips may also come from bartenders, employees of target firms, deliverymen, and frequently from another type of needed associate, the *fence,* or dealer in stolen goods. Contacts with lawyers and bondsmen are also maintained, to ensure prompt release on bail if caught and minimum penalty (Shover, 1972, 1973).

Probably at least three-fourths of the losses by theft and burglary are of merchandise, rather than cash (Walsh, 1976: 1). Therefore, professional property predators usually need dependable arrangements for disposing of stolen goods, which may range from a briefcase of jewelry to a truckload of suits and coats. Fences usually appear to be operating legitimate wholesale or retail businesses, or combinations of the two, and frequently buy from proper sources, such as the manufacturers. They are on the lookout for odd-lot bargains, however, and do not ask about the origin; as indicated, they not only advise professional burglars on what goods are marketable, but also suggest possible sources. The typical fence has numerous contacts in legal and illegal circles to procure and dispose of wares, as well as to cope with police and courts whenever necessary (Klockars, 1974). The selling of stolen goods on a wholesale basis, in truckload lots, is often done by large-scale organized-crime groups (discussed later in this chapter), which often are also involved in various other illegal sales and services, such as loansharking and gambling.

Safecrackers were long the elite among professional burglars. These "boxmen" repeatedly outwitted designers of safes and vaults, although storage places for valuables were made increasingly complex after nitroglycerine, acetylene torches, and other devices opened older ones (Chambliss, 1972; Letkemann, 1973). Today's experts foil electronic silent alarms and, in the most sensational burglaries, cut through walls or burrow into basements to bypass security devices. These are group enterprises and are relatively infrequent. Safes with large amounts of cash are now less common because of both the growth of credit and the increased use of an armed delivery service to transfer receipts from stores to banks.

Although auto theft, even more than burglary, is predominantly a juvenile offense, it becomes a profession for some adults. They typically work in groups, have a garage where serial numbers are altered or parts exchanged with components of used cars, and prefer the most expensive but common autos, such as Cadillacs and late models of other popular brands. Many are driven to distant locations for resale. Some professionals pay garage employees to duplicate keys of valuable cars in for service and to note the owner's address. Others acquire autos by making downpayments with false identification and even with a stolen car as a trade-in, or they depart while presumably trying out the new car. Less prosperous thieves specialize in the juvenile crime of stealing cars only to strip them of parts for resale, then abandoning the depleted vehicle (Hall, 1952: 250–56).

Some regular but amateurish burglars concentrate on residence or hotel and motel rooms, frequently with a partner as lookout. Often drug addicted, they begin burglary as part of a varied pattern of delinquency and gradually specialize in it when they need funds almost daily. As they become older, they operate in areas more distant from home, do more planning, and develop skill at entering locked houses and evading alarms (Reppetto, 1974: 24). Still, their take from any separate entry is usually small, and they spend much time disposing of loot, though obliged to sell so cheaply that they must average three to five burglaries per week. Consequently, as Chapter 5 indicated, they are not likely to burglarize for as long as a year without being caught. The most professional burglars get more (usually thousands of dollars) for each offense, travel longer distances (hundreds or thousands of miles) to reduce prospects of having the loot identified as stolen, and therefore suffer far fewer arrests or convictions per crime than less proficient offenders (Mack, 1964; Shover, 1972, 1973). They more often deal with a wholesale fence, the type of professional property predator who (except perhaps for swindlers) makes the largest profit with the least risk.

PROFESSIONAL FRAUD

Getting wealth by deceit takes many forms, and as indicated in Chapter 12, it is done by some persons in almost every legitimate occupation. The professional deceivers are specialized, however, and can be divided into two broad categories according to whether they rely mainly on forging and counterfeiting documents or on verbal misrepresentation and trickery.

Most forgery, as Chapter 10 reported, is of the "naive" variety, by alcoholics and others who sign someone else's name to a check, or their own name when their bank account has no funds, to procure small sums to satisfy their immediate desires. The "systematic check forger" is likely to use stolen or counterfeit check forms, credit cards, and drivers' licenses, and perhaps a stolen check-writing machine and one or more confederates, to travel across the country "laying paper" in each city (B. Jackson, 1972: Chapter 5). Some work alone, change aliases repeatedly, avoid associates, and—often not having been greatly involved with juvenile delinquency—lack social support in rationalizing their behavior. Because this lone style produces intense anxiety not alleviated by others, "systematic check forgery . . . contains the seeds of its own destruction, or . . . generates its own 'psychopathology'" (Lemert, 1967: 132).

The mobility of the professional forger creates unique risks, especially with the development of computerized national records describing wanted persons, readily accessible to any police agency. Whenever such an offender is caught, unless previously deft at disguises, several counties (often in different states) file detainers (papers requesting detention of the accused for extradition to another jurisdiction), which the court forwards to the prison where the sentence is being served. Therefore, completion of one sentence is usually followed by transfer to another court for a new trial until such time as old charges are not pressed, a rare occurrence unless restitution is made on all forged checks or many years have elapsed. Contrastingly, a lawbreaker in just one county can be tried on all charges simultaneously and receive concurrent sentences; or some charges might be dropped in exchange for pleading guilty to others.

Counterfeiting of currency, and sometimes of other negotiable documents, has since ancient times led to repeated innovation in methods of legitimate printing and of detection, as well as in criminal techniques. Much illicit printing is crude but still passes many cashiers, and some is detected only by experts. Gangs of counterfeiters travel widely to distribute their product, and often many people work at converting it to good money or to property for each person printing it. There are international operations in which counterfeit "hard" currency, such as American dollars or Swiss francs, is sold at premium rates in countries with an active black market for such funds, and the foreign money received in exchange is used to buy legitimate hard currency on the black market elsewhere or to purchase merchandise and services. This offense is recurrently a threat to legitimate business until the printing equipment and personnel of multimillion-dollar operations can be intercepted.

Swindling, confidence game, bunco, and *scam* are synonyms for frauds to hoodwink a victim, or *mark,* into unwarranted trust in the offender. Maurer (1940: 17ff). distinguishes 10 steps that have characterized this trickery from ancient to modern times, although not every swindle requires all 10:

1. *Spotting and investigating a prospective victim.* Methods range from advertising in local newspapers about "investment opportunities" to attending lodge conventions or going on tours or to resorts frequented by small-town businesspersons, retirees, or others presumed to be "well heeled" and gullible.

2. *Gaining the victim's confidence.* The *roper,* or "outside" person, feigns traits that the victim respects—prosperity, pru-

dence, and knowledge about ways to get profits. The mark, accordingly, feels fortunate and flattered by such fellowship.

3. *Introducing the victim to the insider.* The roper mentions others as a source of great income. The mark is then introduced to such a "connection," or the roper's story is confirmed by their encountering another seemingly wealthy person, who actually is an accomplice in the swindle.

4. *The insider's explanation or verification.* Confidence teams are often impressively patient and astute in building an illusion—meeting repeatedly, conversing in a relaxed manner, buying drinks, and flattering the mark, to increase good will and confidence.

5. *The "come-on."* The mark is allowed to make some "easy money."

6. *Sizing up how much the victim can invest.* As they celebrate early successes, they shift the conversation to how much they can raise from bank accounts, loans, or other sources to make much more, the roper and perhaps the insider also pretending to be raising money for this purpose.

7. *Sending the victim for the largest sum.* The victim, deluded into thinking that a rare opportunity for a high-profit investment is imminent, goes to get money.

8. *Fleecing the victim.* Presuming that the roper and the insider are doing the same with their funds, the mark makes a maximum investment, but loses it.

9. *Separating from the victim.* Sometimes this is done abruptly—the swindlers simply disappear—but often the roper and even an insider remain for a while to "cool the mark out." As Goffman (1952) pointed out, the mark's anger is not from losing money so much as from his "belief that he is a pretty shrewd person when it comes to making a deal and that he is not the sort of person who is taken in by anything." The swindlers now try to restore this belief as they pretend to have lost money, too, seem to search for a logical explanation of what went wrong, agree with and compliment the mark if he devises such an explanation, and perhaps suggest that they can now learn from their mistakes (some marks are conned repeatedly by the same persons). In this "cooling out," they also create the impression that they all, including the mark, are in danger of arrest if the police find out what they have done, and thus reduce the risk of the victim's calling the police.

10. *Forestalling prosecution.* Legal maneuvers, hiding the loot, or, in some situations, bribery of police or a witness may protect the swindlers.

In a "big con," a fairly elaborate ostensible business is set up, such as an office or store with printed cards, forms and brochures, telephone switchboard, and other paraphernalia of successful commercial organizations. Sometimes a false "bookie joint" is created. The deception may be an alleged access to secret information about stocks, business deals, or land investments, or even inside tips on horses or advance signaling of race results, in which the "insider" is alleged to be placing bets for his confederate and the victim (Leff, 1976: Chapter 4; Nash, 1976).

A common confidence game in Northern states is the traveling furnace-cleaning truck, usually preceded by a door-to-door salesman offering bargain service. The cleaners then report finding damage, which they often create, and charge for inadequate and overpriced repairs, but the homeowners are given the impression they are lucky to have the defects fixed in time. There are many swindles in the sale of carpeting, siding, and other items on credit in which the salespeople, who are swindlers, resell the contracts to other companies and depart. The victims ultimately discover that they have purchased less and for more money than they realized, and sometimes have unwittingly mortgaged their homes in the process. Trade-training courses promising glamorous careers or high-paid technical employment are also sold by some bunco artists, usually unlicensed and unequipped for the instruction they offer. They encourage applicants, in "entrance tests" and in free or cheap early lessons, to expect success in the course, but when a large payment is completed they either cease sending lessons (in correspondence courses) or (in any type of instruction) make assignments and tests so difficult that students drop out or "flunk" out (Blum, 1972b: 298–318).

Some swindlers do most of their business by post, although they thus risk federal prosecution for using the mails to defraud, while others depend heavily on the telephone. Many dealers in merchandise and services mix legitimate sales with those that clearly misrepresent, as Chapter 12 indicated, so that the line between bona fide and illegal business becomes blurred. But the professional con man or woman is devoted primarily to getting money by fraud, and revels in this. Those who have had appreciable legitimate employment, however, have most often been salespersons (Blum, 1972b: Chapter 3).

Carnivals, county fairs, circuses, amusement parks, and boardwalks have long had a variety of confidence games known as "circus grifting," in which mechanical devices are manipulated to let the victims see or get an easy win before it is made more difficult. Sometimes an accomplice acts as a *shill*, a presumably winning customer, to make the game look more attractive. The *shell game* and *three card monte*, as well as the sale of grossly misrepresented and overpriced watches and jewelry, and other standard types of trickery, have been common in these popular gathering places for centuries (Inciardi & Petersen, 1973).

"Short con" games require, at most, one or two confederates and a few props, and they are usually perpetrated rather quickly. Every town and neighborhood suffers the "pigeon drop" regularly, despite a widespread presumption that hardly anyone would "fall" for it. In this scheme the swindlers often seek victims by following depositors from a savings bank. Near an accomplice who poses as a passerby, and in front of the victim, one of the bunco artists pretends to find a wallet or a package of money with documents suggesting that it comes from a criminal source. The finder pretends they all found it and offers to share it, but requests that they advance several hundred or even a thousand or more dollars to show that they are accustomed to handling large sums. The accomplice agrees to this, which makes the mark feel challenged to do likewise, to not appear to be a "piker," and thus, to share the loot. Alternatively, the accomplice feigns telephoning an attorney, whom he quotes as saying they are entitled to the find unless it is claimed in a certain period, but that each must deposit "good faith" funds in cash with the lawyer, and this the confederate agrees to deliver. There are many further variations (Blum, 1972b: 259–77; Nash, 1976: Chapter 3), but in whatever way it is played the swindlers always disappear with both the money they display and the victim's funds. The Los Angeles Police Department claims that a half-million-dollar loss per year is reported from this game alone, and it is perpetrated nationwide.

In the bank-examiner ploy an upright citizen with a savings account gets a telephone call from a person who claims to be a bank examiner; sometimes the caller knows nothing in advance about the victim's finances but cleverly manipulates the conversation so that the location and sometimes other details of the bank account are unwittingly revealed by the victim. The caller explains that a bank employee is pilfering funds, that cooperation of depositors is needed to entrap the thief, and that the plan must be kept secret. The victim is asked to withdraw a large sum, usually several thousand dollars, for which the "examiner" later provides a receipt. Usually the alleged examiner displays authentic-looking identification and a printed receipt form that looks like a check, and perhaps marks the bills in front of the victim before disappearing with them. The victim often waits days or weeks before suspecting and ultimately confirming the fraud.

Confidence games are sometimes mixed with robbery and theft in forms of extortion and blackmail. A very old set of routines is the *badger game,* in which a woman encourages a man to go with her to a bedroom and engages his attention with sexual overtures while her confederate sneaks in to empty the man's wallet. Immediately thereafter she claims to hear her husband coming and rushes the mark out. In some cruder variations a strong male accomplice, claiming to be her outraged husband and perhaps accompanied by a helper, meets them as they enter a dark passage en route to the alleged bedroom, beats up the victim, and robs him. Sometimes a man who appears to be wealthy and married is caught in a compromising situation with such a female by someone who enters with a flash camera and takes their picture, then demands money for it. In another format, intruders pose as detectives making an arrest, then prove willing to accept a bribe. This scheme is also used against men caught in homosexual acts, particularly in public toilet booths, where they are subject to arrest even in states that have decriminalized such behavior in private. Indeed, there are many forms of false arrest or threat of arrest followed by acceptance of a bribe, including posing as health inspectors in restaurants, safety inspectors in buildings, and federal investigators in any kind of business in which an experienced bookkeeper can usually find or imply attempted income tax fraud.

Deception, credulity, and greed are universal among persons with all levels of schooling. The typical con artists are skilled thespians and highly egocentric, taking special pride in duping those of superior education or fortune, but gratified by success with any victim. In defrauding the aged of life savings and widows of inheritances, they appear to epitomize the conception of psychopaths as persons without conscience, having only contempt for those they hoodwink; they very keenly discern the victim's feelings while "completely avoiding any involvement or identification with these feelings" (Turner, 1956: 319). On the other hand, the victims are usually greedy, which is why they are easily taken in by a scheme that promises something for nothing or for very little, often at the expense of an organization or firm. A professional thief once observed:

> The con rackets are comparatively safe because the victim has attempted to do something dishonest and been beaten at it, and therefore he is not in a position to make a complaint. When he does make a complaint, little attention is paid to him; also he always lies about it, claiming he was robbed by violence. Even if the mob is arrested, it is easy to secure a dismissal (Sutherland, 1937:73).

Quite different, in many respects, are the crimes of those who do use violence for monetary gain.

PROFESSIONAL ROBBERY AND OTHER VIOLENCE

The vocational offenders formerly called "bandits," "brigands" (or, if operating from ships, "pirates"), and by Gibbons (1965: 102–4) "professional 'heavy' criminals," have existed almost as long and as universally as military and naval weapons. They were often men from disbanded armed forces, including the private mercenaries of former days and, in some countries, of today. In many politically unstable nations they are former members of revolutionary and guerrilla forces, especially those long unsuccessful, in which whole units gradually shift to full-time brigandage. The distinguishing feature of the type of professional criminal that concerns us here is "proficient use of coercion, force and threat" (Inciardi, 1974: 345) to rob, usually relying on weapons and often on surprise to control victims.

Historian E. J. Hobsbawm describes the "remarkable uniformity and standardization" (1965: 14) of these bands in many countries and eras:

> In one sense banditry is a rather primitive form of organized social protest . . . in many societies it is regarded as such by the poor, who consequently protect the bandit, regard him as their champion, idealize him, and turn him into a myth. . . . Robin Hood, the archetype "who took from the rich to give to the poor and never killed but in self-defence or just revenge," is not the only man of his kind. The tough man, who is unwilling to bear the traditional burdens of the common man in a class society, poverty, and meekness, may escape from them by joining or serving the oppressors as well as by revolting against them. In any peasant society there are "landlords' bandits" as well as "peasant bandits" not to mention the State's bandits, though only the peasant bandits receive the tribute of ballads and anecdotes. Retainers, policemen, mercenary soldiers are thus often recruited from the same material as social bandits. Moreover . . . one sort of bandit can easily turn into another—the "noble" robber and smuggler into the *bandolero*, protected by the local rural boss. Individual rebelliousness . . . mirrors the divisions and struggles within society (1965: 13).

In the United States as in other countries, bandits frequently became legendary folk heroes. In our Western territories during most of the nineteenth century, the wide-open spaces and meager settlement facilitated cattle rustling, as well as robbing of banks, stagecoaches, and railroads. Bandit "hideouts" sometimes grew to small villages hidden in the hills (Inciardi, 1974: 346–56; 1975: Chapter 8). Many disbanded Civil War soldiers, especially from the Confederacy, alienated youth from settler families, and unemployed ranch hands formed

Young Jesse James.

groups to ply these crimes. "Billy the Kid," Jesse James, and "Butch" Cassidy are among the many nineteenth-century bandit gang leaders romanticized in our motion pictures. At first they were resisted only by local sheriffs and vigilantes, but by the end of that century railroad and private police agencies (such as the Pinkerton detectives and Wells Fargo guards) and public forces were sufficiently superior in weapons, organization, and numbers to make commerce and transportation more secure and bandits less successful.

The Great Depression brought a resurgence of tremendous publicity for some bank robbers, such as John Dillinger and the glamorized Bonnie Parker and Clyde Barrow. The FBI, established in 1926, became prominent after a 1934 law made robbing a federal bank or savings-and-loan association a federal offense. This pitted the "G Men" against robbers in dramatic shoot-outs that eventually terminated most of the notorious bank-holdup careers, but left many less flamboyant professional "heavy" criminals still in "business as usual" (Inciardi, 1974: 353ff.; 1975: 96ff.).

Most armed robbery is by nonprofessional loners, often without a real gun (as elaborated in Chapter 9), but professional groups still rob some banks, savings-and-loan institutions, supermarkets, jewelry stores, and other places where large sums of currency or compact wealth is concentrated. Three to five people usually work together, in roles of driver, lookout in the doorway, and one or more inside, to get the money from the establishment. These robberies are carefully planned after observing the place for several days in advance. A stolen car is used and abandoned near another vehicle that has been parked for further flight. Emphasis is placed on startling and intimidating victims by a loud voice, threatening gestures, and angry profanity, to keep them from thinking of resisting or setting off an alarm; meanwhile, the loot is quickly collected (Letkemann, 1973: Chapter 4).

Career robbers are less cohesive than professional thieves, according to Einstadter (1969). They usually form loose teams for each job and separate afterward, becoming independent entrepreneurs once again. Between robberies most indulge in expensive women, drink, and entertainment, as well as in costly clothes and cars; they then often must get money by quick raids or ambushes on liquor stores or other places without the tens of thousands of dollars sought in well-planned operations. They prefer robbing establishments rather than individuals, and taking money from an employee rather than an owner, both because they rationalize that they are depriving a corporation rather than an individual and because an employee is less likely to do something desperate to protect the funds. Improved alarms, automatic cameras at banks, and a larger number of armed public and private police have in recent years considerably increased the risks in both professional and amateur robbery.

Kidnapping has been a recurrent vocational fad, widely copied in various countries for brief periods (with members of wealthy families held for ransom), then declining after major "crackdowns" by law enforcement. It was prominent in the United States during the Depression, but dropped abruptly after the Lindbergh Law of 1932. Enacted because of the notoriety of the kidnap-murder of Lindbergh's infant, this legislation makes it a federal offense to force someone to cross a state boundary, and authorizes the death penalty or life imprisonment if the victim is injured. Any suspicion that an abduction is interstate brings the FBI into the investigation, usually with a large investment of manpower and other resources. In many countries political kidnappings are frequent, directed at gaining release of certain prisoners or other government action, as well as money.

Hijacking, the seizure of a vehicle by force or threat of force, has become prominent from its use as a form of kidnapping in which an airplane is taken over with all its crew and passengers. Much of this is a political tactic—to bargain for concessions from a government, such as flight to what is hoped will be a safer jurisdiction for the hijackers, and sometimes for money and arms as well—but not as a vocation. This crime greatly diminished in the United States after a wave of it resulted, during the early 1970s, in tighter security measures at airports. The most successful type of professional robbery in the United States today is probably the hijacking of trucks. This is done by teams resembling professional burglars in their apparent connections and planning. They seize huge trailers containing all manner of goods —frozen meats, household appliances, clothing, and even gasoline— and have prior arrangements for selling the loot to a fence. Theirs is a federal offense if the goods are in interstate shipment when hijacked or if carried across a state line by the robbers. Usually the trucks are quickly unloaded and abandoned.

The most heinous and coldblooded professional crime of violence is undoubtedly contract murder, assassination for a fee, usually paid partly in advance and partly after death is inflicted. With the proliferation of handguns in some high-delinquency areas, it is alleged that juvenile "hit men" will murder people for $100 or less, imitating the utter callousness of the professional "heavies" seen in television fiction. The relatively few adult hired assassins in the United States, however, as well as many truck hijacking groups and some others who use violence or threat for gain, appear to be connected with large criminal groups that derive most of their income from nonpredatory offenses.

ORGANIZATIONS FOR CRIMINAL SELLING AND COERCION

Whenever the law prohibits sale of a product or service, such as liquor or gambling, for which there is a highly inelastic demand, it thereby (1) bans all law-abiding businessmen from a potentially profitable market, and (2) gives organized violent criminals special advantages in exploiting that market. In illegal commerce, police and courts cannot be asked for help in keeping competition fair, or even for protection against robbers and burglars. Consequently, the most successful entrepreneurs in illicit trade are those most capable of using force to put competitors out of business, coerce customers, combat marauders, hijack merchandise, or seize control of firms. Furthermore, when criminal sellers have a large clientele, they are likely to have popular support and wealth that tempt police and politicians into collusion with them rather than opposition. Indeed, why should one expect these government employees to prosecute avidly when it is highly probable that they or their friends or relatives, as part of the general public, have also patronized such illegal businesses (e.g., bookies, houses of prostitution, and sellers of marijuana)?

Throughout the nineteenth and early twentieth centuries, some criminals invested in saloons and used violence to discourage competition. When the Prohibition Amendment terminated most legal import, manufacture, and sale of alcoholic beverages, however, it thereby permitted criminals to dominate these fields of commerce, at both wholesale and retail levels; in each metropolitan area the previously legitimate businesses of these types had tens or even hundreds of thousands of customers whom they were no longer allowed to serve. Yet because there was no legal regulation of the competition among these illegal responses to the demands of a thirsty public, each bootlegging group sought a monopoly in its area. Achieving such hegemony usually required a large hierarchy of workers and supervisors, including people skilled at violence and at political corruption; these organizations had to become enormously rich and powerful to survive. Repeal of Prohibition in 1933 permitted reentry of law-abiding firms into this lucrative market, but Prohibition violators could now make some of their businesses legal and many also had already diversified their huge capital into other commerce, both licit and illicit (Cressey, 1969; Inciardi, 1974: 361–79; 1975: Chapter 9).

As indicated in Chapter 8, a succession of different ethnic groups dominated American urban crime, the offenders always disproportionately children of recent poor migrants to American slums. In the late nineteenth and early twentieth centuries, Irish ancestry was especially frequent among prisoners from the cities; later, Poles were overrepresented, and in the 1920s Italian descent was conspicuous. Bootlegging in New York, Chicago, and other major centers during the Prohibition era was at first led by former convicts and others of diverse ethnicity (including Irish, Jewish, and German); but by 1930 Italian-Americans—mainly from Sicilian or Neapolitan families—controlled most organized crime in the largest metropolitan areas, especially in the Northeast and Midwest, although people of other national origins were still prominent in some regions.

The ascendance of Italian immigrants and their offspring in illegal businesses during this period resulted from: (1) the arrival of poor Italians at an annual rate of between 100,000 and 265,000 in the first quarter of the twentieth century, except for the years of travel restriction during World War I and for the immigration quotas enforced after 1921 (Italian-Americans were thus a major portion of the delinquent and criminal children of poor immigrants in many urban slums when Prohibition began); (2) traditional use of alcoholic beverages by Italians, though not with much drunkenness, that made violation of the Eighteenth Amendment seem quite proper and normal to them; (3) a subculture brought from rural Sicily and other parts of southern Italy that instilled values especially advantageous in organized crime, and that has been the basis of much recent mythology.

The "Mafia" and American Crime

The term *mafia* in rural Sicily connotes "a way of thinking, a way of life" (Servadio, 1976: xiii) that stresses self-reliance in achieving one's rights, and use or threat of violence for this purpose if necessary. It also includes sentiments of disdain for everything foreign, especially outside authorities, an attitude directed since ancient times to the many invaders of this island, all of whom failed in efforts to control its mountainous interior. A "mafia" also refers in Sicily to an association of persons regarded as evildoers but respected as demonstrating mafia values. Formerly they were small bandit groups that survived by cattle stealing, raids on isolated villages, and extortion, but often gave to the church and the poor, becoming legendary folk heroes (Hobsbawm, 1959: Chapter 3; Hess, 1973). "Permeating the entire system was the atmosphere of *Omerta*. . . . a code of silence which . . . sealed Sicilian lips even in their own defense, and even when the accused were innocent of charged crimes. . . . The suspicion of being a 'stool pigeon,' a *cascittuni*, constituted the blackest mark against a Sicilian's manhood . . ." (Nelli, 1976: 14–15). On the southern mainland of Italy, *fibbia* in Calabria and *Camorra* in Naples had connotations similar to, though not identical with, *mafia* in Sicily.

Mafioso designates a Sicilian man of honor who exemplifies mafia values. The term is not applied to oneself, but when used by others it denotes recognition of the respect that a person commands in his area. A major source of a mafioso's strength is his group of followers, or *cosca*, persons partly or fully dependent on him for livelihood, security, or status, most of whom are often relatives either by blood or by ritual kinship (the *compareggio*, or godparent, bonds). In addition, each mafioso augments his influence by a *partito*, the assortment of higher-placed or more powerful individuals—such as barons, heads of large urban businesses, or government officials—for whom he has done favors, thus obligating them to reciprocity when needed. These networks of relationships link higher- and lower-ranked mafiosi and their separate coscas and partiti in an intricate system of mutual aid and interdependence (Hess, 1973).

The mafiosi are often men of poor peasant or working-class background, without appreciable schooling, who gain power by their wits and audacity. Sometimes, however, they are lawyers or other business or professional persons, usually with rural kinship ties, who apply mafia principles to achieve influence in the towns. This penetration into the cities and diversity of educational levels developed in the late nineteenth and early twentieth centuries, when elections were initiated for many local government offices. The mafiosi arranged to deliver votes of those obligated to or fearing them, and then claimed favors from government agencies or even appointment to public office (Hess, 1973).

Businessmen and landlords could have a dependable income in areas controlled by mafiosi only by purchasing goods or services from the *capo,* or head, of each local mafia group or by making him a partner or simply paying him directly. If they did not, they probably got polite but transparent extortion notes, and if they still did not cooperate their buildings might be burned, their grapevines or fruit trees cut, their goods stolen, or their agents kidnapped and even murdered. If they made amicable local arrangements, however, they could expect some protection from further harassment, and perhaps assistance in making their operations profitable; some absentee landlords even employed mafiosi to intimidate their tenant peasants (Hess, 1973; Nelli, 1976: Chapter 1). Albini (1971: 135) points out that mafia is "a system of patron–client relationships that interweaves legitimate and llegitimate segments of Sicilian society." It filled gaps from the lack of an appreciable middle class, Servadio (1976) claims, when predominantly feudal Siciliy was annexed to a unified Italy in 1860; and except for a brief decline from Mussolini's repression, it did not markedly diminish as a political force on the island until the 1970s.

The mafia system often suffers temporary upheaval in a particular locality. One mafioso sometimes tries to take sources of income from another, or there is conflict for power within a group when a mafioso dies or is unable to control some of his followers. Once these struggles become violent they can result in long-term feuds, with much killing and destruction before a new network of relationships becomes stable. Thus a high rate of crime long prevailed in Sicily and southern Italy as a result of the mafia type of value system and organization (Hess, 1973; Servadio, 1976).

Intact mafia groups were not among Italian immigrants to the United States, but during the late nineteenth century in New Orleans, where they were then concentrated, a few individuals exhibited mafia lifestyles by extortion and by violent feuding between two gangs vying for control of longshoreman work on the docks. Following assassination of the city's chief of police in 1890, the police department and the local press spread lurid false tales of extensive mafia murders. They alleged an Italian conspiracy to control local government on the basis of rumors that the chief was killed by Italians, either in reprisal for his prosecuting a mafioso 10 years earlier or for his arresting only long-shoremen of one gang for dock violence. When in March 1891 a court acquitted a group of accused Italians, rumors that bribes bought the favorable verdict provoked a mob to storm the jail and kill 11 Italian inmates. This event received international notoriety, and sensational writers embellished the local rumors to claim that a unified Mafia crime syndicate operated in Europe and America (Nelli, 1976: Chapters 2 and 3).

Throughout the first quarter of the twentieth century, much publicity was given to extortion in Italian-American communities, frequently involving notes signed *Mano Nero,* or "the Black Hand." This led to rumors of a large organization with this name, although it was apparently a terror-inspiring term adopted by many mafia groups and individual extortionists, and originated earlier among Spanish bandits (Nelli, 1976: Chapter 4).

During the Prohibition prosperity of underworld bootlegging groups, they branched into such other enterprises as operating houses of prostitution and gambling places, as well as "racketeering." The last entails highly organized extortion in which businesses find that unless they pay fees for "protection," they have much to fear from their "protectors." But these fees were often paid from avarice as well as fear, for in exchange the racketeers frequently intimidated would-be competitors from operating in a small-businessman's neighborhood (Lippman, 1931a). Organized criminals also gained control of numerous legitimate firms, both by investment and by forcing entrepreneurs to take them in as partners. To ensure security and further enrich these activities, underworld leaders corrupted many local political agencies by payments, by threats or violence against uncooperative government functionaries, and in some areas, by getting themselves or their followers appointed or elected to public office. In addition, they gained control of some of the older trade unions, using violence and threats against opponents. They then drained the treasuries of these organizations for high salaries and expense accounts, invested pension funds in their businesses or those of their friends and relatives, and, in a few cases, were convicted of making "sweetheart" contracts favorable to employers or holding off strikes in exchange for payoffs from employers (Cressey, 1969; Conklin, 1973; Homer, 1974; Moquin & Van Doren, 1976).

Businessmen paying for such sellouts and government officials accepting graft certainly are as guilty of lawbreaking as the organized criminals, although they are usually avocational offenders (as that concept is used in Chapter 12), since they rarely depend primarily on crime for a livelihood. Nevertheless, these "respectable" persons are often essential to the operations of organized crime, and thus merit equal condemnation (Chambliss, 1971).

When Prohibition was repealed, criminal groups were already entrenched in the import, manufacture, and distribution of alcoholic beverages; thus, they used their experience, skilled personnel, and other resources to open many of the first legal distilleries, breweries, wineries, and wholesale and retail sales firms. Where criminal records of their leaders made them ineligible for licenses in these new businesses, they often corrupted the licensing officials or used "front" persons without known criminal records as nominal heads of the new enterprises.

During the postrepeal years, bookies in criminal organizations both collected and paid off bets on horse races at every track in the nation, on other sports, and in numbers lotteries, all serviced by hundreds of specialized personnel. Loans at usurious rates of interest, with the threat or use of violence if necessary to collect repayment, allegedly became by the 1960s second to gambling as a source of organized-crime income (although traffic in narcotics was a separate and perhaps more affluent criminal business). Throughout the twentieth century, but especially during Prohibition, frequent feuds among "mobs" in organized crime resulted in hundreds of assassinations, many by hired professional "hit men," and in bombings and other violence.

In all the activities described in the preceding paragraphs, the mafia lifestyle was obviously advantageous to Italian-American offenders. Its emphasis on secrecy and mutual aid, on kinship loyalties, on use of threats or violence, and on corrupting by bribes or favors, gave security to illegal businesses. These qualities also existed among others, but appeared to be not nearly as enculturated in the non-Italian ethnic groups engaged in crime. Omerta, the mafia norms of secrecy, made it difficult for the press or officials to gain precise knowledge of Italian-American organized crime, and thus may have fostered much unwitting as well as some deliberate distortion of the facts.

Explaining most crime as the result of conspiracy by a few extremely evil persons has many sources of appeal. It fits with America's Puritan heritage and fundamentalist religions, which ascribe all the world's troubles to the devil. It sells newspapers, magazines, and sensational books, and attracts movie and television audiences. The promise to punish these malefactors is perennially effective in gaining support for law-enforcement budgets, political candidacies, and a variety of other enterprises, such as the crime commissions established in many American metropolises during the post–World War II years (Moore, 1976: Chapters 1 and 2).

The development and propagation of a myth about "the Mafia" accelerated in the 1950s when Senator Estes Kefauver achieved vice-presidential candidacy mainly through the publicity attracted by his Special Committee to Investigate Organized Crime in Interstate Commerce. Although this committee made some contributions to knowledge, particularly regarding the operation of national wire services to relay horse-racing results to local bookmakers, it was especially misled by the speculation of Bureau of Narcotics Director Anslinger (see Chapter 10) that the Mafia was a secret international "government of crime" directed from Italy by exiled narcotics trafficker "Lucky" Luciano. Even the Senator and the Committee's chief counsel were convinced by the end of their investigation that the Mafia had neither international nor national unity, but these views never gained the acceptance given to its depiction as a worldwide syndicate of crime (Moore, 1976: Chapters 4–9).

United States Senate leadership in the investigation and public agitation on organized crime was renewed for about a decade, beginning in 1957 under Senator John L. McClellan. The theme that crime is controlled by a national Italian-American directorate reached a new peak of support in that year when men of this descent—the number variously reported as from 50 to over 100 and most alleged to be affiliated with illegal enterprises in widely scattered parts of the country (but almost all from the Northeast)—were caught in a police raid on a gathering at a New York resort near Apalachin. Vague and inconsistent testimony on this event before McClellan's committee, and the unsuccessful prosecution of several of the arrestees on conspiracy charges, failed to substantiate any of the numerous speculations on the purpose of their meeting, except their claim that they were enjoying a barbecue when the police arrived (Hawkins, 1969; Morris & Hawkins, 1970: Chapter 8; Moore, 1976: 239).

Before another committee headed by Senator McClellan, 60-year-old Joseph Valachi, then serving a 20-year federal sentence for a narcotics offense and a life term for killing another inmate, testified in 1963 that he had never heard of "the Mafia" but had belonged to "Cosa Nostra." He described in considerable detail the organization of illicit businesses by two dozen Cosa Nostra "families," each controlling a different geographical area, and he vaguely referred to a national "commission" superordinate to other groups. Much of this was consistent with previous reports on local Italian-American criminal ties, but there were several contradictions in Valachi's testimony. His own position had been quite low and in only one of these "families," and he was under considerable pressure to support the allegations of his sponsors in federal law enforcement; so his account of the upper levels of criminal heirarchies probably included much that was rumor, speculation, and perhaps fabrication.

Police wiretap recordings of telephone calls by alleged mafiosi and court testimony in several subsequent organized-crime inquiries confirmed the quasi-family structure of criminal organizations within limited geographical areas, but could demonstrate only periodic business and social transactions among families in different regions, rather than a national crime syndicate (Hawkins, 1969; Albini, 1971: Chapter 6). There is evidence that, since Prohibition days, leaders of different organized criminal groups have periodically held conferences to negotiate agreements, and have sometimes designated the head of one group as arbiter of disputes among others—a so-called boss of bosses—but none of these arrangements established complete or long-term national control by any of them (Nelli, 1976: 182–218, 253–65).

Anthropologist Francis Ianni, in the first detailed and intimate study by a social scientist of an Italian-American criminal "family" concludes that within these organizations three informal criteria prevail for accepting the authority of other members. First, those in the oldest generation of each kinship heirarchy are respected as the elders. Second, regardless of age, those whose ancestors entered the kinship network later by marriage or who themselves are newcomers defer to those in the direct lineage of the man who founded the group (in this case, some 60 years earlier). Third, some members gain authority on the basis of recognized expertise, particularly lawyers and accountants (1972: 111). He observes:

> Italian-American crime families are actually a number of lineages linked together into a composite clan. Like clans everywhere, these crime families enter into exchange relations with one another and form alliances which are perpetuated. Like clansmen everywhere, members treat each other as brothers and acknowledge mutual rights and obligations on a kinship pattern, however remote they may be genealogically. Each clan has its own territory. Because of its kinship base and its territoriality, the clan can establish and maintain its own rigid code of familial law and pass authority from one generation to another. As in the great *Mafia* families of Sicily, the "descendants" intermarry continuously, for the clan defines who may and who may not marry whom. As in clans everywhere, the relationship between the intermarrying pair is defined as strengthening the social structure.
>
> This clan pattern of organization also provides a common system of roles, norms, and values which not only regulate the behavior within the family but also structure relationships among families. Some clans obviously form compact, interlocked regional groups with frequent intermarriages cementing the alliances; all are related by some common business interests. . . .
>
> We believe that it is the universality of this clan organization and the strength of its shared behavior system which makes Italian-American criminal syndicates seem so similar. And we believe that it is this similarity which has inclined observers to maintain that the different

crime families constitute some sort of highly organized national or even international crime conspiracy (1972: 17273).

Many specialists on organized crime in the United States projected upon these large illegal businesses their conception of the organization chart which a legitimate firm would require for the same volume of commerce, as well as protection and corruption functions. They thus assumed that the Mafia had a rather formal bureaucratic structure with national unity like that of a giant corporation or a government agency (e.g., President's Commission, 1967). Cressey observes, however, in his introduction to a study that used Italian sources in Sicily (Hess, 1973):

> An "organization" (e.g., the Mafia) implies membership, offices, a hierarchy of authority. "Organization" (e.g. mafia), on the other hand, implies understandings, common methods, parallelisms.
>
> Organization often is obvious even when there is no evidence of *an* organization. But in discussing organization we often go wrong because we find it necessary to use "the" in phrases such as "the establishment," "the military-industrial complex," "the police." By using "the" we create more structure than we know exists. We transform organization to an organization.
>
> . . .mafia organization in Sicily developed, persisted and gathered power despite the absence of a Mafia. Each mafioso personage operates in specifiable ways and maintains a network of relationships. Violence, threat of violence, and fear of violence are the cement that holds the network together. In a village or territory, the location of deference, respect, honour, fear, and other manifestations of power has become predictable. This is organization. But a way of life neither reflects nor anticipates the existence of a Mafia apparatus with inducted members, a division of labor and a hierarchical pattern of authority (viii).

Indeed, both in Sicily and in the United States, the illegality of organized crime and its consequent reliance on memory rather than written records for many solemn agreements and contracts precludes highly formal and bureaucratic procedure in much of its activity. It requires lawyers and bookkeepers for its legitimate transactions with other businesses and with government agencies, sometimes to make illicit commerce appear law abiding or to maintain secret records, but its illegal claims, promises, services, or payments are not documented in the records needed for stable formal organization. (Therefore, of course, they cannot be used for breach-of-contract suits in the courts.)

By the 1970s, Italian-Americans had become a much smaller and rapidly diminishing fraction of the participants in organized crime. Like the other immigrant groups dominating these illicit businesses in America before them, they had become almost completely assimilated into "mainstream" businesses and occupations, and were replaced in criminal selling and coercion by members of the ethnic groups that followed them into urban slums, particularly blacks, Puerto Ricans, Cubans, and Mexican-Americans. These newer groups, many of whose youth also were attracted to crime as a shortcut out of poverty, likewise often employed violence and bribery to expand and secure illicit commerce. Impoverished newcomers to these metropolitan areas, particularly the blacks, were less closely linked by kinship and were not as long enculturated in values conducive to successful law violation as had been the Italian-American "families"; each ethnic group brought to organized crime a different social and cultural history. Nevertheless, the profit and security that a mafia way of life gives to groups of illegal sellers permits many of its features to develop in extremely diverse criminal organizations, and may account for the recent extension of this term to other ethnic groups in crime by such designations as "Black Mafia" and "Mexican Mafia" (Ianni, 1974a, 1974b; Davidson, 1974).

Some features of illegal sales in alcohol, drugs, and prostitution were indicated in Chapters 10 and 11. Two other major services that many Americans procure from criminals, wagering and risky loans, merit special attention here.

Gambling and Crime

Betting for money or other stakes and making decisions by chance have occurred in virtually all human societies since ancient times, although form, dimension, and impact vary. Numerous allusions to such activities are found in the Bible and in early Greek literature. Murals among the ruins of Pompeii depict women casting knuckle bones as though in a modern dice game, and apparent gambling devices have been unearthed by archeologists in many places. Washington, Jefferson, Franklin, and other founding fathers wagered on horse races, sponsored lotteries, and played cards for money, a pastime that became universal in our Western territories. Yet recurrent efforts to suppress gambling as criminal were also ubiquitous, beginning with its ban by the Puritans in Massachusetts (Messick &Goldblatt, 1976).

Both the appeal of gambling and objections to it can be ascribed to what Weber (1905) called "The Protestant Ethic and the Spirit of Capitalism." Risk taking as brave and as meriting reward if it proves fruitful underlies capitalism's glorification of the entrepreneurs who expand it by successful investment. All wagering, after all, has some resemblance to legitimate financial ventures, such as trading on the stock market, starting a new firm, and purchasing land or wholesale commodities, at which the rich can play. Gambling as play, however, clashes with the Protestant Ethic of work and thrift. Indeed, compulsive gambling often appears to be an effort to escape the realities of earning a livelihood. Opponents of betting decry the failure of losers to meet personal or family financial obligations, and they question whether winners contribute any service to society in exchange for their gains. In British common law, wagering is a misdemeanor if the outcome depends mainly on chance, but not if it depends upon judgment or skill, and there are long-cited but disputed rulings calling poker a game of chance and contract bridge one of judgment.

At different times and places throughout the United States, gambling has been unrestricted, almost completely prohibited, and permitted but regulated under local, state, and federal legislation. During the Prohibition era public gambling in almost all its commercial forms was a misdemeanor in about half the states and was permitted only at licensed race tracks in the others. But in 1931 Nevada reacted to the Depression by legalizing nearly "wide-open" gambling, as well as easy divorce, to create a boom in its tourist centers. Meanwhile, illegal betting flourished in other states and continues today even in those that legalized many forms of gambling in the late 1960s or the 1970s.

Like all other laws penalizing popular nonpredatory activity, antigambling legislation almost invariably created a market for organized criminals, fostered corruption of police and other government agencies, and contributed to the public disrespect for the criminal-justice system that is probably conducive to delinquency and predation, as well as to nonvoting and other poor citizenship. The Kefauver Committee in the 1950s and the McClellan Committee in the 1960s were the most dramatic of many local, state, and federal exposés of multimillion-dollar gambling operations, including bookmaking in virtually all major cities and numbers lotteries in their slums. More recently there has been much illegal sports-card betting, in which wagers are made on college and professional basketball and football games, and sometimes on professional baseball.

One can readily surmise where illegal horse-race gambling is widespread even without personally observing it. Do morning and afternoon editions of city newspapers devote space to details and tips on each race at tracks hundreds or thousands of miles away (even having a turf edition in Northern cities during the winter, when no local tracks are open)? Are the *Daily Racing Form* (a national newspaper designed just for horse players) and various horse-race tip sheets sold at streetcorner newsstands? Are numerous daytime bar or coffee-shop patrons intently studying and discussing these publications? By observing these goings on, it was simple to establish that "bookie joints" with leased wires to receive results from distant tracks were operating in Chicago, Boston, and other cities, once even on the same winter day when Chicago's then-chief of police was quoted as saying that organized gambling had been suppressed in that metropolis.

Scores of slot machines confiscated during a raid.

Estimates on the annual volume of illegal gambling business in the United States range from $20 million to over $100 million, but no one can possibly know the total with precision. One certainty, however, is that after the repeal of Prohibition, gambling was the illicit service with the greatest requirement for large-scale organization and political corruption. To prosper, a bookie joint's location must be widely known, and hence it will also be easily known to the police. It requires considerable investment in space and furnishings, for in a busy season it muct accommodate scores or even hundreds of customers and numerous employees. Often it also sells refreshments, possibly through its physical connection with a front-room or ground-floor public tavern or coffee shop. The safest business practice with such an investment is to make arrangements for the necessary payoffs to police and politicians in advance of opening the establishment, thus insuring against raids and closure. The police and precinct or ward officials thereby become licensing agents for illegal gambling, as they were for moonshine under Prohibition. Indeed, criminal organizations involved in bootlegging also sold many other illegal commodities and services before Repeal, and rapidly expanded bookmaking after 1933 (Kornblum, 1976: Chapter 2).

In addition to operating "horse parlors" or numbers shops where people come to bet, illegal gambling organizations also have agents who take bets in taverns, pool rooms, small stores, and other hangouts, phoning them in to a headquarters or delivering them in person, and later distributing winnings. These organizations also accept some bets by telephone, extending credit to losers for a limited time. The agents develop a very personal relationship with the clientele, usually friendly to encourage continued trade, but violent if necessary to ensure payment on losing bets (Scott, 1968: 140–41). When ability to corrupt the police is insufficient to warrant establishing horse parlors or shops, these mobile agents may be the sole public contacts for the bookies and "numbers" lotteries. It is estimated that tens or even hundreds of thousands of persons have jobs in illegal gambling operations.

About two-thirds of American adults place one or more bets per year, according to a 1974 national survey sample prepared for the National Gambling Commission: 44 percent reported betting in a legal commercial place (bingo, lotteries, race tracks, off-track betting—mainly in New York and New Jersey—and jai alai), 11 percent admitted illegal betting (at a bookie, on a sports card, with a numbers game, or at an illegal casino), and 13 percent said that they only bet with friends or coworkers. Most adults occasionally play cards for money; in many jurisdictions this can be construed as violating laws against gambling, but in practice it is rarely prosecuted if done privately. A greater percentage of the rich than the poor gamble, but the poor who wager spend so much larger a proportion of their income that it is estimated that the state income from legalized gambling is over twice as regressive as a sales tax. Gambling is correlated with job dissatisfaction, marital problems, and alcohol consumption, according to the survey responses, but this does not indicate which of these conditions or behaviors is cause and which effect. In Nevada, only four percent of the betting was reported as illegal, but elsewhere the highest rates of criminal gambling occurred in the states with the most legalized gambling, suggesting that publicity for that which is licit may encourage criminal wagering. Illegal gambling was reported predominantly by the poor in central cities, while suburbanites did mostly state-licensed betting (*Institute for Social Research Newsletter,* Summer 1976).

A class distinction in gambling-law violation has always existed, since formerly no off-track gambling was legal and the affluent could most readily go to the race tracks, not to mention their gambling in the financial markets. Therefore, legalization that makes noncriminal betting more readily accessible in the central city seems equitable, but the resulting agencies sometimes do not allow bets as small as numbers runners take, do not offer credit to many bettors whom criminals would trust, may be more impersonal, and report large winnings to the Internal Revenue Service for income-tax collection. It still is unclear how much the early forms of legalized betting outside of Nevada have diverted funds from illegal gambling; at first, they may simply have increased the total amount of wagering, licit and illicit, but ultimate displacement of much criminal betting by that which is legal is expected.

Laws penalizing gambling are difficult to enforce because it is a nonpredatory crime: those who bet, even though they most often lose, collaborate with the bet collector voluntarily. About 80 percent of Americans favor legalization of some form of gambling, according to the above-cited survey, but there is not quite a clear majority for any particular form; bingo, horse tracks, and lotteries are each endorsed by nearly half the people. Indeed, the same study found that only 30 percent of American citizens would report a bookie to the police if they knew about his activities, as compared with 96 percent who assert they would report a robbery, 69 percent a seller of stolen property, and 64 percent someone selling marijuana (*Los Angeles Times*, September 7, 1976).

It appears from the foregoing that illegal gambling will diminish only when licensed gambling is competitive with it. Therefore, public education on the laws of probability and special therapeutic programs for compulsive gamblers may offer much more promise for alleviating social problems from wagering than reliance on the criminal-justice system. Yet legalization of any form of gambling (or of most other formerly punished nonpredatory behavior) usually means a shift from prohibition to regulation rather than to complete permissiveness. In a search for the optimum form of regulation, however, there is much variation from one region to another in ways of making legal betting more attractive than criminal wagering, and in reducing social costs from gambling.

One concern is to keep criminal organizations from taking over legal gambling, as they did the licensed manufacture and distribution of alcoholic beverages after the repeal of Prohibition. This is a recurrent problem in Nevada, which has had several scandals of criminal groups covertly operating licensed gambling establishments, then "skimming"—removing cash received before it is recorded for tax purposes—and bribing officials (Turner, 1965). Nevertheless, the fact that gambling in Nevada is legal permits presumably noncriminal licensees, including the major national hotel chains, to compete with those under criminal aegis, and facilitates policing of all. Another strategy, adopted in New York and several other states, is to socialize gambling by making it a state monopoly. This has suffered the pitfalls of mismanagement, but these appear to have been sufficiently corrected with experience to make state-operated gambling services firmly institutionalized in several states (Weinstein & Deitch, 1974).

All money bet for win, place, or show (first, second, or third) in each horse race is totalled by the track's betting office as three separate "pools" (and still another pool is kept for each special type of bet, such as the "daily double"—picking winners for the first two races). Ten to 18 percent is deducted from each pool for operating expenses, and the remainder is divided among those who made correct predictions: the "win" pool goes to those who picked the winner; the "place" pool to those who bet to come in second, either on the horse that won or on the horse that was second; the "show" pool is for those who picked for third place either the horse that won, the horse that was second, or the horse that "showed" third. Thus if the winner was a favorite the pools may be divided among many bettors and each receives relatively little; but if a "long shot" wins, there are few persons to share the pool and each receives much. The odds (payoff rates for each type of bet on each horse, if it wins, places, or shows) are repeatedly calculated and posted at the track or off-track betting establishment, and will change before the race has begun if the distribution of bets on various horses changes.

To make money from horserace gambling, one must bet with appreciably more wisdom than the average wagerer, in order to make up for the 10 to 18 percent deducted from each pool for the track's income. In gambling in which the outcome depends purely on chance, such as the "one-armed bandit" slot machines and roulette, everyone who bets repeatedly will ultimately have losses greater than winnings, unless there is a defect in the equipment that only the bettor knows about; for the management takes five to 10 percent and no judgment can possibly be of service in guessing the outcome. In lotteries or the numbers game, management takes an even larger percentage, but there are relatively few winners—sometimes one in thousands—so that a few large payoffs are made: thus the average participant's percentage of bets lost in these "rackets" exceeds those in any other form of gambling.

A bookie establishment can gain the same 10 to 15 percent margin that the track makes, generally with fewer expenses, if the bets it takes are distributed similarly to those at the race tracks, for it pays the track's final odds (though it usually posts only the early-announced odds). If a long shot wins at the track and pays well but is the favorite among bookie patrons, the bookie would lose much money, and several precautions are taken to prevent this. First, the bookie usually limits odds for winners to 20 to one, regardless of how much higher track odds may be. Second, when a bookie organization becomes aware of accepting bets distributed much differently from those at the track, it can bet enough "layoff money" at the track on the long shots its customers favor to make most of the income it must pay out should such horses win. This layoff betting may also drive down the odds at the track, especially if done conspicuously so that others follow the lead of alleged "smart money." Third, large criminal organizations act as "bankers" in taking "layoff bets," or one criminal group operates enough "books" to make it probable that the average distribution of bets at all of its establishments does not deviate much from that at the track. Fourth, and most importantly, illegal bookmakers discourage continued patronage by "sharp" bettors and actively recruit trade from the "dumb" ones who play hunches (Scott, 1968: Chapter 7).

Poor people throughout the world tend to bet small amounts regularly on lotteries or numbers; their poverty is exploited by dream peddlers, who spread tales of vast winnings that can abruptly and dramatically move them upward in status (Moquin & Van Doren, 1976: 270–73; Kaplan & Kessler, 1976: Chapter 4). Most gambling, however, is a social diversion and not more costly than the gambler can afford (Zola, 1963; Herman, 1967: 87–104; Scott, 1968: Chapter 6). In all economic classes there are pathological gamblers who become fascinated by high odds, remember winnings and forget losses, and therefore squander more on foolish long shots than they can afford to lose, deluded by the notion that there can be more than chance in playing hunches.

People who saw themselves suffering from compulsive self-destruction by gambling and considered it comparable to alcohol or drug addiction, established in 1957 a Gamblers Anonymous organization in Los Angeles that has since developed several hundred chapters in the United States and abroad. As with the substance abusers who pioneered analogous organizations (see Chapter 10), they believe they have an affliction that can be conquered only by mutual aid. On the Alcoholics Anonymous assumption that "it takes one to know one and to help one," each chapter is controlled by its members. They charge no dues, but solicit donations for their meeting-house rent or other collective expenses, with the suggestion that the payment be at least two dollars, a symbolic figure since that is usually the minimum bet on a horse race. At their gatherings members relate how they shattered marriages, ruined careers, stole, cheated, lost their self-respect, and even attempted suicide as a result of their vain hopes for salvation through winning. Although it has been estimated that there are as many female as male compulsive gamblers, this organization's members are over 90 percent male. They have Gam-Anon auxiliary groups (modeled on AA's "Al Anon") of members' spouses, who help each other in the difficulties of assisting a marriage partner's recovery from addictive wagering. Some psychoanalysts speculate that pathological bettors unconsciously wish to lose rather than win, to punish themselves for acts or thoughts about which they unconsciously feel guilty (see Chapter 6); others believe that the compulsion to wager and lose is actually a desperate ploy for love. Perhaps it simply expresses that widespread perversion of the Protestant Ethic in which "making the fast buck" is placed above all other values and becomes the primary criterion of self-worth. In any case, these unconscious needs, if they exist, seem to be met by the mutual aid that Gamblers Anonymous fosters (Scodel, 1964; Reuters dispatch to *Los Angeles Times,* February 13, 1976).

The fascination of both self-destructive and successful gamblers with long shots is said to be absent in Sweden and some other European countries in which odds are not posted before a race or other sporting event. Although the payments to winners are determined by dividing among them the total amount bet less operating expenses (as in the United States), nobody knows what the payoff rate will be until the contest is over. Thus bettors are often uncertain about whether they are selecting a favorite or a long shot, and this is said to keep wagers modest (Allen, 1952).

Even if legal betting eventually succeeds in competing with illegal wagering and even if education and treatment reduce the number of foolish and compulsive gamblers, any illicit services or products remaining in demand that can be covertly supplied will probably still be sold by organized criminals. A major need that they now provide is the financial credit their customers presume is unavailable from other sources.

Loansharking

Lending money at higher interest rates than the government permits has long been a specialty of organized crime in the United States, and is reputed to be the second or third largest source of its current income. The traditional illicit rate, 20 percent per week for small loans, is called "six for five," as one dollar interest is charged every week for each five dollars owed, and may even be compounded weekly if not paid. Legitimate loan firms would love to receive this rate of interest per year (Kaplan & Kessler, 1976: Chapter 6).

Ianni (1972: 46–47, 66–67) traces current loansharking in the United States to the personal "banks" in Italian immigrant neighborhoods during the first quarter of the twentieth century. Residents were ashamed to let close friends know that they had to borrow money, for it was a sign of failure, but felt—probably correctly—that as poor and non-English-speaking they could not get credit from licensed financial institutions. The immigrant "bank" was simply a more affluent individual who gave money discreetly, as had been the custom of the landowning *patron* with his peasants in their native villages. Yet in these immigrant communities, for a man to be widely known as a lender made him appear wealthier than others and subject to extortion attempts. Both to protect himself, therefore, and to collect on bad loans, the "bank" had to have the traditional mafioso character and value system, and it would help to have a *cosca* of relatives to aid in making threats effective.

These "banks" of course, preferred to avoid the need for violence by making only safe and short-term loans, but their customers rarely had dependable income. If credit was extended to a small businessman who could not repay with full interest, a share in ownership of his shop or firm might eventually be accepted in settlement. Ianni (1972) shows how this type of banking could produce a wealthy kinship group if it protected itself successfully by mafia methods. If it also expanded into bootlegging under Prohibition, then into gambling, and continued its loansharking and business diversification, it could become and remain the dominant organized-crime "family" in its area.

Today the "loanshark" or "juice racket" head usually makes loans at two percent per week to individual "bankers," who take money to the slum neighborhoods from which they come. Some hang out regularly at dice games and bookies to give credit to losers, others cater to cash-short stevedores on the docks, and still others contact anyone living at the margin of their resources but expecting income at regular intervals. Whenever such persons run out of money, a "banker" or his "street man"—who borrows from the "bankers" at three percent per week—is readily available to supply funds in exchange for a "marker," the "IOU" to pay back, usually at five to eight percent per week but at higher rates—even six for five—if it is a small loan to a poor-risk individual (Ianni, 1972: 98–99). The loansharking heads deal directly with larger businesses having difficulty, and also try to protect themselves from prosecution by corrupting public officials with timely loans or gifts (Cressey, 1969: 71–91; Moquin & Van Doren, 1976: 307–15).

"Rich and poor alike come to loan sharks because they do not have enough money to pay their debts," Homer (1974: 154–56) reports, adding:

> Loan sharks thrive in unions where work is seasonal, such as the construction business, and on the docks, where daily work is not guaranteed. People in ghetto areas or in the working class often must turn to loan sharks out of necessity at the end of the month or in a layoff period, for their credit might not be high with regular lending institutions. . . . loans to these individuals rarely exceed two hundred dollars. Businessmen go to loan sharks when loans they have made through legitimate institutions have become due and they cannot borrow from a legitimate source to pay them off. The loan shark may never recoup all of his money, but will loan the businessman more money than a factory worker, for he can take over the individual's business upon non-payment.
>
> More than one or two individuals are usually involved in loan-sharking operations because of the need for capital, contacts who get customers (often bartenders, office workers, etc.), collectors and enforcers.

The potential scope of loansharking is limited by its competition from banks and other legal lending agencies that have lower interest rates. Its competitive appeal, however, comes from its accessibility to people who either think they are, or may in fact be, ineligible for legal credit, or who do not wish to disclose to law-abiding persons that they need to borrow because of illicit activities. Conservative economists, from Thomas Malthus to Milton Friedman, have decried laws making usury a crime, arguing that if supply and demand were permitted to fix interest rates without government interference, there would be an optimum distribution of credit in relationship to risk. Such legitimation of loansharking by established financial agencies, whether or not desirable from other public-interest standpoints, would probably not give these firms recourse to violence as a collection device or the personal relationships in the community distinctive of the loanshark. Usury by organized crime's unlicensed "bankers" will probably continue, therefore, as long as poverty and crime, or the fear and ignorance of new immigrants to the slums, persist; only great reduction of these conditions will drastically shrink the market for the "juice racket."

Cargo and Securities Theft

Hijacking truckloads of merchandise, discussed earlier in this chapter as a form of professional robbery, is closely linked to the even more voluminous theft of goods in transit estimated to total well over $2 billion per year in the United States. The actual removal of products from loading docks, warehouses, piers, airports, parked trucks, and freight trains is often accomplished by a small group of offenders, frequently with one or more accomplices employed in the firm handling the goods in shipment; but the stolen goods are disposed of through a larger organization of criminals, the wholesale fence group. Preferred in such theft are items with an "instant market" to discount and other stores, such as clothing, alcoholic beverages, electric appliances, and automobile accessories. Those profiting most in these large-scale enterprises have the resources, expertise, and willingness to use bribes, threats, or violence against potential witnesses, making it extremely difficult to trace and prosecute them successfully (Dept. of Transportation & LEAA, 1973).

Some of the stolen cargo is compact, such as jewels, drugs, and other concentrated valuables, but an especially serious problem is theft of negotiable stock certificates, bonds, and other securities. Much of this loot, worth several hundred million or possibly over a billion dollars, is annually taken from registered-mail or special couriers at airports or loading ramps, or is removed from brokerage offices and banks by sneak theft, robbery, or burglary, often with collusion of employees. As with stolen cargo, these purloined documents are then distributed through organized criminal groups that purchase them at from two to 15 percent of their market value. Development of systems for the more exclusively electronic transfer of securities, with the paper certificates retained by a central depository that only changes records of ownership, has been suggested as a method of preventing losses in transit, assuming that depository records would not be subject to fraud by criminals breaching its computer system (Percy, 1973; Dept. of Transportation & LEAA, 1973).

These wholesale crimes do not greatly disturb most of the public, but the total dollar value of the loot may exceed that of street robberies and even rival the total from house burglaries. This raises interesting philosophical questions on relative cost to society of such contrasting types of offense. In terms of impact on the national economy, cargo and security predation causes more of a redistribution than a destruction of the gross national product; so its burden on the public is only indirect. It raises the cost of shipment or burglary insurance, physical protection in storage and transfer, and of other business expenses (and perhaps weakens incentives to honesty and hard work). These costs must ultimately be passed on to consumers through higher prices for merchandise or increases in brokerage fees to those making securities transactions. Indeed, to the predators and much of the public, cargo theft that seems to victimize only large corporations and leads to the stolen goods' being sold cheaply at an independent discount store is rationalized as though this were a national benefit, neglecting the fact that the net effect on the average prices paid by consumers is an increase.

Although the value of loot from street robberies or even from house burglaries may not be greater than that of stolen cargo and securities, threatening or violent confrontation on the street and invasion of a home are much more personally disturbing to the victims and their sympathizers, who comprise thousands of times more people than are even aware of the wholesale crimes. Therefore predations against persons are vastly more costly in terms of the total anxiety they create, which justifies their greatest dollar cost to the economy—the policing and correctional expenditures to prevent them. A similarly complex problem of comparison is involved in assessing the social costs of other organized-crime predations against the American business community.

Bankruptcy Scams and Other Business Ventures by Organized Criminals

As already indicated, many organized criminals become businessmen through demanding partnership as settlement for a usurious loan to a struggling firm; sometimes they even "take over" a share in the management and proceeds of a prosperous firm by sheer threat or force. Perhaps most often they use income from crime to make a proper purchase of a legitimate business or to establish one in a bona fide fashion. All of these procedures have frequently been pathways to respectability for offenders, but in some instances they have instead been techniques for perpetrating their largest predations.

It is estimated that in the United States over $10 billion per year is lost by unsuspecting creditors through bankruptcies that are deliberately planned to defraud them, most often by organized criminals. In the simplest type of *scam,* as such an offense is called, the criminal gets managerial power in a firm with a good credit rating, sometimes by buying a controlling interest, sometimes by coercion or deception. This management then has the company purchase on credit all the easily disposable goods that suppliers will sell without advance payment, and resells these goods for much less than cost to other firms owned by the criminal or by his accomplices, who are wholesale fences. Sometimes the prices of resale are proper, but these customers never pay. In any case, the firm's suppliers are stalled rather than paid, and the credit buying continues as long and extensively as possible. Then, when virtually all the firm's assets are gone, they declare bankruptcy (Cressey, 1969: 105–7; de Franco, 1973).

In a more complex scam, a company with a name almost or exactly like one with a good credit rating is established, and as many purchases as possible are made without payment until bankruptcy occurs. Alternatively, a new firm is created and a good credit rating quickly developed by strategic deposits to get bank references, and by small purchases paid for promptly. Then large orders are made on credit with no intent to pay. Frequently a "pencil" or "front" without a criminal record is recruited as nominal head of the firm, to facilitate good credit. He is denied control over purchases and sales but may be a knowing accomplice in the scheme. Shrewd tactics often appease creditors and stall legal action for a long time before bankruptcy is declared. Afterward rulings are appealed and resolution is impeded for years until creditors are content to settle for a small fraction of what is owed them. Deliberate bankruptcy is a crime, but its prosecution is often difficult and the net gain from it is sometimes in the millions (de Franco, 1973).

Even when persons who have supported themselves by crime sincerely wish to conduct a business conventionally, this intention may at times become diluted if they are frustrated in a sale or purchase when using proper practices and perceive that criminal tactics (e.g., threat, violence, or deception) can result in a profitable transaction. Yet as Chapter 12 indicated, illegal methods—especially deception—are far from unknown in the supposedly respectable pursuits of commerce. In the fields sometimes called "marginal business," such as used cars and job-lot wholesale selling, there are especially large numbers of both criminals striving to be respectable and businessmen without official criminal records who engage in legally questionable practices; on the basis of behavior, the two types often are indistinguishable. Indeed, a parolee once insisted to me that he had quit his job in a used-car firm because he could not stand the way his boss cheated the customers, and his account seemed credible. Furthermore, some persons of criminal background have entered and become law abiding in virtually every type of commercial enterprise, and there is perhaps no category of legitimate business entirely free of illegal transactions.

It is unfortunate that almost every government commission and many writers on organized crime deplore the fact that persons who have been in illegal commerce enter legitimate businesses, as though such a move invariably results in scams or other offenses. It is easy to find instances in which such persistence in crime has occurred, and it is appropriate for policing agencies to make legal and discreet checks on this possibility. But the fact of ethnic succession in organized crime is one proof that many people do move from illicit to licit enterprises and, especially, direct their children into law-abiding vocations. It has been mainly through gradual assimilation, as organized criminals and their descendants have become successful in "straight" businesses, that the minority groups once conspicuous in illegal selling and coercion have become less prominent in the criminal world.

New myths soon develop about the unity of the criminal elements in whatever ethnic group is locally conspicuous in organized offenses. The current vogue is to stigmatize them all by a mafia label, as in "Black Mafia," "Mexican Mafia," and "Cuban Mafia." Eventually their progeny will also be assimilated into respectable occupations and they may well be replaced in these offenses by the offspring of newer poor migrants. To break this cycle, we must provide less criminogenic conditions for the impoverished families in our cities, finally ending the misfortune of criminal children in America that so many families have experienced in their first decades here. Yet organized crime may nevertheless remain attractive to them, for illegal commerce was a pathway to the business elite for many members of most immigrant groups in American history. This pattern began with the earliest settlers on this continent, some of whom engaged in such organized crime as piracy and smuggling, and many of whom had been convicts. Indeed, until the American Revolution hundreds and sometimes thousands of offenders were annually sentenced in Britain to transportation to the colonies, and most of these were sold to sea captains as indentured servants, then resold at a profit here.

SUMMARY AND CONCLUSION

Persons who rely on crime for livelihood, like those in legitimate work, tend to develop shared standards of skill and propriety if they maintain regular contact with others in their occupation. Criminals may thus acquire a professional subculture that provides criteria by which to assess themselves, as well as an ideology of conflict with the police and loyalty to each other. As with most human norms, these principles are more consistently honored in speech than in practice.

Not all recidivist property offenders are committed to crime as a vocation, but those who are tend to be more deliberate, specialized, and successful in their offenses than the many who simply return periodically to adolescent patterns of impulsive lawbreaking. The professional offenders include pickpockets, burglars, and auto thieves who work in teams and often maintain stable relationships with lawyers, bail bondsmen, and especially with that most affluent and least punished type of professional criminal, the fence.

Professional fraud includes systematic check forgery, much of which is done alone. Less frequent but of greater impact on the economy is counterfeiting. Confidence games are extremely varied, but most can logically be divided into a sequence of 10 fairly standard stages. Both the bunco artists and their prey tend to lust after "something for nothing," which is the undoing of these victims; but some swindlers cruelly exploit clearly innocent and trusting persons.

Professional violent offenders are more often autonomous individual entrepreneurs than most other types of property predators, but their robberies are usually coordinated team actions. More costly to society are truck hijackings, which, like nonviolent cargo thefts from docks and airports, involve organized crime in wholesale fencing of huge quantities of stolen merchandise. Comparable in dollar value but not in physical volume are their very extensive transactions in stolen financial securities. These are but a few of the very diversified and often large-scale enterprises of gambling, usury, extortion, and illegal selling conducted by similar and frequently overlapping criminal groups.

Ethnic succession has characterized much of American lawbreaking, most distinctly, perhaps, organized crime during the middle third of the twentieth century, when Italian-Americans were conspicuous in leadership roles, especially in major cities of the East and Midwest. Their rise seems to have been aided by a set of values labeled *mafia* in Sicily, and by the fact that the peak of their immigration came just before the Prohibition era. But tales of the national and even international unified direction of crime by a single Mafia syndicate appear to be clearly mythical. The Mafia subculture's emphasis on family loyalty, secrecy, and aggressive individual enterprise—using threats or violence if necessary—often gave advantages to some Italian kinship groups in organized crime when competing with offenders of other national background. In recent times, however, those Italian families formerly in illegal dealings have moved at an increasing rate into purely legitimate business, and they are being replaced in organized offenses by the progeny of later migrants to the slums, many of whom will presumably also use illegal commerce as an avenue to law-abiding businesses and professions for their children.

In two classic articles published just before the repeal of Prohibition, the late Walter Lippman (1931a, 1931b) alluded first to organized crime as "our secret servant," since it caters to the public's demands for alcoholic beverages, houses of prostitution, gambling, and protection of small businesses from competition. Second, these offenders give us a "stultified conscience" because our Puritan heritage does not permit "compromise with the Devil" through legal recognition of our tolerance for these vices, while our democratic heritage does not allow compromise with the Bill of Rights to give our police the despotism necessary to stamp out these vices. As Thurman Arnold wrote in somewhat the same vein: "Most unenforced criminal laws survived in order to satisfy moral objections to established modes of conduct. They are unenforced because we want to continue our conduct, and unrepealed because we want to preserve our morals" (1935: 160).

More recently we have made both of the compromises to which Lippman referred but, fortunately, serious compromises with the Bill of Rights were shortlived. Under the Nixon Presidency, legislation was sought for increased authority for the FBI and United States Attorneys to use wiretapping and electronic eavesdropping to gain evidence against persons alleged to be in organized crime or endangering national security. The resulting powers granted to the Attorney General were more limited than what was requested, and though they produced some convictions of organized criminals, they subsequently were further restricted because the Watergate scandals revealed their abuse in politically motivated probes under the guise of security inquiries. Now their use requires judicial review in advance.

More effective in reducing the ability of professional and organized predators to evade justice has been an increase in the resources and coordination of prosecution efforts against them. Usually criminal cases are so numerous in a metropolis and the defense of ordinary offenders so limited that, by bargaining and delay (mostly on defense initiative if the accused is out on bail, but often on the prosecution's part if the accused is in jail), a consensus is eventually reached on a plea of guilty to a lesser charge. This solution gives the prosecution a high conviction rate and eliminates the need for trials, while reducing the defendant's penalty. When criminals are able to hire outstanding lawyers, pay for any probable bail, and perhaps bribe or intimidate witnesses, the prospect alters; often they can then delay proceedings and impair prosecution to prevent any convictions, or to make the court's findings and penalties trivial compared with the volume and seriousness of offenses committed. This pattern may now be changing, for the federal government, copying a highly successful "Major Offense Bureau" in New York's Bronx County District Attorney's Office, has subsidized "Career Criminal Programs" in 18 metropolitan counties. These give special priority and resources to the prosecution of the most professional offenders by: (1) having clerks screen all criminal cases at intake, using specific criteria for early identification of what appear to be career criminals; (2) assigning a team of carefully selected attorneys to prosecute each of these identified cases from intake to conclusion, in contrast to the usual practices of using a different state's attorney staff at each transaction and of placing junior personnel in charge of most cases at some time; (3) budgeting more funds for investigation and for securing and protecting witnesses. The result of these efforts has generally been a higher conviction rate on the original charges, with prompter and severer penalties, and this approach is rapidly spreading (LEAA, 1976c).

Also diminishing the power of organized crime in some areas is the post-Watergate reform of the electoral process in the federal government, in some states, and to a lesser extent in municipalities. Estimates of organized crime's contributions to political-campaign funds in the United States have run as high as 15 percent (Cressey, 1969: 253). Limits on the size of contributions, the required publication of sources, and even government payment of all campaign costs make corruption by organized crime more difficult.

Probably the most significant blow to illegal sales organizations is our increasing compromise with the tradition of punishing nonpredatory activities as crime, especially when large segments of the population engage in them and find them, if harmful at all, no worse than many other legal self-indulgences. As indicated in discussing substance abuse in Chapter 10, prostitution and homosexuality in Chapter 11, and gambling in this chapter, using the criminal-justice system to try to prohibit such activities not only is ineffective, but also corrupts that system and fosters predation. The social costs of these activities are much more efficiently reduced by a combination of: (1) educational efforts to discourage clearly self-damaging behavior; (2) public-health measures for extreme abusers; (3) alternative employment and recreation opportunities for more of the population; (4) law enforcement that concentrates primarily on the more visible acts that clearly endanger others, such as solicitation of children to deviant conduct and violation of licensing regulations in selling alcohol, in gambling, and in other decriminalized potential abuses. These seem to be the trends of public-policy changes in recent years, although the surviving elements of our prohibition mentality make the complete elimination of markets for organized crime highly unlikely.

PART THREE

CONCLUSION

FOURTEEN

THE FUTURE OF CRIME

Lawbreaking, death, and taxes will probably always be part of the human condition. Durkheim (1895/1938: 67ff.) said that governments must punish offenders to dramatize behavior standards for noncriminals. In "a society of saints, a perfect cloister of exemplary individuals," he adds, what we call "crime" would be unknown, but the faults we consider trivial would there create "the same scandal" that major offenses generate in our society. Although crime will remain, what it includes will alter.

REVISION OF THE CRIMINAL LAW

A major theme of this book has been the importance of qualifying all generalizations on crime to specify the types of offense to which they apply. Central to this emphasis has been the distinction between predatory and nonpredatory lawbreaking, for it dichotomizes what can be said with confidence about change in the criminal law and on counting, explaining, or preventing crime.

The most independent factor in modern social and cultural change and, hence, in alterations of criminal law has been technological evolution, particularly in the modes of production. Agricultural, manufacturing, and commercial innovations create differentiations in social class, roles, and organizations. They occur at an increasingly rapid pace because almost every new scientific discovery or invention, and most new business or work arrangements, make others possible. The growth of knowledge and of productive efficiency is not only cumulative; in addition, each of these trends generates new ways in which people may be victimized.

Because of the processes of inclusion and adaptive upgrading (discussed in Chapter 2), more and more of the victims of predation are becoming influential voting blocs, able to get the government to combat their oppressors. Large-scale predators yield power only piecemeal, but increasingly the criminal law is snaring polluters, contaminators, misrepresenters in selling, and purchasers of political power—all of whom were previously immune to prosecution. Also, some types of sexism once beyond the reach of the law, such as battering or raping one's wife, are now more readily grounds for arrest in many areas. These are but a few of many new trends in the punishment of predation that are likely to grow in the coming years.

Contrastingly, nonpredatory offenses—such as deviant but victimless drug use or sexual activity—are likely to become of less concern to the criminal law. The generalization of values that, as Durkheim (1893) predicted, inevitably follows increased interdependence and contact with unfamiliar social customs, will foster tolerance of diversity in nonpredatory conduct. It also produces what Chapter 2 (following Weber) called a pragmatic rather than an absolute morality in lawmaking. The social costs of unenforceable statutes are increasingly being considered, along with the behavior that legislation seeks to prohibit. These trends of decreasing government penalties for nonpredatory acts are not nearly as steady as the growth in laws against predation, for there are recurrent conservative periods with local reactions against deviant lifestyles and consequent passage of repressive legislation. Nevertheless, the predominant evolutionary tendency in our criminal law allows adults more freedom to "do their own thing" as long as they do not injure others.

Criminal laws have always reflected the relative influence on government of different segments of society. Laws against predations initially focused on offenses of employees rather than employers, and many of the first antidrug statutes were intended to prevent the spread of practices then ascribed to poor minorities. Yet the assertion that behaviors only become crime "when they disturb or threaten in some way the capitalist order" (Quinney, 1977: 53) overlooks: (1) cumulative popular support for statutes against predation; (2) working-class backing for much punishment of nonpredatory conduct (e.g., homosexuality); (3) the growing reach of the inclusion process— for example, to penalize capitalists who defraud consumers, pollute the environment, or try to buy elections.

Radicals may correctly object that the attained inclusion is still a long way from what justice demands. They may relabel it mere cooptation or scoff that it is just throwing a few crumbs to keep the masses in their place. Change in a nation with firmly institutionalized democratic elections is almost always piecemeal. The pieces do add up if accurately assessed over an appreciable span of history, and the rate of increase has accelerated. More rapid change might follow a violent revolution, but that could come only after a long and unlikely cataclysmic crisis. The benefits from revolution would be costlier and more insecure than those attained more gradually by the democratic process (Boulding, 1970: Chapter 6).

Although Marx's forecast of proletariat rebellion seems to be demonstrated by the rising pressure to penalize some capitalists, the pressure actually comes from large segments of all strata. Despite Marxist predictions that an intensified class conflict would accompany the growth of capitalism, studies show that class consciousness has been diminishing in recent decades in the United States. An expanding majority of the population calls itself "middle class" (Morris & Jeffries, 1970) for indeed, contrary to Marx's prediction, less of the population does routinized unskilled labor (Blau, 1974). Furthermore, a sense of the class struggle is most intense among the new unskilled migrants to the city, the uprooted workers of agrarian background. It diminishes as they and their offspring rise in the urban labor force (Leggett, 1968).

The conflict between classes that has become less evident in criminal lawmaking often seems flagrant in the law's application. Most prison inmates are of low economic status and of minority background. This fact suggests that social stratification either causes crime or biases the administration of justice, or both.

COPING WITH THE MAJOR CAUSES OF CRIME

Since crimes have diverse causes, prevention of all offenses would require a multiplicity of policies. Yet the lawbreaking that most concerns the public and the police is predation by adolescents. It is often the precursor of professional criminality. Offenses are adventures for many youths, shortcuts to a sense of adult independence or even of eminence. Therefore, crime appeals especially to those of any age who do not perceive themselves as making a secure transition from childhood to autonomy as law-abiding adults. Teenagers now have the highest arrest rates for murder, robbery, and assault. They have long comprised the majority of arrestees for burglary and theft.

Most predictive of a criminal record, Chapter 8 stressed, is difficulty in school. Secondary to this is the lack of steady employment when out of school. Perpetuating these conditions and transforming them into crime is the separation of youth with these problems from people who are succeeding at education or employment.

Inexorably, social separation fosters cultural differentiation. Young criminals not only deviate from adult customs as do other youth in our age-segregated society (as in the contrasting tastes in substance abuse described in Chapter 10), but they find in each other their social support for lawbreaking. Clustered in cliques or gangs, they collectively engage in offenses they would not dare alone. Gradually, some successful predators seek their livelihood from crime and even take pride in such a career, viewing it as a commendable performance before a real or imaginary audience of lawbreakers.

Most conducive to crime, therefore, are any conditions that impede success at school, that isolate adolescents from adults, and, especially, that bar former offenders from the labor force. These conditions include (1) membership in a family that has had disadvantaged education for generations and (2) neglect by or antagonism from parents, teachers, and employers. Each of these two types of handicap can be overcome, especially if the other is absent. When they occur together, they particularly lure youth to careers in lawbreaking. They place tremendous barriers before successful alternatives to crime, and thus make life as an outlaw more attractive by comparison.

Unfortunately, being in certain minority groups and being poor foster the disadvantages enumerated above, and others as well. Centuries of racial discrimination in education give many black American youth an English vocabulary and syntax at home different from that which the schools demand, although quite adequate for intelligent communication. Furthermore, poverty, broken families, and life in the crowded ghettos often reduce youth's social life with parents or other noncriminal adults but enhance their opportunities for achieving a sense of importance and other rewards through violence, drugs, and illegal sources of income.

Gradually, blacks are overcoming these handicaps. They are catching up with whites in rates of high-school and college completion. This gives them more attractive employment. The effects of these developments are somewhat understated by the small drop in their percentage of total index-crime arrestees, from 36 in 1970 to 33 in 1975, according to the FBI. The actual decline in arrests of blacks *of United States mainland ancestry* must be greater, for the black arrestees now include more migrants from Puerto Rico and other islands of the West Indies.

Supplementing or replacing the mainland blacks as our most handicapped youth are the children of poor Latin-American migrants of diverse racial ancestry. Their new barrios parallel the older black ghettos, and they are handicapped in most American schools by being reared in an environment where English is not spoken. Prospects are that their numbers will increase from a burgeoning illegal immigration, especially in the Southwest. Unfortunately, we have no national data on their contribution to crime in the United States, but statistics from California, New York, and Florida show growth in the proportion of "Latinos" among arrestees.

Conclusions on a group's crime rates, Chapter 4 pointed out, can be seriously biased if the only available evidence comes from arrests. Such statistics reflect not only crimes but also police arrest policy, which may be prejudiced for or against a particular group. Scattered data suggest, however, that ethnic discrimination, arrests, and crime causation have complex interrelationships. Police may often encourage offenses by not trying hard to solve crimes when victim and offender are both of a minority group. Indeed, even if the officers try, their effectiveness is limited by being of a race and neighborhood different from those of the offenders. These crime-fostering conditions probably reduce the rate of arrest for minority-group criminals more than the police increase this rate by too readily making arrests from such groups.

Prejudice probably increases crime rates more by its effects on housing, jobs, and schools than on criminal-justice agencies. The money, time, and energy spent to impede school desegregation could have been used for dispersed housing for minorities in white neighborhoods and for welcoming them there. Busing would then no longer be an issue, and most children would get a better education. Also, if (1) the federally subsidized job programs for youth authorized in 1977 had been continuously provided in earlier decades, to assure that the government was available as an employer of last resort, and if (2) their design and management were continually revised on the basis of research on their effectiveness for moving youth into adult types of employment, we would probably have much lower crime rates and numerous other social benefits.

The problem of ethnic discrimination in teaching, as in policing, is complex. Research by Dornbusch (reported at the 1977 Pacific Sociological Association meetings) indicates that black juniors and seniors in San Francisco high schools are, on the average, four years behind their grade level in reading ability. Many Chicanos have similar retardation. This comes not only from the disadvantages of their home circumstances in learning to read, he suggests, but also from receiving acceptable grades from Anglo teachers regardless of whether or not they make progress in reading. There is little education if reward is not linked to achievement. His questionnaires revealed that black students like their white teachers more than do the white students. As he summarizes, black and Chicano students get F only for extreme truancy or misconduct, D for some attendance, C for attendance and not making trouble, B for attendance and amiability, and A for definite achievement.

American students will get much more equal opportunities for achievement only as they acquire (1) integrated schools in integrated communities and (2) teachers who show they care by making more effort to motivate *all* pupils to learn. Advances toward these objectives will be steps to crime reduction, particularly for minority youth and especially if accompanied by other collaboration of adolescents with law-abiding adults to reduce the age segregation of our society, in and out of school.

Radical criminologists point to our nation's huge number of high-crime-rate youth, who are poorly schooled and thereafter unemployed, as evidence of capitalism's need for a "marginal working class" (Schwendinger & Schwendinger, 1976a, 1976b), a "reserve army of labor," or, alternatively, a "reserve army of the unemployed and unemployable" (Quinney, 1977: 57, 84). The relatively low rates of idleness in Sweden, West Germany, and Japan suggest that these commentators on the economy, like most who generalize mainly from Marx's nineteenth-century impressions, underestimate the potential of government intervention in predominantly capitalist systems. The state can distribute work opportunities and rewards more equitably, yet maintain relatively high levels of productivity and freedom.

Our current crime peak in adolescence, Chapters 8 and 9 indicate, reflects primarily the failure of our communities and the federal government to adjust rapidly enough to the surging pace of (1) age-group segregation, (2) educational upgrading of the labor force, (3) ethnic-group migration, and (4) demand for minority-group equality. As we conclude the 1970s, actions to cope with these and other major causes of crime are accelerating. There is a sound basis for hope that such efforts will result in lower offense rates.

Prominent recent "conservative" writers advocate more certain convictions and penalties in the criminal courts as the primary crime-fighting method. They object to the alternative that we emphasize—changing the conditions that cause offenses. Wilson (1975: xv) says that "the demand for causal solutions is, whether intended or not, a way of deferring any action and criticizing any policy." Probably he would not apply such a statement to this book. Van den Haag (1975: 77–78) asserts that "theories of crime causation . . . help make the occurrence and frequency of criminal conduct intelligible. But none promises to tell much that can be applied to crime control. . . ." The crime-causation theories that he summarizes, however, do not address the major trends in society enumerated here. It is hard to see how the judicial actions he urges can suffice against the crime-causing social factors we have described.

Of course the certainty of punishment that these authors demand would reduce some kind of offenses. The incapacitation in prison that they advocate is undoubtedly necessary to protect society from most professional predators (although additional measures are also desirable, even for them). Deterrence alone may suffice for avocational offenders. But the severe penalties these writers propose seem unlikely to deter youth who: (1) see no prospect of satisfaction in school or of obtaining a job; (2) realistically perceive each separate offense as offering little chance of arrest, but high prospects for immediate esteem among friends and for other rewards that exceed what they can get legitimately. Many of these who have been repeatedly confined from an early age also find the pains of imprisonment not clearly more severe than those they experienced when they tried to "go straight" after release.

Most causes of crime are also causes of recidivism. Many measures for preventing youth offense, such as assurance of employment, should reduce return to crime by those who complete the imprisonment that these authors stress. Also, the programs these authors urge would be politically even more difficult to attain than the work and education programs that we propose and foresee. The analysis of trends and prospects of the criminal-justice system in our changing society, however, will be the topic of another book.

SUMMARY AND CONCLUSION

The types of predation subject to criminal penalty will continue to increase as victims gain more government backing against those who injure their persons, properties, or civil rights. This trend will not reflect the polarization of our society by the class conflict that Marxists predict, but rather the cross-cutting of interest-group alignments in our pluralistic democracy. Yet the inclusion process will expand state protection for the poor and the weak who are in large groups of voters, and will reduce the ability of the wealthy and powerful to victimize them. Simultaneously, the generalization of values will foster more tolerance of deviant conduct that does not injure others and that the criminal-justice system cannot effectively prohibit, although such a trend may occasionally be reversed by puritanical backlash.

The causes of crime vary with the offense, the offender, and the circumstances, so crime prevention by eliminating causes is a complex problem. Yet the victimizations that most disturb people—murders, muggings, breakins, and purse snatchings—are committed disproportionately by adolescents. Such predations can be diminished if we reduce the age segregation in our society, guarantee employment, augment motivation in education, and eliminate discrimination against minorities. Radical criminologists insist that such goals will be attained only when the working class creates a socialist revolution, and probably not by our election process. On the other hand, conservatives either denigrate these goals or question their feasibility. This book has argued that these goals can be achieved within our political and economic system, and that our society is moving toward them.

REFERENCES

ABELSON, HERBERT I., and RONALD B. ATKINSON

1975   Public Experience with Psychoactive Substances. Princeton, N.J.: Response Analysis Corp (distributed only through National Institute on Drug Abuse, Rockville, Md.).

ABRAMS, ARNOLD, JOHN H. GAGNON, and JOSEPH J. LEVIN

1968   "Psychosocial aspects of addiction." American Journal of Public Health 58 (November): 2142-55.

ADAMS, STUART

1961   "Interaction between individual interview therapy and treatment amenability in older Youth Authority wards." Inquiries Concerning Kinds of Treatments for Kinds of Delinquents. Sacramento: Calif. Department of Correction (reprinted as "The PICO Project," in Norman B. Johnston et al., The Sociology of Punishment and Correction. New York: Wiley, 1st ed., 1962 and 2nd ed. 1970).

ADLER, FREDA

1975   Sisters in Crime. New York: McGraw-Hill.

AGAR, MICHAEL

1973   Ripping and Running. New York: Seminar Press.

AICHHORN, AUGUST

1925   Wayward Youth (originally in German; English ed. by Viking Press, New York, 1935).

AKERS, RONALD L.

1964   "Socioeconomic status and delinquent behavior: a replication." Journal of Research in Crime and Delinquency 1 (January): 38-46.

ALBINI, JOSEPH L.

1971   The American Mafia: Genesis of a Legend. New York: Appleton-Century-Crofts.

ALLEN, DAVID D.

1952   The Nature of Gambling. New York: Coward-McCann.

ALLEN, FRANCIS A.

1974   The Crimes of Politics. Cambridge, Mass.: Harvard University Press.

ALLEN, HARRY E., LEWIS LINDNER, HAROLD GOLDMAN, and SIMON DINITZ
  1969   "The social and bio-medical correlates of sociopathy." Criminologica 4 (February): 68-75.

ALLEN, VERNON L., ed.
  1970   Psychological Factors in Poverty. Chicago: Markham.

ALVIANI, JOSEPH D., and WILLIAM R. DRAKE
  1975   Handgun Control. Washington: U.S. Conference of Mayors.

AMIR, MENACHIM
  1971   Patterns of Forcible Rape. Chicago: University of Chicago Press.

ARCHER, DANE, and ROSEMARY GARTNER
  1976   "Violent acts and violent times: A comparative approach to postwar homicide rates." American Sociological Review 41 (December): 937-63.

ARENS, RICHARD
  1967   "The Durham Rule in action: Judicial psychiatry and psychiatric justice." Law and Society Review 1 (June): 41-80.

ARENS, RICHARD, and HAROLD D. LASSWELL
  1969   Make Mad the Guilty. Springfield, Ill.: C.C. Thomas.

ARMOR, DAVID J., J. MICHAEL POLICH, and HARRIET B. STAMBUL
  1976   Alcoholism and Treatment. Rand Report R-1739. Santa Monica, Calif.: Rand.

ARNOLD, THURMAN W.
  1935   The Symbols of Government. New Haven: Yale University Press.
  1937   The Folklore of Capitalism. New Haven: Yale University Press.

ARONOWITZ, DENNIS S.
  1967   "Civil commitment of narcotic addicts." Columbia Law Review 67 (March): 405-29.

ASCH, SOLOMON E.
  1956   "Studies of independence and conformity." Psychological Monographs 70 (Whole No. 416).

AUSUBEL, DAVID P.
  1958   Drug Addiction. New York: Random House.

BABST, DEAN V.
  1964   "Elective governments—A force for peace." Wisconsin Sociologist 3 (January): 9-14.
  1972   "A force for peace." Industrial Research 14 (April): 55-58.

BABST, DEAN V., CARL D. CHAMBERS, and ALAN WARNER
  1971   "Patient characteristics associated with retention in a methadone program." British Journal of Addiction 66: 195-204.

BACH, GEORGE R., and PETER WYDEN
  1974   The Intimate Enemy. New York: Morrow.

BAGLEY, CHRISTOPHER
  1969   "Incest behavior and incest taboo." Social Problems 16 (Spring): 505-19.

BAHR, HOWARD M., ed.
  1970   Disaffiliated Man. Toronto: University of Toronto Press.

BAHR, HOWARD, and THEODORE CAPLOW
  1973   Old Men Drunk and Sober. New York: New York University Press.

BAKAL, CARL
1966   The Right to Bear Arms. New York: McGraw-Hill.

BAKAN, DAVID
1971   Slaughter of the Innocents. San Francisco: Jossey-Bass.

BALES, (ROBERT) FREED
1942   "Types of social structure as factors in 'cures' for alcohol addiction." Applied Anthropology 1 (April-June): 1-13.

BALL, JOHN C.
1965   "Two patterns of narcotic addiction in the United States." Journal of Criminal Law, Criminology and Police Science 56 (June): 203-11.

BALL-ROKEACH, SANDRA J.
1973   "Values and violence: A test of the subculture of violence thesis." American Sociological Review 38 (December): 736-49.
1975   "Reply to Magura: Issues and non-issues in testing a subculture thesis." American Sociological Review 40 (December): 836-38.

BANDURA, ALBERT
1969   Principles of Behavior Modification. New York: Holt, Rinehart and Winston.
1973a   Aggression. Englewood Cliffs, N.J.: Prentice-Hall.
1973b   "Social learning theory of aggression," in Knutson, 1973.

BARD, MORTON
1970   Training Police as Specialists in Family Crisis Intervention. Washington: U.S. Government Printing Office.

BARNETT, ARNOLD, DANIEL KLEITMAN, and RICHARD C. LARSON
1975   "On urban homicide: A statistical analysis." Journal of Criminal Justice 3 (Summer): 85-110.

BASSIOUNI, M. CHERIF
1969   Criminal Law and Its Processes. Springfield, Ill.: C.C. Thomas.
1974   "A survey of the major criminal justice systems in the world," in Glaser, 1974.

BAZELON, DAVID L.
1974   "Psychiatrists and the advisory process." Scientific American 230 (June): 18-23.

BECKER, HOWARD S.
1953   "Becoming a marijuana user." American Journal of Sociology 59 (November): 235-42.
1955   "Marijuana use and social control." Social Problems 3 (July): 35-44.
1963   Outsiders. New York: Free Press.
1967   "History, culture and subjective experience: An exploration of the social bases of drug-induced experiences." Journal of Health and Social Behavior 8 (September): 163-76.
1973   "Consciousness, power and drug effects." Society 10 (May-June): 26-31.

BEDAU, HUGO ADAM
1964   The Death Penalty in America. Garden City, N.Y.: Doubleday.

BENEDICT, RUTH
1934   Patterns of Culture. Boston: Houghton Mifflin.

BENJAMIN, HARRY, and R.L.L. MASTERS
1964   Prostitution and Morality. New York: Julian Press.

BERKOWITZ, LEONARD
1962   Aggression. New York: McGraw-Hill.

REFERENCES   485

BERKOWITZ, LEONARD, and JACQUELINE MACAULAY
1971   "The contagion of criminal violence." Sociometry 34 (June): 238-60.

BERNE, ERIC
1964   Games People Play. New York: Grove Press.

BERNSTEIN, CARL, and BOB WOODWARD
1974   All the President's Men. New York: Simon & Schuster.

BETTELHEIM, BRUNO
1950   Love Is Not Enough. New York: Free Press.

BEUTEL, FREDERICK K.
1957   Study of the Enforcement of the Bad Check Laws in Nebraska. Lincoln: University of Nebraska Press.

BIDERMAN, ALBERT D.
1967   "Surveys of population samples for estimating crime incidence." Annals of the American Academy of Political and Social Science 374 (November): 16-33.

BIDERMAN, ALBERT D., and ALBERT J. REISS, JR.
1967   "On exploring the 'dark figure' of crime." Annals of the American Academy of Political and Social Science 374 (November): 1-15.

BIERCE, AMBROSE G.
1906   The Devil's Dictionary (originally published as "The Cynic's Word Book"). Garden City, N.Y.: Doubleday, 1967.

BITTNER, EGON
1967a "The police on skid row: A study of peace-keeping." American Sociological Review 32 (October): 699-715.
1967b "Police discretion in emergency apprehension of mentally ill persons." Social Problems 14 (Winter): 278-92.

BLACK, DONALD J.
1970   "Production of crime rates." American Sociological Review 35 (August): 733-48.

BLAKE, GERALD F., and DAVID A. JOHNSON
(undated) Teaching and Educational Inequality. Unpublished paper, Portland State University Criminal Justice Ph.D. Program.

BLALOCK, H.M.
1971   Causal Model in the Social Sciences. Chicago: Aldine-Atherton.

BLANKENBURG, ERHARD
1976   "The selectivity of legal sanctions: An empirical investigation of shoplifting." Law and Society Review 11 (Fall): 109-30

BLANKENSHIP, RALPH L.
1968   "Police response to signs of mental disturbance among juvenile offenders." Master of Arts dissertation, Urbana, Ill.: University of Illinois.

BLANKENSHIP, RALPH L., and B. KRISHNA SINGH
1976   "Differential labeling of juveniles: A multivariate analysis." Criminology 13 (February): 471-90.

BLAU, PETER M.
1963   The Dynamics of Bureaucracy, rev. ed. Chicago: University of Chicago Press.

1974   "Parameters of social structure." American Sociological Review 39 (October): 615-35.

BLOCK, RICHARD
1975   "Homicide in Chicago: A nine-year study (1965-73)." Journal of Criminal Law and Criminology 66 (December): 496-510.

BLOCK, RICHARD, and FRANKLIN E. ZIMRING
1973   "Homicide in Chicago, 1965-70." Journal of Research in Crime and Delinquency 10 (January): 1-12.

BLUM, RICHARD H., and associates
1972a   The Dream Sellers. San Francisco: Jossey-Bass.
1972b   Deceivers and Deceived. Springfield, Ill.: C.C. Thomas.
1973 (ed.)   Drug Dealers—Taking Action. San Francisco: Jossey-Bass.

BLUMBERG, LEONARD, THOMAS E. SHIPLEY, JR., and IRVING W. SHANDLER
1973   Skid Row and Its Alternatives. Philadelphia: Temple University Press.

BLUMER, HERBERT
1960   Symbolic Interactionism. Englewood Cliffs, N.J.: Prentice-Hall.
1969   "Collective behavior," in Alfred McClung Lee, ed. Principles of Sociology, 3rd ed. New York: Barnes & Noble.

BOGUE, DONALD J.
1963   Skid Row in American Cities. Chicago: University of Chicago Community and Family Study Center.

BOHANNON, PAUL
1960   African Homicide and Suicide. Princeton, N.J.: Princeton University Press.

BONNIE, R.J., and C.H. WHITEHEAD II
1970   "The forbidden fruit and the tree of knowledge: An inquiry into the legal history of American marijuana prohibition." Virginia Law Review 56 (October): 971-1203.
1974   The Marijuana Conviction: A History of Marijuana Prohibition in the U.S. Charlottesville: University of Virginia Press.

BONNIE, RICHARD J., and MICHAEL R. SONNENREICH, eds.
1975   Legal Aspects of Drug Dependence. Cleveland: CRC Press.

BORGAONKAR, DIGAMBER S., and SALEEM A. SHAH
1974   "The XYY Chromosome: Male—Or Syndrome?" in Arthur G. Steinberg and Alexander G. Bearn, eds., Progress in Medical Genetics, Vol. X, New York: Grune & Stratton.

BORGATTA, EDGAR F.
1974   "Psychotropic drug use in American families," in Winick, 1974.

BOULDING, KENNETH E.
1970   A Primer on Social Dynamics. New York: Free Press.

BRANCALE, RALPH, ALFRED VUOCOLO, and WILLIAM E. PRENDERGAST, JR.
1972   "The New Jersey program for sex offenders," in Resnik and Wolfgang, 1972.

BRECHER, EDWARD M.
1977   Treatment Programs for Sex Offenders. LEAA Prescriptive Package: U.S. Department of Justice (advance draft).

BRECHER, EDWARD M., and the EDITORS OF CONSUMER REPORTS.
1972   Licit and Illicit Drugs. Boston: Little, Brown.

BRECHER, EDWARD, and RUTH BRECHER, eds.
1966   An Analysis of Human Sexual Response. New York: Signet Books.

BRIAR, SCOTT, and IRVING PILIAVIN
1965   "Delinquency, situational inducements and commitment to conformity." Social Problems 13 (Summer): 35-45.

BRILL, HENRY, and TETSUYA HIROSE
1969   "The rise and fall of a methamphetamine epidemic: Japan 1945-55." Seminars in Psychiatry 1 (May): 179-94.

BRILL, LEON
1972   The De-Addiction Process. Springfield, Ill.: C.C. Thomas.

BRILL, LEON, and DAVID LESKOWITZ
1972   "Cyclazocine in the treatment of narcotics addiction—Another look," in W. Keup, 1972.

BRILL, STEVEN D.
1976   "Tracing the Southern connection." New York Times Magazine (reprinted in Handgun Control News, February-March 1977).

BRODYAGA, LISA, MARGARET GATES, SUSAN SINGER, MARNA TUCKER, and RICHARDSON WHITE
1975   Rape and its victims. LEAA Prescriptive Package. Washington, D.C.: U.S. Department of Justice.

BROMAN, SARAH H., PAUL L. NICHOLS, and WALLACE A. KENNEDY
1975   Preschool IQ: Prenatal and Early Developmental Correlates. New York: Wiley.

BROOKS, ALEXANDER D.
1974   Law, Psychiatry and the Mental Health System. Boston: Little, Brown.

BROOKS, JAMES
1975   "How well are criminal injury compensation programs performing?" Crime and Delinquency 21 (January): 50-56.

BROWN, BARRY S., and LAURENCE T. CARROLL
1976   "Posttreatment evaluation of drug abusers." National Institute on Drug Abuse, Services Research Branch Notes (June).

BROWN, JAMES W., DANIEL GLASER, ELAINE WAXER, and GILBERT GEIS
1974   "Turning off: Cessation of marijuana use after college." Social Problems 21 (April): 527-38.

BROWN, LES
1971   Television: The Business Behind the Box. New York: Harcourt Brace Jovanovich.

BROWN, RICHARD M.
1969   "Historical patterns of violence in America" and "The American vigilante tradition," in Graham and Gurr, 1969.

BROWN, ROGER
1965   Social Psychology. New York: Free Press.

BROWNMILLER, SUSAN
1975   Against Our Will: Men, Women and Rape. New York: Simon & Schuster.

BRUUN, KETTIL, LYNN PAN, and INGEMAR REXED
　1975　The Gentlemen's Club: International Control of Drugs and Alcohol. Chicago: University of Chicago Press.

BRYAN, JAMES H.
　1965　"Apprenticeships in prostitution." Social Problems 12 (Winter): 287-97.
　1966　"Occupational ideologies and individual attitudes of call girls." Social Problems 13 (Spring): 441-50.

BUCKHORN, ROBERT F.
　1972　Nader: The People's Lawyer. Englewood Cliffs, N.J.: Prentice-Hall.

BUREAU OF THE CENSUS, U.S. DEPARTMENT OF COMMERCE
　1970a 1970 Census of Population. Washington, D.C.: U.S. Government Printing Office.
　1970b Current Population Reports, "Educational attainment." Series No. 207, P. 20, U.S. Government Printing Office (March).

BUREAU OF CRIMINAL STATISTICS (CALIFORNIA)
　1974　Homicide in California, 1973. Sacramento: The Bureau, Department of Justice.

BURGESS, ANN WOLBERT, and LYNDA LYTLE HOLMSTROM
　1974　Rape: Victims of Crisis. Bowie, Md.: Robert J. Brady.

BURT, ROBERT A., and NORVAL MORRIS
　1972　"A proposal for the abolition of the incompetency plea." University of Chicago Law Review 40 (Fall): 66-95.

BURTON, LINDY
　1968　Vulnerable Children. New York: Schocken Books.

CAHALAN, DON, IRA H. CISIN, and HELEN M. CROSSLEY
　1969　American Drinking Practices. New Brunswick, N.J.: Rutgers University Center of Alcohol Studies.

CAHALAN, DON, and ROBIN ROOM
　1974　Problem Drinking among American Men. New Brunswick, N.J.: Rutgers Center of Alcohol Studies.

CAMERON, MARY O.
　1964　The Booster and the Snitch. New York: Free Press.

CAPLAN, NATHAN
　1970　"The new ghetto man: A review of recent empirical studies." Journal of Social Issues 26 (Winter): 59-73.
　1974　"Educational expectations linked to delinquency." Institute of Social Research Newsletter. University of Michigan 1 (Winter): 4.

CAPLOW, THEODORE
　1968　Two against One: Coalitions in a Triad. Englewood Cliffs, N.J.: Prentice-Hall.

CARTWRIGHT, DESMOND S., BARBARA TOMSON, and HERSHEY SCHWARZ
　1975　Gang Delinquency. Monterey, Calif. Brooks/Cole.

CARTWRIGHT, DORWIN
　1971　"Risk taking by individuals and groups." Journal of Personality and Social Psychology 20 (December): 361-78.

CATER, DOUGLASS, and STEPHEN STRICKLAND
　1975　TV Violence and the Child: The Evolution and Fate of the Surgeon General's Report. New York: Russell Sage Foundation.

REFERENCES　　　　　　　　　　　　　　　　　　　　　　　　　489

CAVAN, SHERRI

1966 Liquor License. Chicago: Aldine.

CHAMBERS, CARL D., and LEON BRILL, eds.

1973 Methadone: Experiences and Issues. New York: Behavioral Publications.

CHAMBERS, CARL D., ARTHUR D. MOFFETT, and WALTER R. CUSKEY

1971 "Five patterns of Darvon abuse." International Journal of the Addictions 6 (March): 173-89.

CHAMBERS, CARL D., JAMES A. INCIARDI, and RICHARD C. STEPHENS

1971 "A critical review of pentazocine abuse." Health Services and Mental Health Administration Reports 86 (July): 627-36.

CHAMBERS, CARL D., LEON BRILL, and JAMES A. INCIARDI

1972a "Toward understanding and managing non-narcotic drug abusers." Federal Probation 36 (March): 50-55.

1972b "Barbiturate use, misuse and abuse." Journal of Drug Issues 2 (Fall): 15-20.

CHAMBLISS, WILLIAM J.

1971 "Vice corruption, bureaucracy, and power." Wisconsin Law Review (No. 4): 1150-73.

1972 Box-Man: A Professional Thief's Journey. New York: Harper & Row.

1974 "The state, the law, and the definition of behavior as criminal or delinquent," in Glaser, 1974.

CHAMBLISS, WILLIAM J., and RICHARD H. NAGASAWA

1969 "On the validity of official statistics—A comparative study of white, black and Japanese high school boys." Journal of Research in Crime and Delinquency 6 (January): 71-77.

CHILTON, ROLAND, and JAN DEAMICIS

1975 "Overcriminalization and the measurement of consensus." Sociology and Social Research 59 (July): 318-29.

CHILTON, ROLAND J., and GERALD E. MARKLE

1972 "Family disruption, delinquent conduct and the effect of subclassification." American Sociological Review 37 (February): 93-99.

CHRISTENSEN, HAROLD T.

1960 "Cultural relativism and premarital sex norms." American Sociological Review 25 (February): 31-39.

CHRISTENSEN, HAROLD T., and GEORGE R. CARPENTER

1962 "Value-behavior discrepancies regarding premarital coitus." American Sociological Review 27 (February): 66-74.

CHRISTIANSEN, KARL O.

1968 "Threshold of tolerance of various population groups as illustrated by results from Danish criminological twin study," in A.V.S. Reuck and Ruth Porter, eds. Ciba Foundation Symposium on the Mentally Abnormal Offender. London: J. & A. Churchill.

1974 "Seriousness of criminality and concordance among Danish twins," in Roger Hood, ed., Crime, Criminology and Public Policy. New York: Free Press.

CHURCHILL, WAINWRIGHT

1967 Homosexual Behavior among Males. Englewood Cliffs, N.J.: Prentice-Hall.

CLARK, JOHN P., and LARRY L. TIFFT

1966 "Polygraph and interview validation of self-reported deviant behavior." American Sociological Review 31 (August): 516-23.

CLARK, JOHN P., and EUGENE P. WENNINGER
  1962   "Socioeconomic class and area as correlates of illegal behavior among juve-
         niles. American Sociological Review 27 (December): 826-43.

CLARK, ROBERT E.
  1972   Reference Group Theory and Delinquency. New York: Behavioral Publica-
         tions.

CLASTER, DANIEL S.
  1967   "Comparison of risk perception between delinquents and nondelinquents."
         Journal of Criminal Law, Criminology and Police Science 58 (March): 80-86.

CLECKLEY, H.
  1941   The Mask of Sanity. St. Louis: Mosby (4th ed., 1964).

CLINARD, MARSHALL B., and DANIEL J. ABBOTT
  1973   Crime in Developing Countries. New York: Wiley.
  1976   "Community organization and property crime," in Short, 1976.

CLINARD, MARSHALL B., and RICHARD QUINNEY
  1967   Criminal Behavior Systems. New York: Holt, Rinehart and Winston.

CLINE, VICTOR B., ed.
  1974   Where Do You Draw the Line? Provo, Utah: Brigham Young University Press.

CLOWARD, RICHARD D., and OHLIN, LLOYD E.
  1960   Delinquency and Opportunity. New York: Free Press.

COBB, WILLIAM E.
  1973   "Theft and the two hypotheses," in Rottenberg, 1973.

COHEN, ALBERT K.
  1955   Delinquent Boys: The Culture of the Gang. New York: Free Press.
  1959   "The study of social disorganization and deviant behavior," in Merton et al.,
         1959.

COLEMAN, JAMES S.
  1961   The Adolescent Society. New York: Free Press.

COMITAS, LAMBROS
  1975   "The social nexus of Ganja in Jamaica," in Rubin, 1975.

COMMAGER, HENRY STEELE
  1974   The Defeat of America: Presidential Power and National Character. New
         York: Simon & Schuster.

COMMISSION ON OBSCENITY AND PORNOGRAPHY
  1970   Report. New York: Bantam Books/Random House.

COMSTOCK, GEORGE A., and ELIA RUBINSTEIN, eds.
  1972   Television and Social Behavior. Vol. III of Technical Report of the Surgeon
         General's Scientific Advisory Committee on Television and Social Behavior.
         HEW Publications, HSM 72-9058. Washington, D.C.: U.S. Government Print-
         ing Office.

CONKLIN, JOHN E.
  1972   Robbery and the Criminal Justice System. Philadelphia: Lippincott.
  1973   The Crime Establishment. Englewood Cliffs, N.J.: Prentice-Hall.

CONNOR, RALPH G.
  1962   "The self-concepts of alcoholics," in Pittman and Snyder, 1962.

REFERENCES   491

CONNOR, WALTER D.

1972   Deviance in Soviet Society. New York: Columbia University Press.

COSER, LEWIS

1956   The Functions of Social Conflict. New York: Free Press.

1967   Continuities in the Study of Social Conflict. New York: Free Press.

CRAIG, ROGER

1967   Sexual Psychopath Legislation. Washington, D.C.: President's Commission on Law Enforcement and Administration of Justice.

CRANCER, ALFRED, JR., JAMES M. DILLE, JACK C. DELAY, JEAN E. WALLACE, and MARTIN D. HAYKIN

1969   "Comparison of the effects of marijuana and alcohol on simulated driving performance." Science 164 (May 16, 1969): 851-54.

CREIGHTON, LUCY BLACK

1976   Pretenders to the Throne: The Consumer Movement in the United States. Lexington, Mass.: D.C. Heath.

CRESSEY, DONALD R.

1953   Other People's Money. New York: Free Press. (Republished 1971 by Wadsworth, Belmont, Calif.)

1965   "The respectable criminal." Trans-action 2 (March–April).

1969   Theft of a Nation. New York: Harper & Row.

1972   Criminal Organization. New York: Harper & Row.

CURTIS, LYNN A.

1974   Criminal Violence. Lexington, Mass.: D.C. Heath/Lexington Books.

CUSHMAN, PAUL, JR.

1974   "Relationship between narcotic addiction and crime." Federal Probation 38 (September): 38-43.

DATESMAN, SUSAN K., and FRANK R. SCARPITTI

1975   "Female delinquency and broken homes: A re-assessment." Criminology 13 (May): 33-55.

DAVIDSON, R. THEODORE

1974   Chicano Prisoners: The Key to San Quentin. New York: Holt, Rinehart and Winston.

DAVIS, F. JAMES

1952   "Crime news in Colorado newspapers." American Journal of Sociology 57 (January): 325-30.

DAVIS, KINGSLEY

1976   "Sexual behavior," in Robert K. Merton and Robert Nisbet, Contemporary Social Problems, 4th ed. New York: Harcourt Brace Jovanovich.

DAVIS, SHARON K., and PHILLIP W. DAVIS

1976   "Meanings and process in erotic offensiveness: An expose of exposees." Urban Life 5 (October): 377-96.

DAWLEY, DAVID

1973   A Nation of Lords. Garden City, N.Y.: Doubleday.

DE COURCY, PETER, and JUDITH DE COURCY

1973   A Silent Tragedy: Child Abuse in the Community. Port Washington, N.Y.: Alfred.

DEFLEUR, LOIS B.

1975 "Biasing influences on drug arrest records: Implications for deviance research." American Sociological Review 40 (February): 88-103.

DEFLEUR, MELVIN

1970 Theories of Mass Communication, 2nd ed. New York: McKay.

DE FRANCIS, VINCENT

1971 "Protecting the child victim of sex crimes committed by adults." Federal Probation 35 (September): 15-20.

DE FRANCO, EDWARD J.

1973 Anatomy of a Scam: A Case Study of a Planned Bankruptcy by Organized Crime. Washington, D.C.: U.S. Department of Justice, LEAA.

DELLA FAVE, L. RICHARD

1974 "The culture of poverty revisited: A strategy for research." Social Problems 21 (June): 609-21.

DELORA, JOANN S., and CAROL A. B. WARREN

1977 Understanding Sexual Interaction. Boston: Houghton Mifflin.

DEMAREE, R. G., JANICE F. NEMAN, L. J. SAVAGE, JR., and CHARLES R. KEE, JR.

1975 An Assessment of the Cost Effectiveness of Federally Supported Treatment for Drug Abusers. Report No. 75-18. Fort Worth: Texas Christian University Institute of Behavioral Research.

DEMBO, RICHARD, JAMES SCHMEIDLER, DEAN V. BABST, and DOUGLAS S. LIPTON

1977 "Drug information source credibility among junior and senior high school youths." American Journal of Drug and Alcohol Abuse 1 (March): 43-54.

DENENBERG, R. V.

1974 "Sex offenders treat themselves." Correction Magazine 1 (November-December): 53-64.

DENTLER, ROBERT A., and LAWRENCE J. MONROE

1961 "Social correlates of early adolescent theft." American Sociological Review 26 (October): 733-43.

DEPARTMENT of TRANSPORTATION and LEAA

1973 Cargo Theft and Organized Crime (TD 1.8:C 19/3). Washington, D.C.: U.S. Government Printing Office.

DERSHOWITZ, ALAN M.

1975 "Constitutional dimensions of civil commitment," in Bonnie and Sonnenreich, 1975.

DEUTSCHER, IRWIN, and ELIZABETH J. THOMPSON, eds.

1968 Among the People: Encounters with the Poor. New York: Basic Books.

DICKSON, DONALD T.

1968 "Bureaucracy and morality: An organizational perspective on a moral crusade." Social Problems 16 (Fall): 143-56.

DITMAN, KEITH S., GEORGE G. CRAWFORD, EDWARD W. FORGY, HERBERT MOSKOWITZ, and CRAIG MACANDREW

1967 "A controlled experiment on the use of court probation for drunk arrests." American Journal of Psychiatry 124 (August): 160-63.

DIX, GEORGE E.

1976 ''Differential processing of abnormal sex offenders: Utilization of California's Mentally Disordered Sex Offender Program.'' Journal of Criminal Law and Criminology 67 (June): 233-43.

DOLE, VINCENT P.

1974 ''Medicine and the criminal justice system.'' Annals of Internal Medicine 81 (November): 687-89.

DOLE, VINCENT P., and MARIE E. NYSWANDER

1976 ''Methadone maintenance treatment: A ten-year perspective.'' Journal of the American Medical Association 235 (May 10): 2117-19.

DONNELLY, RICHARD C., JOSEPH GOLDSTEIN, and RICHARD D. SCHWARTZ

1962 Criminal Law. New York: Free Press.

DOSHAY, LEWIS J.

1943 The Boy Sex Offender and His Later Career. New York: Grune & Stratton.

DOUGLAS, JACK D.

1977 ''A sociological theory of official deviance and public concerns with official deviance,'' in Douglas and Johnson, 1977.

DOUGLAS, JACK D., and JOHN M. JOHNSON, eds.

1977 Official Deviance. Philadelphia: Lippincott.

DRAPKIN, ISRAEL, and EMILIO VIANO, eds.

1975 Victimology: A New Focus. 5 Vols. Lexington, Mass.: D. C. Heath.

DRUCKER, PETER F.

1972 ''How to take the profit out of hard drugs.'' Saturday Review 55 (May): 26-27.

DUNBAR, ELLEN RUSSELL

1975 Politics and Policy Change. Ph.D. dissertation in Urban Studies, University of Southern California.

DUPONT, ROBERT L.

1974 ''Drug-abuse education a failure so far.'' Los Angeles Times, January 25, editorial section.

DURKHEIM, EMILE

1893 The Division of Labor in Society, trans. by George Simpson. New York: Free Press, 1947.

1895 The Rules of Sociological Method, 8th ed., trans. and ed. by Sarah A. Solovay and John H. Mueller, and ed. by G. E. G. Catlin. New York: Free Press, 1938.

DUSTER, TROY

1970 The Legislation of Morality. New York: Free Press.

EBERTS, PAUL, and KENT P. SCHWIRIAN

1968 ''Metropolitan crime rates and relative deprivation.'' Criminologica 5 (February): 43-52 (reprinted in Glaser, 1970).

EDELHERTZ, HERBERT

1970 The Nature, Impact and Prosecution of White-Collar Crime. Publication ICR 70-1. Washington, D.C.: U.S. Department of Justice, LEAA.

EDELHERTZ, HERBERT, and GILBERT GEIS

1974 Public Compensation to Victims of Crime. New York: Praeger.

EINSTADTER, WERNER J.
1969 "The social organization of armed robbery." Social Problems 17 (Summer): 64-83.

EISENSTADT, S. N.
1956 From Generation to Generation. New York: Free Press.

EISSLER, R. K., ed.
1949 Searchlights on Delinquency. New York: International Universities Press.

ELDREDGE, LAURENCE
1974 "The nationwide uproar over pardoning Nixon: Watergate trials are endangered." Los Angeles Times, opinion section, September 15.

ELLIOTT, DELBERT S.
1966 "Delinquency, school attendance and dropout." Social Problems 13 (Winter): 307-14.

ELLIOTT, DELBERT S., and HARWIN L. VOSS
1974 Delinquency and Dropout. Lexington, Mass. D. C. Heath.

ELLIS, DESMOND P., and PENELOPE AUSTIN
1971 "Menstruation and aggressive behavior in a correctional center for women." Journal of Criminal Law, Criminology and Police Science 62 (September): 388-95.

ELLIS, HERBERT C., and STANLEY M. NEWMAN
1971 "'Gowster,' 'Ivy-leaguer,' 'hustler,' 'conservative,' 'mackman' and 'continental': A functional analysis of six ghetto roles," in Leacock, 1971.

EMPEY, LAMAR T. and LUBECK, STEVEN G.
1971 Explaining Delinquency. Lexington, Mass.: D. C. Heath.

EMRICK, CHAD D.
1975 "A review of psychologically oriented treatment of alcoholism." Journal of Studies on Alcohol 36 (March): 88-108.

ENGLAND, RALPH W., JR.
1957 "What is responsible for satisfactory probation and post-probation outcome?" Journal of Criminal Law, Criminology and Police Science 47 (March-April): 667-76.

ERICKSON, MAYNARD L.
1971 "The group context of delinquent behavior." Social Problems 19 (Summer): 114-29.
1972 "The changing relationships between official and self-reported measures of delinquency: An exploratory predictive study." Journal of Criminal Law, Criminology and Police Science 63 (September): 388-95.
1973 "Group violations, socioeconomic status and official delinquency." Social Forces 52 (September): 41-52.

ERICKSON, MAYNARD L., and LAMAR T. EMPEY
1965 "Class position, peers and delinquency." Sociology and Social Research 49 (April): 268-82.

ERIKSON, ERIK
1963 Childhood and Society, 2nd ed. New York: Norton.
1968 Identity: Youth and Crisis. New York: Norton.

ERIKSON, KAI T.
 1966   Wayward Puritans. New York: Wiley.

ERLANGER, HOWARD
 1974a "The empirical status of the subculture of violence thesis." Social Problems
        22 (December): 280-92.
 1974b "Social class and corporal punishment in childrearing: A reassessment."
        American Sociological Review 39 (February): 68-85.
 1975   "Is there a 'subculture of violence' in the South?" Journal of Criminal Law
        and Criminology 66 (December): 483-90.

ERLANSON, OTTO
 1941   "The scene of a sex offense as related to the residence of the offender."
        Journal of Criminal Law and Criminology 31 (July-August): 339-42.

ERSKINE, HAZEL
 1972   "The polls: Gun control." Public Opinion Quarterly 36 (Fall): 455-69.

ESPOSITO, JOHN C., and LARRY J. SILVERMAN
 1970   Vanishing Air: Ralph Nader's Study Group Report on Air Pollution. New
        York: Grossman.

ESSELSTYN, T. CONWAY
 1968   "Prostitution in the United States." Annals of the American Academy of
        Political and Social Science 376 (March): 123-35.

EYNON, THOMAS G., and WALTER C. RECKLESS
 1961   "Companionship and delinquency onset," British Journal of Criminology 2
        (October): 162-70.

EYSENCK, H. J.
 1964   Crime and Personality. Boston: Houghton Mifflin.

FARBER, BERNARD
 1968   Mental Retardation. Boston: Houghton Mifflin.

FARLEY, REYNOLDS
 1977   "Trends in racial inequalities: Have the gains of the 1960s disappeared in the
        1970s?" American Sociological Review 42 (April): 189-208.

FEDERAL BUREAU OF INVESTIGATION (FBI)
 1939   Ten Years of Uniform Crime Reporting, 1930-1939. Washington, D.C.: U.S.
        Department of Justice.
 1976   Crime in the United States, 1975: Uniform Crime Reports. Washington, D.C.:
        U.S. Department of Justice (similar reports for preceding years also are
        cited).

FEDERAL HOME LOAN BANK BOARD
 1977   "Fraud and embezzlement: Increase of 17 percent leads rise in crimes
        against financial institutions." Federal Home Loan Bank Board Journal 10
        (March): 19-20.

FEENEY, FLOYD, and ADRIANNE WEIR
 1975   "The prevention and control of robbery." Criminology 13 (May): 102-5.

FERDINAND, THEODORE N.
 1967   "The criminal patterns of Boston since 1849." American Journal of Sociol-
        ogy 73 (July): 84-99.

FESHBACH, S.
1961   "The stimulating versus cathartic effects of a vicarious aggressive activity." Journal of Abnormal and Social Psychology 63 (September): 381-85.

FESHBACH, S., and R. D. SINGER
1971   Television and Aggression. San Francisco: Jossey-Bass.

FINESTONE, HAROLD
1957a   "Narcotics and criminality." Law and Contemporary Problems 22 (Winter): 69-85 (reprinted in O'Donnell and Ball, 1966).
1957b   "Cats, Kicks and Color." Social Problems 5 (July): 3-13.

FINGARETTE, HERBERT
1975   "Addiction and criminal responsibility." Yale Law Journal 84 (January): 413-44.

FISHER, GENE A., and MAYNARD L. ERICKSON
1973   "On assessing the effects of official reactions to juvenile delinquency." Journal of Research in Crime and Delinquency 10 (July): 177-94.

FLAMMANG, C.J.
1975   "Interviewing child victims of sex offenders," in Schultz, 1975.

FLEISHER, BELTON M.
1966   The Economics of Delinquency. Chicago: Quadrangle Books.

FONTANA, VINCENT J.
1973   Somewhere a Child Is Crying. New York: Macmillan.

FORD FOUNDATION
1972   Dealing with Drug Abuse. New York: Praeger.

FOULKS, D.
1967   "Dreams of the male child." Journal of Abnormal Psychology 72 (December): 457-67.

FRANTZ, JOE B.
1969   "The frontier tradition: An invitation to violence," in Graham and Gurr, 1969.

FREASE, DEAN E.
1973   "Delinquency, social class and the schools." Sociology and Social Research 57 (July): 443-59.

FREEMAN, LINTON C., and ROBERT F. WINCH
1957   "Societal complexity: An empirical test of a typology of societies." American Journal of Sociology 62 (March): 461-66.

FREUD, SIGMUND
1940   An Outline of Psychoanalysis, trans. by James Strachey. New York: Norton, 1949.

FRIEDENBERG, EDGAR Z.
1959   The Vanishing Adolescent. New York: Dell.

FRISBIE, LOUISE V.
1969   Another Look at Sex Offenders in California. California Mental Health Research Monograph No. 12. Sacramento: Department of Mental Hygiene.

FUJII, EDWIN T.
1974   "Public investment in the rehabilitation of heroin addicts." Social Science Quarterly 55 (June): 39-51.

REFERENCES   497

GAGNON, JOHN H.

1965 "Female child victims of sex offenses." Social Problems 13 (Fall): 176-92.

1974 "Sexual conduct and crime," in Glaser, 1974.

GAGNON, JOHN H., and WILLIAM SIMON

1973 Sexual Conduct. Chicago: Aldine.

GAMSON, WILLIAM A.

1961 "A theory of coalition formation." American Sociological Review 26 (June): 373-82.

1975 The Strategy of Social Protest. Homewood, Ill.: Dorsey Press.

GASTIL, RAYMOND D.

1971 "Homicide and a regional culture of violence." American Sociological Review 36 (June): 412-27.

GEBHARD, PAUL H., JOHN H. GAGNON, WARDELL B. POMEROY, and CORNELIA V. CHRISTENSON

1965 Sex Offenders. New York: Harper & Row and Paul B. Hoeber.

GEIS, GILBERT

1959 "Sociology, criminology and criminal law." Social Problems 7 (Summer): 40-47.

1968 (ed.) White Collar Criminal: The Offender in Business and the Professions. New York: Atherton.

1972 Not the Law's Business. NIMH Crime and Delinquency Issues Monograph. DHEW Publication No. (HSM) 72-9132. Washington, D.C.: U.S. Government Printing Office.

1974 "Avocational crime," in Glaser, 1974.

1977 "Forcible rape: An introduction," in Duncan Chappell, Robley Geis, and Gilbert Geis, Forcible Rape: The Crime, the Victim, and the Offender. New York: Columbia University Press.

GEIS, GILBERT, TED L. HOUSTON, and RICHARD WRIGHT

1976 "Compensating Good Samaritans." Crime Prevention Review of the Attorney General of California 3 (April): 28-35.

GELFAND, D.M., D.P. HARTMANN, P. WALDER, and B. PAGE

1973 "Who reports shoplifters?" Journal of Personality and Social Psychology 25 (February): 276-83.

GELLES, RICHARD J.

1972 The Violent Home. Beverly Hills, Calif.: Sage.

GERARD, DONALD L., and GERHART SAENGER

1966 Out-Patient Treatment of Alcoholism. Toronto: University of Toronto Press.

GERTH, H.H., and C. WRIGHT MILLS

1946 From Max Weber. New York: Oxford University Press.

GIBBONS, DON C.

1965 Changing the Lawbreaker. Englewood Cliffs, N.J.: Prentice-Hall.

GIGEROFF, ALEXANDER K., J.W. MOHR, R.E. TURNER

1968 "Sex offenders on probation: The exhibitionist." Federal Probation 32 (September): 18-21.

GIL, DAVID

1971 Violence against Children. Cambridge, Mass.: Harvard University Press.

GILLIS, JOHN R.

1974 Youth and History. New York: Academic Press.

GLASER, DANIEL

1956 "Criminality theories and behavioral images." American Journal of Sociology 61 (March): 433-44.

1962 "The differential association theory of crime," in Arnold Rose, Human Behavior and Social Processes. Boston: Houghton Mifflin.

1969 The Effectiveness of a Prison and Parole System, rev. ed. Indianapolis: Bobbs-Merrill.

1970 (ed.) Crime in the City, New York: Harper & Row.

1971 Social Deviance. Chicago: Markham/Rand McNally.

1972 Adult Crime and Social Policy. Englewood Cliffs, N.J.: Prentice-Hall.

1973 Routinizing Evaluation: Getting Feedback on Effectiveness of Crime and Delinquency Programs. NIMH Crime and Delinquency Issues Monograph, DHEW Publication No. (HSM) 73-9123, Washington D.C.: U.S. Government Printing Office.

1974 (ed.) Handbook of Criminology. Chicago: Rand McNally.

1975 Strategic Criminal Justice Planning. NIMH Crime and Delinquency Issues Monograph, DHEW Publication No. (ADM) 75-195. Washington, D.C.: U.S. Government Printing Office.

GLASER, DANIEL, and KENT RICE

1959 "Crime, age and employment." American Sociological Review 24 (October): 679-86.

GLASER, DANIEL, BERNARD LANDER, and WILLIAM ABBOTT

1971 "Opiate addicted and nonaddicted siblings in a slum area." Social Problems 18 (Spring): 510-21.

GLASER, DANIEL, and MAX S. ZEIGLER

1974 "Use of the death penalty v. outrage at murder." Crime and Delinquency 20 (October): 333-38.

GLASSER, WILLIAM

1965 Reality Therapy. New York: Harper & Row.

GLUCKMAN, MAX, ed.

1962 Essays on the Rituals of Social Relations. Manchester, England: University of Manchester Press.

GLUECK, SHELDON, and ELEANOR H. GLUECK

1950 Unravelling Juvenile Delinquency. New York: Commonwealth Fund.

1956 Physique and Delinquency. New York: Harper.

GOFFMAN, ERVING

1952 "On cooling the mark out: Some aspects of adaptation to failure." Psychiatry 15 (November): 451-63 (reprinted in Arnold Rose, Human Behavior and Social Processes. Boston: Houghton Mifflin, 1962).

1961 Asylums. Garden City, N.Y.: Doubleday.

1963 Behavior in Public Places. New York: Free Press.

1967 Interaction Ritual. Garden City, N.Y.: Doubleday.

GOLD, MARTIN

1963 Status Forces in Delinquent Boys. Ann Arbor: Institute of Social Research, University of Michigan.

1970   Delinquent Behavior in an American City. Belmont, Calif.: Brooks/Cole.

GOLD, MARTIN, and ELIZABETH DOUVAN, eds.
1969   Adolescent Development. Boston: Allyn & Bacon.

GOLDBERG, PETER B., and JAMES V. DELONG
1972   "Federal expenditures on drug abuse control," in Ford Foundation, 1972.

GOLDMAN, HAROLD, SIMON DINITZ, LEWIS LINDNER, THOMAS FOSTER, and HARRY ALLEN
1974   A Designed Treatment Program of Sociopathy by Means of Drugs: A Summary Report. Monograph No. 29. Columbus, Ohio: Ohio State University Program for the Study of Crime and Delinquency, College of Administrative Science, School of Public Administration.

GOLDSTEIN, ABRAHAM S.
1967   The Insanity Defense. New Haven: Yale University Press.

GOLDSTEIN, AVRAM
1975   "The status of methadone maintenance," in Problems of Drug Dependency. Washington National Academy of Science.
1976   "Heroin Addiction." Archives of General Psychiatry 33 (March): 853-76.

GOLDSTEIN, JOSEPH, and JAY KATZ
1963   "Abolish the insanity defense—Why not?" Yale Law Journal 72 (April): 853-76.

GOLDSTEIN, MICHAEL J., HAROLD S. KANT, and JOHN J. HARTMAN
1973   Pornography and Sexual Deviance. Berkeley: University of California Press.

GOODE, ERICH
1970   The Marijuana Smokers. New York: Basic Books.
1972   Drugs in American Society. New York: Knopf.

GOODE, WILLIAM J.
1971   "Force and violence in the family." Journal of Marriage and the Family 33 (November): 624-36 (reprinted in Steinmetz and Straus, 1974).

GORDON, NORMAN B.
1973   "The functional status of the methadone maintained person," in Luiz R.S. Simons and Martin B. Gold, Discrimination and the Addict, Beverly Hills, Calif., 1973.

GORDON, ROBERT A.
1967   "Issues in the ecological study of delinquency." American Sociological Review 32 (December 1967): 927-44.

GOULD, LEROY C.
1969   "The changing structure of property crime in an affluent society." Social Forces 48 (September): 50-59.

GOULD, LEROY C., ANDREW L. WALKER, LANSING E. CRANE, and CHARLES W. LIDZ
1974   Connections: Notes from the Heroin World. New Haven: Yale University Press.

GOULDNER, ALVIN
1954   Wildcat Strike. Yellow Springs, Ohio: Antioch Press.
1970   The Coming Crisis of Western Sociology. New York: Basic Books.

GOVE, WALTER R.
1970   "Societal reaction as an explanation of mental illness: An evaluation." American Sociological Review 35 (October): 873-84.

GRAHAM, HUGH DAVIS, and TED ROBERT GURR

1969   Violence in America. New York: New American Library (also published in Washington, D.C., by the U.S. Government Printing Office as a Task Force Report of the National Commission on the Causes and Prevention of Violence).

GRAVES, WILLIAM F.

1956   "A doctor looks at capital punishment." Medical Arts and Science: Journal of the Loma Linda University School of Medicine, (4th Quarter): 137-41 (reprinted in Bedau, 1964).

GREEN, MARK J., ed.

1973   The Monopoly Makers: Ralph Nader's Study Group Report on Regulation and Competition. New York: Grossman.

GREEN, MARK J., BEVERLY C. MOORE, JR., and BRUCE WASSERSTEIN

1972   The Closed Enterprise System: Ralph Nader's Study Group Report on Antitrust Enforcement. New York: Grossman.

GRUPP, STANLEY E.

1970   "The 'Marihuana Muddle' as reflected in California arrest statistics and dispositions." Law and Society Review 5 (November): 251-69.

1971   "Prior criminal record and adult marihuana arrest dispositions." Journal of Criminal Law, Criminology and Police Science 62 (March): 74-79.

GUSFIELD, JOSEPH R.

1963   Symbolic Crusade. Urbana: University of Illinois Press.

HACKNEY, SHELTON

1969   "Southern violence," in Graham and Gurr, 1969.

HALL, JEROME

1952   Theft, Law and Society, rev. ed. Indianapolis: Bobbs-Merrill.

HALL, REIS H., MILDRED MILAZZO, and JUDY POSNER

1966   A Descriptive and Comparative Study of Recidivisim in Pre-Release Guidance Center Releases. Washington, D.C.: Bureau of Prisons, U.S. Department of Justice.

HANNEMAN, GERHARD J.

1973   "Communicating drug-abuse information among college students." Public Opinion Quarterly 37 (Summer): 171-91.

HANNERZ, ULF

1969   Soulside. New York: Columbia University Press.

HARDT, ROBERT H.

1968   "Delinquency and social class: Bad kids or good cops," in Deutscher and Thompson, 1968.

HARDT, ROBERT H., and SANDRA J. PETERSON

1968   "Neighborhood status and delinquent activity as indexed by police records and a self report survey." Criminologica 6 (May): 37-47.

HARE, R. D.

1970   Psychopathy: Theory and Research. New York: Wiley.

HARGREAVES, DAVID

1967   Social Relations in a Secondary School. New York: Humanities Press.

REFERENCES   501

HARMS, ERNEST, ed.

1973 Drugs and Youth: The Challenge of Today. New York: Pergamon Press.

HARTMAN, A. ARTHUR, and ROBERT NICOLAY

1966 "Sexually deviant behavior in expectant fathers." Journal of Abnormal Psychology 71 (June): 232-34.

HAWKINS, GORDON

1969 "God and the Mafia." Public Interest 14 (Winter): 24-38, 40-51.

HAWKS, DAVID

1974 "The epidemiology of narcotic addiction in the United Kingdom," in Josephson and Carroll, 1974.

HELFER, RAY E., and C. HENRY KEMPE, eds.

1968 The Battered Child. Chicago: University of Chicago Press.

HELLER, CELIA S.

1966 Mexican American Youth. New York: Random House.

HELLMAN, ARTHUR D.

1975 Laws against Marijuana: The Price We Pay. Urbana: University of Illinois Press.

HELMS, DENNIS J., THOMAS LESCAULT, and ALFRED A. SMITH

1975 "Cocaine: Some observations on its history, legal classification and pharmacology." Contemporary Drug Problems 4 (Summer): 195-215.

HENLY, JAMES R., and LARRY D. ADAMS

1973 "Marijuana use in post-collegiate cohorts." Social Problems 20 (Spring): 514-20.

HERMAN, ROBERT D., ed.

1967 Gambling. New York: Harper & Row.

HESS, HENNER

1973 Mafia and Mafiosi: The Structure of Power. Westmead, England and Lexington, Mass.: Saxon House/D.C. Heath.

HEWITT, L. E., and R. L. JENKINS

1946 Fundamental Patterns of Maladjustment. Illinois Department of Public Welfare.

HIBBERT, CHRISTOPHER

1963 The Roots of Evil. Boston: Little, Brown.

HILGARD, ERNEST R., and GORDON R. BOWER

1975 Theories of Learning, 4th ed. Englewood Clifs, N.J.: Prentice-Hall.

HIMMELWEIT, H. T., A.N. OPPENHEIM, and P. VINCE.

1958 Television and the Child. London: Oxford University Press.

HINDELANG, MICHAEL J.

1971a "Extroversion, neuroticism and self-reported delinquent involvement." Journal of Research on Crime and Delinquency 8 (January): 23-31.

1971b "Age, sex, and the versatility of delinquent involvments." Social Problems 18 (Spring): 522-35.

1971c "The social vs. solitary nature of delinquency involvements." British Journal of Criminology 11 (April): 167-75.

1972 "The relationship of self-reported delinquency to scales of the CIP and

MMPI." Journal of Criminal Law, Criminology and Police Science 63 (March): 75-81.

1974a "The Uniform Crime Reports revisited." Journal of Criminal Justice 2 (Spring): 1-17.

1974b "Decisions of shoplifting victims to invoke the criminal justice process." Social Problems 21 (April): 580-93.

1976 Criminal Victimization in Eight American Cities. Cambridge, Mass.: Ballinger.

HIRSCH, CHARLES S., NORMAN B. RUSHFORTH, AMASA B. FORD, and LESTER ADELSON
1973 "Homicide and suicide in a metropolitan county." Journal of the American Medical Association 223 (February, 19): 900-905.

HIRSCHI, TRAVIS
1969 Causes of Delinquency. Berkeley: University of California Press.

HOBBS, A. H.
1943 "Criminality in Philadelphia: 1790-1810 compared with 1937." American Sociological Review 8 (April): 198-202.

HOBSBAWM, E. J.
1959 Primitive Rebels. New York: Norton.

HODGE, R. SESSIONS, V. J. WALTER, and W. GREY WALTER
1953 "Juvenile delinquency: An electrophysiological, psychological and social study." British Journal of Delinquency 3 (January): 155-72.

HOFSTADTER, RICHARD
1955 Social Darwinism in American Thought. Boston: Beacon Press.

HOFSTADTER, RICHARD, and MICHAEL WALLACE, eds.
1970 American Violence. New York: Knopf.

HOLAHAN, JOHN F.
1972 "The economics of heroin," in Ford Foundation, 1972.

HOMANS, GEORGE C.
1974 Social Behavior: Its Elementary Forms, rev. ed. New York: Harcourt Brace Jovanovich.

HOMER, FREDERIC D.
1974 Guns and Garlic: Myths and Realities of Organized Crime. West Lafayette, Ind.: Purdue University Press.

HORNING, DONALD N. M.
1970 "Blue-collar theft: Conceptions of property, attitudes toward pilfering, and work group norms in a modern industrial plant," in Smigel and Ross, 1970.

HOROWITZ, RUTH, and GARY SCHWARTZ
1974 "Honor, normative ambiguity and gang violence." American Sociological Review 39 (April): 238-51.

HOWARD, JAMES L., MYRON B. LIPTZIN, and CLIFFORD B. REIFLER
1973 "Is pornography a problem?" Journal of Social Issues 29 (No. 3): 133-45.

HOWITT, DENNIS, and GUY CUMBERBATCH
1975 Mass Media, Violence and Society. New York: Wiley.

HUDSON, JOE, and BURT GALAWAY, eds.
1975 Considering the Victim. Springfield, Ill.: C. C. Thomas.

HUGHES, GRAHAM

1964 "The crime of incest." Journal of Criminal Law, Criminology and Police Science 55 (September): 322-31.

HULETT, J. EDWARD, JR.

1966 "A symbolic interactionist model of human communication: Part One: The general model of social behavior." AV Communication Review 14 (Spring): 5-33.

HUMPHREYS, LAUD

1970 Tearoom Trade: Impersonal Sex in Public Places. Chicago: Aldine.

1972 Out of the Closets: The Sociology of Homosexual Liberation. Englewood Cliffs, N.J.: Prentice-Hall.

HUNT, LEON G., and CARL D. CHAMBERS

1976 The Heroin Epidemics: A Study of Heroin Use in the U.S., 1965-75. New York: Spectrum Publications.

HUNT, MORTON

1974 Sexual Behavior in the 1970's. Chicago: Playboy Press (reprinted 1975 by Dell Publishing Co.).

IANNI, FRANCIS A. J.

1972 A Family Business: Kinship and Social Control in Organized Crime. New York: Russell Sage.

1974a Black Mafia: Ethnic Succession in Organized Crime. New York: Simon & Schuster.

1974b "New Mafia: Black, Hispanic and Italian styles." Society 11 (March-April): 26-39.

INCIARDI, JAMES A.

1974 "Vocational crime," in Glaser, 1974.

1975 Careers in Crime. Chicago: Rand McNally.

INCIARDI, JAMES A., and DAVID M. PETERSEN

1973 "Gaff joints and shell games: A century of circus grift." Journal of Popular Culture 6 (Spring): 592-606.

INSTITUTE FOR JUVENILE RESEARCH

(Undated) Juvenile Delinquency in Illinois: Highlights of the 1972 Adolescent Survey. Chicago: The Institute of the State Department of Mental Health.

ISBELL, HARRIS, C. W. GORODETZKY, D. JASINSKI, U. CLOUSSEN, F. V. SPULAK, and F. KORTE

1967 "Effects of delta-nine-trans-tetrahydrocannabinol in man." Psychopharmacologica 11 (s): 184-188.

JACKSON, BRUCE

1969 Outside the Law: A Thief's Primer. New York: Macmillan (reprinted 1972 by Transaction Books, distributed by E. P. Dutton).

1972 In the Life: Versions of the Criminal Experience. New York: Holt, Rinehart and Winston (reprinted 1972 by Mentor Books, New American Library).

JACKSON, DON

1972 "Castrations revealed." The Freeworld Times 1 (April-May): 11-14 (reprinted from the California Prisoners Union Anvil, August-September 1971).

JAFFE, JEROME H., CHARLES R. SCHUSTER, BETH B. SMITH, and PAUL H. BLACHLEY

1970 "Comparison of acetylmethadol and methadone in the treatment of long-term heroin users.'' Journal of the American Medical Association 211 (March 16): 1834-36.

JAFFE, JEROME H., and EDWARD C. SENAY
1971 ''Methadone and L-Methadyl Acetele: Use in management of narcotic addicts.'' Journal of the American Medical Association 216 (February): 1303-5 (reprinted in Chambers and Brill, 1973).

JANSYN, LEON R., JR.
1966 ''Solidarity and delinquency in a street corner group.'' American Sociological Review 31 (October): 600-614.

JEFFERY, CLARENCE RAY
1957 ''The development of law in early English society.'' Journal of Criminal Law, Criminology and Police Science 47 (March-April): 647-66.
1967 Criminal Responsibility and Mental Disease. Springfield, Ill.: C. C. Thomas.

JEFFERY, ROBERT, and STEPHEN WOOLPERT
1974 ''Work furlough as an alternative to incarceration: An assessment of its effects on recidivsim and social costs.'' Journal of Criminal Law and Criminology 65 (September): 405-15.

JENSEN, GARY F.
1969 ''Crime doesn't pay: Correlates of a shared misunderstanding.'' Social Problems 17 (Fall): 189-201.
1972 ''Parents, peers and delinquent action: A test of the differential association perspective.'' American Journal of Sociology 78 (November): 562-75.
1976 ''Race, achievement and delinquency: A further look at *Delinquency in a Birth Cohort.*'' American Journal of Sociology 82 (September): 379-87.

JESSOR, SHIRLEY L., and RICHARD JESSOR
1975 ''Transition from virginity to nonvirginity among youth.'' Developmental Psychology 11 (July): 473-84.

JOE, G. W., PHILIP PERSON, JR.,S. B. SELLS, and R. L. RETKA
1972 An Evaluation Study of Methadone and Drug Free Therapies for Opiate Addiction. Preliminary Draft, IBR Report 72-14 Fort Worth: Institute of Behavioral Research, Texas Christian University.

JOHNSON, BRUCE D.
1972 Social Determinants of the Use of Dangerous Drugs by College Students. New York: Wiley.

JOHNSON, GREGORY, and JOHN NEWMEYER
1975 ''Pleasure, punishment and moral indignation.'' Sociology and Social Research 59 (January): 82-95.

JOHNSTON, LLOYD
1973 Drugs and American Youth. Ann Arbor: Institute for Social Research.
1976 Statement to the Press, October 1, 1975, with tables revised August 1976, on ''Monitoring the Future,'' research project of the Institute for Social Research, Ann Arbor, Michigan, updating Johnston, 1973.

JONES, WELTON A., and JOHN E. BERECOCHEA
1973 California Department of Corrections Methadone Maintenance Program: An Evaluation. Sacramento: Department of Corrections, Research Report No. 50.

JOSEPHSON, ERIC, and ELEANOR E. CARROLL
  1974 Drug Use: Epidemiological and Sociological Approaches. Washington, D.C.: Hemisphere Publishing Co., and New York: Wiley/Halsted.

JUDSON, HORACE FREELAND
  1974 Heroin Addiction: What Americans Can Learn from the English Experience. New York: Random House (published in 1973 as "Heroin Addiction in Britain").

JULIEN, ROBERT M.
  1975 A Primer of Drug Action. San Francisco: Freeman.

KADISH, MORTIMER R., and SANFORD H. KADISH
  1973 Discretion to Disobey: A Study of Lawful Departures from Legal Rules. Stanford: Stanford University Press.

KAHANE, REUVEN
  1975 "Informal youth organizations: A general model." Sociological Inquiry 45 (4): 17-28.

KANIN, EUGENE J.
  1957 "Male aggression in dating-courtship relations." American Journal of Sociology 43 (September): 197-204.

KAPLAN, JOHN
  1970 Marijuana—The New Prohibition. New York: Crowell.
  1973 "Drug dealing and the law," in Blum, 1973.

KAPLAN, LAWRENCE J., and DENNIS KESSLER
  1976 An Economic Analysis of Crime. Springfield, Ill.: C. C. Thomas.

KARACKI, LARRY, and JACKSON TOBY
  1962 "The uncommitted adolescent: Candidate for gang socialization." Sociological Inquiry 32 (Spring): 203-15.

KAREN, ROBERT L., and ROLAND C. BOWER
  1968 "A behavioral analysis of a social control agency: Synanon." Journal of Research in Crime and Delinquency 5 (January): 18-34.

KATZ, ELIHU
  1957 "The two-step flow of communication: An up-to-date report on a hypothesis." Public Opinion Quarterly 21 (Spring): 61-78.
  1960 "Communication research and the image of society: Convergence of two traditions." American Journal of Sociology 65 (March): 435-40.

KEISER, R. LINCOLN
  1969 The Vice Lords: Warriors of the Streets. New York: Holt, Rinehart and Winston.

KELLY, DELOS H.
  1974 "Track position and delinquent involvement." Sociology and Social Research 58 (July): 380-86.

KENNETT, LEE, and JAMES L. ANDERSON
  1975 The Gun in America. Westport, Conn.: Greenwood Press.

KERR, K. AUSTIN, ed.
  1973 The Politics of Moral Behavior: Prohibition and Drug Abuse. Reading, Mass.: Addison-Wesley.

KEUP, W.
1972   Drug Abuse: Covert Concepts and Research. Springfield, Ill.: C. C. Thomas.

KINSEY, ALFRED C., WARDELL B. POMEROY, and CLYDE E. MARTIN
1948   Sexual Behavior in the Human Male. Philadelphia: Saunders.

KINSEY, ALFRED C., WARDELL B. POMEROY, CLYDE E. MARTIN, and PAUL H. GEBHARD
1953   Sexual Behavior in the Human Female. Philadelphia: Saunders.

KIRKPATRICK, C., and KANIN, E.
1957   "Male sex aggression on a university campus." American Sociological Review 22 (January): 52-58.

KITCHENER, HOWARD, ANNESLEY K. SCHMIDT, and DANIEL GLASER
1977   "How persistent is post-prison success?" Federal Probation 41 (March): 9-15.

KITSUSE, JOHN I., and AARON V. CICOUREL
1963   "A note on the uses of official statistics." Social Problems (Fall): 131-39.

KITTRIE, NICHOLAS N.
1971   The Right to Be Different. Baltimore: Johns Hopkins University Press.

KLEIN, MALCOLM W.
1971   Street Gangs and Street Workers. Englewood Cliffs, N.J.: Prentice-Hall.

KLEIN, MALCOLM W., SUSAN LABIN ROSENSWEIG, and RONALD BATES
1975   "The ambiguous juvenile arrest." Criminology 13 (May): 78-89.

KLOCKARS, CARL B.
1974   The Professional Fence. New York: Free Press.

KNOX, S. J.
1968   "Epileptic automatism and violence." Medicine, Science and the Law 8: 96-104.

KNUTSON, JOHN F., ed.
1973   The Control of Aggression. Chicago: Aldine.

KOBRIN, SOLOMON
1951   "The conflict of values in delinquency areas." American Sociological Review 16 (October): 653-61.

KOLKO, GABRIEL
1963   The Triumph of Conservatism. New York: Free Press.

KORNBLUM, ALLAN N.
1976   The Moral Hazards. Lexington, Mass.: D.C. Heath.

KOZLOFF, MARTIN A.
1976   "Systems of structured exchange: Changing families of severely deviant children." Sociological Practice 1 (Fall): 86-104.

KOZOL, HARRY L., RICHARD J. BOUCHER, and RALPH F. GAROFALO
1972   "Diagnosis and treatment of dangerousness." Crime and Delinquency 18 (October): 371-92.

KRAMER, HEINRICH, and JAMES SPRENGER
1484   The Malleus Maleficarum, trans. by M. Summers. New York: Dover, 1971.

KRAMER, JOHN C.
1976   "From demon to ally—How mythology has, and may yet, alter national drug policy." Journal of Drug Issues 6 (Fall): 390-406.

KRAUT, ROBERT E.

1976 "Deterrent and definitional influences on shoplifting." Social Problems 23 (February): 358-68.

KROHM, GREGORY

1973 "The pecuniary incentives of property crime," in Rottenberg, 1973.

KROHN, MARVIN, GORDON P. WALDO, and THEODORE G. CHIRICOS

1974 "Self-reported delinquency: A comparison of structured interviews and self-administered checklists." Journal of Criminal Law, Criminology and Police Science 65 (December): 545-53.

KULIK, JAMES A., KENNETH B. STEIN, and THEODORE R. SARBIN

1966 "Disclosure of delinquent behavior under conditions of anonymity and non-anonymity." American Psychologist 21 (July): 651.

KUTCHINSKY, BERL

1973 "The effect of easy availability of pornography on the incidence of sex crimes: The Danish experience." Journal of Social Issues 29 (No. 3): 163-81.

KVARACEUS, WILLIAM C., and WALTER B. MILLER

1959 Delinquent Behavior. Washington, D.C.: National Education Association.

LAMBORN, LEROY L.

1968 "Toward a victim orientation in criminal theory." Rutgers Law Review 22 (Summer): 733-68 (reprinted in Hudson and Galaway, 1975).

LANE, ROBERT E.

1951 "Why businessmen violate the law." Journal of Criminal Law, Criminology and Police Science 44 (July): 151-65.

LANE, ROGER

1969 "Urbanization and criminal violence in the 19th century: Massachusetts as a test case," in Graham and Gurr, 1969.

1976 "Criminal violence in America: The first hundred years." Annals of the American Academy of Political and Social Science 423 (January): 1-13.

LASAGNA, LOUIS, JOHN M. VAN FELSINGER, and HENRY K. BEECHER

1955 "Drug-induced mood changes in man." Journal of the American Medical Association 157 (March 19): 1006-20; (March 26): 1113-19.

LAUER, BRIAN, ELSA TEN BROECK, and MOSES GROSSMAN

1974 "Battered child syndrome." Pediatrics 54 (July): 67-70.

LAW ENFORCEMENT ASSISTANCE ADMINISTRATION (LEAA)

1970 The St. Louis Detoxification and Diagnostic Evaluation Center. Washington, D.C.: U.S. Government Printing Office.

1973 Methadone Treatment Manual. Proscriptive Package Series. Washington, D.C.: U.S. Department of Justice.

1974a Crime in the Nation's Five Largest Cities: Advance Report (April 1974).

1974b Crime in Eight American Cities: Advance Report (July 1974).

1974c Criminal Victimization in the U.S.: January-June 1973 (November 1974).

1975a Criminal Victimization in the Nation's Five Largest Cities (April 1975).

1975b Criminal Victimization in the U.S. 1973 Advance Report, Vol. 1 (May 1975).

1975c Criminal Victimization Surveys in 13 American Cities (June 1975).

1975d Exemplary Projects; Prosecution of Economic Crime. Washington, D.C.: U.S. Government Printing Office.

1976a Survey of Inmates of State Correctional Facilities, 1974: Advance Report. Washington, D.C.: U.S. Government Printing Office.

1976b Criminal Victimization in the U.S.: A Comparison of 1973 and 1974 Findings (No. SD-NCP-N-3). Washington, D.C.: U.S. Department of Justice.

1976c The Major Offense Bureau: Bronx District Attorney's Office, New York. Exemplary Project Report Series. Washington, D.C.: U.S. Department of Justice.

LEACH, BARRY

1973 "Does Alcoholics Anonymous really work?" in Peter G. Bourne and Ruth Fox, Alcoholism. New York: Academic Press.

LEACOCK, ELEANOR B., ed.

1971 The Culture of Poverty: A Critique. New York: Simon & Schuster.

LECLAIR, DANIEL P.

1975 An Analysis of Recidivism among Residents Released from Boston State and Shirley Pre-Release Centers During 1972-1973. Boston: Massachusetts Department of Correction.

LEFF, ARTHUR ALLEN

1976 Swindling and Selling. New York: Free Press.

LEGGETT, JOHN C.

1968 Class, Race and Labor. New York: Oxford University Press.

LEJEUNE, ROBERT, and NICHOLAS ALEX

1973 "On being mugged: The event and its aftermath." Urban Life and Culture 2 (October): 259-87.

LEMERT, EDWIN M.

1953 "An isolation and closure theory of naive check forgery." Journal of Criminal Law, Criminology and Police Science 44 (September-October): 296-307 (reprinted in Lemert, 1967).

1958 "The behavior of the systematic check forger." Social Problems 6 (Fall): 141-49 (reprinted in Lemert, 1967).

1967 Human Deviance, Social Problems and Social Control. Englewood Cliffs, N.J.: Prentice-Hall.

LENIHAN, KENNETH J.

1974 Theft among Ex-prisoners: Is It Economically Motivated? Washington, D.C.: Bureau of Social Science Research.

LENKE, L.

1974 "Criminal police and public opinion towards crimes of violence," in Collected Studies in Criminological Research, Volume XI: Violence in Society. Strasbourg: Council of Europe.

LERMAN, PAUL

1967 "Gangs, networks and subcultural diversity." American Journal of Sociology 73 (July): 63-72.

LETKEMANN, PETER

1973 Crime as Work. Englewood Cliffs, N.J.: Prentice-Hall.

LEVIN, MARK M., and ROSEMARY C. SARRI

1974 Juvenile Delinquency: A Comparative Analysis of Legal Codes in the U.S. Ann Arbor: National Assessment of Juvenile Corrections, University of Michigan.

LEVINE, DAVID
  1970 "Criminal behavior and mental institutionalization." Journal of Clinical Psy-
        chology 26 (July 1970): 279-84.
LEVY, JERROLD E., and STEPHEN J. KUNITZ
  1974 Indian Drinking. New York: Wiley.
LEWIS, MICHAEL
  1970 "Structural deviance and normative conformity: The 'hustle' and the
        'gang,' " in Glaser, 1970.
LEWIS, MICHAEL, ed.
  1976 Origins of Intelligence. New York: Plenum Press.
LEWIS, OSCAR
  1959 Five Families: Mexican Case Studies in the Culture of Poverty. New York:
        Basic Books.
  1961 The Children of Sanchez. New York: Random House.
  1966 La Vida: A Puerto Rican Family in the Culture of Poverty. New York: Random
        House.

LEWIS, VIRGINIA, and DANIEL GLASER

  1974 "Lifestyles among heroin users." Federal Probation 38 (March): 21-28.

LEYENS, JACQUES-PHILLIPE, LEONCIO CAMINO, ROSS D. PARKE, and LEONARD BERKOWITZ
  1975 "Effects of movie violence on aggression in a field experiment as a function
        of group dominance and cohesion." Journal of Personal and Social Psychol-
        ogy 32 (February): 346-60.
LIBAI, DAVID
  1969 "The protection of the child victim of a sexual offense in the criminal justice
        system." Wayne State University Law Review 15 (Fall): 977-1032 (reprinted in
        Schultz, 1975).
LIEBERT, ROBERT M., JOHN M. NEALE, and EMILY S. DAVIDSON
  1975 The Early Window: Effects of Television on Children and Youth. New York:
        Pergamon.
LIEBHAFSKY, H. H.
  1971 American Government and Business. New York: Wiley.
LIEBOW, ELLIOT
  1967 Tally's Corner: A Study of Negro Streetcorner Men. Boston: Little, Brown.
LIGHT, RICHARD J.
  1973 "Abused and neglected children in America: A study of alternative policies."
        Harvard Educational Review 43 (November): 556-98.
LINDEN, ERIC, and J. C. HACKLER
  1973 "Affective ties and delinquency." Pacific Sociological Review 16 (January):
        27-46.
LINDESMITH, ALFRED R.
  1937 The Nature of Opiate Addiction. Ph.D. dissertation in sociology, University of
        Chicago.
  1938 "A sociological theory of drug addiction." American Journal of Sociology 43
        (January): 593-613.
  1959 "Federal law and drug addiction." Social Problems 7 (Summer): 48-57.
  1965 The Addict and the Law. Bloomington, Ind.: Indiana University Press.

1968   Addiction and Opiates. Chicago: Aldine.

LINDNER, LEWIS A., HAROLD GOLDMAN, SIMON DINITZ, and HARRY E. ALLEN
1970   "Antisocial personality type with cardiac lability." Archives of General Psychiatry 23 (September): 260-67.

LINNER, BRIGITTA
1972   Sex and Society in Sweden. New York: Harper & Row.

LIPPMAN, WALTER
1931a   "The underworld: Our secret servant." Forum 85 (January): 1-4.
1931b   The underworld: A stultified conscience." Forum 85 (January): 65-69.

LISKA, A. E.
1973   "Causal structures underlying the relationship between delinquency involvement and delinquent peers." Sociology and Social Research 58 (October): 23-36.

LOEB, RITA
1973   "Adolescent groups." Sociology and Social Research 58 (October):13-22.

LOFTIN, COLIN, and ROBERT H. HILL
1974   "Regional subculture and homicide: An examination of the Gastil-Hackney thesis." American Sociological Review 39 (October): 714-24.

LOPREATO, JOSEPH, and LETITIA ALSTON
1970   "Ideal types and idealization." American Sociological Review 35 (February): 88-96.

LUDES, FRANCIS J., and HAROLD J. GILBERT, eds.
1961   Corpus Juris Secundum. Brooklyn: N.Y.: American Law Book Co.

LYKKEN, DAVID T.
1957   "A study of anxiety in the psychopathic personality." Journal of Abnormal and Social Psychology 55 (July): 6-10.

MACANDREW, CRAIG, and ROBERT B. EDGERTON
1969   Drunken Comportment. Chicago: Aldine.

MCAULIFFE, WILLIAM E.
1975   "A second look at first effects: The subjective effects of opiates on non-addicts." Journal of Drug Issues 5 (Fall): 369-99.

MCAULIFFE, WILLIAM E., and ROBERT A. GORDON
1974   "A test of Lindesmith's theory of addiction: The frequency of euphoria among long-term addicts." American Journal of Sociology 79 (January): 795-840.

MCCAGHY, CHARLES H.
1967   "Child molesters: A study of their careers as deviants," in Clinard and Quinney, 1967.
1968   "Drinking and deviance disavowal: The case of child molesters." Social Problems 16 (Summer): 43-49.

MCCARRY, CHARLES
1972   Citizen Nader. New York: Saturday Review Press.

MCCLELLAND, DAVID, WILLIAM DAVIS, RUDOLF KALIN, and ERIC WARNER
1972   The Drinking Man: Alcohol and Human Motivation. New York: Free Press.

MCDONALD, LYNN
1969   Social Class and Delinquency. Hamden, Conn.: Archon Books.

MCGEADY, PAUL J.
  1974   "Obscenity law and the Supreme Court," in Cline, 1974.

MCGLOTHLIN, WILLIAM H.
  1975   "Sociocultural factors in marihuana use in the U.S.," in Rubin, 1975.

MCGLOTHLIN, WILLIAM H., DOUGLAS ANGLIN, and BRUCE D. WILSON
  1976   An Evaluation of the California Civil Addict Program: Preliminary Report. Los
         Angeles: UCLA, Department of Psychology.

MACK, JOHN A.
  1964   "Full time miscreants, delinquent neighborhoods and criminal networks."
         British Journal of Sociology 15 (March): 38-43.
  1972   "The able criminal." British Journal of Criminology 12 (January): 44-54.

MACK, JOHN A., and HANS-JUERGEN KERNER
  1975   The Crime Industry. Lexington, Mass.: D. C. Heath.

MCKEE, GILBERT J., JR.
  1972   A Cost-Benefit Analysis of Vocational Training in the California Department
         of Corrections. Ph.D. Dissertation in Economics, Claremont Graduate
         School.

MCKINNEY, JOHN C., and LINDA BROOKOVER BOURQUE
  1971   "The changing South: National incorporation of a region." American Sociol-
         ogical Review 36 (June): 399-412.

MCKISSACK, I. J.
  1967   "The peak age of property crimes." British Journal of Criminology 7 (April):
         184-94.

MAESTRO, MARCELLO
  1973   Cesare Beccaria and the Origins of Penal Reform. Philadelphia: Temple
         University Press.

MAGURA, STEPHEN
  1975   "Is there a subculture of violence? (Comment on Ball-Rokeach, ASR Decem-
         ber, 1973)." American Sociological Review 40 (December): 831-36.

MALTZ, MICHAEL D.
  1977   "Crime statistics: A historical perspective." Crime and Delinquency 23
         (January): 32-40.

MANN, JAY, JACK SIDMAN, and SHELDON STARR
  1973   "Evaluating social consequences of erotic films: An experimental ap-
         proach." Journal of Social Issues 29 (No.3): 113-32.

MANNING, PETER K., and LAWRENCE J. REDLINGER
  1976   "Invitational edges of corruption: Some consequences of narcotic law en-
         forcement," in Paul Rock, Politics and Drugs. New York: Dutton/Society
         Books (also in Douglas and Johnson, 1977).

MARMOR, JUDD, ed.
  1965   Sexual Inversion. New York: Basic Books.

MARTIN, DEL
  1976   Battered Wives. San Francisco: Glide Publications.

MARTIN, JOHN
  1959   "Some characteristics of vandals." American Catholic Sociological Review
         20 (Winter): 318-27.

REFERENCES

MARTIN, JOHN BARTLOW
  1953 Why Did They Kill? New York: Ballantine Books.

MASTERS, WILLIAM H., and VIRGINIA E. JOHNSON
  1966 Human Sexual Response. Boston: Little, Brown.
  1970 Human Sexual Inadequacy. Boston: Little, Brown.

MATZA, DAVID
  1964 Delinquency and Drift. New York: Wiley.

MAURER, DAVID W.
  1940 The Big Con. Indianapolis: Bobbs-Merrill.
  1955 Whiz Mob: A Correlation of the Technical Argot of Pickpockets with Their Behavior Pattern. Publication of the American Dialect Society, No. 24. Gainesville: University of Florida.

MEAD, MARGARET
  1928 Coming of Age in Samoa. New York: Morrow.
  1968 "Incest." International Encyclopedia of the Social Sciences. New York: Macmillan and Free Press.

MECHAM, GARTH D.
  1968 "Proceed with caution: Which penalties slow down the juvenile traffic violator?" Crime and Delinquency 14 (April): 142-50.

MEDNICK, SARNOFF A.
  1977 "A bio-social theory of the learning of law-abiding behavior," in Karl O. Christiansen and Sarnoff A. Mednick, Biosocial Bases of Criminal Behavior. New York: Gardner Press.

MEDNICK, SARNOFF A., FINI SCHULSINGER, JERRY HIGGINS, and BRIAN BELL
  1974 Genetics, Environment and Psychopathology. New York: American Elsevier Publishing Co.

MEGARGEE, EDWIN I.
  1966 "Undercontrolled and overcontrolled personality types in extreme antisocial aggression." Psychological Monographs 80 (Whole, No. 611).
  1972 The Psychology of Violence and Aggression. Morristown, N.J.: General Learning Press.

MELLINGER, GLEN D., MITCHELL B. BALTER, HUGH J. PARRY, DEAN I. MANHEIMER, and IRA H. CISIN
  1974 "An overview of psychotherapeutic drug use in the United States," in Josephson and Carroll, 1974.

MENDELSON, JACK H., A. MICHAEL ROSSI, and ROGER E. MEYER, eds.
  1974 The Use of Marijuana: A Psychological and Physiological Inquiry. New York: Plenum Press.

MERCER, JANE R.
  1973 Labeling the Mentally Retarded. Berkeley: University of California Press.

MERTON, ROBERT K.
  1968 Social Theory and Social Structure, 3rd ed. New York: Free Press.

MERTON, ROBERT K., LEONARD BROOM, and LEONARD S. COTTRELL, JR.
  1959 Sociology Today. New York: Basic Books.

MESSICK, HANK, and BURT GOLDBLATT
  1976 The Only Game in Town: An Illustrated History of Gambling. New York: Crowell.

METHADONE MAINTENANCE EVALUATION COMMITTEE

1968 "Progress report of evaluation of methadone maintenance treatment program as of March 31, 1968." Journal of the American Medical Association 206 (December 16): 2712-14.

MILAKOVICH, MICHAEL E., and KURT WEIS

1975 "Politics and measures of success in the war on crime." Crime and Delinquency 21 (January): 1-10.

MILESKI, MAUREEN, and DONALD J. BLACK

1972 "The social organization of homosexuality." Urban Life and Culture 1 (July): 187-202.

MILLER, NICK

1975 Battered Spouses. Occasional Papers on Social Administration No. 57. London: G. Bell.

MILLER, PATRICIA Y., and WILLIAM SIMON

1974 "Adolescent sexual behavior: Context and change." Social Problems 22 (October): 58-76.

MILLER, ROBERT R., and EMMET KENNEY

1966 "Adolescent delinquency and the myth of hospital treatment." Crime and Delinquency 12 (January): 38-48.

MILLER, WALTER B.

1959 "Lower class culture as a generating milieu of gang delinquency." Journal of Social Issues 14 (April): 5-19.

1973 "Ideology and criminal justice policy: Some current issues." Journal of Criminal Law and Criminology 64 (June): 141-62.

1976 "Youth gangs in the urban crisis era," in Short, 1976.

MOFFITT, DONALD, ed.

1976 Swindles: Classic Business Frauds of the Seventies. Princeton, N.J.: Dow Jones Books.

MOLOF, MARTIN J.

1965 Prediction of Future Assaultive Behavior among Youthful Offenders. Research Report No. 41. Sacramento, Calif.: Department of the Youth Authority.

MONAHAN, JOHN

1973 "Dangerous offenders: A critique of Kozol et al." Crime and Delinquency 19 (July): 418-20.

MONDALE, WALTER F.

1975 The Accountability of Power. New York: McKay.

MONEY, JOHN

1972 "The therapeutic use of androgen-depleting hormone," in Resnik and Wolfgang, 1972.

MONTAGU, ASHLEY, ed.

1973 Man and Aggression, 2nd ed. New York: Oxford University Press.

MOORE, WILLIAM HOWARD

1976 The Kefauver Committee and the Politics of Crime 1950-1952. Columbia: University of Missouri Press.

MOQUIN, WAYNE, with CHARLES VAN DOREN
1976   The American Way of Crime. New York: Praeger.

MORGAN, WAYNE
1974   Yesterday's Addicts: American Society and Drug Abuse, 1865-1920. Norman, Okla.: University of Oklahoma Press.

MORRIONE, THOMAS J.
1975   "Symbolic interactionism and social action theory." Sociology and Social Research 59 (April): 201-18.

MORRIS, NORVAL
1968   "Psychiatry and the dangerous criminal." Southern California Law Review 41 (Spring): 514-47.

MORRIS, NORVAL, and GORDON HAWKINS
1970   The Honest Politician's Guide to Crime Control. Chicago: University of Chicago Press.

MORRIS, RICHARD T., and VINCENT JEFFRIES
1970   "Class conflict: Forget it!" Sociology and Social Research 54 (April): 306-20.

MOWRER, O. HOBART
1964   The New Group Therapy. Princeton, N.J.: Van Nostrand.
1975   "Loss and recovery of community," in Hudson and Galaway, 1975.

MOYNIHAN, DANIEL P.
1972   "The schism in black America." The Public Interest No. 27 (Spring): 3-24.

MUEDEKING, GEORGE DAVID, and HOWARD M. BAHR
1976   "A smallest space analysis of skid row men's behaviors." Pacific Sociological Review 19 (July): 275-90.

MURRAY, DOUGLAS R.
1975   "Handguns, gun control laws and firearm violence." Social Problems 23 (October): 81-93.

MURRAY, MARGARET A.
1960   "Witchcraft," in Encyclopedia Britannica, 27th ed. Chicago: Encyclopedia Britannica, Inc.

MUSGROVE, F.
1964   Youth and the Social Order. London: Routledge & Kegan Paul.

MUSTO, DAVID F.
1973   The American Disease: Origins of Narcotic Control. New Haven: Yale University Press.

NADER, RALPH
1965   Unsafe at Any Speed. New York: Grossman.
1973   (ed.) The Consumer and Corporate Accountability. New York: Harcourt Brace Jovanovich.

NADER, RALPH, MARK J. GREEN, and JOEL SELIGMAN
1976   Taming the Giant Corporation. New York: Norton.

NASH, GEORGE
1976   An Analysis of Twelve Studies of the Impact of Drug Abuse Treatment upon Criminality. White Plains, N.Y.: Westchester County Community Mental Health Services.

NASH, JAY ROBERT
    1976   Hustlers and Con Men. New York: M. Evans & Co.

NATIONAL COMMISSION ON THE CAUSES AND PREVENTION OF VIOLENCE
    1969   To Establish Justice, to Insure Domestic Tranquility (Final Report of the Commission). Washington, D.C.: U.S. Government Printing Office.

NATIONAL INSTITUTE OF MENTAL HEALTH (NIMH)
    1967   Alcohol and Alcoholism. PHS Publication No. 1640. Washington, D.C.: U.S. Government Printing Office.
    1970   Report on the XYY Chromosomal Abnormality. PHS Publication No. 2103. Rockville, Md.: The Institute.

NATIONAL PRISONER STATISTICS
    1953   Prisoners Released from State and Federal Institutions, 1952 and 1953. Washington, D.C.: Federal Bureau of Prisons.
    1960   Prisoners Released from State and Federal Institutions, 1960. Washington, D.C: Federal Bureau of Prisons.

NELLI, HUMBERT S.
    1976   The Business of Crime: Italians and Syndicate Crime in the U.S. New York: Oxford University Press.

NELSON , ALFRED T., and HOWARD E. SMITH
    1958   Car Clouting. Springfield, Ill.: C.C. Thomas.

NEWMAN, DONALD J.
    1962   "The effects of accommodations in justice administration on criminal statistics." Sociology and Social Research 46 (January): 144-55.

NEWTON, ANNE
    1976   "Aid to the victim: Part I. Compensation and restitution." Crime and Delinquency Literature 8 (September): 368-90.

NEWTON, GEORGE D., and FRANK E. ZIMRING
    1969   "Firearms and violence in American life" (a staff report of the National Commission on the Causes and Prevention of Violence). Washington, D.C.: U.S. Government Printing Office.

NORDQUIST, CONRAD A.
    1973   Return from Moriah: Management of Spoiled Identity in a Child Abuse Group (unpublished paper).

NORMANDEAU, ANDRE
    1968   "Patterns in robbery." Criminologica 6 (November).

NYE, F. IVAN
    1958   Family Relationships and Delinquent Behavior. New York: Wiley.

NYE, F. IVAN, JAMES F. SHORT, JR., and VIRGIL J. OLSON
    1958   "Socioeconomic status and delinquent behavior." American Journal of Sociology 63 (January): 381-89.

O'DONNELL, JOHN
    1965   "The relapse rate in narcotic addiction: A critique of follow-up studies," in Wilner and Kassebaum, 1965.
    1966   "Narcotic addiction and crime." Social Problems 13 (Spring): 374-85.
    1969   Narcotics Addicts in Kentucky. U.S. Public Health Service Publication No. 1881. Washington, D.C.: U.S. Government Printing Office.

O'DONNELL, JOHN A., and JOHN C. BALL, eds.
  1966 Narcotic Addiction. New York: Harper & Row.

O'DONNELL, JOHN A., HARWIN L. VOSS, RICHARD R. CLAYTON, GERALD T. SLATIN, and ROBIN G. W. ROOM
  1976 Young Men and Drugs—A Nationwide Survey. NIDA Research Monograph No. 5. Rockville, Md.: National Institute on Drug Abuse.

OPLER, MARVIN K.
  1965 "Anthropological and cross-cultural aspects of homosexuality," in Marmor, 1965.

PACKER, HERBERT L.
  1968 The Limits of the Criminal Sanction. Stanford, Calif.: Stanford University Press.

PAGE, JOSEPH, and MARY-WIN O'BRIEN
  1973 Bitter Wages: Ralph Nader's Study Group Report on Disease and Injury on the Job. New York: Grossman.

PALMER, TED
  1974 "The Youth Authority's Community Treatment Project." Federal Probation 38 (March): 3-20.

PANEL FOR THE EVALUATION OF CRIME SURVEYS
  1976 Surveying Crime. Washington, D.C.: National Academy of Sciences.

PARKER, DONN B.
  1976 Crime by Computer. New York: Scribners.

PARSONS, TALCOTT
  1951 The Social System. New York: Free Press.
  1971 The System of Modern Societies. Englewood Cliffs, N.J.: Prentice-Hall.

PARTRIDGE, WILLIAM L.
  1973 The Hippie Ghetto. New York: Holt, Rinehart and Winston.
  1975 "Cannabis and cultural groups in a Colombian Municipio," in Rubin, 1975.

PATTERSON, G. R., J. A. COBB, and ROBERTA S. RAY
  1974 "Training parents to control an aggressive child," in Steinmetz and Straus, 1974.

PAULSEN, MONRAD G.
  1968 "The law and abused children," in Helfer and Kempe, 1968.

PEKANNEN, JOHN
  1973 The American Connection. Chicago: Follett.

PERCY, CHARLES H.
  1973 "Organized crime in the securities market," in Conklin, 1973.

PESCOR, MICHAEL J.
  1943 "A statistical analysis of the clinical records of hospitalized drug addicts." U.S. Public Health Reports, Supplement No. 143. Washington, D.C.: U.S. Government Printing Office.

PETERSILIA, JOAN, PETER W. GREENWOOD, and MARVIN LAVIN
  1977 Criminal Careers of Habitual Felons. Draft Report, Santa Monica, Calif.: Rand Corporation.

PETERSON, DONALD R., HERBERT C. QUAY, and THEODORE L. TIFFANY

1961 "Personality factors related to juvenile delinquency." Child Development 32 (June): 355-72.

PETERSON, MARY BENNETT

1971 The Regulated Consumer. Los Angeles: Nash.

PETTIGREW, THOMAS F., and ROSALIND B. SPIER

1962 "The ecological structure of Negro Homicide." American Journal of Sociology 67 (May): 621-29.

PFOHL, STEPHEN J.

1977 "The 'discovery' of child abuse." Social Problems 24 (February): 310-23.

PHILLIPSON, COLEMAN

1923 Three Criminal Law Reformers: Beccaria, Bentham, Romilly. London: Dent.

PITTMAN, DAVID J.

1974 "Drugs, addiction and crime," in Glaser, 1974.

PITTMAN, DAVID J., and C. WAYNE GORDON

1958 Revolving Door: A study of the Chronic Police Case Inebriate. New Haven: Yale Center of Alcohol Studies.

PITTMAN, DAVID J., and CHARLES R. SNYDER

1962 Society, Culture and Drinking Patterns. New York: Wiley.

PITTMAN, DAVID J., and WILLIAM HANDY

1964 "Patterns in criminal aggravated assault." Journal of Criminal Law, Criminology and Police Science 55 (December): 462-70.

PITTS, JESSE R.

1968 "Social control: The concept." International Encyclopedia of the Social Science. New York: Macmillan and Free Press.

PLANT, MARTIN A.

1975 Drugtakers in an English Town. London: Tavistock.

PLATT, ANTHONY

1969 The Child Savers: The Invention of Delinquency. Chicago: University of Chicago Press.

POLK, KENNETH, and DAVID HALFERTY

1966 "School cultures, adolescent commitments and delinquency." Journal of Research in Crime and Delinquency 4 (July): 82-96 (reprinted in Polk and Schafer, 1972).

POLK, KENNETH, and WALTER E. SCHAFER

1972 Schools and Delinquency. Englewood Cliffs, N.J.: Prentice-Hall.

POWELL, ELWIN H.

1966 "Crime as a function of anomie." Journal of Criminal Law, Criminology and Police Science 57 (June): 161-71.

PRATHER, JANE E., and LINDA S. FIDELL

1975 "Drug usage as an index of stress among women." Paper presented at National Council of Family Relations, Salt Lake City.

PREBLE, EDWARD, and GABRIEL V. LAURY

1967 "Plastic cement: The ten-cent hallucinogen." International Journal of the Addictions 2 (Fall): 271-81 (reprinted in Harms, 1973).

PREBLE, EDWARD, and JOHN J. CASEY, JR.
1969   "Taking care of business—The heroin user's life on the street." International Journal of the Addictions 4 (March): 1-24.

PRESIDENT'S COMMISSION ON LAW ENFORCEMENT AND THE ADMINISTRATION OF JUSTICE
1967   The Challenge of Crime in a Free Society. Washington, D.C.: U.S. Government Printing Office.

PRICE, JAMES E.
1966   "A test of the accuracy of crime statistics." Social Problems 14 (Fall): 214-21.

PRUITT, DEAN G.
1971   "Choice shifts in group discussion." Journal of Personality and Social Psychology 20 (December): 339-60.

QUAY, H.C.
1965   "Psychopathic personality as pathological stimulation seeking." American Journal of Psychiatry 122 (August): 180-83.

QUINNEY, RICHARD
1977   Class, State and Crime. New York: McKay.

RADZINOWICZ, LEON
1966   Ideology and Crime. New York: Columbia University Press.

RAFFALI, HENRI CHRISTIAN
1970   "The battered child." Crime and Delinquency 16 (April): 139-50.

RAINER, JOHN D., SYED ABDULLAH, and LISSY F. JARVIK
1972   "KYY karyotype in a pair of monozygotic twins: A 17-year life-history study." British Journal of Psychiatry 120 (May): 543-48.

RAINWATER, LEE
1970   "The problem of lower class culture." Journal of Social Issues 26 (Spring): 133-48.

RASMUSSEN, PAUL K., and LAUREN L. KUHN
1976   "The new masseuse: Play for pay." Urban Life 5 (October): 271-92.

RECKLESS, WALTER
1943   The Etiology of Delinquent and Criminal Behavior. New York: Social Science Research Council.

RECKLESS, WALTER C., and SIMON DINITZ
1972   The Prevention of Juvenile Delinquency. Columbus, Ohio: Ohio State University Press.

REDDEN, ELIZABETH
1942   Embezzlement: A Study of One Kind of Criminal Behavior with Prediction Tables Based on Fidelity Insurance Records. Lithographed Ph.D. Dissertation in sociology, The University of Chicago.

REDL, FRITZ, and DAVID WINEMAN
1951   Children Who Hate. New York: Free Press.

REED, JOHN S.
1972   The Enduring South: Subcultural Persistence in Mass Society. Lexington, Mass.: D.C. Heath.

REIFEN, DAVID
1958   "Protection of children involved in sexual offenses: A new method of investi-

gation in Israel." Journal of Criminology, Criminal Law and Police Science 49 (September-October): 222-29.

1975   "Court procedures in Israel to protect child-victims of sexual assaults," in Drapkin and Viano, 1975.

REINARMAN, CRAIG, and DONALD MILLER
1975   Direct Financial Assistance to Parolees. Research Report No. 55, Sacramento: California Department of Corrections.

REISS, ALBERT J., JR.
1951   "Delinquency as the failure of personal and social controls." American Sociological Review 16 (April): 196-208.
1952   "Social correlates of psychological types of delinquency." American Sociological Review 17 (December): 710-18.
1961   "The social integration of peers and queers." Social Problems 9 (Fall): 102-20.
1974   Review of Amir, "Patterns in Forcible Rape." American Journal of Sociology 80 (November): 785-90.
1976   "Settling the frontiers of a pioneer in American criminology: Henry McKay," in Short, 1976.

REISS, ALBERT J., JR., and ALBERT L. RHODES
1961   "The distribution of juvenile delinquency in the social class structure." American Sociological Review 26 (October): 720-31.

REISS, IRA L.
1967   The Social Context of Premarital Sexual Permissiveness. New York: Holt, Rinehart and Winston.

REPPETTO, THOMAS A.
1974   Residential Crime. Cambridge, Mass.: Ballinger.

RESNIK, H.L.P., and MARVIN E. WOLFGANG
1972   Sexual Behaviors. Boston: Little, Brown.

REYNOLDS, PAUL DAVIDSON, and DALE A. BLYTH
1975   "Sources of variation affecting the relationships between police and survey based estimates of crime rates," in Drapkin and Viano, 1975.

RHODES, A. LEWIS, and ALBERT J. REISS, JR.
1969   "Apathy, truancy and delinquency as adaptations to school failure." Social Forces 48 (September): 12-22.

ROBIN, GERALD D.
1963   "Patterns of department store shoplifting." Crime and Delinquency 9 (April): 163-72.
1970a   "The nonshareable problem theory of trust violation." Criminologica 7 (February): 48-57.
1970b   "The corporate and judicial disposition of employee thieves," in Smigel and Ross, 1970

ROBINS, LEE N.
1974   The Vietnam Drug User Returns. Special Action Office Monograph, Series A, Number 2. Rockville, Md.: National Institute on Drug Abuse.

ROBINS, LEE N., and SHIRLEY Y. HILL
1966   "Assessing the contribution of family structure, class and peer groups to

juvenile delinquency." Journal of Criminal Law, Criminology and Police Science 57 (September): 325-34.

ROBINSON, W.S.
1950 "Ecological correlations and behavior of individuals." American Sociological Review 15 (June): 351-58.

ROBY, PAMELA A.
1969 "Politics and criminal law: Revision of the N.Y. State Penal Law on prostitution." Social Problems 17 (Summer): 83-109.

RODMAN, HYMAN
1963 "The lower-class value stretch." Social Forces 42 (December): 205-15.
1968 "Stratification, social: Class culture." International Encyclopedia of the Social Sciences. New York: Macmillan/Free Press.

ROEBUCK, JULIAN, and PATRICK MCNAMARA
1973 "Ficheras and free-lances: Prostitution in a Mexican border city." Archives of Sexual Behavior 2 (June): 231-44.

ROEBUCK, JULIAN B., and WOLFGANG FRESE
1976 The Rendezvous: A Case Study of an After Hours Club. New York: Free Press.

ROGERS, JOSEPH W., and M.D. BUFFALO
1974 "Fighting back: Nine modes of adaptation to a deviant label." Social Problems 22 (October): 101-18.

ROOM, ROBIN
1975 "Normative perspectives on alcohol use and problems." Journal of Drug Use 5 (Fall): 358-68.

ROONEY, JAMES F.
1970 "Societal forces and the unattached male: An historical review," in Bahr, 1970.

ROSENBAUM, PAUL A.
1976 "Guilty but insane." Trial 12 (March): 42-43.

ROSENHAN, D.L.
1973 "On being sane in insane places." Science 179 (January 19): 250-58.

ROSSMAN, PARKER
1973 "The pederasts." Society 10 (March-April): 29-35.

ROTTENBERG, SIMON, ed.
1973 The Economics of Crime and Punishment. Washington, D.C.: American Enterprise Institute for Public Policy Research.

ROY, K.K.
1975 "Feelings and attitudes of raped women of Bangladesh towards military personnel of Pakistan," in Drapkin and Viano, 1975: Vol. 5.

RUBIN, SOL, with HENRY WEIHOFEN, GEORGE EDWARDS, and SIMON ROSENZWEIG
1963 The Law of Criminal Correction. St. Paul, Minn.: West Publishing Co.

RUBIN, TED, and JOHN BABBS
1970 "The glue sniffer." Federal Probation 34 (September): 23-28.

RUBIN, VERA ed.
1975 Cannabis and Culture. The Hague: Moulton.

RUBINGTON, EARL
  1968   "The bottle gang." Quarterly Journal of Studies on Alcohol 29 (December): 943-55.

RUSCHE, GEORG, and OTTO KIRCHHEIMER
  1939   Punishment and Social Structure. New York: Columbia University Press.

RUSHFORTH, NORMAN B., CHARLES S. HIRSCH, AMASA B. FORD, and LESTER ADELSON
  1975   "Accidental firearm fatalities in a metropolitan county (1958-1973)." American Journal of Epidemiology 100 (June): 499-505.

RUSSELL, DIANA E.H.
  1975   The Politics of Rape: The Victim's Perspective. New York: Stein & Day.

SADOUN, ROLAND, GIORGIO LOLLI, and MILTON SILVERMAN
  1975   Drinking in French Culture. New Brunswick, N.J.: Rutgers Center of Alcohol Studies.

SAGALYN, ARNOLD
  1971   The Crime of Robbery in the United States. U.S. Department of Justice, National Institute of Law Enforcement and Criminal Justice (1 CR 71-1) Washington, D.C.: U.S. Government Printing Office.

SAGARIN, EDWARD
  1975   "Forcible rape and the problem of the rights of the accused." Intellect Magazine 3 (May-June): 516-20.

SANDERS, CLINTON R.
  1975   "Caught in the con game: The young, white drug user's contact with the legal system." Law and Society Review 9 (Winter): 197-217.

SCHACHTER, STANLEY
  1971   Emotion, Obesity and Crime. New York: Academic Press.

SCHAFER, WALTER E., and CAROL OLEXA
  1971   Tracking and Opportunity. Scranton, Pa: Chandler.

SCHALLER, MICHAEL
  1970   "The Federal prohibition of marijuana." Journal of Social History 4 (Fall): 61-74 (reprinted in Kerr, 1973).

SCHEFF, THOMAS J.
  1964   "The societal reaction to deviance: Ascriptive elements in the psychiatric screening of mental patients in a midwestern state." Social Problems 11 (Spring): 401-13.
  1966   Being Mentally Ill: A Sociological Theory. Chicago: Aldine.
  1968   "Negotiating reality: Notes on power in the assessment of responsibility." Social Problems 16 (Summer): 3-17.

SCHNEIDER, LOUIS, and CHARLES BONJEAN
  1973   The Idea of Culture in the Social Sciences. New York: Cambridge University Press.

SCHRAG, CLARENCE
  1971   Crime and Justice: American Style. NIMH Crime and Delinquency Issues Monographs. DHEW Publication No. HSM-72-9052. Washington, D.C.: U.S. Government Printing Office.

SCHUCK, PETER
  1972   "The curious case of the indicted meat inspectors." Harper's Magazine (September): 1-8.

SCHULTZ, LEROY G., ed.
1975   Rape Victimology. Springfield, Ill.: C. C. Thomas.

SCHUR, EDWIN M.
1965   Crimes without Victims. Englewood Cliffs, N.J.: Prentice-Hall.
1971   Labeling Deviant Behavior. New York: Harper & Row.
1973   Radical Nonintervention. Englewood Cliffs, N.J.: Prentice-Hall.

SCHWARTZ, BARRY
1968   "The effect in Philadelphia of Pennsylvania's increased penalties for rape
       and attempted rape." Journal of Criminal Law, Criminology and Police
       Science 59 (December): 509-15.

SCHWARTZ, GARY, and DON MERTEN
1967   "The language of adolescence: An anthropological approach to youth cul-
       ture." American Journal of Sociology 72 (March): 453-68.

SCHWARTZ, RICHARD D., and JAMES C. MILLER
1964   "Legal evolution and societal complexity." American Journal of Sociology
       70 (September): 159-69.

SCHWENDINGER, HERMAN, and JULIA SCHWENDINGER
1970   "Defenders of order or guardians of human rights." Issues in Criminology 5
       (Summer): 123-57 (reprinted in Ian Taylor et al., Critical Criminology. Lon-
       don: Routledge and Kegan Paul, 1975).
1976a "Delinquency and the collective varieties of youth." Crime and Social Justice
       (Spring-Summer): 7-25.
1976b "Marginal youth and social policy." Social Problems 24 (December): 184-91.

SCODEL, ALVIN
1964   "Inspirational group therapy: A study of Gamblers Anonymous." American
       Journal of Psychotherapy 18 (January): 115-25 (reprinted in Herman, 1967).

SCOTT, MARVIN B.
1968   The Racing Game. Chicago: Aldine.

SEIDMAN, DAVID, and MICHAEL COUZENS
1974   "Getting the crime rate down: Political pressure and crime reporting." Law
       and Society Review 8 (Spring): 457-93.

SEIDMAN, ROBERT B., and WILLIAM J. CHAMBLISS
1974   "Appeals from criminal convictions," in Glaser, 1974.

SEITZ, STEVEN T.
1972   "Firearms, homicide and gun control effectiveness." Law and Society Re-
       view 6 (May): 595-613.

SELLS, S.B.
1976   "Reflections on the epidemiology of heroin and narcotic addiction from the
       perspective of treatment data." Behavioral Research Report No. 76-3. Fort
       Worth: Institute of Behavioral Research, Texas Christian University.

SELLS, S. B., D. DWAYNE SIMPSON, GEORGE W. JOE, and ROBERT G. DEMAREE.
1976   Evaluation of Drug Abuse Treatments Based on the Drug Abuse Program
       Five Years after Termination: Issues and Preliminary Results. Report No.
       76-7. Fort Worth: Texas Christian University, Institute of Behavioral
       Research.

SERBER, MICHAEL, and JOSEPH WOLPE
1972   "Behavior therapy techniques," in Resnik and Wolfgang, 1972.

SERRILL, MICHAEL S.
  1974 "Treating sex offenders in New Jersey: The ROARE program." Corrections Magazine 1 (November-December): 13-24.

SERVADIO, GAIA
  1976 Mafioso: A History of the Mafia from Its Origins to the Present. New York: Stein & Day.

SHAH, SALEEM A., and LOREN H. ROTH
  1974 "Biological and psychophysiological factors in criminality," in Glaser, 1974.

SHAW, CLIFFORD R., and HENRY D. MCKAY
  1931 "Social factors in juvenile delinquency," in National Commission of Law Observance and Law Enforcement, Report on the Causes of Crime, Vol. 2, pp. 195-201.
  1942 Juvenile Delinquency and Urban Areas. Chicago: University of Chicago Press.

SHELDON, WILLIAM H.
  1949 Varieties of Delinquent Youth. New York: Harpers.

SHERRILL, ROBERT
  1973 The Saturday Night Special. New York: Charterhouse.

SHORT, JAMES F., JR.
  1974 "Collective behavior, crime and delinquency," in Glaser, 1974.
  1976 (ed.) Delinquency, Crime and Society. Chicago: University of Chicago Press.

SHORT, JAMES F., JR., and F. IVAN NYE
  1958 "Extent of unrecorded delinquency: Tentative conclusions." Journal of Criminal Law, Criminology and Police Science 49 (December): 296-302.

SHORT, JAMES F., JR., and FRED L. STRODTBECK
  1965 Group Process and Gang Delinquency. Chicago: University of Chicago Press.

SHOVER, NEAL
  1972 "Structures and careers in burglary." Journal of Criminal Law, Criminology and Police Science 63 (December): 540-49.
  1973 "The social organization of burglary." Social Problems 20 (Spring): 499-514.

SIEGAL, HARVEY A., DAVID M. PETERSEN, and CARL D. CHAMBERS
  1975 "The emerging skid row: Ethnographic and social notes on a changing scene." Journal of Drug Issues 5 (Spring): 160-66.

SIMMEL, GEORG
  1955 Conflict and the Web of Group Affiliations, trans. by Kurt H. Wolff and Reinhard Bendix (from G. Simmel, Soziologie, 1908). New York: Free Press.

SIMON, RITA JAMES
  1967 The Jury and the Defense of Insanity. Boston: Little, Brown.

SINCLAIR, ANDREW
  1962 Prohibition. Boston: Little, Brown.

SINGER, MAX
  1971 "The vitality of mythical numbers." The Public Interest 23 (3): 3-9.

SKINNER, B. F.
  1953 Science and Human Behavior. New York: Macmillan.
  1974 About Behaviorism. New York: Knopf.

SKOGAN, WESLEY G.

1974 "The validity of official criminal statistics." Social Science Quarterly 55 (June): 25-38.

1977 "Dimensions of the dark figure of unreported crime." Crime and Delinquency 23 (January): 41-50.

SMIGEL, ERWIN O.

1956 "Public attitudes toward stealing as related to the size of the victim organization." American Sociological Review 21 (June): 320-27.

SMIGEL, ERWIN O., and H. LAURENCE ROSS

1970 Crimes against Bureaucracy. New York: Van Nostrand Reinhold.

SMITH, ADAM

1776 An Inquiry into the Wealth of Nations (the many reprintings include London: Methuen, 1950).

SMITH, R. B., and RICHARD C. STEPHENS

1976 "Drug use and 'hustling': A study of their interrelationships." Criminology 14 (August): 155-76.

SOBLE, RONALD L., and ROBERT E. DALLOS

1975 The Impossible Dream: The Equity Funding Story, Fraud of the Century. New York: G. P. Putnam.

SOKOL, JACOB

1973 "A survey of the inhaling of solvents among teenagers," in Harms, 1973.

SOLOMON, DAVID, ed.

1966 The Marihuana Papers. Indianapolis:Bobbs-Merrill (reprinted 1968 by Signet Books).

SPENCER, HERBERT

1885 Principles of Sociology, 3rd ed. Williams & Norgate.

SPERGEL, IRVING

1964 Racketville, Slumtown, Haulburg. Chicago: University of Chicago Press.

SPILERMAN, SEYMOUR

1971 "The causes of racial disturbance: Tests of an explanation." American Sociological Review 36 (June): 427-42.

SPRADLEY, JAMES P.

1970 You Owe Yourself a Drink: An Ethnology of Urban Nomads. Boston: Little, Brown.

STANFIELD, ROBERT E.

1966 "The interaction of family variables and gang variables in the aetiology of delinquency." Social Problems 13 (Spring): 411-17.

STEADMAN, HENRY J., and GARY KEVELES

1972 "The community adjustment and criminal activity of the Baxstrom patients: 1960-1970." American Journal of Psychiatry 129 (September): 304-10.

STEELE, BRANDT F., and CARL B. POLLOCK

1968 "A psychiatric study of parents who abuse infants and small children," in Helfer and Kempe, 1968.

STEFFENS, JOSEPH LINCOLN

1904 The Shame of the Cities (reprinted, New York: Hill & Wang, 1960).

1931 The Autobiography of Lincoln Steffens. New York: Harcourt Brace.

REFERENCES 525

STEFFENSMEIER, DARRELL J., and ROBERT M. TERRY

1973 "Deviance and respectability: An observational study of reactions to shoplifting." Social Forces 51 (June): 417-26.

STEINMETZ, SUZANNE K.

1974 "Occupational environment in relation to physical punishment and dogmatism," in Steinmetz and Straus, 1974.

STEINMETZ, SUZANNE K., and MURRAY A. STRAUS, ed.

1974 Violence in the Family. New York: Dodd, Mead.

STIMSOM, G. V.

1973 Heroin and Behavior. New York: Wiley/Halstead Press.

STINCHCOMBE, ARTHUR L.

1964 Rebellion in a High School. Chicago: Quadrangle Books.

STOLL, CLARICE STASZ

1974 Female and Male. Dubuque, Iowa: Brown.

STONE, ALAN A.

1975 Mental Health and Law: A System in Transition. NIMH Crime and Delinquency Issues Monograph, DHEW Publication No. (ADM) 75-176. Washington, D.C.: U.S. Government Printing Office.

STONE, CHRISTOPHER

1975 Where the Law Ends: The Social Control of Corporate Behavior. New York: Harper & Row.

STOUFFER, SAMUEL A., LOUIS GUTTMAN, EDWARD A. SUCHMAN, PAUL F. LAZARSFELD, SHIRLEY A. STAR, and JOHN A. CLAUSEN

1950 Measurement and Prediction. Vol. IV of Studies in Social Psychology in World War II. Princeton, N.J.: Princeton University Press.

STRAUS, MURRAY A.

1971 "Some social antecedents of physical punishment: A linkage theory interpretation." Journal of Marriage and the Family 33 (November): 658-63 (reprinted in Steinmetz and Straus, 1974).

1974 "Leveling, civility, and violence in the family." Journal of Marriage and the Family 36 (February): 13-30.

STURUP, GEORG K.

1972 "Castration: The total treatment," in Resnik and Wolfgang, 1972.

SUDNOW, DAVID

1965 "Normal crimes: Sociological features of the penal code in a public defender's office." Social Problems 12 (Winter): 255-76.

SUTHERLAND, EDWIN H.

1937 The Professional Thief. Chicago: University of Chicago Press.

1949 White Collar Crime. New York: Dryden.

1950 "The sexual psychopath laws." Journal of Criminal Law and Criminology 40 (January-February): 543-54.

SUTHERLAND, E. H., and D. R. CRESSEY

1970 Criminology, 8th ed. Philadelphia: Lippincott.

1974 Criminology, 9th ed. Philadelphia: Lippincott.

SUTTER, ALAN G.

1966 "The world of the righteous dope fiend." Issues in Criminology 2 (Fall):

177-222 (also published as "Worlds of drug use on the street scene," in D. R. Cressey and D. A. Ward, Delinquency, Crime and Social Process. New York: Harper & Row, 1969).

SUTTLES, GERALD D.
1968   The Social Order of the Slum. Chicago: University of Chicago Press.
1970   "Deviant behavior as an unanticipated consequence of public housing," in Glaser, 1970.

SYKES, GRESHAM M., and DAVID MATZA
1957   "Techniques of neutralization." American Sociological Review 22 (December): 664-70.

SZASZ, THOMAS S.
1974   Ceremonial Chemistry. Garden City, N.Y.: Doubleday.

TAFT, PHILLIP, and PHILLIP ROSS
1969   "American labor violence: Its causes, character and outcome," in Graham and Gurr, 1969.

TANNENBAUM, FRANK H.
1938   Crime and the Community. Boston: Ginn.

TAYLOR, IAN, PAUL WALTON, and JOCK YOUNG, eds.
1975   Critical Criminology. London: Routledge and Kegan Paul.

TEETERS, NEGLEY K., and JOHN O. REINEMANN
1950   The Challenge of Delinquency. Englewood Cliffs, N.J.: Prentice-Hall.

TEILMANN, KATHLEEN S.
1976   Sources of bias in self-reported delinquency. Ph.D. Dissertation in Sociology, University of Southern California.

TERRY, CHARLES E., and MILDRED PELLENS
1928   The Opium Problem. New York: Bureau of Social Hygiene (reprinted 1970 by Patterson Smith, Montclair, N.J.).

THOMAS, MARGARET H., and RONALD S. DRABMAN
1975   "Toleration of real life aggression as a function of exposure to televised violence and age of subject." Merrill-Palmer Quarterly 21 (July): 227-32.

THORSELL, BERNARD A., and LLOYD W. KLEMKE
1972   "The labeling process: Reinforcement and deterrent?" Law and Society Review 6 (February): 393-403.

THRASHER, FREDERIC M.
1927   The Gang. University of Chicago Press (reissued, 1963).

TOBY, JACKSON
1957a "Social disorganization and stake in conformity: Complementary factors in the predatory behavior of hoodlums." Journal of Criminal Law, Criminology and Police Science 48 (May-June): 12-17 (reprinted in Glaser, 1970).
1957b "The differential impact of family disorganization." American Sociological Review 22 (October): 505-12.
1966   "Violence and the masculine ideal: Some qualitative data." Annals of the American Academy of Political and Social Science 364 (March): 19-36.
1968   "Delinquency: Delinquent gangs." International Encyclopaedia of the Social Sciences. New York: Macmillan/Free Press.

REFERENCES

TOCH, HANS H.
1969 Violent Men. Chicago: Aldine.
1970 "The care and feeding of typologies and labels." Federal Probation 34 (September): 15-19.

TRICE, HARRISON M.
1957a "A study of the process of affiliation with Alcoholics Anonymous." Quarterly Journal of Studies of Alcohol 18 (March): 39-54.
1957b "Sociological Factors in Association with AA." Journal of Criminal Law, Criminology and Police Science 48 (November-December): 378-86.
1966 Alcoholism in America. New York: McGraw-Hill.

TUCHFARBER, ALFRED J., and WILLIAM R. KLECKA
1976 Random Digit Dialing: Lowering the Cost of Victimization Surveys. Washington, D.C.: Police Foundation.

TURNER, JAMES S.
1970 The Chemical Feast: Ralph Nader's Study Group Report on the Food and Drug Administration. New York: Grossman.

TURNER, RALPH H.
1956 "Role-taking, role standpoint, and reference-group behavior." American Journal of Sociology 61 (January): 316-28.
1964 The Social Context of Ambition. San Francisco: Chandler.

TURNER, WALLACE
1965 Gambler's Money. Boston: Houghton Mifflin (reprinted by Signet Books).

TYLER, E. B.
1871 Primitive Culture, 3rd ed. London: John Murray.

ULLMAN, ALBERT D.
1958 "Sociocultural backgrounds of alcoholism." Annals of the American Academy of Political and Social Sciences 315 (January): 48-54.

U.S. DEPARTMENT OF COMMERCE
1974 The Cost of Crimes against Business. Washington, D.C.: U.S. Government Printing Office.
1976 Statistical Abstract of the United States: 1975. Washington, D.C.: U.S. Government Printing Office.

U.S. DEPARTMENT OF LABOR
1977 Unlocking the Second Gate: The Role of Financial Assistance in Reducing Recidivism among Ex-Prisoners. Research and Development Monograph 45. Washington, D.C.: U.S. Employment and Training Administration.

U.S. PRESIDENT'S SCIENCE ADVISORY PANEL ON YOUTH
1974 Youth: Transition to Adulthood. Report of the Panel on Youth of the President's Science Advisory Panel. Chicago: University of Chicago Press.

VAILLANT, GEORGE E.
1966 "A twelve-year follow-up of New York narcotic addicts: The relation of treatment to outcome." American Journal of Psychiatry 122 (January): 727-37.
1973 "A 20-year follow-up of New York narcotic addicts." Archives of General Psychiatry 29 (August): 237-41.

VALENTINE, CHARLES A.
1968 Culture and Poverty. Chicago: University of Chicago Press.

VAN DEN BERGHE, PIERRE L.
  1963   "Dialectics and functionalism: Towards a theoretical synthesis." American
         Sociological Review 28 (October): 695-705.

VAN DEN HAAG, ERNEST
  1975   Punishing Criminals. New York: Basic Books.

VAN GENNEP, ARNOLD
  1908   The Rites of Passage, trans. by Vizedom and Caffee, published by University
         of Chicago Press, 1960.

VAZ, EDMUND W.
  1971   "Explorations in the institutionalization of juvenile delinquency." Journal of
         Criminal Law, Criminology and Police Science 62 (September): 396-406.

VOLD, GEORGE B.
  1958   Theoretical Criminology. New York: Oxford University Press.

VOLKMAN, RITA, and DONALD R. CRESSEY
  1963   "Differential association and the rehabilitation of drug addicts." American
         Journal of Sociology 59 (September): 129-42.

VON HENTIG, HANS
  1943   "The pickpocket: Psychology, tactics and technique." Journal of Criminal
         Law and Criminology 34 (May-June): 11-15.

VON HIRSCH, ANDREW
  1976   Doing Justice: The Choice of Punishments. New York: Hill & Wang.

VORENBERG, JAMES, and IRVING F. LUKOFF
  1973   "Addiction, crime and the criminal justice system." Federal Probation 37
         (December): 3-7.

VOSS, HARWIN L., and JOHN R. HEPBURN
  1968   "Patterns in criminal homicide in Chicago." Journal of Criminal Law, Crimi-
         nology and Police Science 59 (December): 499-508.

VOTEY, HAROLD L., JR., and LLAD PHILLIPS
  1976   "Minimizing the social cost of drug abuse: An economic analysis of alterna-
         tives for policy." Policy Sciences 7 (December): 315-36.

WALDO, GORDON P., and SIMON DINITZ
  1967   "Personality attributes of the criminal: An analysis of research studies,
         1950-65." Journal of Research in Crime and Delinquency 4 (July): 185-202.

WALKER, NIGEL
  1968   Crime and Insanity in England, Vol. 1: The Historical Perspective. Edinburgh,
         Scotland: The University Press.
  1969   Sentencing in a Rational Society (New York: Basic Books, first American
         edition, 1971).

WALLACE, SAMUEL E.
  1965   Skid Row as a Way of Life. Totowa, N.J.: Bedminster Press 1965 (reprinted by
         Harper & Row, New York, 1968).

WALLERSTEIN, JAMES S., and CLEMENT J. WYLE
  1947   "Our law-abiding law-breakers." Probation 35 (April): 107-18.

WALSH, MARILYN E.
  1976   Strategies for Combating the Criminal Receiver of Stolen Goods. Washing-
         ton, D.C.: U.S. Department of Justice, LEAA.

REFERENCES

WARD, COLIN, ed.
  1973   Vandalism. New York: Van Nostrand Reinhold.

WARREN, CAROL A. B.
  1974a "The use of stigmatizing labels in coventionalizing deviant behavior." So-
         ciology and Social Research 58 (April): 303-11.
  1974b Identity and Community in the Gay World. New York: Wiley.
  1976   "Women among men: Females in the male homosexual community." Ar-
         chives of Sexual Behavior 5 (April): 157-69.

WEBER, MAX
  1905   The Protestant Ethic and the Spirit of Capitalism, trans. by Talcott Parsons,
         London: Allen & Ulwin, 1930.
  1922   The Theory of Social and Economic Organization, trans. by Talcott Parsons,
         New York: Oxford University Press, 1947.

WEIL, ANDREW T., NORMAN E. ZINBERG, and JUDITH M. NELSEN
  1968   "Clinical and psychological effects of marihuana in man." Science 162 (De-
         cember 13): 1234-42.

WEINBERG, MARTIN S.
  1970   "The nudist management of respectability: Strategy for, and consequences
         of, the construction of a situated morality," in Jack D. Douglas, Deviance and
         Respectability. New York: Basic Books.

WEINBERG, MARTIN S., and COLIN J. WILLIAMS
  1975   Male Homosexuals. New York: Penguin Books (1974 edition by Oxford Uni-
         versity Press).

WEINBERG, S. KIRSON
  1955   Incest Behavior. New York: Citadel Press.

WEINSTEIN, DAVID, and LILLIAN DEITCH
  1974   The Impact of Legalized Gambling. New York: Praeger.

WEISSMAN, JAMES C., THOMAS A. GIACINTI, and FRANCIS W. LANASA
  1973   "Undetected opiate use: A comparison of official drug user files and private
         methadone clinic's patient records." Journal of Criminal Justice 1 (Summer):
         133-44.

WENK, ERNST A.
  1975   Peer Conducted Research: A Novel Approach to Drug Education. Davis,
         Calif.: National Council on Crime and Delinquency Research Center.

WENK, ERNST A., and ROBERT L. EMRICH
  1972   "Assaultive youth." Journal of Research in Crime and Delinquency 9 (July):
         171-96.

WENK, ERNST A., JAMES A. ROBISON, and GERALD W. SMITH
  1972   "Can violence be predicted?" Crime and Delinquency 18 (October): 393-402.

WERTHMAN, CARL
  1967   "The function of social definitions in the development of delinquent ca-
         reers," in President's Commission on Law Enforcement and the Administra-
         tion of Justice, Task Force Report: Juvenile Delinquency and Youth Crime.
         Washington, D.C., U.S. Government Printing Office (reprinted in Glaser,
         1970).

WEXLER, DAVID B.
  1976   Criminal Commitments and Dangerous Mental Patients: Legal Issues of Con-

finement, Treatment and Release. NIMH Crime and Delinquency Issues Monographs, DHEW Publication No. (ADM) 76-331. Washington, D.C., U.S. Government Printing Office.

WHEELER, CHARLES A.
1974   The Relationship between Psychopathy and the Weak Automatization Cognitive Style, Ph.D. Dissertation in psychology, Florida State University (reprinted as FCI Research Reports 6, No. 2, Federal Correctional Institution, Tallahasse, Fla.).

WHITE, W.C., JR., W. GEORGE MCADOO, and EDWIN I. MEGARGEE
1971   "Personality factors associated with over and undercontrolled offenders." FCI Research Reports 3, No. 5, Federal Correctional Institution, Tallahassee, Fla.

WHITESIDE, THOMAS
1972   The Investigation of Ralph Nader. New York: Arbor House.

WIKLER, ABRAHAM
1965   "Conditioning factors in opiate addiction and relapse," in Wilner and Kassebaum, 1965.
1968   The Addictive States. Vol. 46 of Research in Nervous and Mental Diseases. Baltimore: Williams & Wilkins.

WILEY, NORBERT
1967   "The ethnic mobility trap and stratification theory." Social Problems 15 (Fall): 147-59.

WILKINS, LESLIE T.
1965   Social Deviance. Englewood Cliffs, N.J.: Prentice-Hall.
1972   Criminal Statistics. NIMH Crime and Delinquency Issues Monograph, DHEW Publication No. (HSM) 72-9094. Washington, D.C.: U.S. Government Printing Office.

WILLIAMS, KRISTEN M.
1975   "Criminal justice statistics: Data from a 'nonsystem.'" Paper presented at the 1975 Annual Meeting of the American Society of Criminology, Montreal.

WILLIE, CHARLES V.
1967   "The selective contribution of family status and economic status to juvenile delinquency." Social Problems 14 (Winter): 326-35.

WILNER, DANIEL, and GENE G. KASSEBAUM, eds.
1965   Narcotics. New York: McGraw-Hill.

WILSON, JAMES Q.
1975   Thinking about Crime. New York: Basic Books.

WINICK, CHARLES
1962   "Maturing out of narcotic addiction." United Nations Bulletin on Narcotics 14 (1): 1-7.
1974   (ed.) Sociological Aspects of Drug Dependence. Cleveland: CRC Press.
1975   "Some aspects of the 'tough' New York State drug law." Journal of Drug Issues 5 (Fall): 400-411.

WINICK, CHARLES, and PAUL M. KINSIE
1971   The Lively Commerce: Prostitution in the United States. Chicago: Quadrangle Books.

REFERENCES   531

WISE, DAVID
    1973   The Politics of Lying. New York: Random House.

WISEMAN, JACQUELINE P.
    1970   Stations of the Lost: The Treatment of Skid Row Alcoholics. Englewood
            Cliffs, N.J.: Prentice-Hall.

WITKIN, HERMAN A., SARNOFF A.
MEDNICK, FINI SCHULSINGER,
ESKILD BAKKESTROM, KARL O. CHRISTIANSEN,
DONALD R. GOODENOUGH, KURT HIRSCHHORN,
CLAES LUNDSTEEN, DAVID R. OWEN,
JOHN PHILIP, DONALD B. RUBIN,
and MARTHA STOCKING
    1976   "Criminality in XYY and XXY men." Science 193 (August 13): 547-55.

WOLFGANG, MARVIN E.
    1958   Patterns of Criminal Homicide. Philadelphia: University of Pennsylvania
            Press.
    1968   "Lombroso, Cesare." International Encyclopedia of the Social Sciences.
            New York: Macmillan Free Press.

WOLFGANG, MARVIN E., and FRANCO FERRACUTI
    1967   The Subculture of Violence. London: Tavistock.

WOLFGANG, M. E., R. M. FIGLIO, and T. SELLIN
    1972   Delinquency in a Birth Cohort. Chicago: University of Chicago Press.

WON, G., and G. YAMAMOTO
    1968   "Social structure and deviant behavior: A study of shoplifting." Sociology
            and Social Research 53 (October): 44-55.

WOOD, ARTHUR L.
    1969   "Ideal and empirical typologies for research in deviance and control." So-
            ciology and Social Research 53 (January): 227-41.

WRIGHT, JAMES D., and LINDA L. MARSTON
    1975   "The ownership of the means of destruction: Weapons in the U.S." Social
            Problems 23 (October): 93-107.

YABLONSKY, LEWIS
    1962   The Violent Gang. New York: Macmillan.
    1965   The Tunnel Back: Synanon. New York: Macmillan.
    1968   The Hippie Trip. New York: Pegasus.

YALE LAW JOURNAL
    1972   "The rape corroboration requirement: Repeal not reform." Yale Law Journal
            81 (June): 1343-66.

YOUNG, FRANK W.
    1967   "Incest taboos and social solidarity." American Journal of Sociology 72
            (May): 589-600.

YOUNGER, EVELLE J.
    1976   Child Abuse. Information Pamphlet No. 3. Sacramento: California Depart-
            ment of Justice.

ZALBA, SERAPIO R.
    1971   "Battered children." Trans-action 8 (July-August): 58-61.

ZEITLIN, LAWRENCE R.

1971   "A little larceny can do a lot for employee morale." Psychology Today 5 (June): 22-26, 64.

ZELLER, ROBERT H.

1966   Lowering the Odds on Student Dropouts. Englewood Cliffs, N.J.: Prentice-Hall.

ZETTERBERG, HANS L.

1963   On Theory and Verification in Sociology, rev. ed. Totowa, N.J.: Bedminster Press.

ZIMRING, FRANKLIN E.

1968   "Is gun control likely to reduce violent killings?" University of Chicago Law Review 35 (Summer 1968): 721-37.

1975   "Firearms and federal law: The Gun Control Act of 1968." Journal of Legal Studies 4 (January): 133-98.

ZOLA, IRVING KENNETH

1963   "Observations on gambling in a lower-class setting." Social Problems 10 (Spring): 353-61 (reprinted in Herman, 1967).

ZURCHER, LOUIS A., JR., R. GEORGE KIRKPATRICK, ROBERT G. CUSHING, and CHARLES K. BOWMAN

1971   "The anti-pornography campaign: A symbolic crusade." Social Problems 19 (Fall): 217-38.

NAME INDEX

Abbott, Daniel J., 225, 491
Abbott, William, 191–92, 499
Abdullah, Syed, 141, 519
Abel, Gene, 399
Abelson, Herbert I., 335, 483
Abrams, Arnold, 297, 483
Adams, Larry D., 324, 502
Adams, Stuart, 170, 483
Adelson, Lester, 214, 503, 522
Adler, Freda, 353, 355, 483
Agar, Michael, 297, 483
Aichhorn, August, 110, 111, 114, 130, 483
Akers, Ronald L., 182, 483
Albini, Joseph L., 449, 453, 483
Alex, Nicholas, 253, 509
Allen, David D., 462, 483
Allen, Francis A., 428–29, 483
Allen, Harry E., 145, 147, 153, 484, 500, 511
Allen, Vernon L., 191, 484
Alston, Letitia, 114, 511
Alviani, Joseph D., 214, 260, 263, 484
Amir, Menachim, 361, 367, 484, 520
Anderson, James L., 201, 213, 261, 262, 507
Anglin, Douglas, 306, 512
Anslinger, Harry J., 295, 303, 322, 452
Aquinas, Thomas, 105, 106
Archer, Dane, 231, 484
Ardrey, Robert, 239
Arens, Richard, 44, 484
Armor, David J., 289–90, 484
Arnold, Thurman W., 421–22, 469, 484
Aronowitz, Dennis S., 305, 484
Asch, Solomon E., 172, 484
Atkinson, Ronald B., 335, 483
Austin, Penlope, 150, 495
Ausubel, David P., 292–93, 484

Babbs, John, 327, 522
Babst, Dean V., 29, 311, 484, 493
Bach, George R., 240, 484
Bagley, Christopher, 370, 377, 484
Bahr, Howard M., 282, 484, 515
Bakal, Carl, 213, 261, 485
Bakan, David, 248, 485
Bakkestrom, Eskild, 141, 532
Bales, (Robert) Freed, 280, 285–86, 288, 485
Ball, John C., 296, 485, 497, 517
Ball-Rokeach, Sandra J., 215–16, 485, 512
Bandura, Albert, vii, 231, 233, 239, 240, 243, 404, 485
Bard, Morton, 228, 485
Barnett, Arnold, 210, 485
Bassiouni, M. Cherif, 41, 256, 485
Bates, Ronald, 74, 507
Bazelon, David L., 42, 43, 46, 485
Bearn, Alexander G., 487
Beccaria, Cesare, 37–38, 108, 512, 518
Becker, Howard S., 22, 33, 293, 321, 322, 485
Bedau, Hugo Adam, 485
Beecher, Henry K., 293, 508
Bell, Brian, 149, 513
Benedict, Ruth, 215, 217, 485
Benjamin, Harry, 352, 357, 485
Bentham, Jeremy, 38, 108, 518
Berocochea, John E., 312, 506
Berkowitz, Leonard, 231, 233, 486, 510
Berne, Eric, 112, 130, 486
Bernstein, Carl, 77–78, 486
Berrigan, Philip, 428
Bettelheim, Bruno, 110, 486
Beutel, Frederick K., 284, 486
Biderman, Albert D., 70, 73, 486
Bierce, Ambrose G., 30, 486
Bittner, Egon, 48, 486
Blachley, Paul H., 314, 505

Black, Donald J., 58, 385, 486, 514
Blackstone, William, 38
Blake, Gerald F., 163, 486
Blalock, H. M., 171, 486
Blankenburg, Erhard, 415, 486
Blankenship, Ralph L., 45, 46, 486
Blater, Mitchell B., 326, 513
Blau, Peter M., 427, 477, 487
Block, Richard, 208, 211, 230, 487
Blum, Richard H., 297, 298, 302,
    440, 441, 487, 506
Blumberg, Leonard, 282, 487
Blumer, Herbert, 127, 227, 292,
    487
Blyth, Dale A., 68, 520
Bogue, Donald J., 282, 487
Bohannon, Paul, 215, 487
Bonger, Wilhelm, 109
Bonjean, Charles, 215, 523
Bonnie, Richard J., 322, 487, 493
Boozer, Geraldine, 399
Borgaonkar, Digamber S., 140–41,
    153, 487
Borgatta, Edgar F., 326, 487
Boucher, Richard J., 393, 508
Boulding, Kenneth E., 476, 487
Bourne, Peter G., 509
Bourque, Linda Brookover, 222,
    512
Bower, Gordon R., 115, 502
Bower, Roland C., 308, 506
Bowman, Charles K., 390, 533
Brancale, Ralph, 393, 402, 487
Brecher, Edward M., 295, 326,
    327, 331, 336, 355, 372, 377,
    395–405, 488
Brecher, Ruth, 355, 488
Briar, Scott, 127, 131, 488
Brill, Henry, 330, 488
Brill, Leon, 307, 310, 311, 315,
    332, 488, 490, 505
Brill, Steven D., 261, 488
Brimmer, Andrew F., 193
Brodyaga, Lisa, 363, 488
Broman, Sarah H., 136, 153, 488
Brooks, Alexander D., 43, 44, 45,
    488
Brooks, James, 257, 258, 488
Broom, Leonard, 514
Brown, Barry S., 310, 314, 488
Brown, James W., 324, 488
Brown, Les, 236, 488
Brown, Richard M., 201, 488
Brown, Roger, 172, 488

Brownmiller, Susan, 369, 489
Bruun, Kettil, 295, 296, 489
Bryan, James H., 351, 352, 489
Buckhorn, Robert F., 424, 489
Buffalo, M. D., 120, 131, 521
Burger, Warren E., 387
Burgess, Ann Wolbert, 359, 360,
    362, 363, 366, 489
Burgess, E. W., 224
Burt, Robert A., 49, 489
Burton, Lindy, 373, 489

Cahalan, Don, 273, 279, 280, 489
Cameron, Mary O., 119, 414, 415,
    489
Camino, Leoncio, 233, 510
Caplan, Nathan, 163, 229, 489
Caplow, Theodore, 15, 282, 484,
    489
Carpenter, George R., 490
Carroll, Eleanor E., 502, 506, 513
Carroll, Laurence T., 310, 314, 488
Cartwright, Desmond S., 175, 489
Cartwright, Dorwin, 172, 490
Casey, John J., Jr., 91, 93, 297, 302,
    519
Cater, Douglass, 236, 490
Cavan, Sherri, 276, 281, 490
Chambers, Carl D., 283, 298, 311,
    315, 330, 332, 334, 484, 490,
    504, 505, 524–25
Chambliss, William J., 14, 19, 20,
    22, 52, 72, 331, 333, 436, 451,
    490, 523
Chappell, Duncan, 498
Chase, Stuart, 423
Chilton, Roland J., 24, 166, 490
Chiricos, Theodore G., 71, 508
Christensen, Harold T., 409–10,
    490
Christenson, Cornelia V., 364, 366,
    370, 371, 372, 375, 377, 379,
    381, 391, 394, 498
Christiansen, Karl O., 141, 148,
    153, 490–91, 513, 532
Churchill, Wainwright, 383, 491
Cicourel, Aaron V., 73, 76, 507
Cisin, Ira H., 273, 326, 489, 513
Clark, John P., 71–72, 183–84, 188,
    191, 196, 491
Clark, Robert E., 125, 131, 491
Claster, Daniel S., 92, 491
Clausen, John A., 143, 526

Clayton, Richard L., 294, 329, 332, 517
Cleckley, H., 143, 491
Clinard, Marshall B., 225, 491, 512
Cline, Victor B., 389, 491
Cloussen, U., 320, 504
Cloward, Richard D., 176–77, 196, 319, 491
Cobb, J. A., 240, 251–52, 517
Cobb, William E., 91, 491
Cohen, Albert K., 124, 180, 186, 187–89, 491
Coke, Edward, 41
Coleman, James S., 171, 491
Comitas, Lambros, 321, 491
Commager, Henry Steele, 428, 491
Comstock, George A., 234, 491
Comte, August, 135
Conklin, John E., 216, 254, 255, 450, 492, 518
Connor, Ralph G., 281, 492
Connor, Walter D., 57, 492
Coser, Lewis, 227, 231, 492
Cottrell, Leonard S., 514
Couzens, Michael, 60, 523
Craig, Roger, 391, 392, 492
Crancer, Alfred, Jr., 321, 492
Crane, Lansing E., 297, 500
Crawford, George G., 288–89, 494
Creighton, Lucy Black, 424, 492
Cressey, Donald R., 125, 131, 142, 308, 417, 418, 447, 450, 454, 463, 466, 470, 492, 527, 529
Crossley, Helen M., 273, 489
Cumberbatch, Guy, 234, 236, 504
Curtis, Lynn A., 212, 361, 368, 492
Cushing, Robert G., 390, 533
Cushman, Paul, Jr., 311, 492
Cuskey, Walter R., 334, 490

Dallos, Robert E., 420, 525
Darwin, Charles, 108–9, 134, 503
Datesman, Susan K., 166, 492
Davidson, Emily S., 233, 510
Davidson, R. Theodore, 455, 492
Davis, F. James, 236, 492
Davis, Kingsley, 352, 492
Davis, Phillip W., 379, 381, 493
Davis, Sharon K., 379, 381, 493
Davis, William, 281, 512
Dawley, David, 177, 217, 493
DeAmicis, Jan, 24, 490

de Bracton, Henry, 41
DeCourcy, Judith, 247, 493
DeCourcy, Peter, 247, 493
DeFleur, Lois B., 74, 493
DeFleur, Melvin, 235, 493
De Francis, Vincent, 370, 371, 373, 493
de Franco, Edward J., 466, 493
Deitch, Lillian, 459, 530
Delay, Jack C., 321, 492
Della Fave, L. Richard, 191, 218, 493
DeLong, James V., 300, 500
DeLora, Joann S., 377, 379, 383, 493
Demaree, Robert G., 309, 314, 493, 524
Dembo, Richard, 341, 493
Denenberg, R. V., 396, 389, 400, 493
Dentler, Robert A., 182, 183, 493
Dershowitz, Alan M., 305, 493
Deutscher, Irwin, 493, 501
Dickson, Donald T., 295, 296, 322, 494
Dille, James M., 321, 492
Dinitz, Simon, 113, 145, 147, 153, 484, 500, 511, 519, 530
Ditman, Keith S., 288–89, 494
Dix, George E., 393, 494
Dole, Vincent P., vii, 310–11, 312, 494
Domhoff, G. William, 78
Donnelly, Richard C., 385, 494
Dornbusch, Sanford, 479
Doshay, Lewis J., 369, 494
Douglas, Jack, D., 426, 428, 494, 513, 530
Douvan, Elizabeth, 157, 500
Drabman, Ronald S., 234, 527
Drake, William R., 214, 260, 263, 484
Drapkin, Israel, 494, 520, 522
Drucker, Peter F., 320, 494
Dunbar, Ellen Russell, 22, 494
Duncan, Otis Dudley, 183
DuPont, Robert L., 341, 494
Durham, Monte, 42–46, 54
Durkheim, Emile, 17, 26, 434, 474, 476, 494
Duster, Troy, 22, 292, 494

Eberts, Paul, 188, 223, 495

Gluckman, Max, 158, 499
Glueck, Eleanor H., 125, 141, 161, 167, 169, 170, 196, 499
Glueck, Sheldon, 125, 141, 161, 167, 169, 170, 196, 499
Goffman, Erving, 45–46, 92, 118, 130, 172, 379, 439, 499–500
Gold, Martin B., 71, 126, 157, 162, 168, 185, 500
Goldberg, Peter B., 300, 500
Goldblatt, Burt, 455, 514
Goldman, Harold, 145, 147, 153, 484, 500, 511
Goldstein, Abraham S., 41, 42, 500
Goldstein, Avram, vii, 302, 317–19, 500
Goldstein, Joseph, 49, 385, 494, 500
Goldstein, Michael J., 388, 500
Goode, Erich, 272, 321, 500
Goode, William J., 248, 500
Goodenough, Donald R., 141, 532
Gordon, C. Wayne, 282, 518
Gordon, Norman B., 310, 500
Gordon, Robert A., 182, 293–94, 500, 511
Goring, Charles, 135
Gorodetzky, C. W., 320, 504
Gould, Leroy C., 297, 416, 500
Gouldner, Alvin, 38, 419, 501
Gove, Walter R., 45, 501
Graham, Hugh Davis, 488, 497, 501, 508, 527
Graves, William F., 231, 501
Green, Mark J., 424, 501, 516
Greenwood, Peter W., 414, 433, 518
Grossman, Moses, 249, 508
Grupp, Stanley E., 324, 501
Gurr, Ted Robert, 488, 497, 501, 508, 527
Gusfield, Joseph R., 23, 24, 501
Guttman, Louis, 143, 526

Hackler, J. C., 167, 169, 196, 511
Hackney, Shelton, 218–19, 220, 501, 511
Halferty, David, 162, 518
Hall, Jerome, 20, 26, 437, 501
Hall, Reis H., 94, 501
Hand, Learned, 429
Handy, William, 204, 518
Hanneman, Gerhard J., 341, 501

Hannerz, Ulf, 226, 501
Hardt, Robert H., 166, 184, 189, 196, 501–2
Hare, R. D., 139, 143, 145, 146, 147, 151, 153, 502
Hargreaves, David, 163, 502
Harms, Ernest, 502, 519, 525
Hartman, Arthur A., 370, 502
Hartman, John J., 388, 500
Hartman, D. P. 415, 498
Hawkins, Gordon, 49, 50, 452, 453, 502, 515
Hawks, David, 315, 502
Haykin, Martin D., 321, 492
Helfer, Ray E., 247, 502, 517, 526
Heller, Celia S., 215, 502
Hellman, Arthur D., 325, 502
Helms, Dennis J., 328–29, 502
Henly, James R., 324, 502
Hepburn, John R., 212, 529
Herman, Robert D., 461, 502, 523, 533
Hess, Henner, 448–49, 454, 502
Hewitt, L. E., 114, 130, 502
Hibbert, Christopher, 106, 502
Higgins, Jerry, 149, 513
Hilgard, Ernest R., 115, 502
Hill, Robert H., 220, 222, 511
Hill, Shirley Y., 162, 166, 521
Himmelweit, H. T., 234, 502
Hindelang, Michael J., 19, 62, 79, 113, 142, 160, 171, 216, 415, 503
Hirose, Tetsuya, 330, 488
Hirsch, Charles S., 214, 503, 522
Hirschhorn, Kurt, 141, 532
Hirschi, Travis, 70, 74, 92, 126, 131, 162, 163, 165, 167, 168, 169, 170, 171, 172, 173, 182, 183, 187, 191, 197, 503
Hobbs, A. H., 76, 503
Hobsbawm, E. J., 232, 443, 448, 503
Hodge, R. Sessions, 139, 153, 503
Hofstadter, Richard, 134, 201, 503
Holahan, John F., 320, 503
Holmstrom, Lynda Lytle, 359, 360, 362, 363, 366, 489
Homans, George C., 427, 503
Homer, Frederic D., 450, 463, 503
Hood, Jacqui, 248
Hood, Roger, 491
Horning, Donald N. M., 419, 503
Horowitz, Ruth, 226, 503
Houston, Ted L., 260, 498

McGeady, Paul J., 388, 512
McGlothlin, William H., vii, 297, 306, 322, 323, 340, 512
Mack, John A., 92, 434, 437, 512
McKay, Henry D., 171, 186–87, 191, 196, 520, 524
McKee, Gilbert J., Jr., 94, 512
McKinney, John C., 222, 512
McKissack, I. J., 163, 512
M'Naghten, Daniel, 41–46, 54
McNamara, Patrick, 356, 521
Maestro, Marcello, 37, 512
Magura, Stephen, 216, 484, 512
Malthus, Thomas R., 37, 464
Maltz, Michael D., 58, 512
Manheimer, Dean I., 326, 513
Mann, Jay, 388, 512
Manning, Peter K., 427, 513
Manson, Charles, 47, 236, 242, 244
Markle, Gerald E., 166, 490
Marmor, Judd, 384, 513, 517
Marston, Linda L., 213, 215, 532
Martin, Clyde E., 72, 507
Martin, Del, 358, 513
Martin, John, 189, 513
Martin, John Bartlow, 365, 513
Marx, Karl, 19, 21, 109, 181, 218, 427, 476, 479, 481
Masters, R. L. L., 352, 357, 485
Masters, William H., 355, 362, 400, 513
Matza, David, 92, 118, 130, 513, 527
Maurer, David W., 433–34, 435, 438–40, 513
Mead, Margaret, 157, 375, 513
Mecham, Garth D., 28, 513
Mednick, Sarnoff A., vii, 141, 144–45, 148–49, 153, 513, 532
Megargee, Edwin I., 239, 241, 513, 531
Mellinger, Glen D., 326, 513
Mendelson, Jack H., 321, 513
Menninger, Karl, 43
Mercer, Jane R., 49, 514
Merten, Don, 160, 523
Merton, Robert K., 122, 223, 491, 492, 514
Messick, Hank, 455, 514
Meyer, Roger E., 321, 513–14
Milakovich, Michael E., 58, 514
Milazzo, Mildred, 94, 501
Mileski, Maureen, 385, 514

Miller, Donald, 94, 520
Miller, James C., 17, 523
Miller, Nick, 358, 514
Miller, Patricia Y., 349, 514
Miller, Robert R., 45, 514
Miller, Walter B., 31, 175, 189–91, 224, 231, 244, 508, 514
Mills, C. Wright, 21, 498
Mitchell, B. Balter, 326, 513
Moffett, Arthur D., 334, 490
Moffitt, Donald, 420, 514
Mohr, J. W., 379, 499
Molof, Martin J., 269, 514
Monahan, John, 393, 514
Mondale, Walter F., 429, 515
Money, John, 404, 515
Monroe, Lawrence J., 182, 493
Montagu, Ashley, 239, 515
Moore, Beverly C., Jr., 424, 501
Moore, William H., 78, 451–52, 515
Moquin, Wayne, 450, 461, 463, 515
Morgan, Wayne, 291, 515
Morrione, Thomas J., 127, 515
Morris, Norval, 49, 50, 452, 489, 515
Morris, Richard T., 476, 515
Moskowitz, Herbert, 288–89, 494
Mowrer, O. Hobart, 402, 515
Moynihan, Daniel P., 193, 515
Muedeking, George D., 282, 515
Murray, Douglas R., 261, 515
Murray, Margaret A., 106, 515
Musgrove, F., 160, 515
Musto, David F., 22, 295, 296, 302, 329, 515

Nader, Ralph, 20, 78, 423–24, 430, 489, 496, 501, 516, 517, 528, 531
Nagasawa, Richard H., 72, 490
Nash, George, 311, 313, 314, 516
Nash, Jay Robert, 440, 441, 516
Neale, John M., 233, 510
Nelli, Humbert S., 448, 449, 450, 453, 516
Nelsen, Judith M., 321, 530
Nelson, Alfred T., 435, 516
Neman, Janice F., 314, 493
Newman, Donald J., 73, 516
Newman, Stanley M., 231, 495
Newmeyer, John, 31, 505

Reiss, Ira L., 350, 520
Reppetto, Thomas A., 437, 520
Resnik, H. L. P., 399, 487, 515, 520, 524, 526
Retka, R. L., 314, 505
Reuck, A. V. S., 490
Rexed, Ingemar, 295, 296, 489
Rhodes, A. Lewis, 162, 184, 188, 191, 196, 520
Rice, Kent, 77, 181, 499
Reynolds, Paul Davidson, 68, 520
Robin, Gerald D., 415, 418, 419, 520–21
Robins, Lee N., 162, 166, 294, 521
Robinson, W. S., 222, 521
Robison, James A., 269, 531
Roby, Pamela, 353, 521
Rock, Paul, 513
Rodman, Hyman, 190, 521
Roebuck, Julian B., 276, 356, 521
Rogers, Joseph W., 120, 131, 521
Romilly, Samuel, 38, 518
Room, Robin, 279, 280, 281, 294, 329, 332, 489, 517, 521
Rooney, James F., 282, 521
Rose, Arnold, 499, 500
Rosenbaum, Paul A., 50, 521
Rosenhan, D. L., 46, 521
Rosenzweig, Susan Labin, 74, 507
Rosenzweig, Simon, 45, 522
Ross, H. Laurence, 418, 503, 521, 525
Ross, Phillip, 202, 527
Rossi, A. Michael, 321, 513
Rossman, Parker, 357, 521
Roth, Loren H., 138, 141, 150, 153, 524
Rottenberg, Simon, 491, 508, 521
Roy, K. K., 366, 522
Rubin, Donald B., 141, 532
Rubin, Sol, 45, 522
Rubin, Ted, 327, 522
Rubin, Vera, 321, 323, 491, 512, 517, 522
Rubington, Earl, 283, 522
Rubinstein, Elia, 234, 491
Rusche, Georg, 106, 522
Rushforth, Norman B., 214, 503, 522
Russell, Diana E. H., 409, 522

Sadoun, Roland, 278, 522
Saenger, Gerhart, 289, 498

Sagalyn, Arnold, 254, 522
Sagarin, Edward, 361, 522
Sanders, Clinton R., 325, 522
Sarbin, Theodore R., 71, 508
Sarri, Rosemary C., 40, 510
Savage, L. J. Jr., 314, 493
Scarpitti, Frank R., 166, 492
Schachter, Stanley, 145–46, 147, 153, 240, 522
Schafer, Walter E., 162, 163, 196, 197, 519, 522
Schaller, Michael, 295, 322, 522
Scheff, Thomas J., 45, 48, 522–23
Schmeidler, James, 341, 493
Schmidt, Annesley 414, 507
Schneider, Louis, 215, 523
Schrag, Clarence, 172, 523
Schuck, Peter, 426, 523
Schulsinger, Fini, 141, 149, 513, 532
Schultz, Leroy G., 359, 497, 510, 523
Schur, Edwin M., 120, 130, 385, 523
Schuster, Charles R., 314, 505
Schwartz, Barry, 368, 523
Schwartz, Gary, 160, 226, 503, 523
Schwartz, Richard D., 17, 385, 494, 523
Schwarz, Hershey, 175, 489
Schwendinger, Herman, 5, 165, 479, 523
Schwendinger, Julia, 5, 165, 479, 523
Schwirian, Kent P., 188, 223, 495
Scodel, Alvin, 462, 523
Scott, Marvin B., 458, 460–61, 523
Seidman, David, 60, 523
Seidman, Robert B., 52, 523
Seitz, Steven T., 261, 524
Seligman, Joel, 424, 515
Sellin, Thorsten, vii, 160, 211, 216, 532
Sells, S. B., vii, 298, 309, 314, 505, 524
Senay, Edward C., 314, 505
Serber, Michael, 405, 524
Serrill, Michael S., 402, 524
Servadio, Gaia, 448, 449, 524
Shah, Saleem A., vii, 138, 140–41, 150, 153, 487, 524
Shandler, Irving W., 282, 487
Shaw, Clifford R., 171, 186–87, 191, 196, 524

Sheldon, William H., 141, 524
Sherrill, Robert, 261, 262, 263,
    264, 524
Shipley, Thomas E., Jr., 282, 487
Short, James F., Jr., 72, 92, 118,
    124, 170, 175, 182, 196, 217,
    514, 517, 520, 524
Shover, Neal, 436, 437, 524
Sidman, Jack, 388, 512
Siegal, Harvey A., 283, 524–25
Silverman, Larry J., 424, 496
Silverman, Milton, 278, 522
Simmel, Georg, 227, 525
Simon, Rita James, 44, 525
Simon, William, 349, 352, 389–90,
    498, 514
Simmons, Luiz R. S., 500
Simpson, D. Dwayne, 309, 314,
    524
Sinclair, Andrew, 24, 525
Singer, Max, 79, 525
Singer, R. D., 233, 497
Singer, Susan, 363, 488
Singh, B. Krishna, 45, 486
Skinner, B. F., 88, 124, 239, 251,
    525
Skogan, Wesley, G., 62, 68, 525
Slatin, Gerald T., 294, 329, 332,
    517
Smelser, Neil, 14
Smigel, Erwin O., 416, 418, 503,
    521, 525
Smith, Adam, 17, 37, 420, 525
Smith, Alfred A., 328–29, 502
Smith, Beth B., 314, 505
Smith, Gerald W., 269, 531
Smith, Howard E., 435, 516
Smith, R. B., 297, 525
Snyder, Charles R., 518
Soble, Ronald L., 420, 525
Sokol, Jacob, 327, 525
Solomon, David, 322, 525
Sonnenreich, Michael R., 487, 493
Speck, Richard, 47, 140, 231
Spencer, Herbert, 109, 214, 525
Spergel, Irving, 177, 525
Spier, Rosalind B., 220, 518
Spilerman, Seymour, 231, 525
Spradley, James P., 282, 525
Sprenger, James, 107, 508
Spulak, F. V., 320, 504
Stambul, Harriet B., 289–90, 484
Stanfield, Robert E., 168, 526
Star, Shirley A., 143, 526

Starr, Sheldon, 388, 512
Steadman, Henry J., 46, 526
Steele, Brandt F., 250, 526
Steffens, J. Lincoln, 77, 526
Steffensmeier, Darrell J., 415, 526
Stein, Kenneth B., 71, 508
Steinberg, Arthur G., 487
Steinmetz, Suzanne K., 249, 500,
    517, 526
Stephens, Richard C., 297, 334,
    490, 525
Stimson, G. V., 315–16, 526
Stinchcombe, Arthur L., 162–63,
    173, 196, 526
Stocking, Martha, 141, 532
Stoll, Clarice Stasz, 348, 526
Stone, Alan A., 43, 526
Stone, Christopher, 421–22, 425,
    526
Stouffer, Samuel A., 143, 526
Straus, Murray A., 240, 248, 500,
    517, 526
Strickland, Stephen, 236, 490
Strodtbeck, Fred L., 92, 118, 170,
    196, 217, 524
Sturup, George K., 403, 526
Suchman, Edward A., 143, 526
Sudnow, David, 48, 372, 527
Sumner, William Graham, 109
Sutherland, Edwin H., 125, 126,
    131, 142, 392, 421, 442, 527
Sutter, Alan G., 297, 527
Suttles, Gerald D., 174, 175, 196,
    231, 527
Sykes, Gresham M., 118, 527
Szasz, Thomas S., 342, 527

Taft, Phillip, 202, 527
Tannenbaum, Frank H., 175, 433,
    435, 527
Taylor, Ian, 109, 523, 527
Teeters, Negley K., 39, 527
Teilmann, Kathleen S., 71, 527
Ten Broeck, Elsa, 249, 508
Terry, Charles E., 302, 527
Terry, Robert M., 415, 526
Thomas, Garth J., vii, 138
Thomas, Margaret H., 234, 527
Thompson, Elizabeth J., 493, 501
Thorsell, Bernard A., 119, 120,
    130, 527
Thrasher, Frederic M., 122,
    180, 186, 196, 528

Tiffany, Theodore L., 114, 518
Tifft, Larry L., 71–72, 491
Toby, Jackson, 117, 130, 166, 171, 176, 226, 506, 528
Toch, Hans H., 114, 241, 245, 528
Tomson, Barbara, 175, 489
Trice, Harrison, M., 274, 287, 528
Tuchfarber, Alfred J., 70, 528
Tucker, Marna, 363, 488
Turner, James S., 424, 528
Turner, R. E., 379, 499
Turner, Ralph H., 171, 173, 442, 528
Turner, Wallace, 459, 528
Tyler, E. B., 214, 528

Ullman, Albert D., 278, 528

Vaillant, George E., 303, 306–7, 340, 529
Valentine, Charles A., 190, 222, 529
van den Berghe, Pierre L., 16, 529
Van den Haag, Ernest, 480, 529
Van Doren, Charles, 450, 461, 463, 515
Van Felsinger, John M., 293, 508
van Gennep, Arnold, 158, 529
Vaz, Edmund W., 184, 529
Viano, Emilio, 494, 520, 522
Vince, P., 234, 502
Vold, George B., 141, 153, 181, 529
Volkman, Rita, 308, 529
von Hentig, Hans, 435, 529
von Hirsch, Andrew, 108, 529
Vorenberg, James, 312, 529
Voss, Harwin L., 74, 162, 163–64, 167, 170, 196, 212, 294, 329, 332, 495, 517, 529
Votey, Harold L., Jr., 320, 529
Vuocolo, Alfred, 393, 402, 487

Walder, P., 415, 498
Waldo, Gordon P., 71, 113, 508, 530
Walker, Andrew L., 297, 500
Walker, Nigel, 41, 42, 530
Wallace, Jean E., 321, 492
Wallace, Michael, 201, 503
Wallace, Samuel E., 201, 282, 530

Wallerstein, James S., 71–72, 530
Walsh, Marilyn E., 436, 530
Walter, V. J., 139, 503
Walter, W. Grey, 139, 503
Walton, Paul, 109, 527
Ward, Colin, 189, 530
Ward, D. A., 527
Warner, Alan, 311, 484
Warner, Eric, 281, 512
Warren, Carol A. B., 119, 377, 379, 383, 384, 493, 530
Washington, George, 320, 455
Wasserstein, Bruce, 424, 501
Waxer, Elaine, 324, 488
Weber, Max, 21, 27, 426–27, 455, 476, 498, 530
Weihofen, Henry, 45, 522
Weil, Andrew T., 321, 530
Weinberg, Martin S., 379, 383, 530
Weinberg, S. Kirson, 375, 377, 530
Weinstein, David, 459, 530
Weir, Adrianne, 254, 255, 497
Weis, Kurt, 58, 514
Weissman, James C., 300, 530
Wenk, Ernst A., 269, 341, 531
Wenninger, Eugene P., 72, 183–84, 188, 191, 196, 491
Werthman, Carl, 92, 173, 531
Wexler, David B., 46, 531
Wheeler, Charles A., 146, 531
White, Richardson, 363, 488
White, W. C., Jr., 241, 531
Whitehead, C. H., 322, 487
Whiteside, Thomas, 424, 531
Wikler, Abraham, 292–93, 531
Wiley, Norbert, 173, 531
Wilkins, Leslie T., 79, 121, 531
Will, George F., 355–56
Williams, Colin J., 383, 530
Williams, Kristen M., 70, 531
Willie, Charles V., 166, 182, 196, 532
Wilner, Daniel, 517, 531, 532
Wilson, Bruce D., 306, 512
Wilson, James Q., 47, 480, 532
Winch, Robert F., 17, 497
Wineman, David, 110, 130, 143, 520
Winick, Charles, 305, 350–52, 487, 532
Wise, David, 428, 532
Wiseman, Jacqueline P., 282, 283, 286–87, 532

Witkin, Herman A., 141, 532
Wolfgang, Marvin E., 135, 160, 211, 215, 216, 220, 390–91, 399, 487, 515, 520, 524, 526, 532
Wolpe, Joseph, 405, 524
Won, G., 414, 532
Wood, Arthur L., 114, 532
Woodward, Bob, 77–78, 486
Woolpert, Stephen, 94, 505
Wright, James D., 213, 214, 532
Wright, Richard, 260, 498
Wyden, Peter, 240, 484
Wyle, Clement J., 71–72, 529

Yablonsky, Lewis, 175, 308, 533

Yamamoto, G., 414, 532
Young, Frank W., 375, 533
Young, Jock, 109, 527
Younger, Evelle J., 246, 533

Zalba, Serapio R., 248, 249, 533
Zeigler, Max S., 219–20, 499
Zeitlin, Lawrence R., 419, 533
Zeller, Robert H., 164, 533
Zelnik, Melvin, 350
Zetterberg, Hans L., 124, 533
Zimring, Franklin E., 211, 213, 230, 261, 262, 487, 516, 533
Zinberg, Norman E., 321, 530
Zola, Irving Kenneth, 461, 533
Zurcher, Louis A., Jr., 390, 533

SUBJECT INDEX

castration, 403–4
catharsis, 233, 240
cheating, 145–46
   see aso confidence game; forgery
child battering, 245–52, 267–68,
   371
child molestation, *see* sexual
   molestation; incest
chromosomes, 139–41
city crime rates, 62–68, 210–11
   see also slums
circular reaction, 228
civil commitment, 303–7, 391–94
civil disobedience, 428–29
civil-rights movement, 30, 229–32
class, socioeconomic
   and child rearing, 249
   consciousness, 476–77
   and crime definition, 15, 16–21
   and crime explanation, 105–6,
      182–92, 222–25
classical school, 38, 41, 53
classification, *see* typologies
clearance rates, 85–87
coalitions, 15–16, 18–19
cocaine, 328–29, 339
collective behavior, *see*
   polarization
community treatment programs,
   114–15, 397–98, 400–401
compensation, *see* victim,
   compensation
competition, 174–78, 420–22
confidence game, 7–8, 438–42
conflict, 15–16
consensus, 15–16
conservatism, 30–32, 34, 108
consumer's movement, 423–26
consumption, illegal, 9–10
contagion, 231
control theory, 125–26, 128, 131,
   224–25
Controlled Substances Act, 300,
   322, 329, 331, 333–35
corporate crime, 18–20, 77–79,
   420–25
corruption
   of criminal justice, 343–44,
      353–54
   measurement, 77–78
   by organized crime, 450, 470
   political, 426–29
counterfeiting, 438

crime
   causation, 104–95, 480
   cost, 79
   definition, 5, 6–12
   profits, 90–99, 320
   risks, 86–90
   specialization, 160–61, 216, 369,
      433
   statistics, 56–80
   see also specific types of offense
criminology, 5–6, 109, 134, 479
cruelty to wildlife, 8
culture, 160, 214–15, 239
   see also subcultures

delinquency, 39–41, 54, 110–11
Depression, Great, 20, 205, 405
deprivation, relative
   definition, 223
   factor in crime, 30, 188, 229, 416
desensitization, 234
deterrence, 108, 115–20, 130, 269,
   480
   see also punishment
Detroit Plan, 355, 391
differential anticipation, 126–27,
   128, 131
   see also stake in conformity;
      informal controls
differential association, 125, 128,
   131
differential identification, 125, 131
differential reference, 125, 131
differentiation, social
   and adolescence, 158–61
   defined, 16–17, 32–33
   and criminal law, 18–21, 32–33
   and stress, 30
   and value generalization, 25–26
diminished responsibility, 45
disloyalty, 10, 12, 28–29
dissent, 28–29, 36, 231
disorderly conduct, 9, 12
double standards, 349
drinking, *see* alcohol; alcoholism;
   drunkenness
drive reduction, 240
dropouts, 163–65
Drug Enforcement
   Administration, 300–1, 313
drugs, psychotropic
   and crime, 9–10, 12, 272–344

drugs, psychotropic *(Cont)*
  and crime explanations, 107,
    111, 272–72, 297, 320
  definition, 326
  education against, 340–41
  prohibition effects, 341–43
  rates, 71–72, 74–76, 323–24, 326,
    332–35
  selling, 297–98
  see also amphetamines,
    barbiturates, and other
    specific drugs
drunkenness
  as crime, 12, 272, 275
  and ethnicity, 277–78
  decriminalization, 20, 275–76
  patterns, 279–85
  rates, 75–76, 275
  see also alcohol; alcoholism
Durham decision, 42–44

ego, 110–12, 114
electioneering, criminal, 8, 428
electroencephalogram (EEG),
  138–39, 146
embezzlement, 7, 75–76, 416–20
enculturation theory, 186, 188
Enlightenment era, 107–8
ether, 326
ethnicity
  and adolescent crime, 192–93,
    478–79
  and crime rates, 72–73
  and drunkenness, 277–78
  and marijuana use, 321–23
  and opiate use, 296–99
  and organized crime, 447–55
  of rapists, 368
  and robbery, 254
  and violence, 209–10, 216–17,
    224–25, 229–32
evolution
  biological, 108–9, 134–36
  social, 16–27, 158–61
  of statistics, 79
exhibitionists, 379–81
extroversion, 142

family, 165–69, 196, 212, 227–28
Federal Bureau of Investigation
  (FBI), 57–61, 445, 446, 496

felonies, 6, 105
fetishism, 389
Food and Drug Administration,
  300, 313, 331, 422–23
forgery, 75, 283–85, 437–38
formal groups, 178–81, 197
fraud, *see* confidence game,
  forgery
friends, 169–74
frustration–aggression theory,
  239–41
fundamentalism, 30, 32, 34

galvanic skin response (GSR),
  144–47, 148, 153, 234
Gamblers Anonymous, 119,
  461–62
gambling
  arrest rates, 74–76
  as crime, 12, 455–62
  as explanation for crime, 88–99,
    107, 111, 172
gangs
  bandit, 443–44
  delinquent, 113–15, 174–81
  mafia, 452–55
glue-sniffing, 326–28, 339
Good Samaritan Law, 259–60
gun
  control, 19, 260–64
  culture, 201
  ownership, 72, 212–14

Harrison Act, 295–96, 300, 329,
  338, 339
hashish, *see* marijuana
heredity, 134–35, 137, 139–41,
  146–49, 151–53
heresy, 10, 12, 105–106
heroin, *see* opiates
hijacking, 231, 446
homicide
  defined, 7, 12, 205
  deterrence, 269
  explanations, 214–45, 265–67
  professional, 446
  rates, 58, 61–63, 74–77, 202–12,
    264
homosexuality, 9, 72, 382–85, 398
hormones, 149–50, 404

personality
  and alcoholism, 281
  and delinquency, 113–15
  and psychoanalytic theory,
    109–15, 128, 130
  overcontrolled, 241
  psychopathic, 114, 142–47,
    391–94
  of sex assault victims, 373
  and violence, 241–44
peyote, 336
physique, 141–42
pickpockets, 434–35
pilfering by employees, 419
pimps, 351–52
pirates, 443
polarization
  as crime cause, 121–24, 131
  of violence, 227–32
political crime, 28–30, 77–79, 202,
    426–29
pollution, criminal, 8
pornography
  childhood norms, 347
  effects, 388–91
  legal issues, 387–88
  and rape, 369
positive school, 135–36
poverty
  and delinquency, 166, 181–92
  and prostitution, 350–51
  and violence, 217, 222–25
pragmatism, 27–29
predatory offenses
  and addictions, 320, 343
  counting, 57–70
  defined, 6–7, 12
  and differentiation, 16–24,
    31–33, 475–76
  see also assault, burglary, and
    other specific offenses
prediction
  of sex offenses, 393–94
  of violence, 269–70
privacy, criminal invasion of, 8,
    381–82
Prohibition Amendment, 19,
    22–23, 27, 274, 447–51
professional criminals, 432–46,
    467–68
prostitution
  as crime, 12, 32, 33
  explanations, 107, 350–52, 358

prostitution (Cont)
  legalization, 353–56
  male, 357
  and rape, 357, 369
  rates, 74–76, 349–50
psilocybin, 336
psychedelics, 335–37
psychoanalysis, 109–12, 130, 165
psychopathy, 114, 142–47, 391–94
punishment
  capital, 219–20, 231
  certainty, 480
  classical theory of, 37–38
  learning theory of, 115–16
  parental, 168, 248–49
  pragmatic, 28
  see also deterrence

race, see ethnicity
racketeering, 450–51
radicalism, 29–30, 32, 109, 479
rape
  defined, 7, 12, 358–59
  effects, 360, 362
  explanations, 120, 364–68,
    409–10
  law enforcement, 359–60,
    361–63
  rapist types, 364–67
  rates, 58, 61–70, 75, 360–61,
    363–64
  recidivism, 368–69
reality therapy, 112, 130
recidivism
  and adolescence, 115, 414
  causation, 480–481
  of sex offenders, 369, 393
  and stakes in conformity, 118
  of violence, 269
Reformation, 107
reinforcement, 115–18, 130
religion, 105–8
responsibility, legal, see insanity;
    intent; retardation
restitution, 26, 256
restraint of trade, 422
retardation, mental, see
    intelligence
riots, 30, 229–32
ROARE, 402
robbery
  definition, 8, 12, 252

robbery *(Cont)*
    professional, 443–45
    rates, 58, 61–75, 252–55
    yield, 91
    violence, 216, 253

safecracking, 436
scholastics, 105
schools, 159–65, 187–89, 196
secondary deviance (and
        deviation), 118–21, 130
selling, illegal, 9, 12, 94–96
sex
    crimes, 346–410
    education, 369, 399
    liberation, 409
    norm acquisition, 347–48
    offender treatment, 395–405
    and personality, 110–12
    role training, 398–400
sexual molestation, 370–74
shoplifting, 117, 119, 414–16, 435
skid row, 282–83
slum
    crime explanations, 186, 191–93,
        222–25
    crime rates, 62, 68–69
SOANON, 403
sodomy, 382–83, 408
Southern violence, 205–206,
        218–22
specialization in crime, 160–61
stake in conformity (and
        nonconformity), 117–18, 131,
        163, 173, 225, 413–14
status groups, 21–22
status offenses, 10–12, 40–41
statute of limitations, 50–51, 54
stereotypes, 120
stigma, 119–20, 139, 339
strain theory, 121–24, 131, 187–88
structural explanation, 217–18
subcultures
    age, 160
    delinquent, 186–89
    lower class, 189–91
    professional crime, 432–34
    of violence, 215–39, 265–67
substance abuse, 272–344
Sullivan Act, 260–61
superego, 111, 114
symbolic interaction, 127
Synanon, 307–9

swindling, *see* confidence game;
        corporate crime; forgery

terrorism, 231–32, 428–29
therapeutic communities, 307–10,
        395–97, 398–402
theft
    auto, 116–17, 436–37
    cargo, 464–65
    definition, 7, 12
    grand, 116–18, 120
    law on, 19–20
    professional, 434–35, 464–65
    rates, 58, 60–77
    securities, 464–65
    yield, 91
    see also shoplifting
till-tapping, 435
torts, 19, 26, 422
tranquilizers, 326, 333–35
transactional analysis, 112
treason, *see* disloyalty
two-step process, 235–36
typologies
    of crime, 6–12
    of criminal law changers, 22–23
    of delinquency, 111, 113–15,
        128
    of drunkenness, 279–85
    of rapists, 364–68
    of sex crimes, 346

undercontrolled personality, 241
unemployment, 181, 254
    see also poverty
Uniform Crime Reports (UCR)
    description, 8, 57–61, 80
    compared with NCP, 63–68
urbanism, *see* city crime rates;
        slums
usury, 464
vagrancy, 9, 12, 75
value generalization, 16, 25–26, 32,
        409–10, 476
vandalism, 188, 189
venereal disease, 357
victim
    compensation, 256–59, 362
    precipitation, 212, 217
    surveys, 61–70, 80
victimless crimes, *see*
        nonpredatory offences